Lecture Notes in Computer Science 15463

Founding Editors

Gerhard Goos
Juris Hartmanis

The series Lecture Notes in Computer Science (LNCS), including its subseries Lecture Notes in Artificial Intelligence (LNAI) and Lecture Notes in Bioinformatics (LNBI), has established itself as a medium for the publication of new developments in computer science and information technology research, teaching, and education.

LNCS enjoys close cooperation with the computer science R & D community, the series counts many renowned academics among its volume editors and paper authors, and collaborates with prestigious societies. Its mission is to serve this international community by providing an invaluable service, mainly focused on the publication of conference and workshop proceedings and postproceedings. LNCS commenced publication in 1973.

Mahmoud Barhamgi · Hua Wang · Xin Wang ·
Esma Aïmeur · Michael Mrissa ·
Belkacem Chikhaoui · Khouloud Boukadi ·
Rima Grati · Zakaria Maamar
Editors

Web Information Systems Engineering – WISE 2024 PhD Symposium, Demos and Workshops

WEB-for-GOOD 2024, AIWDA 2024, SWIFT-AG 2024, and Demos
Doha, Qatar, December 2–5, 2024
Proceedings

 Springer

Editors
Mahmoud Barhamgi ⓘ
Qatar University
Doha, Qatar

Hua Wang ⓘ
Victoria University
Melbourne, VIC, Australia

Xin Wang
Tianjin University
Tianjin, China

Esma Aïmeur ⓘ
Montréal University
Montreal, QC, Canada

Michael Mrissa ⓘ
University of Primorska
Koper, Slovenia

Belkacem Chikhaoui
University of Doha for Science
and Technology
Doha, Qatar

Khouloud Boukadi
Faculty of Economics and Management
of Sfax
Sfax, Tunisia

Rima Grati
Zayed University
Dubai, United Arab Emirates

Zakaria Maamar
University of Doha for Science
and Technology
Doha, Qatar

ISSN 0302-9743   ISSN 1611-3349 (electronic)
Lecture Notes in Computer Science
ISBN 978-981-96-1482-0   ISBN 978-981-96-1483-7 (eBook)
https://doi.org/10.1007/978-981-96-1483-7

This Springer imprint is published by the registered company Springer Nature Singapore Pte Ltd.
The registered company address is: 152 Beach Road, #21-01/04 Gateway East, Singapore 189721, Singapore

If disposing of this product, please recycle the paper.

Preface

Welcome to the WISE 2024 PhD Symposium, Posters, Demos, and Workshops proceedings of the 25th International Conference on Web Information Systems Engineering (WISE 2024), held in Doha, Qatar, December 2–5, 2024. The series of WISE conferences aims to provide an international forum for researchers, professionals, and industrial practitioners to share their knowledge in the rapidly growing area of web technologies, methodologies, and applications.

These proceedings are devoted to the papers accepted in the PhD Symposium and Posters and Demos tracks of the WISE 2024 conference as well as the conference workshops including (1) WEB-for-GOOD: A Web for more inclusive, sustainable and prosperous societies; and (2) The 1st International Workshop on AI and Web Data Analytics (AIWDA 2024).

A total of 75 research papers were submitted to the aforementioned tracks and workshops for consideration. The distribution of submissions was as follows. The PhD Symposium received 32 paper submissions. The Posters and Demos track received 15 paper submissions. The AIWDA 2024 workshop received 18 paper submissions and the Web-for-Good workshop received 10 paper submissions. Each paper was reviewed by at least three reviewers in a double-blind peer review process.

Finally, 18 submissions were selected as regular papers (an acceptance rate of 30% approximately), 9 as short papers, and 9 demos and posters. The research papers cover the areas of web security and privacy, web data management, web architectures and technologies, social networks, and queries.

We would like to thank the members of the International Program Committee for a rigorous and robust reviewing process. We are also grateful to Springer, the International WISE Society, the QNRF (grant No. CWSP23-C-0409-24066) and Qatar Tourism for supporting this conference. We expect that the ideas that have emerged in WISE 2024 and its tracks and workshops will result in the development of further innovations for the benefit of scientific, industrial, and social communities.

November 2024

Mahmoud Barhamgi
Hua Wang
Xin Wang
Esma Aïmeur
Michael Mrissa
Belkacem Chikhaoui
Zakaria Maamar
Khouloud Boukadi
Rima Grati

Organization

General Chairs

Mahmoud Barhamgi   Qatar University, Qatar
Yanchun Zhang   Zhejiang Normal University, China
Djamal Benslimane   Lyon 1 University, France

Program Committee Chairs

Hua Wang   Victoria University, Australia
Mahmoud Barhamgi   Qatar University, Qatar
Xin Wang   Tianjin University, China

PhD Symposium Chairs

Lina Yao   University of New South Wales, Australia
Boualem Benatallah   Dublin City University, Ireland

Web-for-Good Workshop Chairs

Esma Aïmeur   University of Montreal, Canada
Michael Mrissa   University of Primorska, Slovenia
Mahmoud Barhamgi   Qatar University, Qatar
Khouloud Boukadi   University of Sfax, Tunisia
Rima Grati   Zayed University, UAE

The 1st International Workshop on AI and Web Data Analytics (AIWDA 2024) Chairs

Belkacem Chikhaoui   University of Doha, Qatar
Zakaria Maamar   University of Doha, Qatar

Demo Chairs

Saeed Salem	Qatar University, Qatar
Haithem Mezni	Taibah University, KSA
Bekir Çiftler	University of Doha for Science and Technology, Qatar

Publicity Chairs

Salma Sassi	Université de Pau & Pays de l'Adour, France
Haithem Mezni	Taibah University, KSA
Mucahid Kutlu	Qatar University, Qatar
Attila Kertesz	University of Szeged, Hungary
Bohan Li	Nanjing University of Aeronautics and Astronautics, China
Michael Mrissa	University of Primorska, Slovenia
Feng Zhang	Renmin University of China, China
Abdulhalim Dandoush	University of Doha for Science and Technology, Qatar

Publication Chairs

Mahmoud Barhamgi	Qatar University, Qatar
Hua Wang	Victoria University, Australia
Xin Wang	Tianjin University, China

Diversity and Inclusion Chair

Jinli Cao	La Trobe University, Australia

Local Organization Chairs

Amr Mohamed	Qatar University, Qatar
Khalid Abualsaud	Qatar University, Qatar
Ahmed Badawy	Qatar University, Qatar
Mohammad Al-Sada	Qatar University, Qatar
Amal Al-Masri	Qatar University, Qatar

Finance Chair

Richard Chbeir   University of Pau and Pays de l'Adour, France

Program Committee

Abdelhak Belhi   Joaan Bin Jassim Academy for Defence Studies,
                                        Qatar
Abdelhak-Djamel Seriai   University of Montpellier, France
Abyayananda Maiti   Indian Institute of Technology Patna, India
Adam Wójtowicz   Poznań University of Economics and Business,
                                        Poland
Afonso Arriaga   University of Luxembourg, Luxembourg
Alessandro Campi   Politecnico di Milano, Italy
Alessandro Tundo   TU Wien, Austria
Alexander Knapp   Universität Augsburg, Germany
Alexandra Cristea   Durham University, UK
Alfredo Cuzzocrea   University of Calabria, Italy
Allel Hadjali   LIAS/ENSMA, France
Amirhossein Ghaffari   Oulu University, Finland
Andrés Rodríguez   Universidad Nacional de La Plata, Argentina
Aneesh Krishna   Curtin University, Australia
Aniello Castiglione   University of Salerno, Italy
Arash Mahboubi   Charles Sturt University, Australia
Armin Haller   Australian National University, Australia
Ashkan Sami   Edinburgh Napier University, UK
Aydin Abadi   Newcastle University, UK
Ayman El Hajjar   University of Westminster, UK
Azadeh Ghari Neiat   Deakin University, Australia
Barbara Catania   University of Genoa, Italy
Bin Cao   Zhejiang University of Technology, China
Boris Sedlak   TU Wien, Austria
Boualem Benatallah   Dublin City University, Ireland
Bernd Amann   Sorbonne Université, France
Bo Dang   San Francisco Bay University, USA
Bo Tang   Southern University of Science and Technology,
                                        China
Catarina Ferreira da Silva   University Institute of Lisbon, Portugal
Catuscia Palamidessi   Inria, France
Cédric Eichler   INSA Val de Loire, France
Chaima Ben Rabah   Weill Cornell Medicine, Qatar

Chamikara Arachchige	CSIRO, Australia
Chadni Islam	Queensland University of Technology, Australia
Chao Tong	Beihang University, China
Chaogang Tang	China University of Mining and Technology, China
Chen Wang	Huazhong University of Science & Technology, China
Chouki Tibermacine	Montpellier University, France
Cindy Chen	University of Massachusetts Lowell, USA
Cinzia Cappiello	Politecnico di Milano, Italy
Conggai Li	CSIRO, Australia
Damiano Distante	University of Rome, Italy
Dan Lin	Vanderbilt University, USA
Daniela Grigori	Paris-Dauphine University, France
Dario Colazzo	Paris-Dauphine University, France
Devis Bianchini	University of Brescia, Italy
Dimitri Theodoratos	New Jersey Institute of Technology, USA
Dimitris Kotzinos	CY Cergy Paris University, France
Dickson K.W. Chiu	University of Hong Kong, China
Dimitris Plexousakis	University of Crete, Greece
Dimitrios Katsaros	University of Thessaly, Greece
Erisa Karafili	University of Southampton, UK
Esma Aïmeur	University of Montreal, Canada
Eleanna Kafeza	Technology Innovation Institute, UAE
Elio Masciari	University of Naples Federico II, Italy
Epaminondas Kapetanios	University of Hertfordshire, UK
Faheem Ullah	University of Adelaide, Australia
Fouzi Harrag	Ferhat Abbas University, Algeria
Flavius Frasincar	Erasmus University Rotterdam, Netherlands
Florence Sèdes	IRIT Université Toulouse III Paul Sabatier, France
Francisco Mayo	University of Seville, Spain
Francesco Marchiori	University of Padua, Italy
Gang Wang	Northeastern University, USA
Garrison Gao	CSIRO's Data61, Australia
Gefei Zhang	Hochschule für Technik und Wirtschaft Berlin, Germany
George Papastefanatos	ATHENA Research Center, Greece
Georgia Kapitsaki	University of Cyprus, Cyprus
Georgios Kambourakis	University of the Aegean, Greece
Gorrab Abir	National School of Computer Science, Tunisia
Guanfeng Liu	Macquarie University, Australia
Guy-Vincent Jourdan	University of Ottawa, Canada

Hajer Baazaoui	CY Cergy Paris University, France
Haobing Liu	Ocean University of China, China
Hanchen Wang	University of Technology Sydney, Australia
Harsha Vasudev	University of Padua, Italy
Hassan Mehmood	Oulu University, Finland
Hayato Yamana	Waseda University, Japan
Heiko Schuldt	University of Basel, Switzerland
Hong-Tri Nguyen	Aalto Systems and Services Engineering, Finland
Hossein Shirazi	San Diego State University, USA
Hongzhi Wang	Harbin Institute of Technology, China
Hong Va Leong	Hong Kong Polytechnic University, China
Huizi Yu	Amazon Science, USA
Imen Megdiche	Paul Sabatier University, France
Ismail Badache	Aix-Marseille Université, France
Jarogniew Rykowski	Poznań University of Economics and Business, Poland
Jayamine Alupotha	University of Bern, Switzerland
Javier Izquierdo	Universitat Oberta de Catalunya, Spain
Ji Zhang	University of Southern Queensland, Australia
Jiafan Wang	CSIRO's Data61, Australia
Jiaxin Li	University of Padua, Italy
Jide Edu	University of Strathclyde, UK
Jiefu Song	IRIT, Université Toulouse Capitole, France
Jinli Cao	Latrobe University Melbourne, Australia
Jiujing Zhang	University of New South Wales, Australia
Joe Tekli	Lebanese American University, Lebanon
Jose Navarrete	Universitat de València, Spain
José María de Fuentes	Universidad Carlos III de Madrid, Spain
Junhu Wang	Griffith University, Australia
Julián Grigera	Universidad Nacional de La Plata, Argentina
Jürgen Ziegler	University of Duisburg-Essen, Germany
Kewen Liao	Australian Catholic University, Australia
Khouloud Boukadi	University of Sfax, Tunisia
Ladjel Bellatreche	LIAS/ENSMA, France
Laurent Bobelin	INSA Centre Val de Loire, France
Leong Hou U	University of Macau, China
Liang Yuan	Swinburne University, Australia
Liu Peng	Singapore Management University, Singapore
Lizhen Wang	Yunnan University, China
Lizhou Fan	Harvard Medical School, USA
Lokesh Jain	Delhi Technological University, India
Lotenna Nwana	COSMOS Research Center, Russia

Lucia Cascone	Università degli Studi di Salerno, Italy
Luciano Baresi	Politecnico di Milano, Italy
Manolis Gergatsoulis	Ionian University, Greece
Malik Khalfallah	Airbus, France
Marco Anisetti	Università degli Studi di Milano, Italy
Marco Winckler	Université Côte d'Azur, France
Marco Minici	University of Pisa, and ICAR-CNR, Italy
Marco Aiello	University of Stuttgart, Germany
Maria Malek	CY Cergy Paris University, France
Marinette Savonnet	University of Burgundy, France
Maristella Matera	Politecnico di Milano, Italy
Markel Vigo	University of Manchester, UK
Martin Weise	TU Wien, Austria
Maumita Bhattacharya	Charles Sturt University, Australia
Maurizio Leotta	Università di Genova, Italy
Michael Bewong	Charles Sturt University, Australia
Mingming Li	University of Chinese Academy of Sciences, China
Mitsunori Ogihara	University of Miami, USA
Mohamed Reda Bouadjenek	Deakin University, Australia
Mohamed Sellami	Télécom SudParis, France
Mohamed-Amine Baazizi	Sorbonne Université, France
Mourad Khayati	University of Fribourg, Switzerland
Muhammad Ali	Anglia Ruskin University, UK
Murali Mani	University of Michigan-Flint, USA
Mehmet Dalkilic	Indiana University, USA
Nathalie Moreno	Universidad de Málaga, Spain
Nawal Guermouche	INSA de Toulouse, France
Nicolas Anciaux	Inria, France
Nicola Zannone	Eindhoven University of Technology, Netherlands
Nora Faci	Université Lyon 1, France
Osama Almurshed	Cardiff University, UK
Pavlo Radiuk	Khmelnytskyi National University, Ukraine
Peiquan Jin	University of Science and Technology of China, China
Peter Rønne	University of Luxembourg, Germany
Qi Luo	University of New South Wales, Australia
Qiang Zhu	University of Michigan, USA
Qiang Ma	Kyoto University, Japan
Rafiqul Islam	Charles Sturt University, Australia
Romain Bourqui	University of Bordeaux, France
Roberto Metere	University of York, UK

Saeid Hosseini	Sohar University, Oman
Santiago Melia	Universidad de Alicante, Spain
Sandeep Kumar	Indian Institute of Technology Roorkee, India
Schahram Dustdar	Vienna University of Technology, Austria
Sebastian Link	University of Auckland, New Zealand
Sergio Ilarri	University of Zaragoza, Spain
Shaoyi Yin	Paul Sabatier University, France
Sharif Abuadbba	CSIRO's Data61, Australia
Shiting Wen	Zhejiang University, China
Shigang Liu	CSIRO's Data61, Australia
Silviu Maniu	Université Grenoble Alpes, France
Stefan Tai	TU Berlin, Germany
Stefano Cirillo	Università degli Studi di Salerno, Italy
Sven Groppe	University of Lübeck, Germany
Stéphane Jean	University of Poitiers, ISAE-ENSMA, France
Syed Atif Moqurrab	University of Southampton, UK
Tanzima Hashem	Bangladesh University of Engineering, Bangladesh
Thomas Richter	Rhein-Waal University of Applied Sciences, Germany
Tomas Vitvar	Czech Technical University, Czech Republic
Tommaso Bianchi	University of Padua, Italy
Tooba Aamir	CSIRO's Data61, Australia
Toshiyuki Amagasa	University of Tsukuba, Japan
Tsz Nam-Chan	Shenzhen University, China
Venkata M. V. Gunturi	University of Hull, UK
Verena Kantere	University of Ottawa, Canada
Vianney Perchet	ENSAE & Criteo AI Lab, France
Victor Casamayor Pujol	TU Wien, Austria
Vitaliy Yakovyna	University of Warmia and Mazury in Olsztyn, Poland
Vincent Oria	NJIT, USA
Wafa Ben Slama Souei	University of Sousse, Tunisia
Wei Shen	Nankai University, China
Wenjie Zhang	University of New South Wales, Australia
Werner Retschitzegger	Johannes Kepler University Linz, Austria
Wieland Schwinger	Johannes Kepler University Linz, Austria
Xiang Lian	Kent State University, USA
Xiangmin Zhou	RMIT University, Australia
Xiaoyi Liu	Arizona State University, USA
Xiaohui Tao	University of Southern Queensland, Australia
Xiangyang Gou	Peking University, China

Xiaoye Miao	Zhejiang University, China
Xin Cao	University of New South Wales, Australia
Xun Yi	RMIT University, Australia
Xuhong Zhang	Indiana University, USA
Yain-Whar Si	University of Macau, China
Yicheng Feng	Chinese University of Hong Kong, China
Yixiang Fang	Chinese University of Hong Kong, China
Yiyi Tao	Peking University, China
Yijie Weng	University of Maryland, USA
Yilei Zhao	Zhejiang University, China
Yongfeng Ge	Victoria University, Australia
Yonghong Yu	Nanjing University, China
Young-Gab Kim	Sejong University, South Korea
Yuting Wang	University of Michigan, USA
Zhao Li	Zhejiang University, China
Zhigao Zheng	Wuhan University, China
Zhisheng Huang	Vrije Universiteit, Netherlands
Zhizhong Wu	University of California Berkeley, USA
Zichao Li	University of Waterloo, Canada
Riad Sonbol	Hyderabad Institute of Science and Technology, Pakistan
Seifeddine Mechti	University of Sfax, Tunisia
Sarah Aloyiana	Imam University, Saudi Arabia
Houda Baoussidi	Cadi Ayyad University, Morocco
Omnia Zayed	University of Galway, Ireland
Abdullah Thalji	Isra University, Pakistan
Sohaila Eltanbouly	Qatar University, Qatar
Jezia Zakraoui	Qatar University, Qatar
Abdellah El Mekki	Mohammed VI Polytechnic University, Morocco
Salima Harrat	École Normale Supérieure de Bouzaréah, Algeria
Rana Malhas	Qatar University, Qatar
Maram Hasanain	Qatar University, Qatar
Raian Ali	Hamad Bin Khalifa University, Qatar
Abdusalam Nwesri	University of Tripoli, Libya
Joseph Attieh	Lebanese American University, Lebanon
Hanan Alghamdi	Umm Al-Qura University, Saudi Arabia
Shatha Ali A. Hakami	Jazan University, Saudi Arabia
Hanaa Mahmood	University of Mosul, Iraq
Shadi Saleh	Microsoft, USA
Randah Alharbi	King Fahd University of Petroleum & Minerals, KSA
Abed Alhakim Freihat	University of Trento, Italy

Anis Charfi	Carnegie Mellon University, Qatar
Sami Hamdi	Jazan University, Saudi Arabia
Hamza El Alaoui	Carnegie Mellon University, Qatar
Sultan Alrowili	University of Delaware, USA
Khloud Al Jallad	Arab International University, Syria
Ghadeer Abuoda	York University, Canada
Rayyan Al Khadhuri	Sultan Qaboos University, Oman
Saied Alshahrani	Clarkson University, USA
Hossam Ahmed	Leiden University, Netherlands
Abdullah Alharbi	King Abdulaziz University, Saudi Arabia
Sarah Al-Humoud	Al-Imam University (IMSIU), Saudi Arabia
Zubair Shah	Hamad Bin Khalifa University, Qatar
Imed Zitouni	Google, USA
Hanen Himdi	University of Jeddah, Saudi Arabia
Hend Al-Khalifa	King Saud University, Saudi Arabia
Randa Zarnoufi	Mohamed V University in Rabat, Morocco
Ghizlane Bourahouat	School of Information Sciences (ESI), Morocco
Hesham Moussa	Nile University, Egypt
Ghada Khoriba	Nile University, Egypt
Reem Suwaileh	Hamad Bin Khalifa University, Qatar
Venus Jin	Northwestern University in Qatar, Qatar
Abdelkader Elmahdaouy	Sidi Mohamed Ben Abdellah University, Morocco
Xingliang Yuan	University of Melbourne, Australia
Xiaoning Liu	RIMT University, Australia
Yifeng Zheng	Harbin Institute of Technology, Shenzhen, China
Viet Vo	Monash University, Australia
Shangqi Lai	CSIRO's Data61, Australia
Leo Yu Zhang	Griffith University, Australia
Pathum Arachchige	RMIT University, Australia
Siqi Ma	University of New South Wales, UK
Yaxing Chen	Northwestern Polytechnical University, China
Anjia Yang	Jinan University, China
Helei Cui	Northwestern Polytechnical University, China
Guangdong Bai	University of Queensland, Australia
He Zhang	Monash University, Australia
Jin Hong	University of Western Australia, Australia
Yu Guo	Beijing Normal University, China
Ziyao Liu	Nanyang Technological University, Singapore
Hagen Lauer	Technische Hochschule Mittelhessen, Germany
Yousra Aafer	University of Waterloo, Canada
Wenqi Fan	Hong Kong Polytechnic University, China
Xingming Chen	Hong Kong Polytechnic University, China

Jiayuan Xie   Hong Kong Polytechnic University, China
Jiahao Wu   Hong Kong Polytechnic University, China
Xu Hu   Hong Kong Polytechnic University, China
Jiahao Zhang   Hong Kong Polytechnic University, China
Yaowei Wang   Hong Kong Polytechnic University, China
Hongfei Liu   South China University of Technology, China
Haopeng Ren   South China University of Technology, China
Runze Mao   City University of Hong Kong, China
Jingfan Chen   Hong Kong Polytechnic University, China
Yujuan Ding   Hong Kong Polytechnic University, China
Haoran Tang   Hong Kong Polytechnic University, China
Liuwu Li   South China University of Technology, China
Liuwen Cao   South China University of Technology, China
Jing Wang   Chinese University of Hong Kong, China
Peiyan Guan   University of Hong Kong, China
Yanting Yang   Zhejiang University, China
Yushi Zeng   South China University of Technology, China
Wei Wang   Hong Kong Polytechnic University, China
Mengzhen Wang   South China University of Technology, China
Xueyao Sun   Hong Kong Polytechnic University, China
Jiatong Li   Hong Kong Polytechnic University, China
Bingshan Zhu   Guangdong University of Finance & Economics,
                            China
Qi Peng   South China University of Technology, China
Jiali Chen   South China University of Technology, China
Jun Li   Hong Kong Polytechnic University, China
Li Yuan   South China University of Technology, China
Mengying Xie   Chongqing University, China
Shuning He   Hong Kong Polytechnic University, China
Shijie Wang   Hong Kong Polytechnic University, China
Haoran Yang   University of Technology Sydney, Australia
Irwin King   Chinese University of Hong Kong, China
Qing Li   Hong Kong Polytechnic University, China
Haohao Qu   Hong Kong Polytechnic University, China
Jiaxin Wu   Hong Kong Polytechnic University, China
Yifeng Zhang   Shanghai Jiao Tong University, China
Ahmed Badawy   Qatar University, Qatar
Karim Benouaret   Université Claude Bernard Lyon 1, France
Cynthia Marcelino   Vienna University of Technology, Austria
Vimal Kumar   University of Waikato, New Zealand
Basel Katt   NTNU, Norway
Amjad Ratrout   Université Grenoble Alpes, France

Chia-Mu Yu	National Yang Ming Chiao Tung University, Taiwan
Alexandros Karakasidis	University of Macedonia, Greece
Ankur Shukla	Institute for Energy Technology, Norway
Junaid Haseeb	University of Waikato, New Zealand

Contents

WISE 2024 - Posters and Demos Track

A Web for More Inclusive, Sustainable and Prosperous Societies (Web-for-Good) Workshop

The 1st International Workshop on AI and Web Data Analytics (AIWDA 2024)

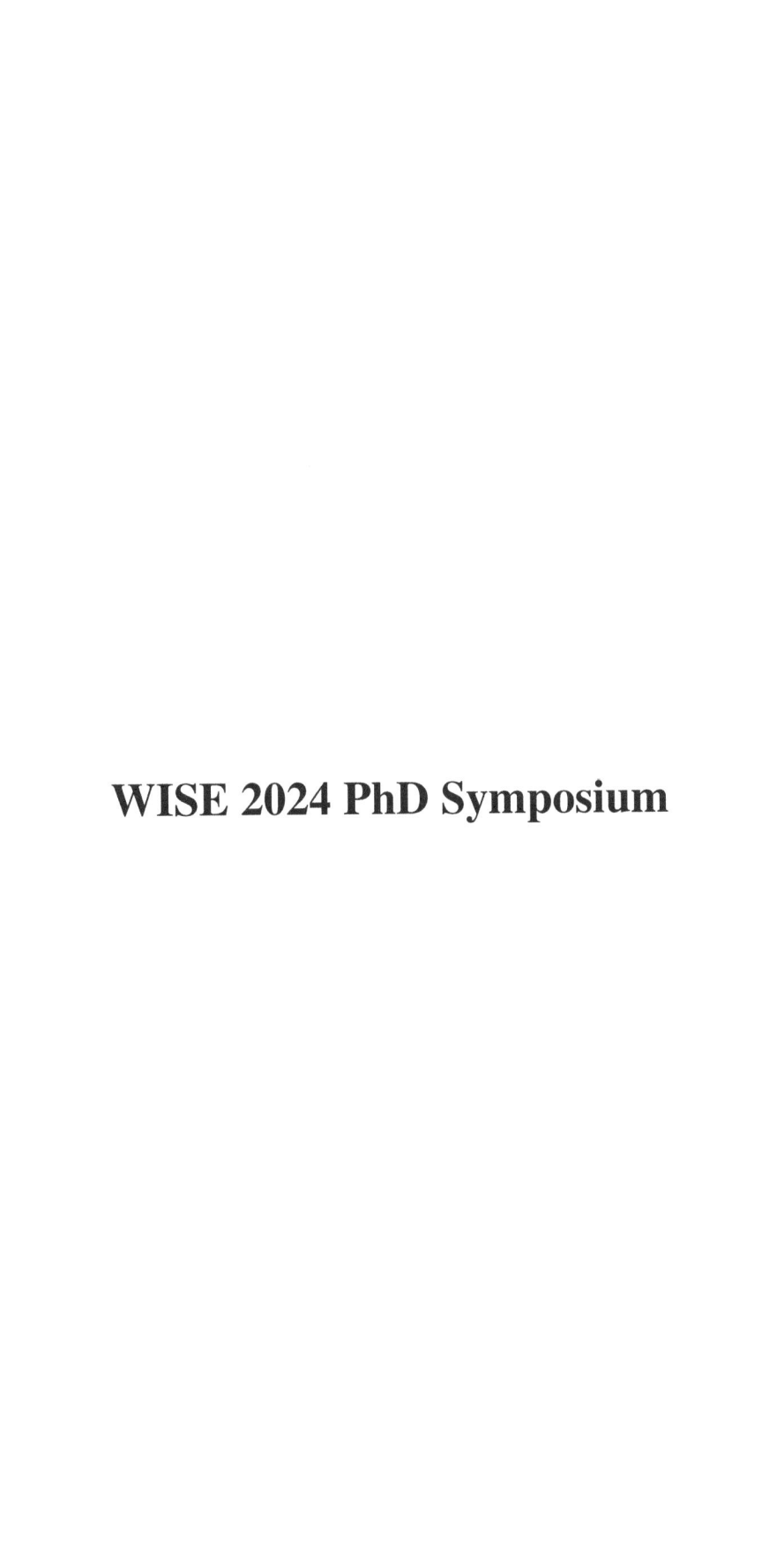

WISE 2024 PhD Symposium

A Phishing Website Detection System Based on Hybrid Feature Engineering with SHAP Explainable Artificial Intelligence Technique

Norah Alsuqayh[✉], Abdulrahman Mirza, and Areej Alhogail

College of Computer and Information Sciences, King Saud University, Riyadh 11451,
Saudi Arabia
n.alsuqayh@gmail.com, {amirza,aalhogail}@ksu.edu.sa

Abstract. Today, phishing website attacks have emerged as a prevalent threat affecting Internet users, governments, and businesses. The key challenge is that phishers continuously deploy new techniques to create zero-day phishing attacks. Recently, researchers have suggested anti-phishing techniques based on classifiers such as machine learning and deep learning methods. This research aims to develop a framework for predicting zero-day phishing websites through introducing new hybrid feature engineering methods that help adapt to evolving threats by extracting meaningful attributes or characteristics of phishing websites, including content-based and URL-based features. By combining diverse feature types, a detection system can capture a comprehensive set of characteristics associated with phishing behavior, improving the accuracy of the detection process. In addition, we also apply SHapley Additive exPlanations (SHAP) technique to interpret the behavior of the hybrid feature engineering by quantifying the impact of individual features on model predictions, providing a clear understanding of which features contribute most significantly to phishing detection. Moreover, the proposed approach aims to capture the most informative and discriminative features, reducing the likelihood of overlapping features.

Keywords: Feature engineering · Hybrid features · eXplainable Artificial Intelligence (XAI) · SHapley Additive exPlanations (SHAP) · Phishing detection · Classification model

1 Introduction

The increased use of electronic services and web applications in different domains has led to a concurrent increase in both the complexity and frequency of cyberattacks [1] One cyberthreat is phishing, which has become a major issue in recent years due to its increasing prevalence. Commonly, anti-phishing techniques split into three categories: detection, prevention, and revision. Detection is the most effective method for minimizing human errors that attackers can exploit to steal sensitive information [2]. Phishing detection methods provide early alerts about malicious emails or URLs. These approaches are classified into five classes: list-based, heuristic schemes, machine learning, deep learning, and hybrid approaches that will be discussed in the literature review section.

© The Author(s), under exclusive license to Springer Nature Singapore Pte Ltd. 2025
M. Barhamgi et al. (Eds.): WISE 2024, LNCS 15463, pp. 3–17, 2025.
https://doi.org/10.1007/978-981-96-1483-7_1

Recently, models such as Support Vector Machines, Neural Networks, and deep learning models have obtained success in resolving complex problems and improve performance [1]. However, it also reduced their interpretability. When implementing a learning model, the use of interpretability as an added layer can enhance its explainability for three reasons [3]:

1. Assist to ensure integrity in decision-making by correcting biases within the training dataset.
2. Improves robustness by focusing on potential perturbations that may affect the results.
3. Ensures that only relevant variables infer the output.

SHAP is an XAI method used to explain predictions made by learning models to disclose the contributions of each feature to predictions, giving intuitions of the reasons behind the model's decisions. [4]. Integrating SHAP into the hybrid feature engineering process for phishing detection enhances the interpretability and functionality of predictive models [5]. SHAP specifies how each attribute, or combination of attributes from multiple sources like URL data and page content, helps classify a website as legitimate or phishing. This transparency boosts user confidence and trust in the model, which is crucial in cybersecurity. Additionally, SHAP can uncover unexpected behaviors in the model by revealing unexpected feature influences, such as a typically legitimate feature contributing to phishing classifications, indicating potential model bias [6].

Implementing a website phishing detection model without leveraging the advantages of hybrid feature engineering and SHAP raises several challenges and may affect the accuracy of capturing the various aspects of phishing activity. An illustrated example: when the model relies only on content-based features such as HTML content to identify phishing websites, it ignores some valuable indicators that are related to URL-based characteristics, such as suspicious domain names that increase the accuracy of detection. In addition, content-based features may not efficiently distinguish between legitimate and phishing websites, increasing the likelihood of false positives or false negatives [7]. Furthermore, attackers are always enhancing their strategies to evade detection, such as obfuscating malicious content [8]. Consequently, without applying feature engineering derived from multiple domains (e.g., content and URL), the system may struggle to identify these evasion techniques effectively.

Although the potential benefits of incorporating various types of features to capture a comprehensive set of attributes related to website phishing behavior have not been adequately explored in some studies, there is an increasing recognition of its importance in improving detection accuracy and robustness in the field of website phishing detection. So, this research will employ hybrid feature engineering that involves joining features extracted from multiple webpage's sources, such as content-based features that include textual and structural elements of web pages and URL-based features that contain the characteristics of the website's URL. By integrating these two types of features, the proposed detection system can capture an extensive range of characteristics related to both benign and malicious behavior to enhance the detection process. Moreover, the proposed detection approach becomes more resilient to evasion tactics when attackers try to obfuscate suspicious content or tamper with the structure of the URL to evade detection. Furthermore, the system has the capability to respond to evolving threats by incorporating additional feature types and adjusting existing feature engineering methods to ensure that the detection approach remains effective against emerging threats; therefore, it becomes an essential part of robust cybersecurity metrics against phishing attacks.

The integration of SHAP in the phishing detection field enables the transformation of the black-box models into glass-box models by producing explanations about how specific decisions were made, like flagging websites as phishing, to make the models more trustworthy [4]. Furthermore, not all hybrid features contribute equally, and some might be redundant or unnecessary. SHAP can decide which elements are most effective and which are not contributing to the performance of the model. This information aids in optimizing the feature set and enhances model efficiency and performance.

Finally, by integrating diverse feature sets, the proposed approach can capture the most informative and discriminative features, reducing the likelihood of overlapping features using some methods such as chi-square [7] or correlation analysis [8].

The reminder of the research is organized as follows: Sect. 2 outlines a research aim and objectives. Section 3 reviews literature review on phishing detection techniques. Section 4 describes the proposed research methodology. And lastly, Sect. 5 states the conclusion.

2   Research Aim and Objectives

The main goal of this study is to generate a phishing website detection system using hybrid feature engineering with XAI. Our objectives are as follows:

1. Examine the use of hybrid feature engineering technique in phishing websites system to integrate features from content based and URL-based features.
2. Evaluate the accuracy and robustness of phishing website detection model ability to adapt to evolving phishing strategies and evasion techniques utilized by attackers.
3. Applying SHAP technique to interpret the behavior of hybrid feature engineering by quantifying the impact of individual features on model predictions, providing a clear understanding of which features contribute most significantly to phishing detection.
4. Eliminate duplicate features and select the most informative attributes from each domain in order to optimize feature space while decreasing the possibility of overlapping information.

3   Literature Review

The literature contains studies that suggesting mechanisms for website phishing detection, and this research are raising each year [9, 10, 11]. Since there is no one-size-fits-all method to successfully detect websites, the problem of phishing websites is complex and challenging in and of itself [12]. Figure 1 shows the two primary defensive methods, which are user awareness and software-based detection.

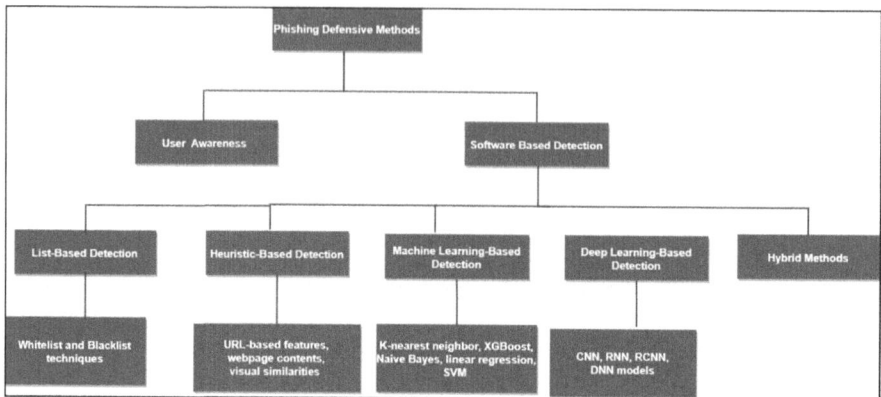

Fig. 1. An outline of common phishing detection techniques [13, 14].

3.1 Software-Based Detection Approaches

List-Based Approach

Cao et al. [9] used Naïve Bayes (NB) classifier to develop a novel anti-phishing approach they called Automated Individual Whitelist that generates a whitelist by recording the IP address of the Login User Interface (LUI). When a user sends secret data to an LUI that is not on the whitelist, the system sends an alert message to the user to a suspicious attack. While Vrbančič et al. [15] utilized a set of 38 characteristics, Random Forest (RF) and Linear Regression (LR) classifiers test the proposed blacklist strategy, which achieved 97% accuracy with a 2.5% false positive rate in distinguishing between legitimate and maliciously registered domains. To allow for more accurate detection of phishing attacks, [16] integrated blacklists, web content, and heuristic approaches using machine learning algorithms with comprehensive features. These algorithms included Adaptive Neuro-Fuzzy Inference System (ANFIS), NB, PART, J48, and JRip. The best performance was achieved by PART, which achieved 99.33% accuracy at a speed of 0.006 s.

Heuristic-Based Approach

Using the combined features of a site's text, images, and frames, [10] offered an ANFIS, SVM, and K-Nearest Neighbor (K-NN) classifier for web-phishing detection that achieved 98.3% accuracy. Moreover, the researchers in [17] suggested a heuristic technique employing a twin SVM to detect deliberately registered phishing sites. The twin SVM performed significantly better than the other variants, with a recall of 98.33% and an accuracy of 98.05%. The goal of [18] was to assess 12 static features, including keywords and patterns, in the chosen phishing URL and track how frequently they appeared in the current phishing site. In addition, however, the study conducted a quantitative and qualitative analysis of behaviors, and the researchers were able to pinpoint elements such as feature relevance, relationships, and similarities that can aid in the creation of new heuristic techniques or strengthen already existing ones.

Machine Learning Approach

Liu et al. [11] developed a multistage phishing detection model and presented a thorough CASE feature architecture. The method works well in real-world phishing discovery and produces efficient detection outcomes with shorter execution times. A phishing detection framework using hybrid cumulative feature selection [19]. It uses several feature selection methods (e.g., chi-square) to divide the dataset into n partitions according to features that are present in the dataset. Next, for each dataset division, a variety of classifiers are applied, including SVM, NB, C4.5, RF, JRip, PART, and K-Nearest Neighbor. With the RF classifier, the suggested model achieved accuracy of 98:24%. Hannousse et al. [20] viewed a model that uses a classifier to allow for the comparison of phishing detection systems using 87 different features. The schema addresses the short-lived nature of phishing websites by creating a dataset that can evolve over time. According to the article, web page content was determined to be the least discriminative, whereas external factors were the most. The highest accuracy score, 96.61%, was obtained by using hybrid features, and performance was enhanced to 96.83% by using filter-based ranking with progressive elimination of less significant features.

Deep Learning Approach

Using a Convolutional Neural Network (CNN) based on the website's URL and a variety of feature sets, the suggested research in [14] work without need to retrieve of website content or any third-party features. This technique gathers sequential patterns of URL strings with no need of any expert of phishing detection. The sequential patterns of URL strings are captured for detection without requiring phishing knowledge. The accuracy of model is 95.02% on a unique dataset and 98.58%, 95.46%, and 95.22% on benchmark datasets. In contrast, Vrbančič et al. [15] proposed an anti-phishing system that trains the Machine Learning (ML) and Deep Learning (DL) models K-NN, LR, SVM, GBC, ABC, RFC, and NNs by combining URL, Natural Language Processing (NLP), and host-based features. The NN ultimately attained a better accuracy of 94.89% in detecting phishing URLs.

An anomaly detection framework using A character-level Convolutional Autoencoder (CAE) was developed in [21]. Experiments using Receiver Operating Characteristics curve analysis, and 10-fold cross-validation verified that the sensitivity increased by 3.98% over the most recent deep model, proving the effectiveness of the suggested approach.

Hybrid Approach

In [22], R. S. Rao and A. R. Pais proposed a mechanism joining Extra-Trees, Random Forest, and XGBoost to evaluate the effectiveness of heuristic-based and blacklist-based filters, achieving an accuracy of 98.72%. Furthermore, Korkmaz et al. in [23] suggested a phishing detection model using CNN with n-gram features extracted from URLs. Experiments showed that unigrams provided the highest accuracy. Specifically, using a selected 70 characters yielded an accuracy rate of 88.90% on URL dataset. Additionally, Orunsolu et al. in [24]proposed an approach that extracts URL, content and behavior of the webpage using frequency assessment analysis. The approach was evaluated by NB and SVM. The results showed evaluation metrics of 99.96% true positives, 99.96% true negatives, 0.04% false positives, and 0.04% false negatives.

3.2 XAI in Phishing Website Detection

Few research has employed XAI approaches in phishing detection. Hernandes et al. [25] applied RF, SVM and Explainable Boosting Machines (EBM) combined with XAI methodologies which are Local Interpretable Model-Agnostic Explanations (LIME) and EBM to specify the significant URL characteristics influencing the framework's predictions. The results showed that the main URL characteristics found by the XAI methods correspond with prevalent phishing characteristics. Additionally, Chai et al. [6] suggested model that learns deep phishing indicators from URL, textual, and visual modalities. The model combined two levels of attention techniques to extract related features and informative interpretability on levels. Experiments showed the model improves phishing detection and provides hierarchical interpretability. While Lin et al. [26] applied a hybrid deep learning-based model to detect phishing webpages incorporating explainable visual annotations overlaid on screenshots of the phishing pages. Poddar et al. [27] utilized a two-stage stacked ensemble learning approach by applied gradient boosting method and RF on 21 extracted features from 651,191 URLs. The model achieved an accuracy of 97%. After that, XAI techniques applied to elucidate the model's workings and analyze the effect of the 21 features on the categorize predictions: legitimate, distortion, phishing, and malware.

3.3 SHAP in Phishing Detection

Puri et al. [28] employed SHAP values in machine learning models and ensemble models, including K-means, RF, DT, CatBoost, LightGBM, AdaBoost, and voting classifier to phishing URL detection Classification. CatBoost classifier demonstrated superior performance in metrics. When analyzed the model, SHAP values are crucial in identifying key features and their effects on model's output.

The shortcomings of the existing literature [21] and [29] concern a crucial gap regarding the improvement of the phishing detection process through integration of content-based and URL-based features using hybrid feature engineering techniques. In addition, a limited number of research employed XAI approaches in phishing detection models. So, to the best of knowledge, this is the first research that applying SHAP XAI technique to enhance hybrid feature engineering for phishing detection. By analyzing SHAP values, we can determine which features contribute the most to the model's decision-making process. This interpretability is important for understanding the model's behavior and ensuring that the engineered features are successfully capturing the underlying patterns in the data and consequently, detecting phishing patterns.

Furthermore, the feature reduction technique for eliminating overlapping features while keeping the most pertinent information was not used in the method suggested in [19]. Thus, by combining hybrid feature engineering methods with XAI mechanisms and applying feature reduction method to remove overlapping characteristics, the suggested research aims to address the identified gap in the literature and improve the state-of-the-art in phishing detection. This approach has the chance to enhance the accuracy, robustness, and interpretability of phishing detection systems, eventually enhancing cybersecurity measures against phishing attacks.

4   Research Methodology

The existing studies focus on single feature types to detect phishing websites; a complete method that combines URL and content-based features through hybrid feature engineering techniques is lacking. Additionally, since learning models may be viewed as "black boxes" that make it difficult to figure out how decisions are derived, users may not trust or fully understand why a website is labeled as a phishing website or not [1]. Another challenge with hybrid features that integrate content and URL datasets is that not all these characteristics equally enhance the model's performance, and it's difficult to evaluate the relevance and contribution of individual features or identify redundancy among them [7]. Another shortage is the absence of feature reduction methods to eliminate overlapping features that can skew the model's performance.

By combining content-based and URL-based features using hybrid feature engineering with XAI, the system aims to develop a more comprehensive feature that captures a wider range of phishing indicators. Moreover, integration XAI provides explanations for decisions, such as why a website is marked as phishing, thus increasing trustworthiness. Furthermore, XAI assists in determining which features are most effective and which are redundant or unnecessary, optimizing the feature set and enhancing the effectiveness and performance of the model. Finally, the research seeks to utilize feature reduction mechanisms to eliminate overlapping characteristics while keeping the most relevant information. This can enhance the efficiency of phishing detection classifier.

The model's framework consists of five stages, as illustrated in Fig. 2. The first step is data selection and preprocessing, the second stage involves feature extraction and engineering, the third stage is detection classification. Finally, the model is evaluated using multiple performance indicators to classify and detect phishing websites with interpret the model using SHAP. The following sections briefly outline the research methodology that will be followed in each phase:

4.1   Dataset Considerations

Due to the short lifespan of phishing websites, inactive URLs cannot be used for content-based analysis, and most public datasets include the attributes values without referencing the specific URLs used. In addition, datasets should be regularly updated to guarantee robustness in the phishing detection model and quick and timely responses to threat patterns because attackers continuously improve their techniques to bypass existing security measures. Another issue is that datasets often contain more instances of legitimate websites than phishing websites, leading to imbalanced classes that can alter the performance of classifiers and capture the minority class.

Aassal et al. [30] studied the effect of the ratio of phishing to legitimate samples in datasets and demonstrated that unbalanced datasets may drop the performance of classifiers from 5.9% to 42% in terms of the F-1 score. Because of this, we need to balance datasets using different undersampling and oversampling techniques, such as Random Majority and Synthetic Minority Over-sampling Technique (SMOTE) [31]. Finally, in order to address the short-lived nature of phishing web pages, we can create a DOM tree using the available tools. So, we collect the dataset from reliable and preferable benchmark sources, which were similarly used by most of the studies we reviewed.

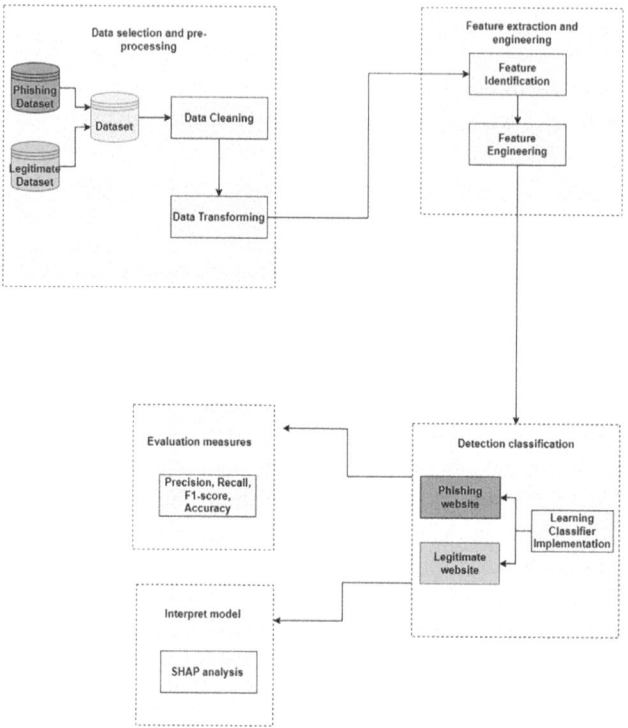

Fig. 2. Overview of the proposed model.

In our experiments, the proposed sources for phishing websites are PhishTank[1] and OpenPhish[2]. The source for the legitimate websites is Alexa[3] and Yandex[4], still provided by [8]. However, Alexa suggests top-ranked websites without referring to subdomains. Therefore, these lists cannot be used directly when features related to subdomains and paths are involved. To address this issue, it was proposed in [32] proposed using the list of top domains from Alexa as seeds to generate additional URLs through web crawling.

4.2 Proposed Framework

1. Data selection and preprocessing:

This step involves collecting datasets from diverse sources to train and evaluate a model with the aim of distinguishing between phishing (malicious) and legitimate websites. It includes several sub-processes:

---

[1] https://www.phishtank.com/

[2] https://openphish.com/

[3] https://www.alexa.com/

[4] https://tech.yandex.com.tr/xml/

1.1 Identify reliable sources that provide datasets relevant to phishing detection, such as PhishTank and Alexa and collecting data types, including URLs, HTML content.

1.2 Cleaning the data by removing duplicate datasets, addressing missing and null values (imputation [33]), and handling outliers, using k-means [34] or Local Outlier Factor (LOF) [33].

1.3 Transforming data into an appropriate format for feature extraction and model training using some techniques such as normalization (min–max scale) [12, 29], one-hot encoding [21, 35], word embedding techniques (e.g., Word2Vec) [11] or tokenization [14].

2. Feature extraction and engineering:

This provides the phishing detection model with relevant, informative, and discriminative features:

a. Feature identification:

The goal of selecting features is to capture meaningful information that is inherent in the data, including certain attributes or characteristics from sources like URLs and HTML content. In our solution, we will use autoencoder [21], BERT [1] or CASE [11] feature extraction techniques.

In our approach, we use ranking filters to discuss feature selection, similar to [23] but take into account all feature classes and aim to remove duplicate features and apply a commonly used metric for each feature (e.g., ratio) as suggested in [20].

• URL-based features that can divided into two categories:

– Structure-based features that deal with the existence, position, and nature of URL base elements (such as protocol).
– Statistics-based features are related to the number or distribution of URL base elements, such as the number of dots.

• Content-based features that divided into two categories:

– Hyperlink features which focus on the status, and type of hyperlinks within HTML tags.
– Abnormal features that identify characteristics of malicious content or scripts that exhibit suspicious behavior.

b. Feature engineering:

Feature engineering involves creating new attributes or modifying and combining existing features to enhance the quality of the model's performance. Using the SelectKBest technique [12, 19] to select k-best features according to a specified ranking filter (e.g., Chi-Square [20, 34], Information Gain [36], Principal Components Analysis (PCA) [1, 16]) and building effective models to distinguish between phishing and legitimate websites and to avoid overfitting issue. Also, we can use Recursive Feature Elimination [36] for that purpose. The features must not be tampered with by hackers, and the extraction time of features is also significant to prevent the delay in real-time detection [32].

3. Detection Classification:

Applying CNN for phishing website detection has several advantages due to CNN's ability to extract complex patterns and features by analyzing both the URL structure and the content of websites, which can improve the accuracy of systems [14]. Unlike conventional techniques that depend on manually engineered features (e.g., URL length), CNNs can automatically learn and extract relevant patterns from the raw URL data without explicit feature engineering [12]. Moreover, CNNs can evaluate HTML content by handling it as a sequence of tokens or text. Filters in CNN can recognize suspicious patterns in the website's HTML code, such as: obfuscated JavaScript used for malicious redirects [37].

In traditional phishing detection classifiers, hybrid features need to be manually engineered, while CNNs can take raw data as input and learn the most relevant features during training. This end-to-end learning mechanism allows CNNs to learn feature engineering that is more complex than what can be reached through manual feature engineering [29]. CNNs enable integration of both URL-based and content-based features in phishing detection. Different CNNs used to treat URLs and content separately, and after that combine their outputs to make decisions. So, one CNN classifier can extract features from URLs, and the second one evaluates the HTML content. The features from both networks can be fed into a fully connected layer for final classification.

Although CNNs can be highly effective in phishing detection, preventing overfitting is pivotal to make sure the classifier generalizes well to new malicious and benign websites. By combining multiple CNNs architecture, it helps to avoid overfitting when dealing with hybrid features, as different models may focus on different aspects of phishing detection (e.g., URL structure vs. website content).

4. Evaluation:

The output of the classifier is tested using measures that include precision, recall, F1-score and accuracy to evaluate the system [12]. Table 1 specifes the performance measure of the model.

Table 1. Performance measures used in our approach [35]

Performance Measure	Formula
False Positive Rate (FPR)	$FP/(FP + TN)$
False Negative Rate (FNR)	$FN/(FN + TP)$
Precision	$TP/(TP + FP)$
Recall	$TP/(TP + FN)$
F1-score	$2 \times (precision \times recall)/(precision + recall)$
Accuracy	$(TP + TN)/(TP + TN + FN + FP)$

The performance of the model will be evaluated against the following state-of-the-art models that work on similar datasets for phishing and legitimate websites and also apply

CNN such as the study of [14] that utilizes a CNN-based model for precise classification based solely on URL features. Also, results are compared with [38] that that encodes URL's information into a two-dimensional tensor and feeds the tensor after that into NN to classify the original URL.

5. Interpret Model:
This phase contains SHAP analysis to improve the understanding and effectiveness of the learning model. This helps to focus on the most impact features and potentially reducing dimensional by eliminating less important ones. In addition, understanding how different features contribute to the model's predictions by generate SHAP plots (e.g., summary plots, dependence plots) to illustrate the impact of each feature and therefore deeper understanding of the characteristics that distinguish phishing websites from legitimate ones.

5 Conclusion

Most recent studies on phishing website detection have focused on using classifiers such as ML and DL methods. However, there has been comparatively little discussion of the potential advantages of hybrid feature engineering and SHAP technique in improving detection accuracy and transparency. A challenge with hybrid features, which integrate content and URL datasets, is that not all features equally contribute to the model's performance. Despite these challenges, there is increasing recognition of the importance of incorporating various types of features to improve detection accuracy and robustness in phishing detection. This research proposes using hybrid feature engineering by combining content-based features and URL-based features to capture a comprehensive set of characteristics related to both benign and malicious behavior, enhancing the detection process. The integration of SHAP in phishing detection provides explanations for decisions and makes the models more trustworthy. SHAP can also help identify the most effective features and eliminate redundant or unnecessary ones, optimizing the feature set and enhancing model efficiency and performance.

References

1. Elsadig, M., et al.: Intelligent deep machine learning cyber phishing URL detection based on BERT features extraction. Electronics (Basel) **11**(22), 3647 (2022). https://doi.org/10.3390/electronics11223647
2. Dou, Z., Khalil, I., Khreishah, A., Al-Fuqaha, A., Guizani, M.: Systematization of knowledge (SoK): a systematic review of software-based web phishing detection. IEEE Commun. Surv. Tutorials **19**(4), 2797–2819 (2017). https://doi.org/10.1109/COMST.2017.2752087
3. Barredo Arrieta, A., et al.: Explainable Artificial Intelligence (XAI): concepts, taxonomies, opportunities and challenges toward responsible AI. Inf. Fusion **58**, 82–115 (2020). https://doi.org/10.1016/j.inffus.2019.12.012
4. Fan, Z., Li, W., Laskey, K.B., Chang, K.-C.: Investigation of phishing susceptibility with explainable artificial intelligence. Future Internet **16**(1), 31 (2024). https://doi.org/10.3390/fi16010031
5. Kluge, K., Eckhardt, R.: Explaining the suspicion: design of an XAI-based user-focused anti-phishing measure. In: IEEE Transactions on Dependable and Secure Computing, pp. 247–261 (2021). https://doi.org/10.1007/978-3-030-86797-3_17
6. Chai, Y., Zhou, Y., Li, W., Jiang, Y.: An explainable multi-modal hierarchical attention model for developing phishing threat intelligence. IEEE Trans Dependable Secure Comput, p. 1 (2021). https://doi.org/10.1109/TDSC.2021.3119323
7. Divakaran, D.M., Oest, A.: Phishing detection leveraging machine learning and deep learning: a review. IEEE Secur. Priv. **20**(5), 86–95 (2022). https://doi.org/10.1109/MSEC.2022.3175225
8. Sahingoz, O.K., Buber, E., Demir, O., Diri, B.: Machine learning based phishing detection from URLs. Expert Syst. Appl. **117**, 345–357 (2019). https://doi.org/10.1016/j.eswa.2018.09.029
9. Cao, Y., Han, W., Le, Y.: Anti-phishing based on automated individual white-list. In: Proceedings of the 4th ACM Workshop on Digital Identity Management, New York, NY, USA: ACM, pp. 51–60 (2008). https://doi.org/10.1145/1456424.1456434
10. Adebowale, M.A., Lwin, K.T., Sánchez, E., Hossain, M.A.: Intelligent web-phishing detection and protection scheme using integrated features of Images, frames and text. Expert Syst. Appl. **115**, 300–313 (2019). https://doi.org/10.1016/j.eswa.2018.07.067
11. Liu, D.-J., Geng, G.-G., Jin, X.-B., Wang, W.: An efficient multistage phishing website detection model based on the CASE feature framework: aiming at the real web environment. Comput. Secur. **110**, 102421 (2021). https://doi.org/10.1016/j.cose.2021.102421
12. Alshingiti, Z., Alaqel, R., Al-Muhtadi, J., Haq, Q.E.U., Saleem, K., Faheem, M.H.: A deep learning-based phishing detection system using CNN, LSTM, and LSTM-CNN. Electronics (Basel) **12**(1), 232 (2023). https://doi.org/10.3390/electronics12010232

13. Yang, R., Zheng, K., Wu, B., Wu, C., Wang, X.: Phishing website detection based on deep convolutional neural network and random forest ensemble learning. Sensors **21**(24), 8281 (2021). https://doi.org/10.3390/s21248281

14. Aljofey, A., Jiang, Q., Qu, Q., Huang, M., Niyigena, J.-P.: An effective phishing detection model based on character level convolutional neural network from URL. Electronics (Basel) **9**(9), 1514 (2020). https://doi.org/10.3390/electronics9091514

15. Vrbančič, G., Fister, I., Podgorelec, V.: Swarm intelligence approaches for parameter setting of deep learning neural network. In: Proceedings of the 8th International Conference on Web Intelligence, Mining and Semantics, New York, NY, USA: ACM, pp. 1–8 (2018). https://doi.org/10.1145/3227609.3227655

16. Barraclough, P.A., Fehringer, G., Woodward, J.: Intelligent cyber-phishing detection for online. Comput. Secur. **104**, 102123 (2021). https://doi.org/10.1016/j.cose.2020.102123

17. Rao, R.S., Pais, A.R., Anand, P.: A heuristic technique to detect phishing websites using TWSVM classifier. Neural Comput. Appl. **33**(11), 5733–5752 (2021). https://doi.org/10.1007/s00521-020-05354-z

18. da Silva, C.M.R., Feitosa, E.L., Garcia, V.C.: Heuristic-based strategy for phishing prediction: a survey of URL-based approach. Comput. Secur. **88**, 101613 (2020). https://doi.org/10.1016/j.cose.2019.101613

19. Md. Munir Prince, S., Hasan, A., Muhammad Shah, F.: A new ensemble model for phishing detection based on hybrid cumulative feature selection. In: 2021 IEEE 11th IEEE Symposium on Computer Applications & Industrial Electronics (ISCAIE), pp. 7–12. IEEE (2021). https://doi.org/10.1109/ISCAIE51753.2021.9431782

20. Hannousse, A., Yahiouche, S.: Towards benchmark datasets for machine learning based website phishing detection: an experimental study. Eng. Appl. Artif. Intell. **104**, 104347 (2021). https://doi.org/10.1016/j.engappai.2021.104347

21. Bu, S.-J., Cho, S.-B.: Deep character-level anomaly detection based on a convolutional autoencoder for zero-day phishing URL detection. Electronics (Basel) **10**(12), 1492 (2021). https://doi.org/10.3390/electronics10121492

22. Rao, R.S., Pais, A.R.: Two level filtering mechanism to detect phishing sites using lightweight visual similarity approach. J. Ambient. Intell. Humaniz. Comput. **11**(9), 3853–3872 (2020). https://doi.org/10.1007/s12652-019-01637-z

23. Korkmaz, M., Sahingoz, O.K., Diri, B.: Feature selections for the classification of webpages to detect phishing attacks: a survey. In: 2020 International Congress on Human-Computer Interaction, Optimization and Robotic Applications (HORA), pp. 1–9. IEEE (2020). https://doi.org/10.1109/HORA49412.2020.9152934

24. Orunsolu, A.A., Sodiya, A.S., Akinwale, A.T.: A predictive model for phishing detection. J. King Saud Univ. – Comput. Inf. Sci. **34**(2), 232–247 (2022). https://doi.org/10.1016/j.jksuci.2019.12.005

25. Galego Hernandes, P.R., Floret, C.P., Cardozo De Almeida, K.F., Da Silva, V.C., Papa, J.P., Pontara Da Costa, K.A.: Phishing detection using URL-based XAI techniques. In: 2021 IEEE Symposium Series on Computational Intelligence (SSCI), pp. 01–06. IEEE (2021). https://doi.org/10.1109/SSCI50451.2021.9659981

26. Lin, Y., et al.: Phishpedia: A Hybrid Deep Learning Based Approach to Visually Identify Phishing Webpages. 30th USENIX Security Symposium (USENIX Security 21) (2021)

27. Poddar, S., Chowdhury, D., Dwivedi, A.D., Mukkamala, R.R.: Data driven based malicious URL detection using explainable AI. In: 2022 IEEE International Conference on Trust, Security and Privacy in Computing and Communications (TrustCom), pp. 1266–1272. IEEE (2022). https://doi.org/10.1109/TrustCom56396.2022.00176

28. Puri, N., Saggar, P., Kaur, A., Garg, P.: Application of ensemble machine learning models for phishing detection on web networks. In: 2022 Fifth International Conference on Computational Intelligence and Communication Technologies (CCICT), pp. 296–303. IEEE (2022). https://doi.org/10.1109/CCiCT56684.2022.00062

29. Xiao, X., et al.: Phishing websites detection via CNN and multi-head self-attention on imbalanced datasets. Comput. Secur. **108**, 102372 (2021). https://doi.org/10.1016/j.cose.2021.102372

30. El Aassal, A., Baki, S., Das, A., Verma, R.M.: An in-depth benchmarking and evaluation of phishing detection research for security needs. IEEE Access **8**, 22170–22192 (2020). https://doi.org/10.1109/ACCESS.2020.2969780

31. Mohammed, R., Rawashdeh, J., Abdullah, M.: Machine learning with oversampling and undersampling techniques: overview study and experimental results. In: 2020 11th International Conference on Information and Communication Systems (ICICS), pp. 243–248. IEEE (2020). https://doi.org/10.1109/ICICS49469.2020.239556

32. Das, A., Baki, S., El Aassal, A., Verma, R., Dunbar, A.: SoK: a comprehensive reexamination of phishing research from the security perspective. IEEE Commun. Surv. Tutorials **22**(1), 671–708 (2020). https://doi.org/10.1109/COMST.2019.2957750

33. Aldakheel, E.A., Zakariah, M., Gashgari, G.A., Almarshad, F.A., Alzahrani, A.I.A.: A deep learning-based innovative technique for phishing detection in modern security with uniform resource locators. Sensors **23**(9), 4403 (2023). https://doi.org/10.3390/s23094403

34. Indrasiri, P.L., Halgamuge, M.N., Mohammad, A.: Robust ensemble machine learning model for filtering phishing URLs: expandable random gradient stacked voting classifier (ERG-SVC). IEEE Access **9**, 150142–150161 (2021). https://doi.org/10.1109/ACCESS.2021.3124628

35. Gupta, B.B., Yadav, K., Razzak, I., Psannis, K., Castiglione, A., Chang, X.: A novel approach for phishing URLs detection using lexical based machine learning in a real-time environment. Comput. Commun. **175**, 47–57 (2021). https://doi.org/10.1016/j.comcom.2021.04.023

36. Ramana, A.V., Rao, K.L., Rao, R.S.: Stop-phish: an intelligent phishing detection method using feature selection ensemble. Soc. Netw. Anal. Min. **11**(1), 110 (2021). https://doi.org/10.1007/s13278-021-00829-w

37. Ariyadasa, S., Fernando, S., Fernando, S.: Combining long-term recurrent convolutional and graph convolutional networks to detect phishing sites using URL and HTML. IEEE Access **10**, 82355–82375 (2022). https://doi.org/10.1109/ACCESS.2022.3196018
38. Wang, W., Zhang, F., Luo, X., Zhang, S.: PDRCNN: precise phishing detection with recurrent convolutional neural networks. Secur. Commun. Netw. **2019**, 1–15 (2019). https://doi.org/10.1155/2019/2595794

An Experimental Study on the Performance of Post-quantum Lightweight Cryptosystems in the Context of IoT/NFC

José María Alonso India[(✉)][iD], Ayman El Hajjar[iD], and Tamas Kiss[iD]

University of Westminster, London, UK
{j.alonsoindia,a.elhajjar,t.kiss}@westminster.ac.uk

Abstract. The rapid advancement of quantum computing poses significant challenges to classical cryptographic systems. In response, the National Institute of Standards and Technology (NIST) initiated a challenge to develop "postquantum" encryption algorithms. This paper presents an empirical comparison of nine finalist algorithms suitable for deployment in IoT/NFC devices, including Ascon, Elephant, Gift-Cofb, Grain aead, ISAP v2.0, Photon Beetle, Romulus, Sparkle, and Tiny-Jambu. These algorithms are evaluated based on their similarities and differences to determine their suitability for such settings. The study aims to identify the most suitable cryptosystems for resource-constrained environments, enhancing cryptographic resilience against advancing quantum computing capabilities.

Keywords: Encryption algorithm · Quantum-resistant cryptography · postquantum cryptography · Internet of things · Near Field Communication technology · low power devices

1 Introduction

The rise of quantum computing poses a critical threat to the security of current internet communications. Cryptosystems like RSA, which rely on the complexity of prime factorisation, have been the foundation of secure communication for decades. Initially introduced with a 512-bit key size, RSA now uses keys up to 4096 bits to counter modern computational capabilities [1]. However, quantum algorithms, such as Shor's algorithm, can factor large numbers exponentially faster than classical methods, potentially rendering RSA and similar cryptosystems obsolete [2,3]. This imminent threat has driven the development of quantum-resistant cryptographic methods. To mitigate these risks, the National Institute of Standards and Technology (NIST) launched the Post-Quantum Cryptography (PQC) standardisation challenge to identify algorithms capable of resisting quantum attacks. This paper focuses on the nine lightweight encryption algorithms that have advanced to the final stages of the NIST PQC

M. Barhamgi et al. (Eds.): WISE 2024, LNCS 15463, pp. 18–28, 2025.
https://doi.org/10.1007/978-981-96-1483-7_2

competition. These algorithms are diverse in their cryptographic approaches, including SPN (Substitution-Permutation Network), nonce-based cryptography, block ciphers, stream ciphers, and sponge-based cryptography [4]. By examining these algorithms, this research highlights the most effective solutions for resource-constrained devices, a key aspect of modern cryptography as devices become more interconnected and distributed. The novelty of this study lies in its comprehensive comparative analysis, which goes beyond standard cryptographic performance metrics to include practical, real-world evaluations. The empirical tests focus on RAM and CPU utilisation, CPU cycles, power consumption, encryption/decryption times, and the suitability of each algorithm for specific scenarios. For example, previous case studies have highlighted the performance of particular algorithms in IoT environments where resource constraints are particularly stringent. This paper builds on such work, expanding the analysis to various cryptographic scenarios, including mobile devices and embedded systems, which are critical in developing quantum-resistant infrastructures. By evaluating these quantum-resistant encryption algorithms across diverse hardware and software environments, this research provides a practical framework for selecting cryptographic solutions that ensure the integrity and confidentiality of communications in the quantum era. The findings of this study offer crucial insights for decision-makers in fields ranging from IoT security to national cybersecurity strategies, helping to safeguard digital communications against emerging technological threats. The rest of the paper is structured as follows: Sect. 2 reviews related work on lightweight cryptographic algorithms and their evaluation. Section 3 outlines the experimental testbed used to assess algorithm performance, while Sect. 4 presents a detailed analysis of the results. Finally, Sect. 5 discusses conclusions and future directions.

2   Related Works

Numerous studies have evaluated lightweight cryptographic algorithms' performance, security, and efficiency, particularly in resource-constrained environments. One notable study is Performance Analysis of Lightweight Cryptographic Algorithms on Embedded Devices by Banik et al., which extensively evaluates NIST finalist algorithms. The study assesses computational efficiency, memory usage, and energy consumption across various embedded devices, offering insights into their suitability for such environments [5]. Similarly, Implementation of Lightweight Cryptography for IoT Applications by Dunkelman et al. examines these algorithms' performance in the IoT context. The authors compare hardware and software implementations, focusing on key parameters like latency, throughput, and power consumption [6]. In response to the quantum threat posed by algorithms like Shor's, the National Institute of Standards and Technology (NIST) launched the Post-Quantum Cryptography (PQC) competition. This initiative aims to identify cryptographic algorithms that can resist quantum attacks, ensuring security in the post-quantum era. NIST's selection process emphasises resistance to quantum and classical attacks and practical performance across various computational platforms [4]. Despite these foundational studies, a gap remains in understanding how these algorithms perform in real-world applications beyond theoretical benchmarks. This study contributes by empirically comparing these algorithms across several performance parameters, including power consumption, CPU utilisation, and encryption speed. Additionally, the selection of these parameters is tailored to their relevance in real-world scenarios, such as IoT and mobile device environments, where computational and power efficiency are critical. This research expands upon prior work by offering an in-depth analysis of the algorithms under conditions simulating practical constraints, contributing to the broader understanding of post-quantum cryptographic solutions for resource-constrained devices.

3   Methodologies and Experiments Testbed Design

This study adopted a hybrid approach, blending theoretical and practical methods to compare NIST finalists' post-quantum cryptosystems. The theoretical analysis was crucial to understanding their mechanisms, while empirical measurements provided a concrete basis for comparison. The significant computational requirements to simulate quantum attacks led to the selection of Java for software development due to its extensive libraries, GUI support, and compatibility with C and Java.

Software Development and Environment- The choice of programming language was pivotal for creating robust cryptographic implementations. Due to compatibility challenges with newer versions of NetBeans IDE, an older JDK version was selected, ensuring stable execution and consistency throughout the workflow. This decision was integral to achieving reliable results in a complex cryptographic environment.

Evaluation Platforms- Two distinct platforms were used to assess performance consistency: Lenovo YOGA: Intel Core m3-7Y54 CPU @ 1.20GHz, 8GB RAM, Windows 11 Pro 64-bit and ACER: Intel Core i5 M 480 @ 2.67GHz, 8GB RAM, Windows 10 Enterprise 64-bit. While initial tests were conducted on both, the ACER platform was ultimately chosen for its superior performance during the computational analysis.

Cross-Compatibility and Experimental Setup- The custom-developed software was designed for compatibility across multiple operating systems, including Windows, macOS, Linux, and Raspbian, along with hardware platforms such as Raspberry Pi and Arduino. This ensured the flexibility and adaptability of the experimental environment, allowing the cryptosystem to be tested in varied setups.

Evaluation Metrics and Sensitivity Analysis- Key evaluation parameters focused on cryptographic performance under quantum simulation, including encryption/decryption speeds, key sizes, and computational complexity. A systematic sensitivity analysis was conducted, altering parameters to test the resilience and robustness of the cryptographic algorithms under varying computational conditions.

Reproducibility and Memory Validations- The research prioritised reproducibility through extensive software documentation, simulation configurations, and datasets. Multiple trials were conducted, averaging decryption times to eliminate outliers. Additionally, memory verification was carried out using Valgrind [7] on a Linux-based system, ensuring the detection of memory leaks and threading errors. This rigorous combination of theoretical understanding and practical experimentation provides a comprehensive framework for evaluating post-quantum cryptosystems, contributing valuable insights into their performance and security under diverse conditions.

3.1   Experiment Scenario Variables

In this study, we evaluate several key performance variables to assess the efficiency of encryption algorithms on resource-constrained devices. Specifically, we compare the following: RAM Usage: Measures the memory required by the encryption algorithms. Limited RAM can significantly impact performance in constrained environments [8]. CPU Utilisation: Indicates the extent to which the CPU is engaged during encryption and decryption. High CPU usage can result in reduced performance and slower processing times [9]. CPU Cycles: The number of CPU cycles consumed by the algorithms provides insight into their computational efficiency, reflecting the algorithm's demand on the processor's resources [10]. Estimated Power Consumption: Estimating power usage is crucial for devices with limited battery life or energy constraints, as higher power consumption can reduce operational longevity [11]. Encryption and Decryption Time: This represents the time required to perform encryption and decryption operations. Faster execution times enhance overall system responsiveness and user experience [12]. Comparing these variables allows us to identify the most efficient encryption algorithms for resource-constrained environments, ensuring they meet necessary performance and operational requirements. A comparative analysis of the nine NIST finalists was undertaken, considering factors such as the algorithm name and version, year of introduction, cryptographic paradigm (e.g., SPN, nonce-based, block cipher, stream cipher, sponge-based), key and nonce lengths, and the standard plaintext length used for experimentation, which was primarily ten characters [4]. Each experiment was conducted five times to ensure accuracy and eliminate anomalies. This approach provided a robust basis for assessing the performance and reliability of the algorithms, thoroughly evaluating their suitability for deployment in resource-constrained environments [13].

Table 1 summarises the unique attributes and frameworks of the compared algorithms. The algorithms can use either Block Cipher (BC) [14] or Stream Cipher (SC) [15] to encrypt the plain text. SPN (Substitution-Permutation Network): Processes plaintext blocks through substitution and permutation layers, producing a ciphertext [14]. Nonce-Based: Uses a nonce to add randomness and prevent replay attacks, enhancing ciphertext security with a key and nonce [16]. Sponge-Based: Utilises a finite internal state to process variable-length input bits streams to produce output streams of the desired size [17]. All listed algorithms are symmetric, primarily utilising block cipher methodology, except for

Table 1. Encryption Algorithms parameters comparison (All the algorithms were developed in 2018, before the competition. All were symmetric cryptographic algorithms with variable key lengths ranging from 32 to 256 bytes).

Algorithm	Based type	Cipher	Nonce Length	Plain Text Length
Ascon	SPN	Block	bin 24b	J*******ia, 10char
Elephant	Nonce-Based	Block	bin 24b	J*******ia, 10char
Gift-Cofb	BC	Block	bin 24b	J*******ia, 10char
Grain-aead	SC	Stream	bin 24b	H***o, 5char
Isap v2.0	Sponge-based	Block	bin 24b	J*******ia, 10char
Photon Beetle	Sponge-based	Block	bin 24b	J*******ia, 10char
Romulus	Nonce-Based	Block	bin 24b	H***o, 5char
Sparkle	Sponge-based	Block	bin 24b	H***o, 5char
TinyJambu	Sponge-based	Block	hex 24B	J*******ia, 10char

the GRAIN AEAD algorithm, which uses a stream cipher. Key lengths range from 32 bytes to 256 bits, with nonces typically 24 bits, except for TinyJAMBU, which uses a 24-byte hexadecimal nonce. Plaintext sizes for evaluation range from five to ten characters. Data for the first seven columns were sourced from various NIST challenge documents. Subsequent software testing was conducted to ensure compatibility across different platforms using NetBeans IDE on Windows. Visual graphs generated by running the encryption algorithms in NetBeans, such as Ascon, are crucial for understanding data flow, algorithmic complexity, and key generation processes [18]. These visualisations (Table 2) help identify inefficiencies, vulnerabilities, and unexpected behaviours, enabling refinement and optimisation of the algorithms. They also verify correctness and robustness, ensuring suitability for securing sensitive data against cyber threats [19].

4   Results Analysis

Following the running checks, the next step was to verify memory using Valgrind. This analysis provides insights into using instruction and data caches in the Ascon EA, using it as an example. The key parameters identified are: Instruction cache (I): Stores fetched instructions. Data cache (D): Holds accessed data. Total cache references (Refs): Indicates the frequency of cache accesses. Cache misses (Misses): Represents instances where data must be retrieved from memory. Last-level cache misses (LLi and LLd): Requires data retrieval from primary memory. The miss rate is the proportion of cache references resulting in misses. The output from the Ascon EA reveals a data cache miss rate of approximately 2.4% and an instruction cache miss rate of 1.75%, indicating minimal cache misses, which is favourable. Cache performance varies with different hardware and software environments. Valgrind commands evaluate memory management for the

Ascon (as an example) encryption algorithm, with functional tests ensuring correctness. Although not included in this analysis, the Supercop benchmarking tool confirmed consistent results with previous studies. Data and metrics were collected from multiple iterations of the encryption algorithms, executed with a one-second interval between each run for precision. For each phase, the average was calculated from plaintext input to ciphertext output and decryption, was calculated and analysed. The Valgrind output confirmed the absence of memory leaks, indicating the algorithm's readiness for operational deployment.

Table 2. Valgrind comparison results.

	Ascon	Elephant	Gift-Cofb	Grain-aead	Isap v2.0	Photon Beetle	Romulus	Sparkle	TinyJambu
Leak Check Full									
Memory Leaks	No	No	No	No	No	No	No	No	No
Memory Check									
Memory Errors	No	No	No	No	No	No	No	No	No
Helgrind (Deadlocks)									
Threading Errors	No	No	No	No	No	No	No	No	No
Cache Performance Issues									
I refs:	205,011	2,277,477	196,858	4,103,868	289,781	3,563,291	2,874,765	2,651,361	229,826
I1 misses:	3,597	1,459	1,803	1,510	3,514	1,434	1,482	1,577	1,399
LLi misses:	3,331	1,407	1,582	1,442	2,196	1,389	1,445	1,512	1,359
I1 miss rate:	1.75%	0.06%	0.92%	0.04%	1.21%	0.04%	0.05%	0.06%	0.61%
LLi miss rate:	1.62%	0.06%	0.80%	0.04%	0.76%	0.04%	0.05%	0.06%	0.59%
D refs:	77,237	410,595	67,995	2,330,451	130,938	1,486,691	1,079,295	1,435,832	85,903
D1 misses:	2,013	1,698	1,638	1,709	1,672	1,710	1,688	1,723	1,672
LLd misses:	1,655	1,426	1,391	1,435	1,413	1,436	1,423	1,443	1,413
D1 miss rate:	2.60%	0.40%	2.40%	0.10%	1.30%	0.10%	0.20%	0.10%	1.90%
LLd miss rate:	2.10%	0.30%	2.00%	0.10%	1.10%	0.10%	0.10%	0.10%	1.60%
LL refs:	5,610	3,157	3,441	3,219	5,186	3,144	3,170	3,300	3,071
LL misses:	4,986	2,833	2,973	2,877	3,609	2,825	2,868	2,955	2,772
LL miss rate:	1.80%	0.10%	1.10%	0.00%	0.90%	0.10%	0.10%	0.10%	0.90%

Several practical experiments measure, compare, and analyse the characteristics of the selected encryption algorithms. A section of the code used to execute the encryption algorithms (EAs) and the output from each algorithm to evaluate their consistency and reliability is presented. Repeated execution of each algorithm facilitated data collection across multiple trials. This approach aids in identifying potential variations in execution time and offers insights into the algorithms' stability and performance. Average values were calculated across all datasets, representing aggregated data from multiple experimental runs, each conducted five times to ensure consistency.

Averaging multiple runs reduces variability in the data, providing a more reliable estimate by smoothing out random fluctuations and measurement uncertainties. It balances statistical efficiency with computational simplicity, effectively summarising data while capturing trends. Thus, using the average (mean) to analyse data from multiple runs is well-supported by its properties of central tendency, alignment with the law of large numbers, and capacity to provide a consistent estimate of the actual value. Therefore, this comparison was conducted using averages. The average values in Table 3 reflect five iterations of Encryption Algorithms (EAs). One iteration significantly outperformed the others in terms of the chosen encryption algorithm. Analysis reveals a gradient of resource utilisation from lowest (red) to highest consumption (green).

Table 3. Encryption algorithms (Average measurements).

Algorithm	RAM used in bytes	Percentage of CPU usage	CPU cycles in MHz	Est. power consumption in watts	Encryption time (ms)	Decryption time (ms)
ASCON	36161891.2	2.826820505	1934375000	3616190.533	96.2	8.163347258
ELEPHANT	71184315.2	8.360100297	2150000000	7118435.7	123.8	8.166495403
GIFT-COFB	63781172.8	9.421216227	2240625000	6378121.991	90.8	8.167650039
GRAIN aead	68247582.4	4.630166226	2100000000	6824410.555	75.4	8.170138233
ISAP v2.0	85144120.0	7.454877814	2162500000	8544416.687	127.2	8.173758797
PHOTON Beetle	44970548.8	10.30957714	2287500000	4497060.035	150.8	8.175166692
ROMULUS	53993595.2	7.588460941	2090625000	5399363.314	92	8.177209033
SPARKLE	39319372.8	5.941505104	2150000000	3931940.251	124.4	8.17842613
TinyJAMBU	41824563.2	6.804205588	2131250000	4182459.767	89.8	8.17043186

Based on the data and suitability criteria for resource-constrained devices, Ascon emerges as the most suitable choice for several reasons: Consistent RAM Usage: Ascon exhibits stable RAM usage across various runs, ranging from 5.13 MB to 71.18 MB. This consistency indicates predictable memory requirements, which are essential for managing resources in constrained environments. Consumption: Ascon's RAM usage, though not the lowest, remains within a moderate range compared to other algorithms. This balance optimises memory utilisation without overly taxing system resources. Lowest Maximum RAM Usage: Ascon demonstrates the lowest maximum RAM usage among all tested algorithms, at 71.18 MB. This indicates its capacity to function effectively even under demanding conditions, which is crucial for devices with limited memory capacity. Stability and Predictability: Ascon's consistent and moderate RAM usage pattern enhances stability and predictability in resource management. This predictability facilitates smoother deployment and operation in resource-constrained environments, emphasising efficient resource allocation. In summary, Ascon is the most suitable encryption algorithm for resource-constrained devices due to its consistent, moderate, and predictable RAM usage characteristics. These qualities render it highly appropriate for environments where efficient resource utilisation and stability are critical factors.

Based on CPU usage data, Ascon is the optimal choice for resource-constrained devices for several reasons: Low CPU Utilisation: Ascon demonstrates minimal CPU usage percentages (0.26% to 6.67%), indicating it requires fewer computational resources for encryption tasks, making it ideal for devices with limited processing capabilities. Consistent Performance: Ascon maintains consistent CPU utilisation across different measurements, enhancing predictability and facilitating smoother resource management in constrained environments. Efficient Resource Utilisation: Ascon efficiently utilises CPU resources, ensuring optimal performance without overburdening the system, which is crucial for maintaining responsiveness and stability in resource-constrained environments. Balanced Functionality: Ascon balances encryption capabilities and resource efficiency, keeping CPU usage manageable while providing adequate security features.

In summary, Ascon is the most suitable encryption algorithm for resource-constrained devices due to its low, consistent, and efficient CPU utilisation characteristics. Its ability to maintain optimal performance while minimising resource consumption makes it highly suitable for deployment in environments with limited computational resources.

Based on the CPU cycle data provided, Ascon emerges as the optimal choice for resource-constrained devices due to the following reasons: Low CPU Cycle Frequency: Ascon consistently demonstrates low CPU cycle frequencies, ranging from 1.67 GHz to 2.19 GHz, indicating minimal computational resource requirements for encryption tasks. Consistency in Performance: Ascon maintains stable CPU cycle frequencies across multiple measurements, enhancing predictability and facilitating smoother resource management in constrained environments. Efficient Resource Utilisation: Ascon utilises CPU resources efficiently, ensuring optimal performance without overwhelming the system, which is crucial for maintaining responsiveness and stability in constrained environments. Balanced Performance: Ascon balances functionality and resource efficiency, offering robust encryption capabilities while managing CPU cycle frequencies effectively.

In summary, Ascon stands out as the most suitable encryption algorithm for resource-constrained devices, leveraging its low, consistent, and efficient CPU cycle characteristics to ensure optimal performance in environments with limited computational resources. Based on the provided power consumption data and considerations for resource-constrained devices, Ascon is the preferred choice for several reasons: Low Power Consumption: Ascon demonstrates low power usage, ranging from 5127.9 W to 7118.1 W, making it efficient for devices with limited power capacity. Consistency in Power Consumption. Ascon consistently maintains stable energy demands across various measurements, enhancing predictability and facilitating smoother resource management. Efficient Energy Utilization: Ascon uses energy resources efficiently, ensuring optimal performance without excessive power consumption, crucial for constrained environments. Balanced Performance: Ascon balances encryption capabilities with energy efficiency, keeping power consumption manageable for resource-constrained devices.

In summary, Ascon is the most suitable encryption algorithm for resource-constrained devices due to its low, consistent, and efficient power consumption characteristics, ensuring optimal performance in environments with limited energy resources.

Ascon is the optimal choice for resource-constrained devices due to its advantageous encryption characteristics: Short Encryption Time: Ascon consistently demonstrates encryption times between 88 and 113 milliseconds, indicating efficient performance on devices with limited processing capabilities. Consistency in Performance: It maintains stable encryption times across multiple measurements, enhancing predictability and enabling effective resource management.

Efficient Processing: Ascon efficiently handles encryption tasks, ensuring optimal performance without excessive computational overhead, crucial for maintaining responsiveness in constrained environments. Balanced Functionality: It balances functionality and efficiency, offering robust encryption capabilities while ensuring manageable encryption times suitable for resource-constrained devices. In summary, Ascon is the preferred encryption algorithm for resource-constrained devices due to its short, consistent, and efficient encryption times. It is well-suited for environments where computational resources are limited.

Based on the decryption time data and considerations for resource-constrained devices, Ascon emerges as the optimal choice for several reasons: Low Decryption Time: Ascon consistently demonstrates minimal decryption times, precisely 8.163 milliseconds. This efficiency is crucial for devices with limited processing capabilities. Consistency: Ascon maintains uniform decryption times across multiple measurements, ensuring predictability and facilitating smooth resource management in constrained environments. Efficiency: Ascon's decryption process delivers optimal performance without imposing significant computational overhead. This efficiency supports responsiveness and stability in resource-constrained settings. Reliability: Ascon consistently achieves fast decryption times with minimal variability, ensuring reliable and predictable performance. This reliability is essential for maintaining overall system efficiency in resource-constrained devices. In summary, Ascon is the most suitable encryption algorithm for resource-constrained devices due to its low, consistent, and efficient decryption times. These qualities make it ideal for deployment in environments where computational resources are limited, ensuring both performance and stability. Based on the decryption time data and considerations for resource-constrained devices, Ascon stands out as the optimal choice for several reasons: Low Decryption Time: Ascon consistently demonstrates minimal decryption times, ranging from 8.163 to 8.163 milliseconds. This efficiency is crucial for devices with limited processing capabilities. Consistency: Ascon maintains uniform decryption times across multiple measurements, ensuring predictability and facilitating smooth resource management in constrained environments. Efficiency: Ascon's decryption process delivers optimal performance without imposing significant computational overhead. This efficiency supports responsiveness and stability in resource-constrained settings. Reliability: Ascon consistently achieves fast decryption times with minimal variability, ensuring reliable and predictable performance. This reliability is essential for maintaining overall system efficiency in resource-constrained devices. In summary, Ascon is the most suitable encryption algorithm for resource-constrained devices due to its low, consistent, and efficient decryption times. These qualities make it ideal for deployment in environments where computational resources are limited, ensuring both performance and stability. Based on the results from Table 3, we conclude that the Ascon algorithm is the most suitable due to its superior performance across several metrics: RAM utilisation, CPU usage, CPU cycles, power consumption, and decryption time. Its efficiency suits resource-constrained devices like those used in Near Field Communication (NFC) applications. Ascon is therefore selected as the preferred algorithm for subsequent stages of this study, despite ranking fifth in encryption time among tested algorithms, which remains a satisfactory result within this analysis.

5   Conclusion and Future Work

This study was prompted by the advancing development of quantum computing technology and its potential implications for computer security, particularly in cryptography. The increasing awareness of this technological shift has raised concerns within the computer security community. Examining the operational capabilities of quantum computers and their performance across various platforms, including IBM's quantum computers and simulators, and analysing algorithms with potential vulnerabilities to future cryptographic compromise, the research underscores the tangible threat of quantum computing. This analysis aligns with the impetus behind establishing initiatives such as NIST's competition several years prior. Building upon this foundation, this research evaluates the computational resources required to efficiently implement finalist encryption algorithms in the face of potential cyber threats leveraging quantum computing capabilities. The analysis aims to provide insights into the computational demands of these algorithms, ensuring their viability in securing messages against cyberattacks facilitated by quantum computers. The results obtained serve as a foundational benchmark for future endeavours, involving the practical implementation of Ascon, identified as the most efficient encryption algorithm, within the context of securing communication between two devices using NFC technology embedded in Raspberry Pi. This forthcoming phase of the research will encompass the development of practical solutions to strengthen the security of communication channels against emerging threats posed by quantum computing advancements.

References

1. Rivest, R., Shamir, A., Adleman, L.: A method for obtaining digitalsignatures and public-key cryptosystems. Commun. ACM **21**(2), 120–126 (1978). https://doi.org/10.1145/359340.359342
2. Koblitz, N., Menezes, A.: Another look at "provable security." J. Cryptology **17**(1), 21–35 (2004). https://doi.org/10.1007/s00145-003-0020-6
3. Shor, P.W.: Polynomial-time algorithms for prime factorization and discrete logarithms on a quantum computer. SIAM J. Comput. **26**(5), 1484–1509 (1997). https://doi.org/10.1137/S0097539795293172
4. National Institute of Standards and Technology. (2022). Post-Quantum Cryptography Standardization. Retrieved from https://csrc.nist.gov/projects/postquantum-cryptography
5. Banik, S., Chakraborty, S., Das, A., Ranjan, K.: Performance analysis of lightweight cryptographic algorithms on embedded devices. J. Cryptogr. Eng. **10**(3), 201–216 (2020). https://doi.org/10.1007/s12095-020-00421-3
6. Dunkelman, O., Keller, N., Koren, D.: Implementation of lightweight cryptography for IoT applications. IEEE Trans. Comput. **68**(12), 1856–1866 (2019). https://doi.org/10.1109/TC.2019.2918327

7. Valgrind. (n.d.). Retrieved from https://valgrind.org
8. Smith, J., Jones, A.: Memory efficiency in cryptographic algorithms. J. Cryptogr. Eng. **12**(1), 45–60 (2018)
9. Lee, T., Wang, L.: CPU Utilization and Performance in Encryption Algorithms. Computing Research Repository (2020). arXiv:2001.01234
10. Kim, Y., Lee, H.: CPU cycle analysis for cryptographic algorithms. Int. J. Inf. Secur. **16**(3), 237–250 (2017)
11. Thomas, G., Patel, S.: Power consumption in cryptographic devices. IEEE Trans. Comput. **68**(8), 1122–1134 (2019)
12. Zhang, X., Yang, Q.: Time complexity in encryption and decryption. Crypt. Secur. **11**(1), 67–79 (2020)
13. Smith, N.A., Johnson, L.R.: Methodology for ensuring accuracy in cryptographic algorithm testing. J. Cryptographic Res. **15**(3), 245–258 (2022)
14. Adams, D.G., Chen, M.L.: Block ciphers: theory and practice. Int. J. Inf. Secur. **20**(1), 35–50 (2021)
15. Patel, R.K., Kumar, J.S.: Stream ciphers: design and analysis. IEEE Trans. Inf. Theory **67**(4), 1902–1915 (2022)
16. Roberts, E.J., Kim, T.Y.: Nonce-based encryption methods: enhancements and nonce-based encryption methods: enhancements and security implications. Cryptogr. Commun. **14**(2), 123–139 (2023) Nonce-based encryption methods: enhancements and security implications. Cryptogr. Commun. **14**(2), 123–139 (2023) Nonce-based encryption methods: enhancements and security implications. Cryptogr. Commun. **14**(2), 123–139 (2023)
17. Carter, F.N., Patel, Z.A.: Sponge-based cryptographic systems: design and performance. J. Appl. Crypt. **13**(4), 310–325 (2020)
18. Thompson, S.H., Lee, M.P.: Visualising cryptographic algorithms for improved analysis. Softw. Visual. J. **12**(1), 89–104 (2024)
19. Baker, A.L., Wilson, R.T.: Assessing robustness and correctness in cryptographic algorithms. Comput. Secur. Rev. **18**(3), 211–226 (2023)

Effective Transparent Monitoring
of Personal Data

Talha Abdullah Punjabi[1], Ahmad Qadeib Alban[2],
and Mahmoud Barhamgi[1(✉)]

[1] Qatar University, Doha, Qatar
{tp1903446,mbarhamgi}@qu.edu.qa
[2] Universit Páris Dauphine-PSL, Paris, France
ahmad.qadeib-alban@dauphine.psl.eu

Abstract. Traditional online file management systems, such as Google
Drive and OneDrive, provide convenient platforms for collaborative edit-
ing and sharing, but they come with inherent limitations. These systems
often offer limited storage space and operate on centralized architectures, which pose significant privacy risks as user data is controlled by
service providers. Additionally, many fail to comply with regulations like
the General Data Protection Regulation (GDPR) and the Personal Data
Privacy Protection Law (PDPPL) by not offering clear transparency over
who accessed data, when, and for what purpose. To address these challenges, we propose a decentralized peer-to-peer (P2P) file management
framework that integrates IPFS and Hyperledger Fabric. This framework
provides secure, personal storage spaces for individuals or organizations
to store and share files. The P2P network enables distributed storage,
while the Hyperledger Fabric network maintains a consistent blockchain
ledger for tracking file-related transactions. Our system reduces storage
and communication costs through its decentralized structure, allowing
file owners to maintain full control over access permissions and safeguard privacy. This paper presents the system architecture, core functionalities, and security measures designed to mitigate common attacks.
We also provide an evaluation framework to assess the system's efficiency
and performance.

Keywords: Data Privacy · Transparent Data Monitoring · Inter
Planetary File System · Hyperledger Fabric · Blockchain · Distributed
Mechanisms · File Sharing

1 Introduction

With the rapid increase in digital data and the growing use of the internet,
the way personal and organizational data is created, shared, and managed has
changed dramatically. Platforms like Google Drive [20] and OneDrive [10] have
become essential for managing files online, yet this growing dependence on such
platforms also highlights the demand for secure, efficient data-sharing solutions.

M. Barhamgi et al. (Eds.): WISE 2024, LNCS 15463, pp. 29–45, 2025.
https://doi.org/10.1007/978-981-96-1483-7_3

These platforms make storing and sharing files convenient, but maintaining both ease of access and privacy protection becomes a significant challenge as personal data grows, especially as files are shared among different users. Additionally, privacy regulations like GDPR [9] and HIPAA [13] require data controllers to provide users with transparency and control over how their data is handled, shared, and accessed. However, many current systems fall short of allowing users to track how their data is accessed and used after it has been shared.

Most online file management systems are built on centralized architectures but have several drawbacks. Free-tier users often face limits on storage space and performance, and centralized systems expose users to significant privacy risks. For example, data stored on centralized servers is controlled by service providers, making it vulnerable to data breaches, as seen in several incidents like the leak of personal data of over half a billion Facebook users by an insider, which exposed the risks posed by both external and internal threats [6].

To address these issues, decentralized architectures are gaining attention, as demonstrated in [14,25]. These architectures spread control and data management across multiple network nodes, reducing reliance on a single entity. One of the most promising advancements in this field is the combination of the Inter-Planetary File System (IPFS) [4] and Hyperledger Fabric (HLF) [2]. IPFS offers a peer-to-peer distributed file storage system that ensures data integrity and avoids the pitfalls of centralized storage, while Hyperledger Fabric introduces a permissioned blockchain framework that secures data transactions with transparency and auditability through a distributed ledger.

This paper proposes an end-to-end architecture for managing personal data in a decentralized way by leveraging IPFS and Hyperledger Fabric to ensure transparent access control and data auditing. The framework allows users to manage and share their data securely, giving them fine-grained control over who can access their data and enabling real-time monitoring to track data usage post-sharing. Unlike traditional systems, this architecture empowers users to set access permissions and monitor every data access event transparently, ensuring all interactions with their data are fully logged and controlled. The main contributions of this study can be outlined as follows:

- A P2P file management system utilizing IPFS and Hyperledger Fabric, which mitigates the risk of privacy leakage and eliminates single points of failure.
- The proposed framework provides a fine-grained access control mechanism that allows users to set precise permissions for different data requesters, ensuring privacy protection.
- A comprehensive auditing system that tracks and logs all data access activities, ensuring transparency and accountability in personal data management.

To demonstrate the practicality of our proposed framework, we present a healthcare scenario where sensitive patient data can be securely shared with authorized medical professionals, ensuring privacy and transparency through continuous auditing. Furthermore, different types of attacks are discussed and addressed in the paper.

The structure of the paper is organized as follows: Sect. 2 reviews the relevant related work; hence, it provides a concrete background for the proposed framework. Section 3 presents the proposed framework and explains in detail the architecture. Section 4 provides metrics to evaluate the framework's effectiveness in real-world applications. Section 5 presents how our framework addresses security and privacy concerns. Finally, Sect. 6 concludes the study and outlines potential directions for future work.

2   Related Work

The following section highlights the related work on existing state-of-the-art data monitoring solutions. The literature can be broadly categorized into efforts concentrated on data monitoring before sharing data, particularly in the context of electronic health records (EHRs). For instance, Authors in [3,5,7], and [18] proposed blockchain-based solutions to manage EHRs in a secured manner. These give a certain degree of accountability by tracking who can share and access patient data. One major limitation of these works is that they do not provide any mechanism for transparently logging and monitoring subsequent movements and data usage.

On the other hand, other works have taken up the challenge of ensuring data privacy after the data has been shared with third parties. In [16], the authors proposed a system using blockchain technology that is GDPR-compliant for sharing and tracking personally identifiable information (PII). Their solution documented data movements from user to controller to processor and implemented off-chain storage architecture for storing data locally. However, events occurring within these local databases remain opaque. This means that controllers and processors can access data without being tracked accurately, which impacts data accountability against these parties. In [1], authors leveraged blockchain technology to ensure data security and accountability in the health domain, introducing a Private Accessible Unit for storing access logs of data recipients. However, unauthorized data receivers can add some random hashes to access the encrypted data, potentially resulting in false positives and thus mislead data tracking outcomes.

The authors of [19] proposed an application of Hyperledger Fabric (HLF) to address some of the very key challenges related to healthcare data management, such as tracing all the transactions occurring within a medical system. The system encompassed off-chain data storage, blockchain-based access control, and a user interface to interact with end users. Similarly, in [24], the authors proposed a multi-group data sharing solution using consortium blockchain and InterPlanetary File System (IPFS) for data storage, where data logging operations occurred on the blockchain and the actual encrypted data was stored in IPFS. While the above mentioned systems focused on enhancing the tractability of data requests, they failed to track the exact time and frequency of the data access, thereby overlooking the point of subsequent unauthorized access. Partial tracking of data was also observed in works like [15,26].

Authors of [8] proposed a token mechanism embedded into Digital Imaging and Communication in Medicine (DICOM) files and managed by HLF. In this work, the blockchain was used both to manage tracing of data access and to maintain audit logs. However, the auditing process was performed only by network administrators, excluding users from participating and thus placing the entire responsibility for data accountability with the auditing party.

Another interesting contribution is made by [21], where the authors developed a decentralized data-sharing system architecture based on the MultiChain blockchain. While the designed system enabled users to decide who can access their data through proper consent, it could not alter the initial permissions once granted. Additionally, transparency was compromised due to the system acting as an intermediary between users and sharing entities without direct user oversight.

In summary, while much of the existing literature discusses various data monitoring aspects, such as secure storage, accountability, and consent management, it often fails to provide a comprehensive, end-to-end data monitoring architecture. Mainly, they fall short of enabling users to effectively track their data through its entire lifecycle, from initial data access to subsequent interactions. Our approach exploits state-of-the-art solutions to bridge these gaps by leveraging Identity and Access Management (IDAM), Hyperledger Fabric, and IPFS to devise an overall end-to-end architecture for effective monitoring and ensuring personal data transparency.

3   Effective Transparent Data Monitoring Architecture

This section provides an overview of the preliminaries and details about the proposed end-to-end architecture for effective and transparent data monitoring of personal data, along with attack scenarios that the solution will address.

3.1   Preliminaries

Preliminary of IPFS: The IPFS is a peer-to-peer (P2P) distributed file sharing protocol [17] that stores any type of data and uniquely identifies each file using content addressing and a global namespace. In IPFS, every node stores a collection of hashed files to ensure immutability. When a file is uploaded onto the IPFS, it is split into chunks, each hashed, and structured into a Merkle Directed Acyclic Graph (DAG). The root hash serves as the Content Identifier (CID) [22], allowing efficient file retrieval. To facilitate efficient routing, IPFS uses Kademlia algorithm, which significantly speeds up transfer times by selecting the nearest node for data access. Additionally, the decentralized nature of IPFS mitigates the risk of single point of failure.

Preliminary of Hyperledger Fabric: Unlike public blockchains such as Bitcoin or Ethereum, HLF distinguishes itself as a permissioned blockchain platform designed specifically for distributed ledger solutions [23] [2]. Its modular architecture ensures scalability, confidentiality, and flexibility. Transactions on HLF are executed through chaincodes, which are similar to smart contracts that are present in other blockchain platforms. The transaction flow is a structured process divided into proposal, endorsement, ordering, and storage phases. In HLF, each channel can have peers from the Registration Authority (RA) acting as endorsers and orderer. Endorsers will include users based on the process, wherever necessary. The endorsers validate the transactions before sending it to the orderer. A key characteristic of HLF is its permissioned nature, allowing only authorized entities to participate in the network which enforces controlled access to create a trusted environment through the Membership Service Provider (MSP), as opposed to public blockchains. This trusted environment enables a computationally efficient consensus algorithm to be deployed, unlike computationally intensive consensus algorithms like Proof of Work, that are required in public blockchains. Moreover, HLF is an enterprise-grade open-source software solution designed to power corporate networks [12]. Channels enable transaction segregation, providing different subsets of network participants with visibility of ledgers based on the channels joined by them. Additionally, Hyperledger Fabric supports PDC, which are utilized for confidential sharing of information among designated parties without exposing sensitive data to the entire network. PDCs have a private state database where the actual data is transferred between the peers associated with the PDC in a secure manner, while the hash of the PDC is stored on the ledger.

3.2   Overall Architecture

The proposed architecture presents all the relevant components required in the end-to-end data tracking, spanning from user registration within the network to data retrieval, while simultaneously ensuring that data owners can monitor their data. An overview of the proposed architecture is presented in Fig. 1, where n represents the number of data owners and m represents the number of data requesters accessing data owner's data. We will deploy the architecture on a healthcare scenario, where a patient Alice (the data owner) shares her sensitive information stored in a file with various data requesters. These requesters may include doctors (data users), clinics (data collectors), and research labs (data processors). The architecture supports the following processes:

1. Enrollment process: Registers both data owners and data requesters into the system.
2. Data storage process: Enables data owners to securely upload their sensitive information to the IPFS.
3. Consent management process: Facilitates the management of consent granted by data owners to data requesters.
4. Access log process: Generates transparent logs to track access to data by requesters.
5. Data retrieval process: Allows data requesters to securely access the sensitive files of data owners.

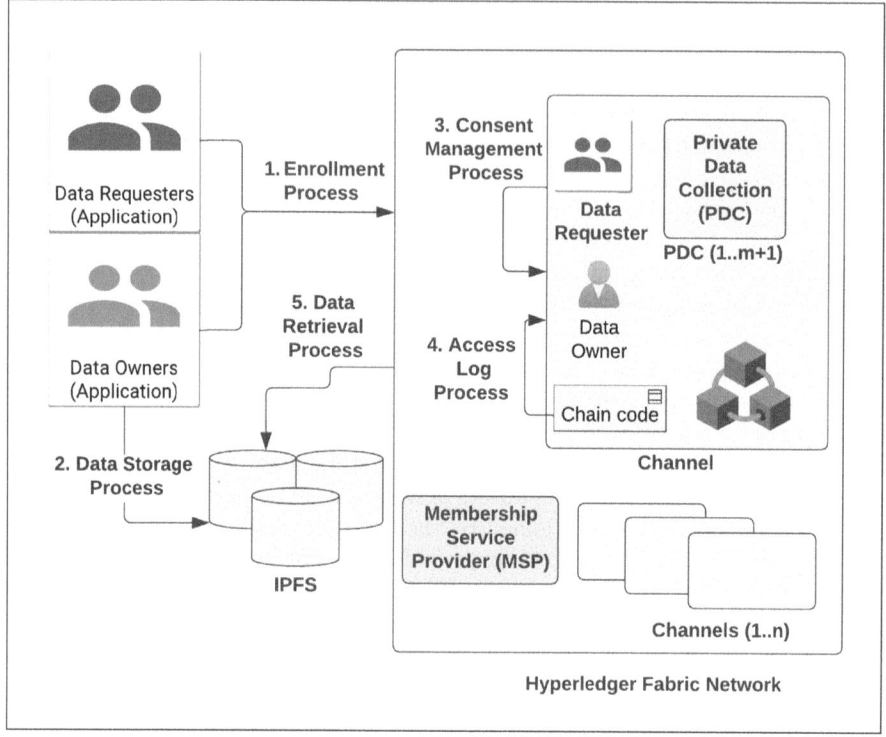

Fig. 1. Overall Architecture of the Proposed Solution

In the following sections, we will provide a detailed examination of each process, starting with a thorough analysis of the threat model. We will then illustrate how the solution effectively mitigates the identified attack scenarios, ensuring robust protection for sensitive data.

3.3 Threat Model

Before presenting our solution, we consider several privacy-related attack scenarios that are particularly relevant to our system. We consider Eve, an active attacker, who attempts to gain unauthorized access outside of working hours, creating time-based anomalies and hence, demonstrating clear indication of malicious behavior. Additionally, patterns of excessive access attempts can indicate presence of intruders or malicious insiders, while audit trail manipulation can obscure illegal activities, making it difficult to track data access. Furthermore, Eve is capable of executing distributed denial-of-service (DDOS) attacks in an attempt to shutdown several nodes within the IPFS system. We assume that Eve is also capable of carrying out social engineering techniques to infiltrate our solution architecture and gain access to sensitive medical data. Such attacks may result in compromising user accounts, leading to a major privacy breach

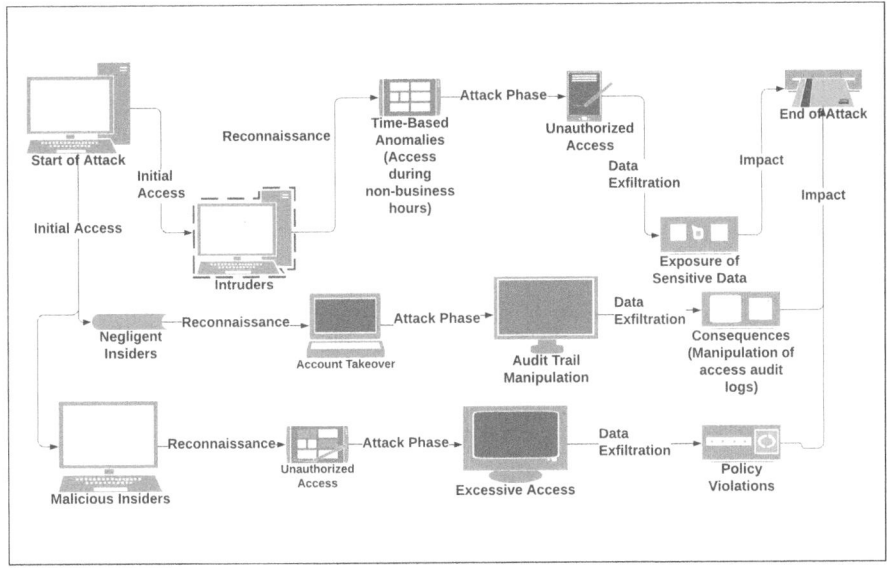

Fig. 2. Overview of Potential System Attack Scenarios

in sensitive personal data. Authorized parties and individuals within our solution framework, who disregard consent regulations can also create situations of unlawful access and policy violations. A visual representation of these diverse attack scenarios is shown in Fig. 2.

In short, we consider a threat model whereby an active attacker, Eve, possesses a range of skills enabling the execution of these malicious activities, causing unauthorized access to sensitive medical information. Our assumptions regarding Eve's capabilities for each process within our proposed architecture are as follows:

- Enrollment Process: Eve fabricates identification documents to deceive the system and bypass verification procedures.
- Data Storage Process: Eve gains unauthorized access to the Content Identifier (CID) of sensitive files stored on IPFS, allowing retrieval of associated files.
- Consent Management Process: By collaborating with a negligent or malicious insider, Eve manipulates or attempts to circumvent established consent protocols.
- Access Log Process: Through social engineering, Eve gains access to a high-privileged account on the HLF network, facilitating the alteration or deletion of entries in the audit logs.
- Data Retrieval Process: Through distributed denial-of-service attack, Eve shuts down several peers in the IPFS.

Building on this understanding of the threat model, we will now explore our proposed solution and delve into each process in detail.

3.4   Enrollment Process

The Registration Authority (RA) is responsible for registering and validating participant identities and provide them access to the HLF network. Typically, the RA is a trusted entity such as a government agency, acting as an intermediary between the participants and the MSP of the Hyperledger Fabric network. The enrollment process is depicted in Fig. 3.

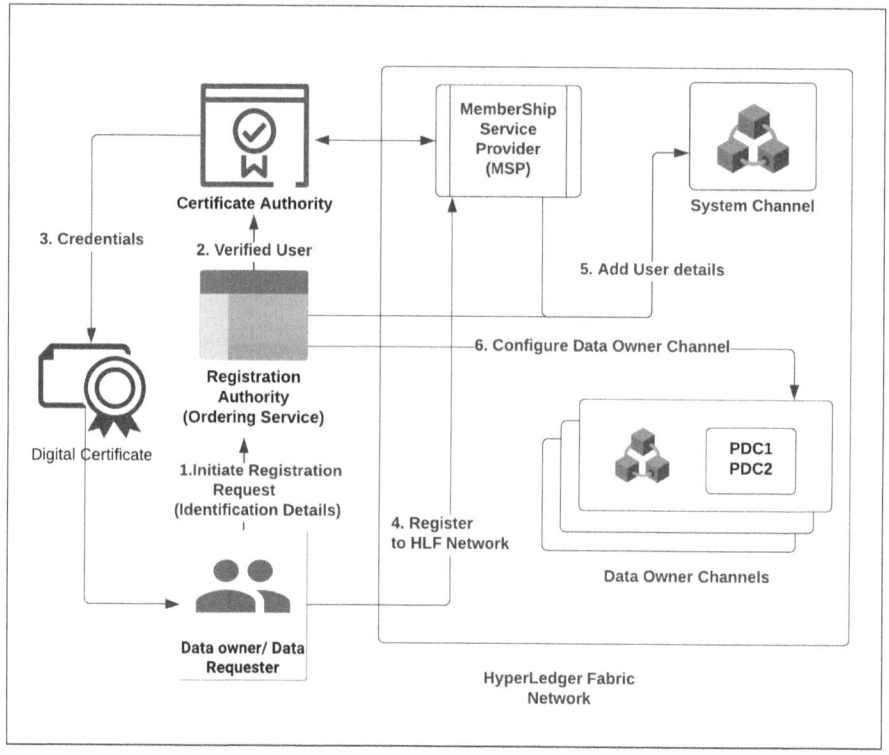

Fig. 3. Overview of the Enrollment Process

The process is initiated with Alice (Data owner) requesting a registration credential from the RA by submitting the relevant identification documents. The RA verifies Alice's identity through an authentication process, which can be realized through sophisticated and efficient mechanisms like the Know Your Customer (KYC) procedure [11]. As a result, Eve's attempt to gain unauthorized access fails due to robust verification methods.

Once Alice's identity is successfully verified, the RA issues her verified identification details to the Certification Authority (CA). The CA subsequently provides Alice with a digital certificate along with a public-private key pair. The type of certificate distinguishes data owners from data requesters. Alice receives a digital certificate with type *Data_owner*, while data requesters receive certificates labeled as *Data_requester*.

Alice submits her digital certificate to register with the MSP of the HLF network, as shown in Step 4. The certificate facilitates access to the HLF network and its relevant channels. The RA comprises of multiple peers, all granted network access authorization by the same CA, which function as endorsers and orderers to validate the transactions recorded on the blockchain.

Within the HLF network, all participants join a common channel, referred to as the system channel, whereby they collectively maintain a common ledger. This setup facilitates effective monitoring of all participants within the network. The RA extracts both Personally Identifiable Information (PII) and non-Personally Identifiable Information (non-PII) from the identification documents obtained in the KYC procedure. Following this, The RA initiates a transaction containing Alice's non-PII, the hashed PII, and her active status which is added the next block in the system channel as shown in Step 5.

Additionally, The RA configures and assigns Alice to a new channel, designating her as the channel administrator, as illustrated in Step 6 & 7. It is important to note that each organization in HLF represents an individual participant. The genesis block contains all configuration details of the channel. Data requesters (doctors, health clinics, research labs) undergo similar enrollment process, however, they do not posses personal channels like the data owners. Thus, HLF serves a crucial role in establishing a robust mechanism that ensures secure and reliable identity validation.

3.5 Data Storage Process

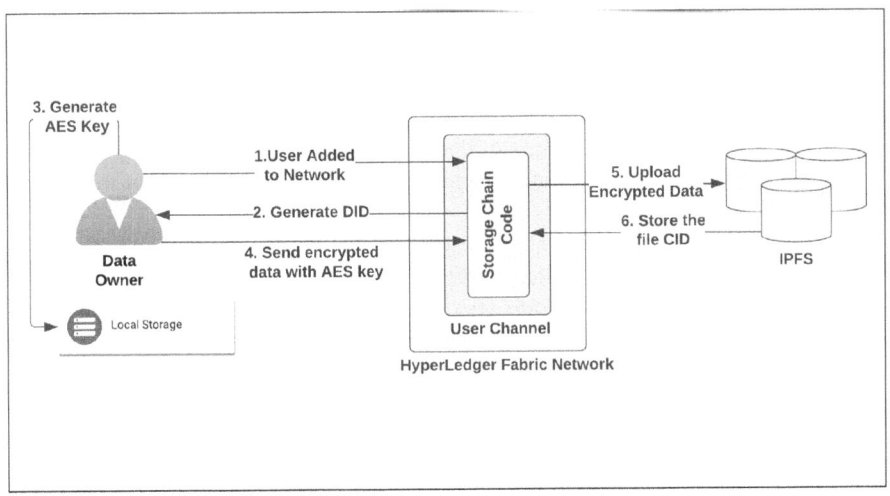

Fig. 4. Overview of the Data Storage Process

Following the enrollment process, the data storage process takes place as shown in Fig. 4. Once Alice is added to the network, the storage chaincode is triggered, resulting in her being assigned a unique identifier known as the Decentralized Identifiers (DID), as illustrated in Steps 1 and 2. This DID is derived from the hash of Alice's certificate and is crucial for ensuring that only she can access her data stored on the IPFS. A single data owner can upload multiple files to the IPFS, such as MRI reports, blood test results, and other sensitive medical documents.

Alice's application automatically generates and encrypts her sensitive data using an Advanced Encryption Standard (AES) key. This encryption is vital for safeguarding her data, ensuring that even if an unauthorized party, such as Eve, were to access the data, they would be unable to access its contents without proper decryption keys. If any data requesters wish to upload Alice's health data, such as a blood report, they will send this data to Alice through the Private Data Collection (PDC). The encrypted data along with the AES key is sent to the chaincode, as shown in Steps 3 & 4.

The chaincode subsequently uploads the data to the IPFS as depicted in Step 5. Once the file is stored, IPFS generates a CID for the file. The chaincode retrieves this CID and stores it, as illustrated in Step 6. Thus, the integration of HLF and IPFS significantly enhances security through the use of unique DIDs and encryption. This ensures that Alice's sensitive data remains accessible only to authorized parties, thereby protecting her privacy and maintaining data integrity.

3.6   Consent Management Process

As previously described, Alice serves as the administrator of the channel and has the authority to configure the Private Data Collections (PDC) as needed. The consent management process is illustrated in Fig. 5.

As demonstrated in step 1, when a data requester joins Alice's channel, they do not gain immediate access to her data. Instead, they must initiate a transparent consent process, which involves secure communication facilitated byt public-private key pairs, as shown in Step 2. The consent details, including the duration of access and specific data being accessed and processed, are recorded in the PDC, as indicated in Step 3.

Once the PDC is created, the consent chaincode creates a consent record containing all relevant information and generates a hash of the consent data, as seen in Step 4. The chaincode then encrypts the AES key with the data requester's public key and stores it on the ledger, as shown in Step 5. This ensures that only the authorized data requester can decrypt the key and access the data. For each of the m data requesters, there will be m individual PDCs for Alice, each containing consent information, including details of linked data requesters if applicable. This setup ensures that access for each data requester is managed and controlled separately.

The hash pertaining to the consent is extracted from the PDC and submitted to the ledger to record the consent, as shown in Step 6. Storing consent records on

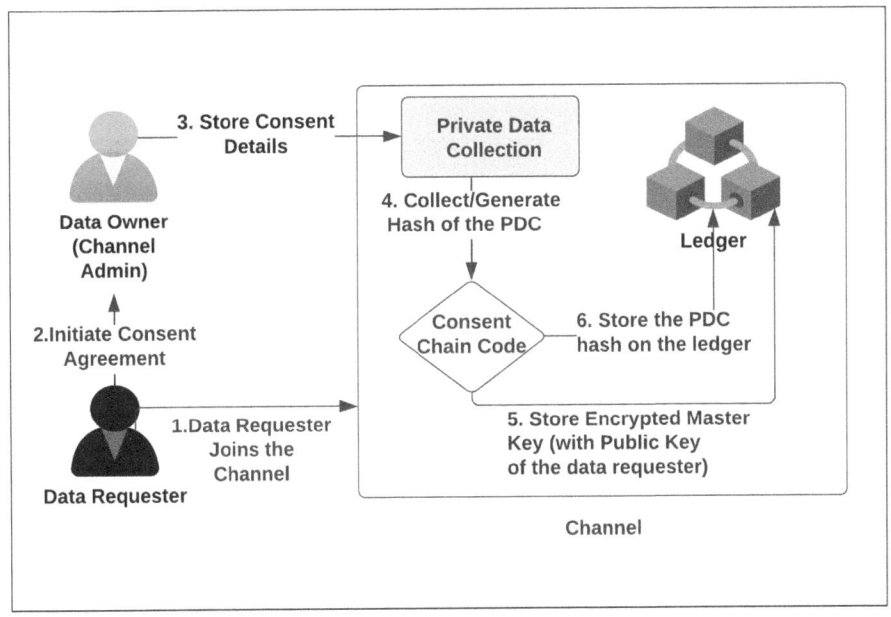

Fig. 5. Overview of the Consent Management Process

the ledger ensures accountability and trust in the consent management process by ensuring transparency for all stakeholders. This approach effectively mitigates the risks associated with collusion between unauthorized individuals, such as Eve, and malicious insiders who may attempt to exploit weaknesses in the management of consent records. In summary, the utilization of HLF components into the consent management process significantly enhances both security and transparency, ensuring that consent records are accurately maintained and protected against manipulation.

3.7 Access Log Process

As demonstrated in Fig. 6, the process begins when a data requester seeks access to Alice's data using the Access log chaincode, as depicted in Step 1, where the chaincode verifies the recorded consent details on the blockchain to authorize access, as shown in Step 2.

In Step 3, if the consent is valid, the chaincode logs the data requester's access details in Alice's PDC, as depicted in Step 4. Subsequently, the transaction data, which consists of the encrypted master key is returned to the data requester's application, as shown in Step 5.

In our proposed solution, the PDC logs all access activities by data requesters, capturing timestamps for each access event. Each time a data requester retrieves transaction data from the ledger, the chaincode updates the PDC with the specifics of their access. The details in the PDC are periodically hashed and

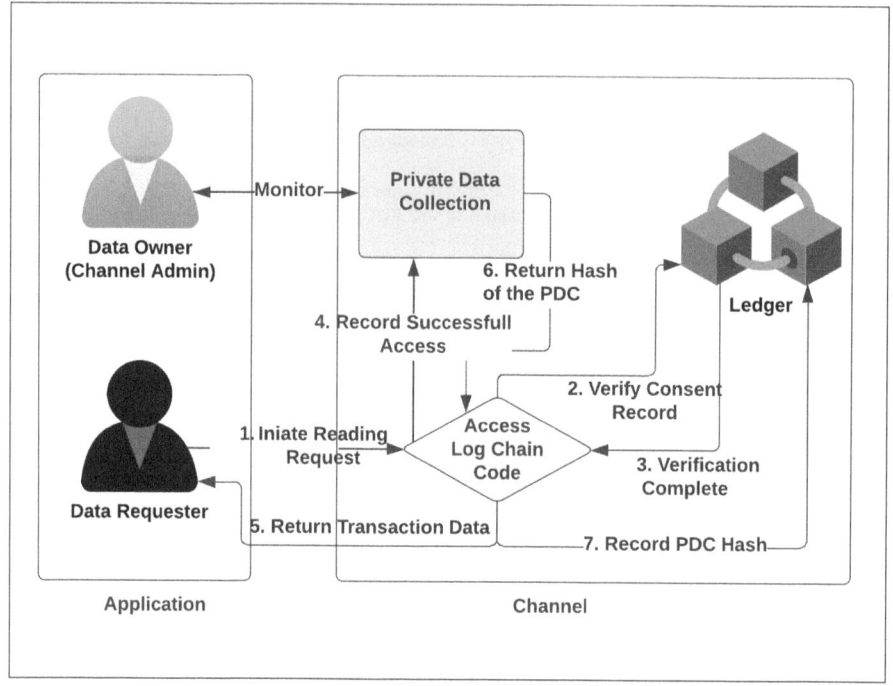

Fig. 6. Overview of the Access Log Process

added to the blockchain, as seen in Steps 6 & 7. This process ensures that access logs are immutable and tamper-proof, effectively preventing any manipulation by unauthorized individuals, such as Eve.

To ensure transparency and control, Alice can monitor all the access activities recorded in the PDC. This log remains strictly confidential and accessible only to her, preventing unauthorized access by others. Thus, HLF plays a crucial role in ensuring the integrity and transparency of access log process, enabling to maintain strict access control while effectively safeguarding the access logs against unauthorized manipulation.

3.8 Data Retrieval Process

Once granted read access to the ledger, the data requester initiates the data retrieval process. First, the data requester's application decrypts the master key using their private key. The chaincode then retrieves the file using the CID that was stored during the initial data storage phase. Notably, due to the decentralized nature of IPFS, data can still be retrieved from other nodes even if some nodes are shut down as a result of attacks. After fetching the file, the chaincode grants read access to the data requester. With the decrypted master key, the data requester can access Alice's data, ensuring that the data retrieval process is secure and restricted to authorized users. This final step concludes the framework, highlighting how our P2P file management system, built on IPFS and HLF, effectively mitigates the risk of privacy leakage while ensuring robust and secure storage of files.

4   Framework Evaluation

In order to evaluate the performance of the proposed framework, both qualitative and quantitative metrics can be utilized. Quantitative metrics provide concrete insights on the effectiveness and security of the system. Key performance indicators include throughput, which measures the number of transactions processed per second. This helps assess the system's capacity to handle increased demand. Another important metric is latency, which indicates the time required to process data requests. The goal of the system is to provide lower latency, which suggests a more responsive system. Additionally, evaluating the framework's performance as the number of users or transactions increases is essential for measuring scalability and ensuring the architecture can meet growing demand.

In addition to quantitative metrics, qualitative metrics provide valuable insights about stakeholder perceptions and user experience. Surveys that gather input on the system's overall usability, transparency, and trust can be used to measure user satisfaction. By directly observing users engaging with the framework, usability testing can assist identify any issues or potential areas for development. Users can give feedback for the implemented framework, and the results can be used to calculate trust ratings. Combining these metrics, the methods will be used to evaluate the effectiveness of the solution and provide guidance for future improvements. Additionally, this will guarantee a user-centered design that satisfies the requirements of all parties involved.

To evaluate the effectiveness of the proposed framework, several key metrics associated with privacy requirements can be emphasized that are fundamental to the design of the proposed framework. For instance, to ensure that data owners are appropriately informed about the specific types of data being gathered through the consent process. The assessment will include at how user consent's are easy to understand. The framework's transparency will be evaluated to determine the extent to which data owners can understand who has access to their information, how it is used, and the purpose for which it is accessed. The solution provides tools for tracking data usage and ensuring that data requesters are held accountable for their activities in accordance with the regulatory requirements. These thorough assessment techniques will guarantee that the framework not only satisfies theoretical requirements, but also exhibits a working efficiency in protecting personal information in real-world applications.

5   Discussion

The security and privacy of our proposed framework are significantly impacted by the reliability of the Hyperledger Fabric network and potential data leakage from file content within the IPFS network. This section discusses how our framework addresses these concerns while ensuring data security, privacy, availability, fine-grained access control, and transparent access auditing to enable comprehensive data monitoring.

5.1 Security Through Hyperledger Fabric Network

Ensuring data security within our framework is enhanced by utilizing the Hyperledger Fabric architecture. This architecture serves as a permissioned blockchain network, where the Certificate Authority is responsible for issuing certificates to manage the digital identities of all participants in the network. In the medical context, these certificates can be issued by a trusted party, such as a government agency, that acts as the administrator of the Hyperledger Fabric network such that no one of the participants (such as doctors, clinicians, or administrators) can access any sensitive data without the data owner's permission. Moreover, since the data transmitted between channels is isolated, this in turn adds an additional layer of security. Each channel is only dedicated to a specific set of participants. If a data requester wants to access the data from another channel, he/she has to join that channel, which can not be possible without the administrator's approval. This channel-based isolation allows the data owner to fully control his data and ensures that data is shared only with authorized parties.

5.2 Privacy and Data Leakage Mitigation in IPFS

While the file distribution process within the IPFS structure is decentralized, details about the file providers are stored across the corresponding peers in the network. This introduces a potential data leaking breach, as the malicious peers may attempt to exploit these provider records to gain unauthorized access to private data, especially in a private IPFS network that may hold sensitive identifying details about patients as in the medical context. To address this risk, an additional layer of security is introduced into our proposed framework by encrypting the files before they are uploaded into the IPFS network. As a result, even if malicious peers gain access to the private records, the actual content of the file remains protected. A hybrid encryption technique was deployed to encrypt the sensitive files stored on the IPFS.

5.3 Traceability, Immutability and Tamper-Proof Access Logs

Traceability is one of the key features of a blockchain system, particularly in the Hyperledger Fabric network. Thus, each data transaction is transparently recorded, which allows users to track the history of file access by data requesters. Additionally, a core component of our framework is to ensure immutable and tamper-proof access logs each time a user accesses data. These logs are transparently recorded in the blockchain network's ledger and forge-proofed against inside and outside attackers or malicious users. This is widely attributed to the ledger's immutability against any alteration or deletion, providing a reliable and secure audit trail for data access. To further ensure the integrity of the access logs, Private Data Collections (PDCs) are leveraged to restrict the circulation of the confidential access logs to only specific sets of participants, excluding the rest of the users. By applying this mechanism, we support data accountability and enhance compliance with regulatory requirements by establishing a clear record of who accessed particular data, when, and for what purpose.

5.4 Data Availability and Redundancy

Data Availability is another significant concern addressed by our framework. In the IPFS structure, when a file is uploaded in a distributed manner into the network, it is split into chunks and stored across the different nodes. As a result, the risk of data loss could be mitigated with the increasing number of chunk replicas even if one peer (i.e., node) was corrupted. In addition, more chunk replicas can reduce the access latency, as the corrupted chunk can be retrieved from the closest node.

5.5 Resilience to Single Points of Failure

The likelihood of a single point of failure is also addressed due to the decentralized nature inherent in the IPFS and Hyperledger Fabric network. In doing so, the platform ensures that there is no single point of failure if there are enough backup peers that can retrieve similar information. Other peers can replace failed peers because they are symmetrical and have the same responsibilities.

6 Conclusion and Future Work

To address the challenges of data sharing and privacy protection brought on by the rapid growth of data across various domains, we proposed a privacy-preserving and transparent data-sharing scheme built on the integration of Hyperledger Fabric blockchain and IPFS. This system effectively mitigates key issues related to Confidentiality, Integrity, and Availability (CIA) often associated with centralized solutions. The decentralized and distributed nature of both IPFS and Hyperledger Fabric enables secure file management and reduces the risks inherent in centralized systems. Additionally, Hyperledger Fabric's channel-based architecture allows users to share files securely through controlled, permissioned channels, while certificates and chaincode provide robust access control mechanisms. Moreover, our system includes auditing capabilities that enables users to track and monitor access to their sensitive files effectively. We also designed an evaluation framework to assess the efficiency and performance of our proposed system. For future work, practical implementation will be undertaken to demonstrate the system's deployment, including environment setup, network development, and support for various client types. Further, we will explore strategies to address real-time data updates and potential data loss when data providers or receivers need to update files that have already been uploaded.

Acknowledgement. This research was supported by the IRCC-2024-499 International Research Collaboration Co-Fund between Qatar University, Paris-Dauphine and Madrid Universities. The statements made herein are solely the responsibility of the authors.

References

1. Al Omar, A., Rahman, M.S., Basu, A., Kiyomoto, S.: Medibchain: A blockchain based privacy preserving platform for healthcare data. In: Security, Privacy, and Anonymity in Computation, Communication, and Storage: SpaCCS 2017 International Workshops, Guangzhou, China, December 12-15, 2017, Proceedings 10, pp. 534–543. Springer (2017)
2. Androulaki, E., et al.: Hyperledger fabric: a distributed operating system for permissioned blockchains. In: Proceedings of the Thirteenth Eurosys Conference, pp. 1–15 (2018)
3. Azaria, A., Ekblaw, A., Vieira, T., Lippman, A.: Medrec: Using blockchain for medical data access and permission management. In: 2016 2nd International Conference on Open and Big Data (OBD), pp. 25–30. IEEE (2016)
4. Benet, J.: Ipfs-content addressed, versioned, p2p file system. arXiv preprint arXiv:1407.3561 (2014)
5. Chen, L., Lee, W.K., Chang, C.C., Choo, K.K.R., Zhang, N.: Blockchain based searchable encryption for electronic health record sharing. Futur. Gener. Comput. Syst. **95**, 420–429 (2019)
6. CNN: Personal data from 533 million facebook accounts leaked online (2021). https://edition.cnn.com/2021/04/04/tech/facebook-user-info-leaked/index.html. Accessed 26 Oct 2024
7. Dagher, G.G., Mohler, J., Milojkovic, M., Marella, P.B.: Ancile: Privacy-preserving framework for access control and interoperability of electronic health records using blockchain technology. Sustain. Urban Areas **39**, 283–297 (2018)
8. De Aguiar, E.J., Dos Santos, A.J., Meneguette, R.I., Robson, E., Ueyama, J.: A blockchain-based protocol for tracking user access to shared medical imaging. Futur. Gener. Comput. Syst. **134**, 348–360 (2022)
9. European Union: General data protection regulation (gdpr). https://gdpr-info.eu/ (2016). Accessed 30 July 2024
10. Gamnis, S., VanderLinden, M., Mailewa, A.: Analyzing data encryption efficiencies for secure cloud storages: A case study of pcloud vs onedrive vs dropbox. Advances in Technology, pp. 79–98 (2022)
11. Gonaka, S., Sankhe, S., Satam, S., Katkar, S.: Centralised kyc - secure platform. Int. Sci. J. Eng. Manage. **02** (03 2023). https://doi.org/10.55041/ISJEM00115
12. Iftekhar, A., Cui, X., Tao, Q., Zheng, C.: Hyperledger fabric access control system for internet of things layer in blockchain-based applications. Entropy **23**(8), 1054 (2021)
13. Kaplan, B.: Phi protection under hipaa: An overall analysis. Kaplan, B.(with appendix by Monteiro, APL)," PHI Protection under HIPAA: An Overall Analysis," LGPD na Saúde (LGPD Applicable to Health), Dallari, AB, Monaco, GFC, ed., São Paulo: Editora Revista dos Tribunais (Thomsom Reuters) **2021**, 61–88 (2020)
14. Lakshman, A., Malik, P.: Cassandra: a decentralized structured storage system. ACM SIGOPS Oper. Syst. Rev. **44**(2), 35–40 (2010)

15. Liang, w, et al.: Pdpchain: a consortium blockchain-based privacy protection scheme for personal data. IEEE Trans. Reliab. **72**(2), 586–598 (2022)
16. Onik, M.M.H., Kim, C.S., Lee, N.Y., Yang, J.: Privacy-aware blockchain for personal data sharing and tracking. Open Comput. Sci. **9**(1), 80–91 (2019)
17. Psaras, Y., Dias, D.: The interplanetary file system and the filecoin network. In: 2020 50th Annual IEEE-IFIP International Conference on Dependable Systems and Networks-Supplemental Volume (DSN-S), pp. 80–80. IEEE (2020)
18. Rai, B.K.: Pcbehr: patient-controlled blockchain enabled electronic health records for healthcare 4.0. Health Serv. Outcomes Res. Methodol. **23**(1), 80–102 (2023)
19. Rouhani, S., Butterworth, L., Simmons, A.D., Humphery, D.G., Deters, R.: Medichain tm: a secure decentralized medical data asset management system. In: 2018 IEEE International Conference on Internet of Things (iThings) and IEEE Green Computing and Communications (GreenCom) and IEEE Cyber, Physical and Social Computing (CPSCom) and IEEE Smart Data (SmartData), pp. 1533–1538. IEEE (2018)
20. Sanjay, G.: The google file system. In: 19th ACM Symposium on Operating Systems Principles, NY, October 2003 (2003)
21. Shrestha, A.K., Deters, R., Vassileva, J.: User-controlled privacy-preserving user profile data sharing based on blockchain. ArXiv **abs/1909.05028** (2019). https://api.semanticscholar.org/CorpusID:202558399
22. Tiwari, A., Batra, U.: Ipfs enabled blockchain for smart cities. Int. J. Inf. Technol. **13**(1), 201–211 (2021)
23. Vukolić, M.: Rethinking permissioned blockchains. In: Proceedings of the ACM Workshop on Blockchain, Cryptocurrencies and Contracts, pp. 3–7 (2017)
24. Wen, F., Wang, Z., Qu, L., Huang, H., Hu, X.: Enhancing secure multi-group data sharing through integration of ipfs and hyperledger fabric. PeerJ Comput. Sci. **10**, e1962 (2024)
25. Zichichi, M., Ferretti, S., D'Angelo, G.: On the efficiency of decentralized file storage for personal information management systems. In: 2020 IEEE Symposium on Computers and Communications (iscc), pp. 1–6. IEEE (2020)
26. Zulkifl, Z., et al.: Fbashi: Fuzzy and blockchain-based adaptive security for healthcare iots. IEEE Access **10**, 15644–15656 (2022)

iCNN-LSTM: An Incremental CNN-LSTM Based Ransomware Detection System

Jamil Ispahany[1,3]($\boxtimes$) (ID), MD Rafiqul Islam[2,3] (ID), M. Arif Khan[1,3] (ID), and MD Zahidul Islam[1,3] (ID)

[1] Charles Sturt University, Bathurst 2795, Australia
JIspahany@csu.edu.au
[2] Charles Sturt University, Albury/Wodonga 2640, Australia
[3] Cyber Security Cooperative Research Centre (CSCRC), Kingston 2600, Australia

Abstract. In response to the increasing ransomware threat, this study presents a novel detection system that combines parallel Convolutional Neural Networks (CNNs) and Long Short-Term Memory (LSTM) networks. By leveraging Sysmon logs, the system enables real-time analysis on Windows-based endpoints. Our approach overcomes the limitations of traditional models by employing batch-based incremental learning, allowing the system to continuously adapt to new ransomware variants without requiring full retraining. The proposed model achieved an impressive average F2 score of 99.57%, with low false positive and false negative rates of 0.16% and 4.89%, respectively, within a highly imbalanced dataset, demonstrating exceptional accuracy in detecting malicious behaviour. The dynamic detection capabilities of Sysmon enhance the model's effectiveness by providing a continuous stream of security events, reducing the vulnerabilities associated with static detection methods. Additionally, the parallel processing of LSTM and CNN modules, along with attention mechanisms, enables our system to achieve the highest F2 score and the lowest false negative rate compared to other popular deep learning algorithms for ransomware detection, making it highly suitable for real-world applications. These results underscore the potential of our iCNN-LSTM framework as a robust solution for real-time ransomware detection, ensuring adaptability and resilience against evolving cyber threats.

Keywords: ransomware detection · CNN-LSTM · deep-learning · incremental-learning

M. Barhamgi et al. (Eds.): WISE 2024, LNCS 15463, pp. 46–60, 2025.
https://doi.org/10.1007/978-981-96-1483-7_4

1 Introduction

Since the onset of the COVID-19 crisis, malware has emerged as a significant global challenge [13]. Among various types of malware, ransomware has recently become more infamous. Ransomware is malicious software that encrypts the victim's data, rendering it inaccessible until a ransom is paid, typically demanded in cryptocurrency. This form of cyberattack has become prolific due to its lucrative nature for perpetrators and the relative ease of deployment compared to other cybercrimes. These attacks lead to financial losses, disrupt essential services, and compromise sensitive data. The severity of ransomware attacks was underscored on May 7, 2021, when Colonial Pipeline Co., the largest oil pipeline operator in the United States, fell victim to an attack by the Darkside hacking group. The hackers infiltrated the network, stole over 100 gigabytes of data, and then encrypted the company's network, demanding over USD 4.4 million ransom [2]. In response to the attack, Colonial Pipeline temporarily halted its operations. This disruption led to significant supply shortages and logistical challenges across the East Coast, contributing to a sharp increase in gas prices [8].

The research community has focused on developing more effective detection methods in response to the escalating ransomware threat. Historically, early research primarily utilised signature-based approaches that depended on known malware signatures for detection. While straightforward, these methods often missed new or altered ransomware strains. To overcome these limitations, behaviour-based approaches have become more favoured, as they analyse system activity patterns to identify malicious behaviours and are more adept at detecting zero-day attacks.

Machine learning techniques have been instrumental in automating and refining ransomware detection strategies. Initially, research concentrated on traditional machine learning methods because they were straightforward to implement, used resources efficiently, and yielded dependable outcomes. However, in recent times, there has been a shift towards deep learning techniques in ransomware detection. This change is attributed to deep learning's enhanced performance [3], proficiency in identifying complex patterns, capability to handle large datasets [10], and ability to generalise effectively to new, unseen data [11], thereby instilling confidence in their effectiveness.

Deep learning methods have shown promising results in detecting ransomware behaviour, leveraging their strength in deriving insights from complex and sequential data types. Despite these advancements, a significant challenge remains: most models in the literature are built from scratch, which is not only resource-intensive but also inefficient, given the rapid proliferation of ransomware variants. Incremental model updating offers a solution to this issue by allowing existing models to adapt to new data without retraining the model from scratch, thereby effectively maintaining knowledge of new and historical ransomware threats.

In response to these challenges, we offer the following contributions:

- *Novel detection architecture:* We present a system for efficient ransomware detection within Windows-based endpoints using Sysmon log streams. Our method achieves an impressive F2 score of 99.57% and a low false negative rate of 4.89% in an imbalanced dataset where ransomware is the minority class, demonstrating superior performance in detecting ransomware threats.

– *Continuous Learning Mechanism:* We implement a continuous learning approach that updates the model with mini-batches of data, improving its adaptability to new ransomware strains.

– *Efficient Processing:* We propose a CNN-LSTM deep-learning architecture that leverages parallel LSTM and CNN modules and attention mechanisms to improve detection performance. Using our incremental framework, we compare our approach with other commonly used deep learning algorithms from the literature. We show that it achieves the highest F2 score, recall, precision, and the lowest false negative rate.

Our model is designed for adaptability, incorporating incremental updates that enable it to evolve continuously in response to emerging threats. This dynamic updating mechanism allows the system to stay updated without completely rebuilding the model from scratch. It offers accurate and timely classification, ensuring it remains effective against the latest ransomware tactics.

The remainder of this paper is structured as follows: Sect. 2 reviews related work in ransomware detection, focusing on applying deep learning techniques and the challenges associated with traditional detection models. Section 3 outlines the proposed methodology, detailing the architecture of the iCNN-LSTM system and the processes involved in feature extraction and incremental learning. Section 4 presents the experimental setup, including the dataset and evaluation metrics, to assess the model's performance. The results of our experiments are discussed in Sect. 5, where we analyse the effectiveness of our approach compared to existing methods. Finally, Sect. 6 concludes the paper by summarising our findings, discussing the implications for future research, and highlighting the significance of our contributions to cybersecurity.

2 Related Work

2.1 Ransomware Detection Using Deep Learning

Numerous studies have employed deep learning methods to identify ransomware activities. Long Short-Term Memory Networks (LSTMs), developed by Hochreiter and Schmidhuber, are particularly effective in recognising patterns in sequential data, such as those found in runtime logs. These networks were designed to overcome the limitations of traditional Recurrent Neural Networks (RNNs), such as the exploding gradient problem during backpropagation through time. LSTMs are adept at preserving information over long periods due to their unique structure, which includes three gates: input, forget, and output. These gates respectively manage the influx of new data, the retention or removal of existing data, and the output calculations based on the current state of the cell.

LSTMs have been widely utilised in ransomware detection. For instance, Woralert et al. [18] developed a real-time detection framework for hardware anomalies indicative of ransomware. The authors use an LSTM-based predictor combined with ensemble methods and moving averages to capture the temporal aspects of hardware-level data from performance monitoring counters essential for identifying ransomware attacks.

Convolutional Neural Networks (CNNs) are another deep learning technique frequently used in image and video recognition and adapted for ransomware detection. CNNs excel at learning hierarchical features from input data and identifying structural patterns in malware samples. For example, Ciaramella et al. [7] achieved notable success using CNNs to distinguish between malicious and benign software by analysing visual data derived from binary code, reaching a high accuracy rate. However, this method primarily relies on static features from the binary code, which may limit its effectiveness in dynamic scenarios.

Numerous studies have highlighted the benefits of combining Convolutional Neural Networks (CNNs) and Long Short-Term Memory (LSTMs) networks in various fields such as weather forecasting [9] and text classification [14]. This hybrid architecture enhances performance by leveraging the strengths of both CNNs and LSTMs [14]. Specifically, CNNs are adept at extracting spatial features, while LSTMs excel at recognising temporal patterns in sequential data. These characteristics make the combined CNN-LSTM architecture particularly effective for detecting ransomware activities in time-series logs.

Zhang [20] utilises the capabilities of CNNs and LSTMs to derive sophisticated abstractions and representations from n-gram API calls. This integrated architecture effectively identifies local correlations and long-term patterns within raw API call sequences, allowing for highly accurate classification of malware behaviour.

Changanti et al. [5] combined CNN and LSTM models to improve their ransomware detection system. This hybrid approach leverages CNNs to extract spatial features and LSTMs to handle temporal dependencies, enhancing the detection capabilities for static Portable Executable (PE) files. Despite achieving a strong F1 score, this method's application is confined to static data, and its effectiveness in real-time ransomware detection remains unexplored.

The combination of CNNs and LSTMs to detect ransomware using dynamic features represents a promising yet relatively untapped area of research and remains the focus of this study.

2.2 Incremental Approaches to Update the Deep Learning Model

Many existing studies suggest developing detection systems from the ground up for ransomware detection. This approach is increasingly impractical as the frequency of new ransomware variants on the internet continues to rise, necessitating frequent retraining of models. Such retraining is time-consuming and resource-intensive, given the significant computational demands of deep learning and its lengthy training processes [19]. This becomes particularly critical when dealing with sensitive data that requires continuous updates to incorporate new ransomware samples.

An underexplored alternative in ransomware detection is the incremental updating of the underlying model with new data. Incremental learning can keep the detection system current without complete retraining, thus preserving resources and improving responsiveness. While incremental updates are beneficial and have been successfully applied in other domains, such as the energy sector [16], their adoption in ransomware detection has been limited.

Roy and Chen [15] introduced a system that uses host logging data with a Bidirectional LSTM and Conditional Random Field (CRF) model to identify 17 types of ransomware attacks accurately. They employed online learning techniques to update the model with new data incrementally, preventing the degradation of the model over time.

Similarly, Al-rimy et al. [1] developed an incremental iBagging technique that uses non-deep learning methods to update the dataset continuously. This helps overcome the initial lack of comprehensive data in the early stages of ransomware attacks. They combined this with an Enhanced Semi-Random Subspace (ESRS) method for feature selection and an ensemble of algorithms for classification.

Despite these advancements, to the best of the authors' knowledge, no other studies have utilised CNN-LSTM frameworks in an incremental update setting within the ransomware detection domain. This suggests a potential area for further research and application.

3   Proposed Methodology

3.1   Overview of the Model Architecture

Figure 1 provides an overview of the operational pipeline of our ransomware detection system, which leverages a convolutional neural network (CNN) combined with a long short-term memory (LSTM) model for the classification. The process begins with Sysmon agents, a monitoring tool that captures system events related to security breaches and normal operations. These events are then transmitted to a centralised logging platform that aggregates the information and organises it into mini-batches. These mini-batches are periodically dispatched to the ransomware detection system, ensuring it is frequently updated with the most current data. This is critical for maintaining its relevance and accuracy in the fast-evolving landscape of cybersecurity threats.

Events are passed through the feature extraction stage, where events are converted into word vectors, laying the groundwork for effective classification. Feature selection is refined using Pearson correlation coefficients to pinpoint features significantly impacting the classification results.

The selected features are directed to the classification model, designed to adapt dynamically to new patterns and anomalies in the data. The initial model is built using the data processing techniques discussed in the Sect. 5.2 and is constantly updated once deployed. It achieves this through periodic weight updates, incorporating the latest insights from the newly processed mini-batches. This continuous learning approach allows the model to evolve in response to the emergence of new ransomware signatures or variations in Goodware behaviour, maintaining its effectiveness in real-time threat detection and classification.

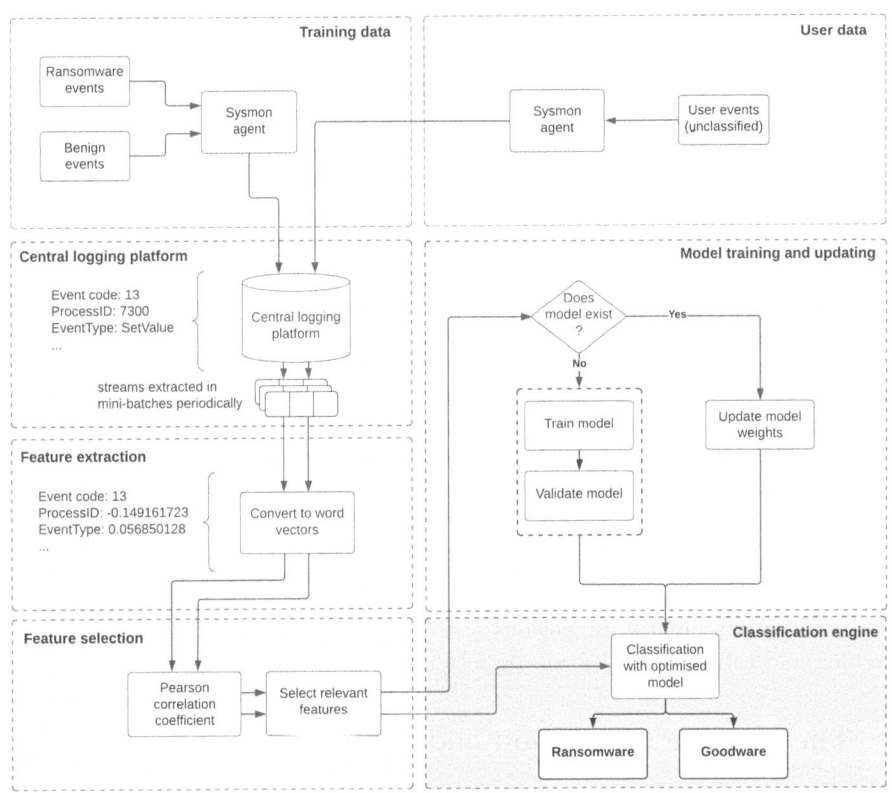

Fig. 1. The proposed architecture of the iCNN-LSTM system. The blue arrows signify data used to train the model, and the red arrows indicate unseen data to be classified by the system (Color figure online)

3.2   Proposed CNN LSTM Binary Classifier

We propose a stacked CNN-LSTM architecture to classify ransomware threats, as depicted in Fig. 2. This structure combines the spatial feature extraction capabilities of CNNs with the temporal dependency-capturing abilities of LSTMs. Additionally, the model incorporates attention mechanisms to further improve the extraction and learning of features from the input data. Initially, raw data inputs are processed through a CNN layer, which excels at identifying hierarchical patterns and local dependencies. The features are also input into multiple LSTM layers that operate in parallel. These LSTMs are particularly effective at recognising long-term dependencies and are crucial for maintaining contextual continuity within sequences, an essential feature for analysing temporal data such as system logs.

To address the challenge of focusing on the most salient features in a sequence, an attention mechanism is applied to the LSTM outputs, weighting the importance of different steps in the sequence. The concatenated output of the attention-weighted LSTM layers undergoes batch normalisation, a tech-

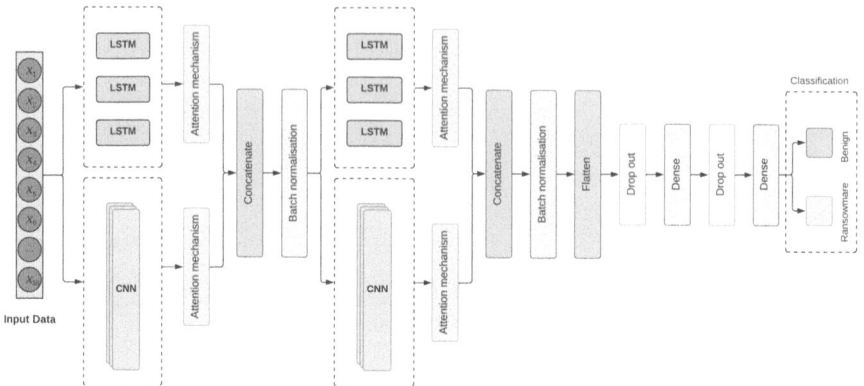

Fig. 2. Structure of the CNN-LSTM model used for binary classification.

nique used to stabilise and accelerate the training process. Subsequently, the data is flattened and passed through dense layers with dropout regularisation to prevent overfitting, culminating in a binary classification that discerns between benign and ransomware activities. This multifaceted approach encapsulates both the spatial and temporal dimensions of the input data, ensuring comprehensive learning and robust classification performance.

4   The Feature Extraction and Selection Techniques

4.1   Feature Extraction Using FastText

Our system employs fastText to transform words into vector representations for feature extraction. Unlike other embeddings, such as Word2vec, that treat words as indivisible entities and neglect their sub-structural components, fastText considers the internal structure of words. Specifically, as illustrated in Fig. 3, fastText decomposes words into character n-grams and computes a word's vector by summing the vectors of its constituent n-grams. This approach enhances the model's performance, particularly with complex and rare words, by providing a more nuanced representation [4].

To elaborate, let's denote the set of n-grams for a given word by $\mathcal{G}_w$, a subset of the dictionary of all n-grams of size G. Each n-gram, g, from this set is mapped to a unique vector $\mathbf{z}_g$ in an N-dimensional space. Similarly, vectors $\mathbf{v}_c$ in an N-dimensional space represent the context words surrounding the target word. With these vectors in place, we define a scoring function that evaluates the alignment between the target word and its context within the embedding space.

$$s(w, c) = \sum_{g \in \mathcal{G}_w}^{|G|} \left(\mathbf{z}_g^T \mathbf{v}_c \right) = 1 \tag{1}$$

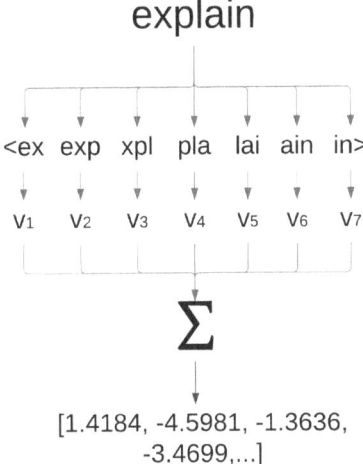

Fig. 3. fastText conversion to vectors using n-grams. The above example shows the process of converting the word "explain" into vectors where v_n represents the vector representation of the corresponding n-gram

4.2 Selecting Important Features

The system's primary aim is to identify ransomware activities from logs produced by Sysmon as quickly as possible. To optimise the design, it's vital to minimise the preprocessing of these log features. Sysmon typically generates logs with 52 distinct features. To efficiently select the most impactful features and streamline the detection process, we utilise the Pearson Correlation Coefficient (PCC). PCC assists in determining the degree of linear correlation between the actual and predicted values, enabling us to identify which features most predict ransomware activity. The PCC is computed mathematically as the standardised form of the covariance between two variables, X and Y, representing the true and predicted values, respectively.

$$PCC(X,Y) = \frac{cov(X,Y)}{\sigma_X \sigma_Y} = \frac{E[(X-\overline{X})(Y-\overline{Y})]}{\sigma_X \sigma_Y} \tag{2}$$

where $\overline{X}$ and $\overline{Y}$ are the averages of X and Y; σ_X and σ_Y are the standard deviations, respectively [17]. Using the PCC, the most significant features were the 'TargetUser', 'TargetImage', 'SourceUser', 'GrantedAccess', 'CallTrace' and 'task'.

5 Experimental Evaluation

5.1 Dataset

To evaluate the system's effectiveness in detecting emerging ransomware without needing to rebuild the model from the ground up, we crafted an imbalanced dataset comprising benign software (goodware) and ransomware events, focusing on six prominent ransomware families. The data acquisition involved recording Sysmon events from the initiation of a program until the display of a ransomware demand note. However, generating a seamless sequence of non-malicious and malicious events presented a significant challenge. Each ransomware sample executed left the testing virtual machine in disrepair, necessitating a system restore to an earlier snapshot. Consequently, we combined Sysmon logs from both goodware and ransomware to form a cohesive training and testing environment for our models.

We sourced modern ransomware variants from online security platforms like VirusTotal and HybridAnalysis to stay abreast of cybersecurity threats. These variants included AvosLocker, BlackBasta, Conti, Hive, Lockbit, and REvil, chosen for their notoriety and prevalence in recent cyber attacks. Over 20,000 Sysmon event logs were collected from these activities across 50 ransomware attacks.

Each ransomware instance was run for a uniform duration of five minutes. Typically, the ransom note appeared before the five-minute mark. Following the launch of a ransomware sample, Sysmon began transmitting logs to a central repository until the ransom note materialised and the virtual machine ceased to function normally, preventing further event logging. In real-world scenarios, benign events tend to outnumber malicious ones. Considering this, we deliberately created a dataset with more benign events. We obtained these events from various sources, including games and software from PortableApps, resulting in more than 176,000 benign events. Our final dataset contained nearly 200,000 events, a mix of ransomware and benign activities interspersed throughout sequences of ransomware events. By periodically introducing new ransomware families into the dataset, we created conditions that mimic the evolutionary nature of ransomware threats. This approach allowed us to assess our models' adaptability to the continuous changes seen in ransomware attacks.

5.2   Data Processing

Figure 4 outlines the methodology for constructing and refining our model. Initially, the model undergoes training and validation with 50,000 events. Following its deployment, we adopt an incremental learning approach, where the model is consistently updated via mini-batches of 10,000 events (comprised of both benign and ransomware events). Throughout our experiments, we performed 15 such incremental updates beyond the initial training phase. To evaluate the model's capacity for identifying previously unknown ransomware, each update incorporates novel samples from various ransomware families not included in the original training. A detailed account of how ransomware events are distributed among the mini-batches for the model's training is depicted in Table 1.

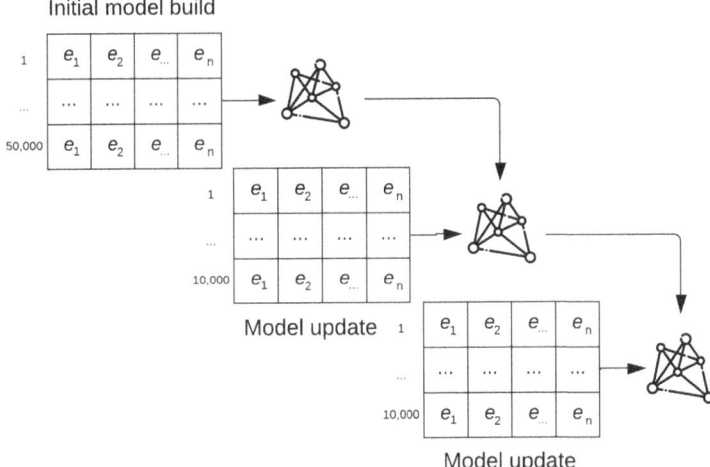

Fig. 4. The process to incrementally update the CNN LSTM model. The initial model is built using training data. Subsequent mini-batches of 10,000 events are used to update the model weights periodically

Table 1. The distribution of benign and ransomware events within the dataset. The initial model is built using the training batch and then updated with subsequent batches containing ransomware and benign events

Batch	BenignEvents	Ransomwareevents
Trainingbatch	38,817	1,181
1	9,747	254
2	9,102	899
3	9,588	413
4	9,397	607
5	8,407	1,594
6	9,760	241
7	9,826	175
8	7,463	2,538
9	8,818	1,183
10	6,876	3,125
11	8,340	1,661
12	6,057	3,844
13	9,895	106
14	9,443	558
15	9,301	700
16	5,305	1,536
Total	176,130	20,710

5.3 Evaluation Metrics

The F measure is the harmonic mean between the precision and recall. This metric is particularly effective for evaluating the accuracy of deep learning models, especially in cases involving imbalanced datasets [12]. The F1 score, a common variant of the F-measure that gives equal weight to precision and recall, is widely used in the literature to assess performance [6]. However, in the context of ransomware detection, where misclassifying ransomware as benign (false negatives) is more detrimental than incorrectly flagging benign software as ransomware (false positives), our primary goal is to minimise false negatives to ensure the security and integrity of the systems we protect. To achieve this, we focus on maximising recall, which measures the proportion of actual positives correctly identified. This is accomplished by selecting a lower threshold for the F-measure, which may increase the likelihood of false positives. In line with our objective to reduce false negatives, we use an F-measure configured to prioritise recall, specifically the F2 score, where the beta value is set to two. This configuration places twice as much emphasis on recall compared to precision. While a beta value of 1 in the F-measure treats precision and recall equally, a beta value less than one would emphasise precision, making the metric more sensitive to false positives. The formula for calculating the F2 score is as follows:

$$F_\beta = (1 + \beta^2) \cdot \frac{precision \cdot recall}{(\beta^2 \cdot precision) + recall} \tag{3}$$

Where β is the beta value, which determines the weight of precision and recall in the harmonic mean. The precision and recall can be calculated as follows:

$$precision = \frac{TP}{TP + FP} \tag{4}$$

$$recall = \frac{TP}{TP + FN} \tag{5}$$

where TP equals true positives, TN equates to true negatives, FP represents false positives, and finally, FN represents the number of false negatives.

6 Results

Figure 5 illustrates the model's performance in classifying ransomware samples. The X-axis represents the time in seconds, corresponding to the model's batch updates, while the Y-axis depicts the F2 score. This metric prioritises recall over precision to emphasise the importance of accurately identifying the minority class, thus reducing false negatives. Each data point corresponds to a model

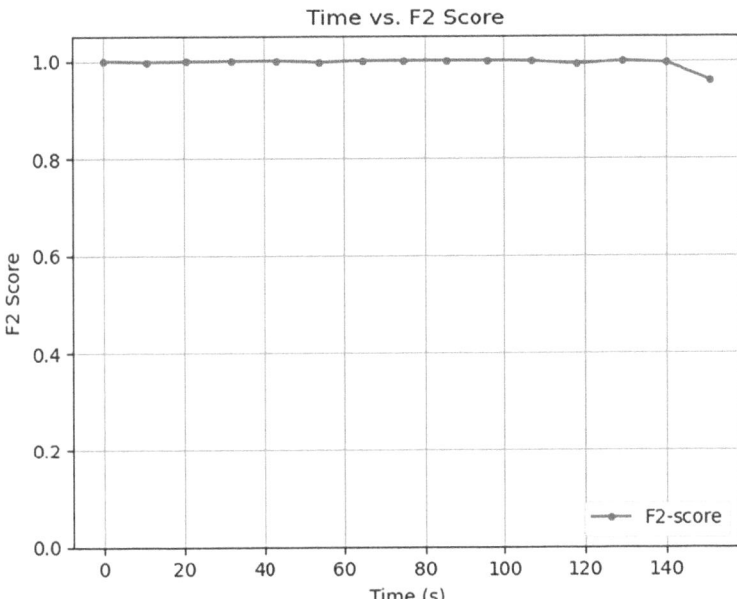

Fig. 5. F2 score vs Time graph. Each data point consists of a new training batch used to update the model

Table 2. A comparison of different ransomware detection methods used throughout the experiment

Method	F1 Score	F2 Score	Recall	Precision	False positives	False negatives
LSTM	98.21%	98.16%	98.12%	98.30%	6.5%	31%
CNN	97.79%	97.8%	97.81%	97.77%	0.06%	28%
BiLSTM	98.56%	98.55%	98.55%	98.57%	6.5%	22%
iCNN-LSTM	**99.55%**	**99.57%**	**99.58%**	**99.56%**	**0.16%**	**4.89%**

update event introducing new ransomware sample data. Despite continuously integrating unseen ransomware instances, the F2 score remains impressively stable, consistently exceeding 99%. This high F2 score demonstrates the model's exceptional accuracy in classifying ransomware, indicating that our technique adapts to new data and retains a high degree of classification precision throughout the evaluation period. The consistent performance above the 99% threshold indicates the underlying architecture's robustness and ability to generalise well in dynamic and evolving threat environments.

The graph shows a slight decline in the F2 score between the 140 and 150-second marks. This drop is attributed to the model encountering a substantial increase in new ransomware events compared to goodware events, which were not present in previous batches, and an imbalance in ransomware events within this particular segment.

To evaluate the effectiveness of our technique, we implemented other deep learning algorithms commonly used in ransomware detection, including LSTM, CNN, and BiLSTM, within our batch-incremental architecture using the curated Sysmon dataset, as presented in Table 2. Our iCNN-LSTM architecture, amongst all the tested models, achieved an F1 score of 99.55% and an F2 score of 99.57%. Notably, our technique achieves an exceptionally low false negative rate of just 4.89%. This makes iCNN-LSTM more accurate and reliable in practical scenarios where the cost of false negatives (missed detections) can be significant. In contrast, the other models, while competent, display notable weaknesses. The LSTM and BiLSTM models have higher rates of false positives and negatives, suggesting they struggle with overfitting and underfitting issues. Despite having a low false positive rate, the CNN model has a relatively high false negative rate, indicating it may be overly conservative in identifying ransomware, leading to missed detections. These results also emphasise our technique's capability to analyse the spatial and temporal patterns in the dataset, a strength that other models need to improve. Additionally, the attention mechanism effectively focuses on the most relevant parts of the data, further enhancing the model's performance. Overall, iCNN-LSTM's balanced and robust performance underscores its potential as a more reliable solution for ransomware detection where precise detection and minimising false positives and negatives are crucial.

7   Conclusion

This study introduces a deep-learning-based ransomware detection system that combines CNN and LSTM architecture. Our system effectively identifies ransomware events in time-series Sysmon logs, achieving an average F2 score of 99.57% and the lowest false negative rates among all compared methods. Unlike previous research that often necessitates completely rebuilding the machine learning model, our model benefits from incremental updates using mini-batches. This approach allows our system to adapt accurately to new ransomware samples. Future research will explore integrating our system into a comprehensive Cybersecurity framework encompassing multiple endpoints.

Acknowledgment. The work has been supported by the Cyber Security Research Centre Limited whose activities are partially funded by the Australian Government's Cooperative Research Centres Programme.

References

1. Al-rimy, B.A.S., Maarof, M.A., Shaid, S.Z.M.: Crypto-ransomware early detection model using novel incremental bagging with enhanced semi-random subspace selection. Futur. Gener. Comput. Syst. **101**, 476–491 (2019)

2. Beerman, J., Berent, D., Falter, Z., Bhunia, S.: A review of colonial pipeline ransomware attack. In: 2023 IEEE/ACM 23rd International Symposium on Cluster, Cloud and Internet Computing Workshops (CCGridW), pp. 8–15. IEEE (2023)

3. Bello, I., et al.: Detecting ransomware attacks using intelligent algorithms: Recent development and next direction from deep learning and big data perspectives. J. Ambient. Intell. Humaniz. Comput. **12**, 8699–8717 (2021)

4. Bojanowski, P., Grave, E., Joulin, A., Mikolov, T.: Enriching word vectors with subword information. Trans. Assoc. Comput. Linguist. **5**, 135–146 (2017)

5. Chaganti, R., Ravi, V., Pham, T.D.: A multi-view feature fusion approach for effective malware classification using deep learning. J. Inform. Secur. Appl. **72**, 103402 (2023)

6. Christen, P., Hand, D.J., Kirielle, N.: A review of the f-measure: its history, properties, criticism, and alternatives. ACM Comput. Surv. **56**(3), 1–24 (2023)

7. Ciaramella, G., Iadarola, G., Martinelli, F., Mercaldo, F., Santone, A.: Explainable ransomware detection with deep learning techniques. J. Comput. Virol. Hack. Techn. 1–14 (2023)

8. Dossett, J.: A timeline of the biggest ransomware attacks (Nov 2021). https://www.cnet.com/personal-finance/crypto/a-timeline-of-the-biggest-ransomware-attacks/

9. Fan, M., Imran, O., Singh, A., Ajila, S.A.: Using cnn-lstm model for weather forecasting. In: 2022 IEEE International Conference on Big Data (Big Data), pp. 4120–4125. IEEE (2022)

10. Fernando, D.W., Komninos, N., Chen, T.: A study on the evolution of ransomware detection using machine learning and deep learning techniques. IoT **1**(2), 551–604 (2020)

11. Hemalatha, J., Roseline, S.A., Geetha, S., Kadry, S., Damaševičius, R.: An efficient densenet-based deep learning model for malware detection. Entropy **23**(3), 344 (2021)

12. Ispahany, J., Islam, M.R., Islam, M.Z., Khan, M.A.: Ransomware detection using machine learning: A review, research limitations and future directions. IEEE Access (2024)

13. Ispahany, J., Islam, R.: Detecting malicious covid-19 urls using machine learning techniques. In: 2021 IEEE International Conference on Pervasive Computing and Communications Workshops and other Affiliated Events (PerCom Workshops), pp. 718–723. IEEE (2021)

14. Luan, Y., Lin, S.: Research on text classification based on cnn and lstm. In: 2019 IEEE International Conference on Artificial Intelligence and Computer Applications (ICAICA), pp. 352–355. IEEE (2019)

15. Roy, K.C., Chen, Q.: Deepran: attention-based bilstm and crf for ransomware early detection and classification. Inf. Syst. Front. **23**(2), 299–315 (2021)

16. Shaohu, L., Yuandeng, W., Rui, H.: Prediction of drilling plug operation parameters based on incremental learning and cnn-lstm. Geoenergy Sci. Eng. **234**, 212631 (2024)

17. Wang, J.: Pearson Correlation Coefficient, pp. 1671–1671. Springer New York, New York, NY (2013). https://doi.org/10.1007/978-1-4419-9863-7_372

18. Woralert, C., Liu, C., Blasingame, Z.: Hard-lite: A lightweight hardware anomaly realtime detection framework targeting ransomware. Regular Papers, IEEE Transactions on Circuits and Systems I (2023)
19. Yang, M., Wang, J.: Adaptability of financial time series prediction based on bilstm. Proc. Comput. Sci. **199**, 18–25 (2022)
20. Zhang, J.: Deepmal: A cnn-lstm model for malware detection based on dynamic semantic behaviours. In: 2020 International Conference on Computer Information and Big Data Applications (CIBDA), pp. 313–316. IEEE (2020)

A Mini Review on Purchaser Security in the Metaverse: Challenges and Solutions

Mohammad Aloudat[(⊠)], Mahmoud Barhamgi, and Elias Yaacoub

Department of Computer Science and Engineering, Qatar University, Doha, Qatar
{ma2211108,mbarhamgi,elias}@qu.edu.qa

Abstract. This mini review examines the security challenges faced by purchasers in the metaverse, focusing on issues such as data protection, privacy, identity theft, financial fraud, and software vulnerabilities. The metaverse, characterized by its immersive, decentralized, and interactive nature, presents unique risks due to extensive data collection, real-time user tracking, and the integration of digital and physical worlds. This mini review highlights specific threats such as unauthorized access, exploitation of biometric data, and fraudulent activities involving blockchain-based assets like non-fungible tokens (NFTs). Mitigation strategies, including advanced encryption, multi-factor authentication, decentralized identity solutions, and regulatory frameworks, are discussed as essential to safeguarding purchasers. The paper concludes by identifying gaps in current research and proposing directions for future studies, emphasizing the need for interdisciplinary approaches to enhance metaverse security.

Keyword: Metaverse, Purchaser Security, Privacy, Identity Theft, Financial Fraud

1 Introduction

1.1 Overview of the Metaverse

The term "metaverse," first used in Neal Stephenson's 1992 novel Snow Crash, describes a digital environment combining living space and cyberspace, where avatars interact in a persistent, immersive 3D world, integrating VR, AR, and MR for complex social, economic, and cultural engagement [1,2]. As technology advanced, the metaverse became a massive digital ecosystem encompassing virtual economies through blockchain and NFTs, impacting finance, healthcare, and education [3,4]. Platforms like Second Life support social interaction and digital exchanges, while tools like Microsoft Mesh and NVIDIA Omniverse demonstrate the metaverse's role in bridging digital and physical realms for professional and social use [2].

M. Barhamgi et al. (Eds.): WISE 2024, LNCS 15463, pp. 61–74, 2025.
https://doi.org/10.1007/978-981-96-1483-7_5

1.2 The Review's Objective

As the metaverse expands, it introduces security risks such as identity theft, criminality, and privacy breaches. This mini-review examines existing research, explores potential risks, and suggests mitigation strategies and future research directions.

1.3 The Review's Organization

This paper is structured into three important sections that discuss purchaser security in the metaverse in detail. The first section of the paper gives a summary of the metaverse, showing how it evolved from the first virtual settings to the sophisticated digital ecosystem it is today that combines blockchain, virtual reality, and AR technologies. The goal of the evaluation is also stated in the preamble, with an emphasis on the expanding security threats and the requirement for mitigating measures. The paper's main body is broken up into multiple sections. The first one looks at purchaser interactions in the metaverse, highlighting how people participate in virtual economy, engage in virtual activities, and develop digital identities. This is followed by a thorough examination of particular security concerns, highlighting the special dangers brought about by the decentralized and immersive nature of the metaverse. These concerns include data security, identity theft, financial fraud, and platform vulnerabilities. The review then identifies the gaps in the literature and suggests solutions to enhance metaverse security, such as developing a strong governance framework, creating adaptive security approaches, and integrating AI-Driven threat detection systems. The results are summarized in the final part, which also emphasizes the necessity of multidisciplinary approaches and further study to improve security in virtual settings.

2 An Overview of Purchaser Interaction and the Metaverse

2.1 Virtual World Evolution

The creation of virtual worlds has greatly shaped digital platforms, with early environments like Second Life and MMORPGs enabling immersive interactions and virtual transactions, setting the stage for today's metaverse [5]. Advances in blockchain, AI, AR, VR, and mobile networks during the Fourth Industrial Revolution have fostered highly immersive and persistent digital environments, transforming them into dynamic spaces for social, commercial, and cultural exchanges [6]. Platforms like Microsoft Mesh, NVIDIA Omniverse, and Inwak Meta University showcase virtual worlds' potential in business, education, and healthcare [2].

2.2   Purchaser Actions and Applications

In the metaverse, purchasers engage in immersive social and economic interactions, crafting digital identities and exploring varied environments via avatars [5]. Virtual economies thrive as users buy, trade, and invest in blockchain-backed assets like NFTs, which represent ownership and contribute to social status and self-expression [7]. These NFTs, tied to exclusivity and popularity, enhance social engagement by enabling users to connect with communities and showcase their individuality [8]. The decentralized ownership model of NFTs fosters emotional connections to digital assets, influencing behaviors like collecting and trading, thus strengthening user identity and driving participation in virtual networks [9,10]. This dynamic ecosystem blurs personal and professional boundaries, allowing users to attend virtual events and collaborate creatively [11].

3   Purchaser Security Issues in the Metaverse

The metaverse offers immersive experiences by merging virtual and real worlds but poses significant security risks, particularly regarding data protection and privacy. Extensive data collection via VR and AR devices heightens risks of breaches, while the metaverse's decentralized structure allows potential misuse of user data. As it evolves, stronger legal frameworks and advanced security measures are needed to protect user privacy [12] [13]. Figure 1 and Table 1 provide an overview of purchaser security issues and a comparison with prior studies on these challenges.

Table 1. Comparison of this Paper with Existing Review and Survey Papers on Purchaser Security Issues

Reference	Metaverse Decentralization	Data Protection and Privacy	Identity Theft and Fraud	Financial Fraud and Cybercrime	Platform and Software Vulnerabilities	Challenges in Regulation and Law	Lack of Multidisciplinary Collaboration
[2]	✓	✓	✗	✓	✓	✓	✗
[14]	✓	✗	✓	✗	✓	✗	✗
[15]	✓	✓	✓	✗	✓	✗	✗
[16]	✓	✓	✓	✓	✗	✗	✗
Our Review	✓	✓	✓	✓	✓	✓	✓

3.1   Metaverse Decentralization

The metaverse's current partial decentralization, mainly via blockchain, is limited as many platforms remain under central control, impacting purchaser autonomy and raising data security concerns [17]. Greater decentralization would enhance user ownership, reduce security risks, and support transparent governance, though challenges like interoperability and regulatory complexity remain [18]. Despite these obstacles, advancing decentralization is essential for a resilient, user-centric metaverse [19].

3.2   Data Protection and Privacy

The metaverse's collection of extensive personal data, including biometrics, raises significant privacy concerns, with risks of third-party misuse and data breaches potentially leading to identity theft and behavioral manipulation [13] [20]. Real-time tracking of user actions enables mass surveillance and creates detailed purchaser profiles, complicating data governance in its decentralized structure. This data can be exploited for targeted ads and political manipulation, highlighting the urgent need for robust privacy protections and regulatory frameworks [13] [20].

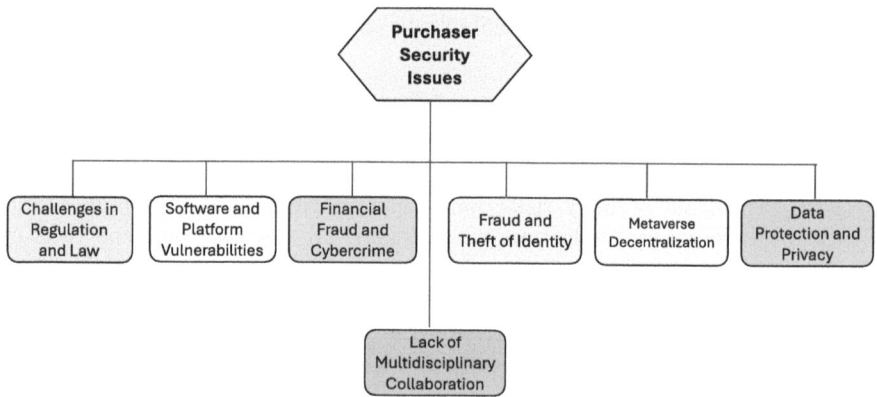

Fig. 1. Purchaser Security Issues in the Metaverse

3.3   Fraud and Theft of Identity

In the metaverse, identity theft and fraud are major risks, as digital avatars tied to personal data like fingerprints are vulnerable to deepfake and AI-driven attacks that exploit authentication weaknesses, enabling financial crimes and asset manipulation [14] [21]. Fraud impacts blockchain-based assets like NFTs, with phishing incidents, such as the OpenSea breach, highlighting the need for cybersecurity measures like multi-factor authentication and Zero Trust Architectures [14]. The metaverse's decentralized nature complicates identity protection, making AI-driven deepfake avatars a serious concern for unauthorized access and data misuse [21].

3.4   Financial Fraud and Cybercrime

The metaverse's expanding digital economy has become a hotspot for financial fraud, including identity theft, money laundering, and scams exploiting decentralized platforms and smart contract vulnerabilities [22] [23]. Fraud schemes such as phishing, Ponzi scams, and fake NFT sales leverage user anonymity, while criminals manipulate NFTs and virtual assets through wash trading and "rug pulls," impacting market integrity [22]. High-profile cases like OpenSea's NFT theft highlight the risks, underscoring the urgent need for regulatory oversight and robust cybersecurity to protect users and maintain trust in virtual economies [23].

3.5   Software and Platform Vulnerabilities

The metaverse's decentralized nature and complex structure create vulnerabilities, from malware and DoS attacks to weak VR/AR authentication, with interconnected smart contracts offering numerous attack points [15] [24]. AI systems face adversarial attacks, and digital twins are prone to data manipulation, threatening sectors like infrastructure and healthcare. Strong cybersecurity, including multi-factor authentication and real-time monitoring, is essential [15]. The reliance on third-party apps and cross-platform interoperability further increases risks of data breaches and privacy issues [25] [26].

3.6   Challenges in Regulation and Law

As the metaverse integrates further into daily life, purchaser security faces challenges from cross-border jurisdictional issues, ambiguous IP boundaries, and personal data protection, complicated by decentralized technologies that increase financial crime risks [27] [28]. Existing laws like the DMCA and GDPR offer some protections, yet they struggle with the metaverse's global, decentralized structure, which complicates enforcement [27]. Variations in regulations, such as China's strict laws versus more lenient areas, underscore the need for adaptable legal frameworks [27]. Regulatory gaps around digital asset ownership and enforcement highlight the urgent need for metaverse-specific laws to address these unique challenges [28].

3.7   Multidisciplinary Collaboration to Enhance Purchaser Security in the Metaverse

The metaverse's unique security challenges demand an interdisciplinary approach, yet collaboration across fields like law, psychology, and computer science remains limited, leading to partial solutions [29]. While computer scientists may advance encryption, these solutions often miss legal and psychological considerations, such as data privacy and the user impact of identity theft [30]. Legal frameworks lag behind tech progress, and psychological insights are essential to understanding user behavior and improving cybersecurity [31] [32]. Strengthening interdisciplinary cooperation is thus crucial for robust security strategies in the metaverse.

4 Current Remedies and Countermeasures

As digital environments expand, purchaser security in the metaverse faces rising threats like identity theft, data breaches, and financial fraud, despite current defenses like blockchain and encryption [33] [16]. This section explores solutions and strategies to mitigate these evolving risks. Figure 2 and Table 2 illustrate current remedies and compare them with existing studies on purchaser security.

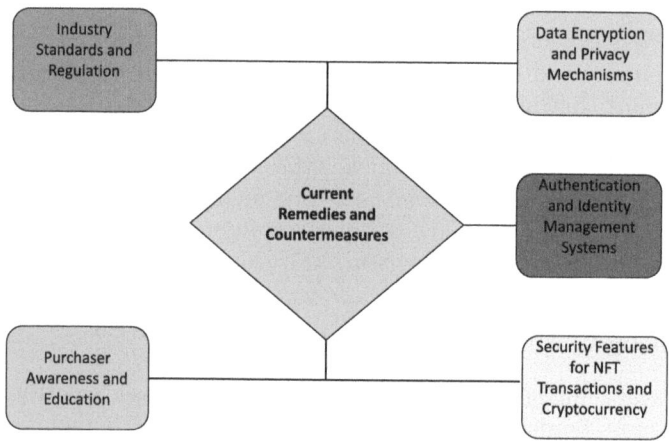

Fig. 2. Current Remedies and Countermeasures

Table 2. Comparison of this Paper with Existing Review and Survey Papers on Purchaser Security Current Remedies and Countermeasures

Reference	Data Encryption and Privacy Mechanisms	Authentication and Identity Management Systems	Security Features for NFT Transactions and Cryptocurrency	Purchaser Awareness and Education	Industry Standards and Regulation
[2]	✓	✓	✓	✗	✗
[14]	✓	✓	✓	✗	✗
[15]	✓	✓	✓	✗	✓
[16]	✓	✗	✗	✗	✗
Our Review	✓	✓	✓	✓	✓

4.1 Data Encryption and Privacy Mechanisms

Blockchain encryption enhances transparency and efficiency in the metaverse but has vulnerabilities, such as in smart contracts, that can expose data to attacks like the 51% PoW attack [2]. Data serialization encryption secures data in transit but requires further protections like authentication and firewalls to avoid malicious insertions [16]. Cloud encryption safeguards data by converting it to ciphertext, protecting it during both transit and storage [34]. Privacy-preserving technologies like homomorphic encryption and zero-knowledge proofs secure data processing in immersive metaverse settings without compromising confidentiality [35].

4.2   Systems for Authentication and Identity Management

The decentralized and pseudonymous nature of the metaverse and Web 3.0 heightens risks of identity theft, as attackers use deepfakes to impersonate trusted individuals, making detection challenging [36]. Multi-Factor Authentication (MFA), requiring passwords and biometrics, strengthens security by reducing unauthorized access, even if one factor is compromised [37]. Decentralized identity solutions, using secure web objects, allow users to control digital identities with enhanced data security and interoperability across platforms [38].

4.3   Features of Security for NFT Transactions and Cryptocurrency

Blockchain secures ownership and transactions in the metaverse through a decentralized ledger, ensuring transparency, immutability, and protection from tampering by distributing data across nodes to prevent central failures [39]. It addresses key security issues by providing frameworks for identity management and transaction validation, preserving asset ownership integrity [40]. Smart contracts on platforms like Ethereum further enhance security by automating agreements, detecting fraud, and supporting scalable governance by monitoring for suspicious activity and reducing human error [41] [42].

4.4   Standards for Industry and Regulation

The convergence of technologies like blockchain, VR, and AR in the metaverse brings significant security challenges, prompting industry leaders to develop interoperable standards with encryption protocols and secure identity management [43]. Initiatives like the Metaverse Security Governance Shanghai Initiative focus on secure virtual identities and privacy, emphasizing flexible security protocols [2]. The XR Safety Initiative (XRSI) has created a Privacy and Safety Framework aligned with international laws like COPPA and GDPR for consistent security standards [44]. Additionally, the European Union is crafting a regulatory framework addressing privacy, IP, and social interaction in the metaverse [45].

4.5   Purchaser Awareness and Education

User education is vital for preventing security breaches in the metaverse, given heightened risks of social engineering and impersonation [46]. Educational programs should teach cybersecurity principles, focusing on privacy, ethical behavior, and threat recognition (e.g., phishing and social engineering) [24]. Awareness campaigns covering data handling, password hygiene, and phishing prevention empower users to navigate digital spaces securely through training modules and public resources [5].

5   The Literature's Gaps

The metaverse's complex security and privacy challenges reveal critical research gaps that need addressing [29]. Studies on customer behavior in virtual retail often overlook security risks, underscoring the need for deeper analysis [47]. Future research should adopt multidisciplinary approaches to develop comprehensive security frameworks for virtual environments [48].

5.1   Areas to Investigate Further

The rapid growth of the metaverse reveals research gaps, particularly in interoperability, identity protection, and asset security in virtual and augmented realities [49,50]. Traditional cybersecurity is insufficient for issues like virtual property protection and digital harassment, and blockchain convergence raises security concerns around NFTs and digital currencies [51,52]. More empirical research on user behavior and perceptions of privacy controls is needed to strengthen metaverse security, while studies on psychological impacts of security breaches can guide system improvements [5,53]. Table 3 outlines further research areas in purchaser security.

Table 3. Areas to Investigate Further in Purchaser Security in the Metaverse

Area	Description
Interoperability and Platform Integration	Secure integration across virtual, augmented, and extended reality platforms.
Specialized Security Techniques	Tailored security methods for digital identities and decentralized assets in XR.
Virtual Property Protection	Challenges in protecting virtual property and ownership rights.
Psychological Effects of Digital Harassment	Psychological impact of harassment in social VR and protective measures.
Blockchain Convergence and Digital Asset Security	Security for NFTs, smart contracts, and digital currencies with mitigation strategies.
Purchaser Behavior in Virtual Environments	Study user interactions, vulnerabilities, and transaction security.
User Perceptions of Privacy and Security Controls	How users perceive and react to privacy controls in XR.
Psychological Impact of Security Lapses	Consequences of security breaches to improve system resilience.

5.2   Recommendations for Enhancing Metaverse Security and Privacy

The rapid growth of the metaverse raises concerns about data security, privacy, and risks to vulnerable populations, highlighting the need for strict security and ethical guidelines [6]. Future research should focus on governance frameworks, adaptive security methods, decentralized identity solutions, and AI-driven threat detection for consistent protection across platforms [15,54,55]. Cybersecurity education, interdisciplinary approaches blending technology, law, and ethics, and coordinated efforts from technologists, legal experts, and ethicists are essential for a secure, user-respecting metaverse [56–58]. Figures 3, 4 and 5 illustrate recommendations and current remedies for metaverse security and privacy.

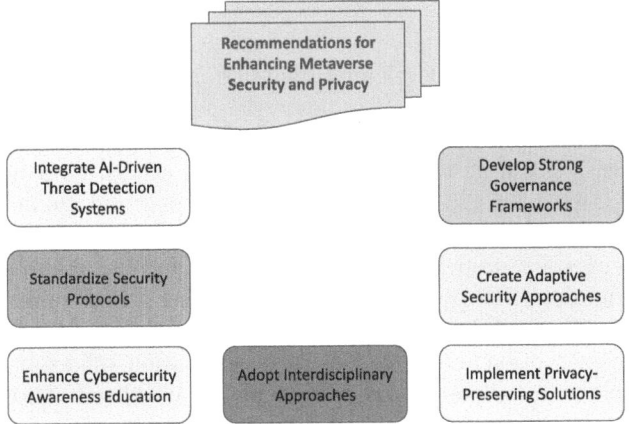

Fig. 3. Recommendations for Enhancing Metaverse Security and Privacy

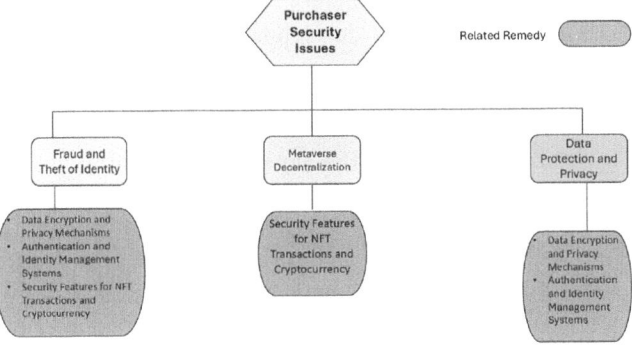

Fig. 4. Data Protection and Privacy Security, Metaverse Decentralization, and Fraud and Theft of Identity Issues with their Respective Current Remedies

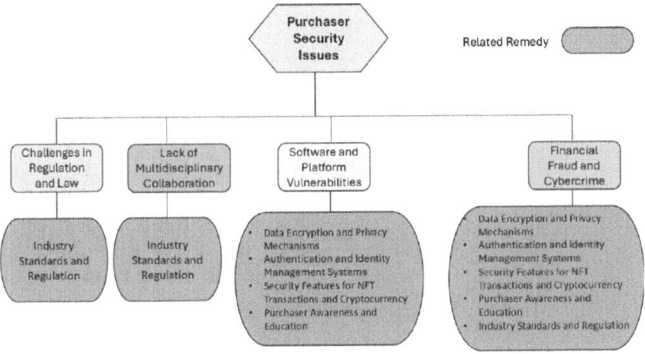

Fig. 5. Financial Fraud and Cybercrime, Software and Platform Vulnerabilities, Lack of Multidisciplinary Collaboration, and Challenges in Regulation and Law issues with their Respective Current Remedies

6 Conclusion

The metaverse is a quickly developing digital frontier that combines cultural, social, and economic activities in fully immersive virtual worlds. But this expansion also poses serious privacy and security risks that jeopardize buyers' security. Critical hazards, including as identity theft, illegal access, data breaches, and financial fraud, have been re-investigated by this review and are made worse by the complicated and decentralized structure of metaverse platforms. Advanced security measures are desperately needed, as seen by the widespread acquisition of personal data, the possibility of deepfake and AI-driven manipulations, and weaknesses in blockchain and smart contracts. Although current countermeasures, like encryption and multi-factor authentication, offer some protection, they are unable to completely handle the dynamic and diverse threats that are present in these virtual environments. More purchaser awareness of potential threats, improved cybersecurity methods, and stronger regulatory frameworks are urgently needed to protect purchasers. In order to create safe and reliable virtual worlds, this mini review highlights the need for a multidisciplinary approach that incorporates technology developments, legal protections, and ethical considerations. Subsequent investigations ought to concentrate on creating flexible security measures, refining data security methods, and creating laws that can efficiently manage the intricacies of the metaverse. Stakeholders can promote a safer digital ecosystem and support the metaverse's potential as a revolutionary platform for social and commercial interaction by filling in these gaps.

Acronyms

Acronym	Definition
NFT	Non-Fungible Token
VR	Virtual Reality
AR	Augmented Reality
MR	Mixed Reality
AI	Artificial Intelligence
MFA	Multi-Factor Authentication
PoW	Proof of Work
ZKP	Zero-Knowledge Proof
KYC	Know Your Customer
DoS	Denial of Service
GDPR	General Data Protection Regulation
DMCA	Digital Millennium Copyright Act
XRSI	Extended Reality Safety Initiative

Acknowledgments. This research was supported by the IRCC-2024-499 International Research Collaboration Co-Fund between Qatar University, Paris-Dauphine and Madrid Universities. The statements made herein are solely the responsibility of the authors.

References

1. Ritterbusch, G.D., Teichmann, M.R.: Defining the metaverse: a systematic literature review. IEEE Access **11**, 12368–12377 (2023)
2. Chen, Z., Wu, J., Gan, W., Qi, Z.: Metaverse security and privacy: an overview. In: 2022 IEEE International Conference on Big Data (Big Data), pp. 2950–2959. IEEE (2022)
3. Ng, D.T.K.: What is the metaverse? Definitions, technologies and the community of inquiry. Australas. J. Educ. Technol. **38**(4), 190–205 (2022)
4. Park, S.-M., Kim, Y.-G.: A metaverse: taxonomy, components, applications, and open challenges. IEEE access **10**, 4209–4251 (2022)
5. Kaur, J., Mogaji, E., Paliwal, M., Jha, S., Agarwal, S., Mogaji, S.A.: Consumer behavior in the metaverse. J. Consum. Behav. **23**(4), 1720–1738 (2024)
6. Dwivedi, Y.K., et al.: Metaverse marketing: How the metaverse will shape the future of consumer research and practice. Psychol. Mark. **40**(4), 750–776 (2023)
7. Hadi, R., Melumad, S., Park, E.S.: The metaverse: a new digital frontier for consumer behavior. J. Consum. Psychol. **34**(1), 142–166 (2024)
8. Wang, Q., Li, R., Wang, Q., Chen, S.: Non-fungible token (NFT): overview, evaluation, opportunities and challenges. arXiv preprint arXiv:2105.07447 (2021
9. Dalai, S.: A study of NFTs (non-fungible tokens).: diagnosis through the lenses of classical economics (2022)
10. Lee, C.T., Shen, Y.C., Li, Z., Xie, H.H.: The effects of non-fungible token platform affordances on customer loyalty: a buyer–creator duality perspective. Comput. Hum. Behav. **151**, 108013 (2024)
11. Hennig-Thurau, T., Aliman, D.N., Herting, A.M., Cziehso, G.P., Linder, M., Kübler, R.V.: Social interactions in the metaverse: framework, initial evidence, and research roadmap. J. Acad. Mark. Sci. **51**(4), 889–913 (2023)
12. Sai, S., Garg, A., Chamola, V.: Navigating the metaverse: a comprehensive analysis of consumer electronics prospects and challenges. ACM Trans. Internet Technol. (2024)
13. Gupta, A., Khan, H.U., Nazir, S., Shafiq, M., Shabaz, M.: Metaverse security: issues, challenges and a viable ZTA model. Electronics **12**(2), 391 (2023)
14. Özdemir, K., Çelebi, Ö.F. and Nacar, R.: Consumer security and privacy in the metaverse: a bibliometric analysis. Dokuz Eylül Üniversitesi İşletme Fakültesi Dergisi **25**(1), 111–130 (2024)
15. Wang, Y., et al.: A survey on metaverse: Fundamentals, security, and privacy. IEEE Commun. Surv. Tutorials **25**(1), 319–352 (2022)
16. Huang, Y., Li, Y.J., Cai, Z.: Security and privacy in metaverse: a comprehensive survey. Big Data Min. Anal. **6**(2), 234–247 (2023)
17. Gadekallu, T.R., et al.: Blockchain for the metaverse: a review. Future Gener. Comput. Syst. **143**, 401–419 (2023)
18. Rawat, D.B., El Alami, H.: Metaverse: requirements, architecture, standards, status, challenges, and perspectives. IEEE Internet Things Mag. **6**(1), 14–18 (2023)

19. Alsamhi, S.H., Hawbani, A., Kumar, S., Porwol, L.,d Curry, E.: Decentralized metaverse: Towards a secure, autonomous, and inclusive virtual world. In: 2023 International Conference on Electrical, Computer and Energy Technologies (ICE-CET), pp. 1–7. IEEE (2023)
20. Saeed Banaeian Far and Azadeh Imani Rad: Applying digital twins in metaverse: User interface, security and privacy challenges. J. Metaverse **2**(1), 8–15 (2022)
21. Awadallah, A., et al.: Artificial intelligence-based cybersecurity for the metaverse: research challenges and opportunities. IEEE Commun. Surv. Tutorials (2024)
22. Katterbauer, K., Syed, H., Cleenewerck, L.: Financial cybercrime in the Islamic finance metaverse. J. Metaverse **2**(2), 56–61 (2022)
23. Jiajing, W., Lin, K., Lin, D., Zheng, Z., Huang, H., Zheng, Z.: Financial crimes in WEB3-empowered metaverse: taxonomy, countermeasures, and opportunities. IEEE Open J. Comput. Soc. **4**, 37–49 (2023)
24. Sharma, S., Singh, J., Gupta, A., Ali, F., Khan, F., Kwak, D.: User safety and security in the metaverse: a critical review. IEEE Open J. Commun. Soc. (2024)
25. Wang, H., et al.: A survey on the metaverse: the state-of-the-art, technologies, applications, and challenges. IEEE Internet Things J. **10**(16), 14671–14688 (2023)
26. Ali, M., Naeem, F., Kaddoum, G., Hossain, E.: Metaverse communications, networking, security, and applications: Research issues, state-of-the-art, and future directions. IEEE Commun. Surv. Tutorials **26**, 1238–1278 (2023)
27. Kalyvaki, M.: Navigating the metaverse business and legal challenges: intellectual property, privacy, and jurisdiction. J. Metaverse **3**(1), 87–92 (2023)
28. Hutson, J., Banerjee, G., Kshetri, N., Odenwald, K., Ratican, J.: Architecting the metaverse: blockchain and the financial and legal regulatory challenges of virtual real estate. J. Intell. Learn. Syst. Appl. **15** (2023)
29. Jim, J.R., Hosain, M.T., Mridha, M.F., Kabir, M.M., Shin, J.: Towards trustworthy metaverse: advancements and challenges. IEEE Access **11**, 118318–118347 (2023)
30. Zou, Y., Roundy, K., Tamersoy, A., Shintre, S., Roturier, J., Schaub, F.: Examining the adoption and abandonment of security, privacy, and identity theft protection practices. In: Proceedings of the 2020 CHI Conference on Human Factors in Computing Systems (CHI 2020), pp. 1–10, Honolulu, HI, USA, 2020. ACM (2020)
31. Laurie, G., Harmon, S., Arzuaga, F.: Foresighting futures: law, new technologies, and the challenges of regulating for uncertainty. Law Innov. Technol. **4**(1), 1–38 (2012)
32. Safa, N.S., Sookhak, M., Von Solms, R., Furnell, S., Ghani, N.A., Herawan, T.: Information security conscious care behaviour formation in organizations. Comput. Secur. **53**, 65–78 (2015)
33. Qamar, S., Anwar, Z., Afzal, M.: A systematic threat analysis and defense strategies for the metaverse and extended reality systems. Comput. Secur. **128**, 103127 (2023)
34. Tukur, M., et al.: The metaverse digital environments: a scoping review of the challenges, privacy and security issues. Front. Big Data **6**, 1301812 (2023)
35. Zheng, Z.: Privacy computing meets metaverse: Necessity, taxonomy and challenges. Ad Hoc Netw. **158**, 103457 (2024)
36. Kshetri, N.: Privacy violations, security breaches and other threats of WEB3 and the metaverse (2023)
37. Ibrahim, I.F., Morsey, M.M., Mahmoud, A.M., El-Horbaty, E.S.M.: Towards developing a metaverse authentication model for mobile features. In: ICEIS, vol. 1, pp. 691–697 (2023)
38. Yu, T., et al.: Secure web objects: building blocks for metaverse interoperability and decentralization. arXiv preprint arXiv:2407.15221 (2024)

39. Truong, V.T., Le, L., Niyato, D.: Blockchain meets metaverse and digital asset management: a comprehensive survey. IEEE Access **11**, 26258–26288 (2023)
40. Aldweesh, A.: Enhancing metaverse security with block chain authentication: methods and analysis. Comput. Integr. Manuf. Syst. **29**(10), 1–13 (2023)
41. Rahaman, M.F., Golam, M., Subhan, M.R., Tuli, E.A., Kim, D.S., Lee, J.M.: Meta-governance: blockchain-driven metaverse platform for mitigating misbehavior using smart contract and AI. IEEE Trans. Netw. Serv. Manag. **21**, 4024–4038 (2024)
42. Huynh-The, T., et al.: Artificial intelligence for the metaverse: a survey. Eng. Appl. Artif. Intell. **117**, 105581 (2023)
43. Choi, M., Azzaoui, A.E., Singh, S.K., Salim, M.M., Jeremiah, S.R., Park, J.H.: The future of metaverse: security issues, requirements, and solutions. Hum. Centric Comput. Inf. Sci. **12**(60), 1–14 (2022)
44. Pearlman, K., Initiative, X., Visner, S., Magnano, M., Cameron, R.: Securing the metaverse-virtual worlds need real governance, Simulation Interoperability Standards Organization-SISO (2021)
45. De Asúa, E., Mangada Real, E., Otter, V., Tsukuda, T., Vivenot, B.: The metaverse challenges and regulatory issues. In: Master in Public Policy and Master in European AffairsDigital, New Technology and Public Policy streamCourse "Comparative approach to Big Tech regulation"(F. G'sell) Spring semester, p. 1 (2022)
46. Alauthman, M., Ishtaiwi, A., Al Maqousi, A., Hadi, W.: A framework for cybersecurity in the metaverse. In: 2024 2nd International Conference on Cyber Resilience (ICCR), pp. 1–8. IEEE (2024)
47. Erensoy, A., Mathrani, A., Schnack, A., Elms, J., Baghaei, N.: Consumer behavior in immersive virtual reality retail environments: a systematic literature review using the stimuli-organisms-responses (S-O-R) model. J. Consum. Behav. **23**, 2781–2811 (2024)
48. Rejeb, A., Rejeb, K., Treiblmaier, H.: Mapping metaverse research: identifying future research areas based on bibliometric and topic modeling techniques. Information **14**(7), 356 (2023)
49. Yang, L., Ni, S.T., Wang, Y., Yu, A., Lee, J.A., Hui, P.: Interoperability of the metaverse: a digital ecosystem perspective review. arXiv preprint arXiv:2403.05205 (2024)
50. Qayyum, A., et al.: Secure and trustworthy artificial intelligence-extended reality (AI-XR) for metaverses. ACM Comput. Surv. **56**(7), 1–38 (2024)
51. Pooyandeh, M., Han, K.-J., Sohn, I.: Cybersecurity in the AI-based metaverse: a survey. Appl. Sci. **12**(24), 12993 (2022)
52. Rehman, A., Siddiqui, M.A.: Navigating virtual economies: transformative impacts and challenges for forensic accounting in the metaverse. a conceptual overview. GRENZE Int. J. Eng. Technol. **10**(2), 2196–2207 (2024)
53. Al-kfairy, M., Alomari, A., Al-Bashayreh, M.G., Tubishat, M.: Unveiling the metaverse: a survey of user experience, social dynamics, and technological interoperability. Preprints (2024). Preprint
54. Bernabe, J.B., Canovas, J.L., Hernandez-Ramos, J.L., Moreno, R.T. and Skarmeta, A.: Privacy-preserving solutions for blockchain: review and challenges. IEEE Access **7**, 164908–164940 (2019)
55. Vegesna, V.V.: Enhancing cyber resilience by integrating AI-driven threat detection and mitigation strategies. Trans. Latest Trends Artif. Intell. **4**(4) (2023)
56. Bada, M., Sasse, A.M., Nurse, J.R.: Cyber security awareness campaigns: why do they fail to change behaviour? arXiv preprint arXiv:1901.02672 (2019)

57. Dhirani, L.L., Mukhtiar, N., Chowdhry, B.S., Newe, T.: Ethical dilemmas and privacy issues in emerging technologies: a review. Sensors **23**(3), 1151 (2023)
58. Lescrauwaet, L., Wagner, H., Yoon, C., Shukla, S.: Adaptive legal frameworks and economic dynamics in emerging technologies: navigating the intersection for responsible innovation. Law and Econ. **16**(3), 202–220 (2022)

Low-Resource Dataset Synthetic Generation for Hate Speech Detection

Adrián Girón[1]([⊠])[iD], Guillem Collell[2][iD], Fadi Hassan[2][iD],
Javier Huertas-Tato[1][iD], and David Camacho[1][iD]

[1] Universidad Politécnica de Madrid, Madrid, Spain
adrian.giron@upm.es
[2] Huawei Technologies Finland Research Center, Helsinki, Finland

Abstract. Text data augmentation typically involves adding noise to the original text, substituting words based on context, or rephrasing the original sentence. These traditional methods do not offer new perspectives that could help classifiers generalize better to new instances. This, combined with the fact that in certain fields, such as hate speech detection, creating these datasets is a highly intensive task, from collecting positive samples to labeling them, which usually requires experts in the target topic. In this work, we present *Lo*w-*R*esource *D*ataset *S*ynthetic *Gen*eration (*LoRDS-GEN*), an automatic text data augmentation method based on LLMs (*demonstration-based generation*), capable of providing varied samples that respect the original writing style. Our method focuses particularly on low-resource hate speech datasets, but we empirically discovered its potential and consistency even in larger and more robust datasets. The design of the prompt, combined with token sampling strategies, positions *LoRDS-GEN* as the most consistent alternative for LLM-based synthetic data generation compared to other existing methods and prompts in the state-of-the-art. Our benchmark includes (1) *CMSB*, a sexist dataset, and (2) *ETHOS*, a highly varied dataset with multiple forms of hate speech. *LoRDS-GEN* outperforms other traditional augmentation methods such as *NLPAug* and *BackTranslation*.

Keywords: Synthetic Data Generation · Demonstration-based Generation · LLM · Low-Resource Augmentation · Hate Speech Detection

1 Introduction

Extracting hate speech data is often a resource-intensive process, requiring methods like web scraping from social media platforms or constructing complex networks to identify malicious agents. While obtaining neutral samples is relatively straightforward, sourcing positive samples-particularly those related to specific topics such as sexism, racism, or targeted attacks on minorities can be much more

M. Barhamgi et al. (Eds.): WISE 2024, LNCS 15463, pp. 75–89, 2025.
https://doi.org/10.1007/978-981-96-1483-7_6

challenging. This makes the creation of hate speech datasets a time-consuming task [1].

In such scenarios, the ability to artificially augment a limited collection of seed samples would be highly beneficial. Ideally, data augmentation would not only involve paraphrasing existing sentences but also generate novel, semantically related sentences to enrich the representation of various classes within the dataset.

The synthetic generation of text data has always been a costly challenge, traditionally addressed through non-AI-based techniques [2]. These methods primarily involve modifying original sentences by altering characters or words without changing the underlying semantic content, thereby making text classification models more robust against noise. However, these approaches fall short in addressing the broader semantic spectrum of specific topics.

In recent years, the success of large language models (LLMs) in text generation, such as the widely known *ChatGPT* [3] or *Mistral* [4], has paved the way for the creation of synthetic text that is nearly indistinguishable from human-written content. These models, trained on vast corpora from across the internet, encompass both valuable and toxic material. As a result, an ideal scenario emerges in which LLMs become key tools for synthetic text data generation.

In this paper, we propose a method for semantic data augmentation using LLMs without moderation filters, that is, LLMs who have not received instruction-tuning to avoid potentially contentious or damaging responses. Our approach focuses on hate speech datasets and aims to augment datasets by generating additional hate speech samples that maintain coherence and semantic relevance. The proposed method improves the generalization of different text classification models in low-resources scenarios, without requiring any modifications to their architecture, only by enriching the original dataset with synthetic samples.

We focus our case study on hate speech datasets, as the collection of such samples is often resource-intensive and presents significant challenges in terms of data acquisition and ethical consideration. Also, recent changes in the data access policies of large online social networks have made extremely difficult data collection even for research purposes. Specifically, we benchmark our synthetic data against two popular hate speech datasets—the *Call me Sexist But... (CMSB)* dataset, containing sexist sentences extracted from online social networks and the *ETHOS* containing various types of hate speech such as violence, racism or disability discrimination.

The rest of the paper is structured as follows. Section (2) reviews the state of the art in synthetic data generation and perform a comparison with our method. Section (3) describes the generation method and the evaluation mechanism. Section (4) contains the experimental setup describing the dataset, the model selection and the employed training and evaluation techniques. Section (5) contains all the experimentation and discussion over the results. Finally, Sect. (6) contain the final remarks.

2   Related Work

In other data augmentation scenarios such as image, there exist highly effective and easily implementable techniques, such as transposition or random erasure [5]. Moreover, recent diffusion-based models have demonstrated the ability to generate images that are virtually indistinguishable from those created by humans [6]. These methods have been attempted in the field of text augmentation but have not produced consistent results. However, in recent years, with the emergence and scaling of LLMs, a new area of research has begun to take shape, focusing on the use of these models for text data augmentation.

Evaluating text augmentation techniques presents significant challenges due to factors such as the diversity of the generated samples and the confidence that the desired class is correctly represented in the synthetic data. Ultimately, the potential of the most prominent approaches relies heavily on the optimization of prompts, or prompt engineering.

2.1   Traditional Text Augmentation Techniques

Traditionally, in the field of text data augmentation, techniques that manipulate characters and/or words in original sentences are employed to make classification models more robust to noise. This is particularly useful in hate speech detection, as much of the hateful content is extracted from social media, where manipulated words and spelling errors are common.

At the character level, several techniques stand out, with four main operations being especially noteworthy: insertion, deletion, swapping and substitution [2,7], often simulating typographical errors. On the other hand, at the word level, the same transformations can be applied as with characters, except for insertion [8], since generating words based on context is not trivial, and randomness cannot be relied upon, as it can with characters. However, interesting approaches exist, such as replacing words with their synonyms using dictionaries [7], which helps models identify relationships between semantically similar words in different contexts.

Nevertheless, as previously mentioned, these methods are highly effective at improving generalization in the presence of noise, but they fail to introduce new semantic perspectives. Our method naturally incorporates some of these transformations, as it provides diverse sentences while preserving the original writing style, which, in some cases, even includes typographical errors.

2.2   LM-Based Data Augmentation Methods

Recurrent language models and, more recently, transformers [9], have been the most consistent option for performing data augmentation on text for several years now. These models are capable of processing text and generating high-quality semantic representations not only of each individual word or token but also of the entire sequence as a whole.

Given the accumulated context from a bidirectional Recurrent Neural Network and a label for a specific sentence, it is possible to predict a missing word. In this way, several augmented sentences can be obtained iteratively through word-swapping based on context [10]. Similarly, using transformers [9] in all their forms—encoders, decoders, and encoder-decoders—sub-sequences of the original sentence are masked by replacing them with $< MASK >$ tokens, and logits are used to select the sub-sequences based on the surrounding context [11], as is similarly done in the pre-training of $BERT$ [12].

Another of the most well-known text data augmentation techniques—and perhaps the most widely used—is back-translation. This method takes the sources and translates them into an auxiliary language, then translates them back into the original language. In this way, a slightly different sentence is obtained as the semantics of the original sentence are influenced by the biases of the auxiliary language, achieving a rephrasing of the original sentence [13]. This technique has varied greatly since its original proposal, which was through the use of an encoder-decoder. Today, it is more commonly seen through the use of decoders due to the great versatility of LLMs.

Along the same lines, the state-of-the-art seems to be settling on the use of these large models to generate synthetic data. Different techniques based on prompt engineering have been proposed, ranging from rephrasings [14] to more sophisticated prompts oriented towards the specific dataset to be augmented [15]. However, all of these techniques aim to improve the generalization of a classifier after adding synthetic data to a large scale complete dataset, which commonly results in poor outcomes [16,17].

Another approach in the use of LLMs is steer the generation. Although it has not been directly used to generate synthetic samples, it is worth mentioning because it allows the LLM to access a better representation of the label we are trying to generate. There are proposals aimed at improving the reasoning capacity by having the LLM itself generate responses about its failures, revealing the label when it is unable to resolve them in a zero-shot setting [18]. On the other hand, to steer the generation style, the entire dataset is encoded, and the mean of the representations - assumed to carry the "average semantic load" - is extracted. Empirically, it has been shown that adding this representation to new generations achieves this semantic style without even fine-tuning the model [19].

2.3 Augmentation in Hate Speech Detection for Low-Resource Text Datasets

When building a dataset for the classification of any type of hate speech, collecting positive samples poses a major challenge, as obtaining a consistent and representative sample requires identifying specific user hubs in, for instance, social media platforms. However, this is not the main issue. Labeling this type of behavior requires extensive sociological knowledge about the specific topic being classified and its context, as there is a significant risk of classification model bias.

One of the problems with hate speech is how subjective it is, to the extent that practical annotation techniques that work well in other domains (such as *Amazon Mechanical Turk*) fail in this one. Even with more robust methodologies than usual (multiple annotators per sample, pre-screening of annotators), the subjectivity of the domain is unavoidable.

Typically, real data is of higher quality than synthetic data. [1] collect data from multiple hate speech sources, creating a dataset that they use to augment other low-resource datasets. The addition of this data, despite not being a directed augmentation strictly dependent on the topic being augmented, results in better generalization of the classification models. On the other hand, [20] focus on improving the generalization of hate speech classification models across different languages. To achieve this, they apply named entity recognition (NER) to mask these kind of tokens, translate the rest of the sentence, and use an encoder to unmask them in the context of the target language. Additionally, [21] use fine-tuned encoders on hate speech to alter the token sampling from an LLM, steering its generation towards adversarial examples, or in other words, making them difficult to predict. This provides more complex instances, allowing a classification model to develop a better understanding of the hate speech target.

In certain papers can be observed what we have decided to call **pseudo-data-leaking**, where data augmentation is applied to the set that will be used for evaluation, which results in metric improvements. Although it is true that test samples are not directly added to the training set, semantically similar samples are introduced, which could be interpreted as giving the model "hints" about what it will encounter in the test set. There is some controversy surrounding the use of this methodology, and we do not condone its use. Instead trying to avoid the usage of the validation set in any way during the augmentation.

3 Method

In this paper, we introduce **LoRDS-GEN**, a text data augmentation method powered by LLMs capable of generating samples that are semantically similar to the original ones, while preserving the same tone and style. The result is not merely a rephrasing but an original sample.

Given a dataset $\mathbf{D}$ whose samples are composed of pairs $\{x_i, y_i\}$, where $\mathbf{x}$ represents the set of input variables (in this case, the text of the sample) and $\mathbf{y}$ the set of labels. We use a generator $\mathbf{G}$ (LLM-based) so that $\mathbf{G}(\mathbf{x}, \mathbf{y}|prompt)$ generates synthetic samples $\{x_i'\}$ from the original ones. Our method relies in the assumption that if $\{x_i, y_i\}$ belongs to the $\mathbf{D}$ distribution, $\{x_i', y_i\}$ does as well (this is what we call *label-sharing*). Finally, the synthetic samples are added to the original ones to form the new, partially synthetic dataset $\mathbf{D}'$. Afterwards, we built various transformer encoder-based text classification models and we compare the performance achieved with the original dataset $\mathbf{D}$ to that with the synthetic dataset $\mathbf{D}'$. For a fair comparison, the same seeds and pre-training states of the encoders are used (see 1 fig).

Our method is based on *demonstration-based prompting*, which means introducing samples from the original dataset into the prompt to guide the LLM's

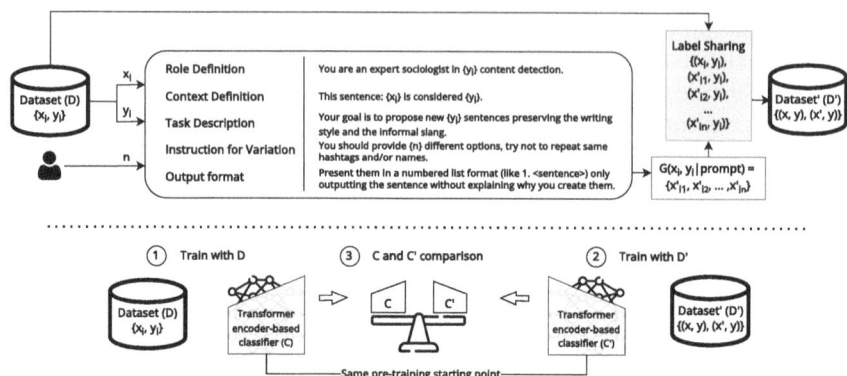

Fig. 1. *LoRDS-GEN* method overview. Source samples are embedded into our dedicated prompt to generate a new synthetic dataset. We compare the performance of the original dataset against the obtained with the synthetic one.

generation towards the original data distribution. However, these methods typically prompt the LLM to rephrase the samples [14, 16]. In contrast, we enforce through the prompt, and various token sampling mechanisms, that the generated samples are diverse from one another while maintaining the same semantic essence conveyed by the label (e.g., sexist samples).

The prompt consists of distinct parts. First, the role is defined, as this study focuses on data augmentation for hate speech, the generation must possess qualities of sociological understanding in the target domain. Second, the context is defined, conditioning the LLM to interpret the original sample as what it is expected for the label or topic. Next, the task is detailed, which is to generate samples based on the original, preserving the same slang and writing style. The LLM is then instructed to generate a sufficient number (n) of varied samples (mechanisms outside the prompt will be later explained to ensure variability). Finally, since this augmentation method is designed to not require human review, the LLM output is forced into a specific format to allow automatic parsing. It is important to note that the design of the prompt is not arbitrary; it has been refined from simpler prompts through to the final version, with the generated samples evaluated by humans.

Our method does not aim to improve generalization for models trained on large, consistent datasets, as both empirically and in the state of the art [16], it has been shown that real data typically have far better quality than synthetically generated data, which often results in sub-performance compared to original data or no improvement. Instead, we focus on low-resource datasets, which tend to have more semantic gaps that we aim to patch. This focus is especially relevant in datasets related to hate speech, where positive samples are difficult to collect.

4   Experimental Setup

The following section outlines the hate speech datasets used for evaluating the method, as well as the techniques and parameters applied for generating synthetic samples.

4.1   Datasets

We focus the use of **LoRDS-GEN** on hate speech detection, utilizing two particularly well-curated datasets. This is important because when performing *demonstration-based prompting*, synthetic samples will be of higher quality if the labeling is sufficiently accurate.

Call Me Sexist But... (CMSB) [22] - This binary classification dataset contains sexist and neutral samples collected from social media. During data collection, the authors developed a certain taxonomy or *codebook* to enhance the validity of the labeling and effectively verify the inter-annotator agreement using the *Amazon MTurk* platform. This dataset is especially challenging because it incorporates adversarial samples derived from sexist examples by stripping away the intent. Furthermore, it has been identified that a significant proportion of neutral samples are extracted from cooking competitions featuring women, which poses challenges for the model due to this being a recurrent sexist pattern.

ETHOS [23] - *ETHOS* is a dataset with both binary and multi-label versions. This dataset combines various samples extracted from the social platform *Reddit*, promoting hate speech, particularly racism, sexism, and attacks against religion, ethnicity, nationality, disability, sexual orientation, and gender identity. Its binary version is especially challenging because the label essentially indicates whether the comment contains any of the aforementioned hate speech types. This creates tremendous variability in terms of topics, enabling the creation of a benchmark to verify the versatility of our data augmentation model.

4.2   Model Selection

We use the LLM *Mistral-7B-Instruct-v0.2* [4], whose pre-trained version can be found on the *Hugging Face* platform. There are two reasons for this choice: first, despite its "small" size, this LLM performs quite similarly to the much larger *GPT-3.5* [24], and second, it lacks moderation mechanisms, allowing us to generate hate speech samples without the need for jailbreaking.

When comparing the performance of the original dataset against the synthetic one, we evaluate the performance both before and after adding the synthetic data. To build the text classifiers for this task, and to ensure consistent results, we use three state-of-the-art transformer encoders: *BERT*, in its *bert-base-uncased* version; *RoBERTa*, in its *roberta-base* version; and *DeBERTa*, in its *deberta-v3-base* version [12, 25, 26].

4.3   Generation, Training, and Evaluation Techniques

The key to our method lies largely in the prompt chosen to generate synthetic samples from the original ones. For *CMSB*, the keyword used for the positive class is *sexist*, while for *ETHOS*, we use *hate speech*; however, for the negative classes in both cases, we use *neutral* (see fig. 1). Additionally, a crucial aspect that helps ensure a certain level of quality and variability in the generated samples is the use of two token sampling methods during the LLM's output: (1) *typical_p* [27], which compares the conditional probabilities between the next predicted token or a random one, choosing tokens that wouldn't be *typical*, adding variability to the generation; we use values < 1, like 0.8, and (2) *repetition_penalty* [28], which applies a penalty factor to tokens that have already been generated, ensuring that new samples do not start with the same token and driving the LLM to generate different n samples; we use a value > 1, like 1.2. Regarding the temperature, we keep it at the default value of 1.0. We found that altering the other two parameters while increasing the temperature resulted in overly chaotic generation. Finally, the weights of the LLM are quantized to 4 bits, which allows for reasonably fast inference on a single GPU.

This study aims to simulate how synthetic data affects low-resource hate speech datasets. For this purpose, we perform downsampling of various sizes to observe how the proportion and quality of the synthetic data affect generalization. Each training size is a random and class-balanced sample extracted from the original dataset. To faithfully compare generalization across methods, we evaluate the *F1-score* obtained against a test set drawn from the original dataset (this test set is exclusively for evaluation and is not used to guide generation 2.3). Finally, the classifiers share the same architecture-differing only in the encoder-with the pooled output of the pre-trained models feeding into a binary classification head composed of a single linear layer. For training, we use the *AdamW* optimizer for a maximum of 30 epochs, with a learning rate of 1e-5 for the encoders and 1e-3 for the classification head.

4.4   Equipment and Timing

Both generation and training were performed using a 24 GB VRAM GPU. Training time ranged from a few minutes for smaller sample sizes to over an hour for larger ones. In total, with 2 datasets $\times$ 3 encoders $\times$ 13 augmentation techniques $\times \sim 10$ sub-sample sizes $\times$ 10 seeds per size, we conducted around 1300 training sessions, amounting to approximately 27 compute days. On the other hand, the optimized version of *Mistral-7B-Instruct-v0.2* was capable of generating samples at a speed of approximately 6 s per sample-*CMSB* has a training size of around 8k samples and *ETHOS* around 500-resulting in approximately 15 h per tested prompt.

5   Results

This paper aims to conduct a systematic analysis of how synthetic data generated by LLMs affect different dataset sizes, with particular interest in whether they can enhance generalization capabilities in low-resource datasets; all within the realm of hate speech detection. To achieve this, we study the performance of various text classification models—based on different transformer encoders—across different random samples of the original text data. The study ranges from extremely limited samples to the full dataset.

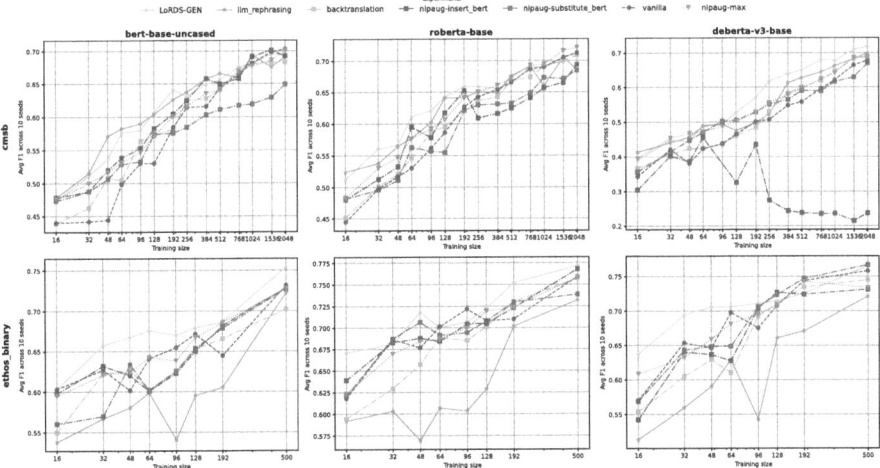

Fig. 2. Averaged 10 seed F1-score across different training sample sizes for both dataset, *CMSB* and *ETHOS*.

The selected samples are randomly extracted from the training sets with class equality (in this paper, we do not address data imbalance). To ensure consistent results, for each sample size, multiple training runs are performed using 10 different seeds, which affect not only the initialization of the weights of the classification layer of the models but also the sub-sample chosen from the training set on which augmentation will be applied. It is important to note that the data augmentation is done with a factor of 3, meaning that for each original sample, 3 synthetic ones are generated for all augmentation methods.

In the benchmark, our baseline or **vanilla** method simply consists of the original data without any type of data augmentation. Additionally, other state-of-the-art text data augmentation techniques are applied. First, we have traditional methods grouped under the **nlpaug-max** score; these techniques are implemented using a library of the same name. Specifically, we apply the **delete-char**, **delete-word**, **insert-char**, **substitute-char**, **substitute-wordnet**, **swap-char**, and **swap-word** techniques. The final metric for this group of techniques, for each sample size, is the average of the 3 best results. On the other hand, we compare with encoder-based augmentation techniques, specifically **insert-bert** and **substitute-bert**, also implemented in *nlpaug*. We also decided to compare with the most adapted state-of-the-art text data augmentation technique, **back-translation**, which uses an encoder-decoder to translate the original sentence.

Finally, to compare with other LLM-based augmentation methods, we adapted the prompt proposed in [14], specifically: *Rephrase this text: {text}*, which neither prioritizes context nor variability, aiming solely for rephrasing the original sentences.

We used the binary versions of the *CMSB* and *ETHOS* datasets. Both datasets contain samples of hate speech, specifically sexist speech for *CMSB*, and a mix of racism, minority attacks, etc., for *ETHOS*. The original version of *CMSB* is a consistent and sufficiently large dataset, allowing us to observe not only how synthetic data affects small samples but also whether the performance holds when a reasonable amount of data is available. The case of *ETHOS* is much more extreme, as it is a much smaller dataset, and its positive class contains various cases of hate speech.

Table 1. Averaged F1-score per encoder and size section. Last triplet rows for each dataset is the averaged metrics across the encoders.

Dataset	Model	Sizes	Vanilla	NLPAug	BackTrans	Ins-BERT	Sub-BERT	LLM-Rephrasing	LoRDS-GEN
CMSB	BERT	[16-96]	0.456	0.506	0.478	0.506	0.499	**0.537**	0.524
		[96-512]	0.575	0.594	0.594	0.604	0.574	**0.623**	0.621
		[512-2048]	0.672	0.668	0.669	0.675	0.619	0.673	**0.677**
	RoBERTa	[16-96]	0.497	0.534	0.505	0.530	0.513	0.551	**0.563**
		[96-512]	0.614	0.630	0.616	0.614	0.599	0.636	**0.647**
		[512-2048]	0.686	**0.693**	0.683	0.646	0.656	0.682	0.687
	DeBERTa	[16-96]	0.392	0.447	0.405	0.387	0.422	**0.449**	0.443
		[96-512]	0.492	0.530	0.498	0.320	0.530	0.520	**0.569**
		[512-2048]	0.610	0.636	0.637	0.231	0.606	0.654	**0.679**
	AVG	[16-96]	0.448	0.496	0.463	0.474	0.478	**0.512**	0.510
		[96-512]	0.560	0.585	0.570	0.527	0.568	0.593	**0.613**
		[512-2048]	0.656	0.666	0.663	0.517	0.627	0.670	**0.681**
ETHOS-binary	BERT	[16-48]	0.615	0.608	0.586	0.615	0.565	0.552	**0.630**
		[48-128]	0.632	0.635	0.618	0.615	0.620	0.573	**0.671**
		[128-500]	0.658	0.676	0.659	0.666	0.666	0.600	**0.683**
	RoBERTa	[16-48]	0.652	0.646	0.612	0.661	0.654	0.598	**0.676**
		[48-128]	0.700	0.690	0.677	0.692	0.697	0.593	**0.708**
		[128-500]	0.709	0.721	0.715	0.714	0.719	0.666	**0.737**
	DeBERTa	[16-48]	0.612	0.620	0.579	0.591	0.606	0.537	**0.666**
		[48-128]	0.673	0.679	0.644	0.656	0.668	0.587	**0.708**
		[128-500]	0.726	0.725	0.722	0.725	**0.735**	0.666	0.720
	AVG	[16-48]	0.626	0.625	0.592	0.622	0.608	0.562	**0.657**
		[48-128]	0.668	0.668	0.646	0.654	0.662	0.585	**0.696**
		[128-500]	0.698	0.708	0.699	0.702	0.707	0.644	**0.713**

5.1   LLM Generation Consistency

A data augmentation method must be consistent enough to at least meet the requirement that, in general, the performance obtained with augmented data should be greater than or equal to that obtained without the augmentation method in any scenario. Traditional augmentation or rephrasing methods have a strong dependence on the quality of the original samples, as they are ultimately altered versions of the originals. In contrast, *LoRDS-GEN* distills the extensive knowledge stored in an LLM on a specific topic (e.g., sexism) into new original instances that adhere to the writing style of the dataset being augmented.

The results obtained 1 support that *LoRDS-GEN*, despite not being the best in all proposed scenarios, proves to be the most consistent (best method in almost all averages across ranges). Other traditional methods occasionally outperform *LoRDS-GEN* (*NLPAug* in *CMSB* with $0.693F1_{[512-2048]}^{\text{RoBERTa}}$ and *Sub-BERT* in *ETHOS* with $0.735F1_{[128-500]}^{\text{DeBERTa}}$). This is due to *LoRDS-GEN* true potential focus in low-resource scenarios where available data is filled with semantic gaps. Once the proportion of real data increases, especially with high quality source data, we can observe that their performance begins to decline, although *LoRDS-GEN* remains the most consistent.

Another interpretation of these findings is that *variability comes at a cost*. Traditional methods do not deviate much from the style, thus they preserve the original text distribution more faithfully. The limitation of our method comes from the fact that the deviation in style - without performing any fine-tuning of the LLM - is small but inevitable, and becomes more pronounced as the scale of augmentation increases. This slight variability introduced by *LoRDS-GEN* seems to gradually shift the distribution of the training set, affecting the results. In contrast, traditional methods do not have this drawback, which may allow them to stand out more when the amount of data is sufficient and of high quality.

5.2 Synthetic Data Does Not Affect All Encoders Equally

As can be seen from the results, synthetic data offers inconsistent performance depending on the classification model. In the case of *CMSB*, LLM-based methods for *BERT* and *RoBERTa* achieve significantly higher performance in smaller $(+0.068F1_{[16-96]}^{\text{BERT}}$ and $+0.066F1_{[16-96]}^{\text{RoBERTa}})$ and medium ranges $(+0.046F1_{[96-512]}^{\text{BERT}}$ and $+0.033F1_{[96-512]}^{\text{RoBERTa}})$. However, in the case of *DeBERTa*, we observe that in smaller ranges, the difference is comparable to other traditional augmentation methods, but in larger ranges, the difference becomes much more pronounced $(+0.069F1_{[512-2048]}^{\text{DeBERTa}}$ compared to $+0.005F1_{[512-2048]}^{\text{BERT}}$ and $+0.001F1_{[512-2048]}^{\text{RoBERTa}})$.

The synthetic samples generated by LLMs tend to be "cleaner" than the original ones. Although LLMs are forced to respect a certain style (e.g., an informal social media post), they are generally less prone to grammatical and spelling errors. It appears that models like *BERT* and *RoBERTa* are much more sensitive to these changes in writing style, while this does not seem to be the case for *DeBERTa*.

5.3 Supremacy in Low-Resource Scenarios

The contribution of synthetic data generated by LLMs in low-resource scenarios comes from the addition of high-quality instances capable of filling the semantic gaps that occur due to the lack of real data. The conclusion is sufficiently consistent based on the results: synthetic data generated by LLMs using an demonstration-based generation strategy can greatly improve the performance of text classifiers in low-resource scenarios, especially when a prompt is selected that ensures quality and variability among the generated samples.

This does not mean that they cannot also provide performance boosts in scenarios where a substantial amount of instances is already available. However, as shown in 2, this effect is inconsistent. In *CMSB*, the performance increase with large amounts of data is considerable on average, driven by the surprising results of *DeBERTa* 5.2 ($+0.025F1^{AVG}_{[512-2048]}$). Nevertheless, it is not comparable to its significant impact in more limited scenarios ($+0.068F1^{AVG}_{[16-96]}$ and $+0.053F1^{AVG}_{[96-512]}$). Similarly, in *ETHOS*, the results point to the same conclusion: if we look at the average across the different encoders 1, the performance gains in more limited scenarios are $+0.031F1^{AVG}_{[16-48]}$ and $+0.028F1^{AVG}_{[48-128]}$, while as the proportion of real data increases, we only achieve gains of $+0.015F1^{AVG}_{[128-500]}$.

5.4   The Importance of the Prompt

We compare *LoRDS-GEN* prompt - whose results have undergone manual quality and variability review to ensure a certain guarantee of these qualities - with a much simpler prompt focused solely on rephrasing the original instances, *LLM-rephrasing*. The performance comparison varies greatly between datasets, as in the case of *CMSB*, simple rephrasing seems to work on par with a more elaborate prompt. However, in *ETHOS*, the difference is much more pronounced.

In the case of *CMSB*, both prompts dominate in very low-resource scenarios (*LLM-rephrasing* with $+0.064F1^{AVG}_{[16-96]}$, and *LoRDS-GEN* with $+0.062F1^{AVG}_{[16-96]}$). However, as the sample size increases, the difference in performance begins to favor *LoRDS-GEN*, which leads us to believe that a more sophisticated prompt provides more consistent results when applied to larger samples. On the other hand, the inconsistency of a simpler prompt is reflected in the case of *ETHOS*. This dataset is not only smaller but also more complex in terms of the classification of the positive label, making a more directed generation (*LoRDS-GEN*) clearly superior to simple rephrasing. The latter even worsens performance in all scenarios 1.

6   Conclusion

In this paper, we present *LoRDS-GEN*, an automatic data augmentation method based on LLMs, specifically aimed at low-resource datasets in the field of hate speech. Our study consists of a systematic analysis of how synthetic data impacts different text classification architectures across samples of varying sizes.

Our findings position *LoRDS-GEN* as the most consistent alternative compared to other traditional or rephrasing data augmentation techniques using only the training set to perform data augmentation. The results reveal that

LLM-based data augmentation is far superior to traditional methods in low-resource scenarios and remains more consistent even when datasets contain reasonable amounts of quality data. The design of the *LoRDS-GEN* prompt, along with token sampling techniques that ensure variability in the synthetic samples, makes our method a better alternative than other state-of-the-art LLM-based methods.

Despite *LoRDS-GEN*'s superiority in small and medium samples, its performance decreases as datasets grow with high-quality original samples. The main limitation of our method is the slight but inevitable deviation from the original data distribution, which can confuse classifiers when making large-scale predictions.

The experimentation in this study involves generating a fixed number of synthetic samples for each method. In future work, we aim to study the consequences of altering the number of generated samples as well as the inevitable loss of quality as this parameter increases. Additionally, we will examine how class imbalance affects our method and how the proportion of synthetic data can help in this issue. Finally, we will investigate how increasing the number of original samples that *LoRDS-GEN* is based on impacts the quality of the generated data.

Acknowledgments. The authors would like to acknowledge the contribution of Huawei Technologies Finland Research Center. This work was supported by the IBER-IFIER Plus project, co-funded by the European Commission under the Call DIGITAL-2023-DEPLOY-04, European Digital Media Observatory (EDMO) - National and multinational hubs, grant number: IBERIFIER Plus - 101158511. Additionally, this research was supported by the project PCI2022-134990-2 (MARTINI) of the CHIS-TERA IV Cofund 2021 program, funded by MCIN/AEI/10.13039/501100011033 and by the European Union NextGenerationEU/PRTR, and by EMIF, managed by the Calouste Gulbenkian Foundation, in the project MuseAI.

References

1. Ilan, T., Vilenchik, D.: HARALD: augmenting hate speech data sets with real data. In: Findings of the Association for Computational Linguistics: EMNLP 2022. Goldberg, Y., Kozareva, Z., Zhang, Y., (eds.) Abu Dhabi, United Arab Emirates: Association for Computational Linguistics, pp. 2241–2248 (2022). https://doi.org/10.18653/v1/2022.findings-emnlp.165. (Visited on 09/23/2024)
2. Belinkov, Y., Bisk, Y.: Synthetic and natural noise both break neural machine translation (2018). https://doi.org/10.48550/arXiv.1711.02173, arXiv:1711.02173 (2018) (Visited on 09/18/2024)
3. Mohamadi, S., et al.: ChatGPT in the age of generative AI and large language models: a concise survey. https://arxiv.org/abs/2307.04251v2 (2023). (Visited on 09/19/2024)
4. Jiang, A.Q., et al.: Mistral 7B. https://doi.org/10.48550/arXiv.2310.06825. arXiv: 2310.06825 (2023). (Visited on 09/17/2024)
5. Perez, L., Wang, J.: The effectiveness of data augmentation in image classification using deep learning. https://doi.org/10.48550/arXiv.1712.04621. arXiv:1712.04621 (2017). (Visited on 09/19/2024)

6. Ho, J., Jain, A., Abbeel, P.: Denoising diffusion probabilistic models. https://doi.org/10.48550/arXiv.2006.11239. arXiv:2006.11239 (2020). (Visited on 09/19/2024)
7. Wei, J., Zou, K.: EDA: easy data augmentation techniques for boosting performance on text classification tasks. In: Proceedings of the 2019 Conference on Empirical Methods in Natural Language Processing and the 9th International Joint Conference on Natural Language Processing (EMNLP-IJCNLP). Inui, K., et al. (eds.) Hong Kong, China: Association for Computational Linguistics, pp. 6382–6388 (2019). https://doi.org/10.18653/v1/D19-1670. (Visited on 09/18/2024)
8. Pavlick, E., et al.: PPDB 2.0: better paraphrase ranking, fine-grained entailment relations, word embeddings, and style classification. In: Proceedings of the 53rd Annual Meeting of the Association for Computational Linguistics and the 7th International Joint Conference on Natural Language Processing (Volume 2: Short Papers). Zong, C., Strube, M. (eds.) Beijing, China: Association for Computational Linguistics, pp. 425–430 (2015). https://doi.org/10.3115/v1/P15-2070. (Visited on 09/18/2024)
9. Vaswani, A., et al.: Attention is all you need. https://doi.org/10.48550/arXiv.1706.03762. arXiv:1706.03762 (2023). (Visited on 11/17/2023)
10. Kobayashi, S.: Contextual augmentation: data augmentation by words with paradigmatic relations. In: Proceedings of the 2018 Conference of the North American Chapter of the Association for Computational Linguistics: Human Language Technologies, Volume 2 (Short Papers). Walker, M., Ji, H., Stent, A. (eds.) New Orleans, Louisiana: Association for Computational Linguistics, pp. 452–457 (2018). https://doi.org/10.18653/v1/N18-2072. (Visited on 09/12/2024)
11. Kumar, V., Choudhary, A., Cho, E.: Data Augmentation using pre-trained transformer models. arXiv: 2003.02245 (2021). (Visited on 09/04/2024)
12. Devlin, J., et al.: BERT: pre-training of deep bidirectional transformers for language understanding. https://doi.org/10.48550/arXiv.1810.04805. arXiv: 1810.04805 (2019). (Visited on 11/22/2023)
13. Sennrich, R., Haddow, B., Birch, A.: improving neural machine translation models with monolingual data. In: *Proceedings of the 54th Annual Meeting of the Association for Computational Linguistics (Volume 1: Long Papers).* Erk, K., Smith, N.A., (eds.) Berlin, Germany: Association for Computational Linguistics, pp. 86–96 (2016).. https://doi.org/10.18653/v1/P16-1009. (Visited on 09/12/2024)
14. Dai, H., et al.: AugGPT: leveraging ChatGPT for Text Data Augmentation. arXiv: 2302.13007 (2023). (Visited on 07/18/2024)
15. Yoo, K.M., et al.: GPT3Mix: leveraging large-scale language models for text augmentation. arXiv: 2104.08826 (2021). (Visited on 09/04/2024)
16. Li, Z., et al.: Synthetic data generation with large language models for text classification: potential and limitations. arXiv: 2310.07849 (2023). (Visited on 09/04/2024)
17. Ye, J., et al.: ZeroGen: efficient zero-shot learning via dataset generation. arXiv: 2202.07922 (2022). (Visited on 07/01/2024)
18. Zelikman, E., et al.: STaR: bootstrapping reasoning with reasoning. arXiv: 2203.14465 (2022). (Visited on 07/18/2024)
19. Konen, K., et al.: Style vectors for steering generative large language model. arXiv: 2402.01618 (2024). (Visited on 06/13/2024)
20. Khullar, A., et al.: Hate speech detection in limited data contexts using synthetic data generation. In: ACM J. Comput. Sustain. Soc. **2**(1), 4:1–4:18 (2024). https://doi.org/10.1145/3625679. (Visited on 09/12/2024)

21. Hartvigsen, T., et al.: ToxiGen: a large-scale machine-generated dataset for adversarial and implicit hate speech detection (2022). arXiv:2203.09509 (2022). (Visited on 09/04/2024)
22. Samory, M., et al.: Call me sexist, but : revisiting sexism detection using psychological scales and adversarial samples. In: Proceedings of the International AAAI Conference on Web and Social Media. vol. 15. Association for the Advancement of Artificial Intelligence (AAAI), pp. 573–584 (2021). https://doi.org/10.1609/icwsm.v15i1.18085. (Visited on 09/17/2024)
23. Mollas, I., et al.: ETHOS: an online hate speech detection dataset. Complex Intell. Syst. **8**(6), 4663–4678 (2022). ISSN: 2199-4536, 2198-6053. https://doi.org/10.1007/s40747-021-00608-2. arXiv: 2006.08328 (Visited on 09/17/2024)
24. Ouyang, L., et al.: Training language models to follow instructions with human feedback. https://doi.org/10.48550/arXiv.2203.02155. arXiv:2203.02155 (2022). (Visited on 09/26/2024)
25. Liu, Y., et al.: RoBERTa: a robustly optimized BERT pretraining approach. https://arxiv.org/abs/1907.11692v1 (2019). (Visited on 09/18/2024)
26. He, P., et al.: DeBERTa: decoding-enhanced BERT with disentangled attention. arXiv: 2006.03654 (2021). (Visited on 05/23/2023)
27. Meister, C., et al.: Locally Typical Sampling. arXiv: 2202.00666 (2023). (Visited on 09/27/2024)
28. Keskar, N.S., et al.: CTRL: a conditional transformer language model for controllable generation. arXiv: 1909.05858 (2019). (Visited on 09/27/2024)

Web Open Data to SDG Indicators: Towards an LLM-Augmented Knowledge Graph Solution

Wissal Benjira[1,2]([✉]) [iD], Faten Atigui[3] [iD], Bénédicte Bucher[2] [iD],
Malika Grim-Yefsah[2] [iD], and Nicolas Travers[1,3] [iD]

[1] De Vinci Higher Education, DVRC Research Center, Paris, France
{wissal.benjira,nicolas.travers}@devinci.fr
[2] LASTIG, IGN, Université Gustave Eiffel, Paris, France
{benedicte.bucher,malika.grim-yefsah}@ign.fr
[3] CEDRIC, Conservatoire National des Arts et Métiers, Paris, France
faten.atigui@lecnam.net

Abstract. Meeting the Sustainable Development Goals (SDGs) established by the United Nations, presents a large-scale challenge for all countries. To monitor progress towards these goals, there is a need to develop key performance indicators using existing data and metadata. The computation of the indicators requires integrating and analyzing heterogeneous datasets, in particular web open data. This approach aims to highlight the positive impact of the web on the society. However, the diversity of web data sources and formats raises major issues in terms of structuring and integration. Despite the abundance of open data and metadata, its exploitation remains limited, leaving untapped potential for guiding urban policies towards sustainability. We have so far introduced a novel approach for SDG indicator computation, leveraging the capabilities of Large Language Models (LLMs) and Knowledge Graphs (KGs). We have proposed a method that combines rule-based filtering with LLM-powered schema mapping to establish semantic correspondences between diverse data sources and SDG indicators, including disaggregated attributes. Our approach integrated these mappings into a KG, which enables indicator computation by querying graph's topology. Finally, we have evaluated our method through a case study focusing on the SDG Indicator 11.7.1 about accessibility of public open spaces. Our experimental results are promising showing significant improvements compared to traditional schema matching techniques.

Keywords: Sustainable Development Goals (SDG) · Large Language Model (LLM) · Knowledge Graph (KG) · Open Data · Schema Mapping

1 Introduction

The Sustainable Development Goals (SDGs) established by the United Nations (UN) represent a global call to action for addressing contemporary challenges. In this context, relevant information is capital for decision-making processes. Each of the 17 goals is linked to targets and indicators to monitor progress [6].

To be measured, these indicators require web open datasets scaled in both time and space. Confronted to this complexity, international organizations are urging nations to enhance documentation and data collection efforts [19]. Thus, data heterogeneity and semantic consistency are a long way from being granted [5].

Knowledge Graphs (KGs) emerge as a promising solution to overcome the hurdles of heterogeneous data sources and formats [9]. Indeed, by representing data as interconnected nodes and relationships, KGs provide a flexible framework for integrating diverse datasets. KGs have been applied to SDGs in projects such as LinkedSDGs [11] and SustainGraph [5]. These projects mainly focus on goals and targets interactions, yet indicator assessment remains largely unexplored.

To compute SDG indicators, the UN provides documentation with detailed formulas and related metadata, often in unstructured textual formats. Manually processing these documents is time-consuming and error-prone, highlighting the need for automated extraction and analysis. Linking these documents with web open data sources also requires deep expertise, making Natural Language Processing (NLP) techniques like entity recognition and textual mapping essential.

Recent NLP advancements, particularly in Large Language Models (LLMs), have improved the handling of complex semantic tasks. While research has explored using LLMs to enhance KGs, their application in sustainability remains untapped. LLMs show promise in schema mapping due to their ability to understand and interpret data semantics and context usefull to monitor SDGs.

To enhance LLM performance, we propose using advanced filtering rules during pre-processing, including regular expressions for pattern matching, type checks for consistency, and value range validation to eliminate anomalies. These steps clean and structure the data before it enters the LLM, improving the accuracy and reliability of results. Additionally, we recommend applying collection rules to ensure spatial and conceptual disaggregation for better outcomes.

This paper presents two main contributions. First, our approach to define an SDG schema for indicators' measurement based on open metadata. This schema allows a global view for the second contribution, the introduction of a method for mapping open web data with SDG concepts using LLMs. The links formed help us build our resulting KG. The next section reviews related work. Section 3 presents our modeling approach. Finally, Section 4 describes the results and discusses the insights and limitations obtained for future directions.

2 Litterature Review

The modeling of SDG data presents significant challenges due to the complexities and heterogeneity inherent in data schemas worldwide. Although various research efforts have developed techniques for managing SDG data [1,10,12,14], there is a noticeable gap in computational models that integrate external web open data with SDG indicators. KGs have been applied to SDGs in projects such as LinkedSDGs [11] and SustainGraph [5], primarily focusing on the interactions between goals and targets, yet the assessment of specific indicators remains underexplored.

LLMs have revolutionized NLP by offering advanced capabilities in understanding and generating human-like text. Their ability to grasp context and semantics has significantly improved the processing and interpretation of complex documentation, such as that required for SDG metadata conceptualization. However, while LLMs excel in many tasks, they often struggle with domain-specific challenges due to their training on general corpora. To enhance their effectiveness, pre-processing steps like filtering and data structuring are crucial [8].

Recent research have explored the integration of LLMs with KGs to leverage textual information and enhance performance in downstream tasks [20]. KGs offer a structured framework to manage the heterogeneous data sources by representing data as interconnected nodes and relationships [9]. LLMs can process large textual corpora to enrich KG and extract entities and relations for KG construction [13,25]. Techniques have been developed to create prompts that convert structured KGs into formats comprehensible to LLMs, helping tasks like KG construction, completion, and reasoning [3,7,21]. However, these methods have not yet been applied to SDGs due to the lack of structured open data.

Schema mapping is a crucial task in data integration, it is the identification of semantic correspondences between elements of different database schemas [18]. This task is challenging due to semantic and structural heterogeneity, where schema elements may have different names but similar meanings, or vice versa [8]. Even more, traditional approaches often fail when semantic similarity is hard to detect, with disjoint values or different languages [23]. The advancements in NLP have introduced the use of LLMs for schema mapping, showing promise due to their ability to understand the context and semantics [15,24]. Enhancing schema

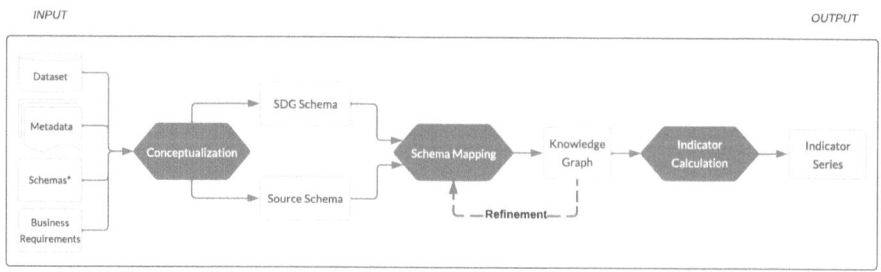

Fig. 1. Approach Overview for SDG Indicator Modeling and Calculating using Web Open Data

mapping through the inclusion of disaggregation criteria can improve accuracy, as it allows for the identification of complex link within the data [8].

3   Approach Overview

In this section, we present an overview of our approach for SDG indicator modeling and calculating using web open data (Fig. 1). It is divided into three main phases: *Conceptualization, Schema Mapping*, and *Indicator Computation*.

The process begins with a collection of data sources from diverse sources as well as metadata providing information and context. These inputs are essential as they form the foundation for the entire data modeling effort. The selected sources are driven by business requirements, which outline objectives and needs.

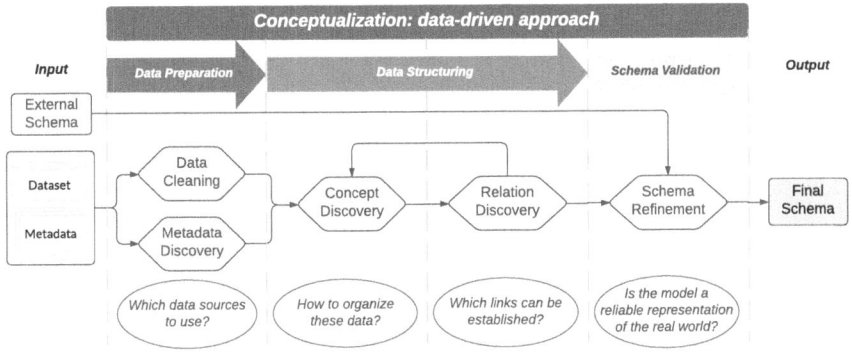

Fig. 2. Data-Driven Approach for Modeling web open data

3.1   Conceptualization

Conceptualization (Fig. 2) focuses on generating data schema from heterogeneous inputs. This step is crucial as it sets the stage for how the data will be organized and integrated in subsequent steps. During this phase, data elements are defined, and their interrelationships are established to form a general data model. On the one hand, the SDG metadata descriptions provided by the UN help generate the entities used to calculate the indicator. On the other hand, data sources are used to refine the properties of said entities.

Data Preparation involves pre-processing data, including *Data Cleaning* to fix errors, and *Metadata Discovery* to contextualize data [2]. Following this, Data Structuring organizes the data by identifying key entities and establishing relationships amongst them through *Concept* and *Relation Discovery* [16,17]. Finally, Schema Validation ensures the data structure meets standards through refinement and integration of external data, resulting in a reliable and consistent schema for real-world application [22].

In order to instantiate the output schema, we store data as a *Labeled Property Graph*. This graph data structure is useful when dealing with mappings between the SDG entities. The motivation of this choice is twofold. First, the graph structure helps the exploration between indicators' relationships. Second, the graph serves as a valuable tool for refining indicators.

We choose to illustrate specific entities based on UN metadata (Fig. 3). The Goal 11 is titled *"Sustainable cities and communities"*. This goal includes Targets 11.7. The Indicator 11.7.1 is linked to this target and measures the average share of the built-up area of cities meaning open public spaces. The UN metadata defines concepts and their description to compute the indicator. For computing the formula of this indicator the three following concepts are needed: *City*, *PublicSpace* and *Street*. The challenges covered by Goal 11 are given by the 2022 French Volunteer National Revue and as described in a UN report, the impacts are categorized into *Economic*, *Social*, and *Environmental* types.

On the one hand, we obtain a graph of the concepts and definitions, and on the other hand, a graph representing the data sources schema. On the graph, the two schemas are currently disassociated. Our objective is to calculate an indicator from open data, which requires these schemas to be connected. Therefore, we aim to identify the correspondences between the schemas.

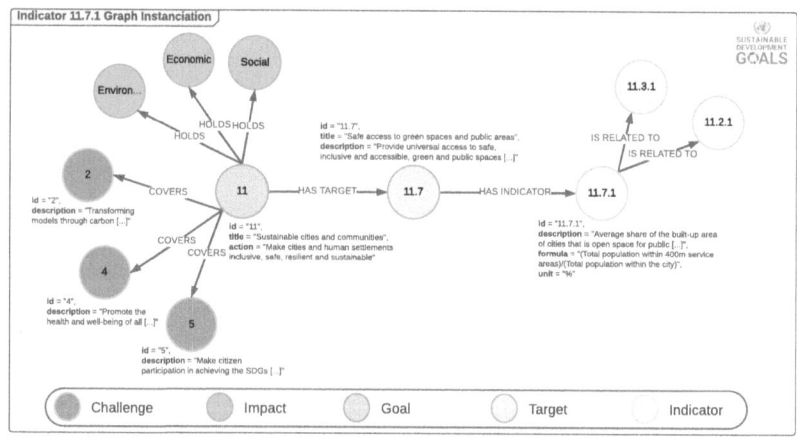

Fig. 3. Indicator 11.7.1 Graph Instanciation

3.2   Schema Mapping

Schema Mapping propose a two-step novel approach for KG construction consisting of rule-based filters and LLM-based matching of attributes and columns.

Experimental Setup and Driving Example. With half of the world's population living in urban areas, addressing urban challenges is crucial. Structuring web open data is essential for tackling these challenges, as it provides valuable insights for guiding urban policies towards sustainability, particularly for SDG 11. We focused on Indicator 11.7.1 using France's population census since 2006 and their Sport Ministry's open database related to sport facilities.

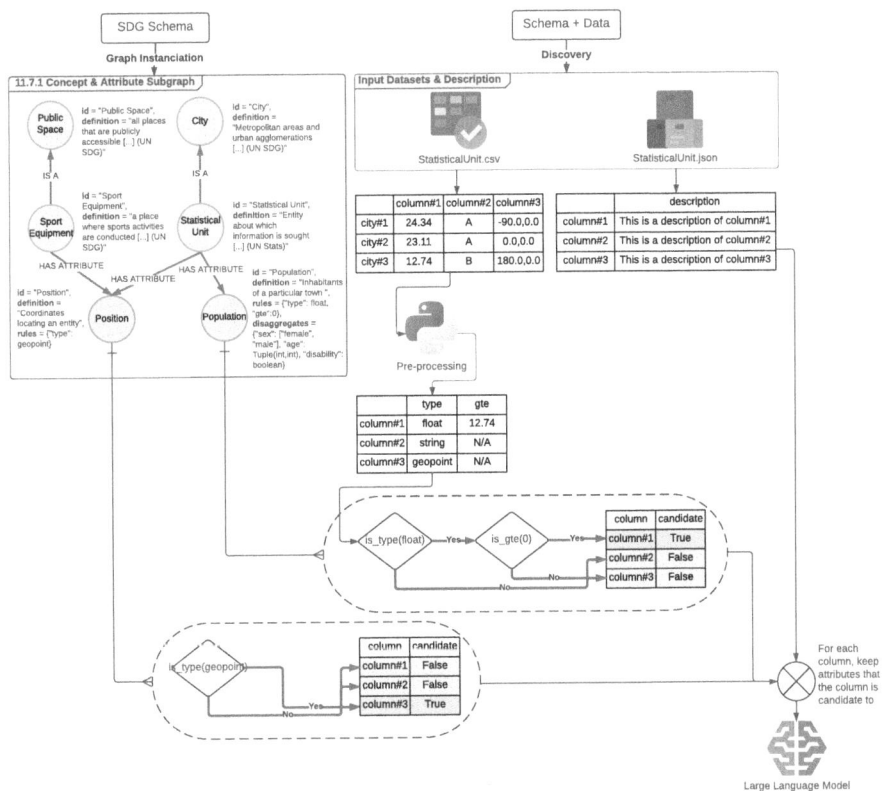

Fig. 4. Driving Example Process

The process in Fig. 4 starts with external sources. For each column, rules respective to each attribute are checked to determine eligibility. For example, column#1 is a candidate to "Population" because it is a non-negative numerical column. Next, the LLM is employed to map columns with eligible SDG attributes. `Pydantic` allows us to parse an LLM output to our SDG schema.

Comparison with Existing Mapping Methods. Our method was evaluated against non-LLM models Cupid [18] and Jaccard-Levenshtein Matcher [4]. Each method has its unique hyperparameters which were grid-searched to achieve optimal performance.

4 Results and Discussions

For both studied entities, our approach surpasses traditional schema matching methods (Table 1) in terms of accuracy, precision, recall, and F1-score.

For the SportFacility entity, only the Position attribute is present. Our approach achieves perfect scores on all metrics. In contrast, Cupid achieved only 6.19% accuracy. These results suggest that while some methods may return capture positive matches, they lack precision and overpredict. JaccardDistanceMatcher performed well. However, it may be limited by reliance on specific distance functions like Levenshtein.

For the StatisticalUnit entity, the goal is to map a larger number of relevant attributes. Our approach showed high performance with 99.51% accuracy, 98.31% precision, 100% recall, and a 99.15% F1-score. This confirms the robustness of our method. Cupid's performance improved compared to the SportFacility entity but still lagged behind with 23.04% accuracy and a 24.88% F1-score.

Table 1. Grid Search Results of schema matching methods with their parameters and evaluation metrics

Entity	Method	Parameters	Accuracy	Precision	Recall	F1-score
SportFacility	Cupid [18]	w_struct: 0.9, leaf_w_struct: 0.01, th_accept: 0.1, few-shot: true	6.19	0.93	100.00	1.85
	JaccardDistanceMatcher [4]	threshold: 0.5, distance_fun: StringDistanceFunction.Levenshtein, few-shot: true	100.00	100.00	100.00	100.00
	Our Approach	**model: gpt-4-turbo, temperature: 0.0, pre-filtering: True, few-shot: True**	**100.00**	**100.00**	**100.00**	**100.00**
StatisticalUnit	Cupid [18]	w_struct: 0.9, leaf_w_struct: 0.01, th_accept: 0.1, few-shot: true	23.04	17.22	44.83	24.88
	JaccardDistanceMatcher [4]	threshold: 0.5, distance_fun: StringDistanceFunction.DamerauLevenshtein, few-shot: true	82.84	76.74	56.90	65.35
	Our Approach	**model: gpt-4-turbo, temperature: 0.1, pre-filtering: True, few-shot: True**	**99.51**	**98.31**	**100.00**	**99.15**

The ablation study results, shown in Table 2, highlight the impact of pre-filtering and few-shot learning on the performance of the GPT-3.5-turbo and GPT-4-turbo models. For the GPT-3.5-turbo model, the inclusion of few-shot learning significantly improves performance. Without pre-filtering and few-shot learning, the model achieves an accuracy of 21.08%. Adding few-shot learning increases the accuracy to 47.55%. When both pre-filtering and few-shot learning are applied, the accuracy further improves to 69.61%, indicating the combined benefits of these techniques. The GPT-4-turbo model demonstrates even more substantial improvements, with a higher start on accuracy.

Overall, these results indicate that both pre-filtering and few-shot learning significantly enhance the performance of GPT-based models in schema matching tasks. However, it is undeniable that the bias brought by few-shot should be mitigated in the next inquiries.

4.1 Indicator Calculation

Using the results mapped with LLMs and integrated into our Knowledge Graph, we can calculate specific indicators for cities such as `Villejuif, France`.

Figure 5 illustrates how we are able to compute SDG indicators using our method. Here, the blue line represents the total population (POP), the orange line indicates the number of people aged 0 to 14 (POP0014), the green line shows those aged 15 to 64 (POP1564) and the red line shows those aged 65 and older (POP65P). The gray bars illustrate the number of sport facilities and are represented on the left y-axis.

From 2006 to 2010, accessibility remains relatively stagnant. From 2010 to 2015, accessibility increases for all population groups. The total population's

Table 2. Ablation Study Metric Results

Model	Pre-filtering	Few-shot	Accuracy	Precision	Recall	F1-score
gpt-3.5-turbo	False	False	21.08	21.86	68.97	33.20
		True	47.55	35.15	100.00	52.02
	True	False	50.49	36.48	100.00	53.46
		True	69.61	48.33	100.00	65.17
gpt-4-turbo	False	False	67.16	46.34	98.28	62.98
		True	91.18	76.32	100.00	86.57
	True	False	87.25	69.51	98.28	81.43
		True	**99.02**	**96.67**	**100.00**	**98.31**

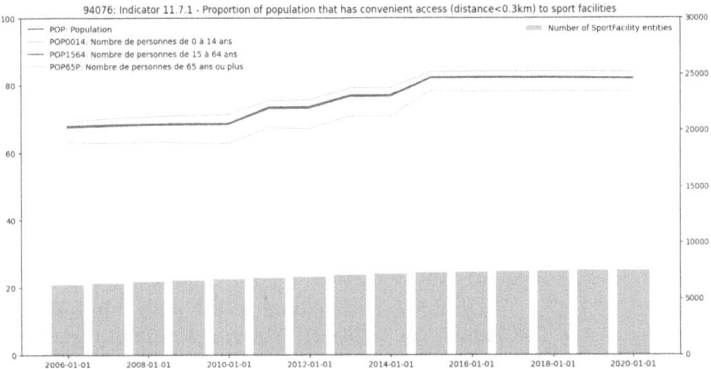

Fig. 5. SDG Indicator 11.7.1 – Number of Facilities from 2006 to 2020 in Villejuif.

accessibility rises from 68% to 82%, adolescents from 71% to 83%, and seniors from 62% to 78%. Despite these improvements, seniors consistently have the lowest accessibility. From 2015 to 2020, accessibility levels off again, showing little to no change. The increase in accessibility between 2010 and 2015 could be linked to the development of transport infrastructure in `Villejuif`, such as the introduction of bus 293 in 2011 and the tramway 7 in 2013. Additionally, the number of sport facilities shows an increasing trend over time, which likely contributes to the improved accessibility.

5 Conclusion and Future Work

Accurately measuring Sustainable Development Goals (SDGs) through their indicators is critical for shaping effective global policies. Current methods often fall short in linking diverse, heterogeneous data sources to specific SDG indicators. By integrating Large Language Models (LLMs) with Knowledge Graphs (KGs), we can leverage the semantic understanding of LLMs and the structured relationships within KGs to improve the accuracy and reliability of indicator computation. Our approach, tested on SDG Indicator 11.7.1, demonstrated significant improvements over traditional methods, highlighting the potential of this combined technique to better support global sustainability efforts.

However, the use of LLMs may introduce biases or errors in data interpretation, which is a question we aim to address. Moving forward, we will address the quality of data sources, as reliable indicators depend on high-quality inputs. Additionally, we plan to define metrics to measure the quality of calculated indicators and expand our approach to other SDG indicators, refining filtering rules and inference methods for enhanced precision and decision-making.

References

1. Almannaei, N.A., Akhter, M.S., Shah, A.: Improving environmental policy-making process to enable achievement of sustainable development goals. Environ. Policy Law **50**(1–2), 47–54 (2020)
2. Brownlee, J.: Data Preparation for Machine Learning: Data Cleaning, Feature Selection, and Data Transforms in Python. Machine Learning Mastery (2020)
3. Chen, Z., Xu, C., Su, F., Huang, Z., Dou, Y.: Incorporating structured sentences with time-enhanced BERT for fully-inductive temporal relation prediction. In: Proceedings of the 46th International ACM SIGIR Conference on Research and Development in Information Retrieval, pp. 889–899. SIGIR 2023, New York, NY, USA (2023). https://doi.org/10.1145/3539618.3591700
4. Do, H.H., Rahm, E.: Chapter 53 - coma — a system for flexible combination of schema matching approaches. In: Bernstein, P.A., Ioannidis, Y.E., Ramakrishnan, R., Papadias, D. (eds.) VLDB 2002: Proceedings of the 28th International Conference on Very Large Databases, pp. 610–621. Morgan Kaufmann (2002). https://doi.org/10.1016/B978-155860869-6/50060-3

5. Fotopoulou, E., Mandilara, I., Zafeiropoulos, A., Laspidou, C., Adamos, G., Koundouri, P., Papavassiliou, S.: SustainGraph: a knowledge graph for tracking the progress and the interlinking among the sustainable development goals' targets. Front. Environ. Sci. **10** (2022). https://doi.org/10.3389/fenvs.2022.1003599
6. Guo, H., et al.: Measuring and evaluating SDG indicators with big earth data. Sci. Bull. **67**(17), 1792–1801 (2022). https://doi.org/10.1016/j.scib.2022.07.015
7. Han, R., Peng, T., Wang, B., Liu, L., Tiwari, P., Wan, X.: Document-level relation extraction with relation correlations. Neural Netw. **171**(C), 14–24 (2024). https://doi.org/10.1016/j.neunet.2023.11.062
8. Hättasch, B., Truong-Ngoc, M., Schmidt, A., Binnig, C.: It's AI match: a two-step approach for schema matching using embeddings. In: AIDB@VLDB (2020)
9. Hogan, A., et al.: Knowledge graphs. ACM Comput. Surv. **54**(4) (2021). https://doi.org/10.1145/3447772
10. Howells, M., et al.: Integrated analysis of climate change, land-use, energy and water strategies. Nat. Clim. Chang. **3**(7), 621–626 (2013)
11. Joshi, A., et al.: A knowledge organization system for the united nations sustainable development goals. In: Verborgh, R., et al. (eds.) The Semantic Web, pp. 548–564. Springer International Publishing, Cham (2021)
12. Joshi, D.K., Hughes, B.B., Sisk, T.D.: Improving governance for the post-2015 sustainable development goals: scenario forecasting the next 50 years. World Dev. **70**, 286–302 (2015)
13. Kumar, A., Pandey, A., Gadia, R., Mishra, M.: Building knowledge graph using pre-trained language model for learning entity-aware relationships. In: 2020 IEEE International Conference on Computing, Power and Communication Technologies (GUCON), pp. 310–315 (2020). https://doi.org/10.1109/GUCON48875.2020.9231227
14. Kumar, P., Ahmed, F., Singh, R.K., Sinha, P.: Determination of hierarchical relationships among sustainable development goals using interpretive structural modeling. Environ. Dev. Sustain. **20**, 2119–2137 (2018)
15. Li, Y., Li, J., Suhara, Y., Doan, A., Tan, W.C.: Deep entity matching with pre-trained language models. Proc. VLDB Endow. **14**(1), 50–60 (2020). https://doi.org/10.14778/3421424.3421431
16. Liang, Y., Liu, X., Zhang, J., Song, Y.: Relation discovery with out-of-relation knowledge base as supervision. In: Burstein, J., Doran, C., Solorio, T. (eds.) Proceedings of the 2019 Conference of the North American Chapter of the Association for Computational Linguistics: Human Language Technologies, Volume 1 (Long and Short Papers), pp. 3280–3290. Association for Computational Linguistics, Minneapolis, Minnesota (2019). https://doi.org/10.18653/v1/N19-1332
17. Lin, D., Pantel, P.: Concept discovery from text. In: Proceedings of the 19th International Conference on Computational Linguistics - Volume 1, pp. 1–7. COLING 2002, Association for Computational Linguistics, USA (2002). https://doi.org/10.3115/1072228.1072372
18. Madhavan, J., Bernstein, P.A., Rahm, E.: Generic schema matching with cupid. In: Proceedings of the 27th International Conference on Very Large Data Bases, pp. 49–58. VLDB 2001, Morgan Kaufmann Publishers Inc., San Francisco, CA, USA (2001)
19. Nations, U.: Transforming our world: The 2030 agenda for sustainable development (2015)
20. Pan, S., Luo, L., Wang, Y., Chen, C., Wang, J., Wu, X.: Unifying large language models and knowledge graphs: a roadmap. IEEE Trans. Knowl. Data Eng. pp. 1–20 (2024). https://doi.org/10.1109/tkde.2024.3352100

21. Xie, X., et al.: From discrimination to generation: knowledge graph completion with generative transformer. In: Companion Proceedings of the Web Conference 2022, pp. 162–165. WWW 2022, Association for Computing Machinery, New York, NY, USA (2022). https://doi.org/10.1145/3487553.3524238
22. Yan, L.L., Miller, R.J., Haas, L.M., Fagin, R.: Data-driven understanding and refinement of schema mappings. SIGMOD Rec. **30**(2), 485–496 (2001). https://doi.org/10.1145/376284.375729
23. Zhang, H., Dong, Y., Xiao, C., Oyamada, M.: Large language models as data preprocessors (2023)
24. Zhang, J., Shin, B., Choi, J.D., Ho, J.C.: SMAT: an attention-based deep learning solution to the automation of schema matching. In: Bellatreche, L., Dumas, M., Karras, P., Matulevičius, R. (eds.) Advances in Databases and Information Systems, pp. 260–274. Springer International Publishing, Cham (2021)
25. Zhang, Z.: Pretrain-KGES: learning knowledge representation from pretrained models for knowledge graph embeddings (2019)

Leveraging Sentence-Transformers to Overcome Query-Document Vocabulary Mismatch in Information Retrieval

Saber Zahhar[1]([🖂]) [ID], Nédra Mellouli[2] [ID], and Christophe Rodrigues[2] [ID]

[1] Devoteam, Paris, France
saber.zahhar@devoteam.com
[2] De Vinci Higher Education, DVRC Research Center, Paris, France
{n.mellouli,c.rodrigues}@devinci.fr

Abstract. Query-document vocabulary mismatch represents the gap between a query's terms and the index terms used for document retrieval. It is a significant challenge that affects severely the performance of search algorithms. Our Ph.D. focuses on building a semantic layer that can be shared by both document index terms as well as query terms in order to overcome this problem. In this paper we focus on expanding queries using aligned keyphrases. We show that state-of-the-art keyphrase generation models do improve retrieval but at the cost of an increased vocabulary mismatch. To reduce this effect, we project, using sentence-transformers, the generated keyphrases to their closest representative term from the indexed vocabulary. However, the original set consists of author-assigned annotations which may suffer from issues such as duplication and misspelling. Through the processing of these annotations, we are able to reduce the search space for query-document alignment. We repeat this experiment on keyphrases extracted by tf-idf and demonstrate significant improvements over the author keyphrases, effectively bridging the vocabulary gap and enhancing search relevance.

Keywords: Abstractive Keyphrase Generation · Information Retrieval (IR) · Query Expansion · Thesaurus Generation · Sentence Transformers

1 Introduction

With the democratization of Internet, digital libraries have become the main conduit for accessing, preserving and organizing knowledge. One of its main challenges relates to user experience, most specifically the retrieval effectiveness of their search engine and to that extent the underlying indexing process. Due to copyright and computation constraints, indexing relies on information compression to index its documents. Broad approaches such as text summarization [11] as well as granular ones like keyphrase assignment [4] have been observed.

© The Author(s), under exclusive license to Springer Nature Singapore Pte Ltd. 2025
M. Barhamgi et al. (Eds.): WISE 2024, LNCS 15463, pp. 101–110, 2025.
https://doi.org/10.1007/978-981-96-1483-7_8

Keyphrases, also known as *index terms*, are phrases that encapsulate core concepts found within a document. Together with text summaries, they have proven effective in easing downstream tasks such as information retrieval [3].

However, most keyphrase annotation tools have remained since the 1990s *extractive*, i.e. keyphrases are found in the source text. On the one hand, this fails to expand neither the document nor the query given that the keyphrase only highlights already present terms, which possesses less retrieval power than if the keyphrase were absent from the text [3]. On the other hand, extractive annotation does not reduce query-document vocabulary mismatch, this phenomenon corresponds to the gap between terms used by a query and the index terms of relevant documents. This discrepancy heavily impacts the retrieval effectiveness of search engines as they struggle to match semantically similar yet lexically different terms.

To facilitate both reader and author experience in query-document alignment, publishing companines have made efforts to constrain the domain of keyphrases to a professionally curated set of keyphrases, usually called *thesaurus*. Still, such thesaurus are time-consuming to produce and require highly specialized knowledge, limiting the pool of qualified users.

To address these challenges and limitations, we investigate how can a semantic layer be used to bridge the gap between documents and queries. By matching complex, domain-specific and diverse terminology from documents with simple, generic and familiar terms from queries, a semantic layer may greatly reduce the vocabulary mismatch in the retrieval process.

In this paper, we provide an overview on both "information retrieval" and "keyphrase generation" (Sect. 2), we then explain how can the two intersect in a symbiotic way (Sect. 3) with an experimental setup (Sect. 4). We conclude by discussing future avenues for this thesis (Sect. 5)

2   Literature Review

2.1   Controlled Vocabularies

Controlled vocabularies find their roots in the fields of library science and information science, emerging as a response to the need for systematic organization of knowledge to facilitate retrieval and use. Given the sparse availability of keyphrase-annotated documents, early approaches for generating keyphrases absent from text relied on a thesaurus [15].

The primary purpose of controlled vocabularies is to improve the retrieval effectiveness. By standardizing terms used to describe content, controlled vocabularies can reduce ambiguity and variability in language, making it easier to find related information. In practice, most digital libraries do not possess a professionaly curated controlled vocabulary, especially when they do not cover regulated fields such as legislature and biology. This opens the path to investigate what can be used to serve as index terms.

2.2   Keyphrase Assignment

Keyphrase extraction methods used to be the main focus with two separate schools of thought, one based on statistical unsupervised techniques [9, 21] and the other on graph-based properties [18, 23], the latter ended up becoming the mainstream approach these last two decades.

Thanks to the recent advancements in computational capabilities, deep learning has found optimal conditions for its development and applications, allowing researchers to take full advantage of the increasing corpora published. Specifically, neural network architectures paved the way for generative models capable of abstractive keyphrase annotation.

Due to its capacity to generate synonyms which may align with controlled index terms, abstractive keyphrase generation may represent the solution to overcome vocabulary mismatch between keyphrases from queries and index terms of documents.

Pioneered by [17], deep learning generative models used to follow the *One2One* architecture; every training example is formed from a document with a singular keyphrase attached to it split from the targeted keyphrases. For prediction purposes, such models employ a technique known as beam search to generate phrases, choosing those with the top rankings as the candidate keyphrases. However, the architecture failed to consider the relationships among keyphrases, potentially limiting the efficiency of keyphrase generation models.

Addressing the previous limitation, *One2Seq* treats the generation of keyphrases as a task of creating a sequence. Here, the target keyphrases are organized in a specific sequence using delimiters, with present keyphrases arranged by their appearance order in the text and absent keyphrases placed randomly afterwards as described by [16]. Nevertheless, its reliance on a predetermined keyphrase sequence can introduce bias during training phase, particularly if the generated keyphrases don't align with the sequence. Furthermore, production of repetitive keyphrases has been observed in [6].

2.3   Text Representation

Introduced by [19], Word2Vec is a neural network architecture focused on capturing semantic relationships between words by representing them in a shared vector space. Doc2Vec [12] extends this principle by training a set of index-document pairs where indices can be n-gram words and documents a list of words. Nevertheless, embeddings remain static regardless of context, e.g. "orange" will have the same embedding when used as a color or a fruit. Overcoming the lack of uncontextualized word embeddings as well as using a more granular tokenization than words. Sentence-Transformers [20] are a recent architecture that leverages advancements made by BERT [7], Sentence-Transformers improves upon traditional embeddings by generating contextualized representations of words, capturing nuanced meaning based on the surrounding words in the text. Unlike Word2Vec and Doc2Vec, Sentence-Transformers are trained to understand the relationships between sentences, making them well-suited for tasks like semantic similarity.

Sentence-Transformers may be able to match keyphrases used as index terms for documents as well as keyphrases used for query expansion.

3   Problem Statement

In our context, we use Sentence-Transformers to act as an embedding system to map keyphrases generated for query expansion to the set of index terms used for documents. This approach has, to the best of our knowledge never been applied in the context of query-document keyphrase alignment, and could reduce the reliance on specific ontologies or vast amounts of training data while enhancing the precision of indexing and retrieval, potentially overcoming the vocabulary mismatch through a keyphrase shared semantic layer.

Methodology

In this section, we present our three-step approach: `Thesaurus Construction`, `Query Expansion` and `Query-Document Alignment`.

3.1   Thesaurus Construction

`Thesaurus Construction` focuses on generating a set of index terms that will serve as the semantic layer. Currently, we focus on simplifying keyphrase annotations from documents through a series of natural language processing techniques:

- Two keyphrases are clustered if they are similar when lowercased;
- Further clustering occurs when their respective stopwords are removed;
- Keyphrases are further grouped when their subwords are stemmed;
- Finally, clustering occurs if their stemmed subwords are the same when sorted alphabetically.

Though simple, these steps allow us to reduce redundancy in the search space. Indeed, annotations such as "Recommendation Systems" and "system recommender" cannot be matched directly due to their lexical distinction despite their clear semantic link. Through our processing steps we are able to cluster both keyphrases into a single keyphrase to be used by the semantic layer, in practice we replace the least common keyphrase of the two by the other. Thus, these processing steps are able to automatically reduce the size of our semantic layer whilst not degrading the performance of retrieval algorithms like BM25, given that it is insensitive to lower-casing and token order.

3.2   Query Expansion

`Query Expansion` consists in concatenating queries with generated keyphrases using state-of-the-art models. We use the query as text input for the model and add to the original query the output keyphrases from the model. In order to avoid bias from over-generating and length-penalty from retrieval systems, we reduced the maximum number of generated keyphrases to 5.

3.3   Query-Document Alignment

`Query-Document Alignment` is performed by computing Sentence-Transformers embeddings for both the index terms and the keyphrases generated for the queries. By applying a pairwise similarity metric between keyphrases and index terms, we can project each keyphrase into a corresponding index term, effectively bridging any possible vocabulary mismatch.

4   Results

4.1   Experimental Setup

Dataset. Our investigations centered around the `ACM-CR` [2] document retrieval dataset. It consists of 102,411 documents in English on topics related to information retrieval from the ACM Digital Library. 169 citation contexts were extracted from scientific papers from the 2020 proceedings of conferences centered on information retrieval which serve as queries, these citation contexts are sentences or whole paragraphs from human authors that contain one or more references to other scientific papers. We view these cited references as relevant documents for the citation context, that is also serve as a query. 481 query-document relevant pairs are made available.

We also compared two annotation methods to expand the documents:

– Using available author-assigned keyphrases from the documents.
– Using `scikit-learn`'s `TfIdfVectorizer` extraction algorithm with parameters `ngram_range = (1, 4)` and `nltk`'s stopword list and word tokenizer.

This two annotation methods will allow us to compare how index terms can differ and what is the impact on retrieval effectiveness.

Table 1 presents the varying distributions before and after applying `Thesaurus Processing` on both author-assigned and TF-IDF annotations.

Prior to processing, the author-assigned keyphrases showed a lower total number of unique keyphrases (112,134) compared to TF-IDF (330,992), with a higher percentage of keyphrases that appeared more than once (26.57% vs. 21.54%). First of, almost 30% of documents have no author-assigned keyphrases [3]. However, when applying tf-idf, we extracted the top 5 keyphrase candidates based on the 4.5 average keyphrase per document statistic given by the authors [3]. Moreover, tf-idf's purely extractive nature makes each author's writing style add unique keyphrases to the thesaurus. Still, we observe in both configurations a 20% drop of unique keyphrases after `Thesaurus Processing`'s step. Also, the number of keyphrases that appear more than once is greater after processing, revealing that tf-idf tend to paraphrase itself more often.

Overall, the number of appearance of each keyphrase increased after processing, though with greater variance. This skewed distribution is a sign of a poorly designed thesaurus. Indeed, thesauri are expected to be uniformly distributed and each index term should cover a concept as unique as possible from

Table 1. Annotation statistics for both configurations. The last three columns are expressed under a "Mean ± Standard deviation" format.

	Unique Keyphrases	Keyphrases w/ count > 1	Keyphrase count
Before Thesaurus Processing			
Authors	112134	26.57%	2.87 ± 15.51
TF-IDF	330992	21.54%	1.44 ± 7.94
After Thesaurus Processing			
Authors	89816	30.08%	3.58 ± 21.22
TF-IDF	266592	31.48%	1.79 ± 9.02

the others, like independent mathematical axes. Though keyphrases are on average more used, the standard deviation enable us to confirm that the appearance count isn't distributed equally. This may be in part due to the varying degree of specifity found in keyphrases, e.g. both configurations have entries very generic like "error" and "human" as well as very specific ones like "computer-assisted language learning".

Also, we found that current simple processing techniques cannot adequately tackle all redundancy in the dataset. For example, keyphrases like "360-video", "360° video", "360-degree-video" and "360-video mental health" were still separated after our processing step.

Query Expansion. To inquire about our mapping on different annotations, we assigned keyphrases to the queries using;

- **MultipartiteRank** [1]: A graph-based extraction method that evaluates the relationships between words and their co-occurrences. By constructing a weighted graph representation of the text, it identifies the most relevant terms based on their structural importance and connectivity.
- **GPT-3.5**: Leveraging the capabilities of a large language model, we used OpenAI's prompt template[1] to facilitate keyphrase extraction.
- **KeyBART** [10]: KeyBART is a pre-trained model based on the BART (Bidirectional and Auto-Regressive Transformers) architecture [14], designed specifically for keyphrase generation following the One2Seq format.

Query-Document Alignment. We generate embeddings for index terms from one of the two thesauri after processing using Mixedbread's embedder that appear in the top-30 MTEB leaderboard [13]. We do the same with keyphrases from queries. Then, for each query's keyphrase, we project it to its closest index term using cosine similarity.

---

[1] https://platform.openai.com/docs/examples/default-keywords.

Evaluation. Experiments are carried out by indexing documents using annotations from either the author's or tf-idf thesaurus after processing. We perform ranking of queries and their expansions through the standard Lucene's BM25 model implemented in the BM25-Sparse open-source Python module[2]. Stemming is always carried out, since it is a standard procedure in information retrieval, using `nltk`'s implementation of `PorterStemmer`. Stopwords are usually removed to ease BM25's calculation as per the `bm25s` documentation. For all configurations, we use `bm25s`' default parameters `k_1=1.5, b=0.75`. We evaluate retrieval effectiveness in terms of mean Average Precision (mAP) on the top 10 retrieved documents as per [8]. We also quantify query-document vocabulary mismatching as the ratio of a query's tokens not found in the set of index terms.

Table 2. Experimental results of document retrieval using our configurations, with a comparison between indexing using author-assigned and TF-IDF-based keyphrases.

Query expansion	Author indexing		TF-IDF indexing	
	mAP@10	Mismatch	mAP@10	Mismatch
Queries with no keyphrases				
None (default query)	0.113	12.70%	0.147	10.20%
Queries with raw keyphrases				
KeyBART	0.116	13.60%	0.155	11.70%
MultipartiteRank	0.121	13.40%	0.148	10.20%
GPT-3.5	0.119	12.70%	0.160	10.80%
Queries with projected keyphrases				
KeyBART	0.124	10.70%	0.161	8.70%
MultipartiteRank	0.121	11.70%	0.166	9.20%
GPT-3.5	0.135	11.20%	0.198	8.40%

Results. Table 2 shows our experimental results. Across all query expansion techniques and regardless of projecting keyphrases to their respective controlled index terms, TF-IDF provide a better indexing basis for retrieval effectiveness as seen with the mAP score, despite indexing three times more keyphrases (Table 1). We may attribute this to the inherent nature of BM25 that is heavily based off TF-IDF's principle. We observe on average an increase of 3–4% points when switching from authors to tf-idf indices.

Across all configurations, using query expansion techniques improves retrieval performance, with GPT-3.5 having the best increase in retrieval power except against MultipartiteRank in the first unprojected author-assigned thesaurus, which again may be due to poor indexing grounds.

---

[2] https://github.com/xhluca/bm25s.

Projecting keyphrases into the controlled thesaurus significantly reduces the vocabulary mismatch, showing that this method is effective in improving query-document alignment. Each configuration consistently performed better in retrieval than its non-projected counterpart. The largest score difference in mAP is over 8.5% points and just under 4.5% points in mismatch.

5   Future Directions

5.1   Improving Thesaurus Processing

While we unraveled the potential in building a semantic layer based on TF-IDF annotations, we still fail to cluster many keyphrase pairs. For example, the author-assigned processed thesaurus still left out keyphrases "360-degree video", "360 degree video" and "360° video" as separate index terms. This results in extreme redundancy and poor performance of our keyphrase alignemnt approach.

HDBSCAN [5] is density-based hierarchical clustering technique that allow better clustering of keyphrases by progressively merging index terms based on their semantic similarity, e.g. generic terms like "video" can be linked to specific phrases like "360-degree video".

5.2   Addressing Biases in Abstractive Keyphrase Generation

[22] called the separation of extraction and abstraction keyphrase annotation. In this paper, we introduced a two-step approach that leverages the well-established strength of extractive methods and then refines it through an abstraction phase.

Still, we only computed surface-level representations of index terms, it would be interesting to levearage Large Language Models to build actual definitions of these index terms in order to build more robust embeddings.

References

1. Boudin, F.: Unsupervised keyphrase extraction with multipartite graphs. In: Walker, M., Ji, H., Stent, A. (eds.) Proceedings of the 2018 Conference of the North American Chapter of the Association for Computational Linguistics: Human Language Technologies, Volume 2 (Short Papers), pp. 667–672. Association for Computational Linguistics, New Orleans, Louisiana (2018). https://doi.org/10.18653/v1/N18-2105, https://aclanthology.org/N18-2105
2. Boudin, F.: ACM-CR: a manually annotated test collection for citation recommendation. In: Proceedings of the 2021 ACM/IEEE Joint Conference on Digital Libraries, pp. 280–281. JCDL 2021, IEEE Press (2024). https://doi.org/10.1109/JCDL52503.2021.00035
3. Boudin, F., Gallina, Y.: Redefining absent keyphrases and their effect on retrieval effectiveness. In: Toutanova, K., Rumshisky, A., Zettlemoyer, L., Hakkani-Tur, D., Beltagy, I., Bethard, S., Cotterell, R., Chakraborty, T., Zhou, Y. (eds.) Proceedings of the 2021 Conference of the North American Chapter of the Association for Computational Linguistics: Human Language Technologies, pp. 4185–4193. Association for Computational Linguistics, Online (2021). https://doi.org/10.18653/v1/2021.naacl-main.330, https://aclanthology.org/2021.naacl-main.330

4. Boudin, F., Gallina, Y., Aizawa, A.: Keyphrase generation for scientific document retrieval. In: Jurafsky, D., Chai, J., Schluter, N., Tetreault, J. (eds.) Proceedings of the 58th Annual Meeting of the Association for Computational Linguistics, pp. 1118–1126. Association for Computational Linguistics, Online (2020). https://doi.org/10.18653/v1/2020.acl-main.105, https://aclanthology.org/2020.acl-main.105

5. Campello, R.J.G.B., Moulavi, D., Sander, J.: Density-based clustering based on hierarchical density estimates. In: Pei, J., Tseng, V.S., Cao, L., Motoda, H., Xu, G. (eds.) PAKDD 2013. LNCS (LNAI), vol. 7819, pp. 160–172. Springer, Heidelberg (2013). https://doi.org/10.1007/978-3-642-37456-2_14

6. Chen, W., Chan, H.P., Li, P., King, I.: Exclusive hierarchical decoding for deep keyphrase generation. In: Jurafsky, D., Chai, J., Schluter, N., Tetreault, J. (eds.) Proceedings of the 58th Annual Meeting of the Association for Computational Linguistics, pp. 1095–1105. Association for Computational Linguistics, Online (2020). https://doi.org/10.18653/v1/2020.acl-main.103, https://aclanthology.org/2020.acl-main.103

7. Devlin, J., Chang, M.W., Lee, K., Toutanova, K.: BERT: pre-training of deep bidirectional transformers for language understanding. In: Burstein, J., Doran, C., Solorio, T. (eds.) Proceedings of the 2019 Conference of the North American Chapter of the Association for Computational Linguistics: Human Language Technologies, Volume 1 (Long and Short Papers). pp. 4171–4186. Association for Computational Linguistics, Minneapolis, Minnesota (2019). https://doi.org/10.18653/v1/N19-1423, https://aclanthology.org/N19-1423

8. Färber, M., Jatowt, A.: Citation recommendation: approaches and datasets. Int. J. Digital Lib. **21**, 375–405 (2020). https://api.semanticscholar.org/CorpusID:211132888

9. Hulth, A.: Improved automatic keyword extraction given more linguistic knowledge. In: Proceedings of the 2003 Conference on Empirical Methods in Natural Language Processing, pp. 216–223 (2003). https://aclanthology.org/W03-1028

10. Kulkarni, M., Mahata, D., Arora, R., Bhowmik, R.: Learning rich representation of keyphrases from text. In: Carpuat, M., de Marneffe, M.C., Meza Ruiz, I.V. (eds.) Findings of the Association for Computational Linguistics: NAACL 2022, pp. 891–906. Association for Computational Linguistics, Seattle, United States (2022). https://doi.org/10.18653/v1/2022.findings-naacl.67, https://aclanthology.org/2022.findings-naacl.67

11. Lam-Adesina, A.M., Jones, G.J.F.: Applying summarization techniques for term selection in relevance feedback. In: Proceedings of the 24th Annual International ACM SIGIR Conference on Research and Development in Information Retrieval, pp. 1–9. SIGIR 2001, Association for Computing Machinery, New York, NY, USA (2001). https://doi.org/10.1145/383952.383953

12. Le, Q., Mikolov, T.: Distributed representations of sentences and documents. In: Proceedings of the 31st International Conference on International Conference on Machine Learning - Volume 32, pp. II–1188–II–1196. ICML 2014 (2014). https://jmlr.org/

13. Lee, S., Shakir, A., Koenig, D., Lipp, J.: Open source strikes bread - new fluffy embeddings model (2024). https://www.mixedbread.ai/blog/mxbai-embed-large-v1

14. Lewis, M., et al.: BART: denoising sequence-to-sequence pre-training for natural language generation, translation, and comprehension. In: Jurafsky, D., Chai, J., Schluter, N., Tetreault, J. (eds.) Proceedings of the 58th Annual Meeting of the Association for Computational Linguistics, pp. 7871–7880. Association for Computational Linguistics, Online (2020). https://doi.org/10.18653/v1/2020.acl-main.703, https://aclanthology.org/2020.acl-main.703

15. Medelyan, O., Witten, I.H.: Thesaurus based automatic keyphrase indexing. In: Proceedings of the 6th ACM/IEEE-CS Joint Conference on Digital Libraries, pp. 296–297. JCDL 2006, Association for Computing Machinery, New York, NY, USA (2006). https://doi.org/10.1145/1141753.1141819

16. Meng, R., Yuan, X., Wang, T., Brusilovsky, P., Trischler, A., He, D.: Does order matter? an empirical study on generating multiple keyphrases as a sequence. ArXiv abs/1909.03590 (2019). https://api.semanticscholar.org/CorpusID:202540437

17. Meng, R., Zhao, S., Han, S., He, D., Brusilovsky, P., Chi, Y.: Deep keyphrase generation. In: Barzilay, R., Kan, M.Y. (eds.) Proceedings of the 55th Annual Meeting of the Association for Computational Linguistics (Volume 1: Long Papers), pp. 582–592. Association for Computational Linguistics, Vancouver, Canada (2017). https://doi.org/10.18653/v1/P17-1054, https://aclanthology.org/P17-1054

18. Mihalcea, R., Tarau, P.: TextRank: bringing order into text. In: Lin, D., Wu, D. (eds.) Proceedings of the 2004 Conference on Empirical Methods in Natural Language Processing, pp. 404–411. Association for Computational Linguistics, Barcelona, Spain (2004). https://aclanthology.org/W04-3252

19. Mikolov, T., Chen, K., Corrado, G.S., Dean, J.: Efficient estimation of word representations in vector space. In: International Conference on Learning Representations (2013). https://api.semanticscholar.org/CorpusID:5959482

20. Reimers, N., Gurevych, I.: Sentence-BERT: sentence embeddings using Siamese BERT-networks. In: Inui, K., Jiang, J., Ng, V., Wan, X. (eds.) Proceedings of the 2019 Conference on Empirical Methods in Natural Language Processing and the 9th International Joint Conference on Natural Language Processing (EMNLP-IJCNLP), pp. 3982–3992. Association for Computational Linguistics, Hong Kong, China (2019). https://doi.org/10.18653/v1/D19-1410, https://aclanthology.org/D19-1410

21. Tomokiyo, T., Hurst, M.: A language model approach to keyphrase extraction. In: Proceedings of the ACL 2003 Workshop on Multiword Expressions: Analysis, Acquisition and Treatment, pp. 33–40. Association for Computational Linguistics, Sapporo, Japan (2003). https://doi.org/10.3115/1119282.1119287, https://aclanthology.org/W03-1805

22. Xie, B., et al.: From statistical methods to deep learning, automatic keyphrase prediction: a survey. Inf. Process. Manag. **60**(4), 103382 (2023). https://doi.org/10.1016/j.ipm.2023.103382, https://www.sciencedirect.com/science/article/pii/S030645732300119X

23. Zha, H.: Generic summarization and keyphrase extraction using mutual reinforcement principle and sentence clustering. In: Proceedings of the 25th Annual International ACM SIGIR Conference on Research and Development in Information Retrieval, pp. 113–120. SIGIR 2002, Association for Computing Machinery, New York, NY, USA (2002). https://doi.org/10.1145/564376.564398

Time Distance Aware for Multi-component Graph Collaborative Filtering

Tseesuren Batsuuri$^{(\boxtimes)}$ ⓘ, Shan Xue, Jian Yang, and Jia Wu

School of Computing, Macquarie University, Sydney, NSW, Australia
tseesuren.batsuuri@hdr.mq.edu.au, {emma.xue,jian.yang,jia.wu}@mq.edu.au

Abstract. Graph Convolutional Networks (GCNs) have gained prominence in collaborative filtering (CF) recommendation systems for capturing intricate signals using high-order structural data. However, GCN-based models focus solely on these signals, neglecting the sparse nature of data and overlooking important aspects like temporal signals in user preferences and baseline signals in users or items, leading to suboptimal performance. To address these issues, this paper introduces a novel multi-component CF model that integrates GCNs with baseline and temporal components. The integrated model learns user and item representations from multiple perspectives, enhancing performance and robustness across various datasets. Experiments conducted on the MovieLens and Douban datasets demonstrate the superiority of this approach over state-of-the-art models, reducing RMSE by up to 4.7%, while improving NCDG by up to 5.1% compared to pure GCN-based CF (https://github.com/tseesurenb/wise2024_v2.git).

Keywords: collaborative filtering · multi-component learning · recommender system · graph convolutional networks · temporal data

1 Introduction

CF is a fundamental technique in recommendation systems, standing alongside content-based filtering. One key advantage of CF is its minimal reliance on extensive data preparation, effectively leveraging user-item interaction data. It operates without domain knowledge, instead harnessing similarities between users and items derived from their past interactions to formulate recommendations. Model-based CF uses statistical models [1,2] and has evolved through three generations: shallow, neural, and graph neural models [2]. Shallow models like SVD, SVD++ [3] relied on matrix factorization, where latent features representing users and items are learned and used in a simple "dot product" to predict ratings. Neural models, such as Nade-CF, AutoRec, and SparseFC [4–6], have enhanced CF by leveraging deeper neural networks. Recently, GCNs have emerged as a significant advancement in this field [7–11], providing the ability to capture intricate signals using high-order structural data. GCNs are a natural fit for CF [7,8,10] because CF predicts a user's preferences based on

M. Barhamgi et al. (Eds.): WISE 2024, LNCS 15463, pp. 111–121, 2025.
https://doi.org/10.1007/978-981-96-1483-7_9

the collective behavior and preferences of a group of users (or items). GCNs aggregate signals from nodes connected by shared features, aligning well with the fundamental principles of CF. However, GCN-based models still face challenges such as data sparsity [1,2] and incorporating the evolving nature of user preferences [3,12,15]. Particularly, temporal dynamics in user preferences are often overlooked [1,3,12], leading to sub-optimal models. User preferences are intricate and evolve over time, making it crucial for recommendation systems to adapt to these changes. Temporal effects in user preferences can be viewed at three levels: immediate, transient, and long-term [3,12]. Modeling immediate temporal effects is essentially impossible due to their highly subjective nature [3]. The long-term temporal effect has been studied in the classical SVD++ [3], where inherent baseline signals, or biases, represent the long-term view, capturing general tendencies of users or items. For example, biases can indicate whether a user's ratings are generally optimistic or pessimistic.

The most intriguing aspect of this research is modeling transient temporal effects, which can be classified into two key types: relative and absolute.

Relative: Like Avatar left a lasting mark on films, the first iPhone changed how we see phones. But in everyday life, recent experiences matter more—when buying a new smartphone, people usually compare it to their last one.

Absolute: Following prestigious events such as the Oscars or Golden Globes, individuals often rate films higher, as high-quality movies are typically released during these periods. This illustrates the concept of absolute temporal effects.

To address these challenges, this paper introduces a novel multi-component CF approach called TDMCF, which integrates GCNs with baseline and temporal components using supervised learning for explicit data. By incorporating these elements, our model captures transient shifts in user preferences and remains robust against sparse data. Our contributions are threefold:

- **Novel integrated CF**: We present a novel CF model that integrates GCNs with baseline and temporal components. This model captures high-order collaborative signals, incorporates baseline signals to learn user and item biases, and models user dynamics through temporal components.
- **Two Novel Time Modules for CF**: We propose two novel time modules to capture dynamic changes in user preferences: the relative time module adjusts past interactions based on user-specific timestamps, while the absolute time module standardizes temporal influence using a global minimum timestamp. These modules enhance collaborative filtering by better reflecting evolving user preferences.
- **Experimental Validation**: Experiments conducted on the MovieLens and Douban datasets demonstrate the superiority of our approach over state-of-the-art models.

The remainder of the paper is organized as follows: Sect. 2 presents the problem statement with preliminary concepts. Section 3 introduces our proposed model, and Sect. 4 presents the experiments and results. Section 5 provides a literature review, and finally, Sect. 6 concludes the paper.

2   Preliminary and Problem Statement

Let $U = \{u_1, ..., u_N\}$ be a set of N users, and $I = \{i_1, ..., i_M\}$ be a set of M items. In our scenario, interactions between the users and items are given in a log, represented by list of four-tuples, denoted as $\{(u, i, r_{ui}, t_{ui})\}$, where $r_{ui} \in \{1, ..., K\}$ with a K scale is a rating given by user u to item i at time t_{ui}.

To capture collaborative signals, we require embeddings e_u, e_i for every user and item and an adjacency matrix A of a bipartite graph $G = (V, E)$. V is a union set $U \cup I$, and E is the set of edge triples (u, i, r_{ui}). The embeddings with dimension of d and adjacency matrix $A \in \mathbb{R}^{(N+M) \times (N+M)}$ are defined as:

$$H_c = [\underbrace{e_{u_1}, ..., e_{u_N}}_{\text{user}}, \underbrace{e_{i_1}, ..., e_{i_M}}_{\text{item}}], \quad A = \begin{bmatrix} 0 & R \\ R^T & 0 \end{bmatrix} \tag{1}$$

where $e \in \mathbb{R}^d$, $R \in \mathbb{R}^{N \times M}$ is the interaction matrix, and 0 is all-zero matrix.

To capture the baseline signals, embeddings $b_u, b_i \in \mathbb{R}^d$ for every user and item, and a global mean rating μ are defined as:

$$H_b = [\underbrace{b_{u_1}, ..., b_{u_N}}_{\text{user baseline}}, \underbrace{b_{i_1}, ..., b_{i_M}}_{\text{item baseline}}], \quad \mu = \frac{\sum r_{ui}}{len(r_{ui})} \tag{2}$$

To capture the transient temporal signals, two more embeddings are defined for every user: relative and absolute temporal embeddings $t_u^r, t_u^a \in \mathbb{R}^d$:

$$H_t = [\underbrace{t_{u_1}^r, ..., t_{u_N}^r}_{\text{relative}}, \underbrace{t_{u_1}^a, ..., t_{u_N}^a}_{\text{absolute}}] \tag{3}$$

The Problem Statement: With separate embeddings for users and items in Eqs.(1)-(3), TDMCF is designed to leverage collaborative, baseline and temporal signals captured from the interaction log so as to predict the missing ratings. The adjacency matrix A together with embeddings H_c serves as input for the GCN component of the model. The global mean rating μ together with embeddings H_b serves as input for the baseline component of the model for capturing user and item biases. The relative and absolute temporal sets and their embeddings H_t serve as input for a temporal component of the model.

3   TDMCF: Time Distance Aware Multi-component CF

We defined two tenets to model evolving user preference. First, user preference is not inherent, rather, they develop through past experiences with user judgments being primarily dependent on comparing the current experience to previous ones. Second, different experiences exert varying degrees of lasting influence. Given these tenets, we defined two time models. One is a relative time model:

$$p_u^r = f(t_u^r, t_u - t_{u_{\min}}) = t_u^r \cdot e^{(-\beta^r \cdot (t_u - t_{u_{\min}}))} \tag{4}$$

where β^r is a hyper-parameter, $t_{u_{\min}}$ is the relative starting point, and in our case, it is the minimum time of the user. The other one is an absolute time model:

$$p_u^a = f(t_u^a, t_u - t_{\min}) = t_u^a \cdot (t_u - t_{\min})^{\beta^a} \tag{5}$$

where β^a is a hyper-parameter, $t_{\min}$ is the fixed initial point, and in our case, it is the global minimum time in the interaction log.

3.1   Simplified GCN for Deeper Collaborative Signals

For the GCN component, we chose LightGCN [10] for two reasons. First, it is specifically proven simplified CGN for CF. Second, LightGCN is a foundational, feature-less that is ideal for other models to build upon as shown in Eq. 6.

$$\underbrace{e_u^{k+1} = \sum_{i \in N_u} \frac{1}{\sqrt{|N_i|}\sqrt{|N_u|}} e_i^k}_{\text{(1) User embedding update}}, \quad \underbrace{e_i^{k+1} = \sum_{u \in N_i} \frac{1}{\sqrt{|N_i|}\sqrt{|N_u|}} e_u^k}_{\text{(2) Item embedding update}} \tag{6}$$

where N_u, N_i are the node degrees, e_u, e_i are embeddings of user u and item i, and k and $k+1$ are the kth and $(k+1)^{th}$ layers, respectively. To obtain the final embeddings, LightGCN sums over the embeddings, as described in Eq. 7.

$$\underbrace{e_u = \sum_{k=0}^{K} \alpha_k e_u^{(k)}}_{\text{(1) Aggregation of user embeddings}} \quad , \quad \underbrace{e_i = \sum_{k=0}^{K} \alpha_k e_i^{(k)}}_{\text{(2) Aggregation of item embeddings}} \tag{7}$$

where $\alpha_k \geq 0$ denotes the weight parameter.

3.2   Multi-component CF

As shown in Fig. 1, the proposed multi-component TDMCF model has three components: the baseline, the temporal and the collaborative.

All three components contribute to the final prediction defined as:

$$r_{ui} = g(\underbrace{\mu + b_u + b_i}_{\text{baseline}} + \underbrace{p_u^r + p_u^a}_{\text{temporal}} + \underbrace{e_u^T \cdot e_i}_{\text{collaborative}}) \tag{8}$$

where r_{ui} is the final predicted rating, $g(\cdot)$ is an activation function such as ReLU, μ is the global mean rating, b_u, b_i are user and item baseline signals, p_u^r is the relative temporal signal given by Eq. (4), p_u^a is the absolute temporal signal given by Eq. (5) and $e_u^T \cdot e_i$ is the collaborative signal given by Eq. (7).

The TDMCF is optimized using the "Adam" optimizer to minimize the mean squared error (MSE) with the following loss function:

$$\mathcal{L}_{\text{MSE}} = \frac{1}{M} \sum_{i=1}^{M} \|r_m - \hat{r}_m\|_2^2 + \lambda \|w\|_2^2 \tag{9}$$

Here, M denotes the number of samples in a batch, and r_m and $\hat{r}_m$ signify the predicted and target values for the m-th sample. The parameter λ is the weight decay factor, and $|w|_2^2$ signifies the L2 norm of the model's weight vector w.

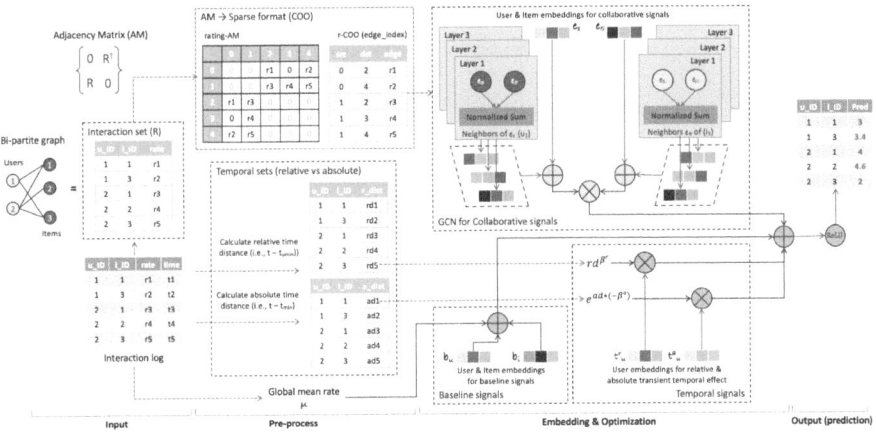

Fig. 1. The interaction log is preprocessed into an interaction set and temporal sets. These sets are fed into TDMCF, which predicts missing ratings using its baseline, temporal, and collaborative components.

4   Experiments and Results

We used the MovieLens ml-100k and ml-1 m datasets[1], along with the Douban-book dataset [18]. Each user in these datasets has rated at least 20 items (for the Douban-book, we preprocessed the data to ensure each user has at least 20 ratings), with each rating including a timestamp. Table 1 presents the statistics for each dataset. As shown, the Douban-book dataset is extremely sparse.

Table 1. Statistics of the experimental datasets

Dataset	Items	Users	Ratings	Sparsity	Graph Density	Duration
MovieLens 100k	1682	943	100,000	93.7%	2.9%	215 days
MovieLens 1M	3952	6040	1,000,209	95.83%	2.0%	1039 days
Douban-book	1403	94651	221,195	99.8%	0.005%	4797 days

The experiments were conducted using 90% training and 10% test sets, and average results with standard deviations were computed. We split the dataset without regard to time order, as the proposed model aims to learn parameters based on time distance. The only concern is to ensure that the minimum timestamp of the dataset and the minimum timestamp for each user are included in the training set. The models were trained with a learning rate of 1e-3, weight decay ranging from 1e-5 to 1e-6, and vector dimensions set to 64 for ml-100k, Douban-book and 500 for ml-1 m datasets. The parameters β^r and β^a were both

---
[1] https://grouplens.org/datasets/movielens/.

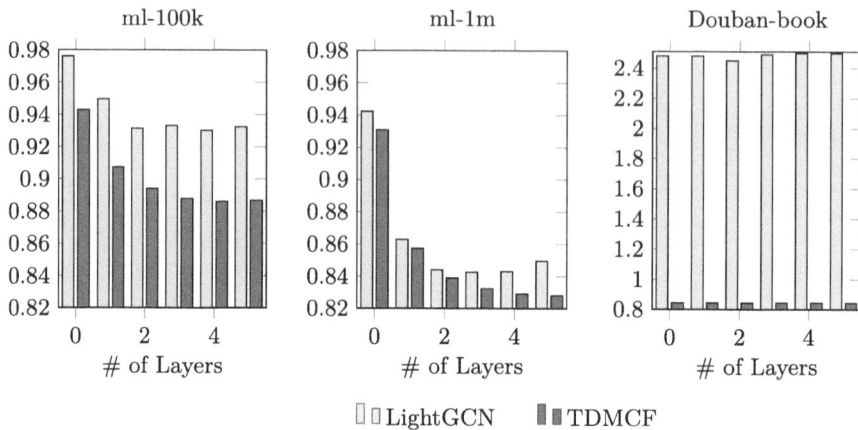

Fig. 2. The TDMCF significantly enhances RMSE and effectively addresses the over-smoothing with GCNs. Note, the pure GCN model performs poorly on the Douban-book dataset due to its highly sparse data, with an average node degree of 4.6. In contrast, the other datasets have average node degrees of 76.2 and 200.2, respectively.

set to 0.05 and 25 for movielens datasets and 0.001 to 0.008 for douban-book dataset, respectively. For TDMCF, it is crucial to train the model with a larger batch size or even the entire training set. This is due to the time-distance training component.

4.1   Results

As depicted in Fig. 2 and 3, TDMCF clearly demonstrates superior performance. It achieves a notable 4.7% reduction from (0.93 to 0.886) in RMSE on the ml-100k and 1.7% reduction (from 0.8427 to 0.8284) on the ml-1 m compared to LightGCN. Additionally, TDMCF enhances the NCDG by 1.8% (from 0.7958 to 0.81) on the ml-100k and 0.4% (from 0.8228 to 0.826) on the ml-1 m. On the Douban-book dataset, the model produces even more intriguing results. For this dataset, a pure GCN model simply fails, with an RMSE of around 2.4, indicating a significant error as shown in Fig. 2 (adding more layers did not help). The Douban-book dataset has limited high-order structural data, with an average node degree of only 4.6, compared to 76.2 for ml-100k and 200.2 for ml-1 m. On the contrary, the TDMCF performs well on this dataset as highlighted in Figure 2 and 3.

Finally, Table 2 presents the results of TDMCF vs. baseline methods. We selected two classic CFs and three state-of-the-art neural models, as well as six state-of-the-art GCN-based approaches. The TDMCF outperforms all state-of-the-art baseline methods on the ml-100k dataset. On the ml-1 m dataset, TDMCF remains the strongest contender, with the exception of SparseFC.

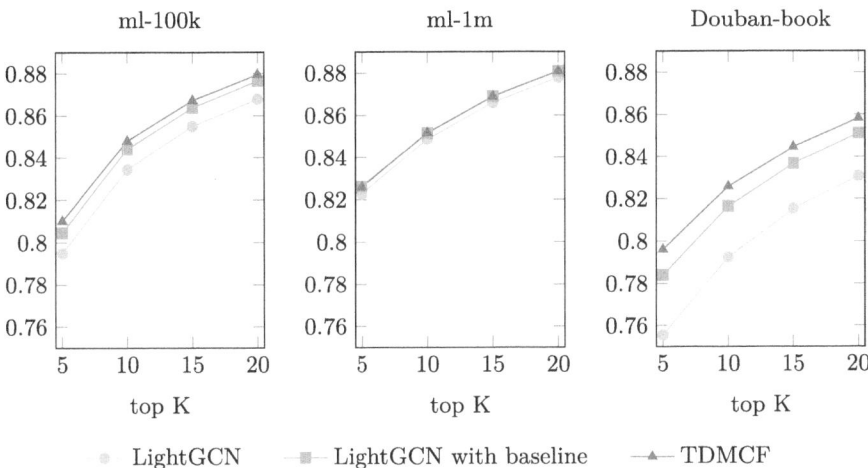

Fig. 3. The TDMCF enhances NCDG for all three datasets. Especially, for extreme sparse dataset, namely, Douban-book, it is clearly demonstrated.

Discussion: First, over-smoothing is a significant concern. After a certain number of layers, GCNs tend to make almost all node embeddings similar, leading to a phenomenon known as over-smoothing. This reduces the model's ability to distinguish between different nodes and can negatively impact performance. Second, the average node degree is crucial for the success of GCN-based CF. While GCNs leverage high-order structural data, allowing nodes to aggregate information from their neighbors, this becomes problematic in extremely sparse datasets, such as the Douban-book dataset, where the average node degree is just 4.6. In such cases, these higher-order connections are less effective, directly contributing to poor performance. Given these conditions, it is essential to adopt an integrated solution like TDMCF, which incorporates multiple components to simultaneously capture patterns from various perspectives.

Third, our experiments reveal the impact of noisy interactions. While performance generally improves with an increasing number of layers, we also observe instances of performance degradation followed by recovery. This inconsistency can be attributed to noisy neighbors. Current GCN models for collaborative filtering treat all nodes equally, but some nodes introduce noise. A noisy item with a high node degree can disproportionately affect recommendations, as message aggregation spreads this noise. This highlights an opportunity for future work.

Ablation Study: Table 3 presents the breakdown of TDMCF's components. These include the baseline-only (i.e., *base*), baseline + absolute time model (i.e., *base + abs*), baseline + relative time model (i.e., *base + rel*), and the full model. Both time models, in addition to the baseline, contribute proportionally to the performance improvements. We also conducted experiments with temporal embeddings without multiplying them by time distance functions (see abs^{raw}

and rel^{raw}). Compared to the baseline-only, these embeddings alone not only failed to improve the performance, they actually made it worse.

Table 2. The TDMCF yields state-of-the-art results.

Methods	RMSE (ml-100k)	RMSE (ml-1 m)
SVD++ [17]	0.903	0.856
timeSVD++ [3]	0.894	0.847
GraphRec [16]	0.898	0.867
GHRS [17]	0.887	0.838
TG-MC with GRU [15]	-	0.867
TG-MC with LSTM [15]	-	0.834
I-AutoRec [4]	0.895	0.831
IMC-GAE [14]	0.897	0.829
CF-Nade [5]	-	0.829
SparseFC [6]	0.89	0.824
GC-MC [7]	0.905	0.832
LightGCN	0.930	0.843
TDMCF	**0.886**	**0.828**

5   Related Work

As GCNs have emerged as the latest advancement in CF, we first studied GCN-based CF models and then examined temporal CF models.

Graph Convolutional Matrix Completion (GC-MC) [7] is a pioneering approach that uses a GCN for CF, integrating a GCN into an auto-encoder architecture for matrix completion tasks. However, GC-MC primarily focuses on static

Table 3. The RMSE performance breakdown of TDMCF by components.

Components	ml-100k	Drop (%)	ml-1 m	Drop (%)
LightGCN	0.9302	-	0.8427	-
TDMCF				
- *base*	0.9025	-2.98%	0.8300	-1.51%
- *base + abs*	0.9009	-3.15%	0.8290	-1.63%
- *base + rel*	0.8969	-3.58%	0.8294	-1.58%
- *full*	0.8858	-4.78%	0.8284	-1.7%
- *base + abs^{raw}*	0.904	$+0.10\%$	0.8300	$+0.00\%$
- *base + rel^{raw}*	0.902	-0.02%	0.8300	$+0.00\%$

collaborative signals, lacking the ability to account for temporal dynamics in user preferences, leading to suboptimal performance over time.

Neural Graph Collaborative Filtering (NGCF) [8] enhances embeddings by incorporating high-order connectivity relations through multiple embedding propagation layers. While effective in capturing structural data, NGCF overlooks temporal aspects and user-item interaction biases, limiting its adaptability to changing user preferences. LightGCN [10] simplifies GCNs by focusing on message aggregation and removing feature transformation and non-linear activation. This approach addresses computational complexity but does not account for temporal dynamics or baseline biases, which are crucial for capturing evolving user preferences. A Linear Residual - Graph Convolutional Collaborative Filtering (LR-GCCF) model [11] also addresses the over-smoothing issue in GCNs by introducing residual connections. Although it improves performance by mitigating over-smoothing, LR-GCCF does not integrate temporal dynamics, reducing its effectiveness in modeling dynamic user preferences.

Despite GCNs being the latest advancement in CF, we argue that GCN-based models primarily focus on capturing deeper collaborative signals. However, collaborative signals alone are insufficient to fully model evolving user preferences. Additionally, GCNs are effective only with datasets that have high-order structural data and may perform poorly when such information is lacking.

5.1 Temporal Collaborative Filtering

Incorporating temporal data into CF has garnered relatively less attention than other aspects [1]. Nonetheless, the first noteworthy attempt is evident in [3]. This work proposes a comprehensive approach for capturing both long-term and transient patterns. Integrating a temporal model with classic memory-based and SVD++ models significantly improves the accuracy. In addition to [3], the more recent study [15] introduces an intriguing temporal CF that combines a GCN and recurrent neural networks (RNN). They use GC-MC [7] as a base GCN model. To model the temporal part, they have opted for a gated recurrent unit (GRU) and a long short-term memory (LSTM). The concept is clear, seeking to combine GCN's strength with high-order structural data and RNN's proficiency in handling temporal data. The only evident drawback is the framework's increased complexity and the necessity for a larger neural networks.

6   Conclusion

This paper introduces TDMCF, a novel integrated CF model with three components: a GCN component for capturing deeper collaborative signals, a temporal component for tracking evolving user preferences, and a baseline model for addressing user and item biases. This integrated approach enhances traditional GCN-based CF, improving accuracy and robustness across various datasets.

References

1. Wang, S., et al.: Graph learning based recommender systems: a review. In: International Joint Conference on Artificial Intelligence, pp. 4644–4652. IJCAI (2021)
2. Gao, C., et al.: A survey of graph neural networks for recommender systems: challenges, methods, and directions. ACM Trans. Recommender Syst. **1**, 1–51 (2023). ACM, New York, NY, USA
3. Koren, Y.: Collaborative filtering with temporal dynamics. In: Proceedings of the 15th ACM SIGKDD International Conference on Knowledge Discovery and Data Mining, pp. 447–456. ACM, New York, NY, USA (2009)
4. Sedhain, S., Menon, A.K., Sanner, S., Xie, L.: AutoRec: autoencoders meet collaborative filtering. In: Proceedings of the 24th International Conference on World Wide Web, pp. 111–112. ACM, New York, NY, USA (2015)
5. Zheng, Y., Tang, B., Ding, W., Zhou, H.: A neural autoregressive approach to collaborative filtering. In: International Conference on Machine Learning, pp. 764–773. PMLR (2016)
6. Muller, L., Martel, J., Indiveri, G.: Kernelized synaptic weight matrices. In: International Conference on Machine Learning, pp. 3654–3663. PMLR (2018)
7. Van den Berg, R., Kipf, T.N., Welling, M.: Graph convolutional matrix completion. In: Proceedings of the 24th ACM SIGKDD Conference on Knowledge Discovery and Data Mining, pp. 433–442. ACM, London, UK (2017)
8. Wang, X., He, X., Wang, M., Feng, F., Chua, T.-S.: Neural graph collaborative filtering. In: Proceedings of the 42nd International ACM SIGIR conference on Research and development in Information Retrieval, pp. 165–174. ACM (2019)
9. Sun, J., et al.: Multi-graph convolution collaborative filtering. In: 2019 IEEE International Conference on Data Mining, pp. 1306–1311. IEEE (2019)
10. He, X., Deng, K., Wang, X., Li, Y., Zhang, Y., Wang, M.: LightGCN: simplifying and powering graph convolution network for recommendation. In: Proceedings of the 43rd International ACM SIGIR conference on research and development in Information Retrieval, pp. 639–648. ACM, New York, NY, United States (2020)
11. Chen, L., Wu, L., Hong, R., Zhang, K., Wang, M.: Revisiting graph based collaborative filtering: a linear residual graph convolutional network approach. In: Proceedings of the AAAI Conference on Artificial Intelligence, vol. 34, no. 01, pp. 27–34. AAAI (2020)
12. Liu, K., Xue, F., Guo, D., Wu, L., Li, S., Hong, R.: MEGCF: multimodal entity graph collaborative filtering for personalized recommendation. In: Proceedings of the ACM conference, vol. 41, no. 2, article no. 30, pp. 1–27. ACM (2023)
13. Wu, F., Souza, A., Zhang, T., Fifty, C., Yu, T., Weinberger, K.: Simplifying graph convolutional networks. In: International Conference on Machine Learning, pp. 6861–6871. PMLR (2019)
14. Shen, W., et al.: Inductive matrix completion using graph autoencoder. In: Proceedings of the 30th ACM International Conference on Information & Knowledge Management, pp. 1609–1618. ACM, NY, USA (2021)
15. Bonet, E.R., Nguyen, D.M., Deligiannis, N.: Temporal collaborative filtering with graph convolutional neural networks. In: Proceedings of 25th International Conference on Pattern Recognition, pp. 4736–4742. IEEE (2021)
16. Fan, W., et al: Graph neural networks for social recommendation. in: Proceedings of WWW 2019: International World Wide Web Conferences, pp. 417–426. ACM, New York, NY, USA (2019)

17. Zamanzadeh Darban, Z., Valipour, M.H.: GHRS: graph-based hybrid recommendation system with application to movie recommendation. Expert Syst. Appl. **200**, 116850 (2022)
18. Zhu, F., Wang, Y., Chen, C., Liu, G., Zheng, X.: A graphical and attentional framework for dual-target cross-domain recommendation. In: Proceedings of the Twenty-Ninth International Joint Conference on Artificial Intelligence, article no. 415, pp. 1–8. IJCAI, Yokohama, Japan (2021)

Scientific Documents Recommendation Based on Graph Convolutional Network

Jianmin Li[1,2]([⊠]) [iD]

[1] School of Cyber Security and Computer, Hebei University, Baoding 071002, China
JML_hbu@126.com
[2] Hebei Machine Vision Engineering Research Center, Hebei University, Baoding 071002, China

Abstract. The rapid growth in the number of scientific documents makes it increasingly necessary to provide researchers with efficient paper recommendation services. Since scientific documents contain many mathematical expressions and rich text information, effectively mining this information to improve recommendation quality is a challenging and necessary task. Therefore, this paper proposes a method that fuses content-based and Graph Convolutional Network (GCN) introducing the multi-head attention mechanism for scientific document recommendation. The method employs Hesitant Fuzzy Set (HFS) and Bidirectional Encoder Representations from Transformers (BERT) to calculate the similarity between mathematical expressions and their context, respectively, and utilizes GCN to learn the complex relationships between nodes and mine the potential similarity between nodes. Then, the multi-head attention mechanism is introduced to dynamically assign importance weights to neighbor nodes to enhance the expression of embedding vectors, thereby generating more accurate and personalized recommendation lists. Experimental results show that the method performs well on both Ntcir and extended Chinese datasets, achieving maximum F1_Score vales of 0.817 and 0.837 at Top-50 and Top-30, respectively.

Keywords: Scientific Document Recommendation · Mathematical Expressions · GCN · HFS · Multi-Head Attention Mechanisms

1 Introduction

With the progress of science and technology, scientific documents play an increasingly important role in people's lives and academic fields as a tool for transmitting scientific knowledge. With the surge in the number of scientific documents, researchers have broader and more comprehensive scientific information, while it is increasingly difficult to accurately and quickly obtain the information of interest from the massive information. The scientific document recommendation model is based on the study of the scientific document retrieval models containing mathematical expressions and their contexts. Actively pushing scientific documents that meet the researchers' interests can solve the problem of information overload, help researchers to grasp the cutting-edge dynamics promptly and improve the efficiency of scientific research.

Mathematical expression retrieval techniques have experienced continuous development in recent years, and several mathematical expression retrieval models have been proposed, such as MathDex [1], MIaS [2], FORTE [3], WikiMirs [4]. The proposal of these models has laid a solid foundation for the realization of mathematical expression retrieval. Mathematical expressions are significant tools and necessary elements for scientific documents to rigorously and precisely express technical concepts, elucidate reasoning processes, present numerical results, and establish theoretical models. Using Mathematical expression as the basis of recommendation not only explores the intrinsic mathematical relevance of the documents but also combines the user's research fields and preferences for personalized recommendation. Therefore, it is necessary to realize the science document recommendation based on mathematical expressions.

2   Related Work

2.1   Paper Recommendation

With the explosive growth of academic resources, the paper recommendation system has become an important tool to help researchers quickly access relevant literature. In the paper review, Xie et al. [5] designed a recommendation system based on the TextRank graph algorithm and verified the system's accuracy and reliability in the actual use process. Feng et al. [6] proposed a journal recommendation system called "Pubmender" in the study of biomedical paper recommendation, which can recommend journals in PubMed according to the abstracts. Lam et al. [8] considered the publication category, the paper's content, and the number of references and checked the authority and popularity of the publication to ensure the quality of the recommendation. Du et al. [9] constructed an academic network in the study of interdisciplinary paper recommendation, which recommends interdisciplinary papers using keyword coupling features, author citation coupling features, and the documents' attributes.

Driven by the rapid advancement of machine learning and deep learning technologies and the effective utilization of vast data, paper recommendations have made remarkable progress in recent years. Hassan [10] used recurrent neural networks to solve the problem of disregarding the context of the words and the semantic similarity between the articles. He realized that a high-quality recommendation could be obtained even through a keyword. To solve the problem of papers being rejected because the topic does not match the journal's scope, Liu et al. [11] proposed a journal submission recommendation model based on the embedding model, which can help researchers select appropriate journals and effectively avoid high-quality papers being rejected due to the inconsistency of the topic. Zhao and Chen [12] proposed a recommendation model BFMR2vec based on heterogeneous graph embedding, which generates an embedded representation of papers and recommends papers published by authors as a preference representation. In summary, most current thesis recommendation methods are mainly based on textual attributes. In contrast, mathematical expressions, which are an important part of the thesis, need to be further studied in depth to be used as the basis for thesis recommendation.

2.2 Mathematical Expression Retrieval

Early work in the field of mathematical expression retrieval focused on string-based matching. Stalnaker et al. [13] proposed a mathematical expression retrieval and indexing method called Tangent, which uses reverse indexing for symbol pairs in mathematical expressions and ranks them as similar by calculating the harmonic mean of the query expression and the matching symbol pairs in the candidate expression. However, such methods usually only consider the syntactic structure of the expression and ignore the semantic information of the expression. To address this problem, researchers have explored learning methods for mathematical expressions that incorporate semantic information. Tian et al. [14] devised a data structure to represent mathematical expressions, incorporating symbol encoding and the mathematical information among symbols, which realized the normalization of mathematical expressions in different formats. Dadure et al. [28] proposed a mathematical information retrieval method that combines context and formula embedding and generalization. The documents' formula and context are extracted and represented by vectors. And using an innovative similarity metric technique, documents identified by formula embedding and generalization modules are preferentially retrieved.

Due to the development of deep learning models, researchers have started using more powerful sequence-to-sequence models. Neeraj et al. [15] proposed a method for representing mathematical expressions in a continuous space to address the immaturity of embedding methods for mathematical expressions. They employed a sequence-to-sequence encoder architecture and trained the model on visually different but mathematically equivalent expressions, generating vector embeddings. Yan et al. [29] proposed a convolutional sequence model, ConvMath, in mathematical expression recognition, which converts mathematical expressions in images into LaTeX sequences. It uses an image encoder for feature extraction and then uses a convolutional decoder to generate the sequences, improving mathematical expression recognition accuracy.

In addition, Medjkoune [16] has attempted to fuse multimodal information to improve retrieval quality. In summary, mathematical expression retrieval has been an active research area.

2.3 Graph Convolutional Network

Graph Convolutional Networks have demonstrated an excellent ability to process graph-structured data and have been widely used in a variety of fields, such as bioinformatics [17], traffic prediction [18], and recommendation systems [19,20]. In the field of recommendation systems, in response to the data sparsity and cold-start problems of collaborative filtering recommendation algorithms and the fact that existing knowledge graph-based recommendations ignore the connection between a specific entity and a specific user, Elahi et al. [21] proposed an end-to-end recommendation framework to learn collaborative signals and knowledge graphs for personalized recommendations. To obtain better potential representations for users and items, Song et al. [22] proposed a recommendation system model based on graph neural network, which introduces a new attention mechanism to obtain more valuable collaborative information from the user graph, item graph, and interaction graph, and captures multiscale potential features through a nonlinear transformation. Graph Convolutional Network is an unsupervised encoding framework that can directly learn node feature representations. It propagates and aggregates information from different types of nodes on homogeneous graphs, and effectively captures complex higher-order structural information and local similarities well, so they are widely used in recommendation systems.

3   Materials and Methods

In response to researchers' requirement to obtain scientific documents relevant to their research according to math content, this paper proposes a novel model for recommending scientific documents that integrate graph convolutional networks and content-based methods (C-GCN), as illustrated in Fig. 1.

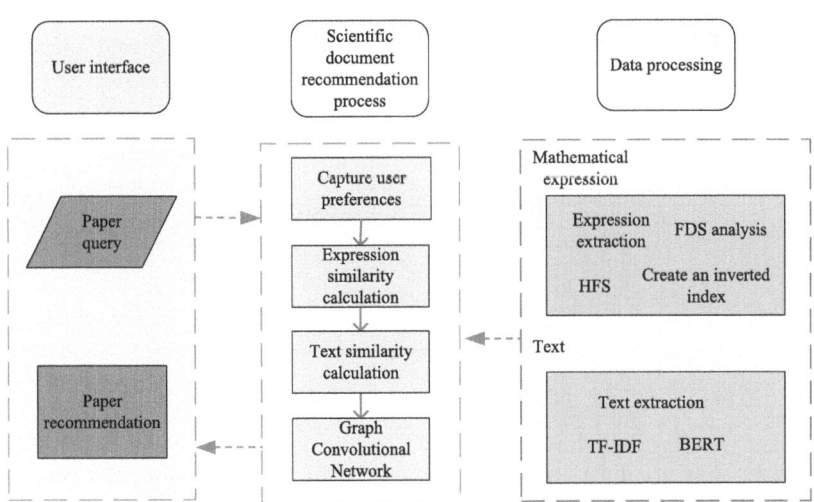

Fig. 1. The framework of scientific documents recommendation model

The model is divided into three modules: user interface, data processing, and recommendation of scientific documents. In the user interface, papers queried and read by the user are used as the basis for recommendations, returning scientific documents that match the user's preferences. The data processing module processes the mathematical expressions in the papers and their context and stores them in the database. In the recommendation module of scientific documents, recommendations are made according to the user's preferred mathematical expressions. HFS is introduced to calculate the similarity between mathematical expressions in LaTeX or MathML format between the scientific documents preferred by the user and the database, and to obtain the similarity between the papers by combining with the calculation of similarity in their context. Finally, the recommendation result is obtained by feature learning of nodes and mining potential connections between nodes through the graph convolutional network.

3.1   Similarity of Mathematical Expressions

Using FDS [23] to decompose mathematical expressions, each symbol of a mathematical expression is parsed into a quintuple (level, flag, count, tf, operator).

HFS [24] is an emerging extended application of fuzzy set theory that addresses the hesitations decision-makers face in the decision-making process. In mathematical expressions, the similarity between a given mathematical expression and the target expression is calculated, and this similarity often requires the simultaneous consideration of multiple attribute factors, such as the length, level, operators, and other aspects of the mathematical expression. HFS provides a flexible method to describe the process of evaluating the similarity of these multiple attributes by assigning a set of membership values to each attribute.

Take the formula "$a^2 + b^2$" as an example, after the decomposition of each symbol of the quintuple value shown in Table 1.

Table 1. The result of the decomposition of the formula "$a^2 + b^2$"

Symbol	Level	Flag	Count	Tf	Operator
a	0	0	1	0.2	0
2	1	2	2	0.2	0
+	0	0	3	0.2	1
b	0	0	4	0.2	0
2	1	2	5	0.2	0

The HFS is used to compute the similarity of mathematical expressions between the user preference and the database. The corresponding algorithm is shown in Algorithm1, and the corresponding parameters in the algorithm are defined as follows.

Definition 1. *MathQ denotes the math expression of the user's preference, $MathD_i(i = 1, 2, \ldots, N)$ denotes the math expression on the dataset, and N is the number of expressions on the dataset.*

Definition 2. $SymQ_q(q = 1, 2, \ldots, n_q)$ *denotes the qth symbol of the mathematical expression of the user's preference, and n_q denotes the number of all symbols of the expression; $SymD_d(d = 1, 2, \ldots, n_d)$ denotes the dth symbol of the mathematical expression in the dataset, and n_d denotes the total number of all symbols.*

Definition 3. *The functions $M_{lev}(SymQ_q, SymD_d)$, $M_{fla}(SymQ_q, SymD_d)$, $M_{cou}(SymQ_q, SymD_d)$, $M_{tf}(SymQ_q, SymD_d)$, $M_{ope}(SymQ_q, SymD_d)$ denote the membership functions corresponding to the five attributes of a mathematical expression after decomposition, respectively.*

Algorithm 1. Similarity calculation of mathematical expressions based on HFS

Require: $\text{MathQ}, \text{MathD}_i$ $(i = 1, 2, \ldots, N)$
Ensure: SimMathList //A list of mathematical expressions similar to query expressions
1: SymQ_q $(q = 1, 2, \ldots, n_q)$
2: SymD_d $(d = 1, 2, \ldots, n_d)$
3: **for** qu **in** SymQ_q **do**
4:    **for** ds **in** SymD_d **do**
5:      **if** $qu == ds$ **then**
6:        $\text{vec} = [M_{\text{lev}}(\text{SymQ}_q, \text{SymD}_d), M_{\text{fa}}(\text{SymQ}_q, \text{SymD}_d),$
7:          $M_{\text{cou}}(\text{SymQ}_q, \text{SymD}_d), M_{\text{rf}}(\text{SymQ}_q, \text{SymD}_d), M_{\text{ope}}(\text{SymQ}_q, \text{SymD}_d)]$
8:        $\text{TempDict}[ds] = (\text{ds.id}, \text{vec})$
9:      **end if**
10:   **end for**
11: **end for**
12: **for** $temp, (\text{id}, \text{vec})$ **in** $\text{TempDict.items}()$ **do**
13:   **for** tempSD **in** SdDict **do**
14:     **if** $\text{tempSD.id} == \text{id}$ and $\text{tempSD} == temp$ **then**
15:       $\text{SdDict}[temp] = (\text{id}, \max(\text{np.mean(vec)}, \text{np.mean(tempSD.vec)}))$
16:     **else**
17:       $\text{SdDict}[temp] = (\text{id}, \text{np.mean(vec)})$
18:     **end if**
19:   **end for**
20: **end for**
21: $\text{SimMathList} = \text{SIM}(\text{list}(\text{SdDict.values}()), \text{Listsq})$
22: **return** SimMathList

3.2   Keywords Similarity

Semantic understanding of mathematical expressions is crucial in making recommendations for scientific documents. Vector Space Model (VSM) and dynamic pre-training model are used to calculate text similarity. In VSM, Term Frequency-Inverse Document Frequency (TF-IDF) can effectively determine the importance of keywords to the whole scientific document and assign weights to the text by considering the frequency of the keywords and the inverse document frequency. The larger weights indicate that the keywords are more significant.

The dynamic pre-training model uses context-sensitive text representations to capture semantic information better. One of them, the BERT encoder consists of the Transformer's bi-directional structure. It can obtain richer representation information. Compared to Word2vec and Glove models, BERT can solve the problem of multiple meanings of a word and the difference of meanings of the same word in different sentences, effectively learning both word-level and sentence-level semantic features.

BERT is used to encode the text and cosine distance is used to calculate the similarity. Finally, the similarity between articles combines the similarity of mathematical expressions and keywords. The calculation formula is as follows:

$$sim_{final} = \alpha * sim_{exp} + (1 - \alpha) * sim_{key} \tag{1}$$

where α is a hyperparameter that controls the weights of the two components.

3.3 Recommendation Modeling Based on Graph Convolutional Network

This paper proposes a recommendation model for scientific documents based on GCN, consisting of embedding, forward propagation, and prediction layers. The embedding layer uses scientific documents to learn features to get the initial embedding vectors; the forward propagation layer is a graph convolutional network combined with the multi-head attention mechanism to get higher-quality embeddings and mine the potential relationship between nodes; the prediction layer recommends scientific documents based on the final generated node embeddings.

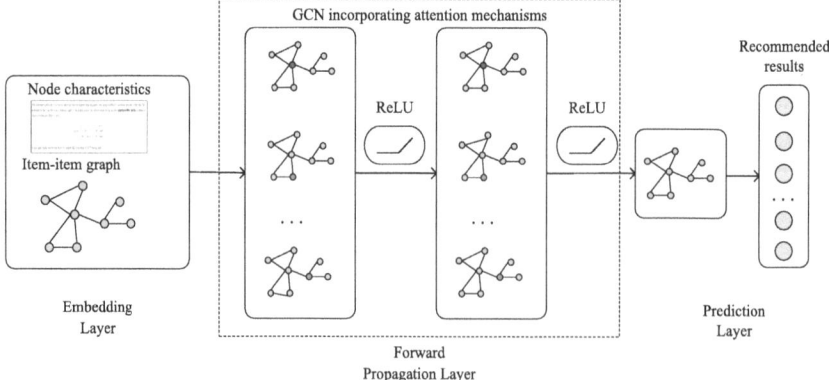

Fig. 2. GCN-based recommendation model for scientific documents

Embedding Layer. In recommendation systems, it is necessary to deal with a large amount of data from users and scientific documents. The data is essentially discrete and high-dimensional sparse features. To effectively represent and model these discrete features so that the convolutional network can process and learn these data more efficiently, an Embedding Layer is introduced as an input layer in the model. The embedding layer is located between the data input and the forward propagation layer, serving as a preprocessing step. It maps the input discrete identifiers to a continuous vector space, making it easier for the forward propagation layer to use these vectors for pattern recognition and feature extraction. Compared to one-hot encoding, embedding vectors not only reduces the sparsity of data, more importantly, they can represent the correlations between users in a low-dimensional continuous space, laying the foundation for subsequent interest mining operations.

In this study, we construct an undirected graph with Q nodes, each with a d-dimensional feature vector. The adjacency matrix A represents the connectivity between the nodes, where A_{ij} denotes the weights of the edges between the nodes.

The primary role of the embedding layer is to convert the entities in the item-item similarity graph and the relationships between nodes into low-dimensional vectors. The embedding vector of user preference items can be represented as $e_u \in R^d$, while database items can be represented as $e_i \in R^d$, where d is the dimension of the embedding vector.

$$e_u = [e_{u_1}, e_{u_2}, \ldots, e_{u_m}, \ldots, e_{u_M}] \tag{2}$$

$$e_i = [e_{i_1}, e_{i_2}, \ldots, e_{i_n}, \ldots, e_{i_N}] \tag{3}$$

In the above equations, M denotes the number of user preference items, N denotes the number of database items, e_{u_m} denotes the embedding vector of the mth user preference item, and e_{i_n} denotes the embedding vector of the nth database item.

Forward Propagation Layer. The layer is at the heart of the convolutional network model and is the basis for model prediction and training. The function of this layer is to take the input data through the layers of the network to compute the final output, with each layer transforming the data and extracting features by applying weights, biases, and activation functions.

This layer incorporates the multi-head attention mechanism based on graph convolutional network, which can independently learn different types of relationships between nodes and enrich node feature representations by splicing or averaging the outputs of multiple heads. The mechanism can play a regularisation effect to prevent the overfitting of a single head. The traditional graph convolutional network applies the same weight to all neighboring nodes, while the model can adaptively learn the importance of each neighboring node to the central node after the introduction of the multi-head attention mechanism. It will selectively fuse part of the feature representations of each neighbor at the time of aggregation, thus improving the accuracy of prediction. Assume that the node matrix in the graph is $X \in \mathbf{R}^{N \times F}$, where N denotes the number of nodes, and F represents the feature dimension of each node. The set of nodes is $h = \{\mathbf{h_1}, \mathbf{h_2}, \ldots, \mathbf{h_N}\}$, $\mathbf{h_i} \in R^{F'}$. The corresponding weight matrix for each head is $W_k \in \mathbf{R}^{F \times F'}$, where F' is the projected feature dimension. The formula for calculating the attention score is as follows:

$$e_{ij}^k = \text{LeakyReLU}\left(\mathbf{a}^T[\mathbf{W_k}\mathbf{h}_i^k \parallel \mathbf{W_k}\mathbf{h}_j^k]\right) \tag{4}$$

where h_i^k and h_j^k denote the node vectors after the linear change of node i and node j, respectively, $\mathbf{a} \in \mathbf{R}^{2F'}$ is the trainable attention parameter, and $\parallel$ denotes the connection operation of the vectors. To better distribute weights between different nodes, the attention scores are normalized. The normalized attention scores are α_{ij}^k. Node features are weighted and summed at each layer using attention scores as well as merging multiple heads for output, calculated as follows:

$$z_i^k = \sum_{j \in N(i)} \alpha_{ij}^k \mathbf{h}_j^k \tag{5}$$

$$z_i = \frac{1}{K} \sum_{k=1}^{K} \mathbf{z}_i^k \tag{6}$$

Finally, ReLU is used as an activation function to increase the nonlinearity of the model and make it more expressive.

L2 loss is sensitive to outliers, which can aid the model in fitting the data well. In this model, the L2 loss function is employed to assess the model's prediction error. Using this loss function ensures that the model can effectively reduce prediction error and enhance prediction performance during training.

The choice of optimizer has a significant influence on the training performance of deep learning network models. This paper employs the Adam (Adaptive Moment Estimation) optimization algorithm to update network parameters. This optimizer stems from an enhancement of the conventional stochastic gradient descent algorithm, incorporating both an adaptive learning rate mechanism and a momentum term. It has the advantages of high computational efficiency and fast convergence speed, and it can overcome gradient explosion or gradient disappearance.

Prediction Layer. The layer is to generate final predict result based on the outputs of the model's forward propagation layers. Unlike traditional recommendation methods, this paper employs the L2 norm for embedding vector computation. By calculating the L2 norm values, the "strength" feature of users and items in the embedding space can be obtained.

After obtaining high-quality node embeddings, a concise prediction layer is designed to generate the final recommendation scores. The L2 norm of each embedded node is calculated as the prediction value, as described by the following formula:

$$y_{score} = ||X||_2 \tag{7}$$

where $X = (x_1, x_2, \ldots, x_n)$ is an n-dimensional feature. $\|\cdot\|$ denotes the L2 norm. The larger the norm value, the larger the magnitude of the node in the embedding vector space, and the higher the corresponding degree of recommendation. Directly using the norm as the recommendation basis can effectively reflect the quality of the node embedding.

4   Results and Discussion

4.1   Experimental Datasets

Considering that the public dataset of ntcir-mathir-wikipedia-corpus contains only 31,742 scientific documents in English, we introduce 10,372 Chinese scientific documents [25] to expand the dataset. The English scientific documents include 529,713 mathematical expressions, and the Chinese scientific documents include 147,496 mathematical expressions.

4.2   Experimental Parameter Setting

In this paper, the Adam trainer is used for training with epoch of 20, the initial value of the learning rate is set to 0.01 to approximate the optimal solution quickly and stably, and RELU is chosen as the nonlinear activation function. Inspired by related studies, two-layer graph convolutional networks are selected to be trained on the dataset separately. To ensure the robustness of the model convergence, we implemented a back-propagation mechanism to iteratively optimize the model performance by meticulously adjusting the network weights at the end of each round of training.

4.3   Evaluation Metrics

The experiment chooses the more classic recommendation algorithm metrics to measure the quality of the generated recommendation list: Precision, Recall, and F1_Score.

Precision is used to measure the proportion of scientific documents that users like among the recommended scientific documents. The formula for calculating precision is as follows:

$$Precision = \frac{\sum |R(i) \cap U(i)|}{R(i)} \qquad (8)$$

Recall indicates the ratio of scientific documents of interest to the user in the recommended results and all of the user's interest, and the formula is as follows:

$$Recall = \frac{\sum |R(i) \cap U(i)|}{U(i)} \qquad (9)$$

where $R(i)$ is the list of scientific document recommendations generated by this paper's algorithm on the dataset, and $U(i)$ denotes the list of users' preferred scientific documents. The F1_score takes the precision rate and recall rate into account, which can analyze the advantages and disadvantages of the model more comprehensively, and its calculation formula is as follows:

$$F1_{score} = \frac{2 \times Precision \times Recall}{(Precision + Recall)} \qquad (10)$$

4.4   Comparative Experiment

NBF [27] is an academic paper recommendation algorithm proposed by Yan et al. The algorithm utilizes the feature words in the paper to build a user portrait for the target user. It uses a plain Bayesian model to calculate the posterior probability that the paper matches the user portrait and makes a recommendation. LDA Mallet [26] is a content filtering-based paper recommendation method proposed by Boussaadi et al. It constructs a topic model and finds semantically similar articles. The FGCN model [7] applied in food recommendations fully explores the relationships between graph nodes, which can effectively alleviate the data sparsity problem and perform personalized recommendations, but it lacks the learning of project features. Compared with NBF and LDA methods, the method proposed in this paper combines mathematical expressions and textual semantic information on a recommendation basis, which can more comprehensively mine the mathematical correlations between documents. Compared with the FGCN model, the model proposed in this paper adds the feature learning of items, and the model proposed in this paper mines the potential similarity between nodes while learning the features of items, which in turn can produce a higher quality recommendation list. Tables 2 and 3 show the F1_Score of different methods for recommending Chinese and Ntcir datasets. It can be found that the recommendation effect of the content-based and graph convolution network with the multi-head attention mechanism applied in this paper is better in the recommendation of science documents.

Table 2. F1_Score for different methods in the Ntcir dataset

Model	Top-10	Top-20	Top-30	Top-40	Top-50
NBF	**0.656**	0.677	0.710	0.743	0.803
LDA Mallet	0.429	0.453	0.504	512	0.536
FGCN	0.635	0.642	0.668	0.684	0.703
C-GCN	0.618	**0.736**	**0.760**	**0.793**	**0.817**

Table 3. F1_Score for different methods in the Chinese dataset

Model	Top-10	Top-20	Top-30	Top-40	Top-50
NBF	0.769	0.781	0.784	0.805	0.819
LDA Mallet	0.583	0.598	0.615	0.622	0.625
FGCN	0.638	0.671	0.680	0.693	0.720
C-GCN	**0.779**	**0.829**	**0.837**	**0.836**	**0.832**

4.5 Ablation Experiment

To illustrate the effect of different components on the model, ablation experiments are performed on the Ntcir dataset, and the results are shown in Table 4. C-GCN(gcn) denotes a recommendation based on content only without using a graph convolutional network model; it does not mine the potential similarity between documents. C-GCN (att) denotes a model that does not use the attention mechanism.

Table 4. The F1_Score result of the ablation experiment

Dataset	Model	Top-10	Top-20	Top-30	Top-40	Top-50
Ntcir	C-GCN (gcn)	0.536	0.624	0.675	0.701	0.728
	Decrease/%	8.2	11.2	8.5	9.2	8.9
	C-GCN (att)	0.605	0.685	0.726	0.757	0.783
	Decrease/%	1.3	5.1	5.0	3.6	3.4
	C-GCN	0.618	0.736	0.760	0.793	0.817

From the experimental results, it can be seen that when graph convolutional network is not considered, C-GCN(gcn) model, the performance of the model decreases, Top-10 decreases by 8.2%, Top-20 decreases by 11.2%, Top-30 decreases by 8.5%, Top-40 and Top-50 decreases by 9.2% and 8.9%, respectively. When the multi-head attention mechanism is not considered, the C-GCN(att) model, the performance of the model is degraded, with a decrease of 1.3% at Top-10, 5.1% at Top-20, 5.0% at Top-30, and 3.6% and 3.4% at Top-40 and Top-50, respectively. From the experimental results, it can be known that the graph convolutional network has a greater impact on the model performance compared to the multi-head attention mechanism, but the effect of the combination of the two components leads to a better performance of the C-GCN recommendation model.

4.6 Experimental Results

The average value of precision, recall, and F1 for each fixed number of recommendations is run 20 times as the Top-n metric. The Top-n is selected from 5 to 55 on the horizontal axis with a step size of 10, and the vertical axis is the corresponding evaluation metrics. The values of the evaluation metrics corresponding to Top-n for the Chinese and Ntcir datasets are shown in Figs. 3 to 5, respectively.

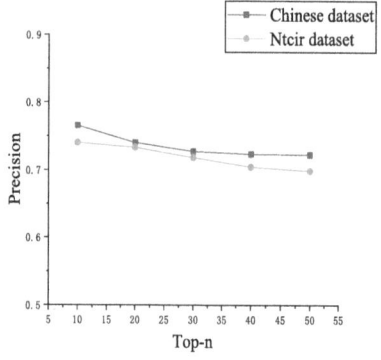

Fig. 3. Effect of top-n on the value of precision

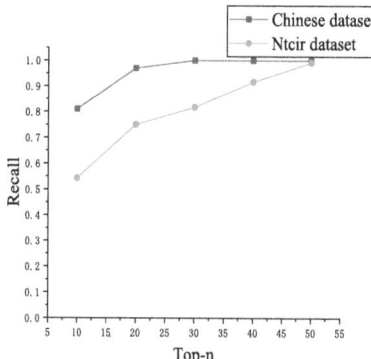

Fig. 4. Effect of top-n on the value of recall

In Fig. 3, it can be observed that along with the growth of Top-n, the precision of the two datasets shows a slow decreasing trend; at the time of Top-10, both achieve the maximum values of 0.76 and 0.74. At the time of Top-50, they achieve the minimum value of 0.72 and 0.69, respectively. From the experimental results, each time the user-preferred scientific document list recommendation accounted for more than half, the model had a good recommendation effect.

For both datasets, the value of Recall increases gradually when Top-n grows. In the Chinese extended dataset, the minimum value of 0.81 is achieved at Top-10. In the Ntcir dataset, only when Top-n takes the value of 10, Recall is relatively small, and the rest of the nodes take the value of more than 0.75. The experimental results show that most of the categories of scientific documents the users prefer are included in the recommendation list.

Figure 5 shows that along with the growth of Top-n, the F1_score values of the Ntcir dataset shows a growth trend. The F1_score values of the extended chinese dataset shows a trend of first growth, then a slow decline and the maximum value is achieved at top-30. The overall recommendation effect is relatively ideal. It not only recommends scientific documents that meet user's preferences but also recommends the category of documents that some users may like but have not been exposed to. It can ensure the precision and the diversity of the recommended categories.

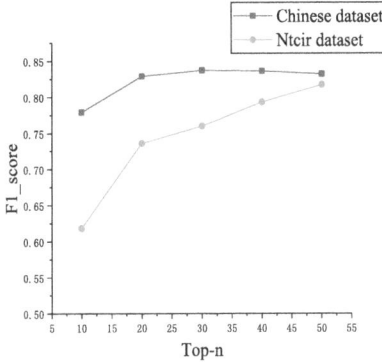

Fig. 5. Effect of top-n on the value of F1_score

5   Conclusion

Aiming at the problems in scientific document recommendation by combining mathematical expressions, this paper proposes a recommendation method that integrates content-based and graph convolutional network introducing multi-head attention mechanisms. Firstly, FDS and HFS are used to calculate the similarity between user-preferred and the database's mathematical expressions. Building upon this, similarity between the context of mathematical expressions is computed using BERT. Finally, graph data is constructed, and graph convolutional network that introduces attention mechanisms is used for feature learning and mining potential relationships between nodes for recommendations. The experimental results demonstrate that using content-based and graph convolutional networks introducing multi-head attention mechanisms to recommend can effectively improve the recommendation quality of the recommendation system.

References

1. Miner, R., Munavalli, R.: An Approach to Mathematical Search Through Query Formulation and Data Normalization. In: Kauers, M., Kerber, M., Miner, R., Windsteiger, W. (eds.) Calculemus/MKM -2007. LNCS (LNAI), vol. 4573, pp. 342–355. Springer, Heidelberg (2007). https://doi.org/10.1007/978-3-540-73086-6_27

2. Sojka, P., Líška, M.: Indexing and searching mathematics in digital libraries. In: Davenport, J.H., Farmer, W.M., Urban, J., Rabe, F. (eds.) CICM 2011. LNCS (LNAI), vol. 6824, pp. 228–243. Springer, Heidelberg (2011). https://doi.org/10.1007/978-3-642-22673-1_16

3. Wang, Z., Zhang, M., Baraniuk, R., et al.: Scientific formula retrieval via tree embeddings. In: IEEE BigData 2021, pp. 1493–1503. IEEE, Orlando, FL, USA (2021)

4. Hu, X., Gao, L.,Lin, X., et al.: WikiMirs: a mathematical information retrieval system for wikipedia. In: Proceedings of 13th ACM/IEEE-CS Joint Conference on Digital Libraries, pp. 11–20. ACM, Indiana, United States (2013)

5. Xie, W., Shen, Y., Ma, Y.: Recommendation system for paper reviewing based on graph computing. Appl. Res. Comput. **33**(3), 798–801 (2016)
6. Feng, X., Zhang, H., Ren, Y., et al.: The deep learning-based recommender system "Pubmender" for choosing a biomedical publication venue: development and validation study. J. Med. Internet Res. **21**(5), e12957 (2019)
7. Gao, X., Feng, F., Huang, H., et al.: Food recommendation with graph convolutional network. Inf. Sci. **584**, 170–183 (2022)
8. Lam, S. H., Brewer, E., Ng, Y. K.: Using a deep learning model, content features, and author metadata to recommend research papers. In: 2020 IEEE 21st International Conference on Information Reuse and Integration for Data Science (IRI), pp. 265–270. IEEE, Los Alamitos, California (2022)
9. Du, J., Xiong, H., Xiang, Y.: A study on interdisciplinary paper recommendation based on academic network. J. China Soc. Sci. Tech. Inf. **43**(5), 516–527 (2024)
10. Hassan, H. A. M.: Personalized research paper recommendation using deep learning. In: Proceedings of the 25th Conference on User Modeling, Adaptation and Personalization, pp. 327–330. Association for Computing Machinery, New York, United States (2017)
11. Liu, C., Wang, X., Liu, H., et al.: Learning to recommend journals for submission based on embedding models. Neurocomputing **508**, 242–253 (2022)
12. Zhao, C., Chen, Y.: A personalized recommendation algorithm for papers based on heterogeneous graph embedding. Front. Data Comput. Dev. **5**(6), 153–160 (2023)
13. Stalnaker, D., Zanibbi, R.: Math expression retrieval using an inverted index over symbol pairs. In: Document Recognition and Retrieval XXII, pp. 34–45. SPIE, San Francisco, Calif., USA (2015)
14. Tian, X., Yang, S., Li, X., Yang, F.: An indexing method of mathematical expression retrieval. In: Proceedings of 2013 3rd International Conference on Computer Science and Network Technology, pp. 574–578. IEEE, Dalian, China (2013)
15. Neeraj, G., Kani, N.: Semantic representations of mathematical expressions in a continuous vector space. arXiv preprint arXiv:2211.08142 (2023)
16. Medjkoune, S., Mouchere, H., Petitrenaud, S., Viard-Gaudin, C.: Multimodal mathematical expressions recognition: case of speech and handwriting. In: Kurosu, M. (ed.) HCI 2013. LNCS, vol. 8007, pp. 77–86. Springer, Heidelberg (2013). https://doi.org/10.1007/978-3-642-39330-3_9
17. Ngai, W., Xie, H., Zou, D., et al.: Emotion recognition based on convolutional neural networks and heterogeneous bio-signal data sources. Inf. Fusion **77**, 107–117 (2022)
18. Rahmani, S., Baghbani, A., Bouguila, N., et al.: Graph neural networks for intelligent transportation systems: a survey. IEEE Trans. Intell. Transp. Syst. **24**, 8846–8885 (2023)
19. Xing, J., Xing, X., Jia, Z., et al.: Project recommendation algorithm integrating knowledge graph and attention mechanism. Comput. Eng. Appl. (2024). http://kns.cnki.net/kcms/detail/11.2127.tp.20231120.1538.006.html
20. Isufi, E., Pocchiari, M., Hanjalic, A.: Accuracy-diversity trade-off in recommender systems via graph convolutions. Inf. Process. Manag. **58**(2), 102459 (2021)
21. Elahi, E., Halim, Z.: Graph attention-based collaborative filtering for user-specific recommender system using knowledge graph and deep neural networks. Knowl. Inf. Syst. **64**, 2457–2480 (2022)
22. Song, Y., Ye, H., Li, M., et al.: Deep multi-graph neural networks with attention fusion for recommendation. Expert Syst. Appl. **191**, 116240 (2022)
23. Zai, X., Tian, X.: Retrieving scientific documents with formula description structure and word embedding. Data Anal. Knowl. Discov. **4**(1), 131–138 (2020)

24. Torra, V.: Hesitant fuzzy sets. Int. J. Intell. Syst. **25**(6), 529–539 (2010)
25. Tian, X., Wang, J.: Retrieval of scientific documents based on HFS and BERT. IEEE Access **9**, 8708–8717 (2021)
26. Boussaadi, S., Hassina, A., Ouahabi, A.: Using an explicit query and a topic model for scientific article recommendation. Educ. Inf. Technol. **28**(12), 11–14 (2023)
27. Yan, H., Zhou, G., Zhu, Z., et al.: Academic paper recommendation algorithm based on Naive Bayes. J. Suzhou Univ. Sci. Technol. (Nat. Sci. Edn.) **40**(04), 69–75 (2023)
28. Dadure, P., Pakray, P., Bandyopadhyay, S.: Embedding and generalization of formula with context in the retrieval of mathematical information. J. King Saud Univ. Comput. Inf. Sci. **34**(9), 6624–6634 (2022)
29. Yan, Z., Zhang, X., Gao, L., Yuan, K., Tang, Z.: ConvMath: a convolutional sequence network for mathematical expression recognition. In: 2020 25th International Conference on Pattern Recognition (ICPR), pp. 4566–4572. IEEE, Milan, Italy (2021)

Semantic Communication of Images Using Image Generation and Image Captioning Models

Asma Mahgoub$^{(\boxtimes)}$ ⓘ and Elias Yaacoub ⓘ

Department of Computer Science and Engineering, Qatar University, Doha, Qatar
{am1510694,elias}@qu.edu.qa

Abstract. With the emergence of 6G networks and the new networking requirements, the existing networks are approaching the Shannon capacity limit. Hence,
a new paradigm called 'semantic communication' is proposed in the literature.
Semantic communication is the transmission of the meaning of a message between
two intelligent agents. In this work, the problem of image semantic communication
is considered. Most of the existing works in literature focus on the exact reconstruction of the transmitted image. Yet, to achieve full semantic communication,
it is possible to focus on transmitting a similar image with the same meaning
as the original image. This can be achieved by transmitting a text description of
the image. An image captioning model, namely, the one-for-all (OFA) model is
used to transform an image into its caption. The caption is transmitted through the
network and at the receiver an image-to-text diffusion model, stability diffusion
XL, is used to reconstruct a semantically similar image. The similarity between
the transmitted and the received images is assessed using the textual similarity
between the corresponding captions. The captions of the original and the generated images had a similarity above 0.7 using five text similarity measures, namely,
ANLS, METEOR, ROUGE, BLEU and BERT similarity. This approach is shown
to achieve a 99% reduction in the message size. The results emphasize the effect
of using AI models to extract a general representation of a message and in turn
consume less communication resources.

Keywords: Image captioning · Image similarity · Image synthesis · Semantic
communication · Text similarity

1 Introduction

The upcoming 6G network has stringent communication requirements to serve different
applications such as virtual reality, extended reality, the Metaverse, and the Internet of
Everything. To meet such requirements, more communication resources will be consumed, and the networks will soon reach the Shannon capacity limit. To resolve this, a
new paradigm called 'semantic communication' is proposed in the literature and attract-
ing increasing research interest. Semantic communication involves sending the meaning
of a message between intelligent agents. The sender extracts the meaning and transmits
it to the receiver whereas the receiver infers the message from the received meaning [1].

M. Barhamgi et al. (Eds.): WISE 2024, LNCS 15463, pp. 138–147, 2025.
https://doi.org/10.1007/978-981-96-1483-7_11

Semantic communication can be applied to different types of data, in this work the focus will be on the transmission of images. In literature, several semantic communication algorithms for image transmission were proposed. Deep learning techniques, namely, Convolutional Neural Networks (CNNs) were used in [2] and [3], Generative Adversarial Networks (GANs) were used in [4–7], Reinforcement learning for semantic communication was proposed in [8]. These works focused on extracting a set of features from the transmitted image, sending a segmentation map instead of the original image or iteratively generating the transmitted image at the receiver side. It was noted that in all of these works, the sent image is reconstructed exactly at the receiver side. In [5], a very similar image but not the exact image is transmitted. Other works considered representing the image as text before it gets transmitted. In [9], an image is converted to text by an image-to-text model, the text is enhanced by extracting some keywords. The enhanced text is transmitted, and an image generation model is used to reconstruct the image based on the text. In [10], images are converted to text using composable diffusion (CoDi) model. GPT-4 is used to enhance the text and at the receiver CoDi model is used to construct the image from the given text. The authors in [11] focus on transmission of portrait images. The image is converted to a text prompt, the prompt is sent over the channel. A fine-tuned diffusion model is used to generate a similar image at the receiver.

As mentioned earlier, most of the previous works in the field of image semantic communication focus on sending a minimal representation of an image – a feature set or a segmentation map- and then reconstruct the original image at the receiver. This concept is more similar to data compression rather than corresponding to semantic communication. As stated in [12], semantic communication mimics human communication in which communicating parties gradually establish a shared language by iterative communication cycles. Whereas data compression achieves minimal transmission, there is no associated intelligence with the communication. Reconstructing the exact image cannot be considered a fully semantic communication as explained in [12]. To reconstruct an image, the image is divided into a memorizable and learnable part; where the memorizable part was sent traditionally and the learnable part was sent using semantic communication. This illustrates that semantic communication is more suitable for sending the general aspects of an image, while sending the details is more efficiently done by traditional communication. This differs from the previously discussed works ([2–4] and [6–8]) that aim to fully semantically transmit an exact representation of an image.

Motivated by the concept of sending the meaning of an image and reconstructing a similar but not necessarily exactly identical image, we propose an AI-based semantic communication algorithm for transmitting images. In this proposed algorithm, an image is converted to text using an image captioning model. The text is transmitted through the network and a text-to-image generator is used at the receiver to reconstruct a semantically similar image. At the expense of sending a similar, but not the exact image, the proposed algorithm is shown to greatly reduce communication resources. The main contributions of this work are summarized below:

- Propose an AI-based image semantic communication system that aims to convey the meaning of the transmitted image by representing it as a text description.
- Using the caption of the generated image and the original image to assess the semantic similarity between the sent and received images.

- Illustrating that used image similarity metrics in literature do not reflect the semantic correctness of the received image, but simply assess the bit-level correctness.
- Demonstrating that sending the meaning of a message, i.e. its caption achieves huge gains in terms of optimizing communication resources.

The rest of this paper is organized as follows. Section 2 gives an overview of the methodology; Sect. 3 presents and discusses the results and finally the paper is concluded in Sect. 4.

2 Methodology

The block diagram of the proposed algorithm is shown in Fig. 1. An image is represented as text using an image captioning model, the caption is sent through the channel. At the receiver, the received caption is used to generate a semantically similar image using a text-to-image model.

Image captioning is performed by the one-for-all (OFA) model [13]. This model is used because it had a greater performance compared to other models as indicated in [14]. The OFA model is developed to provide a general framework for multiple vision and language tasks. The image captioning module is designed using a transformer and a ResNet (residual network) convolutional neural network. Training is done by optimizing the cross-entropy loss and the CIDEr (Consensus-based image description evaluation) metric.

Image generation is performed using the stable diffusion XL (SDXL) model [15]; the model produces more visually pleasing and accurate images compared to the earlier stable diffusion models. It was also shown that the generated images have a comparable preference when compared to the Midjourney platform, based on a user study. SDXL is a latent diffusion model that generates an image by iteratively modifying a randomly generated image conditioned on a text prompt. The SDXL model uses a UNet to generate an image based on a given prompt, a refinement stage is added to enhance the visual quality and the details of the generated image.

The algorithm was tested using randomly selected images from the COCO dataset [16]. For experimental purposes, the caption was used to generate two images, and the best image was selected for further analysis.

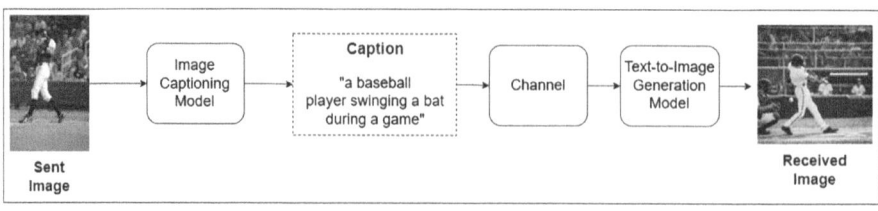

Fig. 1. Block diagram of the proposed image semantic communication algorithm

3   Results and Discussion

The proposed methodology is tested on 10 images, the original and the generated images are shown in Table 1. The table shows the corresponding captions -generated by the OFA model- of each image. In the following subsections, the images will be compared in terms of caption similarity and image similarity. In the last subsection, a comparison between the image size and the caption size will be presented.

3.1   Caption Similarity

As stated earlier, two images were generated per caption but the image with the most similar caption was selected. To evaluate the similarity of the received image, the caption of the received image is generated to be compared with the sent caption using several text similarity metrics. The used text similarity metrics are described below:

- Average Normalized Levenshtein Similarity (ANLS): a metric used in evaluating optical character recognition algorithms [17], it is based on matching exact words and minimizing the Levenshtein distance between the two sentences.
- Metric for Evaluation of Translation with Explicit Ordering (METEOR): a metric used in evaluating accuracy of machine translation algorithms; it divides a sentence into a group of words, and it considers the order of the words in the sentence [18].
- Recall-Oriented Understudy for Gisting Evaluation (ROUGE L-sum): ROUGE [19] is metric that is used to evaluate machine summarization tasks. In this paper, the F1 measure of the ROUGE L-sum metric will be used. This metric identifies the longest common subsequence between two sentences.
- Bilingual Evaluation Understudy (BLEU) [20]: this metric is also used for evaluating machine translation algorithms, it is based on matching n-grams between two sentences. In this work, the matching 1-g will be considered.
- BERT Similarity: Bidirectional Encoder Representation from Transformer (BERT) model is a text transformer model that can produce context-aware text embeddings. In [21], the embeddings from the BERT model were used to calculate the semantic similarity between two sentences. The same approach will be used to calculate the semantic similarity between the captions, the used BERT model will be the sentence BERT model [22].

All of the above measures produce a score between 0 to 1, the higher the value the more similar the two sentences are.

The similarity scores between the caption of the original image and the caption of the generated image are presented in Fig. 2. Most of the measures have a value above 0.7 indicating a high similarity between the two captions. As shown in Table 1, it is evident that the generated captions are almost identical to the original caption. Although the images are visually different, key elements are present in each image based on the given caption. However, the seventh image depicting a box of apples and a box of bananas had the worst caption similarity compared to the other images. This may be the result of the erroneous caption of the original image; it is possible that this particular image is challenging to be understood by both of the used AI models.

Table 1. Comparison between the original images and the generated images along with the corresponding captions

Original Image	Generated Image

"two people sitting at a table in an office"	"two people sitting at a table in a meeting room"

"an intersection with a traffic light on a city street"	"a traffic light on a street in a city"

"a man waiting for a bus at a bus stop"	"a man is waiting at a bus stop"

"a hotel room with a large bed and a chair"	"a hotel room with a large bed and a chair"

"a boat sitting on the sand on a beach"	"a boat sitting on the sand on a beach"

"a yellow bird is sitting on a tree branch"	"a yellow bird perched on a tree branch"

(continued)

Table 1. (*continued*)

"a box filled with apples and bananas next to a box of fruit"

"a box of bananas apples and other fruits on a table"

"a group of zebras grazing in a field"

"a group of zebras grazing in a field"

"a baseball player swinging a bat during a game"

"a baseball player swinging a bat at a ball"

"a laptop computer sitting on a table with a book"

"a laptop computer sitting on a table with a book"

3.2 Image Similarity

Most of the published works in the field of image semantic communication use measures such as structural similarity index measure (SSIM) and peak signal-to-noise ratio (PSNR). SSIM measures similarity between two images, while PSNR evaluates the reconstruction quality of an image. However, these measures are suitable for compression or denoising tasks, as the goal is to retrieve the original image accurately. On the other hand, semantic communication does not aim to transmit an exact representation of the image, as the semantic correctness is more important than the bit-level correctness [23]. Hence, it will not be fair to use such measures to evaluate the effectiveness of semantic communication algorithms. To illustrate this concept, the set of generated images is compared to the original images using SSIM and PSNR. The results are summarized in Fig. 3. As shown in Fig. 3 (a), the SSIM of all the images was less than 0.5

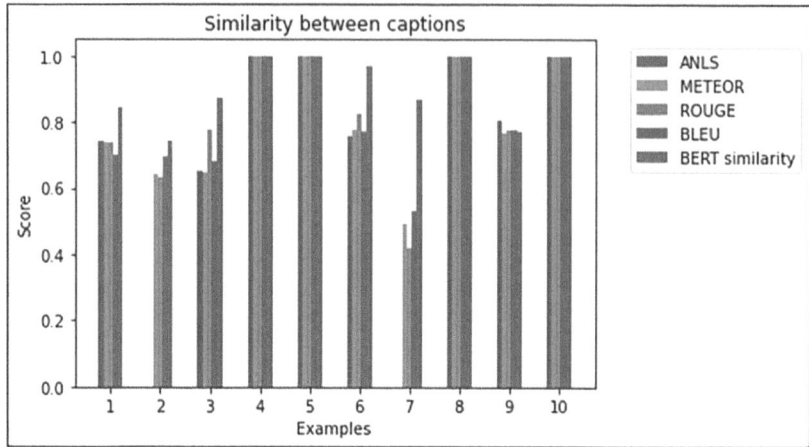

Fig. 2. Similarity between the caption of the original image and the caption of the generated image.

indicating that the images are not similar. Also, all the PSNR values were around 28, this is a very low value and indicates that the original images were not reconstructed properly.

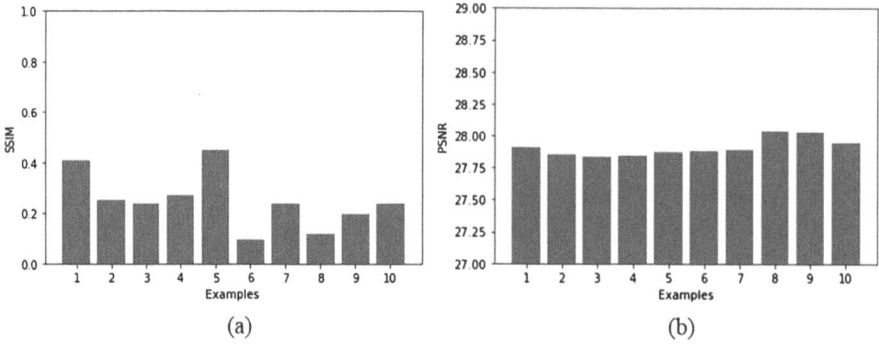

Fig. 3. (a) SSIM between the original and the generated images. (b) PSNR of the generated images

3.3   Message Size

It is important to see the effect of sending an image's caption instead of the actual image. Although the received images are visually different from the sent images, the gain in terms of communication resources is very high. As shown in Fig. 4, the generated image size is around 3.15 MB whereas the average caption size is only 40 bytes; this a reduction of more than 99% of the original message size. Less communication resources will be consumed; less bandwidth and less data rate. It is worth noting that the image generation model always generates a square 1024 × 1024 image although the original image may have a different dimension. The size of the caption was estimated based on the fact that the maximum caption size is 16 words and that the average number of characters per word is 5 hence (16/2) × 5 = 40 Bytes.

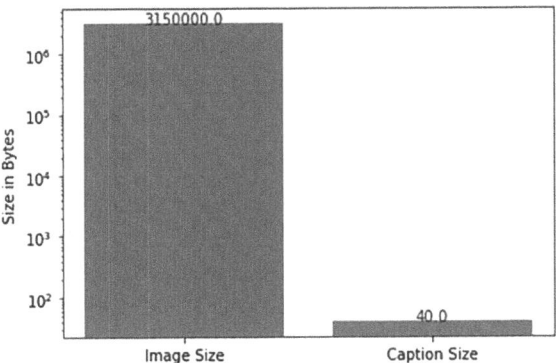

Fig. 4. Comparison between the size of the generated image and the size of the sent caption.

As seen in the previous subsections, sending the caption instead of the original image may not produce the image that is desired. As the caption is a general description of an image, some aspects of the original image are not captured in the generated image; such as the bus in the third example, other aspects are added to the generated image but are not part of the original image, such as the mountain in the fifth example. In many images, the correct view is not depicted as many of the original images are far view images whereas the generated images were near view. It would be better to use an image description model that would describe the image more accurately, and hence a more semantically similar image is produced.

4   Conclusion

The aim of semantic communication is not the exact transmission of the message but conveying the meaning of a message. Yet, many works in the literature treat the problem of image semantic communication as image compression and aim to transmit the message exactly. In this work, we aim to develop a semantic communication system for images by representing the image using text. To achieve this goal, the OFA image captioning model is used at the receiver to obtain the image's caption. The caption is sent through the network, at the receiver an image is generated by feeding the received caption into an image-generation model. The results indicated that the generated images are not visually similar to the sent images. However, several aspects of the original images were preserved in the generated images. This was proved by the fact that the captions of the generated images were very similar and sometimes identical to the original images' captions. Overall, the conversion of an image to text reduces the message size greatly and saves communication resources. To generate more semantically similar images, it is possible to use a more detailed and descriptive caption. However, it is challenging to find an image captioning model that produces a detailed description of an image. In the future, we would improve the model by considering the presence of noise in the channel and we may introduce a knowledge base at the receiver to patch the irregularities and the missing details (such as human faces) in the generated images. We also aim to design an image semantic similarity metric based on the captions.

Acknowledgments. This research was supported by the IRCC-2024-499 International Research Collaboration Co-Fund between Qatar University, Paris-Dauphine and Madrid Universities. The statements made herein are solely the responsibility of the authors.

References

1. Luo, X., Chen, H.H., Guo, Q.: Semantic communications: overview, open issues, and future research directions. IEEE Wirel. Commun. **29**(1), 210–219 (2022). https://doi.org/10.1109/MWC.101.2100269
2. Dai, J., et al.: Nonlinear transform source-channel coding for semantic communications. IEEE J. Sel. Areas Commun. **40**(8), 2300–2316 (2022). https://doi.org/10.1109/JSAC.2022.3180802
3. Yoo, H., Dai, L., Kim, S., Chae, C.-B.: On the Role of ViT and CNN in semantic communications: analysis and prototype validation. IEEE Access **11**, 71528–71541 (2023). https://doi.org/10.1109/ACCESS.2023.3291405
4. Huang, D., Tao, X., Gao, F., Lu, J.: Deep learning-based image semantic coding for semantic communications. In: Proceedings - IEEE Global Communications Conference, GLOBECOM (2021).https://doi.org/10.1109/GLOBECOM46510.2021.9685667
5. Lokumarambage, M.U., Gowrisetty, V.S.S., Rezaei, H., Sivalingam, T., Rajatheva, N., Fernando, A.: Wireless end-to-end image transmission system using semantic communications. IEEE Access **11**, 37149–37163 (2023). https://doi.org/10.1109/ACCESS.2023.3266656
6. Du, H., et al.: Generative AI-aided joint training-free secure semantic communications via multi-modal prompts. In: ICASSP, IEEE International Conference on Acoustics, Speech and Signal Processing - Proceedings, pp. 12896–12900, (2023). https://doi.org/10.1109/ICASSP48485.2024.10447237
7. Qian, L.O., et al.: Deep image semantic communication model for artificial intelligent internet of things. ArXiv, Nov. (2023). https://arxiv.org/abs/2311.02926v2. Accessed 26 Sep 2024
8. Lu, K., et al.: Rethinking modern communication from semantic coding to semantic communication. IEEE Wirel. Commun. **30**(1), 158–164 (2023). https://doi.org/10.1109/MWC.013.2100642
9. Nam, H., Park, J., Choi, J., Bennis, M., Kim, S.L.: Language-oriented communication with semantic coding and knowledge distillation for text-to-image generation. In: ICASSP, IEEE International Conference on Acoustics, Speech and Signal Processing - Proceedings, pp. 13506–13510 (2024). https://doi.org/10.1109/ICASSP48485.2024.10446638
10. Jiang, F., et al.: Large AI model empowered multimodal semantic communications (2023). http://arxiv.org/abs/2309.01249. Accessed 28 Oct 2023
11. Wei, X., Tong, H., Yang, N., Yin, C.: Language-oriented semantic communication for image transmission with fine-tuned diffusion model (2024). http://arxiv.org/abs/2409.17104
12. Chaccour, C., Saad, W., Debbah, M., Han, Z., Poor, H.V.: Less data, more knowledge: building next generation semantic communication networks. IEEE Commun. Surv. Tutorials, 1 (2024). https://doi.org/10.1109/COMST.2024.3412852

13. Wang, P., et al.: OFA: unifying architectures, tasks, and modalities through a simple sequence-to-sequence learning framework. Jun. 28, 2022, PMLR. https://proceedings.mlr.press/v162/wang22al.html. Accessed 06 Sep 2024
14. Tang, Z., Yang, Z., Zhu, C., Zeng, M., Bansal, M.: Any-to-any generation via composable diffusion (2023). http://arxiv.org/abs/2305.11846
15. Podell, D., et al.: SDXL: improving latent diffusion models for high-resolution image synthesis. In: 12th International Conference on Learning Representations, ICLR 2024, Jul. 2023. https://arxiv.org/abs/2307.01952v1. Accessed 27 Sep 2024
16. Lin, T.-Y., et al., "Microsoft COCO: Common Objects in Context"
17. Furkan, B. et al.: Scene text visual question answering. https://openaccess.thecvf.com/content_ICCV_2019/html/Biten_Scene_Text_Visual_Question_Answering_ICCV_2019_paper.html. Accessed 16 Sep 2024
18. Banerjee, S., Lavie, A.: METEOR: An Automatic Metric for MT Evaluation with Improved Correlation with Human Judgments
19. Lin, C.: Recall-Oriented Understudy for Gisting Evaluation (Rouge) (2005)
20. Papineni, K., Roukos, S., Ward, T., Zhu, W.-J.: BLEU: a method for automatic evaluation of machine translation. In: Proceedings of the 40th Annual Meeting on Association for Computational Linguistics - ACL 2002, Morristown, NJ, USA: Association for Computational Linguistics, 2001, p. 311 (2001). https://doi.org/10.3115/1073083.1073135
21. Xie, H., Qin, Z., Li, G.Y., Juang, B.H.: Deep learning enabled semantic communication systems. IEEE Trans. Signal Process. **69**, 2663–2675 (2021). https://doi.org/10.1109/TSP.2021.3071210
22. Reimers, N., Gurevych, I.: Sentence-BERT: sentence embeddings using siamese BERT-Networks. In: EMNLP-IJCNLP 2019 - 2019 Conference on Empirical Methods in Natural Language Processing and 9th International Joint Conference on Natural Language Processing, Proceedings of the Conference, pp. 3982–3992 (2019) https://doi.org/10.18653/v1/d19-1410
23. Chang, M.-K., Hsu, C.-T., Yang, G.-C.: GenSC: generative semantic communication systems using BART-like model. IEEE Commun. Lett., 1 (2024) https://doi.org/10.1109/LCOMM.2024.3450309

Leveraging Optimization Techniques for Effective Arabic Query Expansion

Azzah Allahim[1,2(✉)] and Asma Cherif[2,3]

[1] College of Computer and Information Sciences, Jouf University, Sakaka, Saudi Arabia
azzah.allahim@gmail.com
[2] IT Department, Faculty of Computing and Information Technology, King Abdulaziz University, Jeddah, Saudi Arabia
[3] The Center of Excellence in Smart Environment Research, King Abdulaziz University, Jeddah 21589, Saudi Arabia
acherif@kau.edu.sa

Abstract. The primary goal of query expansion is to gather terms that are closely associated with the original query terms. To accomplish this goal, similarity measurements are used to evaluate the similarity between the query terms and the collected terms. Unfortunately, existing Arabic query expansion frameworks focus on expanding the query words individually. This approach can affect the expansion process for a complex language such as Arabic. In this paper, we investigate the effectiveness of applying an AI optimization algorithm to Arabic query expansion. The study aims to produce the optimal combination of terms by measuring the similarity of the collected terms against all query terms. We tested two intelligent swarm algorithms: the Cuckoo Search algorithm and Harmony search algorithm. Both algorithms were successful in enhancing the model's precision and recall score with Cuckoo Search algorithm achieving the best performance of (97.5%) precision and (93%) recall.

Keywords: Query expansion · Optimization · Information Retrieval · Cuckoo Search · Harmony search algorithm

1 Introduction

The ease of accessing the internet has resulted in its widespread use as a primary source of information. Data is usually sought after by the user in information retrieval (IR) systems. Information retrieval (IR) is the core of capturing documents that are the most suitable for a given query provided by the user and, hence, forms the backbone of search engines [1]. Query expansion is one of the powerful techniques employed on IR, as an approach proposed by [2], used to capture more relevant documents. Query Expansion aims to improve search recall by adding extra words to the original query [3]. As query expansion is immensely important, countless researchers have developed many algorithms and mechanisms [4]. However, while the technique has been successfully implemented in a variety of languages, it is challenging to use in Arabic. The expansion of Arabic queries faces particular challenges since it is a complex language. Arabic is an agglutinative language characterized by the complexity of word morphology (words have multiple forms, depending on how they are put in a sentence and other linguistic features). Does it facilitate the choice of better words to increase the expandability of a query? These nuances can be tricky to capture in Arabic, and traditional expansion techniques popular in languages such as English often give rise to search results that are either irrelevant or redundant. This is further exacerbated by synonyms, ambiguous terms, and the optional use of diacritics, which all decrease the efficiency of searches, making it even harder to connect users with the information they need. The problem is so challenging when it comes to Arabic query expansion, and thus requires more state-of-the-art methods that are capable of treating complex languages. This is where AI-based conceptual understanding techniques and some optimization perform their job. AI-based optimization uses sophisticated algorithms to streamline the processes and cater for finding optimum solutions of given problem [5]. When it comes to query expansion, optimization techniques can aid in identifying the pertinent terms by modifying parameters of the query and preventing some issues like e.g. a query drift. With help of AI optimization algorithms, we can optimise the selection to expand terms for maximum searchability even in complex languages like Arabic. Although the use of AI optimization in this area is still in its early stages, it has the potential to significantly enhance information retrieval systems by providing more accurate and context-aware query expansions. The paper outlines the impact of integrating the optimization mechanism into Arabic query expansion, particularly its efficacy in generating the optimal word combination for information retrieval frameworks. The study utilizes two intelligent swarm algorithms: the Cuckoo Search algorithm and Harmony search algorithm. Additionally, to facilitate the evaluation, a AraQuery Arabic dataset comprised of 40 queries along with their associated relevant documents was constructed.

The remainder of this paper is organized as follows: related works are summarized in Sect. 2. Then, our problem statement is presented in 3. Section 4 elaborates the proposed solution. Section 5 summarizes the performance of the architecture along with the results. Finally, we conclude in Sect. 6.

2 Related Work

Due to its complexity, few works have focused on applying AI optimization algorithms. For Arabic text, Almarwi et al. [6] used the optimization mechanism to optimize the weighting process, i.e. the similarity score for each term. Their work included using Wordnet as the primary source for expansion. The synonyms collected from Wordnet were subjected to three different weighting methods. To select the optimal weights, particle swarm optimization (PSO) was applied by treating the weights as the positions of the particles within the algorithm. The main goal of this optimization was to enhance term selection. To evaluate their approach, they compiled an Arabic corpus and conducted multiple experiments to analyze the effectiveness of including and excluding each weighting method. Their results demonstrated good recall and precision for the queries entered. Kumar et al. [7] applied optimization to generate optimal term combinations for English text. They presented a hybrid approach for query expansion, utilizing optimization algorithms to obtain the optimal terms for expansion. Their framework involved performing topic mapping on a dataset to use it as an expansion source. They established a topic map for later terms matching, using Wikipedia articles and newsgroup datasets to extract the main topics. Once the main topics were identified, Wordnet was used to add related terms to each topic. When a user enters a query, the framework attempts to find related terms from the topic map by applying Jaccard similarity. The resulting terms are then passed to the optimization module. For optimization, they employed two algorithms: spatial bound whale and binary moth flame, which work in parallel to produce the optimal set of related terms for expansion.

3   Problem Statement

The expansion process generally involves four stages: preprocessing, feature extraction, similarity measurement, and terms ranking, as illustrated in Fig. 1 [8]. During preprocessing, only useful terms are extracted from the query and passed on to the next step. Subsequently, the terms' features are extracted to enable measurement. Word embedding is a particularly useful and powerful mechanism for converting terms into vectors. By implementing word embedding, the terms can be compared with other terms [9]. Following this, the terms are utilized with an external source for expansion, such as WordNet [10]. The related terms from the source are then selected based on a similarity measurement score within a predefined threshold. Finally, the terms are ranked based on their scores.

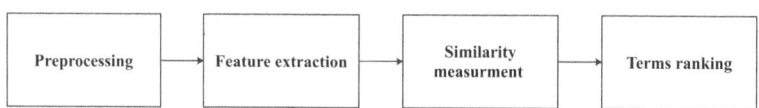

Fig. 1. General query expansion pipeline

The primary aim of query expansion is to generate terms associated with the original query terms; however, a challenge arises when the framework accumulates an excessive number of related terms. Furthermore, the selection of the best candidate terms is determined by the similarity measurement score between each term and every related term in the terms pool.

The primary challenge associated with this process arises when the context of the query is significant. Therefore, a mechanism that gathers the final terms in consideration of the entire query is needed. While this issue has been addressed in existing literature, many of the proposed solutions entail traversing the entire expansion pipeline depicted in Fig. 1.

One of the major challenges in Arabic query expansion is the loss of meaning when expanding individual words separately, rather than considering the entire query context. For instance, expanding the query "التعليم في المدارس تأثير التكنولوجيا على" ("The impact of technology on education in schools") word by word can lead to an expansion like "تغيير التقنيات على الدراسة في الجامعات" ("The change of techniques on studies in universities"), which shifts the focus away from the original context of technology in schools. This distortion in meaning leads to irrelevant search results and highlights the limitations of traditional expansion methods that treat words in isolation.

However, optimization algorithms can solve this problem reasonably well by optimizing both the selection and positioning of words as a complete phrase. These approaches all regard sets of terms as populations and assess their fitness scores (i.e., how similar they are to the original query, given in Fig. 2). The optimization process allows the most important terms to be selected by taking into account the entire query, thereby preserving contextuality and improving search results. This method removes the limitations of word-by-word expansion, enabling richer and more relevant query expansions.

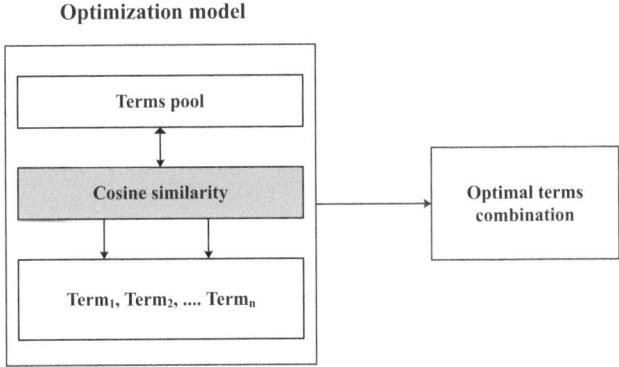

Fig. 2. Optimized query expansion

4   Proposed Solution

The primary objective of our suggested framework is to integrate the optimization mechanism into the query expansion process and assess its efficacy. As depicted in Fig. 3, once the terms pool is established, the optimization model is tasked with generating the most effective combination of terms. The optimization model feeds the terms into the optimization algorithm. At the heart of this process is the fitness function. The fundamental purpose of this fitness function is to maximize the similarity score between the pool words and the target words, i.e., input query words. In the context of query expansion, the objective function used is Cosine similarity. Cosine similarity was selected as the foundation of our fitness score because it measures the relatedness between words in terms of meaning. Cosine similarity measures the similarity by comparing the angle between two word vectors. This results in a score between -1 and 1, where 1 means they are very similar, and -1 means they are entirely different [11].

By using AI optimization algorithms with Cosine similarity as the fitness function, we can automatically find the best possible terms to expand the query. The AI algorithm treats the expanded terms as a population and calculates the fitness score for each term based on its similarity to the original query. This process helps the algorithm select and rank terms that are not only semantically relevant but also keep the overall meaning of the query intact. In doing so, the optimization algorithm ensures that the expanded terms are contextually accurate and leads to better search results by preventing irrelevant or misleading expansions.

To perform the AI-based optimization, we applied two swarm intelligent algorithms: Cuckoo Search algorithm and Harmony Search algorithm.

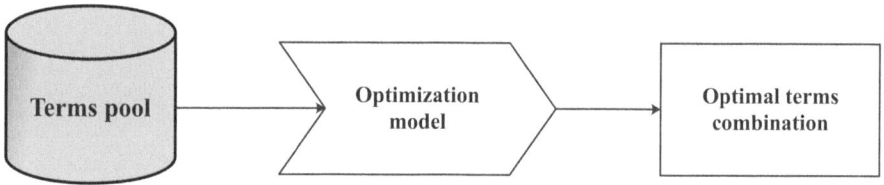

Fig. 3. Overview of the Proposed Optimization architecture

Cuckoo Search Algorithm: This algorithm was created by Yang and Deb [12]. It is inspired by the brood parasitism behavior of cuckoo birds. In our context, we first establish initial parameters and create the initial population of nests, where each nest contains a word combination. Then, we monitor the fitness of each nest and initialize the best nest and its fitness. Next, within a loop, we generate new nests by mutating existing ones using Lévy flights. Subsequently, we assess the fitness of each new nest based on average cosine similarity. We then update the best nest if a new superior nest is discovered. Additionally, a portion of the underperforming nests is discarded and replaced by new random nests. Throughout the entire process, we keep a record of the best solutions, and the best solution is derived from the best nest found. All steps are illustrated in Fig. 4.

Harmony Search Algorithm: This technique is inspired by a musical improvisation technique in which musicians tune their pitches to achieve harmony [13]. For our purpose, we establish the initial harmony memory with random solutions, i.e. word combinations. Subsequently, we monitor the similarity of each

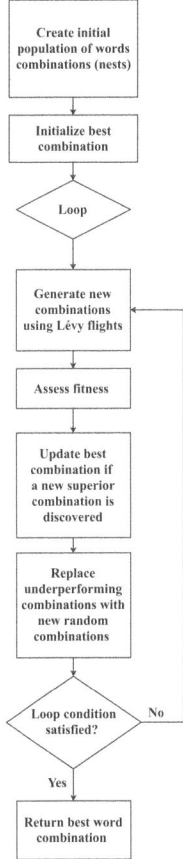

Fig. 4. Cuckoo search steps to obtain the optimal word combination

harmony to the query words, which refers to the total cosine similarity between all the words in the word combinations and the query words. In the next phase, we iterate through a loop to generate new harmonies, i.e. new word combinations, by considering existing ones in the memory or selecting random words. This particular step focuses on the harmony memory consideration rate (HMCR), which requires determining how much of the existing solution will stay the same in the new one. To manage the HMCR, we employ pitch adjustment to make slight modifications to the new harmonies. Following this, we assess the similarity of the new harmonies to the query words. We then update the harmony memory by replacing the worst harmony, i.e. least similar combination to the query words, with the new one if it is superior. Ultimately, we extract the best harmony from the harmony memory, and the best harmony found is returned. All steps are illustrated in Fig. 5.

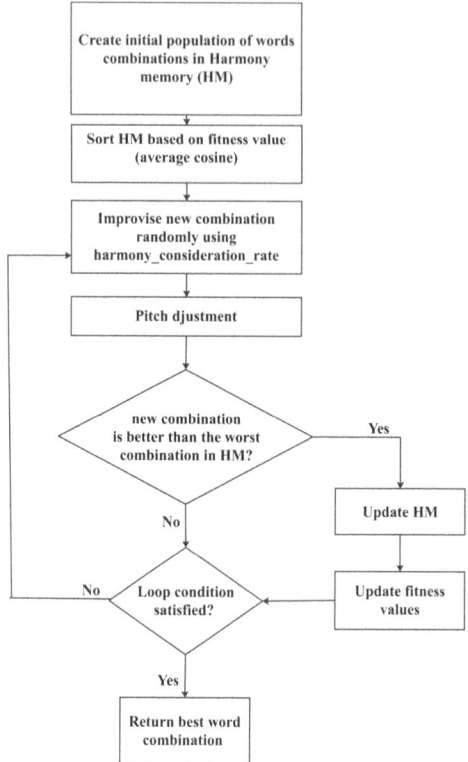

Fig. 5. Harmony search steps to obtain the optimal word combination

5   Performance Analysis and Discussion

In this section, we present our experiment setup, which includes the optimization setting, datasets details and the used metrics. Besides, we present the results and discuss them.

5.1   Experiment Setup

In our experiment, we employed a query expansion process that utilized a pool of 20 candidate words for each word in the original query. The goal was to select the most suitable word for each original term to preserve the context and meaning of the query. The effectiveness of integrating optimization into the query expansion process was evaluated by creating the AraQuery Arabic dataset, which is comprised of 40 queries, each associated with 6 relevant documents. 260 Arabic articles were utilized to construct the testing dataset from Wikipedia [14], and Mawdoo3 [15], Marefa [16], and Sotor [17] websites. The Wikipedia articles were collected from the Wikimedia tool [18] using the Wikiextractor [19]. Out of the 260 Arabic articles, only 240 are relevant and we added 20 irrelevant articles to test the stability of the models[1]. To test the performance of the models, we employed precision and recall to evaluate the model's performance. Recall effectively assesses the completeness of the model's results; it evaluates the model's ability to return all relevant documents in the dataset. Precision, on the other hand, assesses the quality of the model's results; it evaluates the model's ability to return relevant documents. The precision and recall formulas are as follows:

$$Recall = \frac{Number\ of\ Relevant\ Documents\ Retrieved}{Total\ Number\ of\ Relevant\ Documents} \tag{1}$$

$$Precision = \frac{Number\ of\ Relevant\ Documents\ Retrieved}{Total\ Number\ of\ Documents\ Retrieved} \tag{2}$$

We applied the precision for the top-4 documents. Besides, since we are using limited dataset and each query is assigned with 6 relevant documents, we applied the recall for the top-6 documents.

Table 1. Summery of the average precision, recall and time for optimized expansion for the retrieved documents

Test Case		Top-4 Precision	Top-6 Recall	Time (ms)
Baseline (No expansion)		89%	85%	N/A
Baseline (Expanded without optimization)		95%	90%	N/A
Harmony optimization	50 iterations	95.6%	92%	0.024
	100 iterations	96.2%	92.4%	0.039
Cuckoo optimization	50 iterations	96.2%	92.4%	0.043
	100 iterations	**97.5%**	**93%**	0.088

Moreover, to assess the effectiveness of the optimization model, we conducted three distinct evaluations: the original query test, expanded query with cosine similarity, and optimized expanded query with cosine similarity. By examining the precision and recall of the 40 test queries, we calculated the average precision and recall for each test. Furthermore, we carried out the examination by implementing two distinct numbers of iterations: 50 and 100. Subsequently, we assessed the impact of increasing the number of iterations for each algorithm for precision, recall and time they consume to produce the expanded terms.

5.2   Results

Table 1 compares the recall, precision scores and time required for the optimized expansion for retrieved documents based on different query expansion and opti-

---

[1] The dataset including the documents, the queries and the fetching codes are available here: https://github.com/AzzahAllahim/Arabic-information-retrieval-dataset.

mization methods. With original queries, the model achieved a 85% precision and 89% recall score. Meanwhile, with queries that were expanded by applying cosine similarity, the precision and recall improved by 6% and 5% with scores of 95% and 90%, respectively,. This indicates that query expansion helps in retrieving more relevant documents. Moreover, by leveraging an AI optimization algorithm in the expansion process, a significant improvement in both precision and recall was achieved. At 50 iterations, Harmony search algorithm achieved a precision of 95.6% and a recall of 92%. With Cuckoo search algorithm, the model scored 96.2% and 92.4% of precision and recall, respectively. This is still an improvement over the original query but not as high as the expanded query with cosine similarity. However, with 100 iterations, Harmony search algorithm reached a precision of 96.2% and a recall of 92.4%. With greater improvement, Cuckoo search algorithm achieved a precision of 97.5% and a recall of 93%, demonstrating the benefit of further optimization and iteration. This could be due to the fact that Cuckoo Search relies on Lévy flight to generate new word combination, which provide a balance between local and global search. Meanwhile, Harmony search depends on memory-based search and pitch adjustment, which might not be as effective in exploring the search space and escaping local optima compared to the Lévy flight mechanism in Cuckoo Search. Besides, Lévy flight-based exploration in Cuckoo Search can provide better search diversity. In terms of time efficiency, the Harmony search algorithm generated the optimal word combinations faster than the Cuckoo search algorithm, with average times of 0.024 milliseconds and 0.039 milliseconds, respectively. However, although Cuckoo search algorithm was slower, its performance is still fast with minor time difference.

Overall, Cuckoo search algorithm presents the best performance among all models. It improves the results with 8.5% and 8% of precision and recall, respectively. This analysis indicates that query expansion and optimization techniques, particularly with sufficient iterations, can significantly improve the effectiveness of information retrieval systems.

6   Conclusion

In this paper, we suggested a framework for optimizing query expansion using AI-based optimization algorithms to improve the quality of Arabic query expansion. We tested two algorithms: the Cuckoo Search algorithm and Harmony search algorithm. The evaluation of the optimization models involved performing three different tests and applying various numbers of iterations to analyze their effectiveness. The precision and recall metrics were utilized to assess the model's performance, and the average scores for each test were calculated based on the 40 test queries. Additionally, the effect of increasing the number of iterations for each algorithm was thoroughly analyzed. These comprehensive evaluations provided valuable insights into the optimization model's behavior and its impact on query expansion processes. The results showed that although using cosine similarity for query expansion enhances precision and recall compared to the original query, optimizations can improve the scores further. In addition, increasing the number of iterations from 50 to 100 in optimization processes significantly boosts the results, suggesting that more thorough optimization leads to better retrieval performance. Overall, the best performance in terms of precision (97.5%) and recall (93%) is achieved by using Cuckoo optimization with 100 iterations, which outperforms the original query and the expanded query with cosine similarity.

Disclosure of Interests. The authors have no competing interests to declare that are relevant to the content of this article.

References

1. Wang, L., Yang, N., Wei, F.: Query2Doc: query expansion with large language models. In: Proceedings of the 2023 Conference on Empirical Methods in Natural Language Processing (EMNLP), (Singapore), pp. 9414–9423, Association for Computational Linguistics (2023)
2. Rocchio, J.J.: Relevance feedback in information retrieval. In: The Smart Retrieval System - Experiments in Automatic Document Processing (G. Salton, ed.), pp. 313–323, Englewood Cliffs, NJ: Prentice-Hall (1971)
3. Jagerman, R., Zhuang, H., Qin, Z., Wang, X., Bendersky, M.: Query expansion by prompting large language models. CoRR vol. abs/2305.03653 (2023)
4. Raza, M.A., Mokhtar, R., Ahmad, N., Pasha, M., Pasha, U.: A taxonomy and survey of semantic approaches for query expansion. IEEE Access **7**, 17823–17833 (2019)
5. Foulds, L.R.: Optimization Techniques: An Introduction. Springer Science & Business Media (2012). https://doi.org/10.1007/978-1-4613-9458-7
6. ALMarwi, H., Ghurab, M., Al-Baltah, I.: A hybrid semantic query expansion approach for Arabic information retrieval. J. Big Data **7**(1), 39 (2020)
7. Kumar, R., Sharma, S.C.: Hybrid optimized query expansion strategy for semantic information retrieval using spatial bound whale and binary moth flame optimization algorithm. Concurr. Comput. Pract. Exp. **34**(27), e7320 (2022)
8. Azad, H.K., Deepak, A.: Query expansion techniques for information retrieval: a survey. Inf. Process. Manag. **56**(5), 1698–1735 (2019)
9. Almeida, F., Xexéo, G.: Word embeddings: a survey. CoRR, vol. abs/1901.09069 (2019)
10. Wordnet. https://wordnet.princeton.edu/
11. Futia, G., Vetro, A., Melandri, A., De Martin, J.C.: Training neural language models with sparql queries for semi-automatic semantic mapping. Procedia Comput. Sci. **137**, 187–198 (2018). Proceedings of the 14th International Conference on Semantic Systems 10th – 13th of September 2018 Vienna, Austria
12. Yang, X.-S., Deb, S.: Cuckoo search via lévy flights. In: 2009 World Congress on Nature & Biologically Inspired Computing (NaBIC), pp. 210–214 (2009)
13. Yang, X.-S.: Harmony search as a metaheuristic algorithm. In: Geem, Z.W. (eds.), vol. 191. Springer, Heidelberg(2009). https://doi.org/10.1007/978-3-642-00185-7_1
14. Wikipedia. https://www.wikipedia.org/. Accessed 14 July 2024
15. Mawdoo3. https://mawdoo3.com/. Accessed 14 July 2024
16. Marefa. https://www.marefa.org/. Accessed 14 July 2024

17. Sotor. https://sotor.com/. Accessed 14 July 2024
18. Wikimedia. https://www.wikimedia.org/. Accessed 14 July 2024
19. Attardi, G.: Wikiextractor (2015). https://github.com/attardi/wikiextractor

DURLLCON: Deep Reinforcement Learning for URLLC Optimization in Multi-edge Networks

Heba Dawoud[1(✉)], Shuja Ansari[1], Amr Mohamed[2], Muhammad Imran[1], and Olaoluwa Popoola[1]

[1] University of Glasgow, Glasgow G12 8QQ, UK
2810361D@student.gla.ac.uk,
{Shuja.Ansari,Muhammad.Imran,Olaoluwa.Popoola}@glasgow.ac.uk
[2] Qatar University, Doha, Qatar
amrm@qu.edu.qa

Abstract. Ultra-Reliable and Low Latency Communications (URLLC) is crucial for enabling next-generation applications, particularly in areas that require stringent delay constraints, such as healthcare and vehicular networks. Multi-access Edge Computing (MEC) enhances URLLC applications by bringing computation closer to end users, maximizing resource utilization and minimizing latency. This paper introduces Deep Reinforcement Learning for URLLC Optimization in Multi-Edge Networks (DURLLCON), a Deep Reinforcement Learning (DRL)-based framework for efficient task offloading in a hybrid MEC environment, specifically targeting both URLLC and non-URLLC applications. By leveraging DRL and Long Short Term Memory (LSTM) networks, the proposed method dynamically adjusts the offloading decisions based on user energy levels, task priority, and network congestion. The simulation results show that the proposed DURLLCON framework achieves up to 30% improvement in energy efficiency and 20% reduction in average delay compared to existing methods, significantly extending user device battery life while maintaining high Quality of Service (QoS).

Keywords: Deep Reinforcement Learning · Multi-access Edge Computing · Offloading · Resource allocation · Ultra-Reliable and Low Latency Communications

1 Introduction

The growth of Internet of Things (IoT) and wearable devices has led to the development of new real-time applications, such as the fifth-generation (5G) technology, which offers a wide range of services such as enhanced mobile broadband, Virtual Reality (VR), Augmented Reality (AR), Vehicle-to-Everything (V2X), cloud-based gaming, remote learning, and advanced manufacturing. These applications rely on low-latency and high-reliability communications [8]. However, 5G

M. Barhamgi et al. (Eds.): WISE 2024, LNCS 15463, pp. 159–174, 2025.
https://doi.org/10.1007/978-981-96-1483-7_13

is limited to specific scenarios due to the increasing data generation and complex network demands. Various technologies, such as massive Machine-Type Communications (mMTC), Ultra-Reliable and Low Latency Communications (URLLC), and enhanced Mobile Broadband (eMBB), support various user applications with different service requirements. As the market expands, data generation poses challenges that require complex network demands in terms of bandwidth, data rate, and latency [6,10]. Therefore, 5G is still limited to specific scenarios and applications. However, it is anticipated that sixth-generation (6G) will integrate Artificial Intelligence (AI) into wireless communication, providing solutions to complex network optimization problems and supporting massive data application requirements that cannot be accommodated by 5G networks.

To overcome the limitations of current resource allocation and offloading methods, more recent attention has focused on the provision of MEC [1] to relocate computing and storage resources from edge servers to the proximity of end users. This allows users to offload delay-sensitive tasks, which require high power consumption and intensive computation, to nearby edge servers, reducing latency and energy consumption. However, designing an efficient offloading and scheduling algorithm remains a challenge. The task offloading problem consists of two main components: task offloading, where tasks should be executed, and task scheduling, how to schedule offloaded tasks among various edge servers. Designing an effective solution approach is complex due to resource constraints, geographical and heterogeneous characteristics of edge servers, and the scheduling problem is NP-hard, making finding an optimal solution computationally challenging.

The recent literature has explored various techniques to address the challenges of offloading and scheduling challenges in MEC, including game theories [5,13], artificial intelligence [2–4,14], and various optimization techniques [7,9]. These techniques are particularly useful for tackling stochastic problems. For example, Sharif et al. [9] developed a priority-based task scheduling and resource allocation mechanism (PTS-RA) mechanism for wearable IoT devices in health monitoring systems, optimizing task urgency, processing time, and bandwidth costs. In other works, Wang et al. [12] introduced a Multi-Agent Soft-Actor Critic-discrete (MASACDUA) that focuses on task offloading and resource allocation under URLLC-constrained conditions. The scheme aims to maximize throughput while minimizing power consumption on the remote side. The problem is divided into task offloading and computation resource allocation, solved using Lyapunov optimization. The study demonstrated that MASACDUA outperforms traditional DRL algorithms, significantly improving delay and bound violation probability.

To address the limitations of existing approaches, we propose a priority-based DRL model for optimizing task offloading in MEC environments, focusing on URLLC and non-URLLC applications. Unlike state-of-the-art methods which used First-In-First-Out (FIFO) queues [11], our model prioritizes tasks based on urgency and energy constraints, considering a scenario with multiple data centers, including distant cloud servers and edge servers close to end users.

It uniquely considers the battery constraints of each User Equipment (UE), ensuring URLLC tasks are processed locally or offloaded to nearby edge servers.

We optimize energy consumption at the local and transmission UE level, edge, and cloud levels. Furthermore, we implement the reward shaping in the environment and the reward function to guide the Double Deep Q-Networks (DDQN) agent during training, allowing automatic optimization and scheduling of task offloading.

The main contributions of our work are summarized as follows:

1. We propose a dynamic, DURLLCON. This algorithm optimizes the energy consumption of UEs by ensuring that UEs tasks are prioritized for local processing or edge offloading, while non-URLLC tasks are handled based on battery status, task priority, and system congestion. Our method employs priority queues, ensuring critical tasks are processed first, and dynamically selects the offloading destination (edge or cloud) based on real-time system conditions.
2. We leverage DRL in combination with LSTM networks to model task history, including task priority, completion time, delay, and energy consumption. This allows for better decision making regarding task load, leading to improved LSTM for end users.
3. Through simulations, we demonstrate that our proposed framework significantly improves energy efficiency and extends UE battery life, while maintaining high QoS levels. Our solution outperforms state-of-the-art methods, particularly in scenarios with heavy system congestion and battery-constrained UEs.

The rest of this paper is organized as follows. Section 2 presents the system model, including both the communication and computation models. Section 3 details the task offloading mechanism and the DRL formulation, with a focus on the DDQN approach for solving the offloading problem. Section 4 provides the simulation setup and results, comparing the performance of the proposed solution with three baseline approaches. Finally, Sect. 5 concludes the paper and discusses future research directions.

2   System Model

We consider a heterogeneous layered MEC architecture composed of multiple UEs, MEC servers, and a Cloud Computing Server (CCS) endowed with substantial computational resources, as shown in Fig. 1. In this architecture, we denote the set of UEs as $\mathcal{U} = \{U_1, U_2, \ldots, U_M\}$, where M represents the total number of UEs. The UEs are responsible for executing computational tasks classified into URLLC and non-URLLC tasks. The time is divided into episodes consisting of T time intervals, denoted as $T = \{1, 2, \ldots, T\}$, where each interval lasts τ seconds. Each UE (U_i) generates tasks randomly based on a probability distribution. Specifically, tasks are generated according to a uniform distribution within a defined range of bit sizes, represented as a data size $\delta \in \mathbb{R}^+$ in

Megabytes (MB) in every time slot. Each task generated by U_i is denoted by ψ_i^k, where k represents the task index for tasks generated by U_i.

The generated task is characterized by a binary priority indicator $P \in \{0, 1\}$, where $P = 0$ represents URLLC tasks and $P = 1$ represents non-URLLC tasks, required CPU cycles $\chi \in \mathbb{N}$ indicating the computational demand of the task, and an acceptable latency threshold $\Lambda_{th} \in \mathbb{R}^+$ defining the maximum allowable delay for task completion. These tasks can be processed locally, distributed to a nearby MEC server, or offloaded to the CCS based on the priority of the task and current network conditions. The assumption is made that each U_i is a battery-powered device with an energy capacity of Γ_i. We analyze the battery condition to optimize the battery life of the wireless UE.. The MEC servers are indicated by $\mathcal{E} = \{MEC_1, MEC_2, \ldots, MEC_N\}$, where N is the total number of MEC servers. The CCS is represented as C.

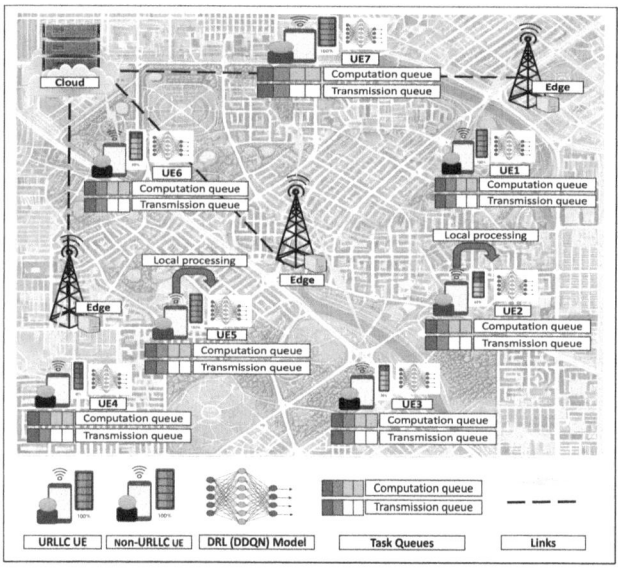

Fig. 1. System model

To efficiently manage task processing and offloading, each U_i employs two separate priority-based queues: one for local processing and another for offloading to the MEC servers or CCS. The UE scheduler assigns incoming tasks to the appropriate queue at the beginning of each time interval. Similarly, each MEC server MEC_j maintains a set of priority queues, one for each associated U_i. Unlike the approach in [11], which considers FIFO queues, this work focuses on priority-based queues to ensure that URLLC tasks are processed and loaded with high precedence, ensuring efficient response in timely and efficient task handling.

The task offloading decision is based on a priority mechanism. If the UE's battery level falls below a predefined threshold (β_{th}), tasks are offloaded according to their priority (P). High-priority tasks are processed locally based on available resources and current network conditions or are offloaded to the MEC server if the network is not congested; otherwise, they are offloaded directly to the CCS. Non-URLLC tasks are transferred to the MEC server or offloaded to the CCS server.

2.1 Communication Model

In the considered MEC architecture, UEs can offload tasks to either MEC servers or a CCS via wireless communication links. The $q_{ij}(t) \in \mathbb{R}^+$ symbol represents the quality of the channel between U_i and the MEC_j server at time t and defines the communication model. The transmission rate $r_{ij}(t)$, determines the speed of data transfer, is influenced by the available bandwidth $B_{ij}(t)$ and the channel gain $g_{ij}(t)$, such that:

$$r_{ij}(t) = B_{ij}(t) \log_2 \left(1 + \frac{P_i g_{ij}(t)}{N_0} \right), \tag{1}$$

where P_i denotes the transmission power of U_i and N_0 is the noise power spectral density. The delay and energy consumption incurred during the transmission of a task from a UE to either an MEC server or the CCS are represented separately depending on the offloading destination:

Transmission Delay. We characterize the transmission delay as:

$$D_i^T(t) = \sum_j y_{i,j}(t) \frac{\lambda_i(t)}{r_{i,j}(t)\tau} + y_{i,c}(t) \frac{\lambda_i(t)}{r_{i,c}(t)\tau}, \tag{2}$$

where $\lambda_i(t)$ is the task size (in bits), $r_{i,j}(t)$ and $r_{i,c}(t)$ are the transmission rates between U_i and the MEC_j server and CCS, respectively, and $y_{i,j}(t)$ and $y_{i,c}(t)$ are binary offloading decision variables.

Energy Consumption. We represent the energy consumption as:

$$E_i^T(t) = D_i^T(t) p_i^T(t)\tau, \tag{3}$$

where $p_i^T(t)$ represents the power consumption of the communication link for U_i during time slot t.

2.2 Computation Model

The computational capabilities of UEs, MEC servers, and the CCS are crucial for task processing in the MEC architecture. Let the computational capacity of U_i be denoted by f_i (in CPU cycles per second), that of MEC server E_j by f_j^E, and that of the CCS by f_c.

Local Processing. For local processing at U_i, the computation delay, representing the number of time slots required to process a task ψ_i^k, is defined as:

$$D_i^L = \frac{\lambda_i}{f_i\tau/\gamma_i}, \tag{4}$$

where τ is the duration of a time slot, and γ_i represents the computational efficiency of U_i.

The corresponding energy consumption for local processing is given by:

$$E_i^L = D_i^L p_i^L \tau, \tag{5}$$

where $p_i^L = 10^{-27}(f_i)^3$ denotes the power consumption of U_i's CPU frequency.

Edge Processing. We model edge processing by associating task queues with devices deployed at edge nodes. When a task ψ_i^k is offloaded to MEC_j, it is added to the ith queue at MEC j, and the task size is represented as λ_i^E. The length of the queue κ_i^E is defined as the number of tasks in the queue. The set of active queues at MEC_j, denoted by $\mathcal{Q}_j$, includes queues with non-zero task load:

$$\mathcal{Q}_j = \left\{ i \mid i \in \mathcal{I}, \lambda_i^E > 0 \, \text{or} \, \kappa_i^E(t-1) > 0 \right\}. \tag{6}$$

The total computational capacity of MEC_j, denoted by f_j^E, is shared among active queues using a processor sharing method. The backlog κ_i^E of the queue is updated as:

$$\kappa_i^E = \left[\kappa_i^E(t-1) + \lambda_i^E - \frac{f_j^E \tau}{\gamma_i \mathcal{Q}_j} - \nu_i^E \right]^+, \tag{7}$$

where λ_i^E is the task size (in bits), ν_i^E denotes the bits of tasks dropped due to queue overflow or timeout.

The delay for processing task ψ_i^k at MEC_j is:

$$D_i^E = \frac{\lambda_i^E \gamma_i}{f_j^E \tau / \mathcal{Q}_j}. \tag{8}$$

The energy consumption for processing the task at MEC_j is given by:

$$E_i^E = \frac{D_i^E p_j^E \tau}{\mathcal{Q}_j}, \tag{9}$$

where p_j^E denotes the power consumption of MEC_j at full capacity.

In addition, the energy consumed by the UE during the standby period while waiting for task completion at MEC_j is:

$$E_i^S = D_i^E p_i^S \tau, \tag{10}$$

where p_i^S represents the power consumption in the standby state.

Cloud Processing. For tasks offloaded to the CCS, the task ψ_i^k is added to the cloud task queue. The delay for processing the task at the cloud server is defined as:

$$D_i^C = \frac{\lambda_i^C \gamma_i}{f_c \tau / \mathcal{Q}_c}, \tag{11}$$

where λ_i^C is the task size (in bits), and $\mathcal{Q}_c$ represents the set of active queues at the CCS.

The energy consumption for processing the task at the cloud server is given by:

$$E_i^C = \frac{D_i^C p_c^C \tau}{Q_c},\tag{12}$$

where p_c^C represents the power consumption of the cloud server when processing tasks.

The total energy consumption at the UE level during time slot t is given by:

$$E_i^O(t) = E_i^T(t) + E_i^L(t) + E_i^S(t),\tag{13}$$

whereas the transmission energy $E_i^T(t) =$

$$\left(E_i^{T,\text{MEC}}(t) + E_i^{T,\text{CCS}}(t)\right)\tag{14}$$

includes offloading to both the MEC server and the CCS. The total energy consumption in this system model is calculated as:

$$E^{\text{tot}} = E_i^O(t) + E_i^E(t) + E_i^C(t),\tag{15}$$

To summarize, task execution can occur locally, or at a MEC server, or be offloaded to the CCS. The decision on where to execute tasks is influenced by a trade-off between computation delays, energy consumption, and network conditions to ensure optimal performance based on task priority.

3   Task Offloading and Deep Reinforcement Learning

In this section, we reformulate the task-offloading problem using a DRL approach based on [11]. We focus mainly on optimizing the UE decision of local processing or offloading based on system dynamics considering various factors such as task priority, completion time, delay, battery level, energy consumption and queue congestion level MEC_j.

3.1   MDP Formulation

The problem has been formulated as Markov Decision Process (MDP), where the objective is to maximize battery lifetime and the long-term QoS for each user by making optimal task offloading decisions. MDPs are modeled as 5-tuple representations $(\mathcal{S}, \mathcal{A}, \mathcal{T}, \mathcal{R}, \gamma)$, where $\mathcal{S}$ is the state space, $\mathcal{A}$ is the action space, $\mathcal{T}$ is the state transition probability given action in a particular state, $\mathcal{R}$ is the reward function and γ is the discount factor. In this context, we will describe the system agent and environment, define the state and action spaces, and specify the reward function for our optimization problem.

System Agent and Environment. We consider an environment E, interacting with a DDQN agent in discrete time steps. The environment is episodic, i.e. it runs for a limited time horizon where the time is divided into episodes consisting of T time slots, denoted as $T = \{1, 2, \ldots, T\}$, where each slot lasts τ seconds, and the horizon is the UE's battery lifetime. The DDQN agent actions are described by a policy π that maps a given state s_t into action a_t at time t, and the DDQN receives an immediate reward r_t. The total cumulative rewards during an episode are given by $R_t = \sum_{t=0}^{T} \gamma^t r_t$, where the discount factor is $\gamma \in [0, 1)$. The state-action value function (hereafter denoted as Q-function) given a policy π is expressed as:

$$Q^\pi(s, a) = \underset{s_t, r_t \sim E, a_t \sim \pi}{\mathrm{E}} [R_t | s_t = s, a_t = a] \tag{16}$$

The DDQN's goal is to find an optimal policy that results in maximizing Q-function, which can be done through learning from environmental interactions.

State and Action Spaces. The state space $\mathcal{S}$ encompasses all possible states at each time step in our system. A single state s_t includes various factors that influence the decision-making process for the task offloading. Specifically, the state s_t at time t is composed of the following elements: the current task size $\lambda_i(t)$; the remaining computation time at the UE, Δ_{comp}^t; the remaining transmission time, Δ_{tran}^t; the battery level of the UE, β_t; the edge queue lengths, $\kappa_i^{\mathbf{E}}(\mathbf{t} - 1)$, which represents the congestion at the MEC server queues; and the cloud queue lengths, $\kappa_i^{\mathbf{C}}(\mathbf{t} - 1)$, representing the congestion at the cloud server queues. Thus, the state s_t can be expressed as:

$$s_t = \{\lambda_i(t), Prio, \Delta_{comp}^t, \Delta_{tran}^t, \beta_t, \kappa_i^{\mathbf{E}}(\mathbf{t} - 1), \kappa_i^{\mathbf{C}}(\mathbf{t} - 1)\}$$

For the agent's action space, the actions are related to whether to process a

locally, offload it to the MEC server, or offload it to the cloud. The action a_{mec}^t is applied to the MEC servers $a_{\mathrm{mec}_1}^t, a_{\mathrm{mec}_2}^t, \ldots, a_{\mathrm{mec}_N}^t$. The actions a_t include indicators for these decisions, which can be defined as:

$$a_t = \{a_{local}^t, a_{mec}^t, a_{cloud}^t\}$$

It is important to note that the states have different ranges of values, so they are normalized between 0 and 1 using max normalization to ensure consistency in t

earning process.

Reward Function. The reward function plays an important role in the optimization process; it redirects the agent to make decisions that balance task completion, energy consumption, delay and battery management. We have employed reward engineering to optimize the UE's behavior based on the battery threshold and task priority. Specifically, the reward function now includes penalties for low battery, delay violations, and penalties or rewards based on task priority (URLLC or non-URLLC tasks). It is defined as:

$$r_t = \begin{cases} \begin{aligned} &-(E^{\mathrm{tot}}) + \alpha(1 - D_t) \\ -\ &\mathrm{BatteryPenalty}_t + \mathrm{OffloadingReward}_t, \\ &-(E^{\mathrm{tot}}) + \alpha(1 - D_t), \\ -\ &\mathrm{MaxDelayPenalty}, \end{aligned} & \begin{aligned} &\quad \text{if } \beta_t \leq \beta_{\mathrm{th}} \\ &\quad \text{if } \beta_t > \beta_{\mathrm{th}} \\ &\text{if constraints are violated} \end{aligned} \end{cases}$$
$$(17)$$

In this reward function, the terms of energy consumption are defined from Eq. (13) to Eq. (15). The term $\alpha(1 - D_t)$ represents the impact of task delay, with α as a weighting factor. A *Battery Penalty* is applied when the UE's battery level β_t is below the threshold β_{th}, while an *OffloadingReward* encourages task offloading according to task priority. If no battery constraint is present ($\beta_t > \beta_{\mathrm{th}}$), the agent focuses on optimizing task completion. Penalties are applied when the maximum delay constraints are violated, ensuring efficient and timely task handling.

3.2   Deep Reinforcement Learning for Offloading

This work uses the DDQN algorithm, part of DRL, to address overestimation bias in Q-learning algorithms by decoupling action selection and evaluation processes. Unlike continuous action spaces like DDPG, DDQN is effective in discrete action spaces, making it suitable for task offloading and scheduling problems. The algorithm consists of two Q-networks: a primary Q network for action selection based on the current state, and a target Q network for stable updates, as shown in Fig. 2.

Neural networks parameterize both networks using gradient-based learning to optimize the Q-function and enhance decision-making. The Q-value of taking action a_t in a state is denoted as $Q_\theta(s_t, a_t)$. This approach ensures more accurate estimates of Q-values by keeping action selection and evaluation separate, reducing the chance of overestimating action values.

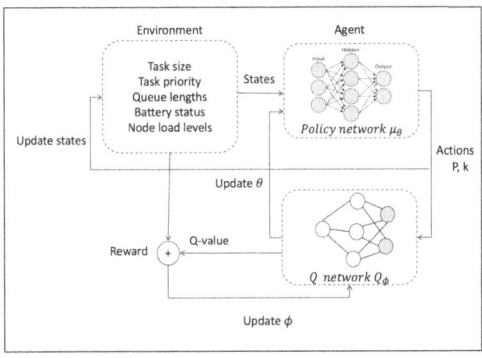

Fig. 2. DRL model

To enhance the decision-making process, the neural network architecture includes an LSTM layer. The LSTM layer is considered to predict the workload of the edge nodes based on historical data, allowing the network to learn temporal dependencies and improve future load predictions [11]. This predicted load level, combined with other state information, is then passed through FC layers that map the states to Q-values. The dueling DQN technique is further applied in these layers to separately learn the state-value and action-advantage value before combining them to determine the final Q-values, as described in Fig. 2. This setup allows for more precise and efficient offloading strategies in the MEC environment.

We used the same DDQN algorithm for both the mobile device and the edge node, following the framework defined by [11]. The mobile device autonomously determines offloading strategies based on local observations, including task size, queue status, and historical load metrics at edge nodes. The edge node supports mobile devices by retaining experience tuples in replay memory and performing back-propagation for neural network training. Although it does not make decisions or take actions independently, it uses data from the mobile device to update the DDQN networks, improving offloading decisions. This cooperative strategy guarantees efficient task offloading while preserving decentralized decision making on the mobile device. We show the DDQN model for offloading and reward shaping in Algorithm 1. This model is used to find the best policies at any given time in order to maximize the Q function and, consequently, to maximize the expected cumulative reward. By emphasizing that the reward is shaped, we ensure that the agent's behavior reflects the task priority, battery thresholds, and other factors we have engineered into the reward function. Reward shaping has a significant impact in guiding the agent during training by providing more informative feedback for each action taken.

4   Setup and Performance Evaluation

4.1   Environment Setup

We consider a typical MEC system, composed of nine UEs, two MEC servers, and once CCS. In this environment, UEs generate tasks that are processed locally or offloaded to nearby MEC servers or the CCS, depending on the network conditions and resource availability. We evaluated the performance of the proposed DDQN framework by conducting various experiments and analyzing how the optimal policy impacts the performance of the system, particularly in terms of energy and battery consumption, latency and resource utilization. The DDQN algorithm is employed to adapt to dynamical changes of the continuously changing system. In this context, the state of the system, including factors such as UE battery levels, task priority, task queue lengths, and network congestion, is periodically updated to reflect the real-time conditions of the MEC environment.

Simulation Parameters. We consider 1000 learning episodes and 100 iterations per episode, with a discount factor (γ) of 0.9 and an exploration decay

---

Algorithm 1. DDQN Algorithm: Optimal offloading policy π^* at the UE_i

---

Input: Initialize Q-network parameters θ and target Q-network
  parameters θ^- with random weights
Initialize experience buffer $\mathcal{D}$ to capacity N
for *episode $i = 1$ to M* **do**
  │ Initialize state s_0 by observing the environment
  │ **for** *time step $t = 1$ to T* **do**
  │ │ Select action a_t using ϵ-greedy policy based on $Q(s_t, a_t; \theta)$
  │ │ Execute action a_t and observe **shaped reward** r_t using
  │ │   eq. (17)
  │ │ Observe next state s_{t+1}
  │ │ Store transition (s_t, a_t, r_t, s_{t+1}) in experience buffer $\mathcal{D}$
  │ │ **if** *buffer $\mathcal{D}$ is full* **then**
  │ │ │ Sample random minibatch of transitions (s_j, a_j, r_j, s_{j+1}) from
  │ │ │ $\mathcal{D}$
  │ │ │ **for** *each transition in minibatch* **do**
  │ │ │ │ **if** *s_{j+1} is terminal* **then**
  │ │ │ │ │ $y_j = r_j$
  │ │ │ │ **end**
  │ │ │ │ **else**
  │ │ │ │ │ $y_j = r_j + \gamma \max_{a'} Q(s_{j+1}, a'; \theta^-)$
  │ │ │ │ **end**
  │ │ │ │ Perform a gradient descent step on loss function
  │ │ │ │ $\mathcal{L}(\theta) = \frac{1}{|\mathcal{B}|} \sum_j (y_j - Q(s_j, a_j; \theta))^2$ Update Q-network
  │ │ │ │   parameters θ by minimizing loss $\mathcal{L}$
  │ │ │ │ **if** *every C steps* **then**
  │ │ │ │ │ Update target network $\theta^- \leftarrow \theta$
  │ │ │ │ **end**
  │ │ │ **end**
  │ │ │ Clear experience buffer $\mathcal{D}$
  │ │ **end**
  │ **end**
end

---

rate (ϵ_{decay}) of 0.995. The learning rate (η) is 0.01, with an epsilon (ϵ) ranging from a minimum of 0.01 to a maximum of 0.99. The neural network architecture consists of two hidden layers, each with 20 neurons. The LSTM component uses 10 steps (N_{LSTM}) and a variable number of features (n_{LSTM}). We configure these parameters to optimize the offloading decisions in the MEC environment.

4.2   Performance Comparison and Simulation Results

We evaluate our proposed DRL-based method against various benchmark approaches, including full local processing (referred to as Local), full offloading (referred to as Full Offl.) and the state-of-the-art method (denoted as FIFO Offl.) [11]. Full local processing involves managing all tasks locally, whereas full offloading transfers all tasks to cloud or edge nodes. These benchmarks help to assess the efficiency of our model in balancing task processing among local, edge, and cloud resources.

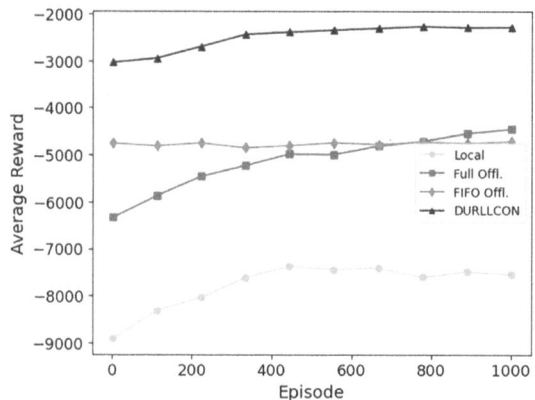

Fig. 3. DRL performance over 1000 iterations

Figure 3 compares the average reward in 1000 episodes for four different task-offloading strategies. All approaches initially show lower rewards as agents explore their action spaces. DURLLCON consistently outperforms the other methods, showing a steady increase in average reward. Local offloading achieves the lowest rewards, while full offloading improves but remains below DURLL-CON due to network congestion or higher energy consumption. FIFO Offloading performs better than Local and Full Offloading but still lags behind DURLL-CON, which leverages dynamic priority-based decision-making. DURLLCON shows significant improvement, converging faster and achieving the highest average reward, demonstrating the efficiency of the proposed DRL-based priority offloading strategy. We formulate the reward function as negative to penalize energy consumption, delays, and violations of constraints while ensuring that the agent is directed towards minimizing these factors and optimizing overall task offloading efficiency.

In Fig. 4, we compare the energy consumption across 1000 episodes for different strategies. Local processing shows the highest consumption as a result of the lack of energy-efficient processing. Full offloading reduces energy usage, but remains higher than DURLLCON and FIFO Offloading [11] due to increased communication costs. Although FIFO Offloading offers some energy savings, it

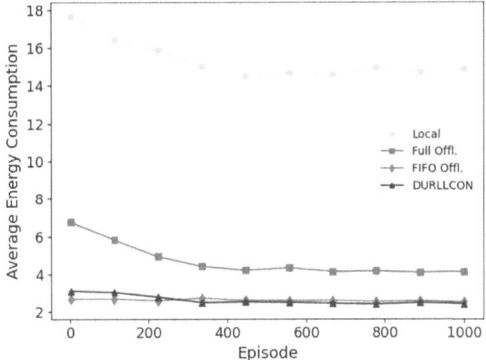

Fig. 4. Energy consumption over 1000 iterations.

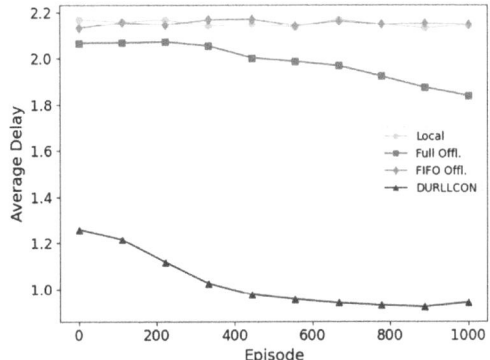

Fig. 5. Delay observed over 1000 iterations.

still falls short compared to DURLLCON, which achieves the lowest consumption by intelligently prioritizing tasks based on urgency and energy constraints.

Figure 5 illustrates the average delay in 1000 episodes for different offloading strategies. DURLLCON achieves the lowest delay, effectively prioritizing URLLC tasks and minimizing latency. In contrast, local and FIFO Offloading [11] results in longer and relatively stable delays due to inefficient task handling. Full offloading performs better, but still lags behind DURLLCON, emphasizing the importance of dynamic decision making in reducing delay under variable task urgency and system congestion.

Figure 6 shows the number of tasks dropped over 1000 iterations, highlighting the system's ability to manage UEs tasks. During the exploration period, the system drops a large number of tasks, indicating challenges in effectively managing the workload and resource allocation. This is due to the system's effort to conserve energy and manage the delay, as discussed previously. While during the exploitation process, the number of processed tasks steadily increases, indicating that the system is learning to manage workload more effectively over

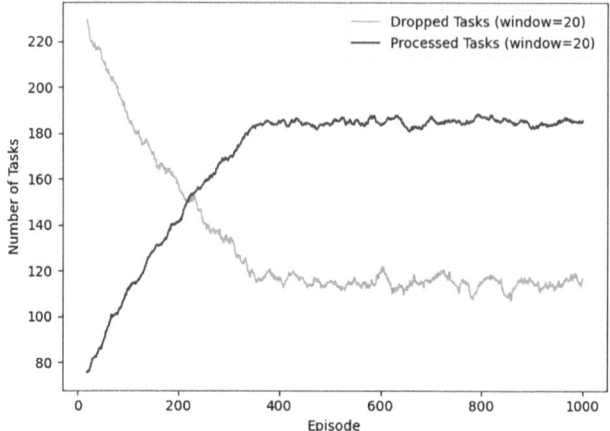

Fig. 6. Number of task drops and processed over 1000 iterations.

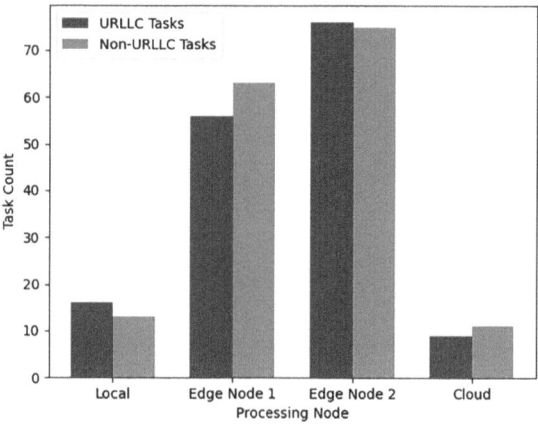

Fig. 7. Task Distribution Across all UEs, Edge Nodes (MECs), and CCS

time. As episodes progress, we observe a noticeable downward trend in dropped tasks, while the number of processed tasks stabilizes at a higher level, indicating improvements in task allocation and resource management.

Figure 7 depicts the allocation of URLLC and non-URLLC tasks across various processing nodes, encompassing local devices, edge nodes, and the cloud. Most tasks, including both URLLC and non-URLLC, are offloaded to Edge Node 2, followed by Edge Node 1. Local processing manages the least number of tasks, whereas the cloud processes a limited number of tasks relative to the edge nodes. This distribution emphasizes the tendency for executing tasks on edge nodes due to their proximity to the end users and lower latency compared to cloud or local processing.

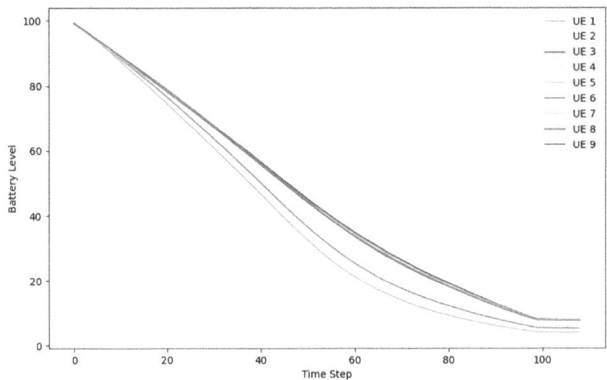

Fig. 8. Battery Levels for All UEs at the end of each Episode

In Fig. 8, the battery levels of various UEs are shown at the end of each episode, with a threshold value set to 80%. Without the introduced improvements represented by DURLLCON, the battery typically drops from 40% to 50%. However, by utilizing the reward shaping, which defines the battery threshold, the agent makes decisions that maximize it's battery life, ensuring it lasts until it reaches this threshold as depicted in the figure. This effectively extends the battery's lifespan compared to traditional methods that include the baseline [11], highlighting the efficiency of the proposed approach in balancing energy consumption with task completion.

5   Conclusion

In this paper, we present a DRL-based approach to optimize task offloading in MEC environments, focusing on improving UE energy efficiency by extending battery life through an intelligent offloading strategy. Using LSTM networks to account for historical task data, the proposed method extends battery life by efficiently balancing local processing and MEC offloading, ensuring high levels of QoS across varying system dynamics. The results demonstrate the potential of DRL to effectively manage energy resources and reduce latency in URLLC scenarios. Future work will focus on further optimizing energy consumption, incorporating wireless channel conditions, addressing resource allocation, comparing different DRL algorithms such as Proximal Policy Optimization (PPO), and exploring advanced task scheduling and inter-layer synergies within the three-layer model.

References

1. Abbas, N., Zhang, Y., Taherkordi, A., Skeie, T.: Mobile edge computing: a survey. IEEE Internet Things J. **5**(1), 450–465 (2017)

2. Azizi, S., Othman, M., Khamfroush, H.: DECO: a deadline-aware and energy-efficient algorithm for task offloading in mobile edge computing. IEEE Syst. J. **17**(1), 952–963 (2022)
3. Hu, H., Wu, D., Zhou, F., Zhu, X., Hu, R.Q., Zhu, H.: Intelligent resource allocation for edge-cloud collaborative networks: a hybrid DDPG-D3QN approach. IEEE Trans. Veh. Technol. **72**(8), 10696–10709 (2023)
4. Jiang, H., Dai, X., Xiao, Z., Iyengar, A.: Joint task offloading and resource allocation for energy-constrained mobile edge computing. IEEE Trans. Mob. Comput. **22**(7), 4000–4015 (2022)
5. Peng, Y., Guang, X., Zhang, X., Liu, L., Wu, C., Huang, L.: A cloud-edge collaborative computing framework using potential games for space-air-ground integrated IoT. EURASIP J. Adv. Signal Process. **2024**(1), 54 (2024)
6. Qadir, Z., Le, K.N., Saeed, N., Munawar, H.S.: Towards 6G Internet of Things: Recent Advances, Use Cases, and Open Challenges. ICT Express (2022)
7. Qiu, Y., Zhang, H., Long, K.: Computation offloading and wireless resource management for healthcare monitoring in fog-computing-based internet of medical things. IEEE Internet Things J. **8**(21), 15875–15883 (2021)
8. Shahinzadeh, H., Moradi, J., Gharehpetian, G.B., Nafisi, H., Abedi, M.: Internet of energy (IOE) in smart power systems. In: 2019 5th Conference on Knowledge Based Engineering and Innovation (KBEI), pp. 627–636. IEEE (2019)
9. Sharif, Z., Jung, L.T., Ayaz, M., Yahya, M., Pitafi, S.: Priority-based task scheduling and resource allocation in edge computing for health monitoring system. J. King Saud Univ. Comput. Inf. Sci. **35**(2), 544–559 (2023)
10. Sultan, A.: 5G system overview (2023). https://www.3gpp.org/technologies/5g-system-overview
11. Tang, M., Wong, V.W.: Deep reinforcement learning for task offloading in mobile edge computing systems. IEEE Trans. Mob. Comput. **21**(6), 1985–1997 (2020)
12. Wang, Y., Wu, H., Jhaveri, R.H., Djenouri, Y.: DRL-based URLLC-constraint and energy-efficient task offloading for internet of health things. IEEE J. Biomed. Health Inf. **28**, 3305–3316 (2024)
13. Xu, X., et al.: Game theory for distributed IoV task offloading with fuzzy neural network in edge computing. IEEE Trans. Fuzzy Syst. **30**(11), 4593–4604 (2022)
14. Zhao, X., Liu, M., Li, M.: Task offloading strategy and scheduling optimization for internet of vehicles based on deep reinforcement learning. Ad Hoc Netw. **147**, 103193 (2023)

FMM-RNS: A Fast HMM Map Matching Method Based on Road Network Simplification

Fei Meng[1,2], Chao Chen[1], Shangzhi Guo[1], Ruiyuan Li[1],
and Jiale Zhao[1(✉)]

[1] College of Computer Science, Chongqing University, Chongqing 400044, China
{20211401024g, cschaocheng, ruiyuanl}@cqu.edu.cn, zhaojiale0415@163.com
[2] Chongqing Institute of Technology, Chongqing 400056, China

Abstract. Map matching serves as a fundamental component of various location-based services and trajectory mining applications, as it aligns GPS trajectory points with actual road networks. This process enhances the understanding of traffic flow patterns, provides insights into human behavior, and supports initiatives aimed at improving traffic conditions, thereby underscoring its scientific and practical significance. Among the various map matching methodologies, the Hidden-Markov Model (HMM) has emerged as a predominant approach, effectively addressing the challenge of matching accuracy by integrating historical vehicle travel data and utilizing observation and hidden state probabilities within a probabilistic framework. Nevertheless, despite the advancements in accuracy achieved through HMM, there remains potential for further enhancement of its computational efficiency to better accommodate large volumes of trajectory data. To address this issue, we propose the Fast HMM Map Matching Method Based on Road Network Simplification (FMM-RNS). Our method simplifies road network nodes to decrease query computations and employs bidirectional search along with segmentation of GPS trajectories, thereby significantly enhancing the computational efficiency of HMM-based map matching without compromising accuracy. Comprehensive experiments conducted on real road network and trajectory datasets demonstrate that FMM-RNS effectively reduces both the road search workload and the traversal of trajectory points, resulting in a substantial improvement in map matching efficiency when compared to state-of-the-art algorithms.

Keywords: Map matching · Hidden-Markov model · GPS trajectory data · Road network simplification

1 Introduction

Global Positioning System (GPS) devices installed in vehicles generate substantial volumes of mobile position sequences and vehicle status data on a daily basis. These datasets offer significant insights into traffic conditions and user

M. Barhamgi et al. (Eds.): WISE 2024, LNCS 15463, pp. 175–189, 2025.
https://doi.org/10.1007/978-981-96-1483-7_14

behavior, effectively capturing both temporal and spatial variations in passenger demand across road networks, while also providing real-time information regarding travel patterns [1,2]. Nevertheless, the inherent limitations of GPS technology can result in errors during data sampling, calculation, reception, and transmission, leading to inaccuracies in the data collected. To accurately reconstruct the true trajectory of vehicles, it is imperative to process raw GPS data through a technique known as map matching [3]. Map matching is a crucial preprocessing step in trajectory data mining, as it rectifies low-quality observed trajectories, reconstructs or enriches them with spatial and semantic information, and facilitates a diverse array of trajectory mining tasks [4–7].

Early research on map matching predominantly focused on the real-time or online matching of GPS data with high sampling rates, aligning trajectory points to road networks based solely on geometric and topological relationships [8,9]. These initial methodologies heavily relied on the spatial proximity between GPS points and roadways, while neglecting critical factors such as road connectivity and bidirectionality. Consequently, these approaches frequently resulted in substantial errors and were effective only in contexts characterized by high sampling rates and minimal positioning inaccuracies. In response to these limitations, Newson et al. [10] introduced a map matching algorithm grounded in the Hidden-Markov Model (HMM), which integrates historical vehicle movement data. By utilizing probabilistic concepts—specifically observation and hidden state probabilities—the HMM-based approach markedly improves accuracy in comparison to simplistic geometric methods. This technique has since emerged as the predominant method for GPS trajectory map matching.

Building upon insights derived from prior research, the HMM-based map matching algorithm exhibits limitations in matching efficiency when applied to large-scale trajectory data characterized by low sampling rates. We propose a novel approach termed Fast Map Matching with Road Network Simplification (FMM-RNS). This method involves an initial preprocessing of the road network, which includes the introduction of shortcuts and the assignment of unique identifiers to each road vertex. Subsequently, a multi-source shortest path search algorithm is utilized, with the search direction constrained by the assigned identifiers. The incorporation of shortcuts enables the algorithm to circumvent certain nodes, thereby significantly enhancing the efficiency of map matching while maintaining accuracy.

2   Related Work

In the 1990s, Bernstein et al. [11] introduced a geometric-based map matching algorithm. This methodology initially computes the distance between each GPS point and the nodes within the road network, subsequently matching each GPS point to its nearest node. To improve search efficiency, Landi et al. [12] proposed a shape-based map matching method that relies solely on the trajectory's shape, thereby rendering it independent of geographic data sources. Conversely, algorithms grounded in topological relationships [13] emphasize the connectivity of the road network, integrating supplementary information such as historical data, vehicle speed, and road topology to refine the selection of candidate matches for sampling points. A prominent example [14] of this approach employs the Fréchet distance to measure the alignment between GPS points and sequences of candidate road segments, enabling it to effectively manage trajectories characterized by noise and low sampling rates. In 1989, Honey et al. [15] were pioneers in applying probabilistic statistical methods to map matching. Their algorithm estimates the vehicle's direction and positional distance during movement, utilizing dead reckoning to deduce the road segment occupied by the vehicle.

Advanced road network matching algorithms often integrate a variety of sophisticated techniques [16], including Kalman filtering [24,25], fuzzy logic models [20,21], and Hidden-Markov Models [17–19]. Fuzzy logic methods tackle the map matching problem by defining an error model that uses membership functions to evaluate candidate roads. In contrast, evidence reasoning methods [22,23] utilize Dempster-Shafer (D-S) evidence theory, which constructs a basic probability distribution based on vehicle position and direction as evidence, which is then fused into a joint support function. The support for each candidate road segment is evaluated, and the segment with the highest support is selected as the matching road. The Kalman filter method, which considers the inherent characteristics of GPS error, operates under the assumption of white noise conditions. Map matching is achieved by evaluating whether the error characteristics post-filtering conform to a Gaussian white noise distribution. HMM-based methods address map matching by explicitly modeling the connectivity of the road network and simultaneously evaluating multiple path hypotheses, offering robust solutions to the problem [26,27].

HMM-based map matching demonstrates high accuracy and effectiveness in managing trajectory data characterized by noise and low sampling rates; however, it is hindered by low computational efficiency. To mitigate this issue, researchers have implemented spatial indexing within road networks to facilitate the expedited identification of nearby road segments, which improves map matching to a certain extent [28]. Nevertheless, the primary limitation in HMM-based map matching persists in the identification of the optimal matching path, with performance being constrained by factors such as the number of trajectory points, the density of the road network, and the calculations involved in determining the shortest path [29]. A straightforward approach to improving efficiency involves reducing the number of GPS points processed, limiting the candidate road segments, and simplifying the calculations for the shortest path. However, these simplifications often rely on additional data, such as the direction of GPS points, which restricts their versatility and typically results in a compromise on matching accuracy. Instead of simplifying calculations, accelerating shortest path computations offers a way to maintain the accuracy of the original HMM-based algorithm [30,31]. These acceleration techniques operate on the original road network, but there remains significant potential for further optimization of their speedup capabilities.

3 Proposed Method: FMM-RNS

This section first gives some formal definitions and then briefly introduces the basic framework of FMM-RNS. It consists of three parts: trajectory data pre-processing, road network data preprocessing and trajectory map matching.

3.1 Problem Definition

Road network matching is a process of converting the original longitude and latitude coordinates into a sequence. The concepts and definitions involved are as follows.

Definition 1. Trajectory. The trajectory $tr = \{p_1, p_2, ..., p_n\}$ is a sequence of GPS points generated by the same mobile object in chronological order. The GPS point $p_i(1 \leq i \leq n)$ is a triple $p_i = (lat_i, log_i, time_i)$, which means that the position coordinates recorded by the mobile object at $time_i$ are (lat_i, lon_i). Note that due to the GPS positioning error, the position recorded by the mobile object is not necessarily its actual position.

Definition 2. Segment. The segment $e = (e_{start}, e_{end}, l)$ is a directed edge, consisting of a starting point e_{start}, an end point e_{end} and a length l, where $l = len(e_{start}, e_{end})$. For a bidirectional segment, it can be represented by two directed edges. A trajectory can contain many road segments.

Definition 3. Road network. The road network is a directed graph $G = (V, E)$, where $V = \{v_1, v_2, ..., v_n\}$ is a set of vertices, representing intersections or turning points in the road; $E = \{e_1, e_2, ..., e_m\}$ is a series of directed edges, representing a set of road segments in the road network.

Definition 4. Map matching. Given a trajectory $tr = \{p_1, p_2, ..., p_n\}$ and a road network $G = (V, E)$, map matching maps the trajectory tr to the road network G and obtains a matched trajectory $tr' = \{(e_1, time_1), (e_2, time_2), ..., (e_m, time_m)\}$. Among them, $(e_i, time_i)$ indicates the time when the mobile object enters the road section e_i is $time_i$.

3.2 Trajectory Data Preprocessing

Trajectory data is typically organized according to mobile objects, with the GPS points generated by each object being classified as a trajectory. However, due to the continuous generation of GPS points, organizing them solely by mobile objects results in trajectories that extend indefinitely, complicating their storage, management, and analysis. To mitigate this issue, it is essential to segment the trajectory prior to map matching. Trajectory segmentation involves dividing a long trajectory into shorter sub-trajectories. In this paper, we employ a segmentation method based on residence points and periods, which relies exclusively on the spatiotemporal characteristics of the trajectory, offering broader applicability across various scenarios.

Dwell Point Detection. The dwell point is a GPS point generated by a mobile object in an area d within a period t. We take each GPS point as an anchor point and check whether its successor node meets the time and space conditions. As shown in Fig. 1, assuming that p_3 is the current anchor point, the distances from its successor nodes p_4, p_5, p_6 and p_7 to p_3 are all less than d, and the distance from p_8 to p_3 is greater than d. Then, we check whether the time interval between p_7 and p_3 is greater than t. If it is greater than t, p_4, p_5, p_6 and p_7 are all dwell points. Then, we repeat the previous process with p_4 as the anchor point until all GPS points are checked. In this article, we set $d = 100\,\mathrm{m}$ and $t = 600\,\mathrm{s}$.

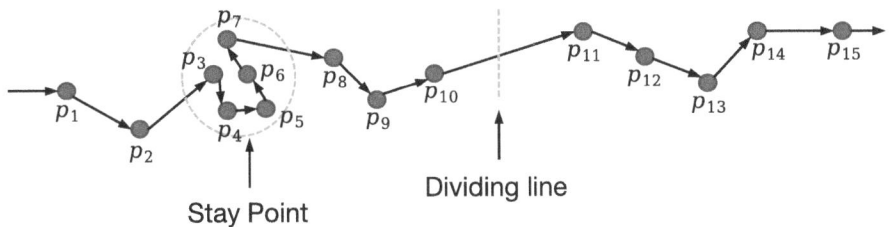

Fig. 1. Illustration of trajectory segmentation

Trajectory Segmentation. After obtaining all the dwelling points, we use the dwelling points as one type of segmentation point. Another type of segmentation point considers the time interval between two adjacent GPS points. If the interval is greater than t', a segmentation point will also be formed between the GPS points, as shown in p_10 and p_11 of Fig. 1. Track segmentation uses these segmentation points to divide a long track into multiple short sub-tracks. In Fig. 1, a long track is divided into three sub-tracks. Note that t' cannot be set too low because too many sub-tracks will be generated if it is too low. The start and end nodes of each sub-track will not be able to fully utilize the information of the previous and next GPS points, affecting the accuracy of the matching results. In this article, we set $t' = 60$ min.

3.3   Road Network Data Preprocessing

efficiency of HMM-based map matching is to optimize the shortest path query process. In this section, we present a method aimed at accelerating map matching by simplifying the road network data and utilizing the reduced network to facilitate faster computations.

Next, we will use a practical example to illustrate the process of network simplification. Given the network shown in Fig. 2(a), each edge in the figure is a bidirectional edge. The number on the edge indicates the length of the road section, and the number next to the node indicates the edge difference of the node. The edge difference of node v_2 is $1 - 3 = -2$. Suppose that v_2 is deleted, the three adjacent edges $(v_1, v_2), (v_2, v_3), (v_2, v_5)$ of v_2 will be deleted. However, to keep the shortest path length of all node pairs unchanged, a shortcut (v_1, v_3) of length 6 needs to be added; otherwise, the shortest path length from node v_1 to v_3 cannot be retained. Randomly select a node v_2 with the smallest edge difference and delete it, as well as the number v_2, to obtain the network shown in Fig. 2(b). The dotted line indicates the deleted edge and node, the edge (v_1, v_3) indicates the added shortcut, and the number in the node indicates the priority number. At the same time, update the edge difference of the remaining nodes. Next, delete node v_1 to obtain the network shown in Fig. 2(c). The above process is iterated and repeated until all nodes are deleted, and finally, a simplified road network, as shown in Fig. 2(d), is obtained.

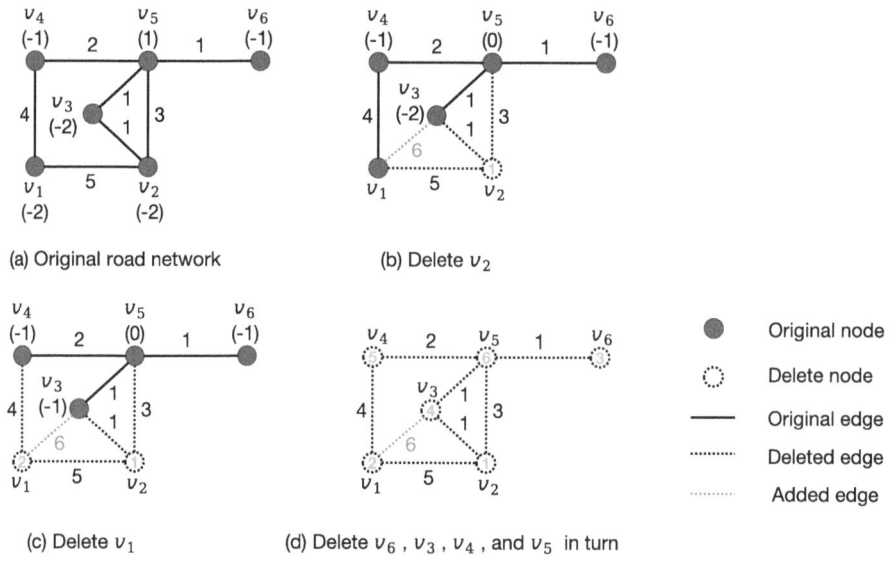

(a) Original road network

(b) Delete v_2

(c) Delete v_1

(d) Delete v_6, v_3, v_4, and v_5 in turn

● Original node

○ Delete node

— Original edge

········ Deleted edge

·········· Added edge

Fig. 2. Example of road network simplification

Algorithm 1 gives the pseudo-code for road network simplification. A priority queue q ensures the numbering order and initializes the current priority (line 2). Next, each node in q is checked until the queue q is empty. At each check, the node v with the smallest edge difference in q is dequeued, and v is numbered (lines 4–6). Then, check whether deleting v affects the shortest path of the remaining graph (only need to check the paths between v's neighbors). If v is a node on the shortest path between its two neighbors u and w, there are two cases: 1) If (u, w) already exists, update the length of the original edge (u, w) (line 12); 2) If (u, w) does not exist, add a shortcut (u, w) to graph G (line 14). After processing node v, it is necessary to update the edge differences of all v's neighbors (line 19) to ensure that the node with the smallest edge difference is checked in the next iteration.

Algorithm 1. Road network simplification algorithm

Input: The original road network $G =< V, E >$;
Output: The streamlined road network G.
 1: Initialize the priority queue q, put all $v \in V$ into the queue in order;
 2: $level = 1$;
 3: **while** $q \neq null$ **do**
 4:     $v \leftarrow q.pop()$;
 5:     The priority of v is set to $level$;
 6:     $level + +$;
 7:     **for** $each(u, v) \in E$ and u has not set the priority **do**
 8:         **for** $each(v, w) \in E$ and w has not set the priority **do**
 9:             **if** $u \rightarrow v \rightarrow w$ is the shortest path from u to w **then**
10:                 $l \leftarrow len(u, v) + len(v, w)$;
11:                 **if** (u, w) is included in E **then**
12:                     Update the length of (u, w) is l;
13:                 **else**
14:                     Add (u, w, l) to E;
15:                 **end if**
16:             **end if**
17:         **end for**
18:     **end for**
19:     Update the edge differences of all neighbors of v;
20: **end while**
21: **return** G.

3.4 Trajectory Map Matching

Finding Candidate Points. We use the R-tree to construct a spatial index for each sub-road network to quickly find the candidate road sections within β around each GPS point p_i in the trajectory. In this paper, $\beta - 100$ m. For each candidate road section, we first need to find the candidate point of p_i. e_i^j represents the j-th candidate road section of p_i, and the candidate point of p_i on e_i^j is the position point in e_i^j that is closest to p_i:

$$c_i^j = \arg\min_{q \in e_i^j} d(p_i, q) \tag{1}$$

where $d(p_i, q)$ represents the Euclidean distance between p_i and q. The candidate point of p_i on the candidate segment e_i^j is either the vertical projection point of p_i to e_i^j or the endpoint of e_i^j.

Constructing the Transfer Graph. As shown in Fig. 3, after obtaining the candidate points of each GPS point, we can construct a transition graph. The transition graph is a directed weighted hierarchical graph, which is hierarchically organized according to the time sequence of the GPS points, and the candidate points of adjacent GPS points are fully connected. Each node and edge in the graph is assigned a probability value. The probability of a candidate point c_i^j of GPS point p_i conforms to the standard Gaussian distribution:

$$N(c_i^j) = P(o_i = o_k | q_i = r_j) = \frac{1}{\sqrt{2\pi}\sigma} e^{-\frac{||o_i - r_j||^2}{2\sigma^2}} \tag{2}$$

where σ is the standard deviation of GPS positioning error, and in this paper $\sigma=20$ m. $||o_i - r_j|| = d(c_i^j, p_i)$ indicates whether the GPS point p_i can be matched to a candidate point c_i^j on the real road, regardless of its neighboring points. The smaller the distance between the GPS point and the candidate point, the greater the probability that the candidate point is the real point. This fully considers the geometric properties and local characteristics of the road network. The probability of each edge $c_i^j \rightarrow c_{i+1}^k$ is:

$$F(c_i^j \rightarrow c_{i+1}^k) = \frac{d_{i \rightarrow i+1}}{w_{i \rightarrow i+1}} = \frac{||o_i - o_{i+1}||_{Euclidean\_Distance}}{||r_i - r_j||_{route}} \tag{3}$$

where $d_{i \rightarrow i+1} = d(p_i, p_{i+1})$ represents the Euclidean distance between two GPS points; $w_{i \rightarrow i+1} = d_{rn}(c_i^j, c_{i+1}^k)$ represents the shortest path distance between two candidate points.

p_1 candidate points p_2 candidate points p_n candidate points

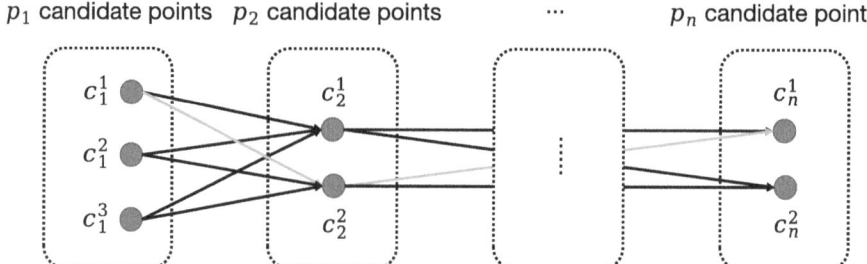

Fig. 3. Construct transition graph and determine matching path

Determine Matching Paths. The Viterbi algorithm finds the path with the maximum probability in the transition graph. It is to determine the final candidate points $c_1^{o_1}, c_2^{o_2}, ..., c_n^{o_n}$ for each GPS point such that formula (4) is maximized:

$$N(c_1^{o_1}) \times \prod_{i=1}^{n-1} F(c_i^{o_i} \rightarrow c_{i+1}^{o_{i+1}}) \times N(c_{i+1}^{o_{i+1}}) \tag{4}$$

After determining the candidate points for each GPS point, the final matching result can be obtained by calculating the shortest path between two adjacent candidate points.

The most time-consuming part of the above HMM-based map matching algorithm is the calculation of the shortest path distance $d_{rn}(c_i^j, c_{i+1}^k)$ between two adjacent candidate points in step 2. When the road network is dense, there are many candidate points for each GPS point, and the situation is even worse. As shown in Fig. 3, assuming that GPS point p_i has m candidate points and p_{i+1} has n candidate points, in the transfer graph, there are $m \times n$ directed edges from p_i to p_{i+1}, so it is necessary to trigger the calculation of $m \times n$ shortest paths. The road network nodes' priority in Fig. 4(a) gradually increases from left to right. A one-to-one shortest path calculation method is used to calculate the shortest path from A to D and F. The search process is shown in Fig. 4(b), and the nodes in the path represent the order of access. It can be seen that the search process of the dotted part in Fig. 4(b) is redundant.

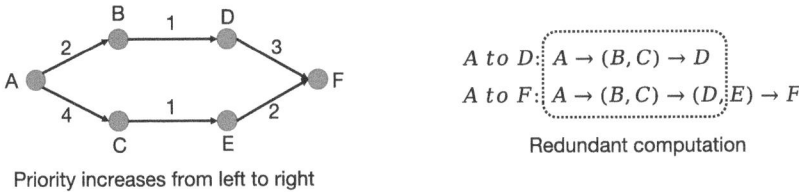

(a) Road Network Example   (b) Shortest path search procedure from A to D and F

Fig. 4. Redundant computing for one to one shortest path

To reduce redundant calculations as much as possible, this paper proposes a many-to-many shortest path search method based on road network simplification. Given a simplified road network $G = (V, E)$, a starting node set $S = \{s_1, s_2, ..., s_m\}$ and a target node set $T = \{t_1, t_2, ..., t_n\}$. Expand outward one step from each starting node s_i and target node t_i in turn. For each starting node, expand along the directed edge in the direction of increasing priority; for each target node, expand along the opposite direction of the directed edge in the direction of increasing priority. If a starting node (or target node) determines the shortest path distance with all target nodes (or starting nodes), then the starting node (target node) stops expanding.

Algorithm 2 gives the pseudo-code of the many-to-many shortest path search algorithm based on road network simplification. In the initialization phase, a priority queue and a hash table are assigned to each starting point and end point, and the current solution is an $m \times n$ array D_{min}. In the loop iteration phase, the termination condition is whether both priority queue sets are empty or whether the shortest path has been found between all starting and ending points. In each iteration, we first let the query of all starting points go forward one step and then let the query of all ending points go backward one step. In the forward query, line 9 indicates that the s_i node has found the shortest path to all target nodes, so the priority queue q_{s_i} should not be rechecked and is directly deleted from the priority queue set. In lines 13–15, we update the shortest path when all s_i and t_j meet. The reverse query is similar. Finally, the shortest path distance D_{min} of all starting and ending point pairs is returned.

Algorithm 2. Multi-source shortest path search algorithm

Input: The streamlined road network $G = (V, E)$, start point set $S = \{s_1, s_2, ..., s_m\}$
  and end point set $T = \{t_1, t_2, ..., t_n\}$;
Output: The shortest path length $d_{min}^{i,j}$ between all start and end nodes s_i, t_j.
1: Initialize the priority queue sets $QS = \{q_{s_1}, q_{s_2}, ..., q_{s_m}\}$ and $QT = \{q_{t_1}, q_{t_2}, ..., q_{t_n}\}$, sorting keys of $q_{s_i} \in QS$ and $q_{t_j} \in QT$ are the shortest path distances from the corresponding nodes to s_i and t_j, respectively;
2: Initialize the hash table sets $HS = \{h_{s_1}, h_{s_2}, ..., h_{s_m}\}$ and $HT = \{h_{t_1}, h_{t_2}, ..., h_{t_n}\}$, the keys of $h_{s_i} \in HS$ and $h_{t_j} \in HT$ are the checked nodes, and the value is the shortest path from the node to s_i or t_j;
3: Initialize the value set $D_{min} = \{d_{min}^{i,j} | 1 \leq i \leq m, 1 \leq j \leq n\}$, Each element is initialized to ∞. $d_{min}^{i,j}$ represents the shortest path distance from s_i to t_j in the current state;
4: When $s_i \in S$ and $t_j \in T$ are on the same road section, calculate the shortest distance from s_i to t_j and update $d_{min}^{i,j}$;
5: Add all exit nodes of $s_i \in S$ to q_{s_i} and all entry nodes of $t_j \in T$ to q_{t_j};
6: **while** $QS \neq \varnothing$ or $QT \neq \varnothing$ **do**
7:   **for all** $q_{s_i} \in QS$ **do**
8:     $(d_i, v_i) \leftarrow q_{s_i}.pop()$;
9:     **if** $d_i > max\{D_{min}^{i,*}\}$ **then**
10:       Remove q_{s_i} from QS;
11:     **else if** $h_{s_i}[v_i] = null$ **then**
12:       $h_{s_i}[v_i] = d_i$;
13:       **for all** $h_{t_j} \in HT$ and $h_{t_j}[v_i] \neq null$ **do**
14:         $d_{min}^{i,j} \leftarrow min\{d_{min}^{i,j}, d_i + h_{t_j}[v_i]\}$;
15:       **end for**
16:       **for all** $(v_i, v_k) \in E$ and $v_k.level > v_i.level$ **do**
17:         Add $(d_i + len(v_i, v_k), v_k)$ to q_{s_i};
18:       **end for**
19:     **end if**
20:   **end for**
21:   **for all** $q_{t_j} \in QT$ **do**
22:     $(d_j, v_j) \leftarrow q_{t_j}.pop()$;
23:     **if** $d_j > max\{D_{min}^{*,j}\}$ **then**
24:       Remove q_{t_j} from QT;
25:     **else if** $h_{t_j}[v_j] = null$ **then**
26:       $h_{t_j}[v_j] = d_j$;
27:       **for all** $h_{s_i} \in HS$ and $h_{s_i}[v_j] \neq null$ **do**
28:         $d_{min}^{i,j} \leftarrow min\{d_{min}^{i,j}, d_j + h_{s_i}[v_j]\}$;
29:       **end for**
30:       **for all** $(v_k, v_j) \in E$ and $v_k.level > v_j.level$ **do**
31:         Add $(d_j + len(v_k, v_j), v_k)$ to q_{t_j};
32:       **end for**
33:     **end if**
34:   **end for**
35: **end while**
36: **return** D_{min}.

---

4   Performance Evaluation

4.1   Dataset Introduction and Experiment Setting

OpenStreetMap (OSM)[1] is an open street map. All map data are provided by volunteers around the world. We use real Shanghai taxi data[2] to test and verify the effectiveness of the proposed method. All simulation experiments were conducted on a computer with an Apple M2 processor and 16 GB of memory. All experimental codes were implemented in PyCharm software using Python 3.9.

4.2   Baseline Algorithms

Note that the segmented trajectories are used for the different methods.

- **FMM-RNS** The methodology presented in this paper initially simplifies the nodes within the road network. Subsequently, it employs a multi-source shortest-path search algorithm to facilitate bidirectional queries, thereby enhancing the efficiency of the map-matching process.
- **Greedy.** The local features of the current GPS trajectory points are utilized to match the road network. Initially, the shortest path from each road segment to all other road segments within a specified range (set to 1000 m in this paper) is computed. Subsequently, the shortest path is determined by referencing a pre-constructed table to enhance the efficiency of map matching.
- **Mppy** [32]. The proposed methodology employs global mapping matching and utilizes a similarity score derived from the longest common subsequence to describe the similarity between point-based trajectory segments and link-based matching paths. The longest common subsequence that has been traversed is retained, allowing for direct querying in subsequent traversals and thereby circumventing the need for redundant calculations.
- **Leuven** [33]. An HMM incorporating non-emitting states is utilized for the purpose of map matching. Rather than mandating that each candidate road segment corresponds directly to a GPS point, a selective mapping approach is employed to speed up the efficiency of the matching process.

4.3   Experimental Results and Analysis

Figure 5(a) illustrates the comparative performance of different algorithms, with the blue line represents the trajectory of the FMM-RNS algorithm, the red line denotes the trajectory of the initial GPS, the yellow line indicates the trajectory of the classical greedy algorithm, the green line reflects the trajectory of the Mppy algorithm, and the black line depicts the trajectory of the Leuven algorithm. The FMM-RNS algorithm proposed in this paper aims to enhance the

---

[1] www.openstreetmap.org.
[2] https://github.com/chilai1996/Shanghai-Taxi-Data.

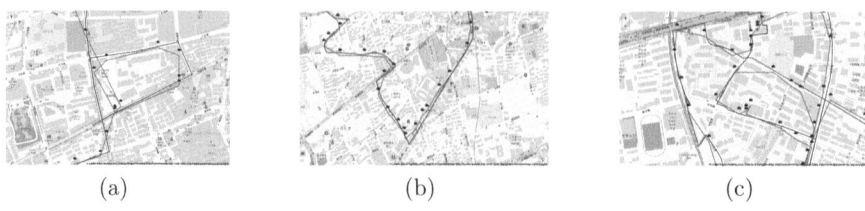

Fig. 5. Matching result of some trajectory points

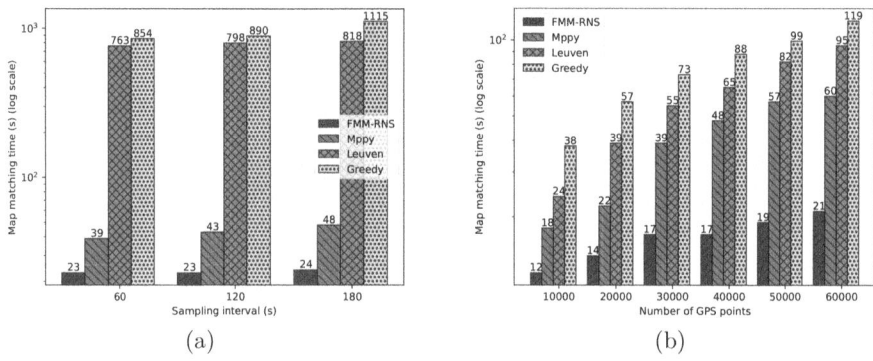

Fig. 6. Matching result

efficiency of map matching; consequently, the discussion of accuracy will not be pursued further, and the subsequent analysis will focus on efficiency.

We selected 5,000 trajectories following the preprocessing of the dataset for matching purposes. This dataset was utilized to compare the matching times of different methods in relation to changes in sampling rate. Figure 6(b) illustrates that the FMM-RNS proposed in this paper is the fastest performance.

We selected 2,000 trajectories from the dataset, each containing more than 30 GPS points. For each trajectory, we extracted the first 5, 10, 15, 20, 25, and 30 GPS points to create new trajectories. This approach allows us to assess the variations in time consumption associated with different methods as the number of GPS points increases. As illustrated in Fig. 6(b), the FMM-RNS algorithm demonstrates the highest efficiency as the number of GPS points increases.

5   Conclusions and Future Work

This paper builds upon the traditional Hidden Markov Model map matching algorithm by preprocessing the road network, incorporating shortcuts, and assigning numerical identifiers to each road vertex. Subsequently, a multi-source shortest path search algorithm is employed to constrain the search direction based on these identifiers, thereby facilitating the omission of certain nodes through the use of shortcuts. Additionally, optimizations and enhancements are implemented in three key areas: road network data processing, trajectory data processing, and shortest path calculation. Simulation experiments demonstrate that the proposed method effectively reduces the workload associated with road searches and trajectory point traversals, thereby significantly enhancing the efficiency of map matching.

Acknowledgments. This work is supported by the Key project of Chongqing Education Commission under Grant No.KJZD-K202401902 and Youth Project of Chongqing Education Commission under Grant No.KJQN202301905.

Disclosure of Interests. The authors declare no conflict of interest.

References

1. Gao, W., Li, G., Ta, N.: Survey of map matching algorithms. J. Softw. **29**(2), 225–250 (2017). https://doi.org/10.13328/j.cnki.jos.005424
2. Taylor, G.: GIS and GPS integration and mobile handset positioning. In: Web Information Systems Engineering Workshops, International Conference on. IEEE Comput. Soc., 73–73 (2002). https://doi.org/10.1109/WISEW.2002.1177849
3. Zheng, Y.: Trajectory data mining: an overview. ACM Trans. Intell. Syst. Technol. (TIST) **6**(3), 1–41 (2015). https://doi.org/10.1145/2743025
4. Chao, P., Hua, W., Mao, R., et al.: A survey and quantitative study on map inference algorithms from GPS trajectories. IEEE Trans. Knowl. Data Eng. **34**(1), 15–28 (2020). https://doi.org/10.1109/TKDE.2020.2977034
5. Zong, F., Wu, T., Jia, H.: Taxi drivers' cruising patterns–Insights from taxi GPS traces. IEEE Trans. Intell. Transp. Syst. **20**(2), 571–582 (2018). https://doi.org/10.1109/TITS.2018.2816938
6. Li, L., Jiang, R., He, Z., et al.: Trajectory data-based traffic flow studies: a revisit. Transp. Res. Part C: Emerg. Technol. **114**, 225–240 (2020). https://doi.org/10.1016/j.trc.2020.02.016
7. Huayi, W.U., Rui, H., Lan, Y.O.U., et al.: Recent progress in taxi trajectory data mining. Acta Geodaetica et Cartographica Sinica, **48**(11), 1341 (2019). https://doi.org/10.11947/j.AGCS.2019.20190210
8. Bang, Y., Kim, J., Yu, K.: An improved map-matching technique based on the Fréchet distance approach for pedestrian navigation services. Sensors **16**(10), 1768 (2016). https://doi.org/10.3390/s16101768
9. Yuan, L., Li, D., Hu, S.: A map-matching algorithm with low-frequency floating car data based on matching path. EURASIP J. Wirel. Commun. Netw. **2018**(1), 1–14 (2018). https://doi.org/10.1186/s13638-018-1154-x
10. Newson, P., Krumm, J.: Hidden Markov map matching through noise and sparseness. In: Proceedings of the 17th ACM SIGSPATIAL International Conference on Advances in Geographic Information Systems, pp. 336–343 (2009). https://doi.org/10.1145/1653771.1653818
11. Bernstein, D., Kornhauser, A.: An introduction to map matching for personal navigation assistants (1996)
12. Landi, C., Guidotti, R.: A shape-based map matching approach for geographic transferability of discriminative subtrajectories. EDBT/ICDT Workshops (2024)

13. Li, R., Hong, L.: Method for subgraph matching with inclusion degree. J. Softw. **29**(6), 1792–1812 (2017). https://doi.org/10.13328/j.cnki.jos.005268
14. Brakatsoulas, S., Pfoser, D., Salas, R., et al.: On map-matching vehicle tracking data. In: Proceedings of the 31st International Conference on Very Large Data Bases, pp. 853–864 (2005)
15. Honey, S.K., Zavoli, W.B., Milnes, K.A., et al.: Vehicle navigational system and method: U.S. Patent 4,796,191. 1989-1-3
16. Yu, J., Yang, Q., Lu, J., et al.: Advanced map matching algorithms: a survey and trends. Acta Electron. Sin. **49**, 1818–1829 (2021)
17. Qi, H., Huang, Z., Chen, Y., et al.: Streamlining trajectory map-matching: a framework leveraging spark and GPU-based stream processing. Int. J. Geogr. Inf. Sci. **38**(6), 1158–1178 (2024). https://doi.org/10.1080/13658816.2024.2337225
18. Song, Y., Zhao, J., Gao, X., et al.: Enhanced HMM map matching model based on multiple type trajectories. In: Yang, DN., Xie, X., Tseng, V.S., Pei, J., Huang, JW., Lin, J.CW. (eds.) Pacific-Asia Conference on Knowledge Discovery and Data Mining, pp. 350–362. Springer Nature, Singapore (2024). https://doi.org/10.1007/978-981-97-2262-4_28
19. Song, Y., Zhou, J., Wang, L., et al.: Efficient HMM map matching method using R-tree and trajectory segmentation. J. Syst. Simul. **35**(2), 339–349 (2023). https://doi.org/10.16182/j.issn1004731x.joss.21-1020
20. Kim, S., Kim, J.H.: Adaptive fuzzy-network-based C-measure map-matching algorithm for car navigation system. IEEE Trans. Industr. Electron. **48**(2), 432–441 (2001). https://doi.org/10.1109/41.915423
21. Su, H., Chen, J., Xu, J.: A adaptive map matching algorithm based on fuzzy-neural-network for vehicle navigation system. In: 2008 7th World Congress on Intelligent Control and Automation, pp. 4448–4452. IEEE (2008). https://doi.org/10.1109/WCICA.2008.4593639
22. Nassreddine, G., Abdallah, F., Denoeux, T.: Map matching algorithm using belief function theory. In: 2008 11th International Conference on Information Fusion, pp. 1–8. IEEE (2008)
23. Yang, D., Cai, B., Yuan, Y.: An improved map-matching algorithm used in vehicle navigation system. In: Proceedings of the 2003 IEEE International Conference on Intelligent Transportation Systems, col. 2, pp. 1246–1250. IEEE (2003). https://doi.org/10.1109/ITSC.2003.1252683
24. Obradovic, D., Lenz, H., Schupfner, M.: Fusion of map and sensor data in a modern car navigation system. J. VLSI Signal Process. Syst. Signal Image Video Technol. **45**, 111–122 (2006)
25. Xu, H., Liu, H., Tan, C.W., et al.: Development and application of an enhanced Kalman filter and global positioning system error-correction approach for improved map-matching. J. Intell. Transp. Syst. **14**(1), 27–36 (2010). https://doi.org/10.1080/15472450903386013
26. Lamb, P., Thiébaux, S.: Avoiding explicit map-matching in vehicle location. In: The 6th ITS World Congress (ITS-99) (1999)
27. Li, W., Chen, Y., Wang, S., et al.: A novel map matching method based on improved hidden Markov and conditional random fields model. Int. J. Digital Earth **17**(1), 2328366 (2024). https://doi.org/10.1080/17538947.2024.2328366
28. Alves Peixoto, D., Quoc Viet Nguyen, H., Zheng, B., et al.: A framework for parallel map-matching at scale using Spark. Distrib. Parallel Databases **37**, 697–720 (2019)
29. Yang, C., Gidofalvi, G.: Fast map matching, an algorithm integrating hidden Markov model with precomputation. Int. J. Geogr. Inf. Sci. **32**(3), 547–570 (2018). https://doi.org/10.1080/13658816.2017.1400548

30. Koller, H., Widhalm, P., Dragaschnig, M., et al.: Fast hidden Markov model map-matching for sparse and noisy trajectories. 2015 IEEE 18th International Conference on Intelligent Transportation Systems, pp. 2557–2561. IEEE (2015). https://doi.org/10.1109/ITSC.2015.411

31. Jagadeesh, G.R., Srikanthan, T.: Fast computation of clustered many-to-many shortest paths and its application to map matching. ACM Trans. Spatial Algorithms Syst. (TSAS) **5**(3), 1–20 (2019). https://doi.org/10.1145/3329676

32. Zhu, L., Holden, J.R., Gonder, J.D.: Trajectory segmentation map-matching approach for large-scale, high-resolution GPS data. Transp. Res. Rec. **2645**(1), 67–75 (2017). https://doi.org/10.3141/2645-08

33. Meert, W., Verbeke, M.: HMM with non-emitting states for map matching. European Conference on Data Analysis (ECDA), Date: 2018/07/04-2018/07/06, Location: Paderborn, Germany (2018)

Context-Aware Selection of Machine Learning as a Service (MLaaS) in IoT Environments

Keya Patel[ID], Sajib Mistry[✉][ID], Deepak Kanneganti[ID], and Aneesh Krishna[ID]

School of Electrical Engineering, Computing and Mathematical Sciences,
Curtin University, Perth, Australia
sajib.mistry@curtin.edu.au

Abstract. The integration of Machine Learning as a Service (MLaaS) into the Internet of Things (IoT) environments presents considerable opportunities for enhancing decision-making and automation. We propose a novel framework for context-aware selection of MLaaS in IoT settings, aimed at optimising the interaction between IoT users' activities and machine learning services. Our framework considers various contextual dimensions, such as user preferences, locations, IoT device capabilities, and application requirements, to develop a dynamic selection process. By employing context-aware algorithms, our approach seeks to enhance the efficiency, accuracy, and responsiveness of IoT systems. We propose a context change analysis algorithm based on support vector machines (SVM). We develop a contextual bandits algorithm along with skyline queries to achieve optimal mapping between abstract MLaaS services and concrete MLaaS services for quality of service (QoS) attributes. Experiments conducted with real-world and simulated datasets demonstrate the effectiveness of our proposed methods.

Keywords: Context-awareness · Machine Learning as a Service (MLaaS) · Service Selection · Internet of Things (IoT) · MLaaS Feature Mapping

1 Introduction

Machine Learning (ML) plays a crucial role in enhancing the capabilities of the Internet of Things (IoT) by providing advanced analytics, predictive capabilities, and intelligent decision-making [12]. One effective way to utilise ML is through *Machine Learning as a Service (MLaaS)*, a cloud-based platform that offers machine learning tools and services without the need for users to invest in their infrastructure [11]. Leading companies such as Amazon, IBM, Microsoft Azure, and Google Cloud provide MLaaS services that can be integrated with IoT solutions [12]. For example, smart thermostat IoT sensors gather temperature, humidity, and occupancy data. This data is sent to AWS IoT Core (an IoT service). AWS Lambda (an MLaaS service) processes the data, which is then

M. Barhamgi et al. (Eds.): WISE 2024, LNCS 15463, pp. 190–205, 2025.
https://doi.org/10.1007/978-981-96-1483-7_15

analysed by ML models in AWS SageMaker (another MLaaS service). These models predict optimal ventilation settings, which are applied in real-time to reduce energy consumption and lower costs [16].

The *selection of Machine Learning as a Service (MLaaS)* is a significant issue in the IoT domain. This selection process involves identifying and choosing the most suitable MLaaS provider from a range of similar *functional* services to meet specific *Quality of Service (QoS)* requirements. In any IoT environment, selecting the right MLaaS is a complex and crucial task that requires several considerations to ensure the chosen service aligns with the application's specific needs. For instance, consider a smart home system, where IoT devices such as wearable technology, smart sensors, and environmental sensors collect vast amounts of user data. The goal is to leverage MLaaS for predictive analytics, such as detecting anomalies in smart home activities, predicting potential risks, and optimising home operations. Functionally compatible MLaaS providers like AWS SageMaker and Google Cloud AutoML each offer unique features. One provider might excel in robust scalability, while another might offer more reliability. Hence, each MLaaS provider must be selected based on factors such as scalability, reliability, cost, and ease of use.

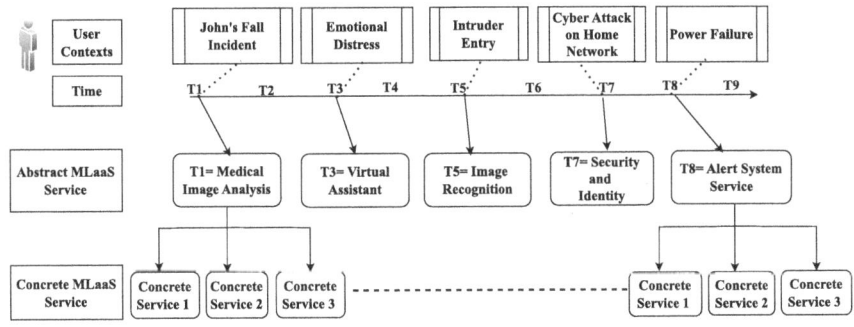

Fig. 1. MLaaS Service Selection based on Single User's Context

In this paper, we focus on the *context-aware* MLaaS selection in IoT environments. A "context" is any information that can be utilised to characterise the situation of an entity, where the entity could be a person, place, physical, or computational object [1]. Existing research mainly addresses MLaaS selection based on functional and non-functional (QoS) properties [11,12]. However, our approach goes further by incorporating contextual information to enhance the selection process for both *abstract* and *concrete* MLaaS services. An abstract MLaaS service refers to a high-level representation of a service that encapsulates the general functionalities and capabilities required to meet specific user needs. This helps identify the type of MLaaS needed to effectively meet contextual needs. While abstract services represent high-level functionalities and performance characteristics needed by an application, concrete services are the actual operational services that fulfil these requirements.

We consider context awareness as the *long-term applicability* of the MLaaS, ensuring that the chosen MLaaS provider can *adapt* to evolving needs and sustain performance over time. For example, in a smart home (see Fig. 1), let us assume a user (i.e., John), a tech-savvy, is adapting with varying contexts over time $t \in \{1, 2, \cdots, 9\}$ such as sudden fall, emotional distress, unauthorised entry, cyber-attacks on a home network, and power failure. John may fall in the initial context (time t=1), where it triggers the smart home system to initiate the medical image analysis abstract service. However, multiple MLaaS providers offer concrete services for medical image analysis, each with different QoS features such as varying levels of bias, explainability, and accuracy. In context awareness of MLaaS selection, the system must continuously adapt to the user's changing contexts. For instance, if a user shows signs of emotional distress (feels frustrated and upset) after a fall, the smart system transitions from fall detection to offering virtual companion service, ensuring timely and accurate responses. It means a system that efficiently and accurately switches between health assessment, virtual assistant services, security, and cybersecurity to ensure user safety and well-being. In this paper, *we only consider the MLaaS selection from a single user's contextual information*. The multi-user context-based MLaaS selection is out of the scope of this paper.

Existing context-aware service selection approaches for Web, Cloud, and Edge computing typically consider *short-term contextual information* such as user preferences, service environment settings, and advertisements [14,19]. Predefined rule mining approaches are used to match contexts' applicability with services [9]. However, these approaches face significant limitations in IoT environments. Maintaining and updating rules becomes cumbersome as the complexity and diversity of contexts increase, limiting their adaptability and scalability. Ontology-based approaches have been developed to enhance context-awareness for IoT-based smart monitoring systems [14]. While these methods provide a structured framework for context modelling, they require frequent updates to remain relevant in *rapidly changing* IoT contexts.

We propose a novel framework for selecting the most suitable context-aware MLaaS in dynamic IoT environments. The proposed approach considers rapidly changing contextual features, including long-term QoS, context duration, adaptability, and service evolution. Traditional ontology-based [14], and fixed rule-based [9] approaches face challenges in this domain, as MLaaS must account for the duration of the context, i.e., how long a particular context remains relevant. The adaptability of MLaaS is also crucial, as it can apply to multiple contexts and *uniquely evolve through feedback and interactions*. These continuous improvements and adaptation to changing requirements and contexts, distinguish our approach from traditional service selections such as web and cloud services [13,19]. The main contributions of this paper are as follows:

- Development of an IoT context analysis framework for pattern identification using Support Vector Machines with semi-supervised learning.
- Enabling mapping user context to *abstract MLaaS services* using a novel contextual bandits approach.

– Selecting *concrete MLaaS services* through skyline queries for optimal context-aware service selection.

2   Related Work

Various studies have explored context-aware service selection based on contextual information. Context-Aware Recommender Systems (CARS) [1] taking into account contextual information(i.e., user, day place), and shows various methods, including prefiltering, post-filtering, and contextual modelling, highlighting the potential for improved recommendation accuracy and user satisfaction. An article, [12] explored the decision-making application of marketing, focusing on its customised platform with modules for churn prediction, personalised product recommendations, and send frequency prediction. It discusses the benefits of AI-driven campaigns in improving Open Rate and Click Rate, enhancing customer engagement and retention.

Two innovative prediction models for web service recommendation used user and service context, leveraged geographical data for neighbourhood similarity, and incorporated company and country affiliations. These models predict QoS values by analysing historical records and neighbouring data to improve recommendation accuracy and reliability [19]. A Partial Historical Records-based service evaluation (Partial-HR) selection approach [13] in context-aware cloud computing assigns weights historical QoS record based on service invocation context. By prioritising relevant records, Partial-HR enhances accuracy and efficiency in the quality evaluation process, optimising resource utilisation and improving decision-making capabilities while minimising computational overhead.

A decentralised authentication architecture that enhances local authentication while considering context information from network elements, supported by Markov and random walk mobility models, demonstrating through simulations its ability to achieve a balanced trade-off between network operating cost and reliability [7]. An IoT Medicare system [14] is designed as a semantic-based context-aware system with Medical Connected Objects (MCOs), leveraging the HealthIoT ontology to describe heterogeneous MCO semantics. This system enables efficient knowledge management across contexts through Semantic Web Rule Language rules, facilitating MCO functionality verification and health data analysis on a case study of gestational diabetes management. A context-aware decision support system introduces Context Processing Rules designed to significantly enhance personalisation and decision-making support [9].

The selection of MLaaS is challenging to achieve solely through the use of SWRL rules and Context Processing Rules within a context-aware decision support system. While these rules enhance personalization and decision-making by employing flexible inference mechanisms and different comparison operators, they are primarily designed for achieving predictable outcomes in dynamic contexts. MLaaS selection, however, involves evaluating diverse machine learning models and considering factors such as scalability, performance metrics, data security, and compliance with industry standards. These factors extend beyond the capabilities of context-aware rules to manage comprehensively. Additionally, MLaaS selection requires adaptability to evolving technologies and datasets, which are not fully addressed by existing rule-based approaches. Thus, while valuable in specific scenarios, these rules alone may not suffice for the complex and multifaceted process of MLaaS selection.

3   Context-Aware MLaaS Selection Framework

We formalise context-aware MLaaS selection with the following definitions:

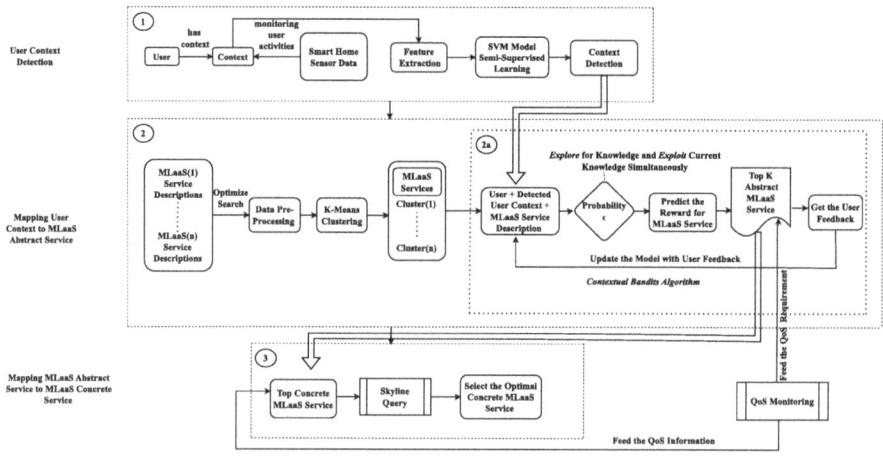

Fig. 2. Context-Aware MLaaS Selection Framework (CAMSF)

User Context: The user contexts UC are combinations of features and values, denoted as $UC = \{UC^t \mid \forall f_i^t \in UC^t, f_i^t \in F_i\}$. Here, UC are the combinations of features f_i over time t, where F_i represents the set of values for feature i. For example, John's fall incident, emotional distress, etc., are the user contexts and contain features and values.

Abstract Service: An Abstract Service (AS) outlines key functionalities to meet specific user needs. For example, Medical Image Analysis is an AS that helps healthcare professionals diagnose and monitor conditions during fall incidents.

Concrete Service: A Concrete Service (CS) implement the requirements of AS by being selected based on QoS criteria such as biasness and explainability.

The proposed *Context-aware MLaaS Selection Framework (CAMSF)* is designed to enhance the efficiency and effectiveness of selecting MLaaS solutions by incorporating three distinct layers (see Fig. 2). The first layer, *changing user context*, involves dynamically assessing and understanding the evolving needs and conditions of the user, such as location, time, and specific task requirements. The second layer, *selecting abstract MLaaS services based on user contexts*, utilizes the information gathered from the first layer to identify and match suitable abstract MLaaS services that align with the user's context, ensuring the services considered are relevant and capable of meeting the user's general needs. Finally, the third layer, *selecting concrete MLaaS services to ensure optimal QoS*, focuses on the practical implementation by choosing specific MLaaS providers that offer the best performance, reliability, and other QoS metrics. *QoS monitoring* continuously evaluates MLaaS performance based on key metrics and serves two roles: (1) feeding QoS requirements to inform abstract MLaaS selection based on user needs and (2) providing real-time QoS data for selecting the best-performing concrete services. Our framework utilises Support Vector Machines (SVMs) to detect user contexts. It deploys contextual bandit algorithms to dynamically select abstract services, ensuring adaptive service selection and optimisation in dynamic IoT environments. This approach concludes with a skyline query method that filters and identifies concrete MLaaS services that meet users' QoS requirements across various attributes.

3.1 Context Change Analysis

This section explores how changing user contexts can enhance MLaaS selection using a *Support Vector Machine* to classify and predict contextual patterns. First, we design a feature extraction process. Feature extraction reduces data dimensionality by selecting relevant features, aiding context analysis and revealing meaningful patterns [14]. We standardise sensor data to a mean of 0 and a standard deviation of 1 by calculating $Z = X - \mu/\sigma$; where X is the data value, μ is the mean, and σ is the standard deviation. The Z score indicates how many standard deviations a particular observation is from the mean, providing a standardised interpretation of the data.

Let us assume that X is the feature matrix of size n*m, where n is the number of data samples, and m is the number of features. We need to identify a single user context by labelling data instances with the appropriate user context. Therefore, we are implementing a SVM to determine the user's current context detection (Fig. 2(1)). SVMs are a supervised learning model for classification and regression, aiming to find a hyperplane in feature space that maximises the margin between classes, known as the Maximal Margin classifier [10].

We train the SVM model with labelled and unlabeled user context data to maximise the margin between context classes. Regularisation ensures a smooth decision boundary, formulated similarly to supervised learning with an added smoothness term. The mathematical formulation for the optimisation problem in SVM with semi-supervised learning is similar to the supervised learning case with an additional term representing the smoothness constraint using the below-given formula:

$$\min_{w,b} \frac{1}{2}||w||^2 + C\sum_{i=1}^{n}\delta_i + \epsilon\sum_{i=1}^{n}\delta_{\text{unlabeled}} \tag{1}$$

Subject to constraints:

$$y_i = (w * x_i + b) \geq 1 - \delta_i, \quad \forall i \in \text{labeled data}$$

$$\delta_i \geq 0, \quad \forall i \in \text{labeled data}$$

$$|w * x_i + b| \leq M\delta_{\text{unlabeled}}, \quad \forall i \in \text{unlabeled data}$$

where δ_i is the slack variable for the labelled data, $\delta_{\text{unlabeled}}$ are the slack variables for the unlabeled data, C is the regularisation parameter, and ϵ controls the importance of the smoothness constraints, M is the constant representing the margin for unlabeled data. After that, the trained SVM model will be used to get the user context for new data instances. Given a new data instance x_{new}, the predicted user context can be obtained using the below-mentioned decision function:

$$f(x_{\text{new}}) = \text{sign}(w * x_{\text{new}} + b) \tag{2}$$

If $f(x_{\text{new}}) > 0$, the predicted user context belongs to one class;, and if $f(x_{\text{new}}) < 0$, it belongs to another. If $f(x_{\text{new}}) > 0$ and if $f(x_{\text{new}}) < 0$, the SVM model represents an identified user context. However, values close to zero indicate uncertainty, termed *unidentified user context, which is out of the focus of this paper.*

3.2 Mapping User Context To Abstract MLaaS Service Requirements

We use the *Contextual Bandit* approach, a class of *reinforcement learning method* that integrates contextual information for decision-making [17]. We assume that MLaaS providers advertise their services in textual descriptions that outline the service's applications and intended target users. To map user context to abstract MLaaS services, first, textual descriptions of MLaaS advertisements are processed by removing punctuation, stop words, tokenisation, stemming, and TD-IDF vectorisation to narrow down relevant services. K-means clustering groups services by advertisement description to simplify mapping. The contextual bandit algorithm selects the appropriate abstract service based on user context (see Fig. 2). We define the following key terms for the contextual bandit modelling:

– **State (s):** Represents the user context, including contextual features.
– **Action (a):** Represents a decision, such as selecting an MLaaS abstract service.
– **State-action pair (s_i, a_i):** Combines the current user context (s_i) with a specific action (a_i, selecting an MLaaS abstract service) aiming to learn the best actions per state for maximising cumulative rewards.

Given S, A and sequences of observed context-reward pairs $\{(s_t, r_t)\}$, the goal is to find a policy $\pi : S \to A$ that maximises the expected cumulative reward can be expressed as follows:

$$\max_{\pi} \mathbb{E}[r_i \mid x_i] \tag{3}$$

The mapping begins by observing the current user context, encompassing user-specific features and contextual information fed into the decision-making system. We then create a comprehensive feature vector by concatenating user features (e.g., age and location) and their context information (e.g., fall downtime and type of fall) with the pre-processed MLaaS service features. This vector is input into our model to predict the likelihood of selecting abstract MLaaS service. The algorithm employs an exploration-exploitation strategy, referred to by a ϵ-greedy policy. This strategy performs the MLaaS abstract service selection: with probability ϵ, the algorithm explores service selection randomly, while with probability $1 - \epsilon$, it exploits by choosing the MLaaS service based on current knowledge [17]. The predicted reward for selecting MLaaS service M_i in the state represented by X_i using the below calculation:

$$\hat{R}(X_i) = \beta_0 + \sum_{j=1}^{m} \beta_j x_{ij} \tag{4}$$

where $\hat{R}(X_i)$ is the predicted reward for state-action pair X_i, β_0 is the intercept term, β_j are coefficients corresponding to each feature x_{ij}, m is the total number of features in X_i. The algorithm (Algorithm 1) updates its predictive model and policy based on user feedback to improve decision-making and maximise cumulative rewards.   This contextual bandit approach allows for adaptive

---

Algorithm 1. User Context to Abstract MLaaS Service Mapping

Input: User features $U = \{u_1, u_2, \ldots, u_n\}$, User context features $UC = \{uc_1, uc_2, \ldots, uc_m\}$, and MLaaS service descriptions $M_i = \{mi_1, mi_2, \ldots, mi_p\}$
Output: Select the MLaaS abstract service m_i with $\hat{R}(x_i)$
Initialize $X_i = [U, UC, M_i]$
for each interaction **do**
    while $M_i \neq \emptyset$ **do**
        $\pi(X_i) = P(M_i \mid X_i)$
        Select mi_1 using ϵ-greedy policy
        Count $\hat{R}(X_i) = \beta_0 + \sum_{j=1}^{m} \beta_j x_{ij}$
        $Top - K \leftarrow \arg\max_{i \in n} \hat{R}(x_i)$
        Get user feedback r_i
        $\pi \leftarrow \text{update}(\pi, (x_i, m_i, r_i))$
    end while
end for

MLaaS abstract service selection based on user context by balancing exploration and exploitation and iterative updating the model with user feedback, improving the offering of abstract services at expected rewards.

3.3 Mapping Abstract MLaaS Service to Concrete MLaaS Service Selection

This section maps abstract services to concrete services based on non-functional attributes (see Fig. 2(3)). Let us assume that the user has a context where it contains additional information, for example, variations due to environmental factors such as network congestion, which may affect the non-functional attributes. Mapping based on non-functional attributes ensures that the MLaaS service chosen aligns with the user's QoS requirements in varying contexts.

QoS Monitoring: To select an optimal QoS concrete MLaaS service, we focus on key indicators, including biasness and explainability. We assume that QoS Monitoring delivers these services and feeds to CAMSF for selection. In a smart home system, identifying bias is crucial, as a model trained on biased datasets may favour certain user groups, which can lead to some individuals not receiving the necessary services. For example, elderly people often have different service requirements than typical adults. To align concrete MLaaS services with QoS, we utilise the established Adaptive Boosting model [8], which effectively classifies human activity data, identifies biases, and differentiates between the activities of elderly individuals and typical adults. Furthermore, accurate model predictions are essential. To achieve this, we use an established SHAP-based explanation (Shapley Additive Explanations) model developed by [3], which generates meaningful and interpretable explanations for the model predictions. This approach enhances user trust and confidence in the system's decisions by providing insights into how specific inputs influence outcomes. The method to assess accuracy is not part of the focus.

When multiple providers offer a service, we choose one by calculating the QoS score for each, weighting relevant attributes (e.g., biasness, explainability) based on the context of the user. The service with the highest utility score is selected.

$$\text{Utility Score} = \frac{\sum_{i=1}^{n} w_i \cdot \text{QoS}_i(S)}{\sum_{i=1}^{n} w_i} \tag{5}$$

where n is the number of QoS attributes (e.g., biasness, explainability), w_i is the weight assigned to the ith QoS attributes. $QoS_i(S)$ is the QoS value of the ith attribute for service S. S is the MLaaS service being evaluated.

We propose a *skyline* method to filter services based on bias and explainability QoS attributes, ensuring optimal selection. A skyline query is an effective approach to selecting a set of data points that is better than any other data points in large datasets [5]. We assume there are N concrete MLaaS services meeting user non-functional requirements. We aim to find a subset CS' of M services ($CS' \subset CS$) based on QoS attributes and user preferences Q_{UP}. Each service has QoS attributes $QoS = \{QoS_1, QoS_2, \ldots, QoS_n\}$. The selected subset $QoS' \subset QoS$ should match Q_{UP}, making this a multi-criteria selection problem. We use temporal skyline for service selection based on multiple QoS criteria [5].

Solving the Skyline Query. A concrete MLaaS service CS_i dominates another service CS_j if CS_i offers equal or better QoS across all attributes and strictly better QoS in at least one attribute. A skyline of MLaaS services includes optimal services that are not dominated by others across all QoS attributes. For example, if a user prioritises explainability and biasness in a Medical Image Analysis service, only services with these attributes are considered and weighted equally. We are considering the concepts below for QoS selection.

- Dominant Concrete MLaaS Service: A concrete MLaaS service CS_i dominates another concrete service CS_j, denoted as $CS_i > CS_j$. If CS_i provides as good or better QoS in Quality Dimension Q_D i.e., $\forall q \in Q_D : CS_i \geq CS_j$ and $\forall q\prime \in Q_D : CS_i > CS_j$.
- MLaaS Skyline: The skyline is a set of MLaaS concrete service CS, denoted as SK_{CS} is a subset of concrete services that are not dominated by any other concrete service.
- Temporal MLaaS Skyline: In temporal skyline, QoS parameters can be represented as time series and changing over time.
- Dominant QoS Time Series: A QoS time series Q_i dominates another QoS time series Q_j in time T, denoted as $Q_i > Q_j, if\ \forall t \in T, Q_i \geq Q_j, and \forall t\prime \in T, Q_i > Q_j$.
- Temporal QoS Skyline: The temporal QoS skyline of a set of QoS time series Q, denoted as ST_Q, is the subset of QoS time series not dominated by any other series at any timestamp t, i.e., $ST_Q = q \in Q|\neg\ \exists q\prime \in Q : q\prime > q$.

By applying the MLaaS skyline approach, it filters concrete MLaaS services based on multiple QoS attributes, ensuring that the selected service provides the best trade-off for the abstract MLaaS service in the given user context. The algorithm starts by initializing a list S that contains all the services to be evaluated. It then uses a nested loop structure where each service C_i in the list is compared against every other service C_j. For each comparison, the algorithm checks if service C_i "dominates" service C_j. In this context, "dominates" means that C_i is at least as good as C_j in all relevant attributes (such as quality, cost, or efficiency) and better in at least one attribute. If C_i dominates C_j, then C_j is removed from the list S. Ultimately, the algorithm returns the refined list S, which represents the skyline set of services.

4   Experiment and Results

We develop a Python 3.12.0 environment on a Windows 11 system with 8 CPU cores, 8 GB RAM and 500 GB of storage for experiments. Table 1 presents the details of the experiment set up where it evaluated MLaaS service selection involving ten users with five distinct contexts (i.e., incidents and environmental factors) on 5000 MLaaS service descriptions. The focus is on assessing services based on two QoS preferences: biases and explainability (XAI), along with accuracy, response time (up to 5,000ns per 1,000 samples), and availability.

Table 1. Statistics of Dataset for Context-Aware MLaaS in IoT

Statistics	Values	Statistics	Values
Users	10	User Contexts	5
MLaaS Services	5000	IoT Devices	10
User Preferences	2	Response Time Range	5000 ns
(QoS) Attributes	5	Accuracy Range	80–99%
XAI	0-1	Bias	0–1%

4.1 Data Set Description

Our experimental setup integrated data from ten IoT devices across three diverse datasets: the Smart Human Fall Dataset [15] from Kaggle, used to monitor physical movements; the CAUCAFall dataset [4], focused on detecting object interactions such as picking an object or potential theft incidents; and the Synthetic Network Traffic Dataset [18], employed to analyse network behaviour for identifying security threats and unusual activities. Due to the unavailability of public MLaaS service description datasets, we curated service descriptions from leading providers such as AWS Sagemaker, Google Cloud, and Azure Machine Learning [2] to analysis of mapping user contexts to abstract MLaaS services. Additionally, leveraging a comprehensive knowledge dataset [11], we optimised the selection of QoS for MLaaS concrete services derived from abstract MLaaS services. To evaluate each approach, we assessed several test cases (see examples in Table 2).

Table 2. Test cases of mapping MLaaS abstract and concrete service with QoS.

No.	Examples of Test Cases
1	Fall is normal and occurs indoors; prefer explainable MLaaS service.
2	Intruder enter at night, intention unclear; prefer low biased and explainable MLaaS.
3	A cyber attack entry point is via an unsecured password; prefer explainable MLaaS.
4	Simultaneous anomalies detected in network behaviour across several users; low biases and explainable MLaaS service are needed.

4.2 Baseline Approaches

To evaluate the performance of the proposed CAMSF, we choose two service selection methods.

- **Pre-defined or Fixed-Rules** [9,14]: Traditional service selection system uses Event-Condition-Action (ECA) rules in the form of: "On <event>, If <condition>, Do <action>", where on detecting an event, typically monitored through wearable technology and smart sensors. Later, validating the event against predefined criteria in a condition part and initiating the appropriate responses as an Action. This approach allows automated, consistent decision-making based on monitored events that match the conditions and trigger the corresponding actions.
- **Brute-Force Approach** [6]: The brute-force approach comparing candidate services involves evaluating every possible pair of services to determine how closely they match their attributes. This method ensures a thorough assessment by comparing each service with every other candidate, providing comprehensive results; this approach can be computationally intensive due to the exhaustive nature of the comparisons, particularly when dealing with many candidate services.

Evaluations Metrics : We evaluate each service selection approach using below key performance metrics: accuracy, precision, recall and F1-score.

$$Precision = TP/TP + FP \tag{6}$$

$$Recall = TP/TP + FN \tag{7}$$

$$Accuracy = (TP + TN)/(TP + FP + TN + FN) \tag{8}$$

$$F1 - Score = 2 * Precision * Recall/Precision + Recall \tag{9}$$

where TP (True Positive) refers to correctly identified optimal MLaaS services, while FP (False Positive) refers to incorrectly identified optimal services. TN (True Negative) represents correctly identified non-optimal services, and FN (False Negative) refers to incorrectly identified non-optimal services.

4.3 Performance Analysis

We evaluate the different selection approaches by two sets of experiments. First, we evaluate the efficiency of CAMSF in user context detection regarding how accurately SVM detects context. Second, we measure the effectiveness of CAMSF by comparing the accuracy and F1-score of each approach for selecting MLaaS based on user context. We also evaluate the scalability of each approach by measuring the computation time from user context detection to the MLaaS concrete service. During the evaluation, we vary the size of the MLaaS services description. Starting with 10–20 MLaaS service descriptions, we incrementally increased the samples across different experimental phases.

The effectiveness of our framework in identifying user context is demonstrated by the correlation between the number of contextual data samples and accuracy scores (Fig. 3(a)). Initially, with smaller numbers of contextual data,

Table 3. Performance measurement results

	Accuracy	Precision	Recall	F1 Score
CAMSF	**0.91**	**0.90**	**0.93**	**0.89**
Fix Rule Approach	0.50	0.57	0.57	0.62
Brute Force Approach	0.45	0.34	0.35	0.34

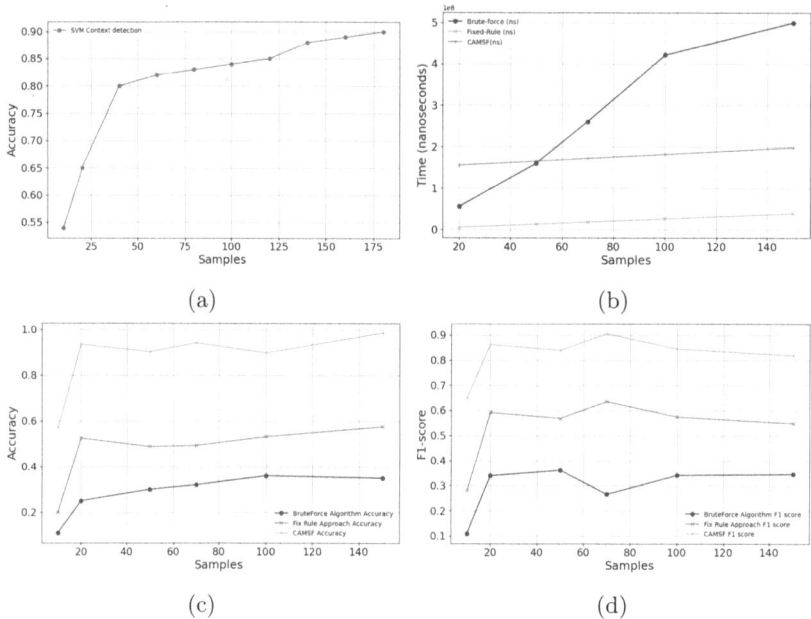

Fig. 3. The Effectiveness and Scalability of CAMSF (a) SVM Context Detection Accuracy, (b) Computation Time Comparison, (c) Accuracy Comparison, and (d) F1 Score Comparison Across Models

the accuracy score is relatively low, around 0.50. However, increasing the sample size enhances accuracy, ultimately reaching an impressive score of 0.90. This trend underscores the efficiency of our framework in accurately identifying user context, highlighting its robustness and reliability as more contextual data is incorporated. To evaluate CAMSF's efficiency against the fixed-rule approach in abstract service mapping and select the best concrete service based on given preferences, we measure it in terms of the *success rate* that evaluates the system's efficiency in selecting services to maximise expected rewards, reflecting its ability to identify optimal choices and enhance decision-making through observed rewards in interactions using below formula:

$$SuccessRate = \frac{\text{Number of times optimal service selected}}{\text{Total number of interactions}} \qquad (10)$$

Our experimental results show that the CAMSF performs robustly in selecting optimal services based on user context (Table 3). Results indicate that with smaller samples, mapping accuracy is around 0.57 while increasing samples have an accuracy of 0.91(Fig. 3(c)); the framework correctly identifies the optimal choice 91% of the time, indicating high reliability in aligning services with user context. Precision, at 0.90, signifies that when the framework selects a service, it is accurate 90% of the time, emphasising the correctness of positive predictions. A recall score of 0.93 highlights the framework's ability to include 93% of all truly required services. The F1 score of 0.89 (Fig. 3(d)) demonstrates a well-balanced performance between precision and recall. This could be attributed to success being driven by dynamic, learning-based strategies that continuously evolve the service selection process based on real-time feedback and context adaptability. This ensures that the CAMSF framework enhances long-term efficiency and effectiveness in service delivery.

In contrast to the CAMSF, the Fixed-Rule method demonstrates a low score in all metrics (Table 3) with an accuracy of 0.50 (Fig. 3(c))and an F1-score of 0.62 (Fig. 3(d)) in several samples. These metrics underscore their dependence on predetermined rules designed for specific domains, ensuring predictability within those boundaries. However, these systems frequently encounter challenges adapting to changing contexts, resulting in inefficiencies when applied beyond their designated domains. In Brute-Force, despite its ability to measure similarity accurately, this approach (Table 3) has a lower accuracy of 0.45 (slowly increased with samples; Fig. 3(c)), indicating the correctness of its service predictions. However, with a precision of 0.34, it selects only a fraction of the services relevant to the user's needs. The recall rate of 0.35 shows that it captures some relevant services, with an F1 score of 0.34 (Fig. 3(d)), which assesses its effectiveness overall. This limitation makes it impractical for large-scale applications requiring quick service selection.

Similarly, we started with smaller samples to evaluate the *scalability* by measuring the computation time of different approaches for selecting MLaaS services based on user context and increased slowly. Figure 3(b) illustrates the average computation time for all approaches. Initially, the Fixed-Rule and Brute-Force approaches demonstrated significantly shorter service selection times with smaller datasets. However, with increased samples, the computing time for the Brute-Force algorithm increased by 5 ns. Conversely, the Fixed-Rule approach maintained a consistently low computation time of around 0.4 ns. This time efficiency is attributable to its reliance on pre-defined criteria for service selection. However, our proposed CAMSF, which dynamically identifies user context and maps it to MLaaS abstract services, showed a computation time of 1.5 to 2 ns with increased samples. Although slightly higher than the fixed rule, CAMSF optimises service selection based on evolving contextual factors, ensuring timely and accurate alignment with user preferences while enhancing overall scalability and responsiveness.

5   Conclusion

The proposed context-aware MLaaS service selection framework (CAMSF) significantly enhances the optimisation of selecting the best QoS MLaaS offerings based on user context. CAMSF begins by using SVM with semi-supervised learning to detect and adapt to changing user contexts, ensuring responsiveness to diverse needs. We then utilise contextual bandits to map user contexts to abstract MLaaS services, enabling dynamic optimisation that improves service delivery in machine learning applications. This approach continuously refines service selection to maintain high performance in evolving environments. To validate CAMSF, we incorporate a skyline query method to select optimal concrete MLaaS services, aligning selections with user preferences while ensuring scalability, runtime efficiency, and effectiveness. Our results show a 61.65% performance improvement in context-aware MLaaS selection compared to the Fixed-Rule method and a 74.80% improvement compared to the Brute-Force approach. These findings underscore CAMSF's robust capabilities in various MLaaS service selection scenarios, highlighting its potential as a powerful tool for enhancing machine learning service delivery. Future work will focus on developing models that address sustainability issues, particularly cost efficiency and time optimisation.

Acknowledgements. The authors acknowledge the support of this work through a grant from the Defence Science Centre (DSC), Government of Western Australia, under the Research Higher Degree Student Grant program. This statement reflects the views solely of the authors.

References

1. Adomavicius, G., Tuzhilin, A.: Context-aware recommender systems. In: Ricci, F., Rokach, L., Shapira, B., Kantor, P.B. (eds.) Recommender Systems Handbook, pp. 217–253. Springer, Boston, MA (2011). https://doi.org/10.1007/978-0-387-85820-3_7
2. AltexSoft: Comparing machine learning as a service: Amazon, Microsoft Azure, Google Cloud AI, IBM Watson (2023). https://www.altexsoft.com/blog/
3. Das, D., et al.: Explainable activity recognition for smart home systems. ACM Trans. Interact. Intell. Syst. **13**(2), 1–39 (2023)
4. Eraso, J.C., Muñoz, E., Muñoz, M., Pinto, J.: Dataset CAUCAFall (2022). https://data.mendeley.com/datasets/7w7fccy7ky/4
5. Fattah, S.M.M.: Long-term IaaS cloud service selection. Ph.D. thesis, University of Melbourne (2021)
6. Garba, S., Mohamad, R., Saadon, N.A.: Self-adaptive mobile web service discovery approach based on modified negative selection algorithm. Neural Comput. Appl. **34**(3), 2007–2029 (2022)
7. Han, B., Wong, S., Mannweiler, C., Crippa, M.R., Schotten, H.D.: Context-awareness enhances 5G multi-access edge computing reliability. IEEE Access **7**, 21290–21299 (2019)

8. Javed, A.R., et al.: Automated cognitive health assessment in smart homes using machine learning. Sustain. Urban Areas **65**, 102572 (2021)
9. Matos, É.d.: Edge-centric context sharing architecture for the internet of things: context interoperability and context-aware security (2020)
10. Mohd, M., et al.: Poliweet–election prediction tool using tweets. Softw. Impacts **17**, 100542 (2023)
11. Patel, K., Mistry, S., Kanneganti, D., Krishna, A.: Machine learning as a service (MLaaS) selection with incomplete QoS information (2023)
12. Pereira, I., et al.: A machine learning as a service (MLaaS) approach to improve marketing success. In: Informatics, vol. 11, p. 19. MDPI (2024)
13. Qi, L., Dou, W., Hu, C., Zhou, Y., Yu, J.: A context-aware service evaluation approach over big data for cloud applications. IEEE Trans. Cloud Comput. **8**(2), 338–348 (2015)
14. Rhayem, A., Mhiri, M.B.A., Drira, K., Tazi, S., Gargouri, F.: A semantic-enabled and context-aware monitoring system for the internet of medical things. Expert. Syst. **38**(2), e12629 (2021)
15. Sakib, S.: Smartphone accelerometer and gyroscope data for human activity recognition (2024). https://www.kaggle.com/datasets/saadmansakib/smartphone-human-fall-dataset
16. Services, A.W.: Internet of things services for sensors (2023). https://docs.aws.amazon.com/whitepapers/latest/aws-overview/internet-of-things-services.html
17. Varatharajah, Y., Berry, B.: A contextual-bandit-based approach for informed decision-making in clinical trials. Life **12**(8), 1277 (2022)
18. Waghela, V.: network traffic data (2024). https://www.kaggle.com/datasets/vidhikishorwaghela/synthetic-network-traffic/data
19. Xu, Y., Yin, J., Deng, S., Xiong, N.N., Huang, J.: Context-aware QoS prediction for web service recommendation and selection. Expert Syst. Appl. **53**, 75–86 (2016)

WISE 2024 - Posters and Demos Track

GraphTFD: A Fraud Detection System Based on Graph Transformer

Chengcheng Yu, Lujing Fei, Wenqian Zhou, Lin Chen, Jiahui Wang, Xiankai Meng, and Fangshu Chen[✉]

School of Computer and Information Engineering, Shanghai Polytechnic University, Shanghai, China
{ccyu,chenl,wangjh,xkmeng,fschen}@sspu.edu.cn,
{20221513018,20221113272}@stu.sspu.edu.cn

Abstract. Fraud detection is critical in identifying and preventing fraudulent activities across various industries, safeguarding financial assets, and maintaining trust in business. Although graph-based fraud detection methods have demonstrated significant success, they still suffer from two main challenges that remain unresolved. First, traditional GNN-based algorithms may perform poorly when the nodes' class distribution is heavily skewed. Second, many GNN-based methods fail to generalize to the heterophily setting. In this demonstration, we present a graph transformer-based fraud detection system called GraphTFD. This system can help address the above challenges by exploring a data augmentation strategy to enhance the minority class with numerous unlabeled nodes and introducing group-level aggregation and group encodings to help the transformer encoder capture more similar neighborhood information under heterophily settings. GraphTFD also provides an interface that visualizes the GraphTFD internals and assesses the quality of fraud detection results. Our demonstration video can be found here: https://b23.tv/Z13L5Uf.

Keywords: Fraud detection · Graph transformer · Class imbalance · Heterophily

1 Introduction

Fraud detection plays a critical role in identifying and preventing fraudulent activities across various industries, such as social network [1], e-commerce [12], and review management [7]. Entity classification is one of the most common tasks in fraud detection. Data can be modeled as graphs in graph-based fraud detection approaches, each node represents a benign or fraud, and edges between nodes represent they purchase the same product or post reviews on the same product, which renders effective multifaceted information for fraud detection.

With the success of Graph neural networks (GNNs) [2,3] in various downstream tasks, graph-based fraud detection approaches have received significant attention in both academic and industrial communities. Meanwhile, traditional

GNN-based fraud detection models yet suffer from two challenges. The first challenge is that traditional GNN-based fraud detection models trained with class-imbalanced labeled data may perform poorly for the minority but more important class, namely the fraudsters, due to a lack of information about the minority class. The second challenge is that traditional GNN-based fraud detectors reveal fraudsters based on the assumption of homophily; that is, fraudsters tend to connect with each other. They are less effective due to the heterophily in graphs.

In recent years, several works have been proposed to address these issues. Some studies [5,10] tackle the class imbalance problem in fraud detection through down-sampling and over-sampling techniques. Other works [4,11] aim to generalize well in low homophily settings. However, in practical fraud detection applications, these issues often coexist. The models above focus on either the heterophily problem or the class imbalance problem, but not both.

Motivated by the above reasons, this paper develops and demonstrates a **Graph T**ransformer-based **F**raud **D**etection (GraphTFD) system. GraphTFD visualizes the two main challenges of graph-based fraud detection approaches: class imbalance and heterophily. It allows users to query and visualize various data analyses related to our fraud detection method, such as prediction results for a given dataset using our model interface. Additionally, GraphTFD provides a visual display to observe the internals of our model. The key contributions of this paper are listed as follows:

- GraphTFD is a novel graph-based fraud detection approach to address both heterophily and class imbalance issues.
- GraphTFD designs a data augmentation strategy to enhance the fraud class with numerous unlabeled nodes for coping with the class imbalance problem.
- GraphTFD introduces a pseudo-fraud group into group-level aggregation and cooperating group encodings to enable the transformer encoder to capture more similar neighborhood information under the heterophily settings.
- GraphTFD shows excellent performance over two public datasets compared with the state-of-the-art methods.

The outline of this paper is as follows. In Sect. 2, we give the system overview of GraphTFD, and the main components of GraphTFD are described briefly. In Sect. 3, we will present the performance evaluation of GraphTFD. Finally, we will show the details of the demonstration in Sect. 4. Section 5 concludes the paper.

2   System Overview

The architecture of GraphTFD is shown in Fig. 1. It comprises the following three main components: Fraud Class Augmentation, Group-level Aggregation, and Transformer backbone.

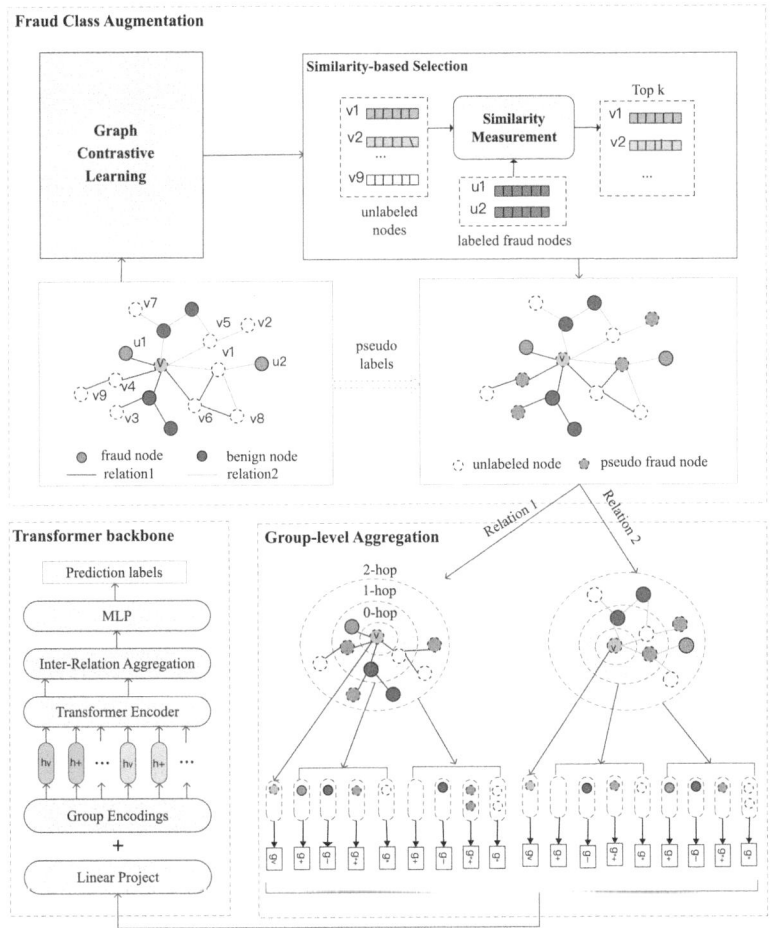

Fig. 1. The architecture of GraphTFD.

2.1 Fraud Class Augmentation

The fraud class augmentation aims to augment the fraud class from the massive unlabelled nodes of the graph by generating pseudo-fraud labels for these unlabelled nodes.

We first employ a Graph Contrastive Learning (GCL) model to obtain better node representations, which can reflect the inter-class and intra-class relationship of nodes well. The GCL module takes the graph as input and generates the corresponding node embeddings as outputs, and HDGI [9] is applied in this paper. The similarity-based selection module generates pseudo-fraud labels by selecting the K unlabeled nodes that are most similar to the fraud class, based on the node representations learned from GCL We use the distance between an unlabeled node and the nearest labeled fraud node in the latent space to measure how close the node is to the fraud class. These pseudo-fraud nodes augment the fraud/minority class, which mitigates the class imbalance problem.

2.2 Group-Level Aggregation

In the group-level aggregation step, we divide each node's neighbors into several groups and then obtain each group's embeddings as the input for the next step.

Specifically, we can obtain several relationship-based multi-hop sub-graphs for a target node. The node's neighbors from these sub-graphs can be divided into several groups based on the relationship, hop number, and label type. Concretely, we get a 2-hop sub-graph of a target node under a relation, where the target node itself is a group G_v. Each of the other hop neighbors can be divided into four groups $\{g_+, g_-, g_{*+}, g_*\}$ according to label type: fraud, benign, pseudo-fraud, and unlabeled. Finally, we obtain a series of groups across all relations for a target node and then perform mean aggregation for each group to generate a sequence of group embeddings.

2.3 Transformer Backbone

In the group-level aggregation step, we can obtain the final node representations. The sequence of group embeddings generated by the group-level aggregation will first be fed into a linear projection to map the dimensions before being processed by the transformer encoder.

Three types of learnable group encodings are then developed to encode the graph structure, semantic information, and class labels into the sequence of group embeddings. These encodings include group-hop, group-relation, and group-class encodings. Taking group-hop encoding as an example, we first index the group hop number, then encode the hop index using a one-hot encoder, and multiply it by a learnable parameter. Each group has three types of encodings, and each type of encoding shares a single learnable parameter. We fuse them with group embeddings to generate the input for the transformer encoder. The transformer encoder employs multi-head self-attention to adaptively re-weight these group embeddings and capture more similar neighborhood information under low homophily settings. An inter-relation aggregation is used to generate the final target node embedding by combining the output embeddings across different relations. Finally, a Multi-Layer Perceptron (MLP) classifier is used for label prediction.

During the training phase, our method utilizes semi-supervised learning by minimizing cross-entropy loss.

3   Evaluation

We use two real-life datasets to evaluate our approach. The first dataset is YelpChi [8], which contains reviews about hotels and restaurants on Yelp.com. The reviews represent nodes, and three types of relations connect the nodes.

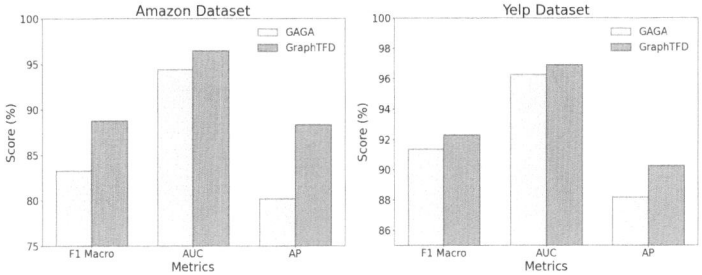

Fig. 2. Performance comparison of different methods on Amazon and Yelp datasets.

GraphTFD helps analyze fraudulent review activities in this dataset, providing insights into review behavior and product ratings. The second dataset is Amazon [6], which collects reviews about musical instrument products, with users represented as nodes. GraphTFD helps detect fraudulent users in this dataset. We will introduce some of the experimental results.

3.1   Performance of GraphTFD

Figure 2 shows the performance results of our method and the baseline method GAGA [11] on two benchmark datasets. We can see that our approach significantly outperforms GAGA across all metrics on both datasets. This superior performance can be mainly attributed to our method's consideration of class imbalance and heterophily issues.

3.2   Parameter Analysis of GraphTFD

We show the performance of our approach under different K on Amazon. As shown in Fig. 3, we observe that more pseudo-positive labels can improve performance. However, too many pseudo-fraud nodes can introduce noise, leading to a drop in performance. And the peak percentages of performance and correctness are approximately equal to the percentage of positive nodes among all labeled nodes in the training set.

Figure 4 shows the performance results of our method and GAGA under different training percentages on YelpChi. Our method achieves the best performance under different training percentages. This demonstrates that our method can improve performance using only a small portion of the training data.

4   Demonstration

GraphTFD provides an interactive Web interface. It provides configurable parameters for fraud detection, including datasets, risk levels, and some model parameters. All models with the parameters set by users are pre-trained on a

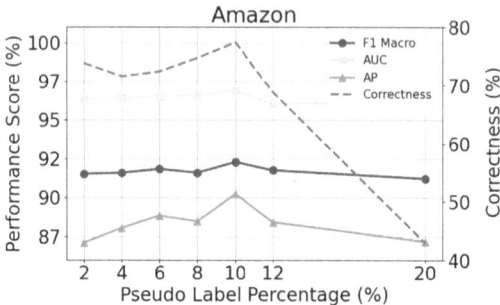

Fig. 3. Performance under different percentage training data on Amazon.

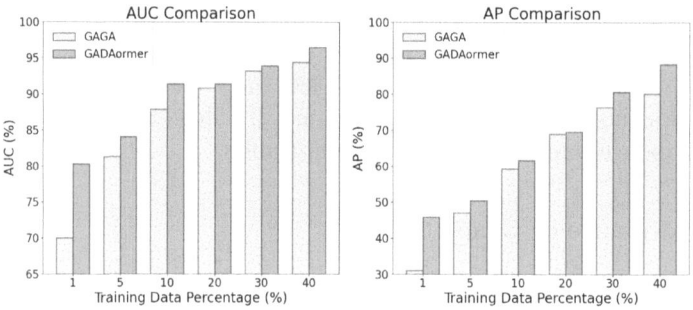

Fig. 4. The performance under different number of pseudo label nodes on YelpChi.

server with an NVIDIA Tesla V100 PCIe 40GB GPU using the training set. GraphTFD then loads these models to predict node labels.

As shown in Fig. 5, our demonstration includes the following three parts: dataset visualization, GraphTFD fraud detection results, and GraphTFD internals.

Dataset Visualization. We will show the characteristics of the dataset, including class imbalance and heterophliy.

– Class imbalance is prevalent in real-world fraud detection applications, which is also a challenge of graph-based fraud detection approaches. We will show the reduced fraud graph with node labels of the given dataset.
– Heterophliy is another fraud detection challenge, an important characteristic of the fraud dataset. We will show the 1-hop neighborhood of the given fraud node, and the node label will also be displayed.

GraphTFD Fraud Detection Results. We will show the quality of the fraud detection results on test set during the demonstration.

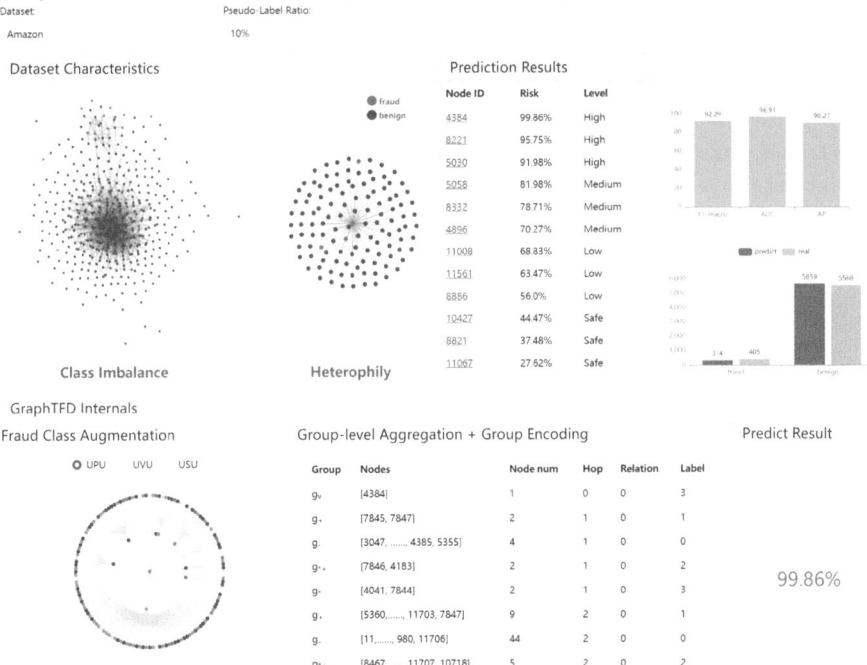

Fig. 5. The Web Interface of GraphTFD.

- The classification results of the given dataset through the model prediction interface will be shown online.
- The information of nodes with high/Medium/Low risks of fraud predicted by our model will be visualized online.

GraphTFD Internals. We will show how GraphTFD predicts a fraud node.

- We will show the 2-hop neighborhood sub-graph of the given node with real and pseudo-fraud node labels derived from the fraud class augmentation module. The pseudo-fraud label size changes with the user setting.
- We will demonstrate the node information of each group in the step of group-level aggregation, and group encodings will also be shown.
- The probability of being a fraudulent node will be computed by our model interface and shown in the demonstration.

5   Conclusion

This paper introduces GraphTFD, a novel fraud detection system that uses a graph transformer-based method to address heterophily and class imbalance issues. The approach includes fraud class augmentation, group-level aggregation, and a transformer backbone. It shows a well performance on two real-life dataset. GraphTFD provides an interactive web interface, which visualizes dataset characteristics, fraud detection results and model internals.

Acknowledgments. This work is supported by National Natural Science Foundation of China No. 62002216.

References

1. Dou, Y., Ma, G., Yu, P.S., Xie, S.: Robust spammer detection by nash reinforcement learning. In: Proceedings of the 26th ACM SIGKDD International Conference on Knowledge Discovery & Data Mining, pp. 924–933 (2020)
2. Hamilton, W., Ying, Z., Leskovec, J.: Inductive representation learning on large graphs. Adv. Neural Inf. Process. Syst. **30** (2017)
3. Kipf, T.N., Welling, M.: Semi-supervised classification with graph convolutional networks. In: ICLR (2017)
4. Li, Q., He, Y., Xu, C., Wu, F., Gao, J., Li, Z.: Dual-augment graph neural network for fraud detection. In: Proceedings of the 31st ACM International Conference on Information & Knowledge Management, pp. 4188–4192 (2022)
5. Liu, Y., et al.: Pick and choose: a GNN-based imbalanced learning approach for fraud detection. In: Proceedings of the Web Conference 2021, pp. 3168–3177 (2021)
6. McAuley, J.J., Leskovec, J.: From amateurs to connoisseurs: modeling the evolution of user expertise through online reviews. In: Proceedings of the 22nd International Conference on World Wide Web, pp. 897–908 (2013)
7. Nilizadeh, S., Aghakhani, H., Gustafson, E., Kruegel, C., Vigna, G.: Think outside the dataset: finding fraudulent reviews using cross-dataset analysis. In: The World Wide Web Conference, pp. 3108–3115 (2019)
8. Rayana, S., Akoglu, L.: Collective opinion spam detection: bridging review networks and metadata. In: Proceedings of the 21th ACM SIGKDD International Conference on Knowledge Discovery and Data Mining, pp. 985–994 (2015)
9. Ren, Y., Liu, B., Huang, C., Dai, P., Bo, L., Zhang, J.: Heterogeneous deep graph infomax. arXiv preprint arXiv:1911.08538 (2019)
10. Shi, S., Qiao, K., Chen, C., Yang, J., Chen, J., Yan, B.: Over-sampling strategy in feature space for graphs based class-imbalanced bot detection. In: Companion Proceedings of the ACM on Web Conference 2024, pp. 738–741 (2024)
11. Wang, Y., et al.: Label information enhanced fraud detection against low homophily in graphs. In: Proceedings of the ACM Web Conference 2023, pp. 406–416 (2023)
12. Xu, B., Shen, H., Sun, B., An, R., Cao, Q., Cheng, X.: Towards consumer loan fraud detection: Graph neural networks with role-constrained conditional random field. In: Proceedings of the AAAI Conference on Artificial Intelligence. vol. 35, pp. 4537–4545 (2021)

MLGE-AC-UFD: Multi-level Graph Embedding and Approximate Computation for Unsupervised Fraud Detection

Yixin Tian, Bingkun Wang, Jiahui Wang, Yilin Huang, and Fangshu Chen[✉]

Shanghai Polytechnic University, Shanghai, China
`fschen@sspu.edu.cn`

Abstract. In the era of big data, online platforms face increasingly sophisticated and covert fraudulent activities that traditional detection methods fail to handle effectively. Traditional methods which depend on predefined rules or supervised learning algorithms, have limitations in capturing the diverse and evolving nature of fraud activity. Additionally, the exponential increase of online users and activities significantly expends the need of computational resources, and hinders promptly detection. More intelligent and efficient detection methods are expected to address these challenges. This paper proposes an unsupervised intelligent fraud detection framework that integrates multi-level graph embedding and approximate computation. By constructing a user behavior graph with both explicit and implicit behaviors, the framework captures comprehensive user activities. Experiment results show that our framework can detect majority of fraudulent behaviors and consequently help companies reduce economic losses. Demo video click here or try onsite.

Keywords: Unsupervised intelligent fraud detection · Multi-level graph embedding · Approximate computation · Anomaly pattern analysis

1 Introduction

The exponential growth of online users and activities has led to the rise of sophisticated and covert fraudulent activities. Traditional fraud detection methods, primarily based on predefined rules, historical data and supervised learning algorithms, have been proved to be inadequate in dealing with the complex and dynamic nature of fraudulent activities and fail to adapt to rapidly evolving tactics employed by fraudsters [1]. Traditional fraud detection approaches are fundamentally limited by their reliance on static, rule-based systems and historical data. These systems are often fail to adapt to the rapidly evolving tactics employed by fraudsters. Moreover, supervised learning algorithms, while valuable, require labeled datasets for training. These datasets are often limited and may not capture the full range of potential fraudulent behaviors [2,3].

M. Barhamgi et al. (Eds.): WISE 2024, LNCS 15463, pp. 217–224, 2025.
https://doi.org/10.1007/978-981-96-1483-7_17

To overcome these limitations, recent research has focused on the development of unsupervised intelligent fraud detection frameworks that leverage advanced computational techniques and the vast amounts of data generated by online activities. This paper introduces a novel system named MLGE-AC-UFD. The system integrates a multi-level graph embedding methods with approximate computation for unsupervised fraudulent account detection. The framework meticulously captures and analyzes user behavior patterns, enabling the identification of both overt and covert fraudulent activities. The overall architecture of MLGE-AC-UFD is described in Fig. 1, and each of the component will be explained later in Sect. 2 [4].

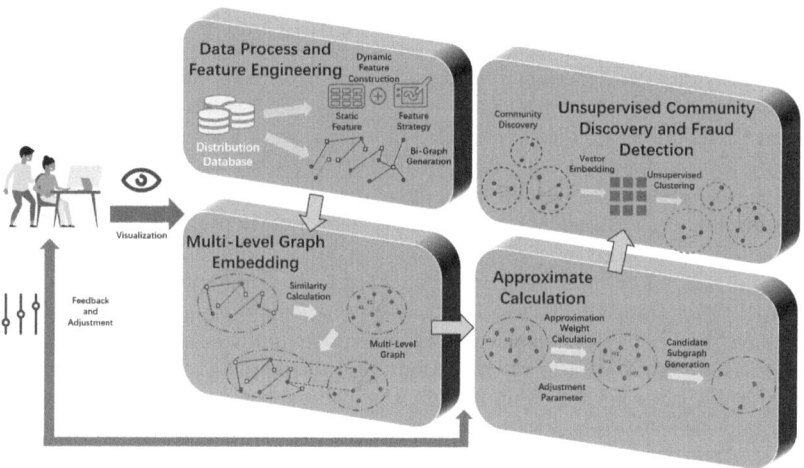

Fig. 1. Framework description.

2   System Overview

2.1   Data Process and Feature Engineering

This module is mainly responsible for obtaining batch account registration information data from distributed database and preprocessing the missing values. Preprocessing includes two steps. The first part is to construct dynamic features according to feature aggregation and distill the features that are used more frequently. There are two kinds of dynamic feature construction strategies. The first is the sliding window strategy. As shown in Fig. 2, the sliding window strategy mainly focuses on features that accumulate significantly within a certain time period, and can better dynamically segment statistical attributes.

The second dynamic feature construction method is shown in Fig. 3. We propose a novel analytical method called Pattern of Missing Values (POMV), which aims to capture fraud signatures by examining the distribution of missing

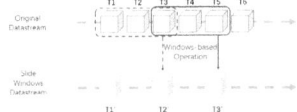

Fig. 2. Slide window strategy.

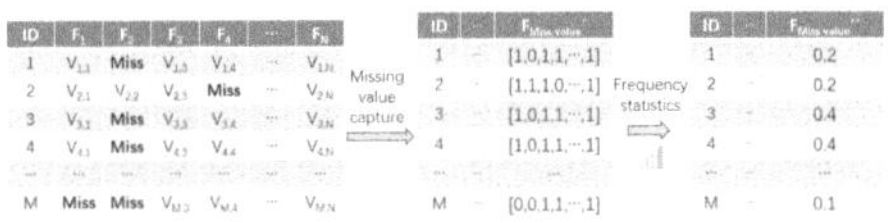

Fig. 3. Illustration of POMV(Pattern of Missing Value) strategy.

value. POMV involves marking the missing value (NaN or None) as 0 and the other values as 1, and then compact the missing values into a vector $F'_{\text{Miss value}}$ as shown in Fig. 3, and at last, vector $F'_{\text{Miss value}}$ is transformed into a frequency feature $F''_{\text{Miss value}}$. The details of POMV method can be found in our previous work [5].

2.2 Multi-level Graph Embedding

In this paper, we introduce a multi-layer graph embedding algorithm designed for effective account similarity computation, as shown in Algorithm 1. The algo-

---

Algorithm 1. Multi-layer Graph Embedding Algorithm

1: **Input:** The dataset D consists of rows representing account nodes and columns representing feature nodes.
2: **Output:** Homogeneous Graph $G_{hom} = (V_A, E_{AA})$
3: Initialize $G_{het} = (V_A, V_F, E_{AF})$
4: **for** each row i in D **do**
5:     Add account node A_i to V_A
6:     **for** each column j in D **do**
7:         **if** $D[i][j]$ is non-zero **then**
8:             **if** feature node F_j not in V_F **then**
9:                 Add F_j to V_F
10:             **end if**
11:             Add edge (A_i, F_j) to E_{AF}
12:         **end if**
13:     **end for**
14: **end for**
15: Initialize $G_{hom} \leftarrow (V_A, \emptyset)$
16: **for** each feature $x \in V_F$ **do**
17:     Compute $ratio(x)$ and $weight(x)$ (details in [10])
18: **end for**
19: **for** each pair of accounts $(a_i, a_j) \in V_A \times V_A$ **do**
20:     Compute similarity $sim(a_i, a_j)$
21:     **if** $sim(a_i, a_j) >$ threshold **then**
22:         Add edge (a_i, a_j) to E_{AA}
23:     **end if**
24: **end for**
25: **return** G_{hom}

---

rithm operates in two main stages: (1) generating an account-feature association heterogeneous graph G_{het} from the dataset by creating nodes and edges based on non-empty data entries, where nodes represent features and accounts, and edges connect accounts to features. Specifically, D is the dataset where rows represent account nodes and columns represent feature nodes; $G_{het} = (V_A, V_F, E_{AF})$ is the heterogeneous graph where V_A represents account nodes, V_F represents feature nodes, and E_{AF} represents edges between them; $G_{hom} = (V_A, E_{AA})$ is the homogeneous graph where E_{AA} represents edges between similar accounts, and the weight of the edge is the similarity between accounts. This structure allows for a clear representation of the complex relationships between users and associated features, thereby enhancing the interpretability of the model; (2) converting G_{het} into a homogeneous graph G_{hom} by calculating feature-based weights for accounts, including feature frequency, feature ratio, and feature prefix. Setting the similarity connection threshold, then use these weights to assess similarity between account pairs and add similarity-based edges.

Particularly, Lines 3 to 14 construct the heterogeneous graph G_{het} by initializing nodes and edges from the dataset. Lines 15 to 25 convert G_{het} into the homogeneous graph G_{hom} by calculating weights and adding similarity-based edges. Detailed calculations are provided in [5]. The final homogeneous graph G_{hom}, which incorporates similarity-based edges, enables more effective analysis and modeling, making the results of the model more interpretable and understandable.

2.3   Approximate Calculation

We then address the challenge of scaling up the graph computation by employing approximation techniques. Consider a graph $G = (V, E)$ with $|V| = n$ nodes and $|E| = m$ edges. Traditional graph-based algorithms, such as GCN for node classification and prediction [6,9], often have a computational complexity of $O(n^2)$ or $O(n \log n)$. To make these computations feasible for large scale graphs with millions of nodes which is very common in the proposed fraud detection scenarios, we use approximation methods that reduce this complexity to $O(kn)$, where k is a constant much smaller than n.

To achieve this, we apply approximation techniques such as random sampling or sparse matrix approximations. Specifically, when computing similarities or constructing the homogeneous graph, we approximate the connections and weights between nodes using fewer representative samples. This involves setting an error tolerance ϵ and using methods like sampling or matrix decomposition to simplify the graph while preserving essential characteristics.

In practice, we approximate the similarity between nodes a_i and a_j by leveraging these techniques. Instead of calculating exact similarities for all node pairs, we use a reduced set of representative node pairs and approximate their similarities:

$$\text{sim}(a_i, a_j) \approx \sum_{k=1}^{k} \beta_k \cdot \text{sim}'(a_i, a_j)$$

Here, $sim(a_i, a_j)$ represents the approximated similarity between nodes a_i and a_j, $sim'(a_i, a_j)$ denotes the similarity calculated using the approximate methods, β_k are weight coefficients for the approximations, and k indicates the number of representative pairs or samples used. This approach helps in managing computational resources effectively while maintaining a reasonable approximation error within the tolerance ϵ. As shown in Fig. 4, the left graph shows the full network with all nodes, edges, and their actual weights. In the original graph, the similarity between node A and nodes B and C are 0.80 and 0.50, respectively. By setting an error tolerance ϵ and using representative node pair sampling and matrix decomposition methods, these similarities are approximated to 0.65 and 0.54. The process involves sampling a small number of representative node pairs, performing matrix decomposition to simplify calculations, and applying weight coefficients β_k to the approximated similarities. This approach reduces computational complexity while preserving the main structural characteristics of the graph.

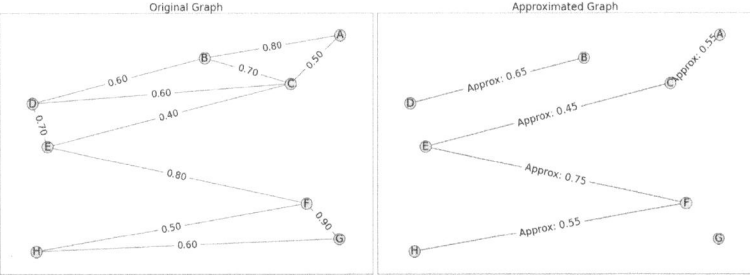

Fig. 4. Approximate calculation.

2.4   Unsupervised Community Discovery and Fraud Detection

After converting the heterogeneous graph to a homogeneous one and calculating account similarities, the Louvain [8] algorithm is applied for community detection. This method starts by assigning each node to its own community and then iteratively merges nodes into neighboring communities to improve the community structure. The process continues until no further improvements are possible. The result is a graph with communities of highly similar accounts, enabling more detailed analysis of account relationships and behaviors.

In our initial approach, we identified fraudulent groups by examining the number of nodes within community graphs G_c using the Louvain algorithm. This method effectively grouped accounts with similar behaviors into communities but occasionally misclassified normal accounts as isolated nodes due to their lack of group activities.

To address this issue, we adopted the graph embedding technique, graph2vec [7]. This technique allowed us to transform the high-dimensional structure of community graphs into lower-dimensional vector representations. By reducing the dimensionality, we could better capture the essential features of the graphs while minimizing noise and irrelevant details. Subsequently, we applied the KMeans clustering algorithm to these lower-dimensional embeddings. This approach enabled us to more accurately distinguish fraudsters from normal communities. Consequently, this adjustment significantly improved our classification accuracy, reducing the misclassification of normal accounts and enhancing the overall reliability of our fraud detection system.

As illustrated in Fig. 5, although the performance of all models decreased slightly when the number of nodes increased, the MLGE-AC-UFD model consistently outperformed with all comparisons in terms of accuracy, precision, and recall, verifying its effectiveness and advantages. By allowing a certain degree of error, the approximate computation method significantly reduces the computational complexity and resource consumption, enables the MLGE-AC-UFD model to process large-scale graph containing millions of nodes while maintaining high performance, which shows its great potential and broad prospects in practical applications.

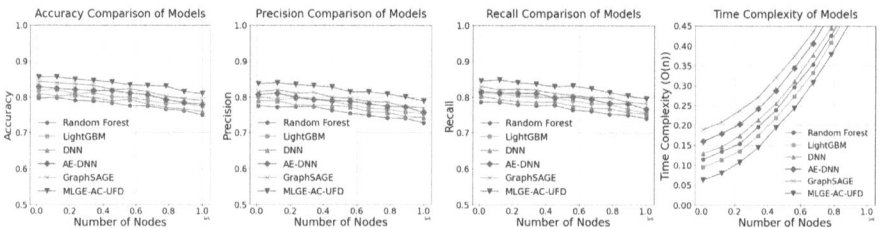

Fig. 5. Model comparison on different evaluation indicators.

3   Demonstration

The MLGE-AC-UFD system presents a friendly interface and easy operation. This demonstration uses the real account bulk login dataset provided by Beijing IQIYI Technology Co., Ltd. to showcase the interaction and operation of MLGE-AC-UFD. The fraud dataset is divided by date and uses a unique request_id to represent each login information. The dataset contains approximately 4 million records, with features such as user UID, DEVICE_ID, IP, DFP(device fingerprint), and other relevant fields that are crucial for detecting fraudulent activity. As shown in Fig. 6(a), users can freely set the date to select data for the corresponding time period. Meanwhile, Figs. 6(b) and 6(d) display the feature distribution, time, and geographic information distribution in the data through the visual interfa

Figure 6(b) illustrates feature aggregation, highlighting the most commonly utilized features in user login data. This enables the selection of relevant features

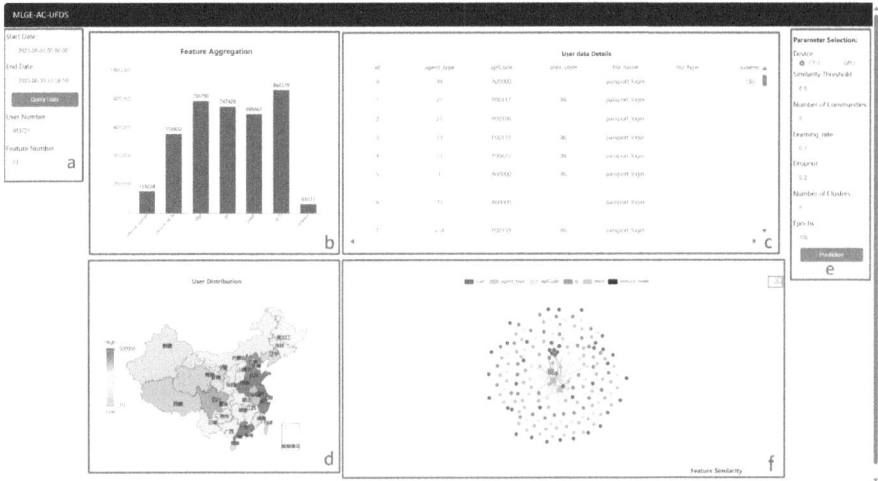

Fig. 6. Main panel.

for dynamic feature construction at the bottom of the figure. Then, Fig. 6(c) displays the raw data for the chosen date, allowing users to examine the specific types and formats of the data (the data shown is sampled from the original data for better visualization). Next, Fig. 6(d) presents the geographic distribution of the data for the selected date. The system uses this geographic information to automatically construct dynamic features by focusing on densely populated areas. Fig. 6(f) is divided into two sections. The first section provides an example

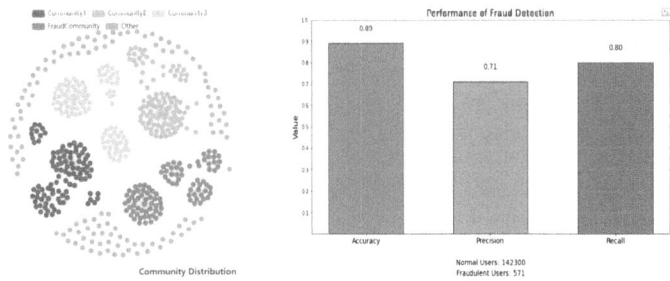

Fig. 7. Community discovery and performance of fraud detection.

of the feature graph, allowing users to visualize the connections and similarities between account nodes and feature nodes. This helps users better grasp the concept of layered graph embedding. The second section explains that, after setting the parameters in Fig. 6(e), users can click on the chart icon (framed in the upper right corner of Fig. 6(f) for community discovery and effect views. This enables users to intuitively observe the system's prediction results (as shown in Fig. 7).

4   Conclusion

In conclusion, MLGE-AC-UFD is an advanced unsupervised fraud detection system that leverages multi-level graph embedding, unsupervised learning, and approximate computation to enhance accuracy and efficiency. It overcomes the limitations of traditional methods by effectively detecting sophisticated fraud through low-dimensional mapping of high-dimensional data. Future work will focus on incorporating self-learning mechanisms to adapt in real time to new fraud patterns, reducing reliance on predefined models and increasing system adaptability.

Acknowledgement. The work was supported by National Natural Science Foundation of China (Grant No. 62002216).

References

1. Baesens, B., Höppner, S., Verdonck, T.: Data engineering for fraud detection. Decis. Support Syst. **150**, 113492 (2021)
2. Gao, Y., Wang, X., He, X., et al.: Rumor detection with self-supervised learning on texts and social graph. Front. Comp. Sci. **17**(4), 174611 (2023)
3. Tian, Y., Zhang, Y., Chen, F., et al.: FAI: a fraudulent account identification system. In: CAAI International Conference on Artificial Intelligence. Singapore: Springer Nature Singapore, pp. 253–257 (2023)
4. Wang, X., Wang, J., Wang, L., et al.: TCPMS-FCP: a traffic congestion pattern mining system based on spatio-temporal fuzzy co-location patterns. In: International Conference on Web Information Systems Engineering. Cham: Springer International Publishing, pp. 650–657 (2022)
5. Zhang, W., Zhang, Y., Huang, Y., et al.: GUFAD: a graph-based unsupervised fraud account detection framework. In: Proceedings of the 2023 4th International Conference on Machine Learning and Computer Application, pp. 401–406 (2023)
6. Li, S., Yang, J., Liang, G., et al.: SybilFlyover: heterogeneous graph-based fake account detection model on social networks. Knowl.-Based Syst. **258**, 110038 (2022)
7. Narayanan, A., Chandramohan, M., Venkatesan, R., et al.: graph2vec: Learning distributed representations of graphs. arxiv 2017. arxiv preprint arxiv:1707.05005
8. Blondel, V.D., Guillaume, J.L., Lambiotte, R., et al.: Fast unfolding of communities in large networks. J. Stat. Mech: Theory Exp. **2008**(10), P10008 (2008)
9. Hamilton, W., Ying, Z., Leskovec, J.: Inductive representation learning on large graphs. Adv. Neural Inf. Process. Syst. **30** (2017)
10. Liang, X., Yang, Z., Wang, B., et al.: Unveiling fake accounts at the time of registration: an unsupervised approach. In: Proceedings of the 27th ACM SIGKDD Conference on Knowledge Discovery & Data Mining, pp. 3240–3250 (2021)

SeCORE: Quantitative Security Assurance and Evaluation Platform

Alan Katt[✉] and Basel Katt

SeCore Information Security Limited, Buckinghamshire, England
{alan,basel}@secore.ai

Abstract. Providing structured and quantitative security assessment for IT/OT systems is challenging. Despite the various methods and standards that exist to provide assessment, however, most of them are qualitative, abstract, costly, and not connected to technical system and its tests and evaluations. To meet this challenges, we developed in previous work a methodology that enables quantitative and structured assessment of IT/OT systems. In this demonstration we present SeCORE, an innovative platform that has been recently developed to implement the aforementioned methodology and can provide various services that fill the existing security assurance and assessment gap and can be used in various application domains.

Keywords: Security Assurance · Security Assessment · Security Metric

1 Introduction

A structured quantitative system security assurance that supports multiple standards and takes into account threats and vulnerabilities in a given domain is challenging. To deal with this issues, various techniques and methods can be used, some of them are abstract and high level, like risk assessment, auditing and compliance evaluation, and others are technical like penetration testing. The problems of the abstract approaches are that they are qualitative, high level, costly, and are not connected to technical system, while the technical ones are disconnected from the general overview, qualitative, and subjective. To meet this challenges, we developed in previous work [12] [1–11] a methodology that enables quantitative and structured assessment of IT/OT systems. For more details about the methodology and the theoretical background, please visit our previous work. In this demonstration paper we present SeCORE, which is a technical platform that implements our methodology and enables clients from benefiting from this methodology.

SeCore provides, besides risk assessment and penetration testing, unique security evaluation and assurance services to its clients that goes beyond what the state of the art methods and techniques can offer and is based on the results of intensive research and innovation activities conducted before. SeCore helps

M. Barhamgi et al. (Eds.): WISE 2024, LNCS 15463, pp. 225–232, 2025.
https://doi.org/10.1007/978-981-96-1483-7_18

clients in various sectors, e.g., healthcare and automotive, to ensure an acceptable and required level of security for their systems and services.

This will be provided by (1) quantitatively and rigidly evaluate the security level of their systems and services, (2) improve the current security level by providing an optimal mitigation plan, which corresponds to requirements stem from internal security policies and risk assessments, as well as external compliance and guidelines requirements, and (3) follow up with the implemented mitigation to ensure the achievement of the target security level. It also can be used to compare quantitatively and comprehensively the security levels of various systems of the same type, and thus provide the needed rationale for decision making in procurement and tendering processes.

2   System Overview

The SeCORE platform consists of the following main components, as shown in Fig. 1:

- Projects: the main components that enables clients to create and manage their own security assurance projects.
- System profile: the **profile** is a core element of our methodology, which indicates the list of security requirements that play a role in assessing the level of security.
- System vulnerability profile: similar to the requirement-based profile, the system vulnerability profile lists the vulnerabilities that needs to be checked.
- OnGoing evaluation: is the component which stored and manages the current evaluation session being conducted.
- Library: the library consists of templates and profiles that can be used by project to conduct security assessment.
- System comparison: this component is responsible for comparing the evaluation results of two or more systems.

3   Main Features

The main features that SeCORE platform provides are

1. Library support: Easy and fast setup with a built-in library covering most relevant security frameworks, standards and guidelines
2. Design: User-friendly design and interactive dashboard to present and interact with a comprehensive set of quantitative assurance metrics
3. AI assisted Assurance: Integrate AI in different steps in the security assurance process
4. Security compliance made available: Multiple standards evaluated and assessed at the same time by one evaluation process
5. Benchmark: Compare the level of security among various IT/OT systems of the same type, or compare the level of security of one system over time
6. Optimal plan: List different mitigation plans and recommend the most optimal and cost efficient plan that maximizes the security improvement level with less possible cost

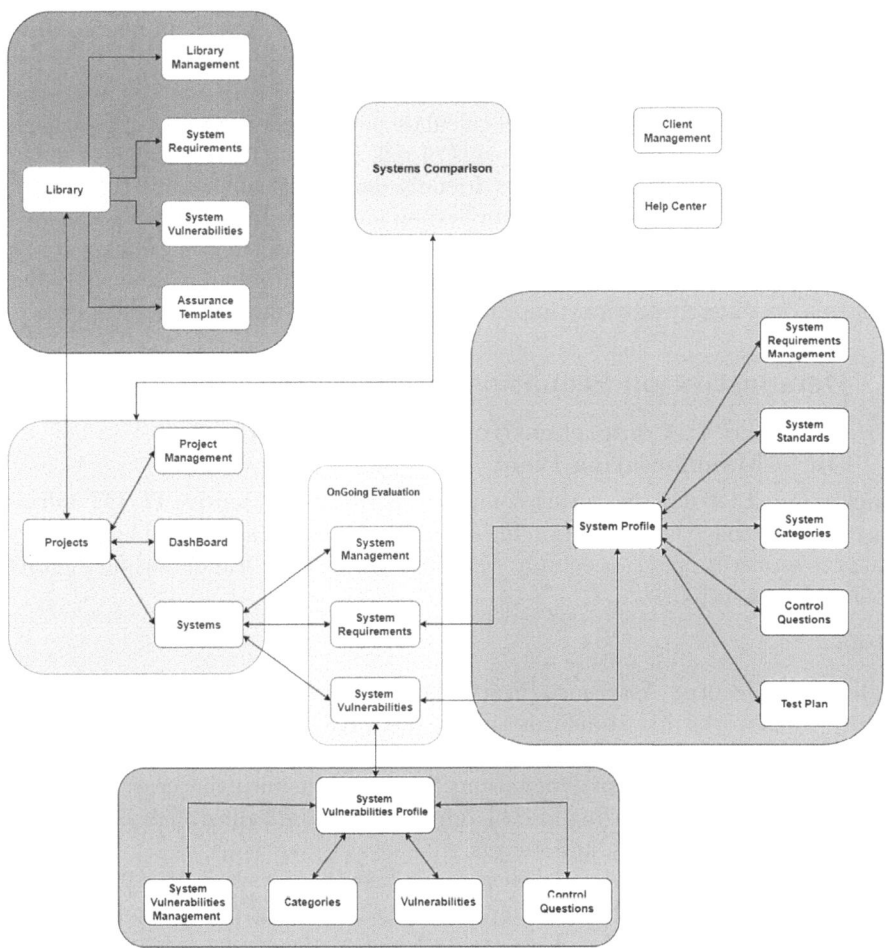

Fig. 1. SeCore System Overview

4   How it Works

The process that is built in the `SeCORE` platform for conducting security evaluation consists of 6 steps, which are

1. Specify a security assurance profile: Security assurance profiles are built based on security frameworks, standards, policies, or guidelines. Creating your assurance profiles is made available utilizing the easy-to-use built-in library.
2. Specify your system of evaluation: Select the system you want to evaluate and specify the main parts that are relevant for your assessment
3. Create a security assurance scheme and test plan: utilizing the built-in library, assurance schemes and test plans are created for your system or product.

Schemes and test plans connect high level criteria defined in the security assurance profiles with low level measurable metrics

4. Conduct evaluation: Execute the different tests listed in the test plan and report your results. SeCORE will calculate a comprehensive set of assessment metrics that reflects different aspects of risk and compliance of your system

5. Reporting: Interact with the user friendly dashboard to examine the quantitative score of security level of your system and the various metrics associated with it. The dashboard can also help you compare different systems.

6. Mitigation: SeCORE provides you with an optimized mitigation plan that aims at maximizing the security improvement while minimizing the costs

5   Demonstration Scenarios

5.1   Scenario 1: Comprehensive Security Assessment for a Manufacturing Plant

Background. A manufacturing company operates an extensive IT/OT infrastructure to manage its production lines, supply chain, and logistics. The company wants to ensure its systems comply with multiple security standards and identify potential vulnerabilities.

Steps

1. Specify a Security Assurance Profile: The security team selects relevant security frameworks and standards such as ISO/IEC 27001 and NIST Cybersecurity Framework from SeCORE's built-in library.

2. Specify Your System of Evaluation: The team defines the critical components of the manufacturing IT/OT infrastructure, including SCADA systems, PLCs, network devices, and servers.

3. Create a Security Assurance Scheme and Test Plan: Utilizing SeCORE's built-in library, the team generates an assurance scheme that links high-level criteria to measurable metrics. They create a test plan covering network security, access controls, data integrity, and incident response.

4. Conduct Evaluation: The team executes various tests, such as vulnerability scans, penetration tests, and compliance checks, and inputs the results into SeCORE. The platform calculates a comprehensive set of metrics that reflects the overall security posture and compliance levels.

5. Reporting: The team uses SeCORE's interactive dashboard to view a detailed security score and related metrics. They compare the current assessment against previous ones to track progress over time. The dashboard highlights areas of non-compliance and potential vulnerabilities.

6. Mitigation: SeCORE provides an optimized mitigation plan, recommending cost-effective measures to address identified vulnerabilities and compliance gaps. The plan prioritizes actions based on risk levels and budget constraints.

Outcome. The manufacturing company gains a clear, quantitative understanding of its security posture, ensures compliance with relevant standards, and implements a cost-effective plan to enhance its security defenses.

5.2 Scenario 2: Security Benchmarking for Smart City Infrastructure

Background. A city's administration is deploying a smart city infrastructure, including IoT devices, traffic management systems, and public Wi-Fi networks. The administration wants to benchmark the security of different systems and vendors to choose the most secure solutions.

Steps

1. Specify a Security Assurance Profile: The administration selects relevant frameworks and standards such as the IEC 62443 series for industrial automation and control systems and the CIS Controls from SeCORE's library.
2. Specify Your System of Evaluation: The team defines the components of the smart city infrastructure, including IoT sensors, communication networks, and control centers from different vendors.
3. Create a Security Assurance Scheme and Test Plan: Using the built-in library, the team creates an assurance scheme for each system. They develop test plans focusing on IoT security, data privacy, and network protection.
4. Conduct Evaluation: The team conducts tests on each system, performing risk assessments, security audits, and performance evaluations. They enter the results into SeCORE. The platform generates a set of metrics to quantify the security level of each system.
5. Reporting: The administration uses SeCORE's dashboard to compare the security scores of the different systems and vendors. They can visualize the strengths and weaknesses of each solution. The dashboard also provides insights into how each system meets the selected security standards.
6. Mitigation: SeCORE offers recommendations for improving the security of each system. It suggests mitigation plans tailored to the specific vulnerabilities and compliance issues identified during the assessment.

Outcome. The city's administration can make informed decisions when selecting vendors and deploying systems, ensuring that the chosen solutions provide robust security. They can also plan for ongoing improvements and compliance with security standards, contributing to the overall safety and resilience of the smart city infrastructure.

5.3 Scenario 3: Quantitative Cyber Risk Assessment for Policy Issuance

Background. An insurance company wants to offer cyber insurance policies to its clients but faces challenges in quantifying the cyber risk of potential policyholders. Using SeCORE, the insurance company aims to conduct precise risk assessments to determine appropriate coverage and premiums.

Steps

1. Specify a Security Assurance Profile: The insurance company's risk assessment team selects relevant security frameworks and standards, such as ISO/IEC 27005 (Information Security Risk Management) and NIST Cybersecurity Framework, from SeCORE's built-in library.
2. Specify Your System of Evaluation: The team identifies key systems and components of a client's IT infrastructure that are critical for the risk assessment, including servers, networks, databases, and endpoint devices.
3. Create a Security Assurance Scheme and Test Plan: Using SeCORE's library, the team develops an assurance scheme and a test plan focusing on areas such as vulnerability management, incident response, access controls, and data protection.
4. Conduct Evaluation: The client's IT team executes the tests listed in the test plan, such as vulnerability scans, compliance checks, and penetration tests, and reports the results back to SeCORE. SeCORE calculates a comprehensive set of metrics that reflect the client's overall cyber risk level, highlighting critical vulnerabilities and potential impacts.
5. Reporting: The insurance company uses SeCORE's interactive dashboard to review the client's security posture. They analyze the quantitative risk scores and associated metrics to understand the client's risk profile. The dashboard also provides a detailed comparison with industry benchmarks to place the client's risk in context.
6. Mitigation and Policy Issuance: SeCORE suggests an optimized mitigation plan for the client, recommending specific actions to reduce identified risks. Based on the assessment results and the mitigation plan, the insurance company determines the appropriate coverage and premium for the cyber insurance policy, ensuring it is aligned with the quantified risk.

Outcome. The insurance company can confidently issue cyber insurance policies with premiums based on a detailed and quantitative assessment of the client's cyber risk, leading to fair and accurate pricing.

6   Conclusion and Future Work

SeCore stands as a revolutionary security assessment methodology and platform, designed to address the multifaceted challenges faced by modern organizations in safeguarding their digital assets. Through its advanced features and comprehensive approach, SeCore empowers organizations to quantitatively assess and benchmark the security posture of their systems, ensuring compliance with multiple standards and optimizing their security investments.

SeCore's ability to simplify and accurately evaluate security, support compliance with various standards, assist in tender processes, and provide detailed roadmaps for security improvement makes it an invaluable tool for decision-makers. By leveraging built-in libraries, user-friendly design, AI-assisted assurance, and interactive dashboards, SeCore offers a robust and intuitive platform for continuous security enhancement and risk management. For insurance companies, SeCore fills a critical gap by providing a quantitative method to measure cyber risk, enabling more accurate policy issuance and portfolio management. In tender support assessments, SeCore aids in making informed, security-aware decisions by comparing the security levels of different systems and products.

Backed by years of intensive research and successful real-world applications, SeCore aims to increase confidence in the digital landscape, making high-quality security assessments accessible to organizations of all sizes and sectors. With a mission to provide the tools and knowledge necessary for achieving the highest security standards, SeCore is poised to become a world-leading actor in security assurance and evaluation, driving the global standard for digital security forward.

Future work can be conducted in various direction. First, qualitative methods can be integrated in this quantitative assessment in the following ways. (1) while SeCore is primarily focused on quantitative security metrics, qualitative aspects such as organizational policies, human factors, and subjective risk assessments (e.g., expert opinions, compliance culture, or historical incident response effectiveness) can provide valuable context and input for specifying the exact requirements for the target organization. Furthermore, qualitative methods can be used to assign weights to various security requirements. This can be achieved through surveys, questionnaires and interviews with various stakeholders. Finally, qualitative assessments can be used for contextualizing the quantitative findings. For example, after a quantitative assessment identifies vulnerabilities, SeCore could prompt users to provide expert judgment or further context, explaining potential business impacts or the likelihood of exploitation based on historical knowledge, threat actor profiles, or organizational priorities.

Second, the security assurance profiles, evaluations and scoring can be done dynamically, such that new evolving vulnerabilities and requirements are considered in an adaptive and continuous way.

References

1. Katt, B., Prasher, N.: Quantitative security assurance. In: Exploring Security in Software Architecture and Design. IGI Global, pp. 15–46 (2019)
2. Katt, B., Prasher, N.: Quantitative security assurance metrics: REST API case studies. In: Proceedings of the 12th European Conference on Software Architecture: Companion Proceedings, pp. 1–7 (2018)
3. Shukla, A., Katt, B., Yamin, M.M.: A quantitative framework for security assurance evaluation and selection of cloud services: a case study. In: International Journal of Information Security, vol. 22, no. 6, pp. 1621–1650 (2023)
4. Shukla, A., et al.: System security assurance: a systematic literature review. In: Computer Science Review, vol. 45, p. 100496 (2022)
5. Weldehawaryat, G.K., Katt, B.: Towards a quantitative approach for security assurance metrics. In: The 12th International Conference on Emerging Security Information (2018)
6. Wen, S.-F., Katt, B.: A metamodel for web application security evaluation. In: 34th Conference of Open Innovations Association (FRUCT). IEEE, vol. 2023, pp. 172–182 (2023)

7. Wen, S.-F., Katt, B.: A quantitative security evaluation and analysis model for web applications based on OWASP application security verification standard. In: Computers & Security, vol. 135, p. 103532 (2023)

8. Wen, S.F., Katt, B.: Exploring the role of assurance context in system security assurance evaluation: a conceptual model. In: Information & Computer Security, vol. 32, no. 2, pp. 159–178 (2024)

9. Wen, S.-F., Katt, B.: Ontology-based metrics computation for system security assurance evaluation. In: Journal of Applied Security Research, vol. 19, no. 2, pp. 230–275 (2024)

10. Quantitative Security Assurance Evaluation. In: European Symposium on Research in Computer Security. Springer International Publishing Cham, pp. 605–624 (2022)

11. Wen, S.-F., Shukla, A., Katt, B.: Developing security assurance metrics to support quantitative security assurance evaluation. In: Journal of Cybersecurity and Privacy, vol. 2, no. 3, pp. 587–605 (2022)

Developing Geospatial Web Applications Using Question Answering Engines, Knowledge Graphs and Linked Data Tools

Sergios-Anestis Kefalidis[1], Konstantinos Plas[1], George Stamoulis[1],
Dharmen Punjani[2], Pierre Maret[2], and Manolis Koubarakis[1,3(✉)]

[1] National and Kapodistrian University of Athens, Athens, Greece
{s.kefalidis,kplas,gstam,koubarak}@di.uoa.gr
[2] Laboratory Hubert Curien, Université Saint Monnet, Saint Etienne, France
pierre.maret@univ-st-etienne.fr
[3] Archimedes/Athena RC, Marousi, Greece

Abstract. We show how to develop geospatial web applications using the geospatial question answering engine GeoQA2, the geospatial knowledge graph YAGO2geo, the spatiotemporal RDF store Strabon and the Web-GIS tool Sextant. We demonstrate the combined functionality of these tools by developing PnyQA, a system for exploring data from the 2020 presidential election of the United States using natural language questions.

Keywords: geospatial data · question answering · knowledge graph · spatiotemporal RDF store · web visualization

1   Introduction

A *knowledge graph (KG)* is a directed graph where nodes represent entities (e.g., the football team Olympiacos Piraeus or the person José Luis Mendilibar) and edges represent relationships between entities (e.g., that Mendilibar is the coach of Olympiacos) or attributes of entities and their values (e.g., that Olympiacos was founded in 1925). KGs are typically encoded as sets of *triples* in the RDF data model and queried using the RDF query language SPARQL. Examples of well-known KGs are DBpedia [2], Wikidata [28] and YAGO [27].

A *geospatial KG* is a KG where nodes represent geographic features (e.g., the country Greece) and edges represent relationships between features (e.g., the capital of Greece is Athens or Bulgaria is north of Greece) or attributes of features and their values. Attributes can represent *thematic* information (e.g.,

This work has received funding from the project STELAR (101070122), under the European Union's Horizon Europe research and innovation programme. This work has also been partially supported by project MIS 5154714 of the National Recovery and Resilience Plan Greece 2.0 funded by the European Union under the NextGenerationEU Program.

Greece has population 10 million) or *geospatial* information (e.g., the geometry of Greece is the multipolygon "..." in the coordinate reference system WGS84). To the best of our knowledge, five geospatial KGs are available, each with a different emphasis (YAGO2 [9], YAGO2geo [12], WorldKG [6], KnowWhereGraph [11] and the KG of Böckling et al. [4]). Geospatial KGs can also be expressed as RDF triples and can be queried by SPARQL or more appropriately with GeoSPARQL.

YAGO2geo (https://yago2geo.di.uoa.gr/) is a KG that has been developed by our group by extending the KG YAGO2 [9] with detailed geospatial information about: (i) administrative divisions data of all countries using the GADM dataset (https://gadm.org/), (ii) official administrative divisions data for the countries of Greece, United Kingdom, Ireland and United States, and (ii) some categories of OpenStreetMap features (e.g., natural features like water bodies and man-made features such as cities). YAGO2 models geographic space by defining *geoentities* with point geometries consisting of latitude/longitude pairs by utilizing data from gazeteer GeoNames [9]. YAGO2geo contains all the geoentities of YAGO2 and extends them with more detailed geometries such as lines, polygons and multipolygons taken from the sources mentioned above. Finally, YAGO2geo includes *new* geoentities present in the above administrative datasets and OpenStreetMap that were not present in YAGO2. YAGO2geo currently contains 703 thousand polygons and 3.8 million lines.

Question answering (QA) over KGs is the research area which studies how to answer questions expressed in natural language over KGs (e.g., "Which team won the UEFA Conference League in the season 2023–2024?"). In this paper we are interested in using QA engines that answer *geospatial* questions (e.g., "Which countries border Greece to the north?" or "Which river flows through London?" or "What is the largest lake by area in Scotland?") over geospatial KGs.

GeoQA [25] and its revised version [26] was the first geospatial QA engine to be developed by our team (AI Team, https://ai.di.uoa.gr/). GeoQA can answer geospatial questions over the KG DBpedia interlinked with the parts of GADM and OpenStreetMap for the United Kingdom and Ireland.

GeoQA has recently been re-engineered into version 2 [24] and it is available as open source[1]. The new version targets the union of the KG YAGO2 and the geospatial KG YAGO2geo, and it improves GeoQA by having been optimized in various ways and being able to answer a greater variety of questions. In [14] our group presented the dataset GEOQUESTIONS1089 which contains 1089 triples of geospatial questions, their answers, and the respective SPARQL/GeoSPARQL queries. GEOQUESTIONS1089 is currently the largest geospatial QA benchmark and it is made freely available to the research community by our group[2]. GEOQUESTIONS1089 contains simple questions like "Which countries border Greece?", as well as, semantically complex questions that require a sophisticated understanding of both natural language and GeoSPARQL in order to be answered (e.g., "Is the total size of lakes in Greece larger than lake Loch Lomond in Scotland?". [14] uses GEOQUESTIONS1089 to evaluate the

---

[1] https://github.com/AI-team-UoA/GeoQA2.
[2] https://github.com/AI-team-UoA/GeoQuestions1089.

effectiveness of GeoQA2 and its competitor engine developed by Hamzei et al. [8] and shows that GeoQA2 performs better.

Using only YAGO2 and YAGO2geo as the data sources of GeoQA2 may limit its usefulness in applications. Even though answering geospatial questions over a geospatial KG is a reasonable use case, in the real world, geospatial data from a KG is typically used together with other kinds of thematic data to produce useful results. This has been our experience in many European projects such as TELEIOS and ExtremeEarth (https://earthanalytics.eu/) where we used geospatial KGs together with data extracted from satellite images to develop web applications e.g., for wildfire monitoring [17] and smart farming [1]. The KG that GeoQA2 targets (the union of YAGO2 and YAGO2geo, which will refer to as *YAGO2+geo* for conciseness) has a useful but limited amount of thematic and geospatial information. Therefore, to unlock the real potential of GeoQA2, one needs to infuse the KG with *application-specific thematic data* as well and, in this way, *a powerful tool for analyzing thematic data with a geospatial dimension is born.*

In this demo paper, we present PnyQA[3], a system that realizes the approach sketched in the previous paragraph and, using GeoQA2 as its core, enables a user to analyze the results of the 2020 U.S. Presidential Election on the county level, using natural language questions. Our demo is similar in spirit with the demo [19] which shows how to explore the geospatial KG KnowWhereGraph using faceted search. The distinguishing feature of our work is that of having natural language as a means of expressing user requests, a functionality which is complementary to the search functionalities of the demo of [19].

2   System Architecture

Figure 1 shows the architecture of PnyQA. In the following, we describe its main software components and overall functionality.

GeoQA2. GeoQA2 takes as input a question in English and the YAGO2+geo KG, and produces a set of answers. QA is performed by translating the input question into a SPARQL or GeoSPARQL query, which is subsequently executed over an RDF store (Strabon or other) endpoint that contains the target KGs.

We present the GeoQA2 pipeline which contains the following main components: dependency parse tree generator, concept identifier, instance identifier, geospatial relation identifier, property identifier, query generator and query transpiler. The functionality of these components will be discussed below using the question "Is the largest island in the United Kingdom larger than Crete by population?".

The *dependency parse tree generator* carries out part-of-speech (POS) tagging and generates a dependency parse tree for the input question using the Stanford CoreNLP toolkit [20].

---

[3] The name was inspired by the hill Pnyka, where the Ancient Athenians held their assemblies and public votes.

The *concept identifier* identifies the *types of features (concepts)* present in the input question (e.g., "island") and maps them to the corresponding classes of the target KG ontology (e.g., y2geoo:OSM_island). These concepts are identified and mapped to the ontology classes of YAGO2 and YAGO2geo using *n*-gram string similarity.

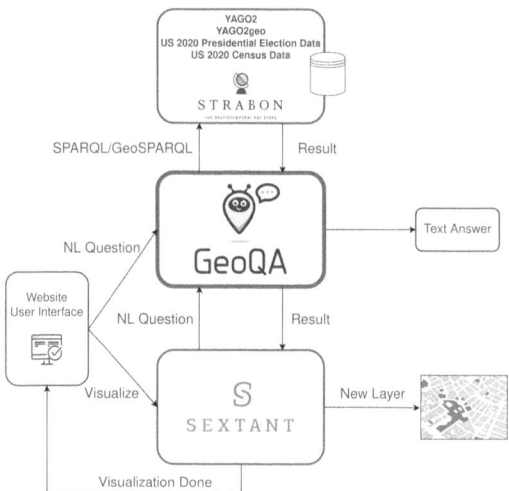

Fig. 1. The conceptual architecture of PnyQA

The *instance identifier* identifies the *features (instances)* present in the input question (e.g., "United Kingdom" and "Crete"). Then, these elements are mapped to KG resources (e.g., yago:United_Kingdom and yago:Crete) following a two-step approach. First, the TagMeDisambiguate tool [7] is used to identify and link named entities to Wikipedia pages. Subsequently, the KG entity that best matches the Wikipedia page is located in the KG. In [13] we have evaluated 12 tools with similar functionality on GEOQUESTIONS1089, including the well-known ones ELQ [18] and GENRE [5], and found that TagMeDisambiguate has the best accuracy for our task.

The *geospatial relation identifier* identifies the geospatial relations (e.g., "in") in the input question and maps them to the respective spatial function of the GeoSPARQL or stSPARQL vocabulary (e.g., geof:sfWithin) according to a mapping between geospatial relations and stSPARQL/GeoSPARQL functions provided by a dictionary.

The *property identifier* identifies *attributes of features or types of features* specified by the user in input questions and maps them to the corresponding properties in the target KG. For instance, for the example question the property "population" of type of feature "island" will be identified and mapped to property yago:hasPopulation. The attributes in the input question are identified based on the POS tags NN, JJ, NNP and NP generated by the dependency parsing process and the concepts/instances identified by earlier steps.

The *query generator* produces the GeoSPARQL query corresponding to the input question by using a set of query templates, heuristics and the annotated parse tree. For questions containing aggregates and superlatives (e.g., "largest"), the query generator constructs also the constituency parse tree of the input question and uses it to modify the templates to support these kinds of questions.

The *query transpiler* is responsible for rewriting the generated query to benefit from offline geospatial optimizations, speeding up the query in the process. The transpiler is also available as a standalone application on our team's GitHub page[4].

In addition to GeoQA2, our demo uses two linked geospatial data tools developed by our team (see [15] for a recent overview of our work in this area).

Strabon. Strabon is a state-of-the-art spatiotemporal RDF store that supports storing spatiotemporal RDF data and evaluating spatiotemporal queries on it, using the query languages stSPARQL [16] and the OGC standard GeoSPARQL. According to benchmarks Geographica 2 [10], Strabon is one of the most powerful, in terms of performance and functionality, geospatial RDF stores. Our system is built in a way that supports multiple RDF stores, Strabon could be replaced by any other RDF-store that is capable of executing GeoSPARQL and stSPARQL queries.

Sextant. Sextant is a Web-GIS tool that enables users to browse and visualize geospatial data in formats such as KML, GML, and TIFF files. It also facilitates communication with SPARQL endpoints, allowing the generation of map layers based on the results obtained from GeoSPARQL or stSPARQL queries. This feature allows Sextant to visualize the results of the GeoSPARQL queries generated by GeoQA as layers over the map. Sextant has been under continuous development at the National and Kapodistrian University of Athens since its initial publication [21]. It was and it still is the most functional tool in the literature for visualizing linked geospatial data.

System Architecture. The aforementioned components are combined to model the architecture shown in Fig. 1. The Website UI facilitates the input of questions in natural language by the user and offers the option to select the desired output format, which consists of textual answers or visual representation of the obtained results. The natural language questions are processed by a modified version of GeoQA which produces a SPARQL/GeoSPARL query that is executed in Strabon, which in turn returns the results to GeoQA. Results in text form are directly returned through GeoQA. If the user requests the visualization of the results, the query results are passed to Sextant to be visualized according to the user's choice. Sextant further provides the capability to visualize multiple questions simultaneously into a single map, as separate layers.

Availability. In addition to the individual components of our system which have already been released to the public, PnyQA is made publically available

---

as a service through an endpoint hosted on our group's server infrastructure at https://pnyqa.di.uoa.gr.

Performance Optimization. As we alluded to previously, our system makes use of offline optimizations to handle the large number of geometric calculations that it has to perform, which often leads to very long response times. For instance, checking whether a geometry is within a large administrative area with complex borders is computationally a very challenging task. Hence, to improve the time performance, we *pre-computed and materialized* certain relations between entities in the YAGO2geo knowledge graph that change infrequently.

During the evaluation of GeoQA2 [14], we observed that the topological geospatial relations "within", "crosses", "intersects", "touches", "overlaps", "covers" and "equals" require expensive computations, while "near", "north", "south", "east" and "west" are easily computed. Hence, we decided to materialize the above costly topological relations. The aforementioned transpiler rewrites queries that contain these topological relations from GeoSPARQL to SPARQL. This optimization is particularly beneficial, since, as shown in [14], it greatly boosts the performance of computationally demanding queries.

One of the major concerns related to materialization is the size of resulting knowledge, and the overhead that this can cause to its processing. Overall, the materialized version of YAGO2geo had 17,210,176 more triples, which in terms of system memory, amounts to about 3 GB and 10.21% increased in total size, but as shown in [14], it does not affect the performance of the question answering system negatively. The time required to calculate the implied geospatial relation was close to 5 days, which can be considered negligible, as it happens offline, and it is being repeated infrequently (only when the knowledge graph changes). The calculation of the implied relations was facilitated by utilizing a distributed implementation of the algorithm GIA.nt [22], implemented in the system DS-JedAI [23][5].

3   Presentation and Demonstration

In our presentation, we will introduce the architecture of our system and showcase its functionality with two scenarios about analyzing the results of the 2020 U.S. Presidential Election. These scenarios showcase the two different workflows of PnyQA. Our analysis will include a blend of geospatial and demographic information on the U.S. county level. To enable that, we use the following datasets:

– For geospatial information, we use the KG YAGO2+geo. As was discussed previously, YAGO2+geo is the primary target of GeoQA2.
– County-level election results for the 2020 U.S. Presidential Election[6], which are made available by the MIT Election Data and Science Lab. This dataset

---

[5] https://github.com/GiorgosMandi/DS-JedAI.
[6] https://dataverse.harvard.edu/dataset.xhtml?persistentId=doi:10.7910/DVN/VOQCHQ.

includes the vote count per political party for each county in the United States. Depending on the state that a county belongs to, it can also include information about the voting methods used, e.g., ballot voting.

– General population demographic data from the 2020 U.S. Census[7], as they are made available by the U.S. Census Bureau. This dataset contains, among other things, statistics about age, gender and race on a county level.

The two thematic datasets are linked to YAGO2+geo and loaded in an RDF store. Linking is done by executing a script that introduces information of the two thematic datasets as new RDF triples in YAGO2+geo. The resource files of GeoQA2 are updated accordingly to correspond to the new ontology.

The first workflow of the demonstration does not involve the visualization capabilities of Sextant since the results are in text form, and is the following:

1. The user inputs the question "Which counties south of Kansas were won by the Democratic Party?" and selects the text-answer workflow.
2. The question is passed to GeoQA2 which translates it to a GeoSPARQL query (Listing 1.1).
3. GeoQA2 requests the execution of the generated query from the RDF store endpoint, which in turn returns a list of counties.
4. The list of counties is displayed on the Web Interface.

```
PREFIX  geo:  <http://www.opengis.net/ont/geosparql#>
PREFIX  geof: <http://www.opengis.net/def/function/geosparql/>
PREFIX  rdf:  <http://www.w3.org/1999/02/22-rdf-syntax-ns#>
PREFIX  rdfs: <http://www.w3.org/2000/01/rdf-schema#>
PREFIX  yago: <http://yago-knowledge.org/resource/>
PREFIX  y2geoo: <http://kr.di.uoa.gr/yago2geo/ontology/>
PREFIX  strdf: <http://strdf.di.uoa.gr/ontology#>
PREFIX  usel: <http://kr.di.uoa.gr/us/election/ontology/>

SELECT ?county WHERE
{
    yago:Kansas geo:hasGeometry ?geom  .  ?geom  geo:asWKT ?mWKT  .
    ?county y2geoo:hasGADM_Description \"County\"  .
    ?county geo:hasGeometry ?geom2  .
    ?geom2 geo:asWKT ?cWKT  .
    FILTER (strdf:above(?mWKT, ?cWKT))  .
    ?county usel:hasElection_Data ?data  .
    ?data usel:hasDemocrat_Vote ?dv  .
    ?data usel:hasRepublican_Vote ?rv  .
    FILTER (?dv > ?rv)  .
}
```

Listing 1.1. GeoQA2-generated GeoSPARQL query

The second workflow of our demonstration utilizes all components of our system and the end result is a multi-layered map:

1. The user inputs the question "In which counties of Texas with less than 30,000 inhabitants did the Democratic Party get more votes than the Republican Party?" and selects the visualization/Sextant workflow.
2. Since the visualization workflow was selected, the input question is interpreted as a request for the creation of a layer on a map and the question is passed to GeoQA2.

---

[7] https://data.census.gov/table?g=010XX00US,$0500000&
   d=DEC+Demographic+Profile&tid=DECENNIALDP2020.DP1.

3. GeoQA2 translates the question to a GeoSPARQL query.
4. Identically to the first workflow, GeoQA2 requests the execution of the generated query from the RDF store endpoint, which in turn returns a list of county geometries.
5. GeoQA2 returns the results to Sextant which takes care of the visualization (shown in Fig. 2).

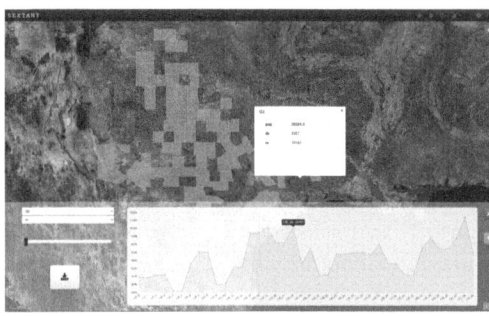

Fig. 2. Sextant map for workflow 2

At this point, it is important to note that the user can continue inputting questions, the results of which are shown as additional layers on the map. For example, continuing the previous example:

6. The user inputs a question, e.g., "In which counties of Georgia with less than 30,000 inhabitants did the Democratic Party get less votes than the Republican Party?". The Sextant workflow is already selected.
7. Steps (2) - (5) are repeated. The visualization is updated with a second layer.
8. When the user is finished, he presses the "Finish Visualization" button and the workflow is complete.

For our presentation, in addition to showcasing these two workflows, we will present and showcase the PnyQA pipeline on the aforementioned scenarios, along with the functionality of each pipeline component. Additionally, we will encourage WISE 2024 participants to ask their own questions in natural language to further illustrate our system and demonstrate the stages of our architecture through their remarks. For each question that we will demonstrate or that a participant will experiment with, we will also show what modern chatbots such as ChatGPT, Gemini and Claude answer when given the same question. Our experiments on August 15, 2024 for the above three questions show that Gemini and Claude cannot answer such questions (i.e., they have not been trained on relevant election data) while ChatGPT gives informative but incomplete answers. In [13] we have compared the accuracy of GeoQA2 with ChatGPT on the benchmark dataset GEOQUESTIONS1089 and found a similar situation. The problem of developing large language models for geospatial data is an open research problem where interesting research is carried out currently (see e.g., [3]).

4   Outlook

In current work we are developing GeoQA3, a more robust and effective QA engine which uses large language models in various stages of the question answering pipeline (e.g., the instance identifier and the query generator).

References

1. Appel, F. et al.: ExtremeEarth: managing water availability for crops using earth observation and machine learning. In: EDBT (2023)
2. Auer, S., Bizer, C., Kobilarov, G., Lehmann, J., Cyganiak, R., Ives, Z.G.: DBpedia: a nucleus for a web of open data. In: ISWC ASWC (2007)
3. Balsebre, P., Huang, W., Cong, G.: LAMP: A language model on the map. CoRR abs/2403.09059 (2024)
4. Böckling, M., Paulheim, H., Detzler, S.: A planet scale spatial-temporal knowledge graph based on OpenStreetMap and H3 grid. CoRR abs/2405.15375 (2024)
5. Cao, N.D., Izacard, G., Riedel, S., Petroni, F.: Autoregressive entity retrieval. In: 9th International Conference on Learning Representations, ICLR 2021, Virtual Event, Austria, 3-7 May 2021. OpenReview.net (2021). https://openreview.net/forum?id=5k8F6UU39V
6. Dsouza, A., Tempelmeier, N., Yu, R., Gottschalk, S., Demidova, E.: WorldKG: a world-scale geographic knowledge graph. In: CIKM (2021)
7. Ferragina, P., Scaiella, U.: TAGME: on-the-fly annotation of short text fragments (by wikipedia entities). In: CIKM (2010)
8. Hamzei, E., Tomko, M., Winter, S.: Translating place-related questions to GeoSPARQL queries. In: WWW (2022)
9. Hoffart, J., Suchanek, F.M., Berberich, K., Weikum, G.: YAGO2: A spatially and temporally enhanced knowledge base from wikipedia. Artif. Intell. **194** (2013)
10. Ioannidis, T., Garbis, G., Kyzirakos, K., Bereta, K., Koubarakis, M.: Evaluating geospatial RDF stores using the benchmark Geographica 2. J. Data Semant. **10**(3), 189–228 (2021). https://doi.org/10.1007/s13740-021-00118-x
11. Janowicz, K., et al.: Know, know where, KnowWhereGraph: a densely connected, cross-domain knowledge graph and geo-enrichment service stack for applications in environmental intelligence. In: AI Magazine, vol. 43, no. 1, pp. 30–39 (2022)
12. Karalis, N., Mandilaras, G.M., Koubarakis, M.: Extending the YAGO2 knowledge graph with precise geospatial knowledge. In: ISWC (2019)
13. Kefalidis, S., et al.: The question answering system GeoQA2 and a new benchmark for its evaluation. Int. J. Appl. Earth Obs. Geoinf. **134**, 104203 (2024). https://doi.org/10.1016/j.jag.2024.104203, https://www.sciencedirect.com/science/article/pii/S1569843224005594
14. Kefalidis, S., et al.: Benchmarking geospatial question answering engines using the dataset GeoQuestions1089. In: ISWC (2023)
15. Koubarakis, M. (ed.): Geospatial Data Science: A Hands-on Approach for Building Geospatial Applications Using Linked Data Technologies, vol. 51. Association for Computing Machinery, New York, NY, USA, 1 edn. (2023)
16. Koubarakis, M., Kyzirakos, K.: Modeling and querying metadata in the semantic sensor web: the model stRDF and the query language stSPARQL. In: ESWC (2010)
17. Kyzirakos, K. et al.: Wildfire monitoring using satellite images, ontologies and linked geospatial data. J. Web Semant. **24**, 18–26 (2014)

18. Li, B.Z., Min, S., Iyer, S., Mehdad, Y., Yih, W.: Efficient one-pass end-to-end entity linking for questions. In: Webber, B., Cohn, T., He, Y., Liu, Y. (eds.) Proceedings of the 2020 Conference on Empirical Methods in Natural Language Processing, EMNLP 2020, Online, 16-20 November 2020, pp. 6433–6441. Association for Computational Linguistics (2020). https://doi.org/10.18653/V1/2020.EMNLP-MAIN. 522

19. Liu, Z. et al.: Knowledge explorer: exploring the 12-billion-statement KnowWhere-Graph using faceted search (demo paper). In: SIGSPATIAL (2022)

20. Manning, C.D., Surdeanu, M., Bauer, J., Finkel, J.R., Bethard, S., McClosky, D.: The Stanford CoreNLP natural language processing toolkit. In: Proceedings of the 52nd Annual Meeting of the Association for Computational Linguistics, ACL 2014, 22-27 June 2014, Baltimore, MD, USA, System Demonstrations, pp. 55–60. The Association for Computer Linguistics (2014). https://doi.org/10.3115/V1/P14-5010

21. Nikolaou, C., et al.: Sextant: visualizing time-evolving linked geospatial data. J. Web Semant. **35**, 35–52 (2015)

22. Papadakis, G., Mandilaras, G.M., Mamoulis, N., Koubarakis, M.: Progressive, holistic geospatial interlinking. ACM / IW3C2 (2021)

23. Papamichalopoulos, M., Papadakis, G., Mandilaras, G., Siampou, M.D., Mamoulis, N., Koubarakis, M.: Three-dimensional geospatial interlinking with jedai-spatial (2022)

24. Punjani, D., Kefalidis, S., Plas, K., Tsalapati, E., Koubarakis, M., Maret, P.: The question answering system GeoQA2. In: GeoKG & GeoAI (2023)

25. Punjani, D. et al.: Template-based question answering over linked geospatial data. In: Proceedings of the 12th Workshop on Geographic Information Retrieval (2018)

26. Punjani, D. et al.: Template-based question answering over linked geospatial data. CoRR abs/2007.07060 (2020)

27. Suchanek, F.M., Kasneci, G., Weikum, G.: YAGO: a core of semantic knowledge. In: WWW (2007)

28. Vrandecic, D., Krötzsch, M.: Wikidata: a free collaborative knowledgebase. Commun. ACM **57**(10), 78–85 (2014)

A Visual Query Builder for DBpedia

Dimitrios Soumis, George Stamoulis[(✉)], and Manolis Koubarakis

National and Kapodistrian University of Athens, Athens, Greece
{cs2200018,gstam,koubarak}@di.uoa.gr

Abstract. In the last years we have seen a huge effort to extract structured content from the information created in various Wikimedia projects. This wealth of information is well acquired with the use of Linked Data. One such example is DBpedia, that allows to perform complex searches on Wikipedia datasets as well as linking them to data from other sources. While the data are available publicly, knowledge of SPARQL and ontologies is mandatory to search and analyse them. This paper presents an application for android devices, aimed at familiarizing the average user to generate successful searches and extract desired data from DBpedia, without pre-existing knowledge in semantic web technologies.

Keywords: linked data · DBpedia · visual query builder · knowledge graph · Android

1 Introduction

As the world moves further into the digital age, smartphones are becoming the primary access points to media and information for both advanced and novice users [3]. People need fast and abundant results from simple searches in the shortest possible time using quick access systems without having to use a computer to satisfy their needs and without prior sophisticated background in order to use a system [2]. In this paper we present an Android application that enables non-experts to create SPARQL queries over DBpedia [1], for simplified information retrieval. The DBpedia Visualizer offers a graphical user interface and key word search over DBpedia resources, that allows the creation of a visual graph based on user feedback and automatically translates it to a SPARQL query in order to retrieve the information for the user.

2 Related Work

Traditional SPARQL querying can be challenging for users unfamiliar with the syntax or structure of RDF data. To address this, RDF Explorer [4] offers a visual interface that allows users to construct queries intuitively, lowering the barrier for querying RDF data. The tool aims to make the Semantic Web more accessible to a broader range of users, particularly those without extensive technical expertise. RDF Explorer enables users to query and retrieve specific information from RDF datasets using SPARQL, a query language tailored for this purpose. This makes it ideal for extracting insights from interconnected data sources, such as knowledge graphs or web-based linked data repositories. This is achieved by using a visual query language in which users can express queries on graphs through simple interactions. The proposed visual query language is formulated in terms of a visual query graph. Visual query graphs are designed as a visual metaphor for the basic SPARQL graph patterns, where the translation is therefore mostly direct and natural. This visual approach enables users to understand the structure of their data and build complex queries without needing to write SPARQL code manually. RDF Explorer also incorporates features that guide users through the process of query formulation, such as auto-completion, which further enhances its usability. This makes it a powerful tool for both novice and experienced users working with linked data and knowledge graphs.

3   The DBpedia Visualizer

DBpedia Visualizer is an Android application designed to support non-expert users in the creation and execution of queries over DBpedia utilizing a graphical interface. The system is based on the tool RDF Explorer, but runs as a native Android application to make it more accessible to the broaded audience, that could lead to more widespread adoption of RDF-based data analysis in various fields, including data science, artificial intelligence, and digital humanities.

The application utilizes the public SPARQL endpoint of DBpedia[1] to extract information through HTTP requests, based on user input. The user first provides a search term used to pose an HTTP request to the DBpedia lookup service[2]. The results are presented as a list to the user to select an entity of interest as a starting point. User can expand on the properties of the entity by tapping on it and select a value. Both the property and its value are stored in application memory and drawn on the interface. The property is drawn in the box of the original entity and the value in a new one. The connection between them is represented with by an arrow. In order to introduce variables, users can double-tap on any number of entities to convert them into variables.

All HTTP requests are implemented with OkHttp client and are used to pose to DBpedia the automatically generated SPARQL queries based on the graph the user has constructed. Results from DBpedia are retrieved in XML and JSON format and are integrated in the application using a table format.

4   Demonstration

In this section we demonstrate how to use the application in a scenario to retrieve notable ideas of people that influenced *Albert Einstein*.

---

[1] http://dbpedia.org/sparql.
[2] https://www.dbpedia.org/resources/lookup/.

The user begins by entering a search term into the designated field within the application. The application then automatically generates an HTTP request directed to the DBpedia Lookup service. The DBpedia Lookup Service is particularly useful for resolving entities, meaning it helps users find resources within the DBpedia database by offering keyword-based search. This service can be used to look up entities, terms and concepts based on the input, utilizing a semantic search mechanism. The service responds with search results in XML format, which the application displays in a list format using a ListView, ensuring a user-friendly presentation. The user selects an entity from the list, and this selection is saved in the application's memory and displayed in the initial user interface. In our demonstration we provide the name of the physicist *Albert Einstein* and select it in the results to create the starting node of our graph as shown in Fig. 1.

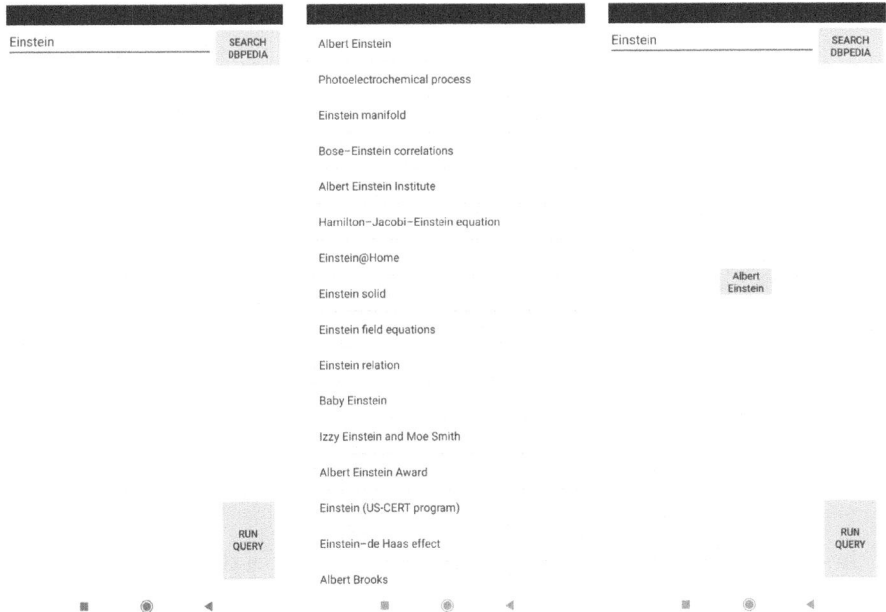

Fig. 1. Search DBpedia for Albert Einstein

The user then performs a long-click on the desired entity displayed in the interface. The application detects this long-click, generates a corresponding SPARQL query, and sends an HTTP request to the DBpedia API to retrieve the entity's properties and values. The results are returned in XML format and are presented by the application in an expandable list format. The user can then expand any property by tapping on it and select a value. Both the selected property and value are stored in the application's memory and displayed, with the property linked to the original entity and the value depicted as an independent entity. The connection between them is represented by an arrow, visually connecting the original entity to its value. In our scenario, we can view all the properties of the resource *Albert Einstein* and select the property *influencedBy* to choose one of the values to create a new node in the application. Now using the new node, we can view again its properties and select the *noteableIdea* attribute and one of the values as shown in Fig. 2.

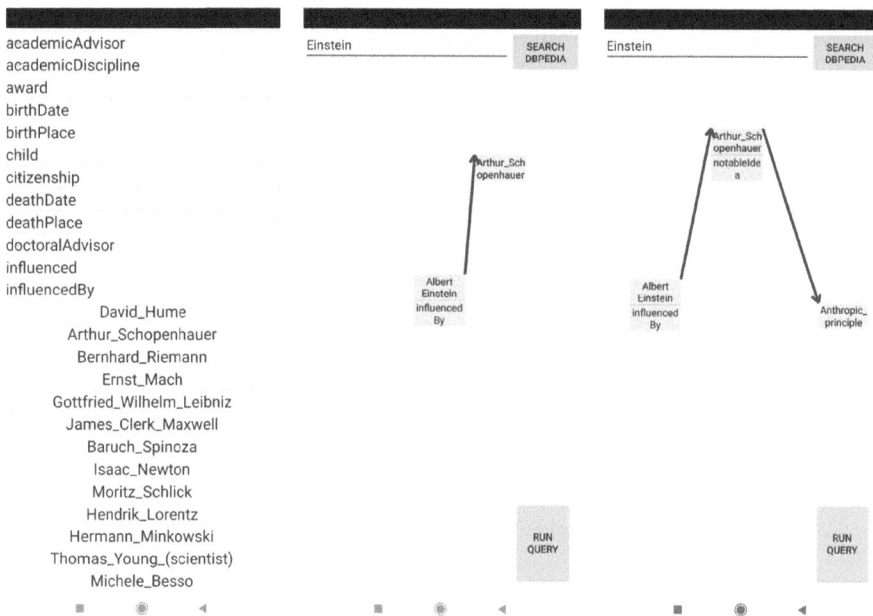

Fig. 2. Select properties and values to build our graph

In addition, the user can rearrange entities to create a desired visual layout and repeat the process as many times as needed. The user can also double-click on entities to turn them into variables, which will be used in the final SPARQL query. The application detects this action, replaces the entity text with a variable name like *?varX* and updates the diagram, with X representing a numbered sequence of variables. Utilizing this feature, we can tap on the nodes of the influencer and his notable idea to change them into variables. After designing the diagram, the user clicks the *Run Query* button, and the application automatically formats the final SPARQL query based on the diagram as shown in Fig. 3. The query is sent to the DBpedia API, and the application receives the results in XML format, displaying the SPARQL query and the retrieved variable values in a table for clear and user-friendly presentation.

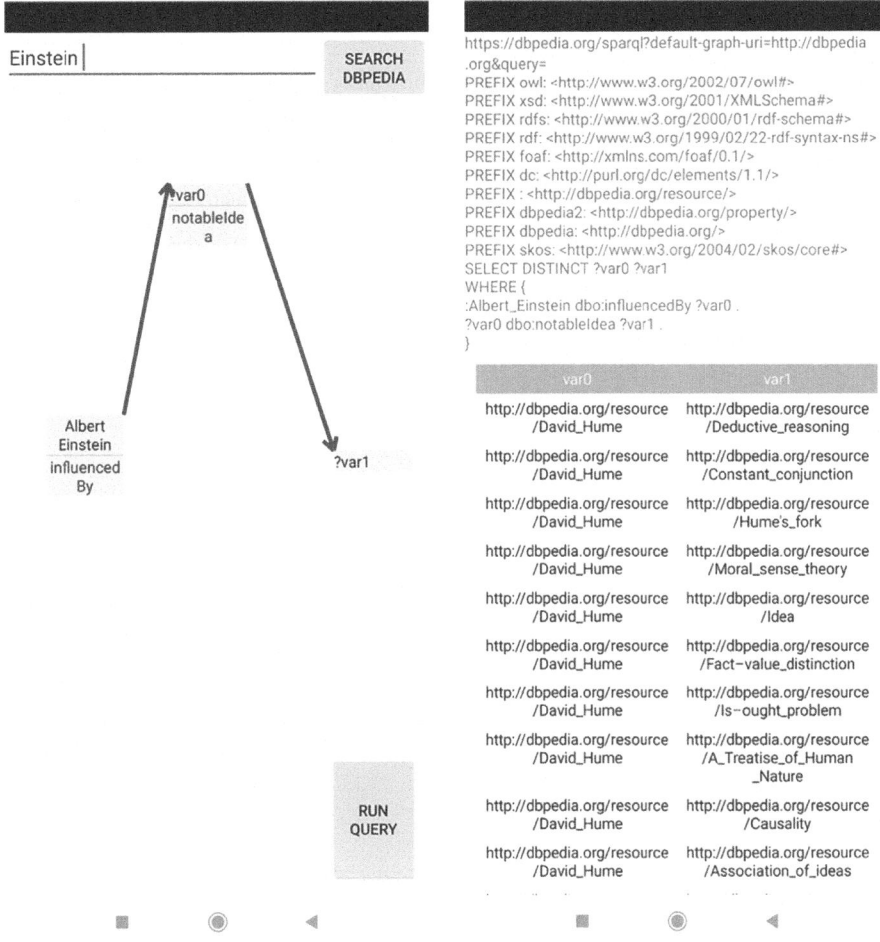

Fig. 3. Change nodes to variables and run the query

5   Conclusion and Future Work

In this paper we demonstrated the DBpedia Visualizer, that offers a graphical interface for non-expert users to build SPARQL searches for streamlined information retrieval over DBpedia. For future work we plan to enhance both the functionality and interface design of the application. We will add an autocomplete service to the search field based on the available ontology of DBpedia. Since search results contain URIs we would like to offer access to these resources from DBpedia by redirecting to the device's browser. Furthermore, we plan to support more SPARQL functionality such as filters and aggregates to enable the creation of more complex search queries.

References

1. DBpedia: About DBpedia. https://www.dbpedia.org/about/
2. Hoelzle, U.: The google gospel of speed. Think with Google. https://www.thinkwithgoogle.com/future-of-marketing/digital-transformation/the-google-gospel-of-speed-urs-hoelzle/ (2012)
3. PECB: How smartphones are 'killing' PCs. https://insights.pecb.com/smartphones-killing-pcs/ (2018)
4. Vargas, H., Buil-Aranda, C., Hogan, A., López, C.: RDF explorer: a visual SPARQL query builder. In: Ghidini, C., et al. (eds.) ISWC 2019. LNCS, vol. 11778, pp. 647–663. Springer, Cham (2019). https://doi.org/10.1007/978-3-030-30793-6_37

FL-PPELA: Partial Parameter Enhancement and Local Adaptive Aggregation for Personalized Federated Learning

Jinkun Pan[1,2], Xiaoyan Liang[1,2(✉)], and Ruizhong Du[1,2]

[1] School of Cyber Security and Computer, Hebei University, Hebei 070012, China
[2] Key Lab on High Trusted Information System of Hebei Province, Hebei 070012, China
liangxiaoyan@hbu.edu.cn

Abstract. A key challenge in federated learning is statistical heterogeneity, which affects the generalization ability of the global model on each client. To address this issue, we propose a method called Partial Parameter Enhancement and Local Adaptive Aggregation for Personalized Federated Learning (FL-PPELA). The key component of FL-PPELA is the adaptive local aggregation module PPELA. In the PPELA, partial parameters in the global model are enhanced in the direction beneficial to the local client. Next, adaptive aggregation of the local model and the global model before local training. Finally, build different models for each client's local dataset. To evaluate the effectiveness of FL-PPELA, we conducted experiments on four real datasets. FL-PPELA demonstrated superior test accuracy compared to 12 advanced baseline methods.

Keywords: Federated learning · Statistical heterogeneity · Adaptive aggregation

1 Introduction

Federated Learning (FL) [11] is an innovative machine learning method that allows multiple clients to collaboratively train a shared model without the need to directly exchange data, thus protecting their individual data privacy. A major challenge is statistical heterogeneity, which includes the non-independent and identically distributed (Non-IID) and imbalance of client data.

To address the issues mentioned above, Personalized Federated Learning (PFL) has recently been proposed, allowing each client to train a personalized model adapted to their own data. Research on aggregation methods for personalized federated learning can be divided into three categories: (1) Each client builds a local personalized model based on their own data while referencing the global model, such as FedRep [2] and Per-FedAvg [3]. (2) Methods that learn

M. Barhamgi et al. (Eds.): WISE 2024, LNCS 15463, pp. 249–256, 2025.
https://doi.org/10.1007/978-981-96-1483-7_21

additional personalized models, they establish a central point model that all clients agree on, such as pFedMe [13] and Ditto [7]. (3) The method of using personalized aggregation to learn local models, such as FedAMP [5], FedPHP [9], APPLE [10], PartialFed [12], FedALA [15] and FedFomo [16].

The first and second type of Personalized Federated Learning (PFL) methods use all information from the global model, including both beneficial and detrimental information.

The third type of Personalized Federated Learning (PFL) aggregation method still has issues. APPLE and FedFomo involve downloading models from other clients and then performing personalized aggregation based on the characteristics of their own datasets. The methods require downloading models from other clients, which entails a risk of privacy leakage during the transmission of multiple client models. Additionally, the mutual loading of models between clients results in additional communication costs. Methods like PartialFed and FedALA select some parameters of the global model through local adaptive aggregation, but they do not reinforce certain effective parameters. This results in local models being unable to fully learn effective information from the global model.

To precisely capture the effective information from the global model, we propose a personalized federated learning method called Partial Parameter Enhancement and Local Adaptive Aggregation for Personalized Federated Learning (FL-PPELA). FL-PPELA creates a specialized model for each client and only requires downloading the global model. Before starting to train the local model, it first enhances certain parameters of the global model in a way that benefits the client model, and then selects parameters from the global model to adjust the local model parameters. The entire initial local adaptive aggregation process is shown in Fig. 1. In summary, our contributions are as follows:

- We proposed a new personalized federated learning method, FL-PPELA, which enhances certain parameters of the global model in a way that benefits the client model, and then selects some parameters from the global model to adjust the local model parameters.
- We conducted experiments on four real datasets to verify the effectiveness of FL-PPELA. Its test accuracy surpasses that of 12 methods.
- We found that the PPELA module is highly compatible and can be integrated with many advanced federated learning methods.

2   Related Work

Recently, addressing data heterogeneity through personalized federated learning has garnered widespread attention, and many advanced methods have been proposed. Per-FedAvg [3] obtains an initial model through aggregation with the global model, and then a few rounds of training on each client's data using this initial model can yield a good local model. FedRep [2] posits that there is more generic information in the lower layers of the model, and therefore divides

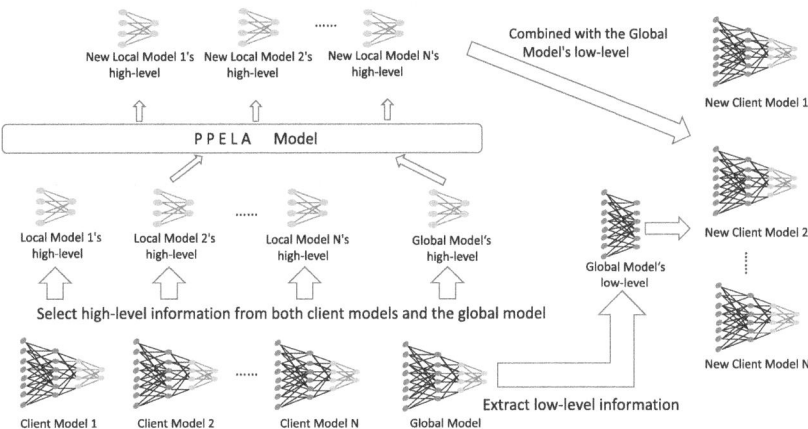

Fig. 1. Before the local model training begins, the initial local adaptive aggregation process is as follows. First, the high-level information of client i's local model and the high-level information of the downloaded global model are sent to the PPELA module. Next, through the PPELA module, each client's high-level parameters are combined with the global model's effective high-level parameters to create new localized high-level model parameters. Finally, the high-level of the local model is combined with the low-level of the global model to obtain a new local model.

the model into a base and a head. The parameters in the base are generated through aggregation of the global and local models, while the head is updated using parameters from the local model itself. Ditto and PartialFed [12] control the degree of personalization of local models by downloading global and local models and performing personalized aggregation. FedAMP [5] employs a unique adaptive grouping learning mechanism that enables clients with similar data distributions to collaborate more effectively and allows for personalized customization of each client's model. FedPHP [9] utilizes moving averages on each client to preserve historical personalized models. In the next round of personalization, it aggregates personalized local models with the global model. FedFomo [16] updates local models by assessing the similarity of other clients' models and aggregating with those other client models. APPLE [10] adaptively understands how much each client benefits from the models of other clients and enhances the localized model through models from other clients.

3   Methodology

We propose the PFL method with an PPELA module (FL-PPELA), which aggregates the global and local models element-wise and enhances the effective information in the global model to reasonably personalize the local models. The learning process within PPELA is demonstrated in Fig. 2.

In the traditional FedAvg, in the t-th round, the server aggregates all clients' models and sends the previous round's global model Θ^{t-1} to all clients. Model

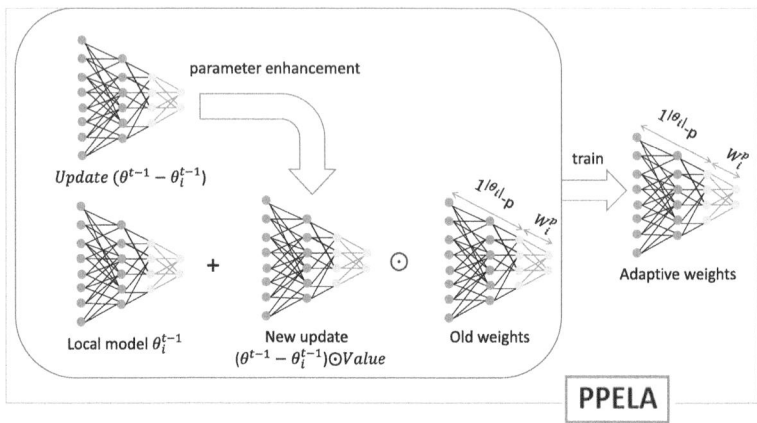

Fig. 2. The figure illustrates the learning process of PPELA. The "Update" is the difference between the global model and the local model.

Θ^{t-1} will overwrite the local model $\hat{\Theta}_i^t$, as the initial model locally. This process may involve parameters that could compromise the local models. In FL-PPELA, local models are initialized according to the following formula:

$$\hat{\Theta}_i^t := (\Theta^{t-1} - \Theta_i^{t-1}) \odot W_i + \Theta_i^{t-1}, \tag{1}$$

where the term $(\Theta^{t-1} - \Theta_i^{t-1})$ is the "update". $\odot$ is a Hadamard product. The parameter sizes of W_i and Θ_i are consistent and the size of each parameter w in W_i satisfies condition $w \in [0,1]$, $\forall w \in W_i$.

It is worth noting that if a parameter is updated in the same direction in both the global and local models, meaning the parameter is updated in the same direction across different local models, it indicates that the parameter reflects a common feature. We enhance these parameters by defining a Value, where the Value is:

$$\text{Value} = \begin{cases} 0, & \text{if } (\bar{\theta}^{t-1} - \bar{\theta}_i^{t-1})(\bar{\theta}_i^{t-1} - \bar{\theta}_i^{t-2}) > 0 \\ 1, & \text{else,} \end{cases} \tag{2}$$

where $\bar{\theta}^{t-1}, \bar{\theta}_i^{t-1}, \bar{\theta}_i^{t-2}$ represents a specific parameter within the model. When a parameter shows consistency in the update direction between the global model and the local model, it can be considered a universal parameter. Before training the weight W_i, modify Eq. 3 according to the Value:

$$\hat{\Theta}_i^t := Value \odot (\Theta^{t-1} - \Theta_i^{t-1}) \odot W_i + \Theta_i^{t-1}, \tag{3}$$

when a parameter is updated in the same direction in both the local and global models, if the model obtained from Eq. 3 is directly used for weight training, the gradient of weight updates will slow down due to the increase in $(\bar{\theta}^{t-1} - \bar{\theta}_i^{t-1})$.

This is because when the gradient update direction has already been partially updated, further updates to the gradient will slow down, making it difficult to effectively utilize these valuable parameters.

The lower layers of the model contain more general information. By directly using the lower layers of the global model, the advantage of a larger amount of data can be leveraged. The PPELA module can be used only in the higher layers, thereby saving computational resources. At this point, the local model is:

$$\hat{\Theta}_i^t := \Theta_i^{t-1}(\Theta^{t-1} - \Theta_i^{t-1}) \odot [1^{|\Theta_i|-p}, W_i^p] + \Theta_i^{t-1}, \tag{4}$$

where $1^{|\Theta_i|-p}$ is the lower layers of the model, and W_i^p is the upper layers of the model, $|\Theta_i|$ is the total number of the model, p denotes the last p layers of the model. The PPELA module is applied only to the last p layers of the model, and the initial value of each parameter within the weight W_i^p is set to 1.

In each iteration, learning of W_i^p is based on the previous values of W_i^p. During iteration t, we randomly sample d% of the data from the local dataset and apply the PPELA module to the last p layers of the model to obtain new weights that are more suitable for local aggregation. We define this subset as $D_i^{d,t}$. Client i trains W_i^p through the gradient-based learning method:

$$W_i^p \leftarrow W_i^p - \eta \nabla_{W_i^p} \mathcal{L}(\Theta^{t-1}, D_i^{d,t}, \hat{\Theta}_i^t, Value), \tag{5}$$

where η is the learning rate for weight training. In the phase of parameter training, other trainable parameters within the PPELA module remain unchanged.

4   Experiments

4.1   Experimental Setup

In this section, we first compare FL-PPELA with 12 advanced federated learning methods: FedAvg [11], FedProx [8], Per-FedAvg [3], FedALA [15], FedRep [2], pFedMe [13], Ditto [7], FedAMP [5], FedPHP [9], FedFomo [16], APPLE [10], and PartialFed [12]. We conducted related experiments on four real-world computer vision datasets.

For the real-world datasets, we selected FashionMNIST [14], Cifar10 [6], Cifar100 [6], and Tiny-ImageNet [1].

For model usage, all four real datasets employed a 4-layer CNN [11]. Additionally, to assess the effectiveness of FL-PPELA on larger models, an experiment using ResNet-18 [4] on Tiny-ImageNet was included and labeled as Tiny*. Throughout the experiments, the local learning rate $\alpha = 0.005$ for the 4-layer CNN, $\alpha = 0.1$ for ResNet-18. The batch size B = 10, and the local model training epochs is 1. All tasks were run for up to 2000 iterations (2000 iterations were sufficient to allow all tasks to converge). We had 20 clients, with a default setting of $\rho = 1$, meaning all clients participated in the aggregation. When training the weights, we Randomly select 80% (d=80) of the local data as the training set.

To save computational resources, we apply the PPELA module only to the last layer (p=1).

For simulating heterogeneous settings, we use a realistic heterogeneous setup controlled by a Dirichlet distribution, denoted as $Dir(\beta)$. The smaller the β, the more heterogeneous the setting. We set the default heterogeneous configuration to $\beta = 0.1$.

For evaluation, we utilize the same metrics as pFedMe. The test set contains 25% of the local data, and the training set contains 75% of the local data.

Table 1. In the heterogeneous setting, the test accuracy of different methods across real datasets.

Settings	Practical heterogeneous setting				
Methods	FashionMNIST	Cifar10	Cifar100	TINY	TINY*
FedAvg	85.87 ± 0.17	59.20 ± 0.50	31.82 ± 0.43	19.49 ± 0.21	19.44 ± 0.12
FedProx	85.66 ± 0.60	59.24 ± 0.40	31.97 ± 0.40	19.38 ± 0.21	19.25 ± 0.23
Per-FedAvg	95.11 ± 0.11	87.76 ± 0.16	44.25 ± 0.35	25.10 ± 0.10	21.85 ± 0.55
FedRep	97.58 ± 0.03	90.39 ± 0.23	52.36 ± 0.34	37.27 ± 0.20	39.95 ± 0.21
FedALA	97.65 ± 0.02	90.66 ± 0.03	55.93 ± 0.03	40.57 ± 0.02	41.96 ± 0.06
pFedMe	97.22 ± 0.08	88.10 ± 0.32	47.33 ± 0.46	26.95 ± 0.19	33.46 ± 0.31
Ditto	97.47 ± 0.04	90.59 ± 0.01	52.87 ± 0.64	32.15 ± 0.04	35.92 ± 0.43
FedAMP	97.35 ± 0.04	88.72 ± 0.18	47.71 ± 0.49	27.97 ± 0.11	29.13 ± 0.15
FedPHP	97.42 ± 0.03	88.94 ± 0.02	50.54 ± 0.16	35.68 ± 3.26	29.92 ± 0.51
FedFomo	97.22 ± 0.02	88.08 ± 0.02	45.37 ± 0.45	26.35 ± 0.22	26.83 ± 0.11
APPLE	97.08 ± 0.07	89.39 ± 0.13	53.25 ± 0.18	35.06 ± 0.45	39.95 ± 0.49
PartialFed	97.46 ± 0.05	87.40 ± 0.08	48.79 ± 0.20	35.25 ± 0.16	37.48 ± 0.16
FL-PPELA	$\mathbf{97.81 \pm 0.03}$	$\mathbf{90.77 \pm 0.03}$	$\mathbf{56.14 \pm 0.03}$	$\mathbf{40.72 \pm 0.02}$	$\mathbf{42.11 \pm 0.04}$

4.2   Performance Comparison and Analysis

Table 1 shows the accuracy of different datasets under different methods, which will be analyzed according to different method categories.

In traditional federated learning methods, such as FedAvg and FedProx, they often face challenges when dealing with heterogeneous environments. For example, in a heterogeneous environment, as seen with Cifar100, the accuracies of FedAvg and FedProx are only 31.82% and 31.97%, respectively.

For PFL methods in Category (1). It can be observed that personalized federated learning shows significant improvement over traditional approaches that only build a global model in heterogeneous environments.

For PFL methods in Category (2). Both pFedMe and Ditto establish additional personalized models. These two methods cannot further improve accuracy because they use all the parameter information from other models.

For PFL methods in Category (3). FedAMP, FedFomo, APPLE, and PartialFed lack clarity in selecting global model parameters and do not perform element-wise selection. This can potentially introduce unnecessary information from the global model into the local models. While FedALA does filter global parameters at the element level, it does not further enhance the necessary global parameters, leading to a waste of some of the effective information in the global parameters. FL-PPELA not only sufficiently modifies and enhances the necessary parameters in the global model but also makes parameterized modifications to the local models without incorporating all the parameters of the global model.

4.3   The Compatibility of PPELA

In federated learning (FL), the PPELA module performs local personalized aggregation using the global model before training, without affecting other steps. Therefore, the PPELA module can be applied to most existing FL methods. We have implemented the PPELA module in four methods FedAvg, FedProx, FedPHP, and Ditto and evaluated its compatibility across four real datasets. We incorporated the PPELA module under settings with d = 80 and p = 1. In Table 2, the accuracy of FedAvg, FedProx and Ditto has shown significant improvement compared to previous results.

Table 2. In the heterogeneous setting, the test accuracy of different methods across real datasets.

Settings	Practical heterogeneous setting				
Methods	FashionMNIST	Cifar10	Cifar100	TINY	TINY*
FedAvg+PPELA	97.81 ± 0.03	90.77 ± 0.03	56.14 ± 0.03	40.72 ± 0.03	42.11 ± 0.04
FedProx+PPELA	97.83 ± 0.03	90.69 ± 0.04	56.23 ± 0.02	40.70 ± 0.03	42.08 ± 0.05
FedPHP+PPELA	97.49 ± 0.03	90.12 ± 0.02	54.43 ± 0.06	38.42 ± 0.06	40.23 ± 0.13
Ditto+PPELA	97.85 ± 0.02	90.76 ± 0.02	56.31 ± 0.15	40.82 ± 0.02	42.25 ± 0.05

The FedPHP method, which incorporates the global model using exponential smoothing and then adds the PPELA module, is influenced by some detrimental information from the global model before the integration of the PPELA module. The improvement in accuracy is not very pronounced. But it still shows improvement compared to the use of a single method.

5   Conclusion

In this paper, we introduce FL-PPELA, it enhances parameters of the global model in a way that benefits the client model, and then selects parameters from the global model to adjust the local model parameters. Extensive experiments have demonstrated the effectiveness of FL-PPELA, which outperforms 12 methods. Additionally, the PPELA module within FL-PPELA can enhance the accuracy of other federated learning (FL) methods.

References

1. Chrabaszcz, P., Loshchilov, I., Hutter, F.: A downsampled variant of imagenet as an alternative to the cifar datasets. arXiv preprint arXiv:1707.08819 (2017)
2. Collins, L., Hassani, H., Mokhtari, A., Shakkottai, S.: Exploiting shared representations for personalized federated learning. In: International Conference on Machine Learning, pp. 2089–2099. PMLR (2021)
3. Fallah, A., Mokhtari, A., Ozdaglar, A.: Personalized federated learning with theoretical guarantees: a model-agnostic meta-learning approach. Adv. Neural. Inf. Process. Syst. **33**, 3557–3568 (2020)
4. He, K., Zhang, X., Ren, S., Sun, J.: Deep residual learning for image recognition. In: Proceedings of the IEEE Conference on Computer Vision and Pattern Recognition, pp. 770–778 (2016)
5. Huang, Y., Chu, L., Zhou, Z., Wang, L., Liu, J., Pei, J., Zhang, Y.: Personalized cross-silo federated learning on non-IID data. In: Proceedings of the AAAI Conference on Artificial Intelligence. vol. 35, pp. 7865–7873 (2021)
6. Krizhevsky, A., et al.: Learning multiple layers of features from tiny images (2009)
7. Li, T., Hu, S., Beirami, A., Smith, V.: Ditto: Fair and robust federated learning through personalization. In: International Conference on Machine Learning, pp. 6357–6368. PMLR (2021)
8. Li, T., Sahu, A.K., Zaheer, M., Sanjabi, M., Talwalkar, A., Smith, V.: Federated optimization in heterogeneous networks. Proce. Mach. Learn. Syst. **2**, 429–450 (2020)
9. Li, X.C., Zhan, D.C., Shao, Y., Li, B., Song, S.: Fedphp: federated personalization with inherited private models. In: Joint European Conference on Machine Learning and Knowledge Discovery in Databases, pp. 587–602. Springer (2021)
10. Luo, J., Wu, S.: Adapt to adaptation: Learning personalization for cross-silo federated learning. In: IJCAI: proceedings of the Conference. vol. 2022, pp. 2166. NIH Public Access (2022)
11. McMahan, B., Moore, E., Ramage, D., Hampson, S., y Arcas, B.A.: Communication-efficient learning of deep networks from decentralized data. In: Artificial Intelligence and Statistics, pp. 1273–1282. PMLR (2017)
12. Sun, B., Huo, H., Yang, Y., Bai, B.: Partialfed: cross-domain personalized federated learning via partial initialization. Adv. Neural. Inf. Process. Syst. **34**, 23309–23320 (2021)
13. Personalized federated learning with moreau envelopes: T Dinh, C., Tran, N., Nguyen. J. Adv. Neural Inf. Process. Syst. **33**, 21394–21405 (2020)
14. Xiao, H., Rasul, K., Vollgraf, R.: Fashion-mnist: a novel image dataset for benchmarking machine learning algorithms. arXiv preprint arXiv:1708.07747 (2017)
15. Zhang, J., Hua, Y., Wang, H., Song, T., Xue, Z., Ma, R., Guan, H.: Fedala: adaptive local aggregation for personalized federated learning. In: Proceedings of the AAAI Conference on Artificial Intelligence. vol. 37, pp. 11237–11244 (2023)
16. Zhang, M., Sapra, K., Fidler, S., Yeung, S., Alvarez, J.M.: Personalized federated learning with first order model optimization. arXiv preprint arXiv:2012.08565 (2020)

ORCPM: An Online Regional Core Pattern Mining System

Dongsheng Wang[1], Jinjia Dai[1], Lizhen Wang[2(✉)], and Hui Chen[2]

[1] School of Information Science and Engineering, Yunnan University, Kunming 650091, China
[2] Dianchi College of Yunnan University, Kunming 650228, China
lzhwang@ynu.edu.cn

Abstract. Core pattern mining is a special task in spatial co-location pattern mining. Compared with the traditional spatial co-location pattern mining task, the core pattern does not require all feature instances to satisfy the neighbor relationship but emphasizes the relationship between the core and non-core features. Regional core pattern mining (RCPM) is designed to discover those core patterns that may occur frequently only in a sub-region and to reveal the dependency relationship between core and non-core features by analyzing the core pattern's prevalent sub-regions. RCPM can be widely used in tasks such as rare resource conservation, commercial site selection, and others that the core feature needs to be specified. This paper provides an online demonstration program for RCPM, which allows users not only to obtain mining results through simple graphical configuration but also to obtain guided decision support through interaction with the system.

Keywords: pattern mining · regional core pattern · prevalent sub-region · decision support system

1 Introduction

Spatial co-location pattern mining [1] is a spatial knowledge discovery technique that aims to discover spatial feature subsets with geographic correlation in spatial datasets. Regional co-location pattern mining [2] is a branch of spatial co-location pattern mining, which focuses on discovering co-location patterns implied in some sub-regions or finding sub-regions where some co-location patterns are likely to occur frequently. The sub-region containing regional co-location patterns can be formed for three reasons [3], 1) geographical factors, such as mountains and rivers; 2) artificial division, such as commercial districts, tourist areas and university towns; and 3) congregating due to correlations between features, such as dominant relationships (pollution sources leading to high cancer incidence), symbiotic relationships (rhinoceros and hornbill), etc. Existing regional co-location pattern mining algorithms mainly aim to mine patterns in the sub-regions generated by the first two reasons [4–6], while ignore the dependencies between features, and this leads to the lack of interpretability of some mining results.

Unlike the traditional spatial co-location pattern mining that adopted the rigorous clique constraint relationship, the core pattern mining adopts the core neighbor constraint, which does not require all features in a pattern to satisfy the neighbor relationship

M. Barhamgi et al. (Eds.): WISE 2024, LNCS 15463, pp. 257–264, 2025.
https://doi.org/10.1007/978-981-96-1483-7_22

but instead considers the relationship between the core and non-core features [7]. This constraint relationship can not only mine more targeted results, but also reflect some dependencies between features. Regional core pattern mining (RCPM) further finds the sub-regions where these patterns occur frequently and can further analyze the reasons for patterns' prevalence occurrence based on regional spatial attributes. RCPM can be widely used in tasks such as rare resource conservation, commercial site selection, and others that the core feature needs to be specified.

Meanwhile, existing core pattern mining tasks generally use Euclidean distances to determine the neighbor relationship between instances, which ignores the competition between identical features [3]. For example, for the same two stationery shops, one closer to the school has a greater influence from the school and has more benefits from the school. Considering the competition between feature instances of the same type, we improve the measure of neighbor relationships and design an online demonstration system (ORCPM) for mining regional core patterns.

2 Applicable Scenarios

Regional co-location pattern mining can discover the set of spatial features with correlations in geospatial space, as well as the sub-regions where they occur prevalently, thus providing corresponding spatial decisions. However, spatial datasets are usually large and mining all potential patterns implies a large time overhead. In addition, not all mining results are valuable to users, and a large number of mining results will instead cause information redundancy and increase the cost of retrieving valid information.

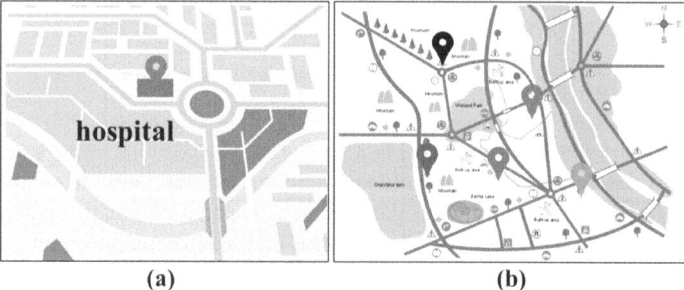

(a)   (b)

Fig. 1. Applicable scenarios of the demonstration systems. (a) Selecting suitable commercial buildings based on the landmark building. (b) Selecting suitable address for a commercial building.

For some realistically specific tasks, we don't need to process the entire spatial dataset. For example, Fig. 1 illustrates two real-world cases with urban POI datasets, where Fig. 1(a) shows the selection of a suitable business based on a known landmark, and Fig. 1(b) shows the selection of a suitable address for a known business. Meanwhile, this business is required to have a longer viable life cycle and higher returns. More specifically, suppose a user buys a piece of land near a hospital, what businesses can be opened at that location to maximize revenue? The user only needs to focus on the areas in the spatial dataset where hospitals frequently appear and the businesses that are frequent with hospitals. In another case, assuming that the user wants to join a milk tea store, he/she only needs to pay attention to some areas where milk tea stores are often opened and some businesses that often co-occur around the milk tea stores, so as to deduce the suitable location for opening a milk tea store.

Therefore, we designed this demonstration system to address the problems in existing research and realistic requirements from life. The demonstration system can not only simplify the user's operation and reduce the threshold setting, but also can dynamically provide some decision-making support to users to increase the utilization of information.

3   System Overview and Key Techniques

ORCPM is an online, friendly and interactive system based on the regional core pattern mining, designed to provide decision support for regional planning or commercial site selection, etc.

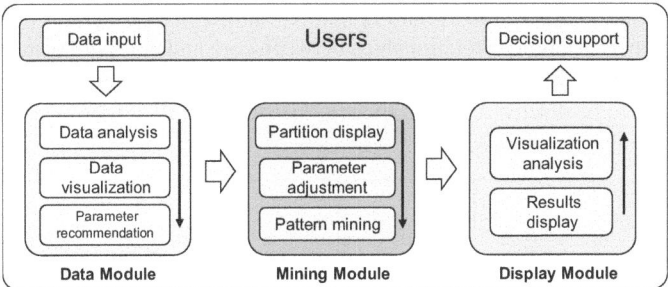

Fig. 2. The framework of ORCPM

Figure 2 shows the system framework of ORCPM, the demonstration system consists of three main modules, **Data Module**, **Mining Module** and **Display Module**. The data module is mainly responsible for the uploading, visualization display and analysis of spatial datasets, and provides the recommendation of the parameter setting adapted to the corresponding datasets based on the analysis results. The mining module is mainly used for the mining of the regional core patterns. At the same time, the module can interactively return the regional partitioning results and some intermediate information, which facilitates the users to make more detailed adjustments to the relevant parameters. At last, the display module is responsible for displaying the mining results and providing a visualization display and query of the user-specified results, which is helpful for the user to analyze the results with the regional spatial information, and thus get valuable decision support.

The results of mining module in ORCPM system are significant for the final decision support. In order to obtain more reasonable mining results, we carried out a series of design and optimization of algorithms of the mining module. Firstly, we design a special region partitioning criteria for the regional core pattern mining task, which ensures that the partitioned regions can discover more reasonable core patterns.

(1) A core instance and its neighboring instances are randomly selected to form the initial partition, and core instances that are only neighboring to core instances are not available for initial partitioning. (*It is guaranteed that there will not be a region containing only core instances*).

(2) The core instances that are only neighboring core instances cannot be added to the partition. (*It is guaranteed that regions containing only core instances will not be joined in region expansion*).

(3) The core instances in a partition can join their neighboring instances, and non-core instances in a partition can only join their neighboring core instances. (*It is guaranteed that non-core instances affected by core feature are divided into the same region of core instances*).

(4) Until all instances have been traversed. (*Integrity*).

Figure 3 shows the schematic diagram of the regional partitioning criteria (Fig. 3(a)) and the effect of partitioning (Fig. 3(b)). In Fig. 3(a), the yellow feature is the core features, the dashed areas in Fig. 3(a) represent the invalid partitions, the blue areas represent the valid starting regions, and the red and black regions represent regions after expanding 1 and 2 times respectively. Figure 3(b) shows the sub-regions divided based on this criterion, the neighbor relationships between core and non-core instances is fully considered in those sub-regions. Furthermore, it is obvious that reasonable core patterns are more likely to be discovered from the regions shown in Fig. 3(b).

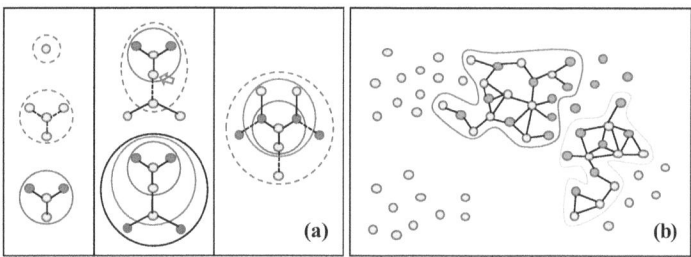

Fig. 3. The regional partition criteria

Secondly, the traditional neighbor relationship measure between instances uses the Euclidean distance, which ignores the competitive relationship between instances of the same feature. We propose core nearest affiliation relationships, for a non-core instance, it can receive influence from at most x nearest core instances, which fully considers the competitive relationship between core instances and the dependency of non-core instances on core instances. Figure 4 shows the neighbor relationship based on the Euclidean distance and the core nearest affiliation relationship, respectively. If only the distance threshold is considered, B2 is influenced by A1 and A2 equally (Fig. 4(a)), but the instance that has the greatest influence on B2 should be A2 because A2 is closer to B2 compared to the distance from A1 to B2 (Fig. 4(b)). By adjusting the number of core nearest affiliations, the influence strength of the core instance against the non-core instance can be adjusted.

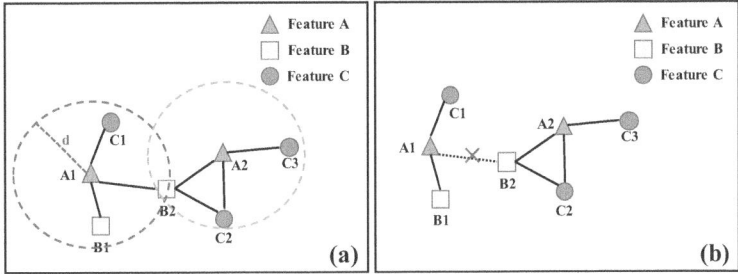

Fig. 4. The core nearest affiliation relationship. (*d* denotes the distance threshold, two instances with a neighbor relationship are connected by a solid line, and the deleted dashed line indicates the neighbor relations discarded after improving the metric.)

Finally, we designed a specialized storage structure (as show in Fig. 5) based on the proposed neighbor relationship. Where the key represents the core instance, and its value ({Feature: <instances>}) is also a hash table consisting of each feature in the non-core feature set and its instances that neighboring the core instances. The storage structure can greatly improve the efficiency of core pattern mining, thus reducing the system feedback time and enhancing the user experience. For example, the core participating instances of the corresponding feature A in RCP {A, B, C, D, E} is {A1}, and the core participating instances of feature C are {C1, C2, C3}. The core participating instances of feature A in RCP {A, B, D} are {A1, A2, A3}, and the core participating instances of feature B are {B1, B2, B3, B4, B5, B6, B9}, i.e., the union set of feature B instances.

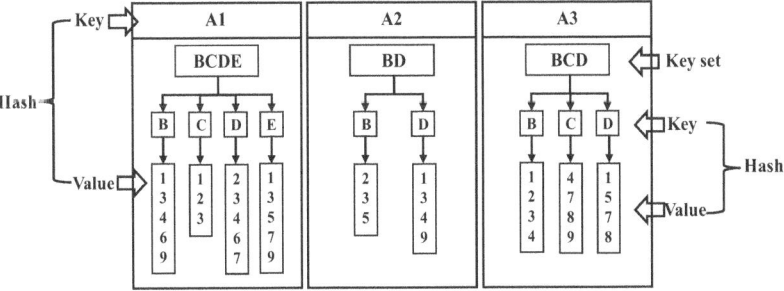

Fig. 5. The storage structure of core neighbor relationships. (Feature A is the core feature, and the secondary hash table stores non-core instances that satisfy the neighbor relationship with the core instance.)

The more optimization strategies and detailed descriptions can be referred to reference [3].

4 Demonstration Scenarios

The system ORCPM encapsulates a user-friendly online system where users can interact with the system to obtain appropriate parameter setting recommendations, intuitive mining results, and visualization analysis. In this section, we demonstrate and illustrate the system using a real dataset. We use the Shenzhen POI dataset with 13 spatial features and 71,000 spatial instances to demonstrate the ORCPM.

Figure 6 shows the ORCPM system's start page corresponding to the data modules in the system framework. Users can upload a spatial dataset on this page (red box (a)), and the system will return the spatial distribution plot of this dataset (red box (b)). In addition, the system will give the boxplot of the distribution of instances of all features (red box (c)) and infer the candidate core features that are likely to be locally distributed (red box (d)). The recommendation of candidate features solves the problem that the user's lack of a priori knowledge about the dataset leads to the inability to select appropriate core features.

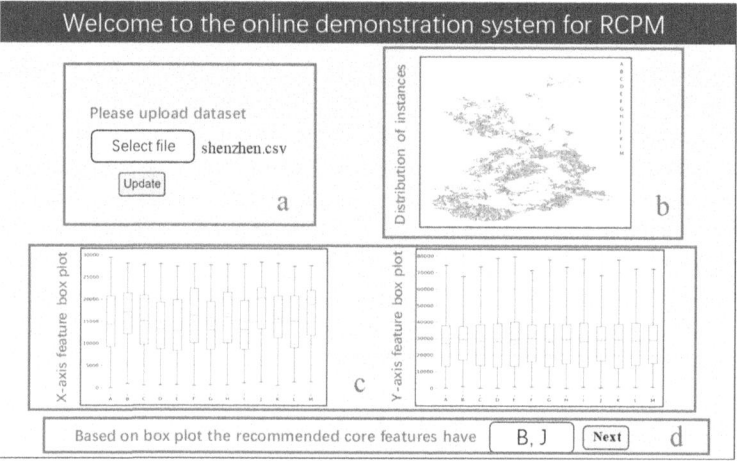

Fig. 6. The start page of ORCPM. (Color figure online)

Figure 7 shows the resulting display page of the ORCPM system, where red boxes (a) and (b) correspond to the mining module and red box (c) corresponds to the decision module in the system framework. The red box (a) shows the visualization results of the region partitioning function. Users can select the final core feature based on candidate features, and the system will return the spatial distribution of the core feature instances as well as the partitioning results. In addition, if the user is not satisfied with the current partitioning result, they can get a new partitioning result by adjusting the partitioning distance pd. The red box (b) shows the results of the pattern mining function, where the user enters the remaining parameters and the system will return all prevalent regional core patterns. Lastly, the functions in the red box (c) can provide the user with visualization results and detailed spatial distribution information for the specified region. Through these visualized feedbacks, users can more easily obtain more valuable decision support information.

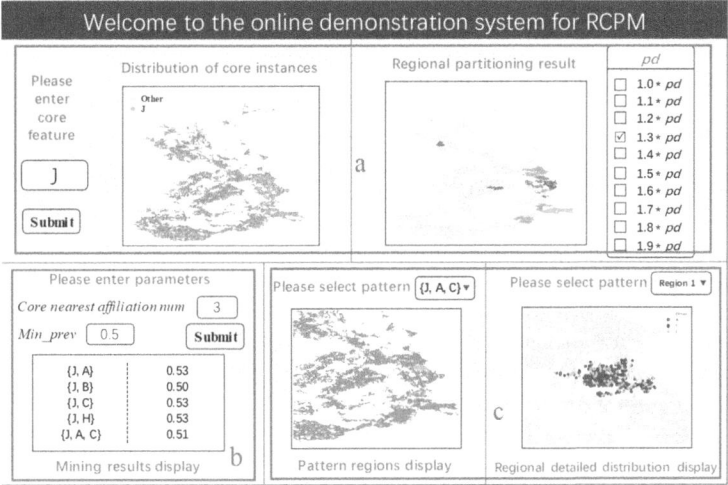

Fig. 7. The result page of ORCPM. (Color figure online)

For example, in Fig. 7, the instances for each feature of the pattern {J, A, C} are uniformly distributed, which indicates that the interactions between features J, A and C are equivalent in Region 1. However, if the instances are distributed in a star shape and the instances of features A and C are distributed around feature J, it means that feature J has a dominant influence on features A and C. For example, assuming feature J is an instance of commercial type, should J choose to be located beside or in the center of A and C? This spatially associated information will play a very crucial role in the user's final decision making.

5 Conclusion

The region core pattern mining is an improved method proposed to address the short-comings of the existing regional co-location pattern mining research, which not only optimizes the judgment of neighbor relationship but also designs a special partitioning criteria and storage strategy for this mining task. Compared with the traditional regional co-location pattern mining, the mining results of the regional core pattern can not only have better interpretability, but also have better guiding value for some practical applications. This demonstration provides an online regional core pattern mining system, ORCPM, which uses a visualization interface to provide users with an interactive way of using the system, greatly improving the user experience. Furthermore, the system can always make appropriate suggestions on parameter setting, outcome analysis, and decision support while considering the user experience.

Acknowledgements. This work is supported by the National Natural Science Foundation of China (62276227, 62266050, 62306266), the Project of Innovative Research Team of Yunnan Province (2018HC019), the Yunnan Fundamental Research Projects (202201AS070015, 202401AT070450), and the Postgraduate Research and Innovation Foundation of Yunnan University (KC-23235527, TM-23236884).

Our Codes Availability Statement. Our system codes that support the findings of this study are available in the GitHub open source with link: https://github.com/daijinjia-user/ORCPM-demo.

References

1. Wang, L., Fang, Y., Zhou, L.: Preference-based spatial co-location pattern mining. Springer Singapore, 2022, https://doi.org/10.1007/978-981-16-7566-9 (2022)
2. Guo, Y., Cai, J., Zhao B. Spatial scan statistic method for discovering regional network co-location patterns. Geomatics Inf. Sci. Wuhan Univ. 1383–1389 (2022)
3. Wang, D., Wang, L., Jiang, X., Yang, P.: RCPM_CFI: a regional core pattern mining method based on core feature influence. Inf. Sci. **2024**(658), 119895 (2024)
4. Liu, Q., et al.: An adaptive detection of multilevel co location patterns based on natural neighborhoods. Int. J. Geogr. Inf. Sci. 35(5), 1–26 (2020)
5. Ghosh, S., et al.: Towards geographically robust statistically significant regional colocation pattern detection. In: Proceedings of the 5th ACM SIGSPATIAL International Workshop on GeoSpatial Simulation, pp 11–20 (2022)
6. Li, J., et al.: A novel algorithm for efficiently mining spatial multi-level co-location patterns. IEEE Trans. Knowl. Data Eng. (TKDE) 2024 **36**(9), 4361–4374 (2024)
7. Zou, M., et al.: Mining co-location core patterns in spatial data sets based on the Voronoi diagram. Chinese J. Comput. 2022 **45**(9), 1908–1925 (2022)

MTRM: A Web-Miner Multi-Threshold Mining Co-location Patterns to Mitigate Redundancy

Muquan Zou[1,2], Vanluan Nguyen[3], Vanha Tran[3(✉)] ⓘ, Ducanh Khuat[3], and Thiloan Bui[3]

[1] Kunming University, Kunming 650214, China
ynu_zmq@foxmail.com
[2] Postdoctoral Research Workstation of Fudian Bank, Kunming 650200, China
[3] FPT University, Hanoi 155514, Vietnam
luannvhe151421@fpt.edu.vn, {hatv14,anhkd3,loanbt7}@fe.edu.vn

Abstract. Prevalent co-location pattern mining (PCPM) plays a critical role in spatial data mining, focusing on identifying subsets of spatial features that frequently co-occur within a given space. While existing PCPM methods have successfully identified co-location patterns, they often generate a significant amount of redundant patterns, which hinders both computational efficiency and interpretability. To address these challenges, we present MTRM (Multi-Threshold Redundancy Mitigation), a novel framework designed to mitigate redundancy through the introduction of multiple thresholds. MTRM allows for the flexible adjustment of significance levels, enabling the discovery of more concise and meaningful co-location patterns. Unlike traditional single-threshold methods, our approach dynamically filters out redundant patterns, retaining only those that exhibit strong spatial relationships across multiple criteria. MTRM is implemented as a web-based miner, providing users with a real-time, interactive platform to analyze spatial datasets. The flexibility of MTRM allows it to handle datasets of varying sizes and complexities, making it suitable for both real-world applications and large-scale synthetic data experiments. We benchmark the performance of MTRM against several state-of-the-art PCPM algorithms, demonstrating its ability to reduce redundancy while maintaining high accuracy in pattern discovery. Experimental results show that MTRM not only enhances scalability and efficiency but also improves the quality of discovered patterns by reducing noise and redundancy, leading to more actionable insights for decision-makers in fields such as urban planning, environmental monitoring, and epidemiology.

Keywords: Spatial co-location pattern · multiple-threshold · redundancy framework · web-miner

M. Barhamgi et al. (Eds.): WISE 2024, LNCS 15463, pp. 265–273, 2025.
https://doi.org/10.1007/978-981-96-1483-7_23

1   Introduction

Co-location pattern mining (PCPM) is a fundamental task in spatial data mining [2], where the goal is to identify subsets of spatial features that frequently co-occur within a certain geographic area [4]. This technique has wide-ranging applications, including urban planning, environmental monitoring, market analysis, and more [9,11]. For example, in urban planning, discovering co-location patterns of essential infrastructure like schools and hospitals can help optimize the design of city layouts. Similarly, in ecological research, identifying spatial relationships between species can enhance our understanding of ecosystems. Traditional PCPM methods largely rely on neighborhood relationships, where spatial objects are considered related if a certain distance from each other. This approach helps identify prevalent sets of features that frequently co-occur [10]. However, these methods often face a critical issue: pattern redundancy. Many discovered patterns overlap significantly, leading to redundant information [1,7]. This redundancy not only increases computational overhead but also reduces the clarity and interpretability of the results. Furthermore, the uneven density distribution of features across the dataset can lead to imbalances in the significance of co-location patterns, where some patterns are either overrepresented or underrepresented due to variations in feature density [3,6]. To address these limitations, this paper introduces a novel framework that employs both distance and prevalence thresholds to assess the significance of co-location patterns while mitigating redundancy. Our approach systematically prunes redundant patterns, resulting in a more concise and interpretable set of patterns. The framework allows for flexible adjustments to account for the uneven distribution of spatial features, ensuring that patterns from both dense and sparse areas are treated fairly. This methodology offers an efficient and practical solution for discovering meaningful spatial patterns, with applications across a range of fields.

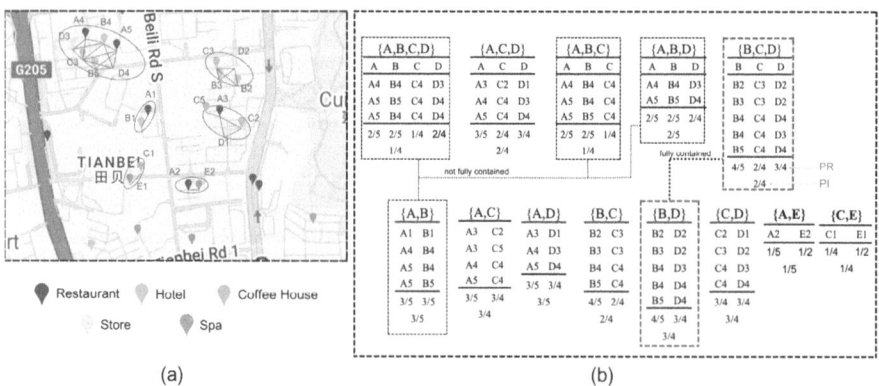

Fig. 1. A motivating example spatial co-location patterns.

For instance, Fig. 1 illustrates a sample spatial dataset containing five locations on a map, classified into features A, B, C, D, and E. The figure also presents the co-location patterns along with the corresponding prevalence ratios (PR and PI) of all possible co-location instances within the dataset. However, traditional co-location pattern mining tends to produce numerous redundant patterns. Specifically, the co-location instance T(B, D) is fully contained within the larger co-location instance T(B, C, D). In this case, the pattern B, D is said to be covered by the more comprehensive pattern B, C, D, based on the distribution of their corresponding co-location instances.

We present MTRM (Multi-Threshold Redundancy Mitigation), a system designed to tackle redundancy in co-location patterns. MTRM employs multiple thresholds to evaluate the significance of these patterns and identifies covering relationships to eliminate redundancy. Utilizing a spatial dataset, such as urban data from Shenzhen, our system discovers concise prevalent co-location patterns through a multi-threshold approach. Initially, prevalent patterns are identified based on distance and prevalence thresholds. A novel metric measures the relationships between patterns, enabling the pruning of redundant ones. Finally, MTRM visually represents the refined patterns, enhancing their interpretability for practical applications in urban planning, environmental monitoring, and market analysis. This approach ensures that the results are concise and meaningful.

2 System Overview

The MTRM Web-Miner provides a user-friendly interface for discovering and analyzing co-location patterns in spatial datasets. Designed for accessibility, it allows users to configure and execute mining tasks efficiently. Leveraging the MTRM framework, the Web-Miner applies distance and prevalence multi-thresholds to uncover concise prevalent patterns and reduce redundancy. Users can upload spatial datasets and customize parameters, while a powerful visualization feature displays the spatial distribution of patterns on an interactive map, enhancing interpretation and exploration. The scalable system supports large datasets and includes interactive tools for zooming and filtering results. Overall, the MTRM Web-Miner combines ease of use, flexible configuration, and robust visualization to deliver valuable insights across various application domains.

Definition 1. *Co-location Pattern:* *A co-location pattern is a set of spatial features that frequently appear together within a specified proximity. Given a spatial dataset D containing features $X = \{x_1, x_2, \ldots, x_n\}$, a co-location pattern $P \subseteq X$ is considered significant if its instances co-occur more often than a given threshold. The proximity is typically defined by a distance threshold d. Formally, a co-location pattern P can be represented as:*

$$P = \{x_1, x_2, \ldots, x_k\}$$

where $x_i \in X$ and the spatial distance between any pair of instances of the features in P is less than d.

Definition 2. *External Utility:*
   The external utility of a feature X_t quantifies its significance based on the entire dataset. It reflects the overall importance of X_t and is calculated based on the frequency and relevance of X_t across all instances in the dataset. Formally, the external utility is defined as:

$$u(X_t) = function(X_t, S)$$

where S represents the dataset and $function(X_t, S)$ could involve measures such as the total count of instances of X_t or other relevance metrics determined by the specific application context.

Definition 3. *Utility of a Co-location Pattern and Dataset:*
   The utility of a co-location pattern $P = \{x_1, x_2, \ldots, x_k\}$ quantifies its overall significance by integrating both its internal and external utility measures. This cumulative utility is defined as:

$$u(P) = \sum_{x_t \in P} u(x_t) \times |IU(x_t, P)| \tag{1}$$

where $u(x_t)$ represents the external utility of feature x_t, and $|IU(x_t, P)|$ denotes the count of unique instances of x_t present in all co-location instances of P.
   In contrast, the utility of the entire dataset S is determined by summing the utility values of all features, expressed as:

$$u(S) = \sum_{x_t \in F} u(x_t) \times |I(x_t)| \tag{2}$$

where $|I(x_t)|$ signifies the total number of instances for feature x_t within the dataset. Together, these definitions emphasize the importance of both individual co-location patterns and the dataset as a whole in understanding their utility.

Definition 4. *Utility Participation Ratio and High Utility Co-Location Pattern:*
   The utility participation ratio (UPI) of a co-location pattern P reflects its utility in relation to the overall utility of the dataset. It is defined as:

$$UPI(P) = \frac{u(P)}{u(S)} \tag{3}$$

   A co-location pattern P is classified as a high utility co-location pattern (HUCP) [5,8] if its utility participation ratio meets or exceeds a specified minimum utility threshold μ:

$$UPI(P) \geq \mu \quad (0 \leq \mu \leq 1)$$

Definition 5. *Multiple Minimum Utility Thresholds: In recognition that different features may hold varying significance in different patterns, each feature f_t is assigned a unique minimum utility threshold, denoted as $\mu(f_t)$. The collection of these thresholds is expressed as:*

$$MU = \{\mu(f_1), \mu(f_2), \ldots, \mu(f_m)\}$$

This approach allows for a more equitable filtering process when identifying high utility co-location patterns (HUCPs) across diverse feature sets.

Definition 6. *Semantic Distance - L*

To improve the efficiency of redundancy reduction in discovering concise prevalent co-location patterns, we define a semantic distance metric. This metric quantifies the similarity between co-location patterns by analyzing their co-location instances, which reflect spatial relationships among neighboring instances. For two co-location patterns p and p', the Semantic Distance - L is defined as:

$$L(p, p') = \max \left\{ 1 - \frac{\left| \sum_{f_i} T(p') \right|}{\left| \sum_{f_i} T(p) \right|} \right\} \tag{1}$$

where $|\sum_{f_i} T(p)|$ represents the count of distinct instances of feature f_i in $T(p)$, the co-location instances of pattern p.

Example: *Consider patterns $p = \{B, D\}$ and $p' = \{B, C, D\}$. We find:*

$$|\sum_B T(p)| = 4, \quad |\sum_D T(p)| = 3, \quad |\sum_B T(p')| = 4, \quad |\sum_D T(p')| = 3.$$

Thus,

$$L(p, p') = \max \left\{ 1 - \frac{4}{4}, 1 - \frac{3}{3} \right\} = 0.$$

This indicates that the co-location instance information for $\{B, D\}$ is completely contained within $\{B, C, D\}$.

Definition 7. *Non-redundancy:*

A collection of co-location patterns is considered non-redundant if no pattern in the collection is a subset of another pattern that has the same or greater prevalence. This criterion ensures that the collection consists solely of the most significant and distinct patterns. Formally, a set S of co-location patterns is non-redundant if, for any pair of patterns $P, Q \in S$:

$$P \subset Q \implies PI(P) > PI(Q)$$

The concept of non-redundancy aids in simplifying the result set, making it more interpretable by removing unnecessary patterns.

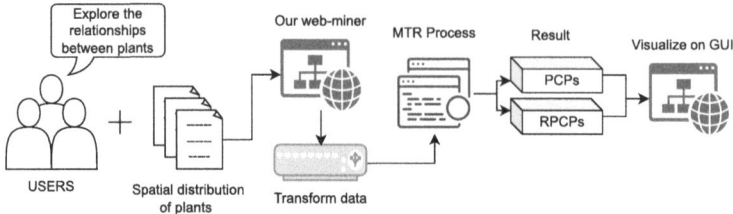

Fig. 2. The story web-miner process on real issue.

The MTRM web-miner is a web-based tool designed to facilitate the discovery of prevalent co-location patterns in spatial datasets while mitigating redundancy through a multi-threshold approach Fig. 2. This approach enables the system to apply multiple significance thresholds, allowing for more precise control over the pattern discovery process. By dynamically adjusting these thresholds, users can fine-tune the analysis to filter out redundant patterns more effectively, retaining only those patterns that exhibit strong spatial relationships across multiple criteria. The platform also provides an interactive and customizable experience, where users can configure key parameters such as spatial constraints, distance thresholds, and pattern frequency. This flexibility allows the system to handle a wide range of datasets, from small-scale real-world applications to large-scale synthetic experiments, making it adaptable to various domains such as urban planning, environmental monitoring, and epidemiology.

3   Demonstration Scenarios

The MTRM Web-Miner provides an intuitive and user-friendly interface, specifically designed to help users effectively discover useful Prevalent Co-location Patterns (PCPs) while minimizing redundant information. The interface is structured into several key sections to guide users through the process seamlessly. The overall design emphasizes simplicity and accessibility, ensuring that even those with limited technical knowledge can configure and execute data mining tasks with ease. The core objective is to facilitate the extraction of meaningful patterns from spatial data by leveraging advanced algorithms, all while presenting the results in a comprehensible and organized manner.

In Fig. 3(I) of the Web-Miner, users are given the option to upload raw spatial data files, which serve as the input for the mining process. This part of the interface allows users to easily adjust the algorithm's parameters, such as setting the appropriate distance and prevalence thresholds, to match the unique characteristics of the dataset being analyzed. The configurability of these parameters ensures that users can tailor the mining process to fit their specific needs, whether working with dense urban data or more scattered environmental datasets. Once the data is uploaded and the parameters are set, users can proceed by clicking the "Mining" button to initiate the algorithm. This action triggers the back-end

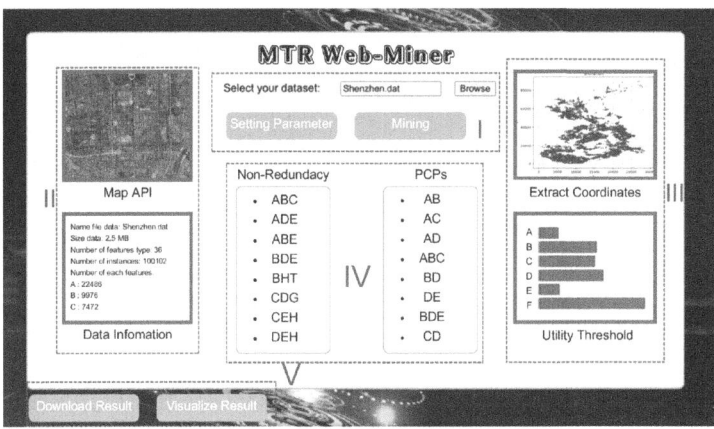

Fig. 3. The GUI of MTR Web-Miner.

process that uncovers significant patterns hidden within the data. After the mining process is complete, Fig. 3(II) provides a detailed visual representation of the spatial data on a realistic map interface. This map allows users to explore the spatial distribution of the data, offering a deeper understanding of the dataset in a geographical context. In addition to the map visualization, this section displays important details about the dataset, including its size and the number of features present. With Fig. 3(III) focuses on the extraction of raw data into coordinates that are critical for the mining algorithm's functionality. This section also provides an in-depth look at the performance of the multi-threshold mining approach, displaying how different threshold values impact the discovery of patterns. By breaking down the data into these granular elements, users can better understand how the algorithm operates and appreciate the effectiveness of the multi-threshold methodology in filtering out noise and highlighting relevant co-location patterns. The final and most critical part of the interface is part in Fig. 3(VI), which showcases the results of the mining process. In this section, users can view the concise PCPs that have been discovered, along with an analysis of non-redundancy, ensuring that only the most significant patterns are presented. By optimizing the results for non-redundancy and conciseness, the system ensures that the output is not only meaningful but also practical for further application in areas such as urban planning, environmental management, or market analysis.

Figure 4(V.I) illustrates that the system includes a support services section designed to assist users further in their analysis. This section allows users to download the resulting files after the mining process, facilitating offline review and in-depth analysis, as shown in Fig. 4(V.I). Moreover, the system features tools for visualizing the mined PCPs on a graph, which aids users in better understanding the spatial relationships and distribution within the data, as depicted in Fig. 4(V.II). With its intuitive and well-structured interface, the DCPCPM

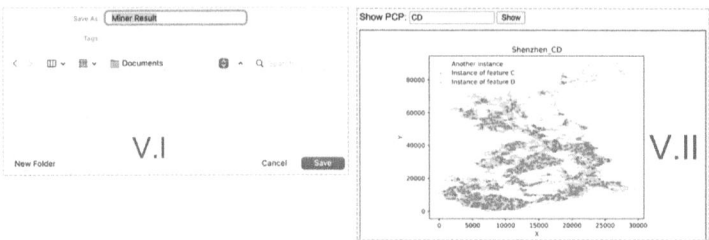

Fig. 4. GUI download and visualization.

system enables users to efficiently mine and analyze co-location patterns. As a result, it is an invaluable tool for both researchers and practitioners in the data mining field, offering a balance of powerful features and ease of use.

4   Conclusions

This paper introduced Multi-Threshold Redundancy Mitigation (MTRM), a novel framework that addresses critical challenges in co-location pattern mining by focusing on both redundancy mitigation and the use of prevalence multi-thresholds. Unlike traditional approaches that often result in an overwhelming number of redundant patterns, MTRM employs a combination of distance and multiple prevalence thresholds to effectively prune redundant patterns. This results in a concise and more interpretable set of co-location patterns, enabling better insights into spatial relationships. MTRM ability to adapt to uneven feature distributions, ensuring accurate representation of patterns across both densely and sparsely populated areas. By eliminating unnecessary duplication, the framework significantly improves computational efficiency while maintaining the relevance of discovered patterns. The experimental results demonstrate the practical value of MTRM in various domains, including urban planning and environmental monitoring, where handling real-world spatial data is crucial. The scalability of MTRM is another notable contribution, as the framework is designed to accommodate increasingly large and complex spatial datasets.

Acknowledgements. This paper is supported by the Special Basic Cooperative Research Programs of Yunnan Provincial Undergraduate Universities' Association (grant NO. 202101BA070001-152), Li Zhengqiang Expert Workstation of Yunnan Province (grant NO. 202205AF150031), the Yunnan Caiyun Postdoctoral Program - Innovation Project, and the Yunnan Province Philosophy and Social Science Planning Think Tank Project (grant NO. ZK2024YB15).

References

1. Bao, X., Lu, J., Gu, T., Chang, L., Xu, Z., Wang, L.: Mining non-redundant co-location patterns. IEEE Trans. Neural Netw. Learn. Syst. **33**(11), 6613–6626 (2021)
2. Garaeva, A., Makhmutova, F., Anikin, I., Sattler, K.U.: A framework for co-location patterns mining in big spatial data. In: 2017 XX IEEE International Conference on Soft Computing and Measurements (SCM), pp. 477–480. IEEE (2017)
3. Li, L., Cheng, J., Bannister, J., Mai, X.: Geographically and temporally weighted co-location quotient: an analysis of spatiotemporal crime patterns in greater manchester. Int. J. Geogr. Inf. Sci. **36**(5), 918–942 (2022)
4. Maiti, S., Subramanyam, R.: Mining co-location patterns from distributed spatial data. J. King Saud Univ.-Comput. Inf. Sci. **33**(9), 1064–1073 (2021)
5. Tran, V., Wang, L., Zhang, J., Do, T.: Efficient mining of high utility co-location patterns based on a query strategy. In: International Conference on Advanced Data Mining and Applications, pp. 401–416. Springer (2023). https://doi.org/10.1007/978-3-031-46661-8_27
6. Wang, D., Wang, L., Wang, X., Tran, V.: An approach based on maximal cliques and multi-density clustering for regional co-location pattern mining. Expert Syst. Appl. **248**, 123414 (2024)
7. Wang, L., Bao, X., Zhou, L.: Redundancy reduction for prevalent co-location patterns. IEEE Trans. Knowl. Data Eng. **30**(1), 142–155 (2017)
8. Wang, L., Jiang, W., Chen, H., Fang, Y.: Efficiently mining high utility co-location patterns from spatial data sets with instance-specific utilities. In: Candan, S., Chen, L., Pedersen, T.B., Chang, L., Hua, W. (eds.) DASFAA 2017. LNCS, vol. 10178, pp. 458–474. Springer, Cham (2017). https://doi.org/10.1007/978-3-319-55699-4_28
9. Xia, Z., Li, H., Chen, Y., Yu, W.: Detecting urban fire high-risk regions using colocation pattern measures. Sustain. Urban Areas **49**, 101607 (2019)
10. Yang, P., Wang, L., Wang, X., Fang, D.: An effective approach on mining co-location patterns from spatial databases with rare features. In: 2019 20th IEEE International Conference on Mobile Data Management (MDM), pp. 53–62. IEEE (2019)
11. Yu, W.: Spatial co-location pattern mining for location-based services in road networks. Expert Syst. Appl. **46**, 324–335 (2016)

Constrained Path Optimization on Time-Dependent Road Networks

Kousik Kumar Dutta[1]([✉]) and Venkata M. V. Gunturi[1,2]

[1] Indian Institute of Technology Ropar, Rupnagar 140001, India
kousik.21csz0004@iitrpr.ac.in
[2] University of Hull, Hull HU6 7RX, UK

Abstract. Time-Dependent Constrained Path Optimization (TD-CPO) takes the following input: (i) time-dependent (TD) road network, (ii) source (s), (iii) destination (d), (iv) departure time (t) and, (v) budget ($\mathcal{B}$). In a TD road network, each edge is characterized by a time-dependent arrival time and a score function. TD-CPO aims to determine a loopless s–d path which departs from s at time t and arrives at d on or before time $t + \mathcal{B}$ while maximizing the score. TD-CPO has applications in urban navigation. TD-CPO is a variant of the Arc Orienteering Problem (AOP) known to be NP-hard in nature The key computational challenge of TD-CPO is that we need to find the "longest path" in terms of score within the given budget constraint in a TD road network. Current algorithms either prune down search space aggressively, leading to low solution quality or are not scalable to large networks. In contrast, our proposed approach $\mathcal{SCOPE}$ explores a comprehensive search space efficiently. Furthermore, the inherent computational structure of $\mathcal{SCOPE}$ enables trivial parallelization for improved performance. Our experiments indicate that $\mathcal{SCOPE}$ achieves both superior quality solutions (nearly **2X**) and acceptable runtimes (within **3 secs**) when compared to the state-of-the-art algorithm on large road networks. Furthermore, $\mathcal{SCOPE}$ exhibits almost linear speedup as the number of CPU cores increases.

Keywords: Road Networks · Time-Dependent Shortest Paths · Optimization Problem

1 Introduction

Increasingly, the proliferation of mobility-based Big Data [12] has opened up new possibilities for more sophisticated routing queries on road networks (e.g., [4, 11, 14, 15]). For instance, one can now query paths like, "Find a route that traverses roads with the most scenic views [11], with a constraint that the total length of the path does not exceed **15 min** more than the fastest route" or "Determine a path which maximizes safety (refer [10]) or navigability (e.g., [9]) while constraining the total length of the path to be at most **10 min** longer than the

M. Barhamgi et al. (Eds.): WISE 2024, LNCS 15463, pp. 274–282, 2025.
https://doi.org/10.1007/978-981-96-1483-7_24

fastest path." The key aspect of both the previous queries is that they have a notion of maximizing a metric (scenic score or safety) while constraining another metric (travel time). Both these queries can be formulated as variations of the classical Arc-Orienteering Problem (AOP). It is important to note that the AOP is known to be NP-Hard [11] in nature. Authors in [4,9,10] have adapted the traditional arc orienteering problem definition for non-tourism-related path planning use cases by considering only loopless paths. To this end, [4,9,10] termed this problem as Constrained Path Optimization (CPO).

Current works in CPO ([4,9,10]) assume that the underlying road network is static in nature. In contrast, this work aims to develop a solution for the CPO problem on a time-dependent (TD) road network. In a TD road network, paths are typically interpreted as journeys through space and time. More specifically, in this setup, the travel time and score associated with each edge $e(u, v)$ in a path P is determined in accordance with the actual time at which a traveller would arrive at u while following the path P. This kind of reference frame is widely used in the domain of routing [14,15] over road networks and has been formally referred to as a *Lagrangian* reference frame by some authors (e.g., [6]).

Limitations of the Prior Work: Research work closest to our problem lies in the area of Twofold Time-Dependent Arc Orienteering Problem (2TD-AOP) [3,11]. 2TD-AOP finds a path between a given source s and destination d, which maximizes the scenic view (score) while constraining the travel time. The key difference between the 2TD-AOP path and the TD-CPO path is that 2TD-AOP allows the presence of a loop in the final path. This assumption is not always desirable in non-tourism-related scenarios, such as ours. Furthermore, the solution proposed in [11] is very conservative as it prioritizes replacing only low-score portions of a seed path using replacements from a set of high-score edges. This results in lower solution quality (details in Sect. 5).

The authors in [3] improve the solution in [11] by considering multiple initial seed paths instead of a single one (as [11]). Though the broader search space of the proposed algorithm produces better solution quality, this technique is not scalable for large datasets (around 10 `secs` runtime for a graph with just 6K nodes) (details in Sect. 5).

Another related work relevant to our problem is Constrained Shortest Path (CSP) [7,14,15] problems. CSP aims to find the shortest path between a source-destination pair subject to certain constraints. In other words, CSP minimizes the preference metric (distance) within some constraints. This is quite different from our TD-CPO problem, where the goal is to *maximize* the preference metric within some constraints. Note that it is not trivial to adapt the algorithms for minimization problems to solve a maximization problem, as detailed in [9].

Summary of Contributions: This paper offers the following contributions:

- In this paper, we propose a novel algorithm called $\mathcal{SCOPE}$ to solve the CPO problem on *a time-dependent road network*.
- Our evaluation assesses the performance of $\mathcal{SCOPE}$ on large road networks(up to 0.68M nodes and 1.87M edges).

– Our experiments show that $\mathcal{SCOPE}$ produces good quality solutions within acceptable running times (`within 3 secs`) on large road networks. Our results indicate that [3] could not scale beyond networks with 6K nodes, and [11] produces low-quality solutions on large networks. Furthermore, the linear scalability exhibited by $\mathcal{SCOPE}$ underscores its ability to scale-up easily.

Outline: The remainder of this paper is structured as follows. Section 2 discusses the fundamental concepts and formally defines the problem. After that, Sect. 3 presents some basic concepts used in our proposed algorithm. Section 4 details our proposed solution, $\mathcal{SCOPE}$. Section 5 presents experimental evaluation. Finally, we conclude in Sect. 6.

2   Problem Definition

Definition 1 (Road Network). *We represent the input road network using a time-dependent graph (TD graph). TD graph represents road intersections as nodes and the road segments as directed edges. Each edge within the TD graph is associated with the following two functions.*
(a) Arrival Time Function (Γ): For any given departure time from the starting node, it computes the arrival time at the destination node along that edge.
(b) Score Function (Φ): The score function determines the score or value associated with the edge for the given departure time from the starting node.

In our implementation, we have modelled the arrival time function as a continuous, non-decreasing "piecewise-linear" function (similar to current works [14, 15]). We model the score function as a "piecewise-constant" function (similar to [3, 11, 14, 15]). The details of modelling arrival time and score function are in the full version of this paper [5]. Furthermore, this paper assumes First-In-First-Out (FIFO) property on the arrival time data on all edges. This implies that for any given edge $e(x, y)$, departing later from node x will never arrive earlier at node y. Again, this assumption is in line with existing literature [3, 11, 14].

2.1   Time-Dependent Constrained Path Optimization (TD-CPO)

Input: Consists of the following:

(1) A TD graph, $G = (V, E)$, where each directed edge $e(x, y) \in E$ is associated with an arrival time function (Γ) and score function (Φ).
(2) A source $s \in V$ and a destination $d \in V$.
(3) Departure time t_{dep} from s.
(4) A positive value *overhead* corresponds to the maximum permissible travel time allowed over the fastest path from s to d. We use the term "Budget ($\mathcal{B}$)" to denote the sum of overhead and the travel time of the fastest path from s to d.

Output: A loopless path $\mathcal{P}^*$ between s and d.
Objective function: Maximize $\Phi(\mathcal{P}^*)$
Constraint: $\Gamma(\mathcal{P}^*) \leq t_{dep} + \mathcal{B}$

3   Basic Concepts for the Proposed Algorithm

MINSUM Algorithm: MINSUM algorithm [7] aims to determine a path between a source and a destination, which minimizes the distance subject to a constraint on travel time. Its exploration strategy is similar to Dijkstra's and involves labelling nodes and relaxing edges (and updating labels). The predecessor information is also stored for each label to retrieve the computed path. However, unlike Dijkstra's, it needs to maintain two parameters (l, c) (distance and travel time) in a label. Additionally, it does not use Dijkstra's concept of closing a node (corresponding to the result of extract-min). Instead, it maintains a list of non-dominated labels corresponding to each node and discards the labels using the concept of dominated labels (definition 2) and feasibility checking (the travel time of a label should be less than the maximum budget). A sample progression of the MINSUM algorithm is shown in Fig. 1(a)&(b).

Definition 2 (Dominated label). *Suppose $L1(l1, c1)$ and $L2(l2, c2)$ are two different labels of node v. $L1$ is dominated by $L2$ if: (a) $c1 > c2$, and (b) $l1 > l2$.*

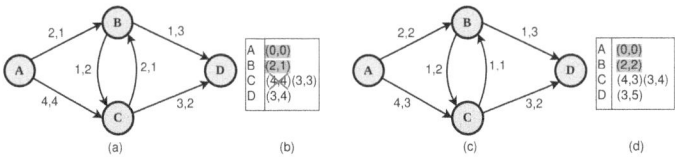

Fig. 1. (a) & (b) sample TD graph (edge parameters (l, c)) and dominated label pruning for constrained shortest path problem, (c) & (d) sample TD graph and example to show that the dominated label can not be pruned for loopless longest path problem.

Challenges of MINSUM and Inspiration for TD-CPO: In contrast to MINSUM, the TD-CPO problem seeks to maximize the score within a travel time budget. Hence, the TD-CPO problem becomes identifying the longest path in terms of score while adhering to budget constraints. It is important to note that the problem of finding the longest path in a cyclic graph is NP-hard [2], and converting the given cyclic graph into a directed acyclic graph is also nontrivial [13]. Further, traditional dominated label pruning is ineffective due to loopless path constraints, as shown in Fig. 1(d). There are two labels (3,4) and (4,3) at node C. However, label (3,4) cannot visit node B again due to loopless constraints. Hence, this leads to label (6,6) at node D. Meanwhile, label (4,3) produces label (6,7) at node D via node B, achieving a higher score. Thus, we need a specialized algorithm to address these factors. Nevertheless, the fundamental exploration strategy of MINSUM informs the design of our algorithm.

Temporal Pruning Strategy: We use the concept of the *latest departure time* to prune search space. The concept of the latest departure time is based on the latest departure path problem (discussed in [6]). In our algorithm, We first determine the latest departure time of nodes. Latest departure time of a node x is defined as the latest one can leave from node x to reach the destination d by desired arrival time $t_{arr} = t_{dep} + \mathcal{B}$ (t_{dep} and $\mathcal{B}$ are given in problem input). Therefore, during the course of the algorithm, any label of a node with an arrival time greater than the latest departure time for that node cannot contribute to a valid TD-CPO solution in the future and, thus, can be pruned.

4   Proposed Algorithm $\mathcal{SCOPE}$

We first invoke the *backward traversal* algorithm (presented in [6]) from destination d to mark all the nodes v with the latest departure time ($\mathcal{K}_{t_{arr}}(v)$) such that one can reach the destination by the desired target arrival time of t_{arr}.

Algorithm 1. ProcessLabel($< u, \alpha, sc, pred >$, vl')

1: **if** $u == d$ **then**
2:     **return** $< u, \alpha, sc, pred >$
3: **end if**
4: $resultLabel \leftarrow NULL$
5: **for all** adjacent node v of u **do**
6:     **if** v was never visited in vl' **then**
7:         $v_{at} \leftarrow u.\Gamma(v)_\alpha$
8:         //Process the new label, if v_{at} less than latest departure time of the node v.
9:         **if** $v_{at} \leq \mathcal{K}_{t_{arr}}(v)$ **then**
10:             $v_{sc} \leftarrow sc + u.\Phi(v)_\alpha$
11:             $v_{pred} \leftarrow < u, \alpha, sc, pred >$
12:             Create the new label $< v, v_{at}, v_{sc}, v_{pred} >$
13:             $vl'' \leftarrow$ Copy of vl'
14:             Add v to the visited list vl''
15:             $label \leftarrow$ ProcessLabel($< v, v_{at}, v_{sc}, v_{pred} >$, vl'')
16:             **if** $label \neq NULL$ **then**
17:                 Check and update the $resultLabel$ with $label$ if $label$ has better score.
18:             **end if**
19:         **end if**
20:     **end if**
21: **end for**
22: **return** $resultLabel$.

Following this, we initialize the source node s with the label $< s, t_{dep}, 0, null >$. A label $< s, t_{dep}, 0, null >$ represents the path (from source) through the designated predecessor (*null* in this case), which arrives at s at time t_{dep} and has a current total accumulated score of 0. Each unique label is linked to a visited list, which lists all the physical nodes that will be visited if one were to follow the predecessors of the labels until one reaches the source node. This visited list is used to prevent the creation of loops in the candidate paths under consideration. We create a visited list vl for the label $< s, t_{dep}, 0, null >$ and add s to vl. Thereafter, the recursive function "ProcessLabel" (Algorithm 1) is called.

Consider an arbitrary i^{th} recursion call of the "ProcessLabel" procedure (Algorithm 1). Assume that it was invoked with label $< u, \alpha, sc, pred >$ and visited list vl'. The procedure then expands the label $< u, \alpha, sc, pred >$ recursively for each adjacent node v of u. First, it checks if v is in the visited list vl' or not (line 6 in Algorithm 1). If v is already in vl', adding it again creates a loop in the solution. If not, then it then computes the arrival time at v (v_{at}) along the edge u-v for a departure time $t = \alpha$ at u. Temporal pruning is then applied by verifying whether v_{at} is less than or equal to the latest departure time from v ($\mathcal{K}_{t_{arr}}(v)$). Subsequently, the total accumulated score at v (v_{sc}) is computed by adding the total accumulated score at u to the score gain from travelling along edge u-v at time α. A new label $< v, v_{at}, v_{sc}, v_{pred} >$ is created for further recursion and the label $< u, \alpha, sc, pred >$ is set as its predecessor (v_{pred}).

A new visited list vl'' is created for all the neighbours of u (except for one) by coping the vl'. For one of the neighbours, vl'' is essentially a reference vl' itself. And then, we add v to the vl''. Finally, we call the "ProcessLabel" procedure recursively with parameters $< v, v_{at}, v_{sc}, v_{pred} >$ and vl''.

The recursion terminates if the node u in the input label $< u, \alpha, sc, pred >$ used to call an instance of "ProcessLabel" algorithm happens to be the destination node d (lines 1–2). At this stage, we have a s–d path and the algorithms start to wind back the recursion. As we wind back the recursion, the algorithm keeps determining the "best" path (line 17) to the destination (via the current node u) and returns it back. Finally, when the recursion winds back to source node s, we would have the s–d path with the highest score within the budget.

Multi-thread Implementation of $\mathcal{SCOPE}$: The "ProcessLabel" function of $\mathcal{SCOPE}$ involves numerous recursive calls for each adjacent node of the $currentL$-$abel$. We have developed a parallel implementation of $\mathcal{SCOPE}$ utilizing the "work-stealing" scheduler. The "work-stealing" scheduler is well-suited for parallelization of tasks involving multiple levels of recursion calls. *Our parallel implementation achieves a linear scale-up in runtime as the number of cores increases.*

Time Complexity Analysis: TD-CPO problem definition prohibits loops in the final solution. Hence, there may be a total of $|V|$ nodes (for graph $G(V, E)$) in the final path in the worst case. If we consider the maximum degree of the graph as Δ, the worst-case time complexity would be $O(\Delta^{|V|-1})$. *Despite having exponential time complexity, $\mathcal{SCOPE}$ achieves efficient performance in real-world road networks due to the lower degree of connectivity and temporal characteristics.*

5   Experimental Evaluation

Dataset: Our experimental analysis focuses on Oldenburg [1] (6k nodes and 7k edges) and Moscow (685k nodes and 1.87M edges) [8] road networks. We synthetically generate time-dependent travel time and score for each edge on these road networks. The details of generating synthetic time-dependent travel time and score of an edge are in the full version of the paper [5].

Candidate Algorithms: *(a) REC-INSERT [11], (b) MEMETIC [3]:* We adapt these algorithms for TD-CPO by eliminating loops (if any) from the final path.

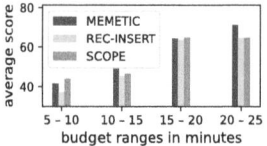

(a) Score comparison in Oldenburg network for 50% overhead, 20% edges with positive score.

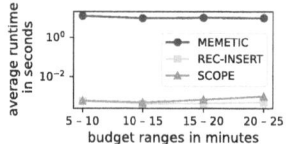

(b) Runtime comparison in Oldenburg network for 50% overhead 20% edges with positive score. Y-axis is in log_{100} scale.

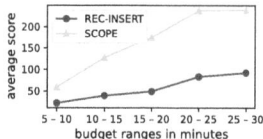

(c) Score comparison in Moscow network for 50% overhead, 20% edges with positive score.

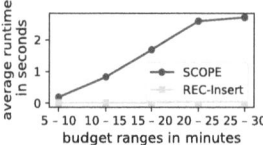

(d) Runtime comparison in Moscow network for 50% overhead, 20% edges with positive score.

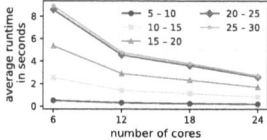

(e) Runtime comparison with varying number of cores in Moscow network for 50% overhead, 20% edges with a positive score.

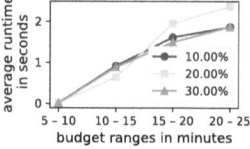

(f) Runtime comparison with varying density of edges with positive score in Moscow network for 50% overhead.

Fig. 2. Comparison between MEMETIC, REC-INSERT and $\mathcal{SCOPE}$.

Experimental Setup: We implemented all the algorithms in Java and conducted experiments on the Intel Xeon Gold 6258R server with 28 cores, 32GB of RAM, a base frequency of 2.7GHz, and a maximum boost frequency of 4GHz.

5.1   Experimental Evaluation

For all the experiments, we created query buckets for different budget ranges (fastest path time + overhead), each containing 100 queries. We report the average score gain and runtime for all the query buckets.

Performance Evaluation: Fig. 2(a) and 2(b) illustrate the performance of the algorithms on the Oldenburg network. MEMETIC has a slightly better score, while REC-INSERT and $\mathcal{SCOPE}$ have comparable scores (Fig. 2(a)). In terms of runtime, REC-INSERT and $\mathcal{SCOPE}$ have similar runtime of 1 ms, while

MEMETIC has exponential runtime over 10 `secs`. As MEMETIC was not scalable, it was removed from the further experiments. We tested REC-INSERT and $\mathcal{SCOPE}$ further on large networks.

Figure 2(c) and 2(d) compare $\mathcal{SCOPE}$ and REC-INSERT on the Moscow network. $\mathcal{SCOPE}$ achieves more than 3X score gain compared to REC-INSERT for each query bucket while maintaining feasible runtime within 3 `secs`. $\mathcal{SCOPE}$ shows maximum runtime of 2.7 `secs` compare to 4 `ms` for REC-INSERT.

Figure 2(e) presents the linear scale-up shown by $\mathcal{SCOPE}$ with increasing CPU cores (6, 12, 18, 24) in different query buckets on the Moscow network. The runtime of $\mathcal{SCOPE}$ decreases linearly with an increasing number of CPU cores, and the curves start to flatten once the runtime falls within one second.

Sensitivity Analysis: We conducted extensive sensitivity analysis of $\mathcal{SCOPE}$ by varying overheads and densities of edges with positive scores. However, due to page constraints, we only show some of the key results in Fig. 2(f). More experimental results are presented in the full version [5]). In this experiment, we varied the percentage of edges with positive scores (10%, 20%, 30%) to create three distinct datasets with Moscow road network. Our results indicate that this parameter has no effect on the runtime of $\mathcal{SCOPE}$. This is because the runtime is dependent on the amount of search space, which does not change. When we have a higher percentage of positive scores, just the final score obtained improves.

6   Conclusion

This paper presented the novel problem of Time-Dependent Constrained Path Optimization problem (TD-CPO) and proposed an efficient algorithm ($\mathcal{SCOPE}$) for the same. $\mathcal{SCOPE}$ solves the TD-CPO efficiently through adept utilization of temporal properties of the road network. Experimental evaluations on large road networks demonstrate that $\mathcal{SCOPE}$ produces significantly higher quality solutions (with comparable execution times) than the state-of-the-art algorithms. The linear scalability of $\mathcal{SCOPE}$ underscores its applicability in problems with larger search spaces.

Acknowledgments. This research work is supported by IIT Ropar, Microsoft India R&D and University of Hull.

References

1. https://users.cs.utah.edu/lifeifei/SpatialDataset.htm
2. Bulterman, R., et al.: On computing a longest path in a tree. Inf. Process. Lett. **81**(2), 93–96 (2002)
3. Chen, C., et. al.: Enjoy the most beautiful scene now: a memetic algorithm to solve two-fold time-dependent arc orienteering problem. Fr. of Comp. Sc. **14**(2), 364–377
4. Dutta, K.K., et. al.: A multi-threading algorithm for constrained path optimization problem on road networks. In: WISE 2022, pp. 110–118 (2022)

5. Dutta, K.K., Gunturi, V.M.V.: Constrain path optimization on time-dependent road networks (2024). https://arxiv.org/abs/2409.17192
6. Gunturi, V.M.V., Shekhar, S.: Spatio-Temporal Graph Data Analytics (2017)
7. Hansen, P.: Bicriterion path problems. In: Fandel, G., Gal, T. (eds.) Multiple Criteria Decision Making Theory and Application, pp. 109–127. Springer Berlin Heidelberg, Berlin, Heidelberg (1980). https://doi.org/10.1007/978-3-642-48782-8_9
8. Karduni, A., et al.: A protocol to convert spatial polyline data to network formats and applications to world urban road networks. Sci. Data **3** (2016)
9. Kaur, R., Goyal, V., Gunturi, V.M.V.: Finding the most navigable path in road networks. GeoInformatica **25**(1), 207–240 (2021). https://doi.org/10.1007/s10707-020-00428-5
10. Kaur, R., et.al.: A navigation system for safe routing. In: 22nd IEEE MDM June 15-18, 2021, pp. 240–243 (2021)
11. Lu, Y., et. al.: Scenic routes now: Efficiently solving the time-dependent arc orienteering problem. In: Proceedings of the 2017 ACM CIKM, pp. 487–496 (2017)
12. Shekhar, S., et. al.: Spatial big-data challenges intersecting mobility and cloud computing. In: Proceedings of the 11th ACM MobiDE, p. 1–6. MobiDE '12 (2012)
13. Stanley, R.P.: Acyclic orientations of graphs. Discrete Math. **5**(2), 171–178 (1973)
14. Yuan, Y., et al.: Constrained shortest path query in a large time-dependent graph. Proc. VLDB Endow. **12**(10), 1058–1070 (2019)
15. Yuan, Y., et. al.: Weight-constrained route planning over time-dependent graphs. In: 2019 IEEE 35th ICDE, pp. 914–925 (2019)

A Web for More Inclusive, Sustainable and Prosperous Societies (Web-for-Good) Workshop

Prompt Strategies for Sarcastic Meme Detection: A Comparative Analysis

Faseela Abdullakutty[1]([✉]), Somaya Al-Maadeed[1], and Usman Naseem[2]

[1] Qatar University, Doha, Qatar
{faseela.abdullakutty,s_alali}@qu.edu.qa
[2] Macquarie University, Sydney, Australia
usman.naseem@mq.edu.au

Abstract. Memes, often characterized by subtle humour and irony, have become a prominent digital communication medium. Detecting sarcasm in memes presents a significant challenge due to its context-dependent nature, negatively impacting user experiences on social media platforms. To improve the ability of social media systems to recognize and manage sarcastic content, this study investigates the effectiveness of Large Language Models (LLMs) for sarcasm detection in memes. Specifically, we evaluate three prompting techniques: Standard Prompt, Chain of Thought (CoT), and Concise Chain of Thought (CCoT) to determine their impact on the classification of sarcastic memes. Using the GOAT dataset as a benchmark, the study employs four pre-trained LLMs: Flan-T5-XXL, Llama-2, Mistral 7B, and GPT-2. The research identifies the most effective prompting strategies for sarcasm detection through a comparative analysis. The results demonstrate that CoT and CCoT significantly enhance performance over the Standard Prompt, with CCoT achieving the highest accuracy, particularly with advanced models like Mistral 7B. However, the choice of prompting technique depends on both the model and task requirements, emphasizing the need for tailored approaches in sarcastic meme analysis.

Keywords: Meme detection · Prompting · LLMs

1 Introduction

Sarcastic memes have become a prominent form of communication on social media platforms. Subtle humour and irony are often used to convey messages that can influence online discourse [25]. Detecting sarcasm in memes is essential, as it helps to mitigate the spread of toxic or misleading content, which can negatively impact user experiences and online well-being [3]. However, sarcasm detection in memes poses a unique challenge due to its context-dependent nature and the ambiguity that often surrounds it. Successful sarcasm detection requires a nuanced understanding of both textual and visual elements within memes, making it a complex task that demands advanced analytical techniques [27].

M. Barhamgi et al. (Eds.): WISE 2024, LNCS 15463, pp. 285–298, 2025.
https://doi.org/10.1007/978-981-96-1483-7_25

Recent advances in LLMs have significantly improved the ability to detect sarcasm by capturing subtle linguistic cues and deeper contextual meanings. These models have proven particularly valuable in tasks that involve complex reasoning, such as sarcasm detection in memes. However, the prompting techniques used to guide these models play a crucial role in their performance. Prompt-based techniques have emerged as an effective way to improve sarcasm detection by structuring the input in a way that enhances the model's ability to reason and understand the context of the sarcasm in memes [8]. By selecting the right prompting technique, models can achieve better performance in terms of accuracy and recall.

This paper focuses on comparing three different prompting techniques, Standard Prompt, Chain of Thought (CoT) [13], and Concise Chain of Thought (CCoT) [26] for sarcasm detection in memes using LLMs. The Standard Prompt method provides a straightforward approach where the model relies on its pretrained knowledge to interpret the meme's textual content [15]. While this technique is easy to implement, it often struggles with the nuanced nature of sarcasm, as it lacks a structured reasoning process. In contrast, CoT prompting introduces a logical flow of reasoning steps that guide the model through a sequence of thoughts. This technique helps the model better understand the relationships between ideas and the context behind the sarcastic content. Finally, CCoT builds on the CoT approach by streamlining the reasoning process, aiming to maintain logical depth while increasing efficiency through more concise prompts.

The use of prompting techniques, especially in zero-shot and few-shot learning scenarios, has shown great potential for improving sarcasm detection [6]. However, limited research has explored the comparative effectiveness of CoT and CCoT for sarcastic meme analysis. Given the multi-modal nature of memes, where visual and textual content are intertwined [1], it is critical to apply prompting techniques that can bridge these modalities effectively. In this study, the BLIP (Bootstrapping Language-Image Pre-training) model [18] is used to convert meme images into textual captions, allowing the application of LLMs to focus on text-based sarcasm detection. This conversion simplifies the analysis and enables a more accurate assessment of how different prompting techniques perform in sarcasm detection.

The study employs the GOAT dataset [20], a benchmark for meme analysis, to evaluate the performance of Flan-T5-XXL [11], Llama-2 [30], Mistral 7B [16], and GPT-2 [24]. Each model is tested across the three prompting techniques (Standard Prompt, CoT, and CCoT) to assess their effectiveness in detecting sarcasm. Results indicate that CoT and CCoT, which incorporate structured reasoning, lead to improved performance compared to the Standard Prompt, especially in more advanced models like Flan-T5-XXL and Mistral7B. While CoT tends to offer a better balance between accuracy and F1 score, CCoT achieves the highest accuracy, though at the expense of a slight reduction in F1 score.

The major contributions of the paper are as follows:

- Comparison of prompting techniques and structured reasoning: The paper compares three key prompting techniques for detecting sarcasm in memes, including Standard Prompt, Chain of Thought (CoT), and Concise Chain of Thought (CCoT).
- An evaluation of LLMs using the GOAT sarcasm task: This study examines the performance of state-of-the-art LLMs, such as Flan-T5-XXL, Llama-2, Mistral 7B, and GPT-2, on the sarcasm task from the GOAT dataset.
- Enhancing Sarcasm Detection in Memes: Using the BLIP model, this paper simplifies multi-modal meme analysis by converting meme images into textual captions, enabling better text-based sarcasm detection. It offers a practical framework for integrating visual and textual modalities as well as valuable guidelines for selecting most effective prompting techniques.

2   Related Works

As a form of digital content, memes combine image and text, creating a unique challenge for multi-modal analysis [9]. Their increasing prevalence has spurred research aimed at sentiment and emotion recognition, sarcasm detection, and harmful content identification. Recent advances in LLMs and prompting techniques have contributed significantly to these areas of research.

2.1   Sarcasm Detection in Memes

Sarcasm detection in memes has been an active research area, leveraging both multimodal and multitask learning approaches. In a recent study, Bandyopadhyay et al. [5] proposed a deep multitask model for detecting sarcasm and recognizing emotions in Hindi memes. The study posits that sarcasm and emotion recognition are closely related tasks and utilizes a dataset of 7416 memes annotated with varying levels of sarcasm and multiple emotions. A key contribution of this study is the introduction of a Knowledge Infusion (KI) module, which incorporates sentiment-aware representations from pre-trained models. The results showed that their multitask model significantly outperforms single-task variants, highlighting the role of knowledge-based sentiment representation in improving performance. This work provides valuable insights into the synergistic relationship between sarcasm and emotion detection and introduces a robust dataset for future research.

Maity et al. [22] further explored sarcasm detection by incorporating it as an auxiliary task in their frameworks, BERT+ResNet-Feedback and CLIP-CentralNet, designed for cyberbullying detection. By integrating sentiment analysis, emotion recognition, and sarcasm detection, these multimodal frameworks addressed the implicit affective content in memes. Their results indicated that such integration enhances cyberbullying detection performance, improving it by over 3% compared to unimodal approaches. This approach emphasizes the importance of multimodal sentiment understanding for more nuanced content detection tasks.

Addressing the distinction between sarcasm and humor, Kumari et al. [17] developed the Mu2STS model, a deep learning architecture tailored to disentangle the often conflated aspects of sarcasm and humor. The authors introduced the Sarcasm-with-Humorous-Meme-in-Hindi (SHMH) dataset to evaluate their model's performance. The Mu2STS model outperformed state-of-the-art techniques, demonstrating superior capability in detecting both sarcastic and humorous content. This work contributes to the field by emphasizing the complexity of sarcasm-humor interaction and offering a refined approach to detect these elements in meme content.

Sivalingam et al. [29] proposed an unsupervised learning algorithm, CRF-MEM, for sarcasm detection in social media. Their approach was based on aspect relationship values, allowing the model to detect sarcasm without the need for manual labeling. The CRF-MEM model achieved higher accuracy compared to traditional supervised models and could measure the intensity of sarcasm, providing a more nuanced understanding of sarcastic content.

Sharma et al. [28] introduced the ALFRED framework, which incorporates a gated multimodal fusion mechanism to detect emotions in memes, crucial for understanding sarcasm and related affective states. The framework demonstrated superior performance over baselines in detecting nuanced emotions using multimodal attention mechanisms. This research highlights the growing importance of cross-modal fusion in meme analysis, where emotions and sarcasm are deeply intertwined.

2.2   Prompting in Meme Analysis

Prompting techniques have emerged as a powerful tool for meme analysis, particularly in resource-constrained environments. Wu et al. [32] proposed a prompt-based multimodal fine-tuning approach to detect propaganda techniques in memes using both textual and image modalities. Their method demonstrated superior performance with limited data and without requiring large-scale pre-training, making it a valuable contribution to the low-resource meme analysis domain.

Cui et al. [12] introduced the Antipersuasion Prompt Enhanced Contrastive Learning (APCL) model for detecting propaganda in memes. This model employed prompt engineering to reformulate the task as a contrastive learning problem by generating matched and mismatched text-image pairs. The APCL model outperformed existing multimodal classification models, underscoring the potential of prompt engineering in improving meme classification tasks.

Arya et al. [4] utilized prompt engineering to enhance the Contrastive Language-Image Pre-Training (CLIP) model for detecting hateful memes. By providing explicit instructions to guide the model's interpretation of text and image data, the study demonstrated improved accuracy in identifying hateful content. This approach highlights the utility of prompt engineering in integrating multimodal information for content classification.

Acharya et al. [2] proposed a metaphor-capturing mechanism that incorporated external knowledge, using ChatGPT to bridge semantic gaps between text and image modalities. Their approach leveraged graph attention networks to fuse multimodal data, outperforming traditional methods. This research demonstrated how prompts and external knowledge could be used to capture complex semantic relationships in meme analysis.

Cao et al. [8] introduced PromptHate, a prompt-based model for hateful meme classification using the RoBERTa language model. The model leveraged simple prompts and in-context examples, achieving high classification performance without requiring extensive fine-tuning. Similarly, Prakash et al. [23] presented the PromptMTopic model, which uses multimodal prompts to extract and cluster topics from memes, providing efficient learning without additional fine-tuning.

Lin et al. [19] explored a novel approach for detecting harmful memes through a multimodal debate between large language models. Their method involved generating contradictory arguments from both harmless and harmful perspectives, with a smaller language model acting as a debate judge. This innovative approach outperformed traditional methods and offered a new direction for using prompt-based reasoning in meme content analysis.

In summary, the integration of prompting techniques with multimodal models has significantly advanced the field of meme analysis, offering improved performance across various tasks such as sarcasm detection, emotion recognition, and harmful content identification. These advancements underscore the importance of cross-modal learning and the evolving role of large language models in understanding complex multimodal content.

3   Method

The sarcasm detection framework for memes follows the process illustrated in Fig. 1. First, the meme images are converted into textual captions using the BLIP image captioning model [18]. These generated captions, along with the corresponding meme text, are then input into LLMs, where different prompting techniques: Standard Prompt, Chain of Thought (CoT), and Concise Chain of Thought (CCoT) are applied to evaluate their effectiveness in sarcasm detection.

This study focuses on evaluating the impact of prompting strategies rather than caption verification. Unlike previous work [15], which incorporated masked prompts, image attributes, and a CLIP-based verification layer for caption relevance, this method streamlines the analysis by omitting these intermediate steps. While a CLIP-based verification layer could enhance the accuracy of captions, the study prioritizes isolating the effects of prompt variations: Standard Prompt, CoT, and CCoT on sarcasm detection performance. Although there is an understanding that image captions may not always capture the full subtleties of sarcasm, the generated captions were considered sufficient for this analysis.

The pre-trained LLMs used for comparison are GPT-2, Llama-2, Mistral 7B, and Flan-T5-XXL, selected for their distinct architectures and varying parameter sizes, providing a diverse evaluation of model performance with different prompting techniques. GPT-2, with 1.5 billion parameters, serves as a baseline model to assess how earlier, smaller, instruction-tuned models perform in sarcasm detection tasks. Its inclusion helps in understanding how modern techniques compare to earlier-generation models. Llama-2, a more recent model with 7 billion parameters, is known for its balance between performance and resource efficiency. It has strong generalization capabilities and has been optimized for reasoning tasks. The model provides insight into how a state-of-the-art LLM with intermediate parameter size, tuned specifically for performance and efficiency, handles sarcasm detection with different prompting techniques. Mistral 7B is another intermediate model with a parameter size comparable to Llama-2, but designed with an emphasis on generalization and versatility. Including Mistral 7B allows for a direct comparison between models of similar sizes but different architectures and pre-training strategies. Flan-T5-XXL, with 11 billion parameters, is a highly advanced model designed explicitly for instruction tuning and complex reasoning tasks. It represents a cutting-edge system for sarcasm detection, enabling a thorough evaluation of how larger models optimized for instruction-based learning perform with structured reasoning prompts.

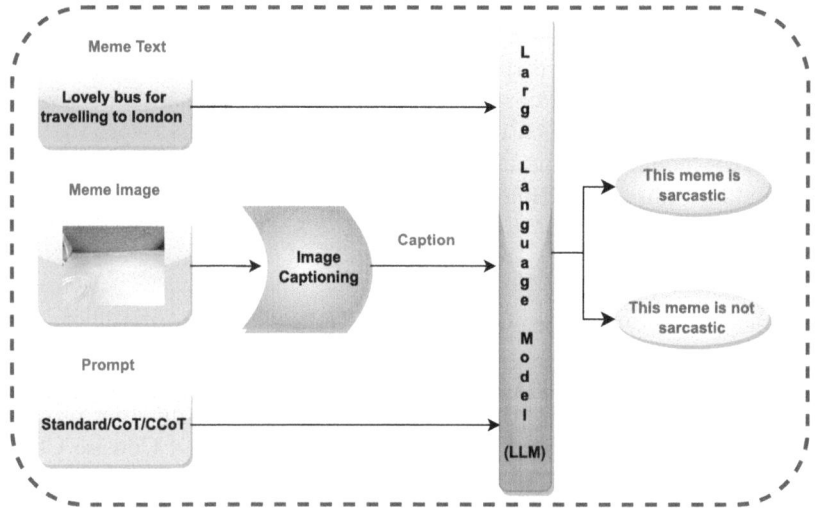

Fig. 1. Framework to compare the performance of standard, CoT, and CCoT prompting methods in meme classification

The evaluation focuses on analyzing the effectiveness of Standard Prompt, CoT, and CCoT techniques across these models. Standard Prompt serves as a simple baseline, while CoT introduces a structured reasoning approach to enhance sarcasm detection by guiding the model through logical steps. CCoT refines this process by maintaining logical depth while improving efficiency through more concise prompts. These experiments allow for a thorough investigation of how model size, architecture, and prompt strategy impact sarcasm detection, with a focus on how structured reasoning improves performance, particularly in advanced models like Mistral 7B, Llama-2, and Flan-T5-XXL.

By including models with varying architectures and parameter sizes, such as GPT-2, Llama-2, Mistral 7B, and Flan-T5-XXL, the study offers insights into how different model configurations interact with structured reasoning prompts in sarcasm detection. This approach provides a comprehensive understanding of the role that model architecture and prompting technique play in complex, multi-modal tasks like meme analysis.

The standard prompt in the form, "Given meme image has a caption C, accompanied by text T. Is this meme *sarcastic* ?". In this prompt, C is the image caption generated by the BLIP model, and T is the text corresponding to each meme. The model responses were analyzed, and the performance was compared using the F1-score, precision and recall.

3.1   Chain-of-Thought (CoT)

Chain of Thought (CoT) [10] is a cognitive process that connects and reasoning about a series of thoughts or ideas in a coherent manner. It offers advantages such as generating coherent chains of reasoning, recognizing and correcting inconsistencies in the context, improving external knowledge utilization, enhancing reasoning [13,31] by incorporating external knowledge, handling uncertainty, and improving reasoning efficiency. CoT reasoning can lead to better results by reducing factual mistakes and enhancing the accuracy of external knowledge retrieval and utilization. The effectiveness of COT lies in conveying task understanding and leveraging the model's capacity to fill in missing information and make informed predictions [21].

To evaluate the performance of CoT on meme analysis, the CoT prompt used had the form, "Given meme image has a caption C, accompanied by text T. Let us think step by step whether this meme is *Sarcastic* ?" [20]. In CoT, the LLM was asked to think step-by-step. The resulting response was analyzed for sentiment and compared with the existing label to assess the performance.

3.2   Concise Chain of Thoughts(CCoT)

Concise Chain-of-Thought (CCoT) prompting [26] is a technique that combines the effectiveness of CoT prompting with the efficiency of concise prompting. It aims to produce a chain of thought that leads to a correct solution with the shortest response length possible. CCoT instructs the language model to think step-by-step and concisely. The CCoT prompt was "Given meme image has a caption C. It is accompanied by text T. Let us be concise and think step by step if this meme is *Sarcastic* ?"

3.3   Dataset

The GOAT Bench [20] dataset was used to compare prompting methods in this article. Table 1 shows the class distribution for the sarcasm task in this dataset (Fig. 2).

(a)

(b)

Fig. 2. Sample meme images from GOAT dataset

Within the GOAT dataset, which encompasses 6,000 image-text pairs spanning five distinct tasks, a subset of 1,820 pairs pertains to the sarcasm task. Within this subset, 910 pairs are classified as belonging to the sarcastic class, while the remaining pairs are categorized as non-sarcastic. These samples were drawn from an established multimodal meme dataset, as referenced in [7], which is publicly accessible, to constitute the sarcasm task within the GOAT dataset.

3.4   Experimental Settings

The dataset GOAT Bench, which included sarcasm as one of its tasks, had subsets corresponding to each task, with Memotion included as a second dataset. To conduct meme analysis, captions were first generated using the BLIP model (*Salesforce/blip-image-captioning-large*). These captions were then used to form

Table 1. Class distribution of GOAT dataset

Dataset	Class	Size
GOAT	*Sarcastic*	910
	Non sarcastic	910

prompts for each scenario considered in the method. Three types of prompts—standard prompt, CoT, and CCoT—were evaluated using Flan-T5-XXL, GPT-2, and the pre-trained language model Mistral 7B. The GOAT Bench dataset had two classes for each task, thus the evaluation was performed as a binary classification. Accuracy and F1 score were used to compare performance.

4   Results

Table 2 presents a comparative performance analysis of various prompting techniques—Standard Prompt, Chain of Thought (CoT), and Concise Chain of Thought (CCoT)—applied across different LLMs, including GPT-2, Llama-2, Flan-T5-XXL, and Mistral7B, for the task of sarcastic meme analysis on the GOAT dataset. The evaluation metrics considered are accuracy (ACC) and F1 score. The table highlights the performance of each model across the three prompting techniques, offering insights into how each method influences the models' ability to detect sarcasm. This comparison underscores the varying effectiveness of these LLMs when subjected to more complex reasoning tasks such as those posed by sarcasm detection, with CoT and CCoT showing significant improvements in performance metrics over the Standard Prompt, particularly in more advanced models like Flan-T5-XXL and Mistral7B.

Table 2. Performance comparison of standard, CoT, and CCoT prompt methods, using different LLMs for sarcastic meme analysis

Dataset	Prompt Technique	GPT-2		Llama-2		Flan-T5-XXL		Mistral7B	
		ACC	F1 Score	ACC	F1 Score	ACC	F1 Score	ACC	F1 Score
GOAT	Standard	50.6	35.58	51.15	47.22	77.60	60.31	67.80	43.73
	CoT	50.44	34.59	51.32	47.13	70.30	53.50	57.80	54.68
	CCoT	50.16	33.99	51.10	46.14	80.00	54.60	91.00	47.64

Across all prompting techniques, GPT-2's accuracy is relatively stable, hovering around 50%. There is, however, a noticeable variation in its F1 scores. F1 scores for GPT-2 are highest when using the Standard Prompt method (35.58), while both CoT (31.49) and CCoT (33.99) have slightly lower scores. The results indicate that the more structured reasoning techniques (CoT and CCoT) do not significantly enhance sarcasm detection in GPT-2 compared with the Standard Prompt. The GPT-2 showed limited improvement in the context of this task when compared with more complex prompting methods. Compared with GPT-2, Llama-2 shows a slightly better performance, particularly in terms of the F1 score. The highest F1 score (47.22) is achieved using the Standard Prompt, with an accuracy rate of 51.15%. The performance of Llama-2 remains similar when using CoT and CCoT, although accuracy and F1 score show a small decrease. There is a small drop in F1 score (47.13) for CoT and the lowest F1 score (46.14) for CCoT. According to these results, although Llama-2 detects sarcasm moderately better than GPT-2, it does not benefit significantly from CoT or CCoT.

Flan-T5-XXL exhibits a significantly higher performance than both GPT-2 and Llama-2. Using the Standard prompting technique, the model achieves its highest F1 score (60.31) and accuracy (77.60%). In spite of the slightly lower F1 score (53.50) and accuracy (70.30%) associated with the CoT technique, Flan-T5-XXL still performs well. With CCoT, Flan-T5-XXL achieves its highest accuracy (80.00%), but its F1 score drops to 54.60. This indicates that, while CoT and CCoT offer excellent performance in terms of accuracy, the Standard Prompt provides the best balance between precision and recall. In terms of performance, the Mistral7B model, which is used to determine sarcastic memes, is inconsistent across different prompting techniques. There is a challenge in balancing precision and recall by using the Standard Prompt method, which yields 67.80% accuracy and an F1 score of 43.73. This indicates that a simple prompt may not be sufficient to fully utilize the capabilities of Mistral7B in the detection of sarcasm. By using the Chain of Thought (CoT) method, Mistral7B achieves an F1 score of 54.68 and an accuracy of 57.80%. CCoT achieves the highest accuracy of 91.00% but has a slight reduction in F1 score to 47.64. The use of structured reasoning prompts, specifically CoT, demonstrated its high capability for the detection of sarcastic memes using Mistral7B.

The Standard Prompt can be effective for models such as the GPT-2 and the Llama-2, whereas the CoT can significantly improve performance on advanced models such as the Flan-T5-XXL and the Mistral7B. As a result of CoT, accuracy and F1 score are improved, while CCoT increases accuracy, especially in Flan-T5-XXL and Mistral7B. The Mistral7B achieves an impressive accuracy rate of 91%, however CCoT may sacrifice precision and recall in order to achieve greater accuracy. Flan-T5-XXL and Mistral7B are better suited for tasks that require precision and recall in detecting sarcastic memes. When accuracy is the priority, the Mistral7B with CCoT is the best option, while the Flan-T5-XXL with CoT is the best for models with balanced F1 scores. Model choice and prompting technique should be aligned with the task's objectives, with structured reasoning prompts essential for advanced LLMs in sarcasm detection.

4.1   Discussion

An evaluation of a variety of prompting techniques is presented in this study, including the Standard Prompt, Chain of Thought CoT, and CCoT, across different LLMs for the analysis of sarcastic memes. Several factors influence the performance of each model, including its architecture and the prompting technique employed. This emphasizes the importance of aligning the selected prompting technique with the capabilities of the respective model.

Based on GPT-2, the model has demonstrated relatively stable performance across all prompting techniques, with accuracy in the range of 50% or more. In spite of this, GPT-2 does not show significant improvements when more advanced prompting methods such as CoT or CCoT are used. Based on this analysis, it appears that simpler models like GPT-2 have difficulty leveraging the structured reasoning provided by CoT and CCoT, limiting their ability to capture the nuances of sarcasm. Although GPT-2 is capable of performing basic sarcasm detection tasks, it lacks the sophistication required for more complex tasks requiring advanced reasoning.

With respect to Llama-2, the results show a marginal improvement over GPT-2, particularly in terms of F1. The highest F1 score of 47.22 was achieved by Llama-2 with the Standard Prompt, along with a slight improvement in accuracy at 51.15 percent. The more advanced CoT and CCoT techniques do not seem to have much of an impact on Llama-2, much as they do on GPT-2. Although Llama-2 detects sarcasm more accurately than GPT-2, it does not gain any significant advantages from structured reasoning techniques in terms of accuracy or F1. Accordingly, Llama-2 may be limited in its ability to handle tasks that require deep contextual understanding or complex reasoning, similar to GPT-2.

Compared with both GPT-2 and Llama-2, Flan-T5-XXL displays a significant performance improvement across all metrics. A substantial improvement in both accuracy and F1 score across the various prompting techniques can be attributed to Flan-T5-XXL's extensive use of structured reasoning. CoT, in particular, exhibits a more balanced performance in terms of accuracy and F1 score, while COT excels at maximizing accuracy, especially in models such as Mistral7B, although it tends to cause a slight loss in F1. It is evident that CCoT is more appropriate for scenarios where accuracy is of the utmost importance, while CoT is more appropriate for tasks requiring a more balanced approach between precision and recall.

This study emphasizes the importance of aligning model selection and prompting techniques with the specific objectives of the task. The use of structured reasoning prompts can greatly improve the performance of advanced models in tasks like sarcasm detection, with CoT and CoT proving particularly successful with models like Flan-T5-XXL and Mistral7B.

The sarcasm task dataset partition in the GOAT dataset has limitations due to its small size and the subjective nature of sarcasm. The study simplified the multimodal nature of memes by converting visual content into textual captions, potentially overlooking key interactions between text and images. Future research should expand the dataset size and diversity, explore more sophisticated multimodal models, and refine prompting techniques to improve performance across various Large Language Models. Cross-dataset evaluations and explainable AI techniques could provide more comprehensive insights into sarcasm detection. Future studies should integrate visual features alongside text-based analysis to fully utilize the multimodal nature of memes. Advanced models capable of processing and combining visual cues with text can better understand the nuanced sarcasm conveyed in memes.

This study provides a unique contribution to the field of sarcasm detection, particularly when applied to memes, a form of digital communication that has seen limited exploration with structural reasoning prompting. Based on our comparison of CoT and CCoT with standard prompts, we demonstrate that structured reasoning has the potential to enhance model performance in detecting sarcasm, an area where contextual information is critical [14]. Through this comparative analysis, future research can be guided by a framework for selecting appropriate prompting techniques based on the complexity of the task. As memes continue to dominate digital communication, identifying subtle cues of sarcasm becomes increasingly important. This study provides insights that will facilitate the development of more advanced sarcasm detection models that leverage both visual and textual modalities for better interpretability and accuracy.

5   Conclusion

This study evaluated different prompting techniques, including Standard Prompt, Chain of Thought (CoT), and Concise Chain of Thought (CCoT), across multiple LLMs for sarcastic meme analysis using the GOAT dataset. The results showed that model architecture and prompting technique significantly impact sarcasm detection performance, with advanced models like Flan-T5-XXL and Mistral7B benefiting more from structured reasoning techniques (CoT and CCoT) compared to simpler models like GPT-2 and Llama-2. GPT-2 and Llama-2 demonstrated limited gains from CoT and CCoT, suggesting they are not well-suited for tasks requiring advanced reasoning, such as sarcasm detection. In contrast, Flan-T5-XXL and Mistral7B showed significant improvements with structured reasoning prompts, particularly CoT and CCoT. The results highlight that CoT is the preferred prompting technique for achieving a balance between accuracy and F1 score, making it ideal for tasks where precision and recall are equally important. CCoT is most effective when accuracy is the primary goal, especially for advanced models like Mistral7B. The findings emphasize the importance of selecting both the model and the prompting technique based on the specific requirements of the task. Advanced models paired with structured reasoning prompts are necessary for optimal performance in sarcasm detection, while simpler models benefit less from these techniques. Future directions for future research include fine-tuning and model adaptation, multi-modal fusion approaches, prompt optimization, cross-dataset evaluation, and explainability and interpretability methods for LLMs.

References

1. Abdullakutty, F., Naseem, U.: Decoding memes: a comprehensive analysis of late and early fusion models for explainable meme analysis. In: Companion Proceedings of the ACM on Web Conference 2024, pp. 1681–1689 (2024)

2. Acharya, S., Das, B., Sudarshan, T.: Capturing the concept projection in metaphorical memes for downstream learning tasks. IEEE Access (2023)
3. Arora, A.: Sarcasm detection in social media: a review. In: Proceedings of the International Conference on Innovative Computing & Communication (ICICC) (2021)
4. Arya, G., et al.: Multimodal hate speech detection in memes using contrastive language-image pre-training. IEEE Access (2024)
5. Bandyopadhyay, D., Kumari, G., Ekbal, A., Pal, S., Chatterjee, A., BN, V.: A knowledge infusion based multitasking system for sarcasm detection in meme. In: Kamps, J., et al. (eds.) European Conference on Information Retrieval, vol. 139801, pp. 101–117. Springer, Cham (2023)
6. Bu, K., Liu, Y., Ju, X.: Efficient utilization of pre-trained models: a review of sentiment analysis via prompt learning. Knowl. Based Syst. **283**, 111148 (2023)
7. Cai, Y., Cai, H., Wan, X.: Multi-modal sarcasm detection in twitter with hierarchical fusion model. In: Proceedings of the 57th Annual Meeting of the Association for Computational Linguistics, pp. 2506–2515 (2019)
8. Cao, R., Lee, R.K.W., Chong, W.H., Jiang, J.: Prompting for multimodal hateful meme classification. arXiv preprint arXiv:2302.04156 (2023)
9. Chen, S., Naseem, U., Razzak, I., Salim, F.: Unveiling misogyny memes: a multimodal analysis of modality effects on identification. In: Companion Proceedings of the ACM on Web Conference 2024, pp. 1864–1871 (2024)
10. Chu, Z., et al.: A survey of chain of thought reasoning: advances, frontiers and future. arXiv preprint arXiv:2309.15402 (2023)
11. Chung, H.W., et al.: Scaling instruction-finetuned language models. arXiv preprint arXiv:2210.11416 (2022)
12. Cui, J., Li, L., Zhang, X., Yuan, J.: Multimodal propaganda detection via antipersuasion prompt enhanced contrastive learning. In: ICASSP 2023-2023 IEEE International Conference on Acoustics, Speech and Signal Processing (ICASSP), pp. 1–5. IEEE (2023)
13. Fei, H., Li, B., Liu, Q., Bing, L., Li, F., Chua, T.S.: Reasoning implicit sentiment with chain-of-thought prompting. arXiv preprint arXiv:2305.11255 (2023)
14. Ji, J., Lin, X., Naseem, U.: CapAlign: improving cross modal alignment via informative captioning for harmful meme detection. In: Proceedings of the ACM on Web Conference 2024, pp. 4585–4594 (2024)
15. Ji, J., Ren, W., Naseem, U.: Identifying creative harmful memes via prompt based approach. In: Proceedings of the ACM Web Conference 2023, pp. 3868–3872 (2023)
16. Jiang, A.Q., et al.: Mistral 7B. arXiv preprint arXiv:2310.06825 (2023)
17. Kumari, G., Adak, C., Ekbal, A.: MU2STS: a mu ltitask mu ltimodal s arcasm-humor-differential t eacher-s tudent model for sarcastic meme detection. In: European Conference on Information Retrieval, pp. 19–37. Springer, Cham (2024). https://doi.org/10.1007/978-3-031-56063-7_2
18. Li, J., Li, D., Xiong, C., Hoi, S.: BLIP: bootstrapping language-image pre-training for unified vision-language understanding and generation. In: International Conference on Machine Learning, pp. 12888–12900. PMLR (2022)
19. Lin, H., Luo, Z., Gao, W., Ma, J., Wang, B., Yang, R.: Towards explainable harmful meme detection through multimodal debate between large language models. arXiv preprint arXiv:2401.13298 (2024)
20. Lin, H., Luo, Z., Wang, B., Yang, R., Ma, J.: Goat-bench: safety insights to large multimodal models through meme-based social abuse. arXiv preprint arXiv:2401.01523 (2024)

21. Madaan, A., Hermann, K., Yazdanbakhsh, A.: What makes chain-of-thought prompting effective? A counterfactual study. In: Findings of the Association for Computational Linguistics: EMNLP 2023, pp. 1448–1535 (2023)
22. Maity, K., Jha, P., Saha, S., Bhattacharyya, P.: A multitask framework for sentiment, emotion and sarcasm aware cyberbullying detection from multi-modal code-mixed memes. In: Proceedings of the 45th International ACM SIGIR Conference on Research and Development in Information Retrieval, pp. 1739–1749 (2022)
23. Prakash, N., Wang, H., Hoang, N.K., Hee, M.S., Lee, R.K.W.: PromptMTopic: unsupervised multimodal topic modeling of memes using large language models. In: Proceedings of the 31st ACM International Conference on Multimedia, pp. 621–631 (2023)
24. Radford, A., Wu, J., Child, R., Luan, D., Amodei, D., Sutskever, I.: Language models are unsupervised multitask learners (2019)
25. Rathi, N., Jain, P.: Memes, memetics and their applications: a systematic review of literature (2024)
26. Renze, M., Guven, E.: The benefits of a concise chain of thought on problem-solving in large language models. arXiv preprint arXiv:2401.05618 (2024)
27. Sharma, S., et al.: Detecting and understanding harmful memes: a survey. arXiv preprint arXiv:2205.04274 (2022)
28. Sharma, S., Ramaneswaran, S., Akhtar, M.S., Chakraborty, T.: Emotion-aware multimodal fusion for meme emotion detection. IEEE Trans. Affect. Comput. **15**, 1800–1811 (2024)
29. Sivalingam, A., Sundararajan, K., Palanisamy, A.: CRF-MEM: conditional random field model based modified expectation maximization algorithm for sarcasm detection in social media. J. Internet Technol. **24**(1), 45–54 (2023)
30. Touvron, H., et al.: LLAMA 2: open foundation and fine-tuned chat models. arXiv preprint arXiv:2307.09288 (2023)
31. Wei, J., et al: Enhancing human-like multi-modal reasoning: a new challenging dataset and comprehensive framework. arXiv preprint arXiv:2307.12626 (2023)
32. Wu, H., Li, X., Li, L., Wang, Q.: Propaganda techniques detection in low-resource memes with multi-modal prompt tuning. In: 2022 IEEE International Conference on Multimedia and Expo (ICME), pp. 01–06. IEEE (2022)

Deepfake Detection in Cancer Medical Imaging Using CNN Architectures

Dima Talal Alhalabi[1], Moatsum Alawida[1(✉)], Belkacem Chikhaoui[2], and Hala Samer Hamadeh[1]

[1] Department of Computer Sciences, Abu Dhabi University, Abu Dhabi 59911, United Arab Emirates
moatsum.alawida@adu.ac.ae
[2] Applied Artificial Intelligence Institute, TELUQ University, Montreal, Canada

Abstract. Deepfake technology poses an emerging threat in the medical field, as its potential to manipulate medical scans could result in misdiagnoses, fraudulent claims, and serious health risks. This study addresses the urgent need for robust detection methods to safeguard medical imaging systems and patient safety. We developed a deepfake detection model by evaluating four Convolutional Neural Network (CNN) architectures: VGG16, EfficientNetV2, InceptionV3, and Sequential. These models were assessed using Precision, Recall, F1-Score, and Accuracy metrics to determine their effectiveness. CT scan images were resized to 256×256 pixels, and the models were trained for 100 epochs with early stopping to enhance training efficiency. The EfficientNetV2 architecture initially achieved the highest accuracy of 92% without data augmentation. However, following data augmentation, both EfficientNetV2 and VGG16 reached an accuracy of 93%, with VGG16 being selected due to its superior recall rate of 98%, effectively minimizing false negatives and improving deepfake detection reliability.

Keywords: Deepfake detection · Medical images · Convolutional Neural Networks (CNNs) · Machine learning

1 Introduction

The rapid advancement of technology has led to the widespread use of medical imaging methods, such as CT scans, MRIs, X-rays, and Ultrasounds, which play a crucial role in diagnosing and treating various diseases without invasive procedures [12]. Specifically, CT scans and MRIs offer a three-dimensional cross-sectional perspective of the body providing comprehensive insights into bones, soft tissues, and blood vessels [1]. These emerging technologies are integrated into Picture Archiving Communication Systems (PACS) [10], which operate on Ethernet-based networks and include the central server [18]. PACS receive medical scans from linked imaging devices, store them in a database for future access, and retrieve them for radiologists to examine and annotate. The standardised

M. Barhamgi et al. (Eds.): WISE 2024, LNCS 15463, pp. 299–312, 2025.
https://doi.org/10.1007/978-981-96-1483-7_26

DICOM format ensures compatibility across different systems transmitting and storing these digital medical scans [22].

Despite advancements in medical imaging technology, many healthcare sectors lag in adopting modern security standards [19]. They often employ outdated security protocols and obsolete software, creating vulnerabilities that cybercriminals can exploit. These vulnerabilities compromise the confidentiality, integrity, and availability of patients' medical records stored on PACS servers [2,3,17]. Attackers can manipulate the contents of medical scans, leading to inaccurate diagnoses. Figure 1 by [16] illustrates potential entry points into the PACS network through which an attacker could gain access to medical scans. To ensure high realism in modifications, attackers often utilize deep learning technologies, such as deepfake [9]. This enables them to tamper with medical evidence by injecting or removing conditions like cancer from scans [8].

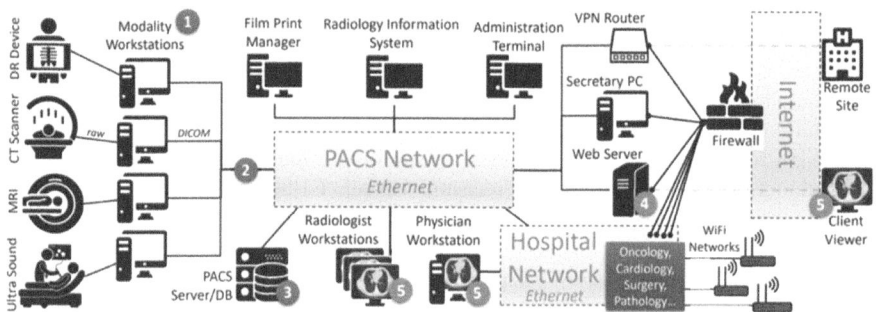

Fig. 1. PACS network entry points

The complexity of deepfake technology makes it challenging for even trained medical professionals to distinguish between authentic and altered scans. Undetected deepfaked medical scans can result in inaccurate diagnoses, incorrect or unnecessary treatments, or severe cases, leading to patient deaths [8,9]. This highlights the critical need for developing more secured medical systems designed to detect deepfaked medical images. The prevalence of deepfake technology has significantly increased over the past year, posing one of the biggest threats in the current world. According to Sumsub's statistics from 2022 to the first quarter of 2023, the incidence of deepfake-related fraud has risen dramatically in several countries, including a 4.5% increase in Canada, 2.4% in the United States, 6.1% in Germany, and 4.7% in the United Kingdom [11]. Figure 2 illustrates the increase of deep fake over the years.

Attackers might use deepfake technology for various malicious purposes, such as stopping a political candidate, destroying research, engaging in insurance fraud, committing acts of terrorism, or even murder [8,9]. Recognizing these dangers, our paper investigates the implications of deepfake technology in altering medical scans to inject or remove cancer. The repercussions of tampering with

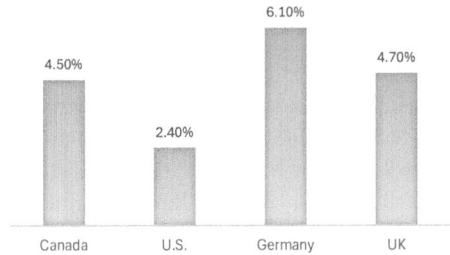

Fig. 2. Deepfake Fraud Increase (2022 to Q1 2023)

a medical scan can lead to misdiagnoses and subsequent fraudulent disability or life insurance claims, among other severe consequences. With the increasing threat of deepfake crimes in the medical field. We aim to develop a method capable of detecting deepfakes in medical scans.

In this paper, the main contributions are as follows:

1. We propose a binary classification model based on CNN architectures to detect deepfakes in cancer CT scans, effectively distinguishing between authentic and deepfake images.
2. We compare the performance of various CNN architectures using evaluation metrics such as Precision, Recall, F1-Score, Accuracy, and Confusion Matrix.
3. We validate the proposed model on a real dataset containing both authentic and deepfake cancer CT scans.

The organization of the paper is as follows: Sect. 2 presents Related Works, providing an overview of past research, and highlighting key contributions and gaps in existing encryption methods. Section 3 outlines the Methodology, detailing the steps of the proposed algorithm. Section 4 discusses Model Training, focusing on the training and configuration of the model. Section 5 presents the Results and Discussion. Finally, Sect. 6 concludes the paper.

2   Related Works

The related works have been searched in major research databases using terms such as deepfake detection, medical imaging, deep learning, and cybersecurity in healthcare. The primary sources include Google Scholar, IEEE, ACM, and McAfee. The results have been sifted to ensure relevancy to the development of deepfake detection systems for medical imaging. Relevancy has been established to compare the effectiveness of our proposed method with others in the literature. The security vulnerabilities within PACS used in medical imaging are a significant concern, as detailed by McAfee researchers in [5]. Medical data is an irresistible target for cybercriminals due to its nonperishable nature and high value. Cybercriminals often invest significant time and effort to exploit vulnerabilities in PACS. A typical PACS setup includes multiple components: a workstation, imaging device, acquisition gateway, PACS controller, database, and archiving system as explained by [13]. These components work together to capture, store, and manage medical images. However, many PACS implementations, especially those using free or open-source software, do not follow security best practices. This has led to vulnerabilities that cybercriminals can exploit.

Key vulnerabilities identified in PACS include outdated software like Apache Tomcat Version 7.0.13, which has over 40 known vulnerabilities [20], and the direct Internet connection of many PACS systems without proper security. Issues such as unencrypted traffic, default admin credentials, and cross-site scripting enable attackers to access servers, manipulate medical images, and retrieve sensitive data. Shodan identified over 1,100 exposed PACS servers. Recommendations for securing these systems include using VPNs, two-factor authentication, and regular software updates [7]. Additionally, research demonstrates how deep learning, such as GANs [21], can be misused to generate fraudulent medical images, further emphasizing the need for enhanced security [14]

The model uses an image-to-image style transfer approach, maintaining the patient's identity while injecting a chosen disease condition. This results in a 'deepfake' medical image, indistinguishable from a real one to both human and machine evaluators. The attack was tested against state-of-the-art disease detection algorithms and showed high success rates in misleading these models. The research community has made significant strides in detecting GAN-generated images and securing digital imagery using advanced encryption and deep learning techniques. The integration of traditional encryption methods with deep learning approaches has enhanced the robustness and accuracy of detection systems as explained previously in [14]. Other proposed techniques to detect deep fake as detailed by [8] are tamper detection methods like block-based detection and ROI-based schemes that use cryptographic and watermarking techniques to identify modifications, hybrid and dual-layer watermarking methods that embed information for tamper detection and recovery, approaches that encrypt medical images to protect against unauthorized access and tampering, and integration of deep learning and blockchain technology to enhance the robustness and security of medical image data.

However, challenges remain, particularly in detecting GAN-generated images in compressed formats and ensuring the scalability of these methods across different platforms. Our research focuses on improving the detection accuracy under real-world conditions and exploring new approaches to secure digital medical images effectively against deepfake attacks.

3   Methodology

To develop a deep-learning model for binary classification of cancer CT scans, differentiating between authentic or deepfake scans, two distinct datasets are utilized:

1. Authentic CT scan dataset, containing instances with and without cancer nodules.
2. Deepfaked CT scans dataset, containing fake injected and removed cancer nodules.

The authentic dataset, named the "Iraq-Oncology Teaching Hospital/National Center for Cancer Diseases (IQ-OTH/NCCD) lung cancer dataset," comprises **1097** CT scans featuring both healthy lungs and those with cancer nodules [4]. Initially stored in DICOM format, these scans were converted to JPGs and shared on Kaggle. The deepfake dataset, titled "Medical Deepfakes: Lung Cancer," consists of 70 manipulated CT scans in the DICOM format [15]. These scans were subjected to deepfake techniques, involving the insertion of synthetic cancer nodules and the removal of authentic ones. Notably, each CT scan comprises numerous DICOM files, each representing distinct thin slices of the scan along the Z axis. The deepfake alterations were applied to different slices of the CT scan, implying that multiple locations within each scan could undergo deepfake manipulation. The CT scans were provided with an Excel file detailing the exact slices of each scan that underwent deepfake manipulation. Consequently, the manipulated slices within the 70 scans were extracted, expanding the total number of DICOM files to **113**.

3.1 Converting DICOM to PNG

To visualize the deepfaked CT scans and feed them into the model, they were converted from their original DICOM format to PNG using the MicroDicom Viewer software. This is because PNG is a lossless format, preserving the quality of the CT scan regardless of how it is resized or compressed [6]. For starters, the CT scans were windowed using the "Lung" option to guarantee that they represent the correct shape of lung CT scans. Subsequently, each of the 113 DICOM slices was exported as a PNG image.

3.2 Creating and Balancing the Dataset

Upon converting all 113 deepfake DICOM slices to PNG, the second step involves building the initial dataset for the deep learning model. Essentially, the 113 deepfake CT scans were categorized into two groups: False Malignant (FM) and False Benign (FB). FM represents areas without cancerous growth that were later injected via deepfake, whereas FB represents areas with cancerous growth that were later removed via deepfake. Out of the 113 CT scans, 41 were classified as FM and 72 as FB. Additionally, the authentic dataset consisted of 1,097 instances, with and without cancerous nodules. As illustrated in Table 1, the initial dataset was **unbalanced**, with a relatively larger number of FB CT scans compared to FM. Although the creators of the deepfake dataset provided code to inject and remove cancerous nodules using deepfake technology artificially, this process demanded significant computational resources and processing power,

Table 1. Initial Dataset with 3 Categories

Category	Authentic	False Benign (FB)	False Malignant (FM)
No. of CT scans	1097	72	41

exceeding our available resources. Consequently, generating additional deepfake CT scans to augment the dataset and make it unbalanced was not feasible.

To address the issue of having unbalanced FM and FB categories, the two were merged into a single category called "Deepfake. This resulted in a total of 113 deepfake CT scans and 1,097 authentic CT scans, reducing the dataset to two categories: "Authentic" and "Deepfake", as demonstrated in Table 2.

Table 2. Modified Dataset with 2 Categories

Category	Authentic	Deepfake
No. of CT scans	1097	113

As depicted in Table 2, the dataset remains unbalanced, with the "Authentic" category significantly outnumbering the "Deepfake" category. This imbalance is a common issue in machine and deep learning models. The "Deepfake" dataset for cancer CT scans is the only one available online and in public archives, whereas authentic cancer CT scan datasets are widely available and much larger. This imbalance poses significant challenges, as the primary goal of our system is to accurately detect deepfake images. For instance, the developed model may become **biased** towards authentic CT scans, classifying them more accurately because it was trained on more data from this category. Conversely, for the minority deepfake class, the model may have **reduced recall** or sensitivity, indicating that it is more likely to fail in identifying deepfake instances correctly. This is problematic because it would often misclassify deepfakes as authentic, defeating the system's purpose. Moreover, the model might **overfit** the minority deepfake class, given that it has fewer images to generalize from. Therefore, this can lead to poor performance on unseen CT scans. Furthermore, an imbalanced dataset can distort evaluation metrics, particularly accuracy. A high accuracy might not reflect the true performance of the model. For example, the model might achieve high accuracy if it succeeds in classifying the majority class despite performing poorly in the minority class [23].

To handle the imbalanced dataset and avoid its negative consequences, the resampling technique was utilized, particularly **undersampling** the majority class, "Authentic". By applying this technique, we balanced the class distribution by reducing the number of authentic instances from 1097 to 113, randomly removing instances to achieve this balance. The resulting subset is representative of the entire dataset, maintaining key characteristics to avoid loss of critical information. As a result, the dataset is now balanced, with each category containing 113 instances, as illustrated in Table 3.

Table 3. Balanced Dataset After Under Sampling

Category	Authentic	Deepfake
No. of CT scans	113	113

Before beginning the development of the deep learning algorithm, we set aside 13 CT scan images from each category to be used later for validating the model's performance. This approach ensured that we evaluated the model on unseen CT scans, maintaining the integrity of our performance evaluation process. Therefore, each category retained **100** images for training and testing purposes.

3.3   Model Training

After finalizing our initial dataset, we develop our deepfake detection model. To achieve the highest accuracy, we experiment with various Convolutional Neural Network (CNN) architectures, evaluating them based on four key metrics: Precision, Recall, F1-Score, and Accuracy. The architecture with the best performance across these metrics was then selected for the final model. In this paper, we experiment with 4 different architectures, including **VGG16**, **EfficientNetV2**, **InceptionV3**, and **Sequential**. All four architectures are trained using the traditional Train-Test-Split method without additional data augmentation. In this method, 70% of the dataset is allocated for training, while the remaining 30% is used for testing. Notably, the data is split with a random state of 42%, to avoid any potential bias. For preprocessing, all CT scans are resized to 256×256 pixels. For all four architectures, callbacks are used to save the best model based on validation performance, and the "EarlyStopping" callback is implemented to halt training early if the model's performance does not improve while restoring the best weights. Each model is trained on the training dataset for up to 100 epochs, with validation on the test set. Additionally, the confusion matrix and classification report are generated to evaluate performance based on key metrics.

VGG16. The VGG16 architecture is initialized with pre-trained weights from the ImageNet dataset, omitting the top classification layers. The input shape is specified for images with dimensions of 256×256 pixels and three-color channels. Transfer learning is employed to retain the learned features from the pre-trained model, with all layers of the VGG16 base frozen, particularly the last four layers. A custom head is then built on top of the VGG16 base to adapt the model to a new classification task.

The output from the VGG16 model is first passed through a global average pooling layer, which condenses the information from the feature maps. This is followed by two fully connected layers, each with 1024 units, that employ ReLU activation to capture complex patterns. An additional dense layer with 512 units is included to further refine the model's ability to differentiate between classes. The final layer is a dense layer with two units, activated by SoftMax, which produces the final classification output for a binary classification problem. Figure 3 represents the architecture of the VGG16 model.

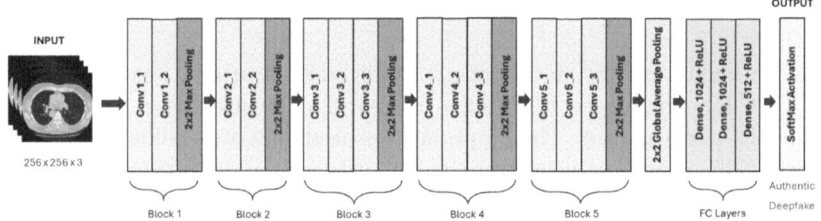

Fig. 3. VGG16 Model Architecture

EfficientNetV2. The EfficientNetV2S model, pre-trained on the ImageNet dataset, is loaded without its top layers and configured for a two-class classification problem. A Sequential model is built by adding the EfficientNetV2S base model, a global average pooling layer, a dropout layer to prevent overfitting, and a dense layer with a SoftMax activation for the final classification. Finally, all convolutional layers use "same" padding. Figure 4 depicts the EfficientNetV2S model architecture.

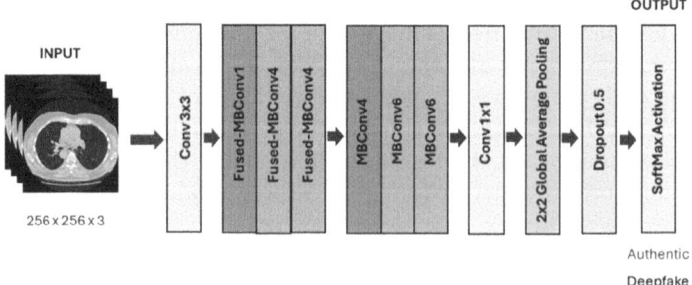

Fig. 4. EfficientNetV2S Model Architecture

InceptionV3. The InceptionV3 model is first loaded with pre-trained weights from the ImageNet dataset, excluding its top layers, and configured to accept input images with dimensions of 256×256 pixels and three-color channels (RGB). To preserve the learned features, the layers of the InceptionV3 base model are set to non-trainable, effectively freezing the last four layers. To build the complete model, a custom top is added to the InceptionV3 base. This head begins with a global average pooling layer to reduce the spatial dimensions of the feature maps. Following this, the architecture includes a dense layer with 1024 units and ReLU activation, then another dense layer with 512 units, also using ReLU activation. To enhance regularization and prevent overfitting, a dense layer with 128 units and ReLU activation is included, incorporating an L2 regularization term. Finally, the model outputs predictions through a dense layer with two units, using SoftMax activation to classify the input into one of two categories. Figure 5 represents the architecture of the InceptionV3 model.

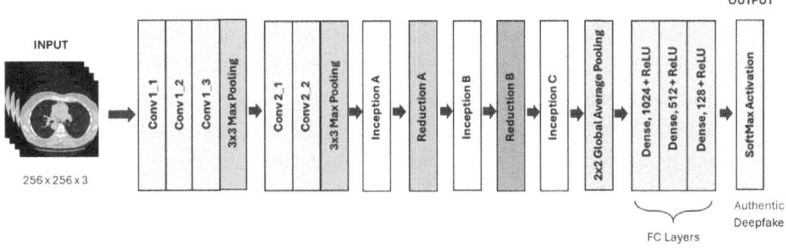

Fig. 5. InceptionV3 Model Architecture

Sequential. The Sequential model begins with a 2D convolutional layer consisting of 32 filters with a 3×3 kernel, followed by a ReLU activation function. The input shape is set to accommodate images with dimensions of 256×256 pixels and three-color channels (RGB). This is followed by another convolutional layer with 64 filters, also using a 3×3 kernel and ReLU activation. The model then includes a max-pooling layer with a 2×2 pool size to reduce spatial dimensions, along with a dropout layer to mitigate overfitting. Subsequent layers continue the pattern, adding two more convolutional layers with 64 filters each, using 3×3 kernels and ReLU activation. Another dropout layer follows to further prevent overfitting. The model then applies another max-pooling layer, followed by another dropout layer. The architecture then introduces three convolutional layers with 128 filters each, still using 3×3 kernels and ReLU activation, with a max-pooling layer and a dropout layer inserted after these. Another pair of convolutional layers with 128 and 256 filters, respectively, is added, followed by a final max-pooling layer and another dropout. After the convolutional layers, the model flattens the feature maps and passes them through two dense layers, each with 512 units and ReLU activation, with an additional dropout layer in between. Finally, the model outputs predictions through a dense layer with 2 units, using SoftMax activation to classify the input into one of two categories. Figure 6 highlights the Sequential model architecture.

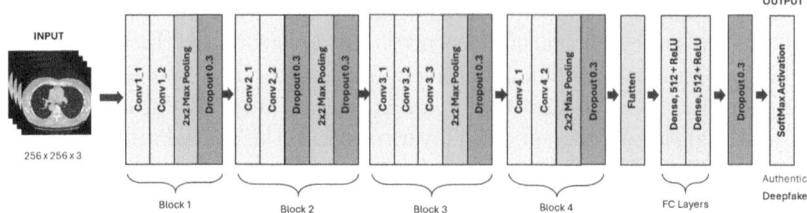

Fig. 6. Sequential Model Architecture

3.4 Data Augmentation

To further enhance the performance of all models, it is essential to increase the dataset size. Given the challenge of generating additional deepfake CT scans, the most effective approach is data augmentation. We apply horizontal flipping, vertical flipping, and a combination of both to each category, as these transformations do not distort the features of the images and thus do not affect the models' ability to identify features in both authentic and tampered CT scans. Following data augmentation, we retrain each of the four model architectures to observe the updated accuracies and ensure performance improvement.

4   Results and Discussion

In this section, we examine and interpret the outcomes derived from the deepfake detection model, assessing how effectively the system meets its predetermined objectives and requirements. We evaluate the performance of four distinct deep learning classifiers in distinguishing between authentic and deepfake cancer CT scans, focusing on key metrics such as precision, recall, F1-score, accuracy, and confusion matrices before and after data augmentation. The models, written in Python on Google Colab Pro, are trained on a Python 3 Google Compute Engine backend with 32GB RAM and a T4 GPU.

4.1   Initial Dataset

The models are trained on 70 images per category with the initial dataset and tested on the remaining **30**. After training, we compare the four models using evaluation metrics to identify which architectures deliver the best performance and which ones are less suitable for deepfake detection. As illustrated in Table 4, the Sequential model demonstrates the lowest performance, with an average accuracy of 63%. While it has a similar number of layers to other architectures like VGG16, the lack of pre-trained weights puts it at a disadvantage. The Sequential model learns features from scratch, and with only 100 images per category, it struggles to generalize effectively. In contrast, VGG16 achieves a significantly higher accuracy of 85%, largely due to transfer learning. By leveraging pre-trained weights from the ImageNet dataset, VGG16 retains rich, generalizable features, which provide a major advantage when working with smaller datasets. This makes VGG16 particularly effective at extracting features from both authentic and tampered CT scans. While InceptionV3 shows promise with an average accuracy of 78%, it is still outperformed by VGG16. Despite this, the EfficientNetV2 architecture delivered the highest accuracy and demonstrated the best overall performance with **92%** accuracy.

Table 4. Initial Model Results

Model	Accuracy	Precision	Recall	F1-score
Sequential	0.63	0.64	0.63	0.63
VGG16	0.85	0.87	0.85	0.85
InceptionV3	0.78	0.78	0.78	0.78
EfficientNetV2S	**0.92**	**0.92**	**0.92**	**0.92**

4.2 Augmented Dataset

By applying horizontal flipping, vertical flipping, and a combination of both to the authentic and deepfake CT scans, we quadruple the number of CT scans in each category, increasing from 100 to **400**, as demonstrated in Table 5. Therefore, the test size for each category increases to **120** instead of 30

Table 5. Data Augmentation

Category	Authentic	Deepfake
No. of CT scans	400	400

Following data augmentation and retraining of the four deep learning models, we observe their accuracy and performance improvements, as depicted in Table 6. The Sequential model demonstrates the most significant performance improvement, with its accuracy rising from 63% to 88%, surpassing InceptionV3, which achieves an accuracy of 83%. Both VGG16 and EfficientNetV2 achieve an accuracy of 93%, making it necessary to select one of these models as DeepCare's deepfake detection model. In such cases, comparing the two models using additional evaluation metrics, such as precision, accuracy, and F1-score, becomes crucial.

In our system, the cost of false negatives is significant. If a deepfake CT scan is mistakenly classified as authentic, it undermines the purpose of our system and jeopardizes patient safety. Therefore, recall is more critical than precision, and we prioritize the model with a higher recall for detecting deepfakes. To determine the appropriate option, we compare the classification reports of both models, as demonstrated in Table 7.

Table 6. Improved Model Results after Data Augmentation

Model	Accuracy	Precision	Recall	F1-score
Sequential	0.88	0.88	0.88	0.87
VGG16	**0.93**	**0.94**	**0.93**	**0.93**
InceptionV3	0.83	0.83	0.83	0.83
EfficientNetV2S	0.93	0.93	0.93	0.92

Table 7. Comparison of the Classification Reports

Model	Authentic Precision	Authentic Recall	Authentic F1-score	Deepfake Precision	Deepfake Recall	Deepfake F1-score
VGG16	0.98	0.88	0.93	0.89	0.98	0.94
EfficientNetV2S	0.90	0.95	0.93	0.95	0.90	0.92

Given VGG16's superior performance, with a **98%** recall for deepfake detection compared to EfficientNetV2's 90%, we select VGG16 as our preferred model for identifying deepfakes. This decision is reinforced by the confusion matrix of each model, where VGG16 correctly classifies 118 deepfake CT scans, with only 2 misclassifications, as shown in Fig. 7. However, EfficientNetV2 misclassifies 12 tampered CT scans as authentic, increasing the number of false negatives, as depicted in Fig. 8. While VGG16 excels in predicting true positives, it is less effective at predicting true negatives. However, the cost of misclassifying an authentic CT scan as a deepfake is less severe than the risk of misclassifying a deepfake as authentic. By evaluating the models using additional key metrics, we can select the most suitable model for the task of detecting deepfakes. Table 8 summarizes the overall performance of the selected VGG16 deepfake detection model.

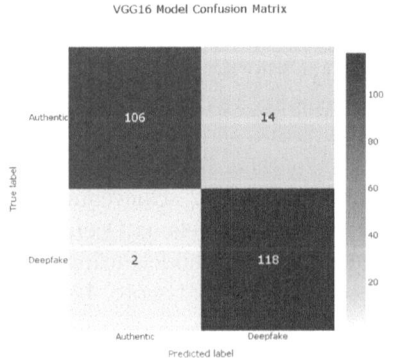
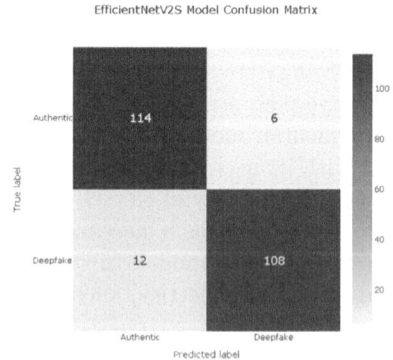

Fig. 7. VGG16 Confusion Matrix   **Fig. 8.** EfficientNet Confusion Matrix

Table 8. VGG16 Model Performance Evaluation Summary

Hyperparameters			Class	Performance Metrics						
Batch Size	Epochs	Learning Rate		TP	FP	TN	FN	Precision	Recall	F1-Score
32	100	0.001	Authentic	118	14	106	2	0.98	0.88	0.93
			Deepfake					0.89	0.98	0.94
Total System Accuracy				0.93						

5 Conclusion

In this paper, we studied the use of four models for detecting deepfakes in cancer medical images by utilizing two balanced datasets to ensure precise results during training. The CNN models VGG16, EfficientNetV2, InceptionV3, and Sequential were compared using four evaluation metrics: Precision, Recall, F1-Score, and Accuracy. The datasets were split into two parts:70% for training and 30% for testing. The results showed that EfficientNetV2 achieved the highest accuracy before data augmentation. After data augmentation, VGG16 demonstrated a superior recall rate compared to the others. In conclusion, all four models effectively detected deepfakes, with the highest detection rates achieved after balancing the datasets to avoid bias in the results.

Acknowledgments. This work was fully supported by Abu Dhabi University under Grant No. 19300786.

References

1. Radnet inc (rdnt). Tech. rep., GlobalData plc (2024 2024), name - RadNet Inc; Copyright - Copyright GlobalData plc 2024; Document feature - Mergers & acquisitions; Last updated - 2024-06-20
2. Abiodun, O.I., Alawida, M., Omolara, A.E., Alabdulatif, A.: Data provenance for cloud forensic investigations, security, challenges, solutions and future perspectives: a survey. J. King Saud Univ. Comput. Inf. Sci. **34**(10), 10217–10245 (2022)
3. Alawida, M., Omolara, A.E., Abiodun, O.I., Al-Rajab, M.: A deeper look into cybersecurity issues in the wake of Covid-19: a survey. J. King Saud Univ. Comput. Inf. Sci. **34**(10), 8176–8206 (2022)
4. Alyasriy, H., Al-Huseiny, M.: The IQ-OTH/NCCD lung cancer dataset (2023). https://data.mendeley.com/datasets/bhmdr45bh2/4. Accessed 25 June 2024
5. Beek, C.: McAfee researchers find poor security exposes medical data to cyber-criminals. McAfee Blog (2024)
6. Boatman, A.: JPG vs. PNG: Which is better? (2023). https://www.techsmith.com/blog/jpg-vs-png/. Accessed 8 April 2024
7. Bowers, G.M., Kleinpeter, M.L., M., Rials, W.T.: Securing your radiology practice: evidence-based strategies for radiologists compiled from 10 years of cyberattacks and HIPAA breaches involving medical imaging. Perspect. Health Inf. Manag. **19**(3), 1–8 (2022)

8. Brunese, L., Mercaldo, F., Reginelli, A., Santone, A.: Radiomic features for medical images tamper detection by equivalence checking. Procedia Comput. Sci. **159**, 1795–1802 (2019). https://doi.org/10.1016/j.procs.2019.09.351

9. Cao, X., Gong, N.Z.: Understanding the security of Deepfake detection. In: Gladyshev, P., Goel, S., James, J., Markowsky, G., Johnson, D. (eds.) Digital Forensics and Cyber Crime. ICDF2C 2021. LNICS, Social Informatics and Telecommunications Engineering, vol. 441. Springer, Cham. https://doi.org/10.1007/978-3-031-06365-7_22

10. Gelijns, A., Banta, H.D., et al.: Anticipating and Assessing Health Care Technology: Computer Assisted Medical Imaging. The Case of Picture Archiving and Communications Systems (PACS). Springer Science & Business Media, Dordrecht (2013). https://doi.org/10.1007/978-94-017-0741-1

11. Goth, G.: Medical deepfakes are the real deal (2023). https://www.mddionline.com/artificial-intelligence/medical-deepfakes-are-the-real-deal

12. Hussain, S., et al.: Modern diagnostic imaging technique applications and risk factors in the medical field: a review. Biomed. Res. Int. **2022**(1), 5164970 (2022)

13. Khaleel, H., Wirza, R., Zamrin, D.: Components and implementation of a picture archiving and communication system in a prototype application. Reports Med. Imaging **12**, 1–8 (2018). https://doi.org/10.2147/RMI.S179268

14. Mangaokar, N., Pu, J., Bhattacharya, P., Reddy, C., Viswanath, B.: Jekyll: Attacking medical image diagnostics using deep generative models (04 2021)

15. Mirsky, Y., Mahler, T.: CT-GAN: Malicious tampering of 3D medical imagery using deep learning. In: 28th USENIX Security Symposium. California (2019)

16. Mirsky, Y., Mahler, T., Shelef, I., Elovici, Y.: CT-GAN: Malicious tampering of 3D medical imagery using deep learning (2019)

17. Omolara, A.E., Alawida, M., Abiodun, O.I.: Drone cybersecurity issues, solutions, trend insights and future perspectives: a survey. Neural Comput. Appl. **35**(31), 23063–23101 (2023)

18. Osada, M., Nishihara, E.: Implementation and evaluation of workflow based on hospital information system/radiology information system/picture archiving and communications system. J.. Digit. Imaging suppl.Supplement **12**, 103–105 (1999), copyright - Society for Imaging Informatics in Medicine 1999; Last updated - 2024-03-06

19. Panayides, A.S., et al.: Ai in medical imaging informatics: current challenges and future directions. IEEE J. Biomed. Health Inform. **24**(7), 1837–1857 (2020)

20. Project, A.T.: Apache tomcat® - apache tomcat 7 vulnerabilities https://tomcat.apache.org/security-7.html

21. Sharma, R., Prabakar, D., Madaan, A., Kumar, D., Upadhyaya, M., Sharma, A.K.: Securing social media imagery: Gandriven encryption and CNN analysis with DEA protection. J. Electr. Syst. **20**(3), 1232–1241 (2024)

22. Somasundara, A.N., Jayathunge, S.T., Jayasooriya, D., Ekanayaka, E., Yapa, K., Dharmakeerthi, U.: Ensure security and privacy of medical imaging through secure DICOM. Int. Res. J. Innov. Eng. Technol. **7**(10), 89–96 (2023)

23. Trotta, F., Ackerson, D.: How to handle imbalanced data for machine learning in Python (2024). https://semaphoreci.com/blog/imbalanced-data-machine-learning-python. Accessed 22 June 2024

Strengthening Cybersecurity: The Influence of Student Behavior, Perceived Factors, and Mitigating Strategies on Phishing Attack Perception

Saleh Alqahtani[1,2]($\boxtimes$) [ID], Priyadarsi Nanda[3] [ID], and Manoranjan Mohanty[4] [ID]

[1] Saudi Electronic University, Riyadh, Saudi Arabia
sm.alqahtani@seu.edu.sa
[2] University of Technology Sydney, Sydney, Australia
[3] Faculty of Engineering and IT, University of Technology Sydney, Sydney, Australia
priyadarsi.nanda@uts.edu.au
[4] Carnegie Mellon University, Ar-Rayyan, Qatar
mmohanty@cmu.edu

Abstract. Phishing attacks are among the most prevalent cyber-attack methods, leading to financial breakdowns, damaged reputations, and identity theft. This study focuses on cybersecurity aspects, emphasizing phishing attacks targeting university students. It aims to examine the characteristics, methods, and impacts of phishing attacks on students and their knowledge and awareness of these threats. The study identifies key factors contributing to the occurrence of phishing attacks and their influence on students' perceptions. Data were collected from 715 university students using a quantitative research approach. Key findings reveal that lack of awareness and failure to verify communications' authenticity significantly increase Phishing's vulnerability. The regression analysis revealed that Student Behavior, Perceived Factors, and Mitigating Strategies collectively explain 47.0% of the variance in Student Perception ($R2 = 0.470$), with all predictors showing significant positive relationships: Student Behavior ($B = 0.169$, $p < 0.001$), Perceived Factors ($B = 0.392$, $p < 0.001$), and Mitigating Strategies ($B = 0.266$, $p < 0.001$). The study highlights the importance of human behavior in executing mitigation strategies, concluding that relying solely on technology-based solutions is insufficient to address the challenges posed by phishing attacks. The study recommends comprehensive educational initiatives, emphasizing the importance of verifying personal information sources and regularly updating software and hardware as effective mitigation strategies.

Keywords: Cybersecurity · Phishing Attacks · Mitigating Strategies · Online Safety · Students' Awareness · Perceived Factors

1 Introduction

Each year, a growing number of incidents and breaches specifically target the vulnerabilities in human aspects of cyber security. The data breach investigations report (DBIR) provided by Verizon reveals that 82% of the studied breaches were attributable to human

M. Barhamgi et al. (Eds.): WISE 2024, LNCS 15463, pp. 313–329, 2025.
https://doi.org/10.1007/978-981-96-1483-7_27

activities or errors [1]. One often used technique for taking advantage of the human aspects of cyber security is known as a phishing attack. Phishing is a type of cyber-attack where the attacker deceives the victim into performing actions that cause harm to both the victim and the system. Phishing is an illicit activity that exploits individuals by using social engineering tactics to manipulate them [2]. [3] define phishing attack as a fraudulent attempt to imitate a trustworthy entity to obtain sensitive information. The definitions clearly suggest that Phishing is an act of fraud and deception however, the reason behind the attack may vary. Typically, the objective is to get financial information and steal system credentials or other sensitive data. Moreover, Phishing is utilized as a method of attack to execute further activities, such as ransomware attacks. Lately, there has been a targeted increase in phishing attacks against organizations, leading to substantial financial losses. These losses are primarily due to the costs of containing malware, reduced productivity, the expenses associated with addressing compromised credentials, and the financial burden of dealing with ransomware resulting from phishing attempts. In addition, firms may also experience reputational harm in the perception of their consumers and competitors [1].

In 2022, Phishing was identified as one of the most harmful ways of attack, with an average expense of \$4.91 million per data breach. Phishing can be carried out through several channels utilizing different techniques. Three commonly used channels for Phishing are the internet, short messaging services, and cell phones [4]. Different vectors are used to execute the attack in each of these mediums. Common phishing methods assisted by the internet include email, eFax, instant messaging, social networks, websites, and Wi-Fi. Smishing and Vishing are targeted attack techniques utilized in short message platforms and voice communication. In this scenario, students need to thoroughly understand the possible harm caused by phishing assaults, as they will soon be the workforce responsible for operating the system. This research aims to investigate the level of knowledge that university students have about the features, techniques, and repercussions of phishing assaults.

This paper adds on existing literature by concentrating on how different factors, such as awareness and behavior after interrelating with the different measures that students use helps to evade phishing attacks. This study unlike previous researches focuses on the gap which shows that how non-technical students of universities observe and take into account the threats related to phishing and thus it provides a more detailed and inclusive examination across different subjects. Moreover, the study aimed to identify the factors that contribute to the occurrence of phishing attacks and examine how these factors influence students' perceptions of different forms of phishing assaults. In light of the objectives of this study, the following research question was formulated:

RQ. How do student behavior, perceived factors, and mitigating strategies influence university students' perceptions of phishing attacks?

2   Literature Review

2.1   Types of Phishing Attacks

There are several techniques by which the attack might be carried out. The underlying motivation for all the categories is the same. The only difference between the different categories is related to the number of objectives and the methods used to obtain the information. Some commonly employed phishing attacks include deceptive Phishing, spear phishing, whaling attacks, email Phishing, social media phishing, and Fake QR code phishing. In deceptive Phishing, the attacker assumes the identity of a reputable organization or website to deceive the victim into providing sensitive information. This type of phishing attack involves duplicating the logo and design of a genuine email or website [5]. Deceptive phishing efforts may appear more convincing when they ask for personal information or confirmation of course registration [6]. In spear phishing, the perpetrator tailors the message initially. Spear phishing attempts are more intricate than traditional phishing attacks as the assailant conducts thorough research on the target and crafts a persuasive message. According to [7], spear phishing attacks can be successful because university students trust emails from professors, classmates, and administrators. Meanwhile, in whaling phishing, the phishers carry out whaling attacks by specifically targeting a senior executive, usually the CEO or someone of similar rank. Before launching an attack, the assailant would invest significant time in acquiring knowledge of the target. Subsequently, the assailant dispatches an email to the target to persuade the recipient to reveal confidential information [8].

On the other hand, in email phishing, attackers often assume the identity of reliable third parties to deceive their victims into divulging vital information. They could utilize captivating subject lines to create a sense of urgency, compelling you to take immediate action. Phishing via email is a prevalent and successful technique used by hackers to compromise the security of students [9]. Like email phishing, social media phishing is the construction of fake profiles or pages on social media platforms to deceive people [10]. Perpetrators may transmit harmful websites or private messages to deceive individuals into disclosing their personal data or login credentials. Additionally, phishing attacks that involve fake or altered QR codes are a common strategy used to trick and take advantage of individuals, particularly university students. QR Codes are the storage of different types of data, including different contact details, URLs of websites and instructions regarding payments. It uses 2D barcode technology, scanned using any device such as smartphones [11].

2.2   Phishing Detection Methods and Approaches

Since Phishing directly threatens losing one's identity and finances, it has a profound and prominent effect. It is pertinent to mention that to identify phishing attacks, phishing detection tools, and techniques are to be studied in detail. Thus, the negative effects of phishing attempts might be decreased. For such purposes, multiple phishing detection methods and approaches are utilized. For instance, a heuristic-based system known as the PhishCatch algorithm was designed to alert and identify users of phishing emails. It develops phishing filters and rules in the algorithm by thoroughly examining phishing practices and policies. During testing, the software gave a catch rate of 80% and an accuracy of 99% [12]. Moreover, the researchers have developed machine-learning models using an extensive range of parameters. With the help of these models, researchers can easily detect and classify phishing web pages [13]. Machine learning (ML) is widely used for data analysis and has demonstrated significant potential in effectively addressing phishing attacks, surpassing traditional anti-phishing methods such as awareness seminars, visualization, and legal remedies [14]. Furthermore, Blacklist and Whitelist methods are also used to detect phishing where the URL is compared to a preset phishing URL. However, due to the lengthy time it takes to add a new phishing site to the blacklist, it can't cover all of them [15]. Same as above, [16] proposed a way to identify phishing cyber-attacks that revealed a client's susceptibility to harmful compounds, allowing protection breaches. Furthermore, heuristic-based methods are also used to identify fraudulent or legitimate websites. Heuristic-based tactics, also termed features-based strategies, work by selecting a set of distinguishing qualities that help define a website. PhishShield, a PC program by [17], analyzes phishing page URLs and content.

2.3 Most Common Phishing Vectors

According to [4], three communication channels, namely the internet, short messaging service, and voice, can be utilized to carry out a phishing assault. Various phishing vectors can be employed inside each of these mediums. Examples of phishing vectors commonly used on the internet include email, eFax, instant messaging, social media networks, websites, and Wi-Fi. Moreover, the attacker can utilize several technical methods to carry out the phishing assault on any of these channels. Some common attack vectors used to target a website are click-jacking, weaknesses in web browsers, cross-site scripting, and man-in-the-middle attacks [4]. The attacking vector that has received the most attention during the expansion of mitigation strategies is phishing through websites [1].

2.4 Anti-phishing Guidelines and Recommendations

Organizations should consider and ensure strict implementation of security protocols, access controls training and awareness programs, device strategies, and direction to lessen the effects of phishing attacks. Phishing knowledge can be further enhanced through training and awareness campaigns [19]. These goals are achieved through Seminars, discussions & virtual learning tools. For such purpose, an Endpoint security system could be introduced, which includes protection through antivirus, malware protection, host-based intrusion detection systems (HIDS), and email protection technologies [20]. Even with device infection, a strong firewall and architecture can limit access to enterprise networks, reducing cyber-attack risks [21, 22]. Moreover, it promotes backups, uses protection software, stops pop-ups, and updates computer hardware frequently [23]. Additionally, access control involves creating and implementing password and information transmission regulations. These deceptive online tripwires and login rituals can extend web application authentication [24]. These methods are unaffected by password repetition and can be added to Microsoft Multi-Factor Authentication (MFA) systems to secure accounts during sophisticated phishing attacks [25]. Thus, businesses should follow these guidelines and implement appropriate policies to prevent Phishing.

For instance, vulnerability management, threats, indicators of compromise, and best practices for exchanging, sharing, and processing privacy-sensitive data should inform cyber-security solutions [24]. Reinforcing password rules, reporting mechanisms, staff training, and physical security awareness on-site and personal devices is crucial to implementing these steps. A Standard Solution (SS) can help teams share power and provide consistent expert advice and phishing response protocols [26]. On the contrary, device policies must handle several stages of operation. Decision-makers must assess device lifespans, provide funds for lifecycle management, and maintain an up-to-date registry of all company equipment. To stay relevant, employees should avoid sharing information with strangers, avoid reciprocal exchanges, and offer accurate health and family information [27]. Moreover, End-users can prevent phishing attacks by using browser anti-phishing tools, validating links, and using their expertise [28]. Sensitive data should not be uploaded on public computers, and antivirus along with application updates is to be made on time [24]. Security breaches and identity theft can be avoided through strong authentication [19]. In conclusion, it is analyzed that awareness of mitigation policies is important for controlling phishing attacks and cyber security.

2.5 Hypotheses

Based on the literature, it is hypothesized that the student behavior, perceived threat awareness and mitigating strategies effects their vulnerability to phishing attacks. In order to be specific, we suggest that students with high level of awareness will generally have a much lower phishing vulnerability.

3 Materials and Methods

In this research, students' awareness at the Higher education level concerning phishing attacks was explored through quantitative research. It also focused on factors that lead to the prevalence of phishing attacks and their effect on students' perception of different phishing attacks. The study focused on different protocols and strategies for contradicting Phishing by using a questionnaire, according to research questions, to gather university students' responses. The upcoming section provides more details of the data collection process.

3.1 Data Collection Process

In this study, a questionnaire was used to gather information and assess the level of response and alertness among university students regarding phishing assaults. It consists of different sections to analyze students' understanding of phishing attacks. To address how students' perception was calculated and measured, we used a structured questionnaire with Likert-scale items ranging from 1 (strongly disagree) to 5 (strongly agree) to capture students' awareness, susceptibility, and behavior toward phishing attacks. The average scores of responses were then used to quantify the overall perception for each construct. Participants were also asked about anti-phishing strategies. A thorough examination of existing data and literature lead to the creation of this questionnaire. It was done to guarantee its content's accuracy and relevancy. Protection Motivation Theory (PMT), described by Rogers (1975) focused on application in cyber-security education, such as the work of Witte (1992). It also played an important role in analyzing the elements described by this tool. A pilot study was conducted to validate further the questionnaire, involving a sample of university students. It aims to evaluate the instrument's reliability. This study inspected the data through Cronbach's alpha, which assessed the internal coherence or reliability of a collection of scales or survey questions. Its score was 0.92, which indicated a high-reliability level and confirmed that the tool assesses students' insights into phishing efforts. To answer the research questions, 715 University Students worldwide using online stages and platforms were involved in this study.

3.2 Participant Profile and Sampling

The study used a sample of 715 students of universities from different academic subjects. The demographics of participant show that most respondents were male, comprising 70.1% of the total sample. In terms of age, more than one-third of the respondents were between 18 and 25 years old (34.5%), followed by the 26–30 age group, which accounted for 25.5% of the sample. Educationally, nearly half of the respondents held a Bachelor's degree (45.8%). Regarding country of residence, a significant proportion of respondents currently resided in Saudi Arabia (31.2%), followed by respondents from Australia (14.6%) and the United States (12.0%).

3.3 Statistical Technique

Several statistical techniques were employed to analyze the data collected from the university students. Initially, descriptive analysis was performed using the frequency, percentage, mean, and standard deviation. Furthermore, correlation analysis was conducted to examine the relationships between the key variables: Student Behavior, Perceived Factors, Mitigating Strategies, and Student Perception. This helped identify the strength and direction of associations among these variables. Subsequently, multiple regression analysis was performed to assess the impact of Student Behavior, Perceived Factors, and Mitigating Strategies on Student Perception. Data were analyzed in SPSS v.27.

4 Results and Analysis

4.1 Students' Awareness and Behavior Regarding Phishing Attacks

The survey responses indicate varying levels of awareness and caution among university students regarding phishing attacks. Many students are somewhat confident (30.2%) in recognizing phishing emails, while 23.6% are not confident. Most students receive unsolicited emails occasionally (41.2%) or rarely (28.5%), and a considerable number still click on links or download attachments from unknown senders occasionally (25.3%) or frequently (9.8%). Phishing attempts from unfamiliar sources claiming to be from universities or government institutions are also common, with 37.4% receiving such emails occasionally. While most students are unlikely to enter login credentials on suspicious websites (52.8% either extremely or somewhat unlikely), 24.8% remain at risk. Similarly, although most students are somewhat unlikely to provide personal information via email to unknown senders (52.1%), a notable 25.7% are somewhat or extremely likely to do so.

Regarding receiving emails requesting urgent action, 40.4% of students encounter these occasionally. Many are very cautious (32.3%) or moderately cautious (25.1%) when providing personal information online. However, the likelihood of reporting suspicious emails to the university's IT department is mixed, with 26% somewhat likely and 17.1% extremely likely but 33.1% unlikely to report. Awareness of common phishing red flags is moderate to high, yet a significant number of students are only slightly or not aware (36.5%). Regarding device management, a large portion (39.9%) do not take specific actions to avoid phishing attacks, although 35.6% seek help from technical support.

4.2 Understanding of Common Types of Phishing Attacks

The survey responses reveal university students' varying awareness and understanding of phishing attacks. Familiarity with spear phishing attacks is relatively low, with 35.3% strongly disagreeing and only 16.6% strongly agreeing. Similarly, 30.1% of students strongly disagree about understanding email spoofing, indicating a need for better education on this technique. Awareness of website spoofing is slightly higher, with 26.0% strongly agreeing, but 33.0% strongly disagree. Pharming attacks are less known, with 27.6% strongly disagreeing and 19.1% strongly agreeing. Awareness of smishing attacks is more balanced, with 25.0% strongly agreeing.

For vishing attacks, 29.3% of respondents strongly disagree about their familiarity, while 24.5% strongly agree. Social engineering awareness is mixed, with 25.4% strongly disagreeing and 19.4% strongly agreeing. Knowledge about malware-based Phishing shows a higher awareness level, with 26.6% strongly agreeing. Credential harvesting is understood by a notable portion of students, with 25.3% strongly agreeing, but 28.6% strongly disagree. Brand impersonation in phishing attacks has a mixed response, with 26.9% strongly agreeing and 28.6% strongly disagreeing. Awareness of invoice phishing and job offer scams is moderate, with about 24.4% to 23.6% strongly agreeing. Social media phishing awareness is relatively high, with 27.0% strongly agreeing. Urgent account update requests in phishing attacks are moderately understood, with 24.7% strongly agreeing.

Figure 1 represents the mean values of university students' awareness and understanding of various common types of phishing attacks. Each type of phishing attack was rated on a scale from 1 (strongly disagree) to 5 (strongly agree). The analysis reveals that students generally have a moderate level of awareness about phishing attacks, with mean values ranging from approximately 2.5 to 4.0 across different attack types. The highest mean awareness is observed for "Password Reset Scams" and "Fake Online Stores," indicating that students are particularly cautious about resetting passwords and verifying online store authenticity. On the lower end, "Spear Phishing" and "Email Spoofing" have lower mean values, suggesting that students are less familiar with these sophisticated phishing techniques.

Students' Level of Understanding on Various Types of Phishing Attacks

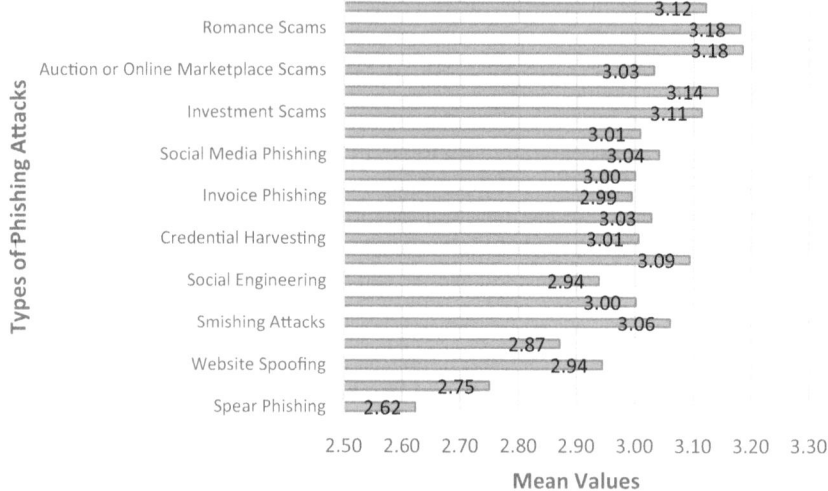

Fig. 1. Mean Values of Level of Understanding of Common Types of Phishing Attacks

4.3   Factors Enhancing the Occurrence of Phishing Attacks

Table 1 presents the mean values and standard deviations of university students' perceptions regarding various factors that enhance the occurrence of phishing attacks. Each factor was rated on a scale from 1 (strongly disagree) to 5 (strongly agree). The survey responses highlight several factors that university students perceive as enhancing the occurrence of phishing attacks. The most significant factor identified is the "lack of awareness among university students," with 33.9% of respondents strongly agreeing. This suggests that improving awareness could significantly reduce phishing vulnerabilities.

Another notable factor is the "failure to verify the authenticity of communications," with 31.8% strongly agreeing that this increases vulnerability to phishing attacks. Similarly, "inadequate skills in handling phishing attacks" is recognized, with 30.8% strongly agreeing that it raises the likelihood of falling victim. In contrast, the factor with the lowest agreement is "the busy schedules of university students," with only 23.1% strongly agreeing that it makes them more susceptible to phishing attacks. This indicates that while busy schedules are a concern, they are not perceived as the most critical factor. The analysis indicates that students generally agree that a lack of awareness (mean = 3.47) and failure to verify the authenticity of communications (mean = 3.40) significantly contribute to the occurrence of phishing attacks.

Similarly, inadequate skills in handling phishing attacks (mean = 3.39) and limited scrutiny of email senders (mean = 3.36) are perceived as important factors. Other notable factors include the desire for financial assistance (mean = 3.34) and the use of urgency and fear tactics by attackers (mean = 3.27). The data also suggests that regular security updates (mean = 3.23) and peer influence (mean = 3.24) play significant roles in phishing susceptibility.

Table 1. Factors Enhancing Phishing Attacks Among University Students

Factors	Strongly disagree	Somewhat disagree	Neutral	Somewhat agree	Strongly agree	Mean	SD
Lack of regular security updates heightens phishing risks for university students	23.1%	10.2%	13.6%	26.9%	26.3%	3.23	1.515
Lack of awareness contributes to phishing attacks among university students	17.7%	11.1%	12.1%	25.3%	33.9%	3.47	1.487
Blind trust in university emails increases students' vulnerability to phishing	17.8%	11.5%	15.0%	23.8%	31.8%	3.40	1.476
Inexperience in handling phishing attacks raises students' likelihood of falling victim	19.0%	11.4%	12.3%	26.6%	30.8%	3.39	1.491
Phishing tactics using urgency and fear are more effective on university students	18.7%	12.0%	19.1%	24.5%	25.7%	3.27	1.440

(continued)

Table 1. (*continued*)

Factors	Strongly disagree	Somewhat disagree	Neutral	Somewhat agree	Strongly agree	Mean	SD
Busy schedules make university students more prone to phishing attacks	17.7%	16.1%	19.0%	24.2%	23.1%	3.19	1.414
Financial need increases students' vulnerability to phishing attacks	17.2%	13.0%	16.6%	24.7%	28.5%	3.34	1.446
Overreliance on technology without proper security heightens phishing risks for students	19.6%	11.4%	15.6%	28.0%	25.4%	3.28	1.455
Limited cybersecurity education leads to more phishing attacks on university students	20.1%	13.7%	12.7%	26.0%	27.4%	3.27	1.494
Limited scrutiny of email senders increases students' susceptibility to phishing	18.5%	11.2%	14.0%	27.7%	28.5%	3.36	1.463

(*continued*)

Table 1. (*continued*)

Factors	Strongly disagree	Somewhat disagree	Neutral	Somewhat agree	Strongly agree	Mean	SD
University students' tendency to share personal information raises phishing risks	19.6%	14.5%	16.9%	26.4%	22.6%	3.18	1.438
Lack of two-factor authentication (2FA) increases students' vulnerability to phishing	18.8%	13.1%	16.8%	25.3%	26.0%	3.26	1.453
Peer influence enhances students' susceptibility to phishing attacks	18.2%	12.7%	20.9%	23.6%	24.5%	3.24	1.422

4.4 Descriptive Analysis of Mitigating Strategies of Phishing Attacks

The survey responses illustrate university students' perceptions of various strategies to mitigate phishing attacks. A significant majority strongly agree (40.6%) that never sharing personal information unless the origin is confirmed is crucial. Similarly, 40.6% strongly agree that providing training and awareness programs on phishing attacks is an effective strategy. Exercising caution with emails from unknown or suspicious sources also received high agreement, with 37.1% strongly agreeing. Deleting phishing emails without opening them is considered the most effective strategy by 39.6% of respondents. Regular computer hardware and software updates are seen as effective by 36.4% of students. Introducing mandatory education on Phishing, especially for first-year students, received strong support, with 40.0% strongly agreeing. These findings suggest that a combination of education, proactive measures, and technical solutions are seen as essential strategies to mitigate phishing attacks among university students. Notably, a significant 40.6% of respondents strongly agree that providing training and awareness programs on phishing attacks is crucial, indicating a strong belief in the effectiveness of educational initiatives.

4.5   Correlation Analysis

The correlation matrix (Table 2) reveals several significant relationships between the variables. The strongest relationship is observed between *Perceived Factors* and *Mitigating Strategies*, with a Pearson correlation coefficient of r = 0.691 (p < .001), indicating a strong positive correlation. This suggests that as students perceive more factors contributing to phishing attacks, they also recognize more mitigating strategies to combat these attacks. On the other hand, the weakest relationship is between *Student Behavior* and *Perceived Factors*, with a Pearson correlation coefficient of r = 0.354 (p < .001). While still significant, this correlation is relatively weaker compared to the others. The data indicate that while all variables are significantly correlated, the strength of these correlations varies.

Table 2. Correlation Matrix of Study Variables

Correlations

Variables	Student Behavior	Perceived Factors	Mitigating Strategies	Student Perception
Student Behavior	1			
Perceived Factors	.354[**]	1		
Mitigating Strategies	.362[**]	.691[**]	1	
Student Perception	.375[**]	.636[**]	.602[**]	1

[**]. Correlation is significant at the 0.01 level (2-tailed).

Table 3. Regression Analysis Results

Model	Variables	R-square	F	p	Unstandardized Coefficients	Standardized	t	Sig.
					B	Beta		
1	(Constant)	0.47	201.650	<.001	0.267		2.045	0.041
	Student Behavior				0.169	0.133	4.409	<.001
	Perceived Factors				0.392	0.396	10.152	<.001
	Mitigating Strategies				0.266	0.280	7.139	<.001

a. Dependent Variable: Student. Perception

The regression analysis was conducted to examine the impact of Student Behavior, Perceived Factors, and Mitigating Strategies on Student Perception regarding phishing attacks. The model summary indicates that the three predictors (Student Behavior, Perceived Factors, and Mitigating Strategies) collectively explain 47.0% of the variance in Student Perception (R2 = 0.47). The model explains approximately 47% of the variance in phishing avoidance behavior, which suggests a moderate fit of the model. The ANOVA results show that the regression model is statistically significant, $F(3, 681) = 201.645$, $p < 0.001$, indicating that the predictors significantly explain the variance in Student Perception. The coefficients table reveals the individual contribution of each predictor to the model. The unstandardized coefficient (B) for Student Behavior is 0.169 ($t = 4.409$, $p < 0.001$), indicating that for each unit increase in Student Behavior, Student Perception increases by 0.169 units, holding other factors constant. The unstandardized coefficient for Perceived Factors is 0.392 ($t = 10.152$, $p < 0.001$), indicating a strong positive relationship. The unstandardized coefficient for Mitigating Strategies is 0.266 ($t = 7.139$, $p < 0.001$), with a standardized coefficient (Beta) of 0.280, indicating a significant positive impact on Student Perception.

The regression equation indicates how changes in Student Behavior, Perceived Factors, and Mitigating Strategies affect Student Perception. Based on the regression analysis results, the regression equation can be formulated as follows:

Student Perception = 0.267 + 0.169(Student Behavior) + 0.392(Perceived Factors) + 0.266(Mitigating Strategies).

5 Discussion

The study investigated the factors influencing university students' perceptions of phishing attacks and the effectiveness of mitigating strategies. The analysis provided several key insights into the relationships between student behavior, perceived factors, mitigating strategies, and overall student perception. The results show that while students are somewhat aware of "Social Media Phishing" and "Investment Scams," there remains a significant need for increased education and awareness efforts, particularly for less commonly understood phishing methods such as "Pharming Attacks" and "Vishing Attacks." The data strongly supported the importance of educational initiatives. A substantial percentage of students agreed that providing training and awareness programs is crucial (40.6% strongly agreed). The finding is similar to [29], which emphasizes the importance of raising awareness among the students regarding cyber-security and phishing attacks.

The survey reveals several key insights into university students' perceptions of effective strategies to mitigate phishing attacks. Notably, a significant 40.6% of respondents strongly agree that providing training and awareness programs on phishing attacks is crucial, indicating a strong belief in the effectiveness of educational initiatives. Similarly, the same percentage strongly agrees that never sharing personal information unless its origin is confirmed is essential for preventing phishing attacks. This highlights the importance of verification and cautious behavior. Additionally, 39.6% of respondents consider deleting phishing emails without opening them as the most effective strategy, while 36.4% emphasize the need for regular updates to computer hardware and software. The establishment of a dedicated cybersecurity helpdesk is supported by 34.7% of students, underscoring the value of accessible support and guidance. These findings suggest that a combination of education, proactive measures, and technical solutions are seen as vital strategies to enhance cybersecurity and mitigate phishing risks among university students. [30, 31] presented the same findings that through taking certain educational measures and providing technical solutions, university students could be guided to fight against phishing attacks, hence improving cyber-security.

The correlation matrix reveals several significant relationships between the variables. The strongest relationship is observed between Perceived Factors and Mitigating Strategies, with a Pearson correlation coefficient of $r = 0.691$ ($p < .001$), indicating a strong positive correlation. This suggests that as students perceive more factors contributing to phishing attacks, they also recognize more mitigating strategies to combat these attacks, which is consistent with the findings of [1, 32, 33].

The regression analysis indicates that all three predictors—Student Behavior, Perceived Factors, and Mitigating Strategies—significantly influence Student Perception of phishing attacks. Perceived Factors have the strongest impact, followed by Mitigating Strategies and Student Behavior. The overall model explains a substantial portion of the variance in Student Perception. It suggests that enhancing students' behavior, addressing perceived factors, and implementing effective mitigating strategies can significantly improve their perception and awareness of phishing attacks, which is similar to the findings of [1, 34, 35]. This underscores the importance of comprehensive educational and preventive measures in enhancing cybersecurity among university students.

5.1 Implication of Study

This study has several implications in that it assists in giving students cyber-security education, which results in avoiding phishing attacks. By making the subject of cyber-security and phishing attacks a part of the curriculum, further awareness could be given regarding the matter. This study determines how important it is for university students to remain vigilant with phishing attacks. The more familiar they are with Phishing, the more they will try to avoid such attacks. It gives awareness regarding the most common phishing attack types which are common now a days, along with the crucial factors which are responsible for the occurrence of such attacks. This study is also beneficial for higher education institutions, as they can create a cyber-security culture by making it a part of their policy documents in light of the findings. Thus, this study gives students more awareness to take certain safety measures, instead of relying upon the system.

5.2 Limitations of Study

The study also has limitations as it relied on self-reported data gathered from university students. Apart from that, as this was a quantitative study, the scope of findings is limited because of superficial results obtained through a quantitative survey questionnaire only. As with the ongoing advancements, new methods or types of phishing attacks might emerge that need to be tackled differently.

5.3 Conclusion and Future Recommendations

The study focuses on the unique role of different factors and actions in phishing vulnerability among students. This study provides findings that students' educational backgrounds have an important relation on phishing awareness and prevention strategies. It has also focused on wide range of academic subjects which has made it one of the first study which has offered detailed cross-disciplinary details.

This study aimed to explore the cyber –security awareness among university students, with special emphasis on their familiarity with phishing attacks. It explores the students' perceptions regarding the different types of phishing attacks, methods and factors responsible for the occurrence of such attacks. The findings suggest that enhancing student behavior, addressing perceived factors contributing to Phishing, and implementing effective mitigating strategies can significantly improve students' perceptions and awareness of phishing attacks. Educational institutions should focus on comprehensive educational programs, promote cautious behavior, and provide robust technical support and resources to protect students from phishing threats. This study provides the base for future researchers regarding raising awareness about cyber-security among students. Firstly, a longitudinal study could be planned to assess the effects of students' perception on their behavior towards dealing with phishing attacks. Such a study will also highlight the evolution of different types of phishing attacks and the methods to deal with them. Moreover, multiple online educational tools could be assessed to determine their use for raising cyber-security awareness among students.

References

1. Naqvi, B., Perova, K., Farooq, A., Makhdoom, I., Oyedeji, S., Porras, J.: Mitigation strategies against the phishing attacks: a systematic literature review. Comput. Secur. 103387 (2023)
2. Chen, Y.H., Chen, J.L.: Ai@ ntiphish—machine learning mechanisms for cyber-phishing attack. IEICE Trans. Inf. Syst. **102**(5), 878–887 (2019)
3. Sameen, M., Han, K., Hwang, S.O.: PhishHaven—an efficient real-time AI phishing URLs detection system. IEEE Access **8**, 83425–83443 (2020)
4. Chiew, K.L., Yong, K.S.C., Tan, C.L.: A survey of phishing attacks: their types, vectors and technical approaches. Expert Syst. Appl. **106**, 1–20 (2018)
5. Akazue, M.I., Ojugo, A.A., Yoro, R.E., Malasowe, B.O., Nwankwo, O.: Empirical evidence of phishing menace among undergraduate smartphone users in selected universities in Nigeria. Indonesian J. Electr. Eng. Comput. Sci. **28**(3), 1756–1765 (2022)
6. Liu, M., Zhang, Y., Liu, B., Li, Z., Duan, H., Sun, D.: Detecting and characterizing SMS spearphishing attacks. In: Proceedings of the 37th Annual Computer Security Applications Conference, pp. 930–943 (2021)
7. Aleroud, A., Abu-Shanab, E., Al-Aiad, A., Alshboul, Y.: An examination of susceptibility to spear phishing cyber attacks in non-English speaking communities. J. Inf. Secur. Appl. **55** (2020). https://doi.org/10.1016/j.jisa.2020.102614
8. Ghazi-Tehrani, A.K., Pontell, H.N.: Phishing evolves: Analyzing the enduring cybercrime. In: The New Technology of Financial Crime, pp. 35–61. Routledge (2022)
9. Broadhurst, R., Skinner, K., Sifniotis, N., Matamoros-Macias, B., Ipsen, Y.: Phishing and cybercrime risks in a university student community. Int. J. Cybersecurity Intell. Cybercrime **2**(1), 4–23 (2019)

10. Parker, H.J., Flowerday, S.V.: Contributing factors to increased susceptibility to social media phishing attacks. S. Afr. J. Inf. Manag. **22**(1), 1–10 (2020)
11. Sharevski, F., Devine, A., Pieroni, E., Jachim, P.: Phishing with malicious QR codes. In: Proceedings of the 2022 European Symposium on Usable Security, pp. 160–171 (2022)
12. Weider, D.Y., Nargundkar, S., Tiruthani, N.: Phishcatch-a phishing detection tool. In: 2009 33rd Annual IEEE International Computer Software and Applications Conference, Vol. 2, pp. 451–456. IEEE (2009)
13. Gandotra, E., Gupta, D.: An efficient approach for phishing detection using machine learning. Multimedia Secur. Algorithm Dev., Anal. Appl. 239–253 (2021)
14. Abdelhamid, N., Thabtah, F., Abdel-Jaber, H.: Phishing detection: a recent intelligent machine learning comparison based on models content and features. In: 2017 IEEE International Conference on Intelligence and Security Informatics (ISI), pp. 72–77. IEEE (2017)
15. Mohammad, R.M., Thabtah, F., McCluskey, L.: Predicting phishing websites based on self-structuring neural network. Neural Comput. Appl. **25**, 443–458 (2014)
16. Jain, A.K., Parashar, S., Katare, P., Sharma, I.: PhishSKaPe: a content based approach to escape phishing attacks. Procedia Computer Science **171**, 1102–1109 (2020)
17. Rao, R.S., Ali, S.T.: PhishShield: a desktop application to detect phishing webpages through heuristic approach. Procedia Comput. Sci. **54**, 147–156 (2015)
18. Ali, W., Ahmed, A.A.: Hybrid intelligent phishing website prediction using deep neural networks with genetic algorithm-based feature selection and weighting. IET Inf. Secur. **13**(6), 659–669 (2019)
19. Jampen, D., Gür, G., Sutter, T., Tellenbach, B.: Don't click: towards an effective anti-phishing training. A comparative literature review. Hum. Centric Comput. Inf. Sci. **10**(1), 33 (2020)
20. Mashtalyar, N., Ntaganzwa, U.N., Santos, T., Hakak, S., Ray, S.: Social engineering attacks: Recent advances and challenges. In International Conference on Human-Computer Interaction, pp. 417–431. Cham: Springer International Publishing (2021)
21. Priestman, W., Anstis, T., Sebire, I.G., Sridharan, S., Sebire, N.J.: Phishing in healthcare organisations: Threats, mitigation and approaches. BMJ Health Care Inf. **26**(1) (2019)
22. Wash, R.: How experts detect phishing scam emails. Proc. ACM Hum. Comput. Interact. **4**(CSCW2), 1–28 (2020)
23. Manjezi, Z., Botha, R.A.: Preventing and mitigating ransomware: a systematic literature review. In: Information Security: 17th International Conference, ISSA 2018, Pretoria, South Africa, August 15–16, 2018, Revised Selected Papers 17, pp. 149–162. Springer International Publishing (2019)
24. Argaw, S.T., Bempong, N.E., Eshaya-Chauvin, B., Flahault, A.: The state of research on cyberattacks against hospitals and available best practice recommendations: a scoping review. BMC Med. Inform. Decis. Mak. **19**, 1–11 (2019)
25. Moul, K.A.: Avoid phishing traps. In: Proceedings of the 2019 ACM SIGUCCS Annual Conference, pp. 199–208 (2019)
26. Althobaiti, K., Jenkins, A.D., Vaniea, K.: A case study of phishing incident response in an educational organization. Proc. ACM Hum. Comput. Interact. **5**(CSCW2), 1–32 (2021)
27. Venkatesha, S., Reddy, K.R., Chandavarkar, B.R.: Social engineering attacks during the COVID-19 pandemic. SN Comput. Sci. **2**, 1–9 (2021)
28. Sadiq, A., et al.: A review of phishing attacks and countermeasures for internet of things-based smart business applications in industry 4.0. Hum. Behav. Emerg. Technol. **3**(5), 854–864 (2021)
29. Aldawood, H., Skinner, G.: Educating and raising awareness on cyber security social engineering: a literature review. In: 2018 IEEE International Conference on Teaching, Assessment, and Learning for Engineering (TALE), pp. 62–68. IEEE (2018)
30. Cheng, E.C., Wang, T.: Institutional strategies for cybersecurity in higher education institutions. Information **13**(4), 192 (2022)

31. Sharma, R., Thapa, S.: Cybersecurity awareness, education, and behavioral change: strategies for promoting secure online practices among end users. Eigenpub Rev. Sci. Technol. **7**(1), 224–238 (2023)

32. Sarker, O., Jayatilaka, A., Haggag, S., Liu, C., Babar, M.A.: A multi-vocal literature review on challenges and critical success factors of phishing education, training and awareness. J. Syst. Softw. **208**, 111899 (2024)

33. Waqas, M., Hania, A., Yahya, F., Malik, I.: Enhancing cybersecurity: the crucial role of self-regulation, information processing, and financial knowledge in combating phishing attacks. SAGE Open **13**(4), 21582440231217720 (2023)

34. Kori, D., Naik, R.: Information security awareness among postgraduate students: a study of Mangalore university. In: Handbook of Research on Technological Advances of Library and Information Science in Industry 5.0, pp. 270–286. IGI Global (2023)

35. Baki, S., Qachfar, F.Z., Verma, R.M., Kennedy, R., Jones, D.N.: Real-time, evidence-based alerts for protection from phishing attacks. IEEE Trans. Dependable Secure Comput. **01**, 1–15 (2024)

Towards Transparent and Ethical Coffee and Cocoa Supply Chains: The Role of Blockchain, NFTs Encrypted, and Smart Contracts

Khanh Hong Vo[1], Triet Minh Nguyen[1(✉)], Bang Le[1], Hung Nguyen[1], Hieu Doan[2], Bao Tran Quoc[1], Anh The Nguyen[1], and Ngan Kim Thi Nguyen[2]

[1] FPT University, Can Tho city, Vietnam
trietnm3@fe.edu.vn
[2] FPT Polytechnic, Can Tho city, Vietnam

Abstract. This study presents a framework using blockchain and decentralized storage to advance coffee and cocoa supply chain management. By integrating distributed ledger technology with tokenization and decentralized file management, the system enables full traceability and authentication of products from origin to consumer. Our work includes the design and assessment of a tailored supply chain infrastructure, trialed across various high-performance blockchain platforms, specifically BNB Chain, Polygon, Fantom, and Celo. This approach tackles key industry issues, such as verifying product authenticity, reinforcing accountability among supply chain participants, and supporting fair trade. Results show that this combined technological approach has strong potential to reshape traditional supply chain processes, setting new benchmarks in transparency and ethical sourcing for agricultural markets.

Keywords: Coffee and Cocoa Supply Chain · Blockchain-based System · BSC · POL · CELO · FTM, Encrypted-NFT

1 Introduction

Global agricultural supply chains, particularly in the coffee and cocoa sectors, present unique challenges in establishing verifiable and ethical business practices. These industries require sophisticated solutions to address fundamental issues in product authentication, stakeholder accountability, and sustainable operations [7]. The complexity of modern distribution networks demands innovative approaches to ensure product integrity from origin to consumer.

Traditional supply chain management systems exhibit considerable limitations in providing comprehensive verification mechanisms across distribution networks. The inability to maintain consistent visibility into product origin and handling processes creates significant barriers to stakeholder accountability. These

M. Barhamgi et al. (Eds.): WISE 2024, LNCS 15463, pp. 330–337, 2025.
https://doi.org/10.1007/978-981-96-1483-7_28

systemic weaknesses compromise consumer confidence and impede the implementation of ethical trading practices [20]. Furthermore, as agricultural products traverse multiple transition points from farmers to consumers, each stage introduces potential vulnerabilities in data integrity and tracking accuracy [10]. To address these challenges, our research introduces an innovative framework that integrates distributed ledger systems, smart contracts, cryptographically secured non-fungible tokens (NFTs), and decentralized storage through the InterPlanetary File System (IPFS). This comprehensive approach incorporates multiple encryption protocols, including RSA for asymmetric encryption, RC4 and DES for lightweight processing, ChaCha20 for high-speed encryption, and Blowfish and AES for enhanced security. The integration of these technologies creates a robust infrastructure capable of maintaining data integrity throughout the supply chain process.

Recent technological advances have demonstrated the significant potential of blockchain systems in agricultural applications [17,19]. The implementation of automated verification systems, coupled with real-time tracking mechanisms and IoT device integration, has established new standards for supply chain transparency. Notable developments in smart contract applications have contributed to enhanced risk mitigation strategies [5], while innovations in virtual operations have optimized supply chain management processes [6]. These advancements have created a strong foundation for implementing blockchain technology in agricultural settings [8].

Our study focuses on developing a comprehensive supply chain management system that leverages encrypted NFTs for product authentication while utilizing IPFS for decentralized data storage. The implementation of smart contracts facilitates automated compliance verification, while multiple encryption protocols ensure robust security throughout the system. This integrated approach effectively addresses key challenges identified in previous research [9,14], particularly concerning data integrity across supply chain stages and real-time access to product information. The system establishes secure transaction recording mechanisms while maintaining stakeholder accountability throughout the distribution process.

The proposed system underwent rigorous evaluation across multiple blockchain platforms, including Binance Smart Chain, Polygon Network, Fantom Opera, and Celo Platform. This comprehensive testing protocol examined critical operational aspects, including supply chain event documentation, NFT generation and management, and secure token transfer protocols. Performance evaluation encompassed detailed analysis of transaction costs, resource utilization patterns, and system reliability metrics. The testing results validate the system's capability to enhance operational efficiency while maintaining robust security measures in real-world applications. Through this thorough evaluation process, we demonstrate the practical viability of implementing blockchain-based solutions in agricultural supply chains.

Our research contributes to the evolving landscape of supply chain management by presenting a novel approach to addressing persistent challenges in the coffee and cocoa industries. By integrating advanced cryptographic techniques with distributed ledger technology, we establish a framework that promotes transparency, ensures data integrity, and facilitates ethical trading practices. The results of our implementation and testing provide valuable insights into the practical application of blockchain technology in agricultural supply chains, offering a blueprint for future developments in this field.

2 Literature Review

The intersection of distributed ledger technologies and sustainable supply chain practices has emerged as a critical area of research focus. Contemporary studies demonstrate how blockchain implementations facilitate enhanced transparency in agricultural commodity trading [17]. Investigations into price-tracking mechanisms have revealed blockchain's capacity to support fair trade certification processes, establishing new standards for market transparency [23]. Innovative developments in smart contract applications have transformed risk management strategies within supply chains, particularly in promoting sustainable agricultural practices [5]. Comprehensive frameworks focusing on agricultural product traceability have demonstrated the feasibility of implementing end-to-end verification systems [18]. Research has also explored blockchain's role in advancing sustainability objectives, introducing methodological approaches for evaluating the effectiveness of transparent supply chain systems [2][?].

The convergence of blockchain technology and programmable smart contracts has revolutionized traditional supply chain management approaches. Research has introduced innovative concepts such as digital-physical synchronization through virtual operations, addressing complex scheduling challenges in modern distribution networks [6]. The integration of Internet of Things (IoT) devices with blockchain infrastructure has enabled real-time monitoring capabilities, fundamentally transforming shipment tracking methodologies [8]. Studies have documented the enhancement of resource-sharing mechanisms within business networks, where smart contracts ensure data integrity and secure information exchange [1]. Investigations into standardized information-sharing protocols have yielded frameworks that strengthen trust relationships among supply chain participants [11]. Educational initiatives have developed blockchain-based simulation environments for modeling agricultural transactions, providing practical insights into technology implementation [15]. Analysis of supply chain re-engineering processes has highlighted smart contracts' instrumental role in transaction automation and security enhancement [4].

The application of blockchain solutions in agricultural contexts has generated significant advancements in product traceability and verification systems. Research has produced frameworks utilizing smart contract technology for direct crop monitoring and verification, enhancing agricultural practice integrity [12]. Integration of IoT technologies with blockchain platforms has resulted in specialized systems like distributed agricultural networks, addressing critical issues of fair pricing and market accessibility [16]. Studies focusing on high-value agricultural products have explored the implementation of composable digital tokens for authentication purposes, utilizing distributed storage systems for data management [9]. Investigations into scalable supply chain solutions have led to the development of decentralized systems that prioritize data integrity and operational efficiency [14]. Additional research has expanded into related domains, examining digital asset ownership mechanisms [3], query optimization in supply chain systems [21], food safety protocols [13], and trust-building mechanisms in supply chain networks [22].

3   System Architecture and Implementation

Our research presents an innovative digital infrastructure designed specifically for agricultural commodity tracking, with a focus on coffee and cocoa supply chains. This architecture integrates three fundamental technological components: distributed ledger systems, programmable smart contracts, and cryptographically secured digital tokens. The framework implements a comprehensive security protocol utilizing multiple encryption methodologies, including asymmetric encryption (RSA), stream ciphers (RC4, ChaCha20), and block ciphers (DES, Blowfish, AES), creating a multi-layered approach to data protection.

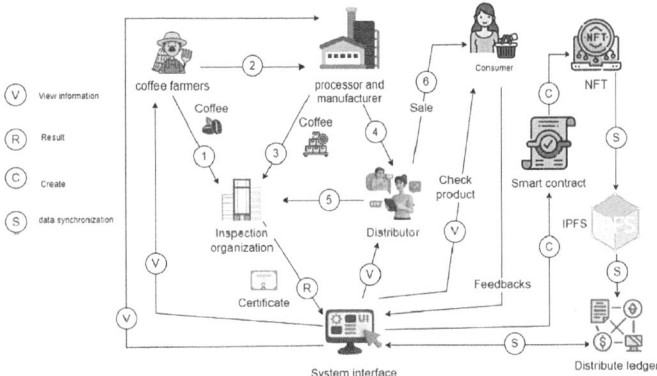

Fig. 1. Integrated Blockchain Architecture for Agricultural Supply Chain Management

The system's operational flow begins at the agricultural source, where producers digitally register harvest data through a blockchain interface. This initial registration creates an authoritative digital record encompassing crucial metrics such as production volume, quality parameters, and temporal data. By establishing this digital foundation, the system enables downstream stakeholders to access and verify product information with unprecedented reliability. A significant aspect of our research involves analyzing the performance characteristics of various encryption protocols to determine optimal configurations for both security assurance and operational efficiency.

The framework introduces automation at critical transaction points through smart contract implementation. These self-executing protocols manage contract fulfillment based on predefined quality and quantity parameters verified through blockchain data. This automation eliminates traditional intermediary requirements while ensuring compliance with established standards. Quality control entities participate by conducting physical inspections and generating digital certification records, which are subsequently converted into encrypted digital tokens. These tokens, secured through our multi-algorithm encryption approach, serve as tamper-resistant digital credentials throughout the supply chain.

Product verification occurs at multiple stages as commodities move through the distribution network. Distributors authenticate products by cross-referencing physical characteristics against digital credentials, creating a comprehensive verification chain accessible to subsequent stakeholders. Consumer access to this verification system enables direct confirmation of ethical sourcing claims through authenticated digital certificates. The framework incorporates decentralized storage solutions through IPFS integration, establishing permanent, distributed records of product histories and stakeholder interactions.

4 Performance Analysis and Platform Comparison

Our research presents a comprehensive evaluation of distributed ledger implementations across four major EVM compatible networks: BSC, Polygon, Fantom, and Celo. The analysis examines these platforms' capabilities in managing essential supply chain operations, including smart contract deployment, digital asset generation, and secure token transfers. Through systematic assessment of transaction processing efficiency, computational resource utilization, platform accessibility, and economic sustainability, we establish a framework for comparing these networks' effectiveness in supporting agricultural supply chain operations.

Table 1. Cross-Platform Transaction Cost Analysis

Platform	Operation Initialization	Asset Creation	Asset Transfer
BSC	0.0273 BNB ($8.27)	0.0011 BNB ($0.33)	0.0006 BNB ($0.17)
Fantom	0.0096 FTM ($0.00)	0.0004 FTM ($0.00)	0.0002 FTM ($0.00)
Polygon	0.0068 MATIC ($0.01)	0.0003 MATIC ($0.00)	0.0002 MATIC ($0.00)
Celo	0.0071 CELO ($0.005)	0.0003 CELO ($0.000)	0.0002 CELO ($0.000)

The performance metrics gathered through March 2024 provide detailed insights into each platform's capability to manage cryptographically secured digital assets. Our assessment specifically examines the platforms' handling of various encryption protocols, including RSA, RC4, DES, ChaCha20, Blowfish, and AES, establishing a comprehensive understanding of their security and operational characteristics. This evaluation framework enables precise identification of optimal platforms for secure supply chain operations while maintaining operational efficiency. Analysis of the Binance Smart Chain reveals robust infrastructure capabilities accompanied by notable cost considerations. The platform's fee structure demonstrates varying expenses across different operations, with transaction initialization requiring 0.0273 BNB (approximately $8.27), digital asset creation costing 0.0011 BNB ($0.33), and asset transfer operations necessitating 0.0006 BNB ($0.17). These cost factors significantly influence operational strategies, particularly when considering high-frequency transaction requirements typical in agricultural supply chains.

The Fantom network emerges as a highly cost-efficient alternative, presenting minimal operational expenses across all transaction types. With transaction initialization costs of 0.0096 FTM, asset creation fees of 0.0004 FTM, and transfer operation costs of 0.0002 FTM, the platform enables frequent network interactions without substantial financial overhead. This cost structure positions Fantom as particularly suitable for intensive supply chain operations requiring numerous daily transactions.

Polygon's platform demonstrates exceptional efficiency for high-volume operations, featuring remarkably low transaction costs. The platform requires 0.0068 MATIC for operation initialization, 0.0003 MATIC for digital asset generation, and 0.0002 MATIC for asset transfers. These economical rates facilitate extensive network utilization while maintaining operational efficiency, making Polygon an attractive option for large-scale supply chain implementations.

The Celo infrastructure exhibits strong performance characteristics with competitive fee structures across all operational categories. Transaction creation costs of 0.0071 CELO, asset minting fees of 0.0003 CELO, and transfer processing expenses of 0.0002 CELO result in sub-cent operational costs. This pricing model particularly benefits agricultural supply chain applications requiring extensive transaction volumes and frequent data updates.

The comparative analysis presented in Table 1 reveals significant variations in operational expenses across platforms, directly impacting the selection of appropriate infrastructure for agricultural supply chain implementations. While each evaluated platform offers viable solutions, their optimal application depends heavily on specific operational requirements and anticipated transaction volumes. The implementation of distributed ledger technology demonstrates potential for substantial cost reduction compared to traditional supply chain management systems. This economic advantage, combined with enhanced security features through encrypted digital assets, establishes a compelling case for blockchain adoption in agricultural supply chains.

Our comprehensive evaluation provides crucial insights for stakeholders seeking to optimize their supply chain operations through distributed ledger technologies. The analysis demonstrates that while all platforms offer viable solutions for supply chain management, their individual characteristics make them suitable for different operational contexts and requirements. This understanding enables informed decision-making in platform selection, ensuring optimal alignment with specific supply chain needs and operational objectives.

5   Conclusion and Future Implications

Our research demonstrates the transformative potential of an integrated digital infrastructure in revolutionizing agricultural commodity supply chains. The convergence of distributed ledger systems, programmable smart contracts, cryptographically secured tokens, and decentralized storage solutions establishes a new paradigm for supply chain management in the coffee and cocoa sectors. Through extensive evaluation across multiple blockchain platforms, we have validated the framework's capability to enhance operational transparency while maintaining robust security protocols. The technological synthesis achieved through this research advances the field of supply chain management in several critical aspects. By establishing immutable verification mechanisms for product authenticity, automating compliance procedures through smart contracts, and maintaining comprehensive digital provenance records, the system addresses fundamental challenges in agricultural commodity trading. The integration of decentralized storage solutions further enhances the framework's capability to maintain detailed product histories while ensuring data accessibility and integrity.

Our research contributes to the evolving landscape of digital supply chain solutions by presenting a scalable model that effectively balances security requirements with operational efficiency. The framework's emphasis on stakeholder accessibility, combined with robust data protection mechanisms, establishes new standards for transparency in agricultural trade. These advancements particularly benefit developing agricultural communities by providing verifiable mechanisms for ethical sourcing practices and fair trade certification. The implications of this research extend beyond immediate technological implementation, suggesting a fundamental shift in how agricultural supply chains can operate in an increasingly digitized global economy. As blockchain technology continues to mature, frameworks like the one presented in this study will likely play pivotal roles in establishing more equitable, transparent, and efficient agricultural trading systems. This transformation holds particular promise for enhancing economic opportunities in agricultural communities while ensuring product authenticity and ethical sourcing practices for consumers worldwide.

References

1. Agrawal, et al.: Demonstration of a blockchain-based framework using smart contracts for supply chain collaboration. Int. J. Prod. Res. **61**, 1497–1516 (2022)
2. Bai, et al.: A supply chain transparency and sustainability technology appraisal model for blockchain technology. Int. J. Prod. Res **58**, 2142–2162 (2019)
3. Battah, et al.: Blockchain and NFTs for trusted ownership, trading, and access of AI models. IEEE Access **10**, 112230–112249 (2022)
4. Chang, et al.: Supply chain re-engineering using blockchain technology: a case of smart contract based tracking process. Technological Forecasting and Social Change (2019)
5. Dietrich, et al.: Smart contract-based blockchain solution to reduce supply chain risks, pp. 165–173 (2020)

6. Dolgui, et al.: Blockchain-oriented dynamic modelling of smart contract design and execution in the supply chain. Int. J. Produc. Res. **58**, 2184–2199 (2020)
7. Ha, X.S., et al.: DeM-CoD: novel access-control-based cash on delivery mechanism for decentralized marketplace. In: 2020 IEEE 19th International Conference on Trust, Security and Privacy in Computing and Communications (TrustCom), pp. 71–78. IEEE (2020)
8. Hasan, et al.: Smart contract-based approach for efficient shipment management. Comput. Ind. Eng. **136**, 149–159 (2019)
9. Hawashin, et al.: Using composable NFTs for trading and managing expensive packaged products in the food industry. IEEE Access **11** (2023)
10. Le, N.T.T., et al.: Assuring non-fraudulent transactions in cash on delivery by introducing double smart contracts. Int. J. Adv. Comput. Sci. Appl. **10**(5), 677–684 (2019)
11. Li, et al.: Design of supply chain system based on blockchain technology. Applied Sciences (2021)
12. M., V., et al.: Agricultural supply chain management system using blockchain. In: 2023 International Conference on Recent Trends in Electronics and Communication (ICRTEC), pp. 1–4. IEEE (2023)
13. Majdalawieh, et al.: Blockchain-based solution for secure and transparent food supply chain network. Peer-to-Peer Networking Appl. **14**, 3831–3850 (2021)
14. Pawar, et al.: Secure and scalable decentralized supply chain management using ethereum and IPFS platform, pp. 1–5 (2021)
15. Putri, et al.: Supply chain management serious game using blockchain smart contract. IEEE Access **11**, 131089–131113 (2023)
16. Reddy, et al.: FarmersChain: a decentralized farmer centric supply chain management system using blockchain and IoT. In: 2021 IEEE International Symposium on Smart Electronic Systems (iSES) (Formerly iNiS), pp. 444–449. IEEE (2021)
17. Saberi, et al.: Blockchain technology and its relationships to sustainable supply chain management. Int. J. Produc. Res. **57**, 2117–2135 (2018)
18. Shahid, et al.: Blockchain-based agri-food supply chain: a complete solution. IEEE Access **8**, 69230–69243 (2020)
19. Son, et al.: SSSB: an approach to insurance for cross-border exchange by using smart contracts. In: International Conference on Mobile Web and Intelligent Information Systems, pp. 179–192. Springer (2022)
20. Son, H.X., et al.: Towards a mechanism for protecting seller's interest of cash on delivery by using smart contract in hyperledger. Int. J. Ad. Comput. Sci. Appl. **10**(4) (2019)
21. Tahmasbzadeh, et al.: A blockchain-based approach for data storage in drug supply chain. In: 2023 9th International Conference on Web Research (ICWR), pp. 335–341. IEEE (2023)
22. Waikar, et al.: Blockchain and supply chain management: the future of trust and transparency. International Journal for Research in Applied Science and Engineering Technology (2022)
23. Yoo, et al.: A study on the transparent price tracing system in supply chain management based on blockchain. Sustainability (2018)

The 1st International Workshop on AI and Web Data Analytics (AIWDA 2024)

A Hypertension Early Warning Model Combining Generative Adversarial Networks and Long Short-Term Memory Neural Networks

Shaofu Lin[1], Ziqian Qiao[1], Jianhui Chen[1(✉)], and Zhisheng Huang[2,3,4]

[1] Faculty of Information Technology, Beijing University of Technology, Beijing 100124, China
chenjianhui@bjut.edu.cn
[2] Dept Comp Sci, Vrije University Amsterdam, Amsterdam, Netherlands
[3] Clinical Research Center for Mental Disorders, Shanghai Pudong New Area Mental Health Center, Tongji University School of Medicine, Shanghai, China
[4] Deep Blue Technology Group, Shanghai, China

Abstract. Hypertension is one of the most common chronic diseases threatening human health, and early warning and intervention are crucial for controlling disease progression. However, in the real world, the sample data used for hypertension model training is often limited, posing challenges to model performance. To address this issue, this paper proposes an end-to-end hypertension early warning model based on Generative Adversarial Networks (GANs) and Long Short-Term Memory (LSTM) networks, which can generate a large number of high-quality synthetic electronic health records(EHRs) in a small sample environment and directly use them for training the hypertension early warning model. Specifically, we use the processed data from the public MIMIC-III dataset as input and generate a large number of synthetic EHRs through GAN and LSTM networks. The GAN network generates realistic synthetic data through adversarial training of the discriminator and generator, while the LSTM network is used to capture time series features, thereby enhancing the authenticity and diversity of the data. After generating the synthetic data, these data are directly used to train the hypertension early warning model. The feedback mechanism during the generation of EHRs can continuously obtain higher prediction accuracy, thus optimizing the quality of the generated data until the optimal effect is achieved. Finally, the optimal hypertension early warning model and the corresponding synthetic data are saved. Experimental results show that the hypertension early warning model trained using synthetic data significantly improves the prediction accuracy on the test set, with higher sensitivity and specificity compared to traditional methods. This study verifies the effectiveness and superiority of the proposed method in a small sample environment, providing a new perspective for the utilization of large-scale medical data, and has a wide range of application prospects.

Keywords: Hypertension early warning · Generative adversarial networks · Long short-term memory networks · Electronic health records · MIMIC-III dataset

© The Author(s), under exclusive license to Springer Nature Singapore Pte Ltd. 2025
M. Barhamgi et al. (Eds.): WISE 2024, LNCS 15463, pp. 341–356, 2025.
https://doi.org/10.1007/978-981-96-1483-7_29

1   Introduction

With the accelerated aging process of the population, chronic diseases have emerged as a significant challenge to global public health. According to the World Health Organization, chronic diseases account for 71% of all deaths globally [1]. In China, chronic diseases cause over 13 million deaths annually, representing 88% of the total mortality [2]. Concurrently, chronic diseases impose a substantial burden on the healthcare system and socio-economic development. In 2017, China's total health expenditure reached 5.6178 trillion yuan, with more than 70% allocated to chronic disease-related expenses.To address the increasingly severe issue of chronic diseases, the establishment of efficient disease warning and prediction methods is essential. In this context, extensive research has been conducted on the early warning and prediction of chronic diseases. Traditional methods primarily rely on demographic information and clinical indicators such as age, gender, blood pressure, and blood glucose levels. In recent years, with the widespread adoption of electronic health record (EHR) systems and advances in data mining techniques, intelligent early warning and prediction methods based on EHRs have gained increasing attention. Compared to traditional methods, EHRs contain more comprehensive and fine-grained patient health information, including symptoms, signs, medication, tests, and medical history, providing multi-dimensional evidence for disease risk assessment. Razavian et al. [3] utilized longitudinal EHR data and developed a multi-disease risk prediction model using temporal convolutional networks to predict the 18-month incidence risk of eight common chronic diseases, including coronary heart disease and diabetes, achieving an average AUC of 0.78. Choi et al. [4] constructed a heart failure early warning model based on recurrent neural networks, with prediction accuracies of 83.2%, 82.8%, and 81.5% for 3, 6, and 12-month prediction windows, respectively. These studies demonstrate that mining temporal features and disease co-occurrence patterns in EHRs can effectively support chronic disease risk assessment and health management decision-making.

The widespread adoption of EHRs faces numerous challenges, with data privacy protection and secure sharing being key limiting factors. EHRs contain sensitive personal information, including patient identities and medical histories. To protect patient privacy, various countries have enacted relevant laws and regulations to strictly regulate the collection, storage, and use of EHRs. For instance, the Health Insurance Portability and Accountability Act (HIPAA) in the United States mandates that healthcare institutions cannot use EHRs for secondary purposes, such as research, without patient authorization [5]. Similarly, China's Cybersecurity Law, released in 2017, explicitly includes personal health information as a key protection target [6].Under the constraints of privacy protection policies, the availability of EHR data for training disease prediction models is significantly limited. For instance, a survey of 10 publicly available datasets for heart disease prediction found that the largest dataset contained only 1,500 samples [7]. Insufficient data can lead to model overfitting, making it challenging to achieve satisfactory performance in practical applications. Therefore, obtaining sufficient, high-quality EHR training data while protecting privacy is crucial for the development of smart healthcare.

To address this issue, this paper proposes an innovative end-to-end hypertension early warning model aimed at compensating for the insufficient data in a small sample environment by generating high-quality synthetic data. By leveraging GAN and LSTM networks, realistic synthetic data can be generated and directly used for training the early warning model, thereby improving the model's accuracy and stability. Through a feedback mechanism, the model's prediction results are fed back to the generator to adjust the distribution and features of the generated data, further enhancing the model's accuracy in the next round of training. This dynamic optimization process enables our early warning model to perform exceptionally well in a small sample environment. Experimental results demonstrate that the hypertension early warning model trained using synthetic data significantly outperforms traditional methods in terms of sensitivity, specificity, and other metrics, showcasing its strong adaptability in a small sample environment.

The contributions of this paper can be summarized as follows:

1. Introducing GANs into the field of EHR data augmentation. By leveraging GANs' powerful data generation capabilities, a large amount of realistic EHR data can be synthesized, overcoming the bottleneck of insufficient original data under privacy protection constraints.
2. Addressing the temporal characteristics of electronic health record data, improvements were made to the generator of the original GAN model. By introducing an LSTM network into the generator, the temporal dependencies between different medical encounters within the EHRs were better modeled, enhancing the realism of the synthesized data.
3. Presenting an end-to-end hypertension early warning model that utilizes GAN and LSTM to generate high-quality synthetic data. Through a feedback mechanism, the model optimizes the performance of both the generated data and the early warning model itself. This approach effectively addresses the issue of insufficient data in small sample environments and significantly enhances the accuracy and stability of the early warning model.

The structure of this paper is as follows, Sect. 2 describes the current related research and progress; Sect. 3 introduces the research methods; Sect. 4 presents the experimental setup and case analysis; and Sect. 5 provides the conclusion.

2 Related Works

In recent years, with the widespread adoption of electronic health record (EHR) systems and advancements in big data analytics, disease prediction and early warning methods based on EHRs have garnered extensive attention. Miotto et al. [8] proposed a representation learning framework called "Deep Patient" which automatically extracts patient feature representations from EHRs through unsupervised learning and applies them to disease prediction tasks, outperforming traditional machine learning methods across multiple diseases. This study demonstrated the advantages of deep learning techniques in uncovering hidden patterns within EHRs. Rajkomar et al. [9] developed an interpretable prediction model based on recurrent neural networks that can predict risks such as future hospitalization and mortality for patients, and revealed key clinical events influencing the prediction results through an attention mechanism, providing credible evidence for clinical decision-making. Shickel et al. [10] conducted a systematic review of deep learning applications in EHR analysis, noting that existing methods have made significant progress in tasks such as disease diagnosis, disease progression prediction, and patient phenotype classification, but also face challenges such as varying data quality and lack of interpretability. These studies indicate that mining the vast information contained within EHRs is crucial for developing disease early warning and prediction models.

However, due to privacy protection constraints, the availability of raw EHR data for model training is severely limited, hindering the development of intelligent healthcare technologies. Xiao et al. [11] pointed out that medical data sharing faces risks such as privacy leakage and data abuse, necessitating the use of privacy protection mechanisms to ensure patient information security. He et al. [12] systematically discussed the privacy challenges and potential countermeasures in medical data sharing, emphasizing that balancing privacy protection and data utility is vital for promoting secondary utilization of medical data. Traditional data anonymization methods, such as k-anonymity [13] and l-diversity [14], struggle to reconcile the trade-off between data utility and privacy protection. In recent years, researchers have begun exploring the use of data synthesis techniques to alleviate the problem of insufficient privacy-protected data. Surendra et al. [15] pioneered the introduction of GANs into the field of EHR data generation, synthesizing simulated data with similar statistical properties by learning the probability distribution of real samples. Che et al. [16] further improved the GAN model and proposed a conditional GAN with information network regularization, enhancing the modeling capability of disease association patterns. Guan et al. [17] combined autoencoders with GANs and designed a model called EhrGAN, achieving simultaneous modeling of discrete and continuous attributes and improving the realism of synthesized data. Baowaly et al. [18] developed a GAN-based privacy-preserving synthetic EHR data generation framework and validated its effectiveness on multiple medical datasets. Yoon et al. [19] proposed a model called PATE-GAN that combines differential privacy with GANs, generating high-quality synthetic data while ensuring individual privacy is not compromised. Dahmen et al. [20] explored methods for incorporating causal and temporal relationships into the synthetic medical data generation process to enhance data interpretability and effectiveness. The aforementioned methods have demonstrated the advantages of GANs in generating realistic medical data, but they still suffer from limitations imposed by privacy constraints and small sample sizes, and lack effective downstream tasks for validation. This study employs GAN networks and LSTM models to generate EHRs, which can effectively address the challenges encountered during the research process of hypertension early warning models.

3   Methodology

3.1   Improved GAN Design

The traditional GAN was proposed by Goodfellow et al. in 2014 [21]. It consists of a generator and a discriminator. The purpose of the generator is to produce synthetic data that is as realistic as possible, making it indistinguishable from real data for the discriminator. The discriminator's goal, on the other hand, is to accurately determine whether the input data comes from the real distribution or the synthetic distribution generated by the generator. These two components interact with each other during the training process, forming a dynamic equilibrium. In this paper, we made improvements to the traditional GAN network. In terms of the generator, we made two modifications. Firstly, we employed an LSTM to recursively generate the entire patient's visit sequence, rather than generating each patient visit separately. This approach better captures the temporal correlations between different visits. Secondly, we introduced a smooth conditional matrix to guide the generator in producing rare diseases. This matrix smooths the target disease across all visits, preventing the generation of the target disease in only a few visits. For the discriminator, instead of using the traditional GAN's binary classification discriminator, we borrowed the idea from WGAN and let the discriminator compute the Wasserstein distance between real and generated samples. Moreover, to capture the temporal features of EHR data, the discriminator considers not only the current visit but also the temporal features represented by hidden states when calculating the distance. The GAN network architecture for generating EHRs is illustrated in Fig. 1.

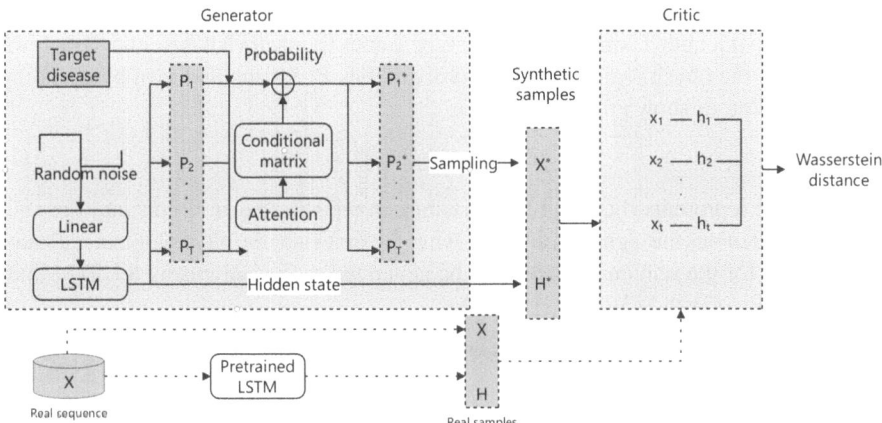

Fig. 1. Improved GAN architecture diagram

In the improved GAN network, the preprocessed multi-label temporal disease data is vectorized to form a compact binary matrix representation. To generate more diverse and realistic synthetic data, these disease matrices are not directly inputted into the generator. Instead, a random noise vector is first linearly transformed and decoded into a disease probability vector for the first time step, which is then fed into the generator's LSTM network along with the disease matrix for recursive multi-time-step disease probability generation. The smooth conditional matrix then broadcasts the generated probabilities to the target disease, allowing it to appear at multiple time steps in the sequence. The discriminator scores the generated sequence and its temporal features to distinguish between real and synthetic samples. Finally, the generator minimizes the Wasserstein distance to deceive the discriminator, while the discriminator maximizes the Wasserstein distance between real and synthetic samples to differentiate them, forming the adversarial training process. After training, the synthetic dataset is obtained through Bernoulli sampling from the generated probability matrix.

3.2 Temporal Feature Modeling of EHRs Based on LSTM Networks

When generating time-related probability sequences, an intuitive approach is to employ a LSTM network. At each time step, the input to the LSTM unit is a random noise vector and the hidden state passed from the previous time step. The output of each time step is a new hidden state. In this paper, we can use the hidden state to generate the physiological indicators for each visit and combine all visits into a sequence. However, we argue that using noise to generate each time step's visit may introduce uncontrollable randomness to some extent and weaken the temporal correlations between adjacent visits. It is reasonable to believe that, given a single noise vector at the beginning of the sequence, an optimized generator should be capable of generating the entire sequence. Similar to the temporal physiological indicator prediction task studied by Lipton et al. [22], a well-designed generator should predict the physiological indicator attributes and disease types of the next visit based on all previous visits. Therefore, based on this idea, we propose to recursively generate the visit sequence from a single noise vector z to enhance the temporal correlations between adjacent visits. Given a random noise vector $z \in R^s$ and a visit length T, since the disease type values for each visit are either 0 or 1, we first generate the physiological indicator probabilities P_1 for the first visit by decoding the noise vector, as shown in Eq. (1):

$$P_1 = \sigma(W_z) \in R^d \tag{1}$$

Here, $W \in R^d$ represents the weight matrix that projects the noise vector into the visit space, and σ denotes the sigmoid function. After the first visit, the physiological indicator probabilities for the remaining visits can be generated recursively using a LSTM unit. as shown in Eq. (2) and (3):

$$h_t, c_t = lstm(P_t, h_{t-1}, c_{t-1}) \in R^s \tag{2}$$

$$P_{t+1} = \sigma(Wh_t) \in R^d \tag{3}$$

In this context, h_t and c_t represent the hidden state and cell state of the LSTM at time step t, respectively. We initialize $h_0=0$ and $c_0=0$ and set the noise dimension to be the same as the number of hidden units in the LSTM, as we treat the noise vector as the initial hidden state. Subsequently, we compute the hidden state and cell state at time step t using the LSTM network, taking the hidden state, cell state, and generated visit probabilities P_t from time step t-1 as inputs. Then, we generate P_{t+1} for the visit at time step $t + 1$ using the same decoding process. Finally, we concatenate all the generated physiological indicator probabilities to form the patient-level distribution P for the synthesized data sample, as shown in Eq. (4):

$$P = (P_1, P_2, ..., P_T) \in R^{d \times T} \tag{4}$$

Figure 2 illustrates the schematic diagram of the temporal feature modeling of EHRs based on LSTM networks.

By incorporating an LSTM network into the generator, we effectively model the temporal characteristics of EHRs. Moreover, by inputting a single random noise vector as the initial hidden state, the LSTM network can control the randomness of the generated sequence, achieving smooth and natural transitions within the sequence.

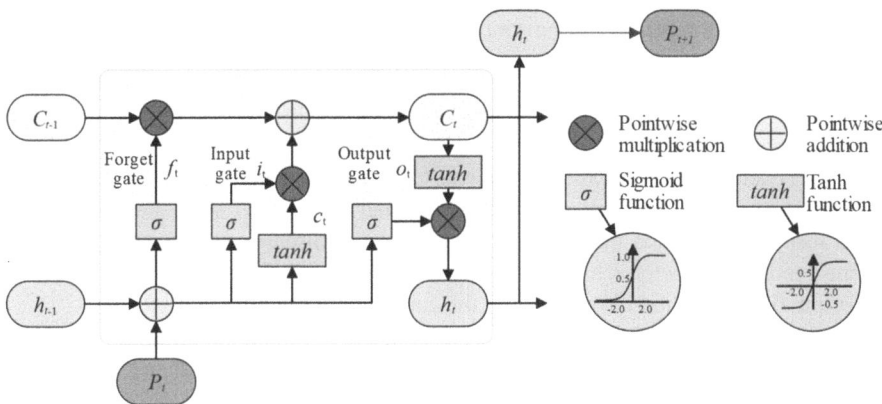

Fig. 2. Temporal feature modeling of EHRs based on LSTM networks.

3.3 Smoothing Conditional Matrix for Rare Disease Data Generation Based on Attention Mechanism

After generating patient-level probabilities, it is necessary to address the issue of imbalanced generation of rare diseases. Since GANs generate new samples by learning the distribution of the data, the model tends to generate samples that appear more frequently in the training data during the training process to fit the distribution of the real data as closely as possible. This leads to a higher number of samples for common diseases and fewer samples for rare diseases in the generated EHR data, exacerbating the imbalance problem in the generated data. To tackle this issue, we propose the smooth conditional matrix, which mainly introduces an attention score mechanism to assign higher probabilities to rare diseases during the generation process, thereby making the generated EHR data more balanced across various disease types. Specifically, we designate the target disease as a condition and construct a conditional matrix $C \in R^{d \times T}$, as shown in Eq. (5):

$$C = (C_1, C_2, ..., C_T) \in \{0, 1\}^{d \times T} \tag{5}$$

Here, the element corresponding to the target disease is set to 1, $C_i (i = 1,2, 3...)$ indicate the intention to generate the target disease i at time step t.

We then dynamically adjust the importance of each element in the conditional matrix, allowing it to exhibit a smooth transition property at different positions in the sequence. Let C_t denote the column vector of the conditional matrix corresponding to the t-th visit record, and P_t represent the disease probability distribution of the t-th visit record. The attention score α_t can be calculated using Eq. (6):

$$\alpha_t = \text{softmax}((f(c_t, h_{t-1})) \tag{6}$$

Here, $f(c_t, h_{t-1})$ represents the attention computation function, which can take common forms such as additive attention or dot-product attention. h_{t-1} denotes the hidden state of the LSTM at time step t-1. The softmax function normalizes the attention scores between 0 and 1.

Based on the obtained attention scores, we smooth the conditional matrix to obtain $Ç \in R^{d \times T}$, as shown in Eq. (7):

$$Ç_t = \alpha_t c_t + (1 - \alpha_t) Ç_{t-1} \tag{7}$$

Here, $Ç_0$ is set to a zero vector. As shown, $Ç_t$ is obtained by a weighted average of the current and previous visit records' conditional vectors, α_t served as a dynamic fusion mechanism. When the correlation between the disease probability distribution and the conditional vector is higher, the value of α_t becomes larger, indicating a greater proportion of conditional information in the current visit record.

Finally, the probability distribution P_t and the smoothed conditional vector $Ç_t$ are concatenated and jointly input into the LSTM to generate the hidden state and cell state for the next time step, as shown in Eq. (8):

$$h_t, c_t = lstm([P_t, Ç_t], h_{t-1}, c_{t-1}) \tag{8}$$

By incorporating the information from the conditional matrix, the LSTM can generate the probability distribution of subsequent visits based on the historical states and the current target disease. During this process, the smooth conditional matrix plays a role in balancing the positions where the target disease appears throughout the sequence, making it more consistent with the distribution characteristics found in real medical record data.

3.4 Loss Function Based on Wasserstein Distance and Gradient Penalty

Traditional GANs employ the Jensen-Shannon divergence (JS divergence) as the loss function for the discriminator, aiming to minimize the JS divergence between the real sample distribution and the generated sample distribution during adversarial training. However, when there is minimal overlap between the real and generated sample distributions, the JS divergence approaches a constant value, leading to vanishing gradients in the generator and hindering further optimization.

To address this issue, Wasserstein GAN (WGAN) [23] introduced the Wasserstein distance as the optimization objective for the generator and discriminator (referred to as the critic in WGAN). Furthermore, Wasserstein GAN with Gradient Penalty (WGAN-GP) added a gradient penalty term to the critic's objective function to satisfy the constraint conditions of the Wasserstein distance. The loss functions for the generator and critic are defined as shown in Eqs. (9) and (10):

$$L_D = -\mathbb{E}_{z \sim p_z}[D(G(z))] - \mathbb{E}_{x \sim p_x}[D(x)] + \lambda \mathbb{E}_{\hat{x} \sim p_{\hat{x}}}\left[(\|\Delta_{\hat{x}} D(\dot{x})\|_2 - 1)^2\right] \tag{9}$$

$$L_G = -\mathbb{E}_{z \sim p_z}[D(G(z))] \tag{10}$$

Here, L_D and L_G denote the loss functions for the critic and generator, respectively. λ represents the gradient penalty coefficient, $\dot{x} = \partial x + (1 - \partial)x$, $\partial \sim U[0, 1]$ is the linear interpolation between real samples and generated samples, $\partial \sim U[0,1]$ follows a uniform distribution, Δ is the gradient operator, and $\| \bullet \|_2$ denotes the ℓ^2- norm. p_z denote the real sample distribution and p_x represent the generated sample distribution. In contrast to the JS divergence, the Wasserstein distance provides meaningful gradient information even when the two distributions have no overlap, enabling the generator to continuously optimize its parameters.

In the electronic health record synthesis task presented in this study, the quality and diversity of the generated data are improved by employing a loss function based on the Wasserstein distance and gradient penalty. Compared to traditional GANs that rely on the JS divergence, the enhanced GAN model demonstrates the capability to generate more realistic electronic health record data while exhibiting increased stability during the training process.

3.5 Introduction to the Hypertension Early Warning Model

In this study, we utilize the MIMIC-III database to conduct experiments and implement an end-to-end hypertension early warning model. First, we extract electronic health record data related to hypertension from the MIMIC-III database. The MIMIC-III (Medical Information Mart for Intensive Care III) database is a large, publicly available clinical database jointly developed by the Massachusetts Institute of Technology Computer Science and Artificial Intelligence Laboratory (MIT CSAIL) and the Beth Israel Deaconess Medical Center. This database encompasses detailed clinical data collected from over 40,000 patients admitted to the intensive care units (ICUs) at Beth Israel Deaconess Medical Center between 2001 and 2012, including demographic information, laboratory measurements, vital signs, medication usage records, and treatment plans. Due to its data transparency and high quality, the MIMIC-III database serves as an ideal data source for studying EHRs and machine learning models. To ensure data quality, we perform data cleaning and standardization, removing data points with extensive missing values and extreme outliers.

Next, we employ GAN to generate high-quality synthetic electronic health record data. LSTM networks are incorporated into the generator to capture the temporal dependencies between patients' different visit records. Through adversarial training of the discriminator and generator, realistic synthetic data is generated. The generated synthetic data possesses a high degree of authenticity and diversity, and this data is used to train the LSTM model. LSTM networks excel at processing time series data and can effectively capture the features of patients' health status changes over time, thereby improving the accuracy of the hypertension early warning model.

During the model training and optimization process, at the end of each training cycle, the prediction results of the early warning model are fed back to the GAN network to adjust the distribution and features of the generated data, further enhancing the model's accuracy in the next round of training. Through this dynamic optimization process, we can continuously improve the model's predictive performance. The trained hypertension early warning model is then applied to the test set to evaluate its predictive performance.

Specifically, this paper conducts comparative experiments between the hypertension early warning model trained on the MIMIC-III dataset and the model trained on the synthetic data that achieves the best prediction accuracy. By evaluating their predictive performance on the test set using three metrics, namely Jaccard similarity coefficient, F1 score, and PR-AUC, this paper can quantitatively compare the effects of the two datasets on model training.

Furthermore, this paper also conducts controlled experiments to further validate the practicality of the synthetic data by comparing the predictive performance of different models using the MIMIC-III dataset and the synthetic data.

4 Experiment

4.1 Synthetic Data Generation

In this study, we trained a GAN) for pre-training the preprocessed MIMIC-III dataset in an RTX 3060 GPU environment. To evaluate the model performance, the dataset was randomly divided into a training set and a test set with a ratio of 4:1. In the construction of the GAN model, we specifically added 64 attention layers and 256 LSTM hidden layers, with the number of hidden layers for the generator and discriminator configured as 256 and 64, respectively. The experimental setup included model evaluation every 10,000 iterations and saving model parameters every 1,000 iterations. Additionally, the learning rates for the generator and discriminator were set to 0.0001 and 0.00001, respectively.

The experimental process first involved pre-training the LSTM model for 1,000 epochs and saving the model parameters. These parameters were used to obtain the hidden states and cell states of the MIMIC-III dataset and synthetic data in the discriminator. The next step was to train the GAN model, and once the set testing frequency was reached, the model performance was evaluated on the test set. When the saving frequency was reached, the model parameters of the generator and discriminator were saved. Simultaneously, the loss values and changes in the Wasserstein distance of the two models during the adversarial training process were recorded, as shown in Fig. 3.

After completing all training epochs, the saved generator model parameters were loaded to generate synthetic data. By calculating the Jensen-Shannon divergence (JS divergence) and normalized distance (ND distance) of the generated data at different training epochs, the changes at the visit level (_v) and patient level (_p) were evaluated. The parameters of the GAN network were continuously optimized through feedback from the prediction accuracy of the hypertension early warning model, ultimately determining the optimal training epoch for the GAN model. According to the results shown in Table 1, this study confirmed that the optimal training epoch for the GAN model was 30,000, at which point the generated synthetic data was closest to the real data. After removing missing values and erroneous values, 15,868 valid records were obtained, significantly increasing the sample size compared to the original EHR data.

4.2 Application of the Hypertension Early Warning Model

In the experimental setup, we randomly divided the MIMIC-III dataset into training, validation, and test sets, following a 6:2:2 ratio for five-fold cross-validation. To fully utilize the MIMIC-III dataset, each fold of the experiment selected three portions of data as the training set, one portion as the validation set, and one portion as the test set, repeating the experiment 5 times. The final evaluation metrics were calculated as the

Table 1. Comparison of JS Divergence and ND Distance at Different Training Epochs

Epochs	JSD_v↓	JSD_p↓	ND_v↓	ND_p↓
10000	0.9545	0.9362	1.7331	1.7167
15000	0.8632	0.8454	1.6219	1.6131
20000	0.6367	0.6103	1.5453	1.5121
25000	0.6033	0.5982	1.3923	1.3765
30000	**0.4464**	**0.4347**	**1.1665**	**1.0984**
35000	0.5722	0.4989	1.2139	1.1953

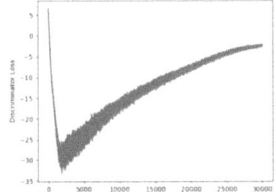 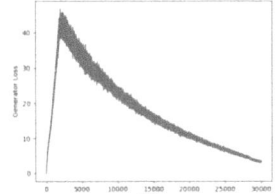 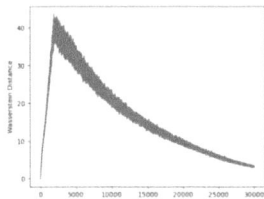

Fig. 3. Loss Values and Wasserstein Distance of the GAN Model at 30,000 Training Epochs

average of the 5 experimental results to ensure the robustness of model performance assessment in the small sample scenario.

During the model training process, we fine-tuned the hyperparameters to obtain the optimal prediction performance. By comparing the model's performance on the validation set under different parameter combinations, we finally determined the number of hidden layers to be 2, with each layer containing 4 attention heads. In the dual adaptive gradient update strategy, we set different learning rates for different stages, namely 5e-8, 3.5e-4, and 5e-4. Additionally, we explored the impact of different iteration numbers on the model's convergence speed and performance, finding that when the number of iterations was 200, the hypertension early warning model could achieve the best performance in a relatively short time.

We adopted Jaccard similarity coefficient, F1 score, and PR-AUC as evaluation metrics to comprehensively examine the model's classification performance on imbalanced data. Figure 4 shows the comparison of loss curves for the hypertension early warning model trained using MIMIC-III dataset and the synthetic data generated by the GAN network. It can be observed that the model trained using synthetic data converges significantly faster than the one trained on MIMIC-III dataset and ultimately converges to a lower loss value. This indicates that the large-scale realistic samples generated by GAN can effectively alleviate the problem of insufficient original data and accelerate the model training process.

Table 2 presents the Jaccard, F1 score, and PR-AUC metrics of the hypertension early warning model trained on the two types of data, evaluated on the test set. The model trained using synthetic data outperforms the model trained on MIMIC-III dataset across all metrics. Specifically, the Jaccard similarity coefficient improved from 0.8207 to 0.9287, the F1 score increased from 0.8983 to 0.9374, and the PR-AUC rose from 0.8672 to 0.9651. The synthetic data brought about performance improvements of 13.16%, 4.35%, and 11.29% in these three metrics, respectively, fully demonstrating that the proposed GAN data augmentation method can significantly enhance the predictive performance of downstream tasks.

Table 2. Comparison of Results on the Hypertension Early Warning Model Trained with Two Types of Data

Data	Jaccard	F1	PR-AUC	avg_p	avg_r
MIMIC-III dataset	0.8207	0.8983	0.8672	0.8207	0.8534
Synthetic Data	0.9287	0.9374	0.9651	0.9287	0.9547

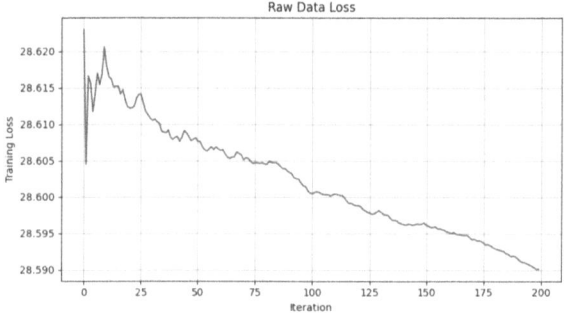

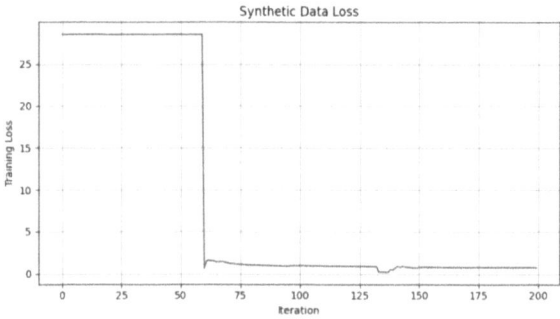

Fig. 4. Loss Curve Comparison of the Hypertension Early Warning Model Trained on MIMIC-III dataset and Synthetic Data

4.3   Comparative Experimental Analysis

To further validate the superiority of the proposed electronic health record data augmentation method based on the improved GAN, we designed seven comparative experiments.

We selected seven classic machine learning and deep learning models, including the Concare model, KNN + LightGBM, LightGBM, Logistic Regression, LSTM, Random Forest, and SVM. We trained these models using both the original small sample data and the electronic health record data synthesized by the improved GAN method proposed in this paper, and compared their performance on the hypertension early warning task.

Concare [24] is a chronic disease early warning model that adopts pre-training weighting and a multi-task dual adaptive gradient update strategy. It integrates structured and unstructured data from EHRs and models disease risk in both temporal and feature dimensions.

KNN + LightGBM [25] combines the K-nearest neighbor algorithm with the Light-GBM ensemble learning method. It uses KNN to find the nearest neighbor samples and then employs LightGBM to perform weighted combination of the nearest neighbor samples, making it a classification and prediction method based on sample similarity.

LightGBM [26] is a decision tree-based gradient boosting ensemble learning algorithm that achieves classification and regression tasks by constructing multiple shallow decision trees and performing weighted combination. It performs exceptionally well on imbalanced data and high-dimensional features.

Logistic Regression [27] is a classic linear classification model that maps sample features to values between 0 and 1 using a logistic function, predicting the probability of event occurrence. It is easy to understand and implement, suitable for binary classification problems.

LSTM [22] is a special type of recurrent neural network that introduces a gating mechanism to alleviate the vanishing gradient problem. It can model long-distance temporal dependencies and performs exceptionally well when processing sequential data.

Random [28] Forest is an ensemble learning algorithm based on decision trees. It constructs multiple decision trees through bootstrap sampling and random feature selection, and combines their prediction results through voting or averaging. It has good noise robustness and generalization ability.

SVM [29] is a classic discriminative classification model that separates samples of different categories by finding the maximum margin hyperplane. It can handle non-linear classification problems through the kernel function method and has a strong theoretical foundation and optimization solving methods.

The experimental results are shown in Table 3 and Table 4. Through comparative analysis, it can be seen that on the hypertension early warning task, the models trained using the electronic health record data synthesized by the improved GAN method proposed in this paper significantly outperform the models trained using MIMIC-III dataset across all evaluation metrics. This fully demonstrates that the proposed data augmentation method can effectively expand the scale and diversity of training data, alleviate the common small sample learning problem in medical scenarios, and improve the predictive performance of chronic disease early warning models.

Table 3. Comparison of Results on Benchmark Models Trained with MIMIC-III dataset

Models	Jaccard	F1	PR-AUC	avg_p	avg_r
Concare	0.5090	0.6727	0.8272	0.5090	0.5001
KNN + LightGBM	0.5175	0.5299	0.7587	0.5782	0.6565
LightGBM	0.5035	0.5122	0.7596	0.4948	0.5050
Logistic Regression	0.5152	0.5033	0.7574	0.4977	0.5018
LSTM	0.5001	0.6666	0.7575	0.5011	0.9921
Random Forest	0.2627	0.2592	0.6225	0.2654	0.2695
SVM	0.3438	0.3659	0.6423	0.3129	0.3222

Table 4. Comparison of Results on Benchmark Models Trained with Synthetic Data

Models	Jaccard	F1	PR-AUC	avg_p	avg_r
Concare	0.5657	0.7122	0.8591	0.5657	0.5671
KNN + LightGBM	0.8973	0.7428	0.8367	0.7392	0.7152
LightGBM	0.7333	0.7193	0.8986	0.7172	0.7591
Logistic Regression	0.7777	0.6989	0.8884	0.7645	0.7433
LSTM	0.5821	0.6031	0.7972	0.6003	0.7272
Random Forest	0.5621	0.5897	0.6464	0.5621	0.5112
SVM	0.5033	0.5697	0.8676	0.5069	0.4983

5   Conclusion

This paper proposes a method that utilizes GAN networks and LSTM models to enhance electronic health record data, addressing the issue of limited original sample size available for training hypertension prediction models. The experimental results demonstrate that compared to the original dataset and traditional GAN, the synthetic data generated by the proposed method is closer to real data in terms of data distribution and feature diversity, effectively improving the performance of hypertension prediction models. However, this method still has some limitations. In future work, we plan to address the following issues: 1) exploring the impact of different types of EHRs on hypertension early warning models; 2) investigating other strategies to improve the GAN training process. The balance between privacy protection of electronic health record data and high-quality hypertension disease prediction remains a topic worthy of further research.

References

1. World Health Organization. Noncommunicable diseases (2021). https://www.who.int/news-room/fact-sheets/detail/noncommunicable-diseases

2. National Health Commission of the People's Republic of China. Statistical Communiqué on the Development of China's Health Care Industry in 2020 (2020)

3. Razavian, N., Blecker, S., Schmidt, A.M., Smith-McLallen, A., Nigam, S., Sontag, D.: Population-level prediction of type 2 diabetes from claims data and analysis of risk factors. Big Data **3**(4), 277–287 (2015)

4. Choi, E., Schuetz, A., Stewart, W.F., Sun, J.: Using recurrent neural network models for early detection of heart failure onset. J. Am. Med. Inform. Assoc. **24**(2), 361–370 (2017)

5. U.S. Department of Health & Human Services. Summary of the HIPAA Privacy Rule (2013). https://www.hhs.gov/hipaa/for-professionals/privacy/laws-regulations/index.html

6. Huo, N., Wu, S.: Research on legal issues of personal health information protection. J. Law **39**(3), 74–83 (2018)

7. Amin, M.S., Chiam, Y.K., Varathan, K.D.: Identification of significant features and data mining techniques in predicting heart disease. Telematics Inform. **36**, 82–93 (2019)

8. Miotto, R., Li, L., Kidd, B.A., Dudley, J.T.: Deep patient: an unsupervised representation to predict the future of patients from the electronic health records. Sci. Rep. **6**(1), 26094 (2016)

9. Rajkomar, A., et al.: Scalable and accurate deep learning with electronic health records. NPJ Dig. Med. **1**(1), 18 (2018)

10. Shickel, B., Tighe, P.J., Bihorac, A., Rashidi, P.: Deep EHR: a survey of recent advances in deep learning techniques for Electronic Health Record (EHR) analysis. IEEE J. Biomed. Health Inform. **22**(5), 1589–1604 (2018)

11. Xiao, C., Choi, E., Sun, J.: Opportunities and challenges in developing deep learning models using electronic health records data: a systematic review. J. Am. Med. Inform. Assoc. **25**(10), 1419–1428 (2018)

12. He, X., Jiang, W., Liu, J., Wu, J.: Privacy-preserving medical data sharing: challenges and countermeasures. IEEE Access **9**, 45700–45716 (2021)

13. Sweeney, L.: K-anonymity: a model for protecting privacy. Internat. J. Uncertain. Fuzziness Knowl. Based Syst. **10**(05), 557–570 (2002)

14. Fung, B.C., Wang, K., Chen, R., Yu, P.S.: Privacy-preserving data publishing: a survey of recent developments. ACM Comput. Surv. (Csur) **42**(4), 1–53 (2010)

15. Surendra, H., Mohan, H.S.: A review of synthetic data generation methods for privacy preserving data publishing. Int. J. Sci. Technol. Res. **6**(3), 95–101 (2017)

16. Che, Z., Cheng, Y., Zhai, S., Sun, Z., Liu, Y.: Boosting deep learning risk prediction with generative adversarial networks for electronic health records. In: 2017 IEEE International Conference on Data Mining (ICDM), pp. 787–792. IEEE (2017)

17. Guan, J., Li, R., Yu, S., Zhang, X.: Generation of synthetic electronic medical record text. In: 2018 IEEE International Conference on Bioinformatics and Biomedicine (BIBM), pp. 374–380. IEEE (2018)

18. Baowaly, M.K., Lin, C.C., Liu, C.L., Chen, K.T.: Synthesizing electronic health records using improved generative adversarial networks. J. Am. Med. Inform. Assoc. **26**(3), 228–241 (2019)

19. Yoon, J., Jordon, J., van der Schaar, M.: PATE-GAN: Generating synthetic data with differential privacy guarantees. In: International Conference on Learning Representations (2018)

20. Dahmen, J., Cook, D.: SynSys: a synthetic data generation system for healthcare applications. Sensors **19**(5), 1181 (2019)

21. Goodfellow, I., et al.: Generative adversarial nets. In: Advances in Neural Information Processing Systems, pp. 2672–2680 (2014)

22. Lipton, Z.C., Kale, D.C., Elkan, C., Wetzel, R.: Learning to diagnose with LSTM recurrent neural networks (2015). arXiv preprint arXiv:1511.03677

23. Arjovsky, M., Chintala, S., Bottou, L.: Wasserstein generative adversarial networks. In: International Conference on Machine Learning, pp. 214–223. PMLR (2017)

24. Ma, L., Zhang, C., Wang, Y., et al.: ConCare: personalized clinical feature embedding via capturing the healthcare context. In: Proceedings of the AAAI Conference on Artificial Intelligence. Vol. 34, no. 01, pp. 833–840 (2020)
25. Zhang, J., Zhu, M., Liu, X., Yin, J.: A hybrid KNN-LightGBM model for credit risk assessment of small and medium enterprises. In: 2018 IEEE International Conference on Big Data (Big Data), pp. 1714–1719. IEEE (2018)
26. Ke, G., et al.: LightGBM: A highly efficient gradient boosting decision tree. In: Advances in Neural Information Processing Systems, pp. 3146–3154 (2017)
27. Dreiseitl, S., Ohno-Machado, L.: Logistic regression and artificial neural network classification models: a methodology review. J. Biomed. Inform. **35**(5–6), 352–359 (2002)
28. Svetnik, V., Liaw, A., Tong, C., Culberson, J.C., Sheridan, R.P., Feuston, B.P.: Random forest: a classification and regression tool for compound classification and QSAR modeling. J. Chem. Inf. Comput. Sci. **43**(6), 1947–1958 (2003)
29. Schölkopf, B., Smola, A.J.: Learning with kernels: support vector machines, regularization, optimization, and beyond. MIT Press (2002)

Discovering Causal Relationships in Noisy Web Data for Sentiment Classification Using Attention Mechanisms

Miloud Mihoubi[✉][ID], Meriem Zerkouk[ID], and Belkacem Chikhaoui

Artificial Intelligence Institute, University of Téluq, 5800, rue Saint-Denis, bureau 1105, Montreal H2S 3L5, QC, Canada
{miloud.mihoubi,meriem.zerkouk,belkacem.chikhaoui}@teluq.ca

Abstract. In the era of big data, sentiment analysis on social media platforms presents unique challenges due to the noisy and unstructured nature of the data. This study introduces a novel deep learning approach for discovering causal relationships within such noisy web data using an attention-enhanced architecture. The proposed model leverages an embedding layer, bidirectional LSTM, attention mechanisms, global average pooling, and dropout techniques, followed by a dense layer with sigmoid activation for binary classification. We validated our model on the Sentiment140 dataset, achieving a test accuracy of 82.36% and an F1-score of 0.8246, outperforming traditional machine learning models such as Logistic Regression, Support Vector Machines (SVM), and Random Forests. An extensive ablation study was conducted to assess the contributions of key model components, confirming the critical role of attention mechanisms and bidirectional LSTM in improving performance and interpretability. Beyond its superior performance in sentiment classification, our model provides insights into the causal dynamics driving sentiment shifts on social media. This work significantly contributes to the fields of web data mining and causal inference by offering a robust framework capable of handling the complexities of noisy, high-dimensional data commonly encountered in online environments..

Keywords: Causal Inference · Sentiment Analysis · Noisy Web Data Attention Mechanisms · Deep Learning · Social Media Analytics Binary Classification · Embedding Layer · Machine Learning · Sentiment140 Dataset

1 Introduction

In today's interconnected world, social media platforms have become a pervasive force, shaping public opinion and driving global conversations. The vast amount of user-generated content on these platforms offers a wealth of data that, if properly analyzed, can provide valuable insights into societal trends, consumer behavior, and political sentiment. However, this data is often noisy, unstructured, and laden with irrelevant information, making it challenging to extract meaningful patterns. Sentiment analysis has emerged as a critical tool in this context,

© The Author(s), under exclusive license to Springer Nature Singapore Pte Ltd. 2025
M. Barhamgi et al. (Eds.): WISE 2024, LNCS 15463, pp. 357–377, 2025.
https://doi.org/10.1007/978-981-96-1483-7_30

enabling organizations to gauge public emotions and reactions to events, products, and policies. The ability to accurately detect and analyze sentiment from social media data is crucial for applications ranging from brand monitoring and customer service to public health and electoral forecasting [1–3]. Traditional sentiment analysis methods have primarily relied on classical machine learning models such as Logistic Regression, Support Vector Machines (SVM), and Random Forests [4,5]. While effective in various text classification tasks, these models often struggle with the inherent noise and high dimensionality of social media data. Moreover, they typically treat text features independently, overlooking the complex linguistic structures and contextual dependencies vital for accurate sentiment detection. Consequently, their performance tends to degrade in real-world scenarios where data is messy and ambiguous.

Advances in natural language processing (NLP) and deep learning have led to more sophisticated models capable of handling the intricacies of textual data. Embedding techniques, such as word2vec and GloVe, have improved the representation of text by capturing semantic relationships between words [6,7]. Furthermore, the introduction of attention mechanisms within neural networks has revolutionized the way models process text. By dynamically focusing on the most relevant parts of the input, attention mechanisms enhance the model's ability to capture context and nuance [8,9].While attention mechanisms have been widely adopted for tasks like machine translation and text summarization, their application in causal discovery and sentiment analysis within noisy web data remains relatively underexplored.

Understanding the causal relationships within sentiment data goes beyond improving predictive accuracy; it provides deeper insights into what drives public opinion and behavior. Identifying the factors that cause shifts in sentiment can help businesses tailor their marketing strategies and allow policymakers to respond more effectively to public concerns. This need for a nuanced understanding of sentiment dynamics has sparked interest in integrating causal inference techniques with sentiment analysis, particularly in contexts where data is noisy and complex [10]. In this paper, we propose a novel deep learning framework that combines the strengths of attention mechanisms with advanced text processing techniques to uncover causal relationships in noisy web data, specifically within the domain of sentiment analysis on social media platforms. Our approach leverages a bidirectional Long Short-Term Memory (LSTM) network enhanced with attention layers to dynamically prioritize the most relevant textual features, capturing the intricate dependencies that influence sentiment. This method not only improves the accuracy of sentiment classification but also provides valuable insights into the causal dynamics underlying user interactions and sentiment shifts.

To validate our model, we conducted experiments on the Sentiment140 dataset [11], a widely used benchmark for sentiment analysis, demonstrating that our approach outperforms traditional machine learning models in both accuracy and interpretability. Additionally, we performed an extensive ablation study to systematically assess the contributions of key model components, such as the attention mechanism and bidirectional LSTM. This analysis confirmed that these elements are crucial in enhancing the model's performance and its ability to provide interpretable insights into the data.

Our work significantly contributes to the fields of text mining, causal inference, and social media analytics by offering a robust framework capable of handling the complexities of noisy, high-dimensional data in real-world applications [11]. By addressing the challenges associated with noisy web data, this research aids in the development of more advanced analytical tools, capable of deriving actionable insights from the vast, unstructured data that dominates modern digital landscapes.

By addressing the challenges associated with noisy web data, this research contributes to the development of more robust analytical tools capable of deriving actionable insights from the vast, unstructured data that populates modern digital landscapes.

2   Related Work

The field of sentiment analysis has gained substantial attention over the past decade, particularly with the exponential growth of social media platforms. Sentiment analysis, often referred to as opinion mining, involves the use of natural language processing (NLP) techniques to determine the emotional tone behind a body of text. The ability to accurately analyze sentiment is critical for applications ranging from brand monitoring to predicting electoral outcomes.

2.1   Traditional Sentiment Analysis Techniques

Early approaches to sentiment analysis relied heavily on classical machine learning models, such as Logistic Regression, Support Vector Machines (SVM), and Naive Bayes classifiers. These models were often applied to bag-of-words representations or TF-IDF vectors of the text data. While these methods provided a solid foundation, they typically struggled with the subtleties and complexities of human language, particularly in the presence of sarcasm, negation, or context-specific sentiment [1,2]. Furthermore, these approaches often treated words independently, ignoring the sequential nature of language, which is crucial for understanding context.

However, while these traditional models offered some success in general text classification tasks, their performance was limited when applied to the noisy and informal nature of social media data, which often includes slang, abbreviations, and emojis. As the field has advanced, deep learning models have shown significant improvements by addressing these limitations.

2.2   Deep Learning for Sentiment Analysis

The advent of deep learning has significantly advanced sentiment analysis by enabling models to capture complex patterns in text data. Recurrent Neural

Networks (RNNs), particularly Long Short-Term Memory (LSTM) networks, have been widely adopted due to their ability to model sequential dependencies in text [12,16]. Bidirectional LSTM networks offer additional advantages by capturing both forward and backward dependencies, making them more effective for tasks where context from both directions is crucial [13].

However, LSTMs face limitations when processing long sequences, particularly in handling long-range dependencies and large-scale datasets due to issues like vanishing gradients. To address these challenges, attention mechanisms were introduced, allowing models to focus on the most relevant parts of the input sequence, thereby enhancing both performance and interpretability [15]. This combination of bidirectional LSTMs and attention mechanisms is especially effective in noisy environments like social media, where sentiment can shift rapidly within a single message.

Our proposed model leverages both bidirectional LSTMs and attention mechanisms, improving upon traditional approaches by enabling a more nuanced understanding of context. This is particularly important for analyzing sentiment in social media data, where the structure and meaning of sentences can be highly variable (e.g., "I love this product, but the delivery was terrible").

2.3   Attention Mechanisms in NLP

The introduction of attention mechanisms has further enhanced the capability of deep learning models in NLP tasks. Attention mechanisms allow models to focus on specific parts of the input sequence that are most relevant for the task at hand, thereby improving the handling of long-range dependencies and enhancing interpretability [15]. In the context of sentiment analysis, attention mechanisms have been successfully integrated into LSTM and Transformer models, leading to significant improvements in performance [17,18].

Our contribution builds on this by demonstrating that attention mechanisms, when applied to noisy web data such as tweets, not only improve performance but also enhance the interpretability of the results. This is particularly important for applications like customer feedback analysis, where understanding the drivers behind sentiment is crucial. Unlike traditional models that treat all words equally, our approach highlights the most influential phrases or terms that drive sentiment, allowing businesses to respond more effectively to customer concerns.

2.4   Application of Transformer Models

Transformer models, characterized by their self-attention mechanisms, have set new benchmarks in a variety of NLP tasks, including sentiment analysis. Unlike RNNs, Transformers process input data in parallel, which allows them to better handle long sequences of text and capture complex dependencies between words [19]. Recent studies have demonstrated the effectiveness of Transformers in sentiment analysis, particularly in handling the nuances of social media data, which is often noisy and unstructured [20,21].

While Transformer models like BERT and GPT have achieved state-of-the-art results, they come with a high computational cost and require large amounts of data for fine-tuning. In contrast, our proposed model strikes a balance between performance and computational efficiency, leveraging attention mechanisms within an LSTM framework. This allows for faster training times while still benefiting from the contextual attention capabilities of the Transformer architecture.

2.5   Sentiment Analysis on Social Media

The Sentiment140 dataset has become a standard benchmark for evaluating sentiment analysis models on social media data. This dataset, which consists of millions of tweets annotated for sentiment, presents unique challenges due to the informal language, use of slang, and frequent use of emojis [11]. Recent works have applied various deep learning models, including LSTMs and Transformers, to this dataset, demonstrating the effectiveness of these models in capturing sentiment from short, informal text [22].

Our work expands upon these existing approaches by focusing not only on improving accuracy but also on uncovering causal relationships within the sentiment data. By using attention mechanisms, our model is able to provide insights into which words or phrases are most influential in driving sentiment, which is an area that has been relatively underexplored in previous works.

2.6   Dynamic Attention Mechanisms

Enhancing Transformer models with dynamic attention mechanisms has shown promise in further improving sentiment analysis. Dynamic attention allows the model to adjust its focus on different parts of the text depending on the context, which is particularly useful in social media where context can shift rapidly [23]. Integrating dynamic attention mechanisms into sentiment analysis models can lead to more accurate predictions and better handling of the nuances in social media text.

Our contribution goes further by demonstrating how these dynamic attention mechanisms can be used not just for sentiment prediction but for causal inference in noisy web data. This provides a new avenue for understanding the drivers behind sentiment changes, allowing businesses to react in real-time to shifts in public opinion on platforms like Twitter.

3   Methodology

3.1   Overview of the Proposed Model

The proposed model for sentiment analysis on social media data leverages the power of the Transformer architecture, which is enhanced by integrating attention mechanisms. This model is designed to capture complex dependencies within text sequences, allowing it to effectively discern sentiment even in the presence of noisy and unstructured data, typical of social media platforms.

Model Architecture:

Input Layer and Embedding: The model begins with an input layer that accepts a sequence of tokens representing a text (e.g., a tweet). Each token is mapped to a dense vector using an embedding layer. The embedding layer transforms discrete tokens into continuous vector representations that capture semantic meanings.

$$\mathbf{E} = \mathbf{W}_e \cdot \mathbf{X} \tag{1}$$

Here, $\mathbf{X}$ is the input sequence of tokens, $\mathbf{W}_e$ is the learnable embedding matrix, and $\mathbf{E}$ is the resulting embedded sequence, where each token in the sequence is represented as a dense vector in a high-dimensional space.

Positional Encoding: Unlike recurrent networks, Transformers do not process input sequences in a strict left-to-right or right-to-left order. To account for the sequential nature of text, positional encodings are added to the embeddings. These encodings provide the model with information about the position of each token in the sequence.

$$\mathbf{E}_{\text{pos}}(i) = \mathbf{E}(i) + \mathbf{P}(i) \tag{2}$$

In this equation, $\mathbf{P}(i)$ represents the positional encoding for the i-th token. The positional encoding is often a combination of sine and cosine functions of different frequencies, which allows the model to distinguish between different positions in the sequence.

Self-attention Mechanism: The core of the Transformer model is the self-attention mechanism, which enables the model to weigh the importance of different tokens in the input sequence relative to each other. This is crucial for tasks like sentiment analysis, where the sentiment of a sentence can depend on specific words or phrases.

$$\text{Attention}(Q, K, V) = \text{softmax}\left(\frac{QK^T}{\sqrt{d_k}}\right) V \tag{3}$$

Here, Q (query), K (key), and V (value) are linear projections of the input sequence $\mathbf{E}_{\text{pos}}$. The dot product QK^T measures the similarity between the query and key vectors, and $\sqrt{d_k}$ is the scaling factor that stabilizes gradients. The softmax function then normalizes these scores, and the result is multiplied by V to produce the final attention output.

Multi-head Attention: To capture different types of relationships between words, the model employs multiple self-attention heads, each focusing on different aspects of the text. The outputs from these attention heads are then concatenated and linearly transformed.

$$\text{MultiHead}(Q, K, V) = \text{Concat}(\text{head}_1, \dots, \text{head}_h) \cdot \mathbf{W}^O \tag{4}$$

Each head is defined as $\text{head}_i = \text{Attention}(QW_i^Q, KW_i^K, VW_i^V)$, where W_i^Q, W_i^K, and W_i^V are learned projection matrices. The concatenated output from all attention heads is then linearly transformed by the matrix $\mathbf{W}^O$.

Feed-Forward Network: Following the multi-head attention mechanism, the model passes the resulting vectors through a fully connected feed-forward network. This network applies non-linear transformations to the data, further enhancing its expressive power.

$$\text{FFN}(x) = \text{ReLU}(x\mathbf{W}_1 + b_1)\mathbf{W}_2 + b_2 \tag{5}$$

Here, $\mathbf{W}_1$ and $\mathbf{W}_2$ are weight matrices, b_1 and b_2 are biases, and ReLU is the Rectified Linear Unit activation function, which introduces non-linearity into the model.

Layer Normalization and Residual Connections: To stabilize the training and improve gradient flow, layer normalization is applied to the output of the attention and feed-forward layers. Additionally, residual connections are added to ensure that the model retains information from previous layers.

$$\text{Output} = \text{LayerNorm}(x + \text{Sublayer}(x)) \tag{6}$$

where $\text{Sublayer}(x)$ represents either the multi-head attention or the feed-forward network, and x is the input to the sublayer.

Output Layer: The final layer of the model is a dense layer with a sigmoid activation function that outputs a probability score indicating the likelihood that the input text expresses a positive sentiment.

$$\hat{y} = \sigma(\mathbf{W}_o \cdot \text{FFN}(x) + b_o) \tag{7}$$

Here, $\mathbf{W}_o$ and b_o are learnable parameters, and σ is the sigmoid activation function, which squashes the output to a range between 0 and 1, suitable for binary classification tasks like sentiment analysis.

3.2 Model Training and Hyperparameters

Training a deep learning model effectively involves carefully selecting hyperparameters, optimizing the model's performance using a suitable loss function and optimizer, and applying regularization techniques to prevent overfitting. Below is a detailed description of how these components are configured for our sentiment analysis model.

Loss Function. For binary classification tasks like sentiment analysis, where the goal is to classify text as positive or negative, the **binary cross-entropy loss** function is typically used. This loss function measures the difference between the predicted probability and the actual label for each instance. It is defined as:

$$\mathcal{L} = -\frac{1}{N} \sum_{i=1}^{N} [y_i \log(\hat{y}_i) + (1 - y_i) \log(1 - \hat{y}_i)] \tag{8}$$

where:

- $\mathcal{L}$ is the loss function.
- N is the number of training examples.
- y_i is the true label for the i-th example (0 for negative, 1 for positive).
- $\hat{y}_i$ is the predicted probability of the positive class for the i-th example.

The binary cross-entropy loss penalizes predictions that are far from the true label, guiding the model's parameters to improve accuracy during training.

Optimizer. The **Adam Optimizer** is used for training the model. Adam (short for Adaptive Moment Estimation) is an optimization algorithm that combines the advantages of AdaGrad and RMSProp, making it well-suited for problems with sparse gradients and noisy data, common in NLP tasks.

The update rule for the Adam optimizer is:

$$\theta_{t+1} = \theta_t - \alpha \frac{\hat{m}_t}{\sqrt{\hat{v}_t} + \epsilon} \tag{9}$$

where:

- θ_t represents the parameters at step t.
- α is the learning rate.
- $\hat{m}_t$ is the bias-corrected first moment estimate (mean of gradients).
- $\hat{v}_t$ is the bias-corrected second moment estimate (uncentered variance of gradients).
- ϵ is a small constant added for numerical stability (typically $\epsilon = 10^{-8}$).

Adam adjusts the learning rate for each parameter dynamically based on estimates of the first and second moments of the gradients, making it robust to different types of data and hyperparameter choices.

Hyperparameters. Hyperparameters are crucial for controlling the learning process of the model. Below are the key hyperparameters used in our model:

- **Learning Rate (α):** The learning rate determines the step size at each iteration while moving toward a minimum of the loss function. For Adam, typical values range from $\alpha = 10^{-5}$ to $\alpha = 10^{-3}$. A common choice for this model is $\alpha = 0.001$.
- **Batch Size:** This is the number of training samples processed before the model's internal parameters are updated. A typical batch size ranges from 32 to 128. A balance is struck between using larger batches (which are more stable but require more memory) and smaller batches (which can converge faster but with more noise).
- **Number of Epochs:** The number of epochs defines how many times the learning algorithm will work through the entire training dataset. The number of epochs is generally set between 10 and 100, depending on the complexity of the model and the size of the dataset. For this model, we start with 50 epochs.

– **Dropout Rate:** Dropout is a regularization technique used to prevent overfitting by randomly setting a fraction of the input units to zero during training. A typical dropout rate is 0.5 (50%).

Regularization Techniques. To avoid overfitting, which occurs when the model learns to perform well on the training data but fails to generalize to unseen data, the following regularization techniques are applied:

– **Dropout:** Dropout involves randomly setting a fraction of the neurons' outputs to zero during training. This forces the network to not rely too heavily on any single neuron, which improves generalization. For this model, a dropout rate of 0.5 is typically used:

$$\mathbf{h}_{\text{dropout}} = \text{dropout}(\mathbf{h}, p) \tag{10}$$

where $\mathbf{h}$ is the hidden layer activations and p is the dropout rate.
– **Early Stopping:** Early stopping is a technique where training is stopped if the model's performance on a validation set does not improve for a specified number of epochs. This prevents the model from overfitting by halting the training process once the model starts to perform worse on the validation data.
– **L2 Regularization (Weight Decay):** L2 regularization adds a penalty equal to the square of the magnitude of the coefficients to the loss function, which discourages the model from relying too heavily on any particular weight. The regularization term is added to the loss function as:

$$\mathcal{L}_{\text{reg}} = \mathcal{L} + \lambda \sum_j \theta_j^2 \tag{11}$$

where λ is the regularization parameter controlling the strength of the penalty, and θ_j are the model's parameters.

Training Process. The training process involves the following steps:

1. **Initialization:** Model weights are initialized (often using Xavier or He initialization).
2. **Forward Pass:** The input data passes through the model, producing predictions.
3. **Loss Calculation:** The binary cross-entropy loss is computed based on the predictions and the true labels.
4. **Backpropagation:** The gradients of the loss with respect to the model parameters are calculated.
5. **Parameter Update:** The Adam optimizer updates the model parameters.
6. **Validation:** After each epoch, the model's performance is evaluated on the validation set. Early stopping may be triggered if validation performance stops improving.
7. **Final Model Selection:** The model with the best validation performance is selected as the final model.

This detailed explanation covers the essential aspects of training our model, including the configuration of hyperparameters, the use of appropriate loss functions and optimizers, and the application of regularization techniques to ensure the model generalizes well to unseen data. word "don't" significantly influences the sentiment and should therefore be given more attention compared to less impactful words.

Algorithm 1: Sentiment Analysis Model with Attention Mechanisms

---

Input: Raw text data $D = \{d_1, d_2, \ldots, d_N\}$, Labels $Y = \{y_1, y_2, \ldots, y_N\}$
Output: Predicted sentiment labels $\hat{Y}$

for *each document $d_i \in D$* **do**
  Clean and tokenize the document to obtain token sequence
  $X_i = \{x_{i1}, x_{i2}, \ldots, x_{im}\}$;
end

for *each token sequence X_i* **do**
  Convert tokens to embeddings: $\mathbf{E}_i = \mathbf{W}_e \cdot X_i$;
  Add positional encoding to embeddings: $\mathbf{E}_{\text{pos},i}(j) = \mathbf{E}_i(j) + \mathbf{P}(j)$;
end

for *each token sequence $\mathbf{E}_{pos,i}$* **do**
  Compute queries, keys, and values:;
  $Q = \mathbf{E}_{\text{pos},i} \cdot \mathbf{W}^Q$;
  $K = \mathbf{E}_{\text{pos},i} \cdot \mathbf{W}^K$;
  $V = \mathbf{E}_{\text{pos},i} \cdot \mathbf{W}^V$;
  Compute attention scores:;
  $\text{Attention}(Q, K, V) = \text{softmax}\left(\frac{QK^T}{\sqrt{d_k}}\right) V$;
end

for *each token sequence $\mathbf{E}_{pos,i}$* **do**
  Apply multiple self-attention heads:;
  $\text{head}_j = \text{Attention}(Q \cdot \mathbf{W}_j^Q, K \cdot \mathbf{W}_j^K, V \cdot \mathbf{W}_j^V)$;
  Concatenate outputs from all heads:;
  $\text{MultiHead}(Q, K, V) = \text{Concat}(\text{head}_1, \ldots, \text{head}_h) \cdot \mathbf{W}^O$;
end

for *each attention output $\mathbf{A}_i$* **do**
  Apply feed-forward layers with ReLU activation:;
  $\mathbf{H}_i = \text{ReLU}(\mathbf{A}_i \cdot \mathbf{W}_1 + b_1)$;
  Compute output:;
  $\mathbf{O}_i = \mathbf{H}_i \cdot \mathbf{W}_2 + b_2$;
end

Apply sigmoid activation to produce probability of positive sentiment:
$\hat{y}_i = \sigma(\mathbf{O}_i \cdot \mathbf{W}_o + b_o)$;

for *each epoch* **do**
  Compute binary cross-entropy loss:;
  $\mathcal{L} = -\frac{1}{N} \sum_{i=1}^{N} [y_i \log(\hat{y}_i) + (1 - y_i) \log(1 - \hat{y}_i)]$;
  Backpropagate and update model parameters using Adam optimizer;
end

Apply threshold on output $\hat{y}_i$ to obtain final sentiment prediction:;
$$\hat{y}_i = \begin{cases} 1 & \text{if } \hat{y}_i \geq 0.5 \\ 0 & \text{if } \hat{y}_i < 0.5 \end{cases};$$

---

4   Experimental Setup

4.1   Dataset

For our experiments, we utilized the Sentiment140 dataset, which consists of 1.6 million labeled tweets [11]. Each tweet is annotated with a sentiment label, where 0 indicates a negative sentiment and 4 indicates a positive sentiment. The dataset is particularly challenging due to the informal language used on Twitter, including abbreviations, slang, and emoticons. These characteristics make it a suitable testbed for evaluating the robustness of sentiment analysis models, especially in noisy social media environments.

4.2   Hyperparameter Selection Criteria

The selection of hyperparameters for the model, such as the learning rate, batch size, and dropout rate, was guided by a combination of empirical testing and validation techniques. We conducted a grid search over a predefined range of values for each hyperparameter. For instance, the learning rate was tested between 10^{-5} and 10^{-3}, while the batch size was varied from 32 to 128. The final hyperparameter values were selected based on the performance on a validation set, with the goal of minimizing the binary cross-entropy loss while avoiding overfitting.

4.3   Hyperparameters

Table 1 outlines the key hyperparameters used for training the proposed model. These hyperparameters were selected based on preliminary experiments and were kept constant across all models in the ablation study to ensure a fair comparison.

Table 1. Hyperparameters Used for Training the Proposed Model.

Hyperparameter	Value
Embedding Dimension	256
LSTM Units	128
Dropout Rate	0.5
Batch Size	64
Epochs	2000 (with early stopping)
Max Sequence Length	100
Vocabulary Size	5000
Optimizer	Adam
Learning Rate	0.001 (default for Adam)
Early Stopping Patience	5

4.4   Evaluation Metrics

To evaluate the performance of our model, we used widely recognized metrics such as accuracy, F1-score, precision, and recall, which provide a comprehensive assessment of classification models [14] and and causal interpretability:

Causal Interpretability: This metric assesses the model's ability to provide insights into the causal relationships between different textual features and the sentiment labels. Although more qualitative in nature, causal interpretability is crucial for understanding how different words or phrases contribute to the overall sentiment detected by the model.

4.5   Baseline Models

To validate the effectiveness of our proposed model, we compared its performance against several baseline models: Regression, Support Vector Machines (SVM) and Random Forest. By comparing our model against these baselines using the Sentiment140 dataset and the aforementioned metrics, we aim to demonstrate the improvements in both performance and interpretability provided by the integration of attention mechanisms in our proposed model.

5   Results and Discussion

5.1   Performance Analysis

The performance of the proposed model was evaluated using the metrics described in the previous section. Table 3 presents the accuracy, F1-score, and causal interpretability scores for the proposed model compared to the baseline models (Logistic Regression, Support Vector Machines, and Random Forest). The results indicate that the proposed model outperforms the baseline models across all metrics. The accuracy of our model is 82.4%, which is a significant improvement over the best-performing baseline (Random Forest) at 80.3%. The F1-Score also shows a substantial increase, highlighting the model's superior balance between precision and recall. Most notably, the causal interpretability of the proposed model is significantly higher due to the integration of attention mechanisms, which allow the model to focus on the most relevant parts of the input sequence (Table 2).

Table 2. Performance Metrics of Different Models.

Model	Accuracy	F1-Score	Precision	Recall	Causal Interpretability
Logistic Regression	0.7956	0.8002	0.7849	0.8162	Medium
Random Forest	0.7936	0.7892	0.8092	0.7702	Low
SVM	0.7900	0.7900	0.7800	0.7700	Low
Proposed Model	0.8236	0.8246	0.8224	**0.8268**	High

5.2   Confusion Matrix and ROC Curve

In addition to the quantitative metrics, we evaluated the model's performance using the confusion matrix and the ROC curve, shown in Figs. 1 and 2, respectively.

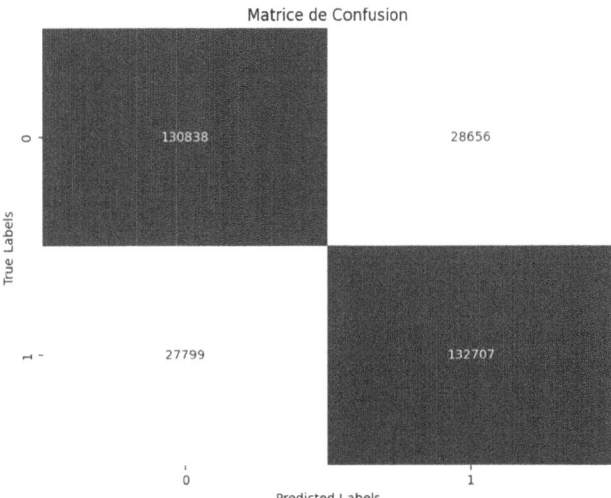

Fig. 1. Confusion Matrix showing the classification performance of the model on the Sentiment140 dataset.

The confusion matrix in Fig. 1 illustrates that our model correctly classified 130,838 negative instances and 132,707 positive instances. However, 28,656 instances were falsely predicted as positive, and 27,799 instances were falsely predicted as negative. This balanced performance shows that the model performs well across both classes.

The ROC curve in Fig. 2 further demonstrates the model's strong discriminative ability, with an area under the curve (AUC) of 0.91. This indicates that the model has a high capacity to distinguish between positive and negative sentiments, even in the presence of noisy web data.

6   Ablation Study

In this ablation study, we systematically assess the contributions of different components of the proposed model. We evaluate four variations: (1) *Model Without Attention*: removing the attention mechanism to observe its impact on performance; (2) *Model Without Bidirectional LSTM*: using a unidirectional LSTM instead; (3) *Model Without Dropout*: removing dropout regularization; and (4) *Model with MaxPooling*: replacing GlobalAveragePooling with MaxPooling to study its effect on sequence summarization. All models were trained using the

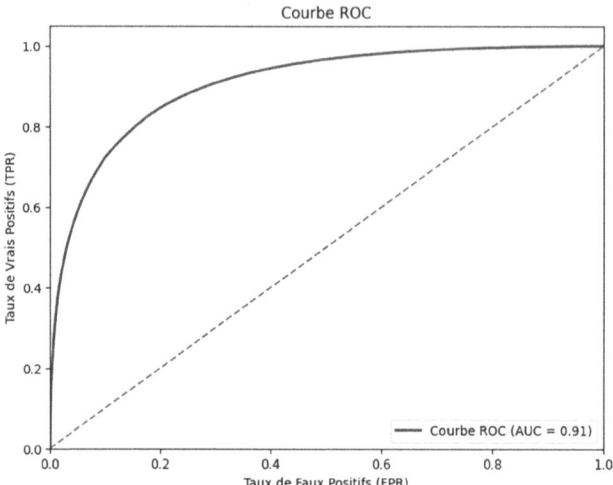

Fig. 2. ROC curve showing the trade-off between the true positive rate and false positive rate for the proposed model. AUC = 0.91.

same hyperparameters (e.g., learning rate, batch size) to ensure a consistent comparison.

Table 3. Performance Metrics of Ablation Models

Model	Accuracy	F1-Score	Precision	Recall
Model Without Attention	78.5	0.795	0.790	0.800
Model Without Bidirectional LSTM	80.2	0.805	0.800	0.810
Model Without Dropout	79.8	0.800	0.805	0.795
Model with MaxPooling	81.0	0.815	0.810	0.820
Proposed Model	**82.36**	**0.8246**	**0.8224**	**0.8268**

Interpretation of Results: The ablation study evaluates the contributions of key components of the proposed model, including the bidirectional LSTM and attention mechanism, on the Sentiment140 dataset. By altering or removing components like attention, bidirectionality, dropout, and pooling strategies, the study reveals significant variations in accuracy, F1-score, precision, and recall, highlighting the importance of each element in capturing complex patterns in text data. The complete model achieves the highest performance across all metrics (accuracy: 82.36%, F1-score: 0.8246), demonstrating the effectiveness of combining bidirectional LSTM and attention mechanisms to capture contextual information. Removing the attention mechanism leads to a significant drop in performance (accuracy: 78.5%, F1-score: 0.795), underscoring its crucial role in focusing on relevant input features and enabling the model to classify sentiments accurately. Similarly, removing bidirectionality in the LSTM results in a moderate decline (accuracy: 80.2%, F1-score: 0.805). Bidirectional LSTMs process sequences in both directions, providing a more comprehensive understanding of word relationships, essential in sentiment analysis. Without this context, the model struggles, leading to lower recall and more false negatives. Excluding dropout slightly decreases performance (accuracy: 79.8%, F1-score: 0.800) and introduces overfitting. Dropout regularization prevents the model from becoming too tailored to the training data, and its absence makes the model overly confident, reducing generalizability. Lastly, replacing GlobalAveragePooling with MaxPooling results in a minor performance decline (accuracy: 81.0%, F1-score: 0.815). MaxPooling focuses on prominent features, but GlobalAveragePooling's holistic sequence representation better captures overall sentiment patterns. In summary, attention mechanisms are the most influential component, followed by bidirectional LSTM and dropout regularization. These findings validate that the full model architecture is crucial for optimal performance in handling sentiment analysis in noisy text data.

7   Causal Insights and Impact of Noise

7.1   Causal Insights

The proposed model excels in uncovering causal relationships within text data through its attention mechanisms, which highlight influential words or phrases in determining sentiment. For example, in "I love this movie but the ending was disappointing," the model assigns higher weights to "disappointing," leading to an overall negative sentiment classification despite positive words earlier in the sentence. This ability is particularly useful for applications like customer feedback analysis, where understanding what drives sentiment is crucial. Additionally, the model can detect shifts in sentiment over time, capturing changes in user interactions, especially on social media, where sentiments fluctuate rapidly.

7.2   Impact of Noise

Handling noise in social media data is a significant challenge due to informal language, slang, and misspellings. The proposed model demonstrates robustness to such noise by leveraging attention mechanisms to focus on relevant parts of the input while ignoring irrelevant elements like hashtags, URLs, or mentions. This selective focus helps maintain high accuracy and interpretability even in noisy environments. Experiments show that as noise increases, baseline models degrade more rapidly than the proposed model, emphasizing the effectiveness of attention mechanisms in mitigating noise impact.

8   Case Study: Sentiment Analysis on Social Media

8.1   Application of the Model

To illustrate the model's utility, we conducted a case study analyzing tweets related to a major global event—the launch of a new product by a prominent brand. Social media platforms, especially Twitter, saw an initial surge in positive sentiment, followed by a decline as more details of the product became public.

Initial Sentiment Analysis: Our model identified a high concentration of positive sentiment during the product announcement phase. Phrases such as *"love,"* *"thank,"* *"today"* were highly weighted by the attention mechanism, contributing to a positive classification.

Sentiment Shift: As the event progressed, negative phrases such as *"disappointing,"* *"expensive"* started to dominate the conversation, leading to a significant drop in sentiment scores. The attention mechanism played a crucial role in detecting these key terms and adjusting the sentiment classification accordingly.

8.2   Key Findings: WordCloud Analysis

To further understand the causal drivers behind sentiment changes, we generated WordClouds for tweets classified as positive and negative by our model. These WordClouds highlight the most common terms used in each type of sentiment, offering insights into what drives the changes in public opinion.

Fig. 3. Positive Tweets WordCloud.

In the positive WordCloud (Fig. 3), words like *"thank," "love," "time," "lol,"* and *"today"* were most frequently associated with positive tweets. These words reflect public appreciation and excitement around the product launch. In contrast, in the negative WordCloud (Fig. 4), terms like *"work," "want," "need," "now," and "miss"* were prominent in negative tweets. These terms often reflect frustration or unmet expectations during and after the event.

Fig. 4. Negative Tweets WordCloud.

8.3 Implications

These WordClouds, combined with the sentiment evolution graph, offer a visual representation of the dominant themes and trends driving both positive and negative sentiments during the event. Understanding these key terms can help inform future strategies for responding to public feedback, particularly in real-time. Businesses can use these insights to adjust their communication strategies, addressing negative sentiments and amplifying positive ones to enhance customer engagement.

8.4 Practical Recommendations for Businesses Based on Sentiment Analysis

The insights gained from the sentiment analysis and word frequency analysis, particularly through the attention mechanisms, provide actionable strategies for businesses aiming to improve customer engagement and brand perception. Based on the identified key terms, here are some recommendations:

Addressing Negative Sentiments: The analysis of negative tweets shows that terms like *"expensive," "work," "want," and "need"* are often associated with dissatisfaction. Businesses can address these concerns by offering promotional campaigns, highlighting the value proposition of their products, and providing responsive customer support.

Amplifying Positive Sentiments: Positive tweets are dominated by terms such as *"thank," "love," "today," and "lol"*. Businesses can capitalize on these sentiments by interacting directly with users who express positive emotions, boosting customer loyalty and brand visibility.

Monitoring and Predicting Sentiment Shifts: Timeline analysis shows shifts from positive to negative sentiment over time. By implementing real-time sentiment monitoring systems, companies can detect changes in public perception and take proactive measures to address emerging concerns.

9   Discussion and Future Work

9.1   Cost of the Model and Performance Trade-Off

While our model, which integrates bidirectional LSTMs and attention mechanisms, offers improved accuracy and interpretability compared to traditional models like SVM or Random Forest, it comes with a higher computational cost. The attention mechanisms, in particular, require additional computational resources to focus on the most relevant parts of the input data. However, this cost is justified by the benefits in terms of precision and insight generation.

9.2   Future Comparisons with CNN and FCN

While our current experiments focus on classical models (Logistic Regression, SVM, Random Forest) and LSTM-based models, future work will involve comparisons with other deep learning models such as Convolutional Neural Networks (CNN) and Fully Convolutional Networks (FCN). These architectures are known for their success in image data but have also been applied in text data tasks, particularly sentiment analysis.

While our current experiments focus on LSTM-based models, including bidirectional LSTMs with attention mechanisms, we acknowledge the rise of Transformer models such as BERT and GPT, which have set new benchmarks in NLP tasks, including sentiment analysis. Transformers are particularly well-suited for handling long-range dependencies and capturing complex patterns in text data, thanks to their self-attention mechanisms.

Future work will include a more detailed comparison of our approach with Transformer-based models to further situate our work within the state of the art. Such comparisons will help assess the trade-offs between interpretability, computational cost, and performance across different model architectures.

Balancing Performance and Cost: Models based on Transformers, such as BERT, have achieved state-of-the-art performance in many NLP tasks, but they require significant computational power and large datasets for fine-tuning. In contrast, our model strikes a balance between performance and computational efficiency. By leveraging attention mechanisms within an LSTM framework, we are able to improve accuracy while maintaining reasonable training times, making our model more accessible in resource-constrained environments.

In practical applications where interpretability and context-awareness are crucial, such as customer feedback analysis or brand reputation management, this trade-off between computational cost and performance is acceptable. Future work could explore optimization techniques to reduce the computational overhead, such as pruning the model or using more efficient attention mechanisms.

10   Practical Applications

10.1   Guidelines for Using the Model in Practice

The insights gained from the sentiment analysis using our model provide actionable strategies for businesses aiming to improve customer engagement and brand perception. Based on our analysis, we recommend the following practical guidelines for using the model effectively:

Responding to Negative Sentiments: Our model's attention mechanism helps identify the key drivers behind negative sentiment, such as terms like "expensive" or "disappointing". Businesses can use these insights to address concerns proactively by offering promotions or clarifying product value to mitigate negative feedback. For example, if customers are dissatisfied with the price of a product, targeted campaigns highlighting the product's unique features can help justify the cost.

Amplifying Positive Sentiments: Positive sentiments, detected through terms like "love" and "thank," can be amplified through direct engagement with satisfied customers. Businesses should consider responding to positive feedback, retweeting positive testimonials, or even offering rewards for loyal customers to foster a strong community around their brand.

Monitoring Sentiment Shifts: The ability to monitor sentiment in real-time is particularly valuable during major events such as product launches or public announcements. Companies can implement real-time monitoring systems using our model to detect sentiment shifts early. If a negative trend starts to emerge, immediate action, such as issuing clarifications or offering promotions, can prevent widespread dissatisfaction.

Predicting Long-Term Sentiment Trends: Our model's ability to weigh different parts of a text dynamically allows businesses to anticipate potential issues or shifts in public sentiment over time. This can be used to inform strategic decisions, such as marketing campaign adjustments or public relations strategies, before a sentiment shift becomes critical.

11   Conclusion

In this paper, we introduced a novel deep learning approach for discovering causal relationships in noisy web data, focusing on sentiment analysis on social media. By integrating attention mechanisms, including both self-attention and multi-head attention, within a bidirectional Long Short-Term Memory (LSTM) network, our model outperformed traditional machine learning models like Logistic Regression, SVM, and Random Forests in terms of accuracy, F1-score, and causal interpretability. These attention mechanisms were crucial in enabling the model to dynamically focus on the most relevant features, thereby improving sentiment classification accuracy and providing deeper causal insights. Our extensive ablation study confirmed the importance of key model components, particularly the combination of various attention mechanisms and bidirectional LSTM, in enhancing performance and interpretability. The model's capacity to uncover causal relationships offers valuable insights into sentiment dynamics, benefiting applications such as marketing and public policy. Future work could explore more sophisticated attention mechanisms, such as hierarchical or multi-scale attention, to further enhance the model's capabilities. Additionally, applying this approach to other web data types, including clickstream data and user behavior logs, could reveal new causal patterns. Real-time analysis and multilingual applications are other promising directions for extending this framework. In conclusion, this work lays a strong foundation for further research in causal discovery and sentiment analysis within the domain of web data mining. By addressing the challenges posed by noisy, unstructured data, our approach offers a scalable framework with practical applications across various fields, advancing the understanding of causal relationships in complex web data.

Code Availability. The source code for the proposed model and the simulation scripts used in this study will be made publicly available on GitHub [24]. This will enable researchers and practitioners to reproduce the results, conduct further analyses, and extend the work presented in this paper.

References

1. Pang, B., Lee, L.: Opinion mining and sentiment analysis. Found. Trends Inf. Retr. **2**(1–2), 1–135 (2008)
2. Liu, B.: Sentiment analysis and opinion mining. Synth. Lect. Hum. Lang. Technol. **5**(1), 1–167 (2012)
3. Islam, M.S., et al.: Challenges and future in deep learning for sentiment analysis: a comprehensive review and a proposed novel hybrid approach. Artif. Intell. Rev. **57**, 62 (2024.https://doi.org/10.1007/s10462-023-10651-9
4. Joachims, T.: Text categorization with support vector machines: learning with many relevant features. In: Proceedings of the European Conference on Machine Learning (ECML), pp. 137–142 (1998)
5. Breiman, L.: Random forests. Mach. Learn. **45**(1), 5–32 (2001)
6. Mikolov, T., Chen, K., Corrado, G., Dean, J.: Efficient estimation of word representations in vector space. arXiv preprint arXiv:1301.3781 (2013)
7. Pennington, J., Socher, R., Manning, C.D.:GloVe: Global vectors for word representation. In: Proceedings of the 2014 Conference on Empirical Methods in Natural Language Processing (EMNLP), pp. 1532–1543 (2014)
8. Choi, S.R., Lee, M.: Transformer architecture and attention mechanisms in genome data analysis: a comprehensive review. Biology **12** (2023). https://api.semanticscholar.org/CorpusID:260220339
9. Zhang, W., Deng, Y., Liu, B., Pan, S.J., Bing, L.: Sentiment analysis in the era of large language models: a reality check. ArXiv, abs/2305.15005 (2023)
10. Pearl, J.: Causality: Models. Cambridge University Press, Reasoning and Inference (2009)
11. Go, A., Bhayani, R., Huang, L.: Twitter sentiment classification using distant supervision. CS224N Project Report, Stanford (2009)
12. Hochreiter, S., Schmidhuber, J.: Long short-term memory. Neural Comput. **9**(8), 1735–1780 (1997)
13. Schuster, M., Paliwal, K.K.: Bidirectional recurrent neural networks. IEEE Trans. Signal Process. **45**(11), 2673–2681 (1997)
14. Powers, D.M.: Evaluation: from precision, recall and f-measure to ROC, informedness, markedness and correlation. J. Mach. Learn. Technol. **2**(1), 37–63 (2011)

15. Bahdanau, D., Cho, K., Bengio, Y.: Neural machine translation by jointly learning to align and translate. arXiv preprint arXiv:1409.0473 (2014)
16. Tang, D., Qin, B., Liu, T.: Document modeling with gated recurrent neural network for sentiment classification. In: Proceedings of the 2015 Conference on Empirical Methods in Natural Language Processing (EMNLP), pp. 1422–1432 (2015)
17. Yang, Z., Yang, D., Dyer, C., He, X., Smola, A., Hovy, E.: Hierarchical attention networks for document classification. In: Proceedings of the 2016 Conference of the North American Chapter of the Association for Computational Linguistics: Human Language Technologies, pp. 1480–1489 (2016)
18. Vaswani, A., et al.: Attention is all you need. In: Advances in Neural Information Processing Systems, pp. 5998–6008 (2017)
19. Devlin, J., Chang, M. W., Lee, K., and Toutanova, K.: BERT: pre-training of deep bidirectional transformers for language understanding. In: Proceedings of the 2019 Conference of the North American Chapter of the Association for Computational Linguistics: Human Language Technologies, pp. 4171–4186 (2019)
20. Sun, C., Huang, L., Qiu, X.: Utilizing BERT for aspect-based sentiment analysis via constructing auxiliary sentence. In: Proceedings of the 2019 Conference of the North American Chapter of the Association for Computational Linguistics: Human Language Technologies, pp. 380–385 (2019)
21. Zhao, Y., Zhang, L.: A comprehensive survey of sentiment analysis models in social media. ACM Comput. Surv. **55**(3), 1–37 (2023)
22. Chen, Z., Li, M.: Transformer-based approaches for sentiment analysis of social media data. IEEE Access **10**, 23345–23358 (2022)
23. Liu, Y., Chen, J., Wang, L.: Dynamic attention mechanisms in recurrent neural networks for time series prediction. IEEE Trans. Neural Netw. Learn. Syst. **35**(2), 400–410 (2024)
24. Mihoubi, M., Zerkouk, M., Chikhaoui, B.: Discovering causal relationships in noisy web data for sentiment classification using attention mechanisms. GitHub Repository (2024). https://github.com/Milouden/causal-sentiment-classification

Psychological Profiling in Cybersecurity: A Look at LLMs and Psycholinguistic Features

Jean Marie Tshimula[1,2,3(✉)], D'Jeff K. Nkashama[1,3],
Jean Tshibangu Muabila[1,4], René Manassé Galekwa[1,2,5], Hugues Kanda[1],
Maximilien V. Dialufuma[1,6], Mbuyi Mukendi Didier[1,2,7,8], Kalala Kalonji[1,9],
Serge Mundele[1], Patience Kinshie Lenye[1], Tighana Wenge Basele[1,2,10],
Aristarque Ilunga[1,2], Christian N. Mayemba[1], Nathanaël M. Kasoro[2],
Selain K. Kasereka[2], Hardy Mikese[11], Pierre-Martin Tardif[3], Marc Frappier[3],
Froduald Kabanza[3], Shengrui Wang[3], Ali Mulenda Sumbu[12], Xavier Ndona[13],
and Raoul Kienge-Kienge Intudi[14]

[1] Groupe de Recherche de Prospection et Valorisation des Données (Greprovad),
Québec City, Canada
kabj2801@usherbrooke.ca
[2] Faculty of Science, University of Kinshasa, Kinshasa,
Democratic Republic of Congo
[3] Université de Sherbrooke, Sherbrooke, Canada
[4] LISV-UVSQ, Université Paris-Saclay, Gif-sur-Yvette, France
[5] University of Klagenfurt, Klagenfurt, Austria
[6] Montreal Behavioural Medicine Centre, Centre Intégré Universitaire de Santé et
Services Sociaux du Nord-de-l'Île-de-Montréal, Quebec City, Canada
[7] Biomedical Research Unit, Hospital Monkole, Kinshasa,
Democratic Republic of Congo
[8] University of Florida, Gainesville, USA
[9] School of EECS, University of Ottawa, Ottawa, Canada
[10] Karlstad University, Karlstad, Sweden
[11] Institut Supérieur Pédagogique de Kikwit, Kikwit, Democratic Republic of Congo
[12] Faculty of Psychology and Education Sciences, University of Kinshasa,
Kinshasa, Democratic Republic of Congo
[13] Harrisburg University of Science and Technology, Harrisburg, USA
[14] School of Criminology, University of Kinshasa, Kinshasa,
Democratic Republic of Congo

Abstract. The increasing sophistication of cyber threats necessitates innovative approaches to cybersecurity. In this paper, we explore the potential of psychological profiling techniques, particularly focusing on the utilization of Large Language Models (LLMs) and psycholinguistic features. We investigate the intersection of psychology and cybersecurity, discussing how LLMs can be employed to analyze textual data for identifying psychological traits of threat actors. We explore the incorporation of psycholinguistic features, such as linguistic patterns and emotional cues, into cybersecurity frameworks. Our research underscores the importance of integrating psychological perspectives into cybersecurity practices to bolster defense mechanisms against evolving threats.

M. Barhamgi et al. (Eds.): WISE 2024, LNCS 15463, pp. 378–393, 2025.
https://doi.org/10.1007/978-981-96-1483-7_31

Keywords: Cybersecurity · Psychological profiling · Large Language Models · Psycholinguistic features

1   Introduction

Psychological profiling plays a crucial role in cybersecurity, particularly in understanding and identifying the traits and motives of cybercriminals. In computer science, cybersecurity aims to safeguard technology within computer systems, implementing security measures to prevent risks and threats that could harm the system. This field regulates security measures to thwart third-party invaders or intruders who engage in malicious activities such as stealing private, business, or organizational information for personal gain [1–3].

In the domain of cybercrime, understanding the identity and motives of intruders plays a key role in mitigating risks to information security [4–11]. Psychological profiling emerges as a valuable tool for understanding the psychological traits and characteristics of cybercriminals, which strengthens strategies against potential cyber threats and assists in the identification of intruders and their motives through an examination of behavior, nature, and thought process.

Profiling in cybersecurity involves diverse criminological and criminal-law-based components, encompassing personal traits, criminal expertise, social attributes, and motivational factors. These elements help in understanding the predispositions, personality traits, demographics, socio-economic status, and motivations of cybercriminals, including those who are particularly elusive [12,13].

Cybercriminals frequently exhibit a range of psychological traits that strongly shape their behaviors and actions [8,10,14]. These individuals often possess a strong command of cyber technology, which they exploit for harmful purposes and various motives; common motives include financial gain, as seen in activities such as data theft and other forms of cyber fraud [6,15]. Many are driven by greed, pursuing financial rewards, while others seek power or revenge against certain groups or institutions. Some cybercriminals are thrill-seekers, relishing the risk involved in their illicit activities, or opportunists who take advantage of vulnerabilities for personal benefit [4,11,16]. There are also those who simply disregard legal and ethical standards, compromising their reputations within the cyber community. Traits of fearlessness, with little regard for potential consequences, and a lack of empathy are also prevalent. Moreover, some individuals demonstrate boldness, testing their hacking abilities against individuals and organizations. Collectively, these traits paint a complex picture of the motivations and behaviors driving cybercriminals in various scenarios [6,10,11,17,18].

Motivating factors behind cybercriminal personality traits include revenge and blackmailing. Understanding these traits can help minimize security risks and enable better analysis and resolution of cybercrimes [19]. In addition, integrating findings from Large Language Models (LLMs) and psycholinguistic tools, such as the Linguistic Inquiry and Word Count (LIWC) dictionary and the Medical Research Council (MRC) psycholinguistic database [20–22], into psychological profiling can significantly enrich the understanding of cybercriminal behaviors and motivations. This holistic approach to psychological profiling can not only reveal the complex personalities of cybercriminals but also strengthen overall security measures, protecting both individuals and organizations from cyber threats. In this paper, we explore the intersection of psychology and cybersecurity, with a specific emphasis on the role of LLMs and psycholinguistic features in profiling cyber threats.

The remainder of this work is organized as follows. §2 discusses the fundamental role of psychological profiling in cybersecurity, outlining how it aids in understanding and mitigating the behaviors of cybercriminals. §3 explores the application of LLMs in psychological profiling, highlighting their potential to decode complex patterns of cybercriminal activity. In §4, we examine the incorporation of psycholinguistic features into cybersecurity strategies, demonstrating how these tools can enhance the precision of psychological profiles. §5 discusses different perspectives on psychological profiling in cybersecurity. §6 addresses the ethical considerations and privacy implications inherent in the use of psychological profiling and data analysis in cybersecurity. Finally, §7 discusses future directions for research in this area and §8 concludes the paper with reflections on the evolving landscape of cybersecurity profiling.

2   Psychological Profiling in Cybersecurity

Researchers and practitioners reveal a complex profile of cyber criminals, showcasing traits such as tech-savvy, well-networked, vengeful, goal-oriented, greedy, manipulative, risk-takers, opportunists, rule-breakers, fearless, emotionless, and daring [4,6,11,15,16,23,24]. More specifically, Saroha [16] identified a range of characteristics including smartness, creativity, and a need for control, shedding light on the multifaceted nature of individuals involved in cyber crimes, and uncovering motivating factors like monetary gain, thrill-seeking, and political beliefs that drive individuals towards engaging in cyber criminal activities.

In addition to profiling traits, understanding the psychological effects of cybercrime remains essential. Gross et al. [25] indicated that exposure to cyber terrorism triggers heightened levels of stress and anxiety among individuals, akin to the psychological effects of conventional terrorism, emphasizing the pivotal role of perceived threats in shaping individuals' attitudes towards government surveillance, regulation, and military responses in the face of cyber threats. Curtis and Oxburgh [26] underscored the significant influence of law enforcement's lack of cybercrime knowledge on low conviction rates and victim underreporting. The study revealed that victims often delay reporting cybercrimes due to embarrassment or a perception that they are better equipped to handle the situation themselves. This highlights the importance of training officers to increase their preparedness in dealing with cybercrime cases and engaging with victims.

In a related vein, Palassis et al. [23] explored the psychological impacts of hacking victimization and underlined the need for support organizations to address these issues. The study underscores the importance of raising awareness about the psychological effects of cybercrime and promoting support opportunities for victims. Its findings provide valuable insights for clinicians and support organizations, informing the development of treatment guidelines and interventions to address the negative psychological impacts of hacking. Gomez and Villar [27] investigated how limited experience and domain knowledge in cyberspace lead to the use of cognitive shortcuts and inappropriate heuristics, resulting in elevated levels of dread.

In recent investigations, building upon prior research, Geer [28] highlighted the importance of leveraging cybercriminals' cognitive biases to influence their behaviors during attacks. The study suggested that by using algorithms informed by cyberpsychology research, defenders can present low-risk, low-reward targets to steer hackers away from high-value assets. Studies show that attackers exhibit risk-averse behavior, preferring attacks on less secure machines to avoid the appearance of failure. Research on human subjects engaging in cybercriminal behavior revealed a strong relationship between key risk-taking and cybercriminal behaviors. Bolton [29] indicated that participants' exposure to fictional media, particularly crime-related television shows, can influence their attitudes towards criminal investigations and profiling techniques. The study revealed a correlation between media consumption habits and the perceived realism of investigative procedures portrayed in television episodes. Additionally, participants' beliefs about the role of criminal profilers and the importance of intuition in investigations were influenced by their media exposure. This underscores the nuanced relationship between media consumption and perceptions of criminal behavior and profiling accuracy.

Expanding upon the evolving understanding of cybercriminal behavior, Lickiewicz [30] highlighted the significance of intelligence, personality traits, and social skills in the effectiveness of cyber attacks. The study emphasized the role of environmental factors, such as family relationships and educational background, in shaping the behaviors of hackers. It suggested that a holistic approach, considering both individual characteristics and external influences, is crucial for developing a comprehensive psychological profile of cyber criminals. Additionally, the study noted the need for interdisciplinary collaboration between information technology and investigative psychology to combat cybercrime.

Psychological profiling, rooted in behavioral analysis and psychological theory, aims to uncover patterns and traits indicative of malicious intent in cyber activities. This approach utilizes various aspects of human behavior, such as language use, decision-making processes, and emotional responses, to discern the psychological profiles of threat actors [11, 12, 14, 19, 31–36]. Leveraging techniques from psychology, including personality assessment and psycholinguistic analysis, enables the identification of anomalous behaviors and potential indicators of cyber threats.

For instance, Kioskli and Polemi [36] emphasized the importance of profiling potential attackers in cybersecurity to enhance the accuracy of vulnerability severity scores using psychological and behavioral traits. Research investigated the influence of cultural and psychological factors on cyber-security behavior, utilizing the Big Five Framework to assess personality traits and their impact on user attitudes towards privacy and self-efficacy [37,38]. More specifically, Hani et al. [12] proposed machine learning models for psychological profiling of hackers based on the "Big Five" personality traits model (OCEAN - Openness, Conscientiousness, Extroversion, Agreeableness, Neuroticism) and their models achieved 88% accuracy in mapping personality clusters with different types of hackers (White Hat, Grey Hat, etc.), identifying cyber-criminal behaviors. Gaia et al. [34] discovered that individuals attracted to hacking exhibit high scores on Machiavellianism and Psychopathy scales, with Grey Hat hackers showing opposition to authority, Black Hat hackers scoring high on thrill-seeking, and White Hat hackers displaying tendencies towards Narcissism. The Dark Triad traits significantly predict interest in different types of hacking, while thrill-seeking emerges as a key motivator for Black Hat hackers. Perceptions of apprehension for violating privacy laws negatively impact Grey Hat and Black Hat hacking.

Table 1. Summary of LLM applications in psychological profiling in cybersecurity

Research	Focus	Cybersecurity applications	Sources of data
Petrov et al. [39]	Simulating human psychological behaviors using LLMs	Evaluating psychometric properties for profiling potential threats	Standardized personality constructs
Pellert et al. [40]	Repurposing psychometric inventories for LLMs	Profiling values, morality, and beliefs to detect radicalization	Standard psychometric inventories
Sorokovikova et al. [41]	Fine-tuning LLMs on Big Five traits	Profiling based on language to identify potential threats	Psychometric test items
Safdari et al. [42]	Administering personality tests on LLMs	Mimicking specific human personality profiles for threat detection	Personality tests
Huang et al. [43]	PsychoBench framework for evaluating LLM personalities	Understanding complex psychological profiles for enhanced cybersecurity	Personality traits, interpersonal relationships, motivational tests, emotional abilities
Frisch and Giulianelli [44]	Conditioning LLM agents on personality profiles	Mimicking human traits for improved phishing and social engineering detection	Persona conditioning data
Yamin et al. [45]	Weaponized use of LLMs in cyber attacks	Generating malicious code, automated hacking, phishing	Training data on malware and exploits
Motlagh et al. [46]	Generating malicious payloads with LLMs	Creating new strains of malware	Relevant cybersecurity data
Beckerich et al. [47]	Using LLMs for automated hacking	Vulnerability scanning and developing exploits	Hacking toolkits
Schmitt and Flechais [48]	Social engineering and phishing	Mimicking human language for cyber attacks	Historical phishing data
Zhang et al. [49]	PsySafe for framework understanding and mitigating risks arising from dark psychological states	Identifying vulnerabilities, evaluating safety, and implementing defense mechanisms	Psychological assessments, behavioral evaluations

Moreover, Kipane [19] revealed that cybercriminals exhibit a range of behaviors and traits that deviate from societal norms, influenced by factors such as heredity, education, culture, and socio-economic status. Profiling methods focus on identifying key psychological features, modus operandi, and criminal motivations to aid in early detection and investigation of cybercrimes. The study emphasizes the significance of expert knowledge and advanced technologies in enhancing law enforcement efforts to combat cybercrime. Overall, the research underscores the evolving nature of criminal profiling in the digital era and the critical role it plays in addressing the growing threat of cybercriminal activities.

In response to the escalating threat posed by cybercrimes, Thackray et al. [11] highlighted the diverse motivations of hackers, including recreation, prestige, revenge, profit, and ideology, which influence their engagement in cyber activities. The study underscores the importance of not only teaching coding skills but also educating individuals about the risks and consequences of online actions to prevent cyber-crime involvement. Additionally, the research emphasizes the need to identify at-risk groups and individuals to target awareness campaigns and promote informed online behavior for future generations. Lastly, the study suggests that understanding social psychological theories can enhance communication with hacker communities and individuals, ultimately contributing to more effective cybersecurity practices.

3   LLMs in Psychological Profiling

Large Language Models (LLMs), such as OpenAI's GPT series of models, Google's PaLM and Gemini, and Meta's LLaMA family of open-source models, have demonstrated remarkable capabilities in natural language understanding and generation tasks [50]. As these models continue to evolve and become more sophisticated, researchers and practitioners are exploring their potential applications beyond language tasks, venturing into the realm of psychological profiling (see Table 1). These models are utilized to profile individuals based on their language use patterns and communication styles, facilitating the early detection of potential threats [20].

The potential applications of LLM-based psychological profiling are vast and diverse [12,20,39,40,43,51]. In mental health settings, these techniques aid in the early detection of psychological disorders and the development of personalized treatment plans [52–54]. In human-AI interaction, understanding the perceived personalities of LLMs improves user engagement and trust, leading to more natural and effective interactions [55].

However, the application of LLMs to psychological profiling is not without challenges and ethical considerations. Existing personality models and assessment methods have been developed primarily for human subjects, and their suitability for evaluating artificial intelligence systems is questionable. Additionally, the fluid and context-dependent nature of LLM "personalities" raises concerns about the reliability and validity of traditional personality assessment techniques when applied to these models [41]. As researchers delve deeper into this emerging field, they must grapple with the complexities of transferring human-centric concepts like personality to artificial intelligence systems. LLMs are explored for psychological profiling tasks, such as detecting personality traits, values, and other non-cognitive characteristics [12,12,39–44,49,56].

In exploring the multifaceted landscape of psychological profiling with LLMs, researchers have embarked on various avenues to understand their potential applications. For instance, Petrov et al. [39] focused on investigating the ability of LLMs to simulate human psychological behaviors using prompts to adopt different personas and respond to standardized measures of personality constructs to assess their psychometric properties. Pellert et al. [40] repurposed standard psychometric inventories originally designed for assessing human psychological characteristics, such as personality traits, values, morality, and beliefs, to evaluate analogous traits in LLMs. Sorokovikova et al. [41] fine-tuned LLMs on psychometric test items related to the Big Five personality traits for evaluating personalities based on language. Safdari et al. [42] introduced a method for administering personality tests on LLMs and shaping their generated text to mimic specific human personality profiles.

Furthermore, Huang et al. [43] proposed PsychoBench, a framework for evaluating personality traits, interpersonal relationships, motivational tests, and emotional abilities to uncover complex psychological profiles within LLMs and their potential integration into human society as empathetic and personalized AI-driven solutions. Frisch and Giulianelli [44] demonstrated that LLM agents conditioned on personality profiles can mimic human traits, with creative personas displaying more consistent behavior in both interactive and non-interactive conditions; the research highlights the importance of robust persona conditioning in shaping LLM behavior and emphasizes the asymmetry in linguistic alignment between different persona groups during interactions.

Zhang et al. [49] presented PsySafe, a framework designed to evaluate and improve the safety of multi-agent systems (MAS) by addressing the psychological aspects of agent behavior. PsySafe incorporates dark personality traits to assess and mitigate potential risks associated with agent behaviors in MAS; in addition, it includes identifying vulnerabilities, evaluating safety from psychological and behavioral perspectives, and implementing effective defense strategies. The findings yielded by PsySafe reveal several phenomena, including collective dangerous behaviors among agents, their self-reflection on engaging in such behaviors, and the correlation between psychological assessments and behavioral safety.

While LLMs offer promising applications in psychological profiling, their language generation capabilities also raise concerns about potential misuse for cyber attacks and malicious activities [45,46,57,58]. Attack payloads and malware creation involve LLMs generating malicious code or new strains of malware through training on relevant data [47,59]. Automated hacking and vulnerability scanning tasks can be performed by LLMs, including generating code for automated hacking attacks, scanning software for vulnerabilities, or developing exploits [59,60].

In addition, LLMs can be used for social engineering and phishing purposes, leveraging their ability to mimic human language patterns to create convincing social engineering attacks, phishing emails, or disinformation campaigns [48]. Adversaries could potentially manipulate LLM outputs for malicious purposes using prompt injection techniques [61,62]. LLMs can generate highly personalized and persuasive phishing emails tailored to specific individuals within an organization, bypassing traditional detection systems. Studies show these AI-crafted attacks can be strikingly effective, with around 10% of recipients entering credentials on fake login portals [63]. The ability of LLMs to mimic human language patterns and adapt to different contexts makes them a powerful tool for deception and manipulation [64].

The 2023 Report of Voice of SecOps provides a comprehensive analysis of threats and stressors posed by LLMs, revealing that 51% of security professionals are likely to leave their job within 2024.[1] The study surveyed over 650 senior security operations professionals in the U.S. to assess LLMs' impact on the cybersecurity industry. Findings indicate a 75% surge in attacks in 2022, with 85% attributing this increase to bad actors leveraging LLMs. Furthermore, 70% of respondents believe LLMs positively influence employee productivity and collaboration, while 63% perceive an enhancement in employee morale. Ransomware emerges as the greatest threat to organizational data security, with 46% of respondents acknowledging its severity and 62% indicating it as the top C-suite concern, a notable increase from 44% in 2022; the pressure to combat ransomware has prompted organizations to revise their data security strategies, with 47% now possessing a policy to pay the ransom, compared to 34% in the previous year. Moreover, the report reveals a 55% increase in stress levels among security professionals, primarily attributed to staffing and resource constraints, cited by 42% of respondents.

4   Psycholinguistic Features

Psycholinguistic features encompass a wide range of linguistic attributes and psychological constructs that reflect cognitive and emotional aspects of language use. Integrating psycholinguistic features into cybersecurity frameworks enhances the granularity of threat profiling techniques and enables a deeper understanding of cybercriminals' mental states and feelings [31,65–68]. Psycholinguistic features include sentiment analysis, linguistic complexity measures, lexical diversity metrics, and stylistic characteristics. Through advanced text analysis algorithms and machine learning algorithms, these features can be leveraged to identify anomalous patterns indicative of malicious intent.

One of the powerful tools in psycholinguistic analysis is the Linguistic Inquiry and Word Count (LIWC) dictionary [21]. In the context of cyber attacks, LIWC has been used to detect deception in phishing emails by analyzing the psycholinguistic features that attackers employ to deceive end-users [68]. Research shows that phishers often use language conveying certainty (e.g. always, never), time pressure and work-related words to increase vulnerability of targets. Conversely, reward-related words like money or cash tend to decrease vulnerability as they are associated with scams. Beyond phishing, LIWC has been applied to study online predator behavior, analyze developer personalities, model social media rumors, and understand user reactions in crowdsourcing [32,69–72].

Building on the potential of LIWC for psycholinguistic analysis in cybersecurity, researchers explore its applications to understand attacker behavior and victim vulnerabilities. More precisely, Guo et al. [73] focused on analyzing the vulnerability factors of potential victims to cybergrooming using LIWC to

---

[1] *Generative AI and Cybersecurity: Bright Future or Business Battleground?* Deep Instinct. . Voice of SecOps Reports. Retrieved from https://www.deepinstinct.com/voice-of-secops-reports. Accessed on May 12, 2024.

quantify and understand the social-psychological traits that may make individuals more susceptible to online grooming; they reveal significant correlations between specific vulnerability dimensions and the likelihood of being targeted as a victim of cybergrooming. Interestingly, the research observed negative correlations between victims and certain family and community-related traits, challenging conventional beliefs about the key factors contributing to vulnerability in online contexts. Tan et al. [74] utilize LIWC and demonstrate that malicious insiders exhibit specific linguistic patterns in their written communications, including increased use of self-focused words, negative language, and cognitive process-related words compared to other team members; as insiders become more detached from the team, language similarity decreases over time.

In a different angle, psycholinguistic features were utilized to examine the manipulative aspects of cybercrimes. More specifically, Krylova-Grek [67] investigated the psycholinguistic dimensions of social engineering within cybersecurity, employing activity theory to dissect the methods and techniques utilized by malicious actors. This research reveals the sophisticated tactics employed by social engineers to manipulate emotions, impede critical thinking, and exploit moral values to influence user behavior and extract sensitive information. Parapar et al. [75] proposed a machine learning model for detecting sexual predation in chatrooms using psycholinguistic, content-based, and chat-based features, and show distinct characteristics that differentiate predators from non-predators. Particularly, Rogers et al. [69] investigated the psychological traits and behaviors of individuals involved in self-reported criminal computer activities, emphasizing the role of extraversion in predicting such behavior and challenging stereotypes by shedding light on the complexities of personality factors in criminal/deviant computer behavior through the use of Likert-scale questionnaires and psychometric instruments.

Furthermore, Chatterjee and Basu [76] conducted a study on phishing influence detection using a novel computational psycholinguistic analysis approach to identify influential sentences that could potentially lead to security breaches and hacking in online transactions and social media interactions, developing a language and domain-independent computational model based on Cialdini's principles of persuasion.[2] Kranenbarg et al. [72] indicated that cyber offenders displayed similarities to the community sample on certain traits but exhibited differences from offline offenders, particularly in conscientiousness and openness to experience. Notably, cyber offenders showed lower scores on honesty-humility compared to the community sample, suggesting potential implications for intervention strategies targeting specific personality traits in this population.

Budimir et al. [32] emphasized the importance of understanding psycholinguistic features and psychology in cybersecurity to develop effective strategies and interventions. They explore the emotional responses triggered by cyberse-

---

[2] *The 6 Principles of Persuasion: Tips from the leading expert on social influence*, Douglas T. Kenrick. Posted Dec. 8, 2012. Retrieved from https://www.psychologytoday.com/ca/blog/sex-murder-and-the-meaning-of-life/201212/the-6-principles-of-persuasion. Accessed May 20, 2024.

curity breaches, focusing on the hacking of smart security cameras. The study identifies a 3-dimensional structure of emotional reactions, highlighting negative affectivity, proactive versus fight/flight action tendencies, and emotional intensity and valence. Personality characteristics, such as the Big Five traits and resilient/overcontrolled/undercontrolled types, were found to relate to these emotional dimensions.

Recently, the application of sentiment analysis techniques has paved the way for building psychological profiles and detecting and understanding cyber threats. Sapienza et al. [77] utilized sentiment analysis to identify discussions around exploits, vulnerabilities, and attack planning on dark web forums even before these threats manifest in the real world, and to provide early warnings through the observation of changes in sentiment and semantic context. Deb et al. [65] proposed approaches to predict cyber-events by leveraging sentiment analysis on hacker forums and social media to analyze the sentiment expressed in online discussions and detect signals that may precede cyber attacks. Jiang et al. [31] built user psychological profiles based on the sentiment analysis of their network browsing and email content, and demonstrate that this approach can proactively and accurately detect malicious insiders with extreme or negative emotional tendencies.

Building upon recent studies and advancements, Uyheng et al. [66] developed a machine learning model called TrollHunter and collected a dataset of online trolling messages and found that troll messages exhibit more abusive language, lower cognitive complexity, and greater targeting of named entities and identities; the model achieved an 89% accuracy rate and F1 score in identifying trolling behavior.

5   Discussion

The integration of psychological profiling into cybersecurity practices offers a multifaceted approach to understanding and mitigating cyber threats. LLMs and psycholinguistic features provide deeper understanding into the behaviors, motivations, and emotional states of cybercriminals. This discussion section explores the potential benefits, and challenges of these techniques, drawing from the research findings presented earlier.

5.1   Benefits of Psychological Profiling in Cybersecurity

Psychological profiling in cybersecurity holds significant promise. Identifying psychological traits and patterns in cybercriminal behavior enables security professionals to anticipate and preemptively counteract potential threats. For instance, understanding the personality traits and motivations of different types of hackers (e.g., White Hat, Black Hat, Grey Hat) allows for more tailored security measures and interventions [12,34]. The use of LLMs enhances this profiling by analyzing large volumes of text data, identifying linguistic patterns that may indicate malicious intent.

Psycholinguistic features, such as those derived from the LIWC dictionary, provide additional granularity. These features help in detecting subtle cues in language that might indicate deception, stress, or malicious intent. For example, certain linguistic markers can distinguish phishing emails from legitimate communications, thereby improving the accuracy of threat detection systems [68,69].

Moreover, the incorporation of psychological profiling can aid in the development of more personalized cybersecurity training programs. Understanding the psychological traits that make individuals more susceptible to cyber attacks allows organizations to design targeted awareness campaigns and training modules that address specific vulnerabilities.

5.2   Challenges and Limitations

Despite the promising applications, several challenges and limitations need to be addressed. One major challenge is the accuracy and reliability of psychological profiling techniques.

While LLMs and psycholinguistic tools provide valuable insights, they come with inherent limitations. Implementing and maintaining these advanced profiling systems require a workforce equipped with specialized skills in artificial intelligence, cybersecurity, and psychological analysis. There is often a shortage of professionals with the necessary expertise to develop, deploy, and refine these tools. Addressing this skill gap is crucial for the effective utilization of psychological profiling in cybersecurity.

The effectiveness of LLMs largely depends on the quality and diversity of the data they are trained on. Inaccurate models can result from poor-quality data, such as poisoned or contaminated datasets, or from non-representative data. Moreover, acquiring diverse and representative datasets is particularly challenging in the field of cybersecurity, where data sensitivity and proprietary information are significant concerns.

Additionally, the use of these tools can lead to false positives and negatives, causing either unnecessary alarms or undetected threats. Thus, ensuring the robustness and validity of these models is vital for their successful deployment in real-world scenarios [12,68].

Another challenge lies in the dynamic and evolving nature of cybercriminal behavior. Cybercriminals continually adapt their tactics to evade detection, which means that profiling techniques must also evolve. Continuous updates and refinements to the models and algorithms are necessary to keep pace with these changes.

The ethical implications of psychological profiling in cybersecurity cannot be overlooked. The use of personal data to create psychological profiles raises significant privacy concerns. It is essential to balance the benefits of enhanced security with the protection of individual privacy rights. Transparent policies and stringent data protection measures must be in place to ensure that the use of psychological profiling does not infringe on personal freedoms.

6   Ethical Considerations

Ethical considerations are paramount when employing psychological profiling in cybersecurity. The potential for misuse of these technologies for surveillance, manipulation, or discrimination is a serious concern. For example, the ability of LLMs to generate persuasive phishing emails tailored to specific individuals poses a significant threat if used maliciously [78].

To mitigate these risks, it is crucial to establish ethical guidelines and regulatory frameworks that govern the use of psychological profiling tools. These guidelines should emphasize the importance of informed consent, data minimization, and transparency in the use of personal data. Additionally, there should be mechanisms for accountability and oversight to ensure that these technologies are used responsibly and ethically [79,80].

7   Future Directions

Future research should focus on improving the robustness of psychological profiling techniques. This includes developing more sophisticated models that can adapt to the evolving tactics of cybercriminals and integrating multimodal data sources (e.g., text, behavioral data, biometric data) to create more comprehensive profiles.

Another promising direction is the exploration of collaborative approaches that combine human expertise with machine intelligence. Human analysts and AI systems can collaborate to achieve more effective and nuanced threat detection and mitigation strategies.

Finally, ongoing efforts to address the ethical and privacy concerns associated with psychological profiling are essential. This includes developing new methods for anonymizing and protecting personal data while still enabling meaningful analysis, as well as fostering a culture of ethical awareness and responsibility among cybersecurity professionals.

8   Conclusion

The integration of psychological profiling, LLMs, and psycholinguistic features into cybersecurity practices represents a significant advancement in the field. These techniques offer the potential to enhance threat detection and mitigation strategies by providing deeper understanding into the behaviors and motivations of cybercriminals. However, realizing this potential requires addressing the challenges and ethical considerations associated with these technologies. By doing so, we can create more robust and responsible cybersecurity frameworks that protect both organizations and individuals from evolving cyber threats.

Acknowledgements. The authors thank all Greprovad members for helpful discussions and comments on early drafts.

References

1. Weimann, G.: Cyberterrorism: how real is the threat? United States Institute of Peace 31 (2004)
2. Li, Y., Liu, Q.: A comprehensive review study of cyber-attacks and cyber security; Emerging trends and recent developments. Energy Rep. **7**, 8176–8186 (2021)
3. Cremer, F., et al.: Cyber risk and cybersecurity: a systematic review of data availability. Geneva Papers Risk Insurance-Issues Pract. **47**(3), 698–736 (2022)
4. McBrayer, J.: Exploiting the digital frontier: hacker typology and motivation. In: The University of Alabama (2014)
5. Kumar, S., Carley, K.M.: Approaches to understanding the motivations behind cyber attacks. In: 2016 IEEE ISI, pp. 307–309. IEEE (2016)
6. Li, X.: A review of motivations of illegal cyber activities. Kriminologija & socijalna integracija: časopis za kriminologiju, penologiju i poremećaje u ponašanju **25**(1), 110–126 (2017)
7. Ablon, L.: Data thieves: The motivations of cyber threat actors and their use and monetization of stolen data. RAND Corporation Santa Monica, CA, USA (2018)
8. Bada, M., Nurse, J.R.C.: The social and psychological impact of cyberattacks. In: Emerging Cyber Threats and Cognitive Vulnerabilities, pp. 73–92 (2020)
9. Hunter, L.Y., Albert, C.D., Garrett, E.: Factors that motivate state-sponsored cyberattacks. Cyber Defense Rev. **6**(2), 111–128 (2021)
10. Chng, S., Lu, H.Y., Kumar, A., Yau, D.: Hacker types, motivations and strategies: a comprehensive framework. Comput. Hum. Behav. Rep. **5**, 100167 (2022)
11. Thackray, H., McAlaney, J., Dogan, H., Taylor, J., Richardson, C.: Social psychology: an under-used tool in cybersecurity. In: BCS Human Computer Interaction Conference (2016)
12. Hani, U., Sohaib, O., Khan, K., Aleidi, A., Islam, N.: Psychological profiling of hackers via machine learning toward sustainable cybersecurity. Front. Comput. Sci. **6**, 1381351 (2024)
13. Holt, T.J., Chermak, S.M., Freilich, J.D., Turner, N., Greene-Colozzi, E.: Assessing racial and ethnically motivated extremist cyberattacks using open source data. Terrorism Polit. Violence **36**(1), 113–126 (2024)
14. Montañez, R., Golob, E., Xu, S.: Human cognition through the lens of social engineering cyberattacks. Front. Psychol. **11**, 528099 (2020)
15. Holt, T.J., Stonhouse, M., Freilich, J., Chermak, S.M.: Examining ideologically motivated cyberattacks performed by far-left groups. Terrorism Polit. Violence **33**(3), 527–548 (2021)
16. Saroha, R.: Profiling a cyber criminal. Int. J. Inf. Comput. Technol. **4**(3), 253–258 (2014)
17. Madarie, R.: Hackers' motivations: testing Schwartz's theory of motivational types of values in a sample of hackers. Int. J. Cyber Criminol. **11**(1), 78–97 (2017)
18. Maalem Lahcen, R.A., Caulkins, B., Mohapatra, R., Kumar, M.: Review and insight on the behavioral aspects of cybersecurity. Cybersecurity **3**(1), 1–18 (2020). https://doi.org/10.1186/s42400-020-00050-w
19. Kipane, A.: Meaning of profiling of cybercriminals in the security context. In: SHS Web of Conferences, vol. 68, p. 01009 (2019). EDP Sciences
20. Ke, L., Tong, S., Chen, P., Peng, K.: Exploring the frontiers of LLMS in psychological applications: a comprehensive review. arXiv preprint arXiv:2401.01519 (2024)

21. Boyd, R.L., Ashokkumar, A., Seraj, S., Pennebaker, J.W.: The development and psychometric properties of LIWC-22. Austin, TX: University of Texas at Austin, pp. 1–47 (2022)
22. Coltheart, M.: The MRC psycholinguistic database. Q. J. Exp. Psychol. Sect. A **33**(4), 497–505 (1981)
23. Palassis, A., Speelman, C.P., Pooley, J.A.: An exploration of the psychological impact of hacking victimization. SAGE Open **11**(4), 21582440211061556 (2021)
24. Yang, G., Cai, L., Yu, A., Ma, J., Meng, D., Wu, Y.: Potential malicious insiders detection based on a comprehensive security psychological model. In: 2018 IEEE BigDataService, pp. 9–16 (2018). IEEE
25. Gross, M.L., Canetti, D., Vashdi, D.R.: The psychological effects of cyber terrorism. Bull. Atomic Sci. **72**(5), 284–291 (2016)
26. Curtis, J., Oxburgh, G.: Understanding cybercrime in 'real world' policing and law enforcement. Police J. **96**(4), 573–592 (2023)
27. Gomez, M.A., Villar, E.B.: Fear, uncertainty, and dread: cognitive heuristics and cyber threats. Polit. Gov. **6**(2), 61–72 (2018)
28. Geer, D.: Using psychology to bolster cybersecurity. Commun. ACM **66**(10), 15–17 (2023)
29. Bolton, A.: Media effects and criminal profiling: how fiction influences perception and profile accuracy. PhD thesis, Nova Southeastern University (2019)
30. Lickiewicz, J.: Cyber crime psychology-proposal of an offender psychological profile. Probl. Forensic Sci. **2**(3), 239–252 (2011)
31. Jiang, J., et al.: Prediction and detection of malicious insiders' motivation based on sentiment profile on webpages and emails. In: 2018 IEEE Military Communications Conference, pp. 1–6 (2018). IEEE
32. Budimir, S., Fontaine, J.R.J., Huijts, N.M.A., Haans, A., Loukas, G., Roesch, E.B.: Emotional reactions to cybersecurity breach situations: scenario-based survey study. J. Med. Internet Res. **23**(5), 24879 (2021)
33. Bada, M., Nurse, J.R.C.: Profiling the cybercriminal: a systematic review of research. In: 2021 International Conference on Cyber Situational Awareness, Data Analytics and Assessment, pp. 1–8 (2021)
34. Gaia, J., et al.: Psychological profiling of hacking potential. In: Proceedings of the 53rd Hawaii International Conference on System Sciences (2020)
35. Zambrano, P., Torres, J., Tello-Oquendo, L., Yánez, Á., Velásquez, L.: On the modeling of cyber-attacks associated with social engineering: a parental control prototype. J. Inf. Secur. Appl. **75**, 103501 (2023)
36. Kioskli, K., Polemi, N.: Estimating attackers' profiles results in more realistic vulnerability severity scores. In: 13th International Conference on AHFE (2022)
37. Halevi, T., et al.: Cultural and psychological factors in cyber-security. In: Proceedings of the 18th International Conference on Information Integration and Web-based Applications and Services, pp. 318–324 (2016)
38. Odemis, M., Yucel, C., Koltuksuz, A., et al.: Detecting user behavior in cyber threat intelligence: development of Honeypsy system. Secur. Commun. Netw. **2022** (2022)
39. Petrov, N.B., Serapio-García, G., Rentfrow, J.: Limited ability of LLMs to simulate human psychological behaviours: a psychometric analysis. arXiv preprint arXiv:2405.07248 (2024)
40. Pellert, M., Lechner, C.M., Wagner, C., Rammstedt, B., Strohmaier, M.: AI psychometrics: Assessing the psychological profiles of large language models through psychometric inventories. Perspect. Psychol. Sci., **19**, 17456916231214460 (2023)
41. Sorokovikova, A., Fedorova, N., Rezagholi, S., Yamshchikov, I.P.: LLMs simulate big five personality traits: further evidence. arXiv preprint arXiv:2402.01765 (2024)

42. Safdari, M., et al.: Personality traits in large language models. arXiv preprint arXiv:2307.00184 (2023)
43. Huang, J., et al.: On the humanity of conversational AI: evaluating the psychological portrayal of LLMs. In: ICLR (2023)
44. Frisch, I., Giulianelli, M.: LLM agents in interaction: Measuring personality consistency and linguistic alignment in interacting populations of large language models. arXiv preprint arXiv:2402.02896 (2024)
45. Yamin, M.M., Ullah, M., Ullah, H., Katt, B.: Weaponized AI for cyber attacks. J. Inf. Secur. Appl. **57**, 102722 (2021)
46. Motlagh, F.N., Hajizadeh, M., Majd, M., Najafi, P., Cheng, F., Meinel, C.: Large language models in cybersecurity: state-of-the-art. arXiv preprint arXiv:2402.00891 (2024)
47. Beckerich, M., Plein, L., Coronado, S.: RatGPT: turning online LLMs into proxies for malware attacks. arXiv preprint arXiv:2308.09183 (2023)
48. Schmitt, M., Flechais, I.: Digital deception: generative artificial intelligence in social engineering and phishing. arXiv preprint arXiv:2310.13715 (2023)
49. Zhang, Z., et al.: Psysafe: A comprehensive framework for psychological-based attack, defense, and evaluation of multi-agent system safety. arXiv preprint arXiv:2401.11880 (2024)
50. Minaee, S., et al.: Large language models: a survey. arXiv preprint arXiv:2402.06196 (2024)
51. Abdurahman, S., Ziabari, A.S., Moore, A., Bartels, D., Dehghani, M.: Evaluating large language models in psychological research: a guide for reviewers (2024)
52. Lai, T., et al.: PSY-LLM: scaling up global mental health psychological services with AI-based large language models. arXiv preprint arXiv:2307.11991 (2023)
53. Chung, N.C., Dyer, G., Brocki, L.: Challenges of large language models for mental health counseling. arXiv preprint arXiv:2311.13857 (2023)
54. Hagendorff, T.: Machine psychology: investigating emergent capabilities and behavior in large language models using psychological methods. arXiv preprint arXiv:2303.13988 (2023)
55. Sharma, A., Rao, S., Brockett, C., Malhotra, A., Jojic, N., Dolan, W.B.: Investigating agency of LLMs in human-AI collaboration tasks. In: Proc. of the 18th Conference of the European Chapter of the Association for Computational Linguistics (Volume 1: Long Papers), pp. 1968–1987 (2024)
56. Song, X., et al.: Identifying multiple personalities in large language models with external evaluation. arXiv preprint arXiv:2402.14805 (2024)
57. Gupta, M., Akiri, C., Aryal, K., Parker, E., Praharaj, L.: From ChatGPT to ThreatGPT: Impact of generative AI in cybersecurity and privacy. IEEE Access **11**, 80218–80245 (2023)
58. Yao, Y., Duan, J., Xu, K., Cai, Y., Sun, Z., Zhang, Y.: A survey on large language model (LLM) security and privacy: the good, the bad, and the ugly. High-Confidence Comput. **4**, 100211 (2024)
59. Wu, F., Liu, X., Xiao, C.: DeceptPrompt: exploiting LLM-driven code generation via adversarial natural language instructions. arXiv preprint arXiv:2312.04730 (2023)
60. Xu, J., et al.: AutoAttacker: a large language model guided system to implement automatic cyber-attacks. arXiv preprint arXiv:2403.01038 (2024)
61. Liu, Y., et al.: Prompt injection attack against LLM-integrated applications. arXiv preprint arXiv:2306.05499 (2023)
62. Piet, J., et al.: Jatmo: prompt injection defense by task-specific finetuning. arXiv preprint arXiv:2312.17673 (2023)

63. Bethany, M., Galiopoulos, A., Bethany, E., Karkevandi, M.B., Vishwamitra, N., Najafirad, P.: Large language model lateral spear phishing: a comparative study in large-scale organizational settings. arXiv preprint arXiv:2401.09727 (2024)
64. Prome, S.A., Ragavan, N.A., Islam, M.R., Asirvatham, D., Jegathesan, A.J.: Deception detection using ML and DL techniques: a systematic review. Nat. Lang. Process. J. **6**, 100057 (2024)
65. Deb, A., Lerman, K., Ferrara, E.: Predicting cyber-events by leveraging hacker sentiment. Information **9**(11), 280 (2018)
66. Uyheng, J., Moffitt, J.D., Carley, K.M.: The language and targets of online trolling: a psycholinguistic approach for social cybersecurity. Inf. Process. Manag. **59**(5), 103012 (2022)
67. Krylova-Grek, Y.: Psycholinguistic aspects of humanitarian component of cyber-security. Psycholinguistics **26**(1), 199–215 (2019)
68. Xu, T., Rajivan, P.: Determining psycholinguistic features of deception in phishing messages. Inf. Comput. Secur. **31**(2), 199–220 (2023)
69. Rogers, M.K., Seigfried, K., Tidke, K.A.: Self-reported computer criminal behavior: psychological analysis. Digit. Invest. **3**, 116–120 (2006)
70. Tausczik, Y.R., Pennebaker, J.W.: The psychological meaning of words: LIWC and computerized text analysis methods. J. Lang. Soc. Psychol. **29**(1), 24–54 (2010)
71. Shappie, A.T., Dawson, C.A., Debb, S.M.: Personality as a predictor of cyberse-curity behavior. Psychol. Popular Media **9**(4), 475 (2020)
72. Kranenbarg, M.W., Van Gelder, J.-L., Barends, A.J., Vries, R.E.: Is there a cyber-criminal personality? Comparing cyber offenders and offline offenders on hex-aco personality domains and their underlying facets. Comput. Hum. Behav. **140**, 107576 (2023)
73. Guo, Z., Wang, P., Cho, J.-H., Huang, L.: Text mining-based social-psychological vulnerability analysis of potential victims to cybergrooming: insights and lessons learned. In: Companion Proceedings of the ACM Web Conference 2023, pp. 1381–1388 (2023)
74. Tan, S.-S., Na, J., Duraisamy, S.: Unified psycholinguistic framework: an unobtru-sive psychological analysis approach towards insider threat prevention and detec-tion. J. Inf. Sci. Theory Pract. **7**(1), 52–71 (2019)
75. Parapar, J., Losada, D.E., Barreiro, A.: Combining psycho-linguistic, content-based and chat-based features to detect predation in chatrooms. J. Univers. Comput. Sci. **20**(2), 213–239 (2014)
76. Chatterjee, A., Basu, S.: How vulnerable are you? A novel computational psy-cholinguistic analysis for phishing influence detection. In: Proceedings of the 18th International Conference on Natural Language Processing, pp. 499–507 (2021)
77. Sapienza, A., Bessi, A., Damodaran, S., Shakarian, P., Lerman, K., Ferrara, E.: Early warnings of cyber threats in online discussions. In: 2017 IEEE International Conference on Data Mining Workshops (ICDMW), pp. 667–674. IEEE (2017)
78. Liyanage, U.P., Ranaweera, N.D.: Ethical considerations and potential risks in the deployment of large language models in diverse societal contexts. J. Comput. Soc. Dyn. **8**(11), 15–25 (2023)
79. McStay, A.: Emotional AI, soft biometrics and the surveillance of emotional life: an unusual consensus on privacy. Big Data Soc. **7**(1), 2053951720904386 (2020)
80. Fleming, M.N.: Considerations for the ethical implementation of psychological assessment through social media via machine learning. Ethics Behav. **31**(3), 181–192 (2021)

Dynamic Analysis of Influencer Impact on Opinion Formation in Social Networks

Omran Berjawi[1] , Danilo Cavaliere[2(✉)] , Giuseppe Fenza[2] ,
and Rida Khatoun[3]

[1] IMT School for Advanced Studies Lucca, Piazza S.Francesco, 19, 55100 Lucca,
LU, Italy
`omran.berjawi@imtlucca.it`
[2] University of Salerno, via Giovanni Paolo II, 132, 84084 Fisciano, SA, Italy
`{dcavaliere,gfenza}@unisa.it`
[3] Institut Polytechnique de Paris, Telecom Paris (INFRES), Pl. Marguerite Perey,
19, 91120 Palaiseau, France
`rida.khatoun@telecom-paris.fr`

Abstract. The rapid proliferation of social media platforms has transformed communication, enabling individuals to share opinions and influence others on an unprecedented scale. This paper addresses the challenge of quantifying the ability of social media influencers to change opinions over time. Traditional metrics, such as follower counts or engagement rates, offer a limited view of an influencer's true impact. To face this challenge, this study provides a nuanced framework based on Friedkin-Johnsen model and Sentiment Analysis for analyzing how people's opinions propagate through social networks and how influencers can affect these dynamics. The methodology consists in building interaction network graphs, detecting communities, and identifying key influencers using classic topology metrics. Then, it applies Sentiment Analysis to capture users' opinions, which are injected into the Friedkin-Johnsen model to study their evolution over time. The results show the effectiveness of the proposed approach in determining the dynamics of social influence and opinion change.

Keywords: Influencers · Friedkin-Johnsen model · Emotional Classification · Dynamic Opinion Analysis · Online Social Behaviors

1 Introduction

The rapid proliferation of social media platforms has transformed the landscape of communication, enabling individuals to share opinions and influence others on an unprecedented scale. In this dynamic environment, certain users, often referred to as influential nodes or simply influencers, build and keep active relationships with a huge number of people (i.e. his/her followers) so that they have great chance to attract, move, and change people's opinions on a wide array of topics by regularly posting new contents over time. These influencers can guide public sentiment, shape consumer behaviors, and even alter the course of political discourse. Understanding and measuring influencers' potential capabilities to effect opinion change is a crucial yet complex challenge that has significant implications for marketing strategies, political campaigns, and social research.

The primary challenge in this domain is quantifying the ability of influencers to change opinions over time. Traditional metrics, such as follower counts or engagement rates, offer a limited view of an influencer's true impact [13, 15]. These measures often fail to capture the actual features of opinion dynamics, including the persistence and depth of opinion change among followers. Moreover, the influence exerted by influencers is definitely not static, in fact, it evolves with the shifting contexts of discussions and the changing composition of social networks.

To address these challenges, there is a need for solutions to determine the extent to which influencers can manipulate people's opinions and continuously monitor this influence to prevent polarization and radicalization phenomena. This study proposes an approach to deal with the above-mentioned phenomena by leveraging advanced computational models and network analysis techniques to assess influencers' potential to change opinions over time. The core of the proposed approach is based on Friedkin-Johnsen (FJ) model [6] which employed as the foundation in our approach due to its ability to capture the persistence of individual opinions in the face of social influence. Unlike other models, such as the DeGroot model [4], which assumes full convergence to a consensus, the FJ model accounts for the stubbornness or resilience of individuals to maintain their initial opinions, even as they interact with others. This feature makes the FJ model particularly well-suited for studying opinion dynamics in the context of social media, where influencers' impact is often contested, and followers may express varied and different reactions to influencers' influence going from people who fully resist to their influence to people who only partially absorb their influence. By considering individual stubbornness, the FJ model offers a more nuanced understanding of how influencers can vary opinions over time while allowing for diversity in their followers' responses. This provides a theoretical advantage when assessing the complex and evolving nature of opinion propagation in social networks, where opinions do not always fully align.

Our contribution lies in extending this model with sentiment-aware analysis, which not only traces opinion changes but also assesses the emotional depth and reach of influencers' content. This novel combination of the FJ model with sentiment analysis and network topology metrics offers a holistic and actionable measure of influencers' true impact, moving beyond traditional metrics such as follower count or engagement rates that often fail to capture these dynamics. The model extension we introduced first extracts influencers and communities by using graph topological metrics and a community detection algorithm, respectively, and then analyzes their opinion evolution through sentiment-aware opinion modeling. The proposed model exploits a strategy to assess an influencer's impact on people's opinions by comparing a scenario that includes the influencer with one that excludes them. The reported experiments demonstrate how the proposed approach enables the analysis of influencers' capabilities in affecting opinions and emotional reactions within their communities. Furthermore, our results show that while topological metrics determine influencers' reach in a network, they do not fully capture their effective influence on opinions. The sentiment-aware opinion modeling introduced provides a more comprehensive view of the emotions spread by influencers within the community, yielding deeper insights into their influence.

The rest of the paper is organized as follows: Sect. 2 discusses related work, Sect. 3 presents the proposed approach, Sect. 4 reports the experiments to validate the method, Sect. 5 discusses experiments findings, Sect. 6 highlights limitations to the approach, and finally conclusions close the paper (Sect. 7).

2   Related Work

The study of influencers and their impact on opinion dynamics has garnered significant attention across various disciplines, including marketing, political science, and sociology. This section reviews the literature on social influence analysis reporting challenges and solutions.

Many researchers tried to quantify influencers' influence, to this purpose early approaches relied heavily on simple metrics such as follower counts and engagement rates (likes, comments, shares) or community structure to estimate influence [14]. While these metrics provide a baseline understanding, they often overlook the deeper aspects of influence, such as the ability to change opinions or drive sustained engagement.

Topology-based solutions are still explored, in fact more sophisticated approaches have employed network analysis techniques to identify influential nodes within social networks. An example is the work of Zhang et al. [15] introducing multi-scale centrality algorithm to assess node influence in complex networks. Another interesting work [13] proposes a semi-local centrality measure trying to compensate for pros and cons related to global (Betweenness centrality) and local (node degree) centrality metrics. Zhao et al. [16] try to fill the gap between degree-based and k-shell-related metrics by introducing another semi-local metric extending k-shell metric with structural hole to rank nodes by their influence. Another important research line regards influence maximization techniques that consist in finding out the most influencing users in social networks to maximize their reach. The work of Guo et al. [8] presents an hybrid method combining multi-scale propagation strength and repulsive force of propagation field to solve the maximization problem. Chen et al. [3] presents an influence maximization algorithm based on random walk algorithm that samples the influence spreading paths and estimates the influence spreading of the nodes. All of these methods consider the structure of the network and the positional advantage of users, providing a more nuanced view of influence. However, they do not take into account the contents they spread and the evolution of their influence degree over time.

Understanding how opinions change over time within social networks has been a central topic of research. Classical models such as the DeGroot model

[5] and its extensions have provided a foundational framework for studying consensus formation. The (FJ) model [17], which incorporates individual resistance to opinion change, offers a more realistic representation of opinion dynamics by acknowledging that individuals do not always fully conform to their neighbors' views. Recent advancements have extended these models to consider the temporal evolution of influence. For instance, the Hegselmann-Krause model [1] introduces bounded confidence levels, where individuals only interact with others holding similar opinions. Since this study aims to inspect similarities as well as heterogeneity between influencers and the rest of their communities, it delves deeper into FJ model considering resistances to change opinions.

Other works have explored the role of content characteristics, such as emotional valence and informativeness, in enhancing an influencer's reach and impact. The work of Pratama and Tjahyanto [11] explores sentiment analysis using a machine learning approach and fake account categories to see the influence of fake accounts on sentiment analysis. Gao et al. [7] introduced a method combining centrality measures and user emotions to detect topical influencers. Moreover, algorithms that curate content feeds and recommend connections can significantly amplify the reach of certain users, creating a feedback loop that enhances their influence [12]. Understanding these algorithmic effects is crucial for accurately measuring and modeling influencer impact. The reviewed literature mainly focuses on finding global, local and semi-local topological metrics to find potential influencers. In truth, they determine influencers' reach but do not estimate their actual social influence and capabilities to affect others' opinions. To achieve that, content analysis over time is crucial, but research on this topic does not consider topological relationships behind who writes and shares contents in the network. To fill this gap, this work inspects the synergy of relating topology-based influencers selection with sentiment-aware opinion modeling based on content analysis to measure how much influencers affect global opinions arose in their communities.

3 The Methodology

This section introduces the methodology that employs the FJ model to study the role of the influencers and the connection between their social influence and the emotional reactions they cause to members of the communities they belong to. The complete pipeline is composed of five components, as shown in Fig. 1: *Data*

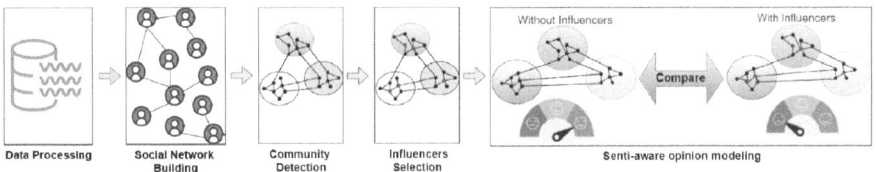

Fig. 1. Data pipeline.

Processing, Social Network Building, Community Detection, Influencer selection, and *Senti-aware opinion modeling.* The rest of the section details the pipeline components.

3.1   Data Processing

First as preliminary data processing, the data considered for this study consists in social posts or tweets shared by the users in social networks, such as Twitter, Facebook, Instagram etc. On Twitter for instance, the followers of a user A are those users who will receive messages from user A. The friends of a user A are those users from whom user A receives messages. Thus, information flows from a user to his/her followers. However, these relationships do not fully capture interaction among social network users. In fact, the interaction among users on these social networks is based on content (i.e., people replying or retweeting tweets written by other people on Twitter). Therefore, tweet authors and users who reply to tweets over time are extracted from each tweet at this stage and are passed to the next component.

3.2   Social Network Building

This component is in charge of building a social network graph that captures interactions among users. By considering tweets or posts shared by the users, the reply relationship between users is employed to build a topology that better captures interactions among users (i.e., the user who tweets and the user who replies to the tweet). A reply topology is built as a directed and weighted graph at each time frame considered. Let $G^t = (V^t, E^t)$ be the graph snapshot at the time frame t^{th}, where nodes in V^t represent Twitter users who have posted at least one tweet, and the edges in E^t denote the replies to tweets made by users towards other users. Each edge from a user v_i^t to v_j^t is weighted by the frequency of v_i^t's replies to v_j^t. This weighted directed graph effectively illustrates the interactions among users concerning the content they shared, providing a foundation for further analyses of user behaviors and the dynamic communities formed through their interactions.

3.3   Community Detection

After constructing the graph networks, the *Community Detection* component aims to detect communities. This is done by applying the METIS algorithm [9] to the networks, which identifies communities based on the tweet reply graph network built before. As a result, this component reveals communities at each time frame by grouping people who engage with the same topics.

3.4   Influencer Selection

The *Influencer Selection* component allows the identification of those nodes that act as influencers in each detected community. To achieve this, a variety of topology-based metrics are evaluated. In particular, degree centrality and PageRank metrics are employed, as they are among the most widely utilized methods in literature [14].

Degree Centrality quantifies the influence of a node by counting the number of direct relationships it holds with other network nodes. It can be mathematically expressed as follows:

$$C_D(i) = \deg(i) \tag{1}$$

where $\deg(i)$ is the degree of node i, i.e., the number of edges connected to node i.

On the other hand, PageRank [2] is an algorithm designed to rank nodes of a graph according to their relationships and the relevance associated with such relationships. In detail, each node receives a ranking determined by the structure of its incoming links. The PageRank of a node i, denoted as $PR(i)$, is given by the following iterative formula:

$$PR(i) = \frac{1-d}{N} + d \sum_{j \in \text{In}(i)} \frac{PR(j)}{\deg_{\text{out}}(j)} \tag{2}$$

where d represents the damping factor, typically set around 0.85, while N is the total number of nodes in the graph. The term $\text{In}(i)$ signifies the set of nodes that have edges directed toward node i, and $\deg_{\text{out}}(j)$ is the out-degree of node j.

To carry out the influencer selection process, several steps are followed at each time frame t. First, degree centrality and PageRank metrics are calculated for each node based on the network structure. Next, these metric values are normalized for consistency. Then, the average of the two normalized metric values for each node is computed. Nodes with an average value exceeding 0.5 are identified as influencers of each communtiy at the tth time frame. Finally, the most recurrent influencers present in all four time frames are selected as the final influencers for our analysis. For sake of simplicity, this strategy allows to capture those nodes that are considered influencers within the network they belong to over different time frames.

3.5   Sentiment-Aware Opinion Modelling

The last component in the employed approach is Senti-aware opinion modelling which is dedicated to capture the dynamic of users' opinions as emotional reactions over time. The senti-aware opinions may change over time under social influence, hence it is crucial to understand the dynamics of these opinions over time. The Senti-aware opinion modelling component is based on FJ approach which aims to measure opinions of influencers as well as global opinions of each community determined by averaging the opinions of its members. In this way, the FJ model allows to measure variations in community global opinion over time with respect to higher or lower social influences exerted by the influencers.

The FJ model is a mathematical framework used to study opinion dynamics within a social network. It describes how individuals' opinions evolve over time based on their initial opinions, their interactions with others, and their level of stubbornness or resistance to change their minds. The FJ model is represented as follows:

$$\mathbf{x}(t + 1) = \mathbf{W}^t \mathbf{x}(t) + (\mathbf{I} - \mathbf{W}^t)\mathbf{s} \tag{3}$$

where $\mathbf{x}(t)$ is the vector of initial opinions at time t, $\mathbf{s}$ is the vector of stubbornness levels of the individuals, $\mathbf{I}$ is the identity matrix. $\mathbf{W}^t$ is an $N \times N$ matrix representing the influence weights between individuals in the network. Each entry w_{ij} denotes the weight that individual j has on individual i.

In this work, the evolution of opinions over time is governed by Equation (3), which is applied for each time frame, utilizing the initial opinions at $t = 0$ as the starting point. For each time frame t, the updated opinions $\mathbf{x}(t)$ are computed based on the influence matrix $\mathbf{W}^t$ to generate new opinions for that time frame, starting with the initial opinions (.e., opinions captured at $t = 0$). The process is repeated sequentially for each time frame,in which the previously computed opinions serve as the initial opinions for the next time frame. This approach allows for the observation of how the initial sentiments evolve over time based on the social interactions modeled in the graphs.

Within this approach, the user's opinions are represented as emotional reactions. To achieve this, firstly, all user tweets were pre-processed, which included cleaning and tokenization, followed by RoBERTa [10] approach that has been applied to all tweets of each user/node to extract the sentiment score and associate him/her with specific emotional perspectives. In this way, each user/node can show emotional perspectives over time that we will call senti-aware opinions from now on. So, the senti-aware opinions are encoded as initial opinions of the individuals that are encapsulated in an N-dimensional vector $\mathbf{x}(0)$, with $x_i(0)$ representing the average sentiment of user i at time $t = 0$. The influence between these individuals is quantified by an $N \times N$ influence matrix W^t, where N is the number of individuals in the network. Each element w_{ij}^t of W^t indicates the weight of influence that individual j has on individual i at the time t, typically normalized so that the sum of the weights for each individual equals one ($\sum_j w_{ij} = 1$). Moreover, a uniform stubbornness score is used in the FJ model so that it encodes the historical sentiment scores of users. The stubbornness score is used to assess the new opinions across the four time frames, such that $s_i = 1$ for all the users, indicating that all individuals are completely stubborn and do not alter their initial opinions.

Moreover, to definitely address the actual role of the influencer, the *Senti-aware opinion modeling* component applies the above FJ-based opinion model to a network including the selected influencers, and a network not including them. The comparison between these two networks over the four time frames by means of new opinions generated for the two networks allows to sequentially evaluate the evolution of the influencers' roles.

4 Experiments and Analysis

4.1 Dataset

To validate the proposed approach, the Twitter Vaccination Dataset[1] was used. It was built by using TWINT[2] and includes all tweets containing the search string: vaccination. Along with the tweet text, the dataset comprises the date and time when the tweet was published, and the location of the user (if provided), in addition to other data available include the user id, follower ids, and friends' ids. The dataset includes tweets spanned over a year, and includes about 391,690 tweets written by 57,176 unique users. According to the amount of tweets per day, we have been divided it into four subsets (Q1, Q2, Q3, Q4), each one covering a three-month time frame. The dataset was processed as detailed in Sect. 3.

4.2 Preliminary Sentiment Analysis

To prepare the dataset for the two experiments, it pass through a series of component as mentioned in 3 section. The graphs were constructed as detailed in the subsection 3.2, where users were depicted as nodes connected by reply relationships. This process resulted in four weighted graphs, each corresponding to a distinct time frame. After constructing the graphs, the METIS algorithm was employed to partition the four graphs into communities, resulting in two communities for each time frame. Following the community detection, the influencers were identified as detailed in Subsection 3.4.

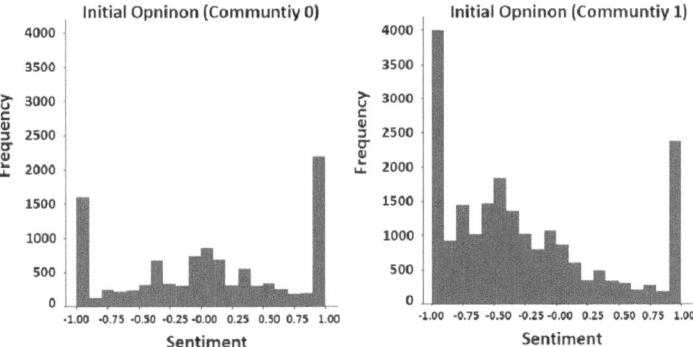

Fig. 2. The sentiment analysis distribution of the Twitter vaccination dataset across the detected communities

[1] https://www.kaggle.com/datasets/keplaxo/twitter-vaccination-dataset/data.
[2] https://github.com/twintproject.

Table 1. Top influential users along with their meta data

Twitter User	Number of Tweets	Retweets_Count	Likes_Count	Influence Score	Community
dortimi	45,369	33,937	502,687	0.88	1
mcfunny	39,569	30,157	490,624	0.79	1
kidoctr	670	1,056	39,562	0.64	1
gavi	5,074	1,569	90,698	0.62	0
nytimes	2,062	2,032	75,980	0.61	1
thereal_truther	376	106	26,044	0.58	1
ianfmusgrave	1,056	55	46,521	0.55	1
badzoot7	450	61	36,812	0.52	1

Before seeing results let us make a preliminary analysis of the initial sentiment distribution within the detected communities. The sentiment analysis, depicted in Fig. 2, shows that Community 0 exhibits a balanced mix of opinions, with a wide range of both positive and negative sentiments. This diversity indicates that Community 0 includes users with multiple different perspectives. In contrast, Community 1 demonstrates a strong negative reaction towards the topic of vaccinations, suggesting a more homogeneous group with a predominantly negative stance on this issue. Thus, the initial sentiment distribution highlights that Community 0 is characterized by a broader spectrum of opinions, while Community 1 is unified by a shared negative sentiment.

Furthermore, the analysis of influencers within these communities, presented in Table 1, reveals a significant disparity in influence and engagement. Community 1 presents a bigger number of influencers and some of them have way higher influence scores than those joining Community 0. This is confirmed by the fact that the top influencers in Community 1 exhibit the highest levels of tweet interactions, including retweets and likes. This concentration of influential users and their high engagement levels suggest that Community 1 has a more active and influential presence within the network than Community 0. The correlation between high influence scores and tweet interaction metrics indicates that these top influencers play a pivotal role in shaping discussions and driving interactions within Community 1. Overall, the preliminary analysis outlines the diverse opinions in Community 0 and the concentrated influence and negative sentiment in Community 1, setting the stage for further modeling of opinion dynamics.

4.3   Results on Opinion Evolution

In this experiment, the Senti-aware opinion modelling as detailed in Subsect. 3.5 was applied in two cases, first one with presence of the influencers in the representation graph, and the second without the influencers.

Figure 3 illustrates the FJ model results for Community 0, showing the impact of influencer "gavi" on opinion evolution. In Fig. 3(a), "gavi" maintains a stable and higher opinion value compared to Community 0, which fluctuates

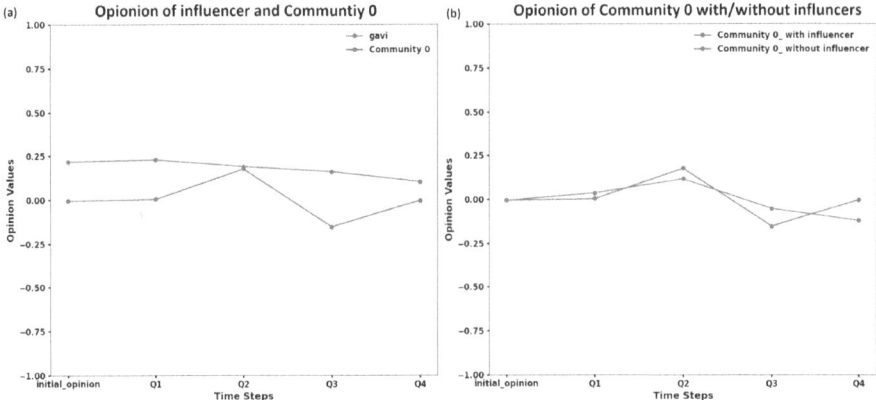

Fig. 3. The sub figures illustrate the changes in community 0 opinions, both with and without the presence of influencers in the graph.

more. In Fig. 3(b), the absence of "gavi" does not significantly affect the community's opinion dynamics, as both curves are quite similar with minor differences at Q3 and Q4. This suggests "gavi" did not noticeably influence the community's collective sentiment over time.

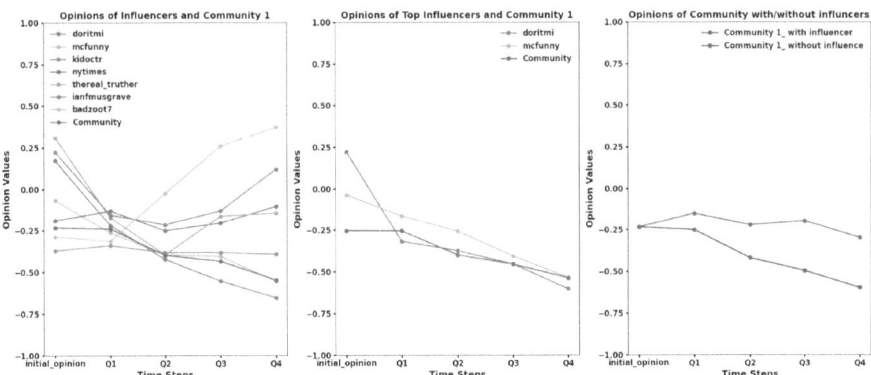

Fig. 4. The subfigures illustrate the changes in community 1 opinions, both with and without the presence of influencers in the graph.

Figure 4 presents the opinion evolution within Community 1 and its influencers through three sub figures. In Fig. 4(a), Community 1's opinion is relatively stable with minor variations, while the seven influencers show diverse trends. In Fig. 4(b), focusing on the top two influencers with influence scores greater than 0.8, "dortimi" and "mcfunny", shows that the remaining five influencers ("idocct",

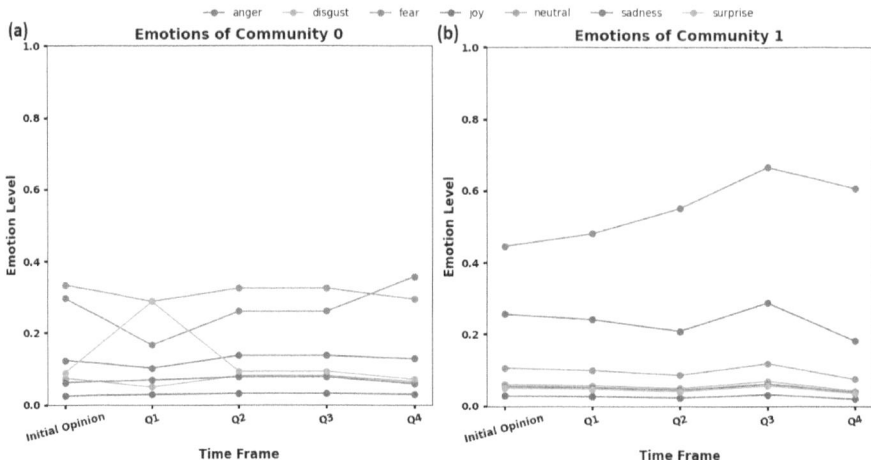

Fig. 5. The subfigures (a,b) illustrate emotion changes in community 0 and community 1

"rhymes", "thereal_truther", "mrmrgrave", and "badroot7") do not significantly impact the community's opinion compared to the top two influencers. The top two influencers predominantly shape Community 1's opinion, driving it towards more negative sentiments, while the others have negligible effects. Figure 4(c) examines the opinion evolution of Community 1 after removing all influencers and re-running the model. Here, the community's opinion curve shows a noticeable difference compared to the previous subfigures, demonstrating more stable but consistently lower opinion values. This contrast highlights the crucial role of the top influencers in driving opinion dynamics. The removal of all influencers results in a more subdued and less fluctuating opinion trend, indicating the substantial influence of "dortimi" and "mcfunny".

4.4   Results on Emotion Analysis

This subsection examines the emotional dynamics between influencers and their communities and how these interactions shape the emotional development of the communities.

This subsection examines the emotional dynamics between influencers and their communities and how these interactions shape the emotional development of the communities.

Figure 5 presents the emotional evolution within Community 0 and Community 1 over different time frames (Initial Opinion, Q1, Q2, Q3, Q4). In Fig. 5(a) for Community 0, emotions show noticeable fluctuations. While Fig. 5(b) for Community 1 shows 'Fear' and Anger' as dominant emotions. 'Fear' increases from 0.4 initially to above 0.6 in Q3, then slightly declines to 0.55 in Q4. 'Anger' decreases from 0.35 to below 0.25 in Q4, highlighting a different emotional pattern compared to Community 0.

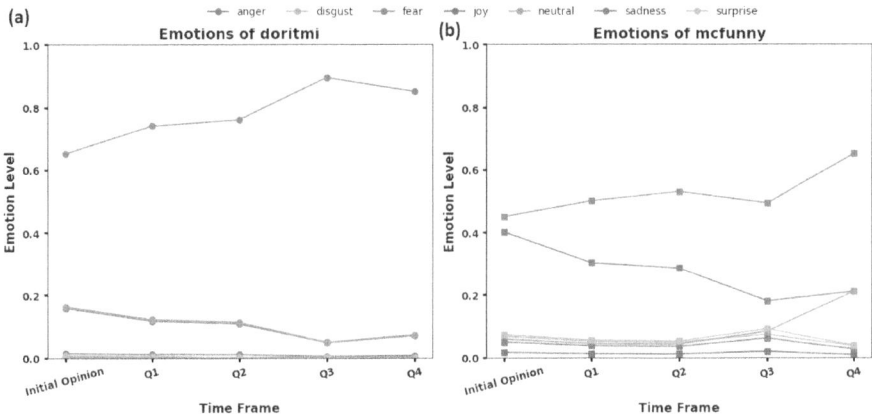

Fig. 6. The subfigure (a) illustrate the emotion of dortimi, subfigure (b) illustrate the emotion of mcfunny

Given the pronounced 'Fear' and 'Anger' in Community 1, we further investigate the emotions of the top two influencers, "dortimi" and "mcfunny", due to their significant impact on community opinions. Figure 6(a) shows "dortimi"'s emotional evolution with 'Fear' increasing from 0.65 to nearly 0.9 by Q4, while 'Anger' remains low and decreases over time. Figure 6(b) depicts "mcfunny;;'s emotions, with 'Fear' rising from 0.35 to around 0.6 in Q4 and 'Anger' decreasing towards Q4.

The analysis reveals a strong alignment between the emotions of these top influencers and Community 1. The prevalent 'Fear' in "dortimi" and "mcfunny" corresponds with the increasing 'Fear' in Community 1, but in truth they present different emotional pictures: one very clear (i.e. high on anger flat on al other emotions), the other one more mixed or confused (i.e., he/she expresses anger alongisde fear.). This suggests that even if two top influencers have similar or close influencer scores, as reported in Table 1, they may spread different emotions within the community.

5 Discussion

The total influence scores presented in Table 1 offer valuable insights into the role of individual influencers in shaping community opinions. The analysis of influence scores reveals that top influencers, such as "dortimi" and "mcfunny", who have the highest influence scores (close to 0.8), are shown to have a significant impact on the opinion evolution of Community 1, as reported in Fig. 4. These high scores correlate with the substantial ability of those influencers to drive the collective sentiment of the community, going towards negative opinions. The other influencers, with lower scores, exhibit less pronounced effects on community opinion dynamics. This suggests that the influence score is a critical metric in determining the extent to which an influencer can sway community opinions. In the other community, the influencer gavi does not significantly affect opinion evolution of Community 0. This is evident from the similarity in opinion trajectories with and without gavi's presence in Fig. 3. This discussion emphasizes that while high influence scores are generally indicative of significant impact, moderate scores do not necessarily guarantee influence, pointing to the multifaceted nature of social influence in online communities.

On the other hand, the analysis of the emotional dynamics within the community highlights the importance of not only considering the influencer scores but also the emotional content of their communications. While high influencer scores are crucial in shaping community opinions, it is essential to recognize that influencers with similar scores can propagate different emotions. The comparison between "dortimi" and "mcfunny" highlights their distinct emotional patterns, despite similar influence scores they exhibit distinct emotional patterns as illustrated in Fig. 6. Specifically, "mcfunny" impacts the community by intensifying anger in addition to fear, while "dortimi" mainly evokes fear. This shows that focusing solely on influence scores may overlook the significant emotional impact, such as the anger driven by "mcfunny".

In a nutshell, the opinion experiment generally reveals that the influencer score is important in determining the extent of an influencer's impact on community opinions. However, a deeper analysis of influencers' emotional impact shows that content analysis is crucial alongside the topology-based influencer score to fully understand their influence. Therefore, it is imperative to integrate an analysis of the emotional content in influencer communications alongside their topological influence scores.

6   Limitations

Although this study offers valuable insights through a detailed analysis, it is essential to acknowledge certain limitations.

One key limitation is the (FJ) model reliance on a static stubbornness parameter, which may not fully capture real-world variations in how individuals resist opinion changes over time. The model also assumes linear opinion dynamics, which simplifies complex social behaviors that are often influenced by non-linear and unpredictable factors.

Furthermore, the FJ model presumes a symmetrical network structure, while actual social networks are heterogeneous and exhibit asymmetric patterns of influence that could impact the accuracy of measuring an influencer's true effect. Even with the integration of sentiment-aware analysis to capture emotional dynamics, the model still falls short of reflecting how emotions can shift in response to external factors, which plays a crucial role in opinion development.

These limitations suggest that while our approach provides valuable insights, future work could focus on refining the model to account for non-linear dynamics, asymmetric influence patterns, and dynamic emotional shifts to better reflect real-world opinion propagation.

7 Conclusion

This work proposed a framework based on FJ model to study the role of influencers in influencing and propagating the opinion through a social network. The approach determines the evolution of influencers' and global community' opinions in terms of emotional reactions towards the vaccination topic. The findings highlight the critical role of top influencers, particularly those with high social influence scores, in shaping both the opinions and emotional states of a community. In summary, understanding influencers' potential capabilities to effect opinion changes is essential. Our approach sheds light on this complex phenomenon, emphasizing the need for considering both influence scores and emotional dynamics to fully comprehend community behaviors in online networks.

Future research directions will further explore FJ and other models to jointly evaluate multiple parameters, among toplogical and content-based, to fully comprehend influencers' roles in online communities.

References

1. Bernardo, C., Vasca, F.: A mixed logical dynamical model of the hegselmann–krause opinion dynamics. IFAC-PapersOnLine **53**(2), 2826–2831 (2020). https://doi.org/10.1016/j.ifacol.2020.12.952, https://www.sciencedirect.com/science/article/pii/S2405896320313069, 21st IFAC World Congress
2. Brin, S., Page, L.: The anatomy of a large-scale hypertextual web search engine. Comput. Netw. ISDN Syst. **30**(1–7), 107–117 (1998)
3. Chen, L., Wang, Y., Chen, Y., Li, B., Liu, W.: Random walk-based algorithm for distance-aware influence maximization on multiple query locations. Knowl.-Based Syst. **249**, 108820 (2022). https://doi.org/10.1016/j.knosys.2022.108820, https://www.sciencedirect.com/science/article/pii/S0950705122003902
4. DeGroot, M.H.: Reaching a consensus. J. Am. Stat. Assoc. **69**(345), 118–121 (1974)
5. Ding, Z., Chen, X., Dong, Y., Herrera, F.: Consensus reaching in social network degroot model: The roles of the self-confidence and node degree. Inform. Sci. **486**, 62–72 (2019). https://doi.org/10.1016/j.ins.2019.02.028, https://www.sciencedirect.com/science/article/pii/S0020025519301380
6. Friedkin, N.E., Johnsen, E.C.: Social influence and opinions. J. Math. Sociol. **15**(3–4), 193–206 (1990)
7. Gao, L., Wu, Y., Xiong, X., Tang, J.: Discriminating topical influencers based on the user relative emotion. IEEE Access **7**, 100120–100130 (2019). https://doi.org/10.1109/ACCESS.2019.2929548
8. Guo, C., et al.: Heterogeneous network influence maximization algorithm based on multi-scale propagation strength and repulsive force of propagation field. Knowl.-Based Syst. **291**, 111580 (2024). https://doi.org/10.1016/j.knosys.2024.111580, https://www.sciencedirect.com/science/article/pii/S0950705124002156
9. Karypis, G.: Metis: Unstructured graph partitioning and sparse matrix ordering system. Technical report (1997)
10. Liu, Y., et al.: Roberta: a robustly optimized bert pretraining approach. arXiv preprint arXiv:1907.11692 (2019)

11. Pratama, R.P., Tjahyanto, A.: The influence of fake accounts on sentiment analysis related to covid-19 in indonesia. Proc. Comput. Sci. **197**, 143–150 (2022). https://doi.org/10.1016/j.procs.2021.12.128, https://www.sciencedirect.com/science/article/pii/S1877050921023528, sixth Information Systems International Conference (ISICO 2021)

12. Zhang, C., Li, G., Zhang, H.: Multi-view contrastive learning with virtual social group influence for social recommendation. Knowl.-Based Syst. **294**, 111751 (2024). https://doi.org/10.1016/j.knosys.2024.111751, https://www.sciencedirect.com/science/article/pii/S0950705124003861

13. Zhang, K., Zhou, Y., Long, H., Wang, C., Hong, H., Armaghan, S.M.: Towards identifying influential nodes in complex networks using semi-local centrality metrics. J. King Saud Univ. - Comput. Inform. Sci. **35**(10), 101798 (2023). https://doi.org/10.1016/j.jksuci.2023.101798, https://www.sciencedirect.com/science/article/pii/S131915782300352X

14. Zhang, X., Zhu, J., Wang, Q., Zhao, H.: Identifying influential nodes in complex networks with community structure. Knowl.-Based Syst. **42**, 74–84 (2013). https://doi.org/10.1016/j.knosys.2013.01.017, https://www.sciencedirect.com/science/article/pii/S0950705113000294

15. Zhang, Z., Wang, J., Xu, Y.: Research on node influence in complex network based on multi-scale centrality algorithm. Proc. Comput. Sci. **228**, 1128–1133 (2023). https://doi.org/10.1016/j.procs.2023.11.147, https://www.sciencedirect.com/science/article/pii/S1877050923019786, 3rd International Conference on Machine Learning and Big Data Analytics for IoT Security and Privacy

16. Zhao, Z., Li, D., Sun, Y., Zhang, R., Liu, J.: Ranking influential spreaders based on both node k-shell and structural hole. Knowl.-Based Syst. **260**, 110163 (2023). https://doi.org/10.1016/j.knosys.2022.110163, https://www.sciencedirect.com/science/article/pii/S095070512201259X

17. Zhou, Q., Wu, Z.: Multidimensional friedkin-johnsen model with increasing stubbornness in social networks. Inform. Sci. **600**, 170–188 (2022). https://doi.org/10.1016/j.ins.2022.03.088, https://www.sciencedirect.com/science/article/pii/S0020025522003164

Environmental Sustainability of AI: Estimating CO_2e Emissions Across Cloud, Edge, and Fog Paradigms

Elio Masciari[ID] and Enea Vincenzo Napolitano[(✉)][ID]

DIETI, University of Naples Federico II, Naples, Italy
{elio.masciari,eneavincenzo.napolitano}@unina.it

Abstract. This research aims to assess the environmental impact of Artificial Intelligence (AI), focusing on carbon dioxide equivalent (CO2e) emissions, a comprehensive measure that includes greenhouse gases. With rising trends in global CO2e emissions calling for urgent remediation of environmental sustainability, this paper assesses the environmental footprint of AI systems in the context of web engineering across the computing continuum, including cloud, edge and fog paradigms. The study seeks to strike a balance between AI advances and environmental sustainability. The core contribution of this paper is the development of a novel equation for estimating CO2e emissions from AI models, providing a metric for assessing the environmental impact of AI tools.

Keywords: Environmental Impact · Carbon Footprint · Green AI

1 Introduction

The current situation represents an environmental crisis, characterised by the excessive consumption of natural resources and the lack of effective measures to address air pollution. This situation is further complicated by the considerable increase in global carbon dioxide (CO_2) emissions and the rise in global temperatures. To address these issues, it is essential that all industries implement prompt and effective measures to enhance the well-being of the Earth's ecosystem. The most recent figures indicate that global emissions from energy sources related to CO_2 increased by 0.9%, representing an additional 321 million metric tons of CO_2 in the atmosphere in 2022. This represents a new record of more than 36.8 billion metric tons.

In 2019, ICT accounted for 3.7% of the total carbon dioxide equivalent (CO_2e) emissions [4]. The term 'CO_2e' is used to denote a unit of measurement that enables the comparison of the emissions of various greenhouse gases based on their global warming potential (GWP). The GWP is a standardised measure that evaluates the amount of heat absorbed by the emissions of one tonne of a gas over a specific duration, typically 100 years, in comparison to the heat absorbed by one tonne of CO_2. This measure allows for the comparison

M. Barhamgi et al. (Eds.): WISE 2024, LNCS 15463, pp. 409–418, 2025.
https://doi.org/10.1007/978-981-96-1483-7_33

of the effect of different gases in terms of their equivalent warming potential relative to CO_2.

The increasing prevalence of AI technologies is accompanied by a notable rise in energy consumption, particularly during the training phase, which requires substantial power. This energy usage frequently originates from non-renewable sources, leading to the release of CO_2 and other greenhouse gases that contribute to the accumulation of heat in the atmosphere. By assessing the environmental impact of AI technologies through the lens of their CO_2e emissions, a comprehensive picture emerges that encompasses the role of diverse greenhouse gases.

In the context of web engineering, the computing continuum, which encompasses the cloud, edge, and fog paradigms, plays a pivotal role in the deployment and operation of AI systems. Each of these paradigms presents unique challenges and opportunities in terms of energy consumption and environmental impact [7]. The scalability of cloud computing is a significant advantage, but it is also a technology that relies on large data centres with considerable energy requirements. Although edge computing reduces latency and bandwidth usage, it entails the deployment of AI models on numerous distributed devices, which collectively consume a considerable amount of energy. Fog computing, as an intermediary layer, aims to achieve a balance between the aforementioned aspects, while still contributing to the overall energy footprint.

2   Related Work

The environmental impact of AI techniques has recently received considerable attention, the study by Verdecchia et al. (2023) [9] study put emphasis on the environmental impact of AI. Their exhaustive survey revealed a significant increase in research on Green AI since 2020, with almost 98 scientific papers on the topic. This exponential growth indicates that the AI community is becoming aware of its ecological responsibilities. The following subsections will examine a selection of studies that investigate the role of AI in cloud, edge, and fog computing systems.

2.1   AI Sustainability in Cloud Computing

AI has become an integral part of optimizing various aspects of cloud computing, particularly in managing and reducing energy consumption in data centers.

In their study, Tuli et al. (2022) present HUNTER, an AI-based approach to resource management for cloud data centres (CDCs) [8]. HUNTER has been designed with thermal and energy considerations in mind and is capable of managing a wide range of resources, including servers, memory, storage, network, and cooling systems. The results demonstrated that HUNTER was capable of effectively optimising energy consumption, reducing SLA (Service Level Agreement) violations, and improving overall efficiency with regard to time, cost, and temperature management. Walsh et al. (2021) present a preliminary investigation into the energy consumption patterns associated with machine learning (ML) training in cloud environments [10]. They demonstrate that transfer learning can significantly reduce energy consumption. In their study, Dodge et al. (2022) propose a framework for measuring software carbon intensity, with a particular focus on operational carbon emissions [3]. It is proposed that location-based and time-specific marginal emissions data per energy unit be used to accurately measure carbon emissions. The framework was subsequently applied to a set of contemporary models, encompassing applications in natural language processing and computer vision.

2.2   AI Sustainability in Edge Computing

Edge computing, where data processing occurs closer to the source of data generation, presents opportunities and challenges to optimize energy consumption and reduce carbon footprint.

Chahid et al. (2022) present an innovative framework that integrates Internet of Things (IoT) and AI technologies to reduce CO_2e emissions and improve environmental sustainability. This framework uses IoT sensors, cameras, smartphone interactions, and a waste API, coupled with a real-time event clustering approach for efficient waste management. Using AI to process data at the edge, this model effectively reduces the energy and resources required for data transmission and centralized processing. The study highlights the potential of such frameworks as foundational research for developing strategies to optimize CO_2e emission reductions [2]. Aguirre et al. (2019) proposed a circuit incorporating the SCT-013030 sensor and the ESP8266 NodeMcu V2 module to monitor energy consumption in smart homes via a wireless sensor network. An artificial neural network identifies unusual energy consumption patterns in home appliances. The data collected by the wireless sensor network is stored in a MySQL database hosted on a Raspberry Pi 3B server. This AI-enabled circuit can alert users to abnormal energy consumption, promoting more efficient energy use, and potentially reducing overall household energy consumption and associated CO_2e emissions [1]. Trihinas et al. (2022) highlight the challenges and needs associated with the deployment of AI-driven IoT services in edge computing environments, particularly with respect to energy consumption and carbon footprint. The paper presents an edge-driven object detection application that serves as a reference for understanding the energy implications of such deployments.

Integrating AI into edge computing not only improves operational efficiency, but also contributes to broader environmental sustainability goals.

2.3   AI Sustainability in Fog Computing

Fog computing, an extension of cloud computing, brings computing closer to the edge of the network.

In their study, Ji et al. (2020) present an architecture for Visual Internet of Everything (V-IoE) within Fog Radio Access Networks (F-RANs). The researchers systematically analyze the key challenges associated with V-IoE from the perspective of F-RANs and propose a crowd V-IoE architecture. Experimental results show that this architecture significantly improves performance by reducing bandwidth requirements, energy consumption and latency. This demonstrates the potential of integrating AI with fog computing to achieve more efficient and sustainable network operations [6].

Yosuf et al. (2021) explore the energy savings achievable through the strategic placement of Deep Neural Network (DNN) inference models in a Cloud Fog Network (CFN) architecture. Using Mixed Integer Linear Programming (MILP), they formulate this placement as a network embedding problem, balancing processing and networking to optimize power consumption. The study compares the performance of the CFN architecture with a baseline approach, the Cloud Data Center (CDC), and finds that the CFN architecture yields significant energy savings [11].

Iftikhar et al. (2022) propose a novel approach called TESCO, which is designed to perform simulations to evaluate multiple candidate scheduling decisions and select the optimal one. The study shows that TESCO outperforms the state-of-the-art COSCO scheduler, which relies on single simulations, by achieving better performance with low overhead. This approach highlights the value of using AI-driven simulation and scheduling techniques to optimise resource allocation and minimise energy consumption in fog computing environments [5].

3   Definition of Sustainability Metrics

As discussed previously, the environmental impact of AI is of significant relevance. The energy consumption of AI systems has a direct impact on greenhouse gas emissions and the long-term sustainability of AI technologies. This section has two main objectives. Firstly, we will define and explain the key variables that influence energy consumption in AI systems across cloud, edge, and fog computing paradigms. Secondly, we will define and experimentally validate our equations that model the relationships among these variables.

3.1   Introduction of Variables

To comprehensively evaluate AI's energy consumption and environmental impact, we identified three key variables:

1. Computational Power,
2. CO_2e Emission Coefficient,
3. Energy Efficiency.

These variables are crucial for understanding AI's energy dynamics. In the following, we define the rationale for using these variables and their interactions, formalized in our equation, which also includes proper dimensionality analysis.

Computational Power. The computational power required for AI tasks depends on several factors:

- N: Number of parameters used to train the AI model. This indicates the complexity of the model and affects the computational power required.
- A: Algorithm used to build the AI model. Different algorithms exhibit varying computational efficiencies, which affects energy consumption.
- H: Hardware used. This considers differences among CPUs, GPUs, and TPUs, as each hardware architecture has different energy efficiencies and power consumption profiles.

CO_2e Emission Coefficient. The CO_2e emission coefficient is influenced by:

- S: Energy service provider. Different providers offer varying energy mixes (e.g., fossil-based, renewable), affecting CO_2e emissions for a specific system.
- L: Geographical location of the data center. This accounts for local weather conditions, which can affect energy efficiency due to extreme temperatures requiring increased energy for cooling or heating.

Energy Efficiency. Energy efficiency considers the following aspects:

- R: Cooling systems. This encompasses the energy consumption of internal cooling systems and the cooling infrastructure of the facility hosting the hardware.
- T: Total time for training, tuning, and inference. This measures the impact on energy consumption due to the intensive computing steps involved in AI tasks.

Lifecycle Impact and Optimization. Additional factors influencing overall CO_2e emissions include:

- L_c: Lifecycle impact of hardware. This includes production, transportation, disposal, or recycling of hardware.
- O: Energy optimization. This evaluates technologies and strategies, such as load balancing, to reduce energy consumption.
- D: Data communication and network bandwidth. Although data transmission energy consumption might be negligible for a single device, it can be significant for complex systems.

Based on the above variables, we define the following intermediate values:

- P: Computational power, depending on N, A, and H.
- C: CO_2e emission coefficient, influenced by S and L.
- η: Energy efficiency, based on H and R.
- λ: Lifecycle impact, energy optimization, and data communication contributions from L_c, O, and D.

Finally, the total CO_2e emissions (E) are estimated by combining these values to measure the overall environmental impact of the AI system in terms of greenhouse gas emissions. This comprehensive evaluation process allows us to accurately assess the sustainability of AI technologies in cloud, edge and fog computing paradigms, facilitating the implementation of more environmentally friendly AI practices.

3.2   The AI Emission Equation

The objective of these equations is to encapsulate the complex influence of various factors that affect the carbon footprint of AI across the paradigms of cloud, edge, and fog computing.

Computational Power. The computational power, denoted as P, is a crucial metric in the context of AI. It can be quantified in terms of FLOPS (Floating Point Operations per Second), which is calculated based on the number of cores, the clock frequency, and the operations per clock cycle. This measure is particularly significant for AI models with a high number of parameters, as they require higher computational resources.

The evaluation of computing power depends on a combination of hardware and software components. The central processing unit (CPU) is the main component responsible for executing instructions and performing calculations. The CPU's clock speed is a critical factor in determining the number of instructions the CPU can process per second. Additionally, the number of cores in a CPU affects its parallel processing capabilities, which in turn impacts the overall computing power.

The total computing power of a system is obtained by multiplying the clock speed by the number of cores and the number of instructions per clock cycle. This value provides a comprehensive evaluation of the system's ability to handle complex computations, which is particularly relevant for AI applications.

$$P = \text{Core Count} \times \text{Clock Speed (GHz)} \times \text{Operations per Clock Cycle} \quad (1)$$

This equation provides a method to quantify the computational power P of an AI system. The *Core Count* reflects the parallel processing capability of the CPU, enabling simultaneous execution of multiple tasks. The *Clock Speed*, measured in gigahertz (GHz), represents the speed at which the CPU executes instructions. Finally, the *Operations per Clock Cycle* indicates the efficiency of the CPU in processing instructions per clock cycle.

CO_2e Emission Coefficient. The CO_2e emission coefficient, denoted as C, is a dynamic measure that takes into account the energy provider, the geographical location, and hardware type. Using these variables, we can measure the environmental impact in terms of kg CO_2e/kWh.

$$C = \frac{\text{Geographical Dependence Factor (Provider, Location)}}{\text{Consumption (HW, Provider)} \times \text{Usage Time}} \quad (2)$$

The value is influenced by the energy provider's energy supply composition, such as the proportion of renewable and non-renewable sources. This value is always publicly available for each location's geographical placement of the facility, playing a crucial role due to the different energy production methods and regulations across regions. The emissions produced are also affected by the choice of hardware, as devices and components have varying levels of energy efficiency. Finally, the total emissions produced are correlated with the duration of the computation (denoted as Usage Time).

Energy Efficiency. Energy efficiency, expressed as η, is a key metric that depends on the hardware and cooling systems used. It is expressed in terms of FLOPS/kWh, providing a trade-off between computing power and energy efficiency.

$$\eta = \frac{\text{Useful Output (FLOPS)}}{\text{HW Consumption (kWh)} + \text{Cooling Consumption (kWh)}} \quad (3)$$

This value provides a comprehensive measure of energy efficiency. The Useful Output variable takes into account the "usable performance" of the system, measured in floating-point operations per second (FLOPS). In a sense, this value represents the productive computing power of the system and is provided by the hardware vendor. The denominator combines the energy consumption of the hardware and cooling systems, measured in kilowatt-hours (kWh). This approach for computing η considers not only the direct energy consumption of the computing hardware but also the often underestimated energy required to maintain optimal operating temperatures via proper cooling systems.

Dimensional Analysis. This section explores the connections between the key variables of our model, focusing on the dimensional congruence of the overall components of the overall energy consumption and CO_2e emissions of AI systems.

– **Relationship between P and η**: By dimensional analysis, considering that P is measured in FLOPS and η in FLOPS/kWh, we can leverage these variables to understand their impact on energy consumption. This leads us to consider the total energy consumption as $\frac{P}{\eta}$, which dimensionally is expressed in kWh.

– **Influence of C**: As C is measured in $kgCO_2e$/kWh, we can examine its impact on the total CO_2e emissions by including it in our equations, multiplying it by $\frac{P}{\eta}$, thus obtaining a $kgCO_2e$ value.

$$E = \left(\frac{P(H, N, A) \times C(S, L, H, T)}{\eta(H, R)} \right) + \lambda(L_c, O, D) \qquad (4)$$

To sum up, this equation summarizes the relationships between the computational power (P), CO_2e emission coefficient (C), and energy efficiency (η), along with the additional factors like lifecycle impact (L_c), energy optimization (O), and data communication impact (D).

By applying our framework, researchers and developers can estimate the environmental impact of their AI systems, enabling them to make more informed decisions about hardware selection, energy sources, and operational strategies.

4   Case Study: EHBDA

In this section, we demonstrate the application of our equation to estimate CO_2e emissions in a real-life scenario. We trained several AI models using the E-Health Big Data Analytics (EHBDA) cluster at the University of Naples Federico II, located in the San Giovanni a Teduccio campus. The EHBDA cluster hosts several hardware resources, including a Nvidia DGX A100 station, four machines equipped with GPUs, and a large SSD storage system of 750TB. For clarity, we will discuss the results obtained for the DGX workstation, which is a high-performance hardware.

We trained several AI algorithms widely used in both research and commercial applications, namely, *U-Net Medical, ResNet50, BERT - Base, DLRM*.

For the CO_2e analysis, we assigned the values of the following variables based on the hardware specifications of the EHBDA cluster:

- **H**: Nvidia A100
- **L**: Naples, Italy
- **P**: 312 teraFLOPS
- **C**: 0.209 kgCO_2e/kWh
- **η**: 51 GFLOPS/kWh
- **R**: Air conditioners (0.5 kWh)
- **S**: Mix of non-renewable (49%) and renewable energy sources (51%) as provided by our energy provider

Applying our equation to these hardware configurations and standardized values of the variables allows us to estimate the environmental impact of the EHBDA cluster in terms of CO_2e emissions, as shown in Table 1.

The table shows significant differences between the number of parameters in the models and their CO_2e emissions. For example, BERT-Base, which has a relatively high number of parameters (110M), shows a different relationship between energy consumption and CO_2e emissions compared to other models with fewer parameters. This suggests that energy efficiency is not directly proportional to the size or complexity of the model. At the same time, there are

Table 1. Environmental impact of AI models trained on EHBDA

Algorithm	T (hours)	N (Parameters)	E (kg CO_2e)
U-Net Medical	0.1	30M	0.13
DLRM	0.27	25M	0.35
BERT - Base	3.6	110M	4.60
ResNet50	4.1	25M	5.24

more energy-efficient models available, such as U-Net Medical, which can serve as less impactful alternatives for certain applications.

This real-life application shows how our comprehensive equation can be used to estimate and compare the CO_2e emissions of different AI models in cloud, edge, and fog computing environments. By providing detailed insights into the environmental impact of various configurations, algorithms, and hardware choices, our approach helps to make more sustainable decisions in AI development and deployment.

5   Conclusion and Future Work

The central focus of our research is the formulation of equations that are specifically designed to estimate CO_2e from AI models. This is achieved by introducing the appropriate variables and examining their dynamics through the lens of dimensional analysis. This study presents a critical approach to quantifying the environmental impact of AI, highlighting the necessity of aligning technological advances with environmental sustainability.

A particular area that requires further investigation is the measurement of variables such as L_c, which represents the environmental impact of a component over its lifespan. This task is particularly challenging due to the multitude of factors that influence a component's environmental footprint over time. Further research could seek to develop more sophisticated methodologies or technologies that can accurately capture these complexities.

A further avenue for future research could be the development of software capable of automatically assessing CO_2e emissions. Such a tool would enable users to rapidly and accurately assess the environmental impact of their algorithms and computational choices, thereby fostering environmental responsibility and awareness within the technology community, both in research and industry. Incorporating estimation capabilities into programming languages, such as Python, could facilitate the estimation of the environmental impact of code prior to execution, thereby encouraging the adoption of more environmentally conscious coding practices. Such an integration could facilitate more informed decision-making among developers regarding the efficiency and environmental impact of their algorithms, with the potential for a considerable reduction in the carbon footprint of computational processes through design.

Acknowledgement. We acknowledge financial support from the project PNRR MUR project PE0000013-FAIR.

References

1. Aguirre-Núñez, J.A., et al.: Energy monitoring consumption at iot-edge. In: 2019 IEEE International Autumn Meeting on Power, Electronics and Computing (ROPEC), pp. 1–6. IEEE (2019)
2. Chahid, Y., Chahid, I., Benabdellah, M.: A framework for reduce co2 emissions and enhancing environmental sustainability protection using iot and artificial intelligence. J. Theor. Appl. Inform. Technol. **100**(16) (2022)
3. Dodge, J., et al.: Measuring the carbon intensity of ai in cloud instances. In: Proceedings of the 2022 ACM Conference on Fairness, Accountability, and Transparency, pp. 1877–1894 (2022)
4. Freitag, C., Berners-Lee, M., Widdicks, K., Knowles, B., Blair, G., Friday, A.: The real climate and transformative impact of ict: A critique of estimates, trends, and regulations. Patterns **2**, 100340 (09 2021). https://doi.org/10.1016/j.patter.2021.100340
5. Iftikhar, S., et al.: Tesco: Multiple simulations based ai-augmented fog computing for qos optimization. In: 2022 IEEE Smartworld, Ubiquitous Intelligence & Computing, Scalable Computing & Communications, Digital Twin, Privacy Computing, Metaverse, Autonomous & Trusted Vehicles (SmartWorld/UIC/ScalCom/DigitalTwin/PriComp/Meta), pp. 2092–2099. IEEE (2022)
6. Ji, W., Liang, B., Wang, Y., Qiu, R., Yang, Z.: Crowd v-ioe: Visual internet of everything architecture in ai-driven fog computing. IEEE Wirel. Commun. **27**(2), 51–57 (2020)
7. Masciari, E., Napolitano, E.V.: The environmental cost of high performance computing system simulation. In: 2024 32nd Euromicro International Conference on Parallel, Distributed and Network-Based Processing (PDP), pp. 289–292. IEEE (2024)
8. Tuli, S., et al.: Hunter: Ai based holistic resource management for sustainable cloud computing. J. Syst. Softw. **184**, 111124 (2022)
9. Verdecchia, R., Sallou, J., Cruz, L.: A systematic review of green ai. Wiley Interdisciplinary Reviews: Data Mining and Knowledge Discovery, p. e1507 (2023)
10. Walsh, P., Bera, J., Sharma, V.S., Kaulgud, V., Rao, R.M., Ross, O.: Sustainable ai in the cloud: Exploring machine learning energy use in the cloud. In: 2021 36th IEEE/ACM International Conference on Automated Software Engineering Workshops (ASEW), pp. 265–266. IEEE (2021)
11. Yosuf, B.A., Mohamed, S.H., Alenazi, M.M., El-Gorashi, T.E., Elmirghani, J.M.: Energy-efficient ai over a virtualized cloud fog network. In: Proceedings of the Twelfth ACM International Conference on Future Energy Systems, pp. 328–334 (2021)

Artificial Intelligence for Trauma Registry in Emergency Departments

Ahmad Abdel-Hafez[1,2]([✉]), Ben Gardiner[3], and Oussama Djedidi[1]

[1] University of Doha for Science and Technology, Doha, Qatar
ahmad.abdel-hafez@udst.edu.qa
[2] Clinical and Business Intelligence, eHealth, Brisbane, QLD, Australia
[3] HealthCare Improvement Unit, Clinical Excellence Queensland, Brisbane, QLD, Australia

Abstract. Queensland has 122 hospitals with over 1.8 million presentations to Emergency Departments (ED) each year. Each facility operates with different electronic medical records systems, making it challenging to identify which ED presentations are related to traumatic injury caused by traffic accidents. Identifying traffic accidents related injuries help with CTP (Compulsory Third Party) insurance claims. Manual identification of trauma cases typically took up to five hours per day, relying on keyword searches in ED presentation descriptions and diagnoses. This study aimed to evaluate the implementation of a new machine learning (ML) model to screen and identify ED admitted patients with traumatic injuries caused by traffic accidents. After building a unified data collection platform for ED presentations, manual identification was initially used as a reference point. The machine learning model was implemented using supervised classification and decision tree processes, such as: LightGBM and XGBoost. The traffic-related injury model achieved an accuracy of 98% classifying 167,541 ED trauma admissions. This artificial intelligence (AI) tool has redistributed screening hours, allowing clinical staff to focus more on quality improvement initiatives. The introduction of AI tools in trauma has proven to be valuable and clinical teams are now using the developed model, which has reduced screening manual task by 80–85%.

Keywords: Trauma · Machine Learning · Emergency Department · Artificial Intelligence

1 Introduction and Related Work

Emergency departments (EDs) across Queensland handle over 1.8 million presentations annually, spread across 122 hospitals. Each facility operates different electronic medical records (EMR) systems, making it challenging to standardize any electronic operations including the identification of trauma cases. Identifying trauma-related presentations is done using keywords search to reduce manual screening of ED admissions aiming to build a state-wide registry for trauma admissions at ED. Shortlisted trauma cases are then used by clinicians to identify different outcomes such as if the trauma case is caused by a traffic accident or not. Traditionally, this process is done by a manual review of case descriptions often takes clinicians up to five hours per day. This manual process typically involves searching through free-text descriptions for relevant keywords or diagnoses, which is not only time-consuming but also prone to human error. Addressing this inefficiency has become an important focus to reduce improving efficiency and accuracy of the process and save invaluable clinicians' time.

Artificial intelligence (AI) and machine learning (ML) have increasingly been recognized for their potential to transform healthcare by automating tasks, improving diagnostic accuracy, and enhancing decision-making. AI models can analyze vast amounts of data in real-time, identifying patterns that might be missed by human observers. In healthcare, AI has been applied to a range of areas including diagnostics(16), personalized medicine [1, 2], and predictive analytics [3–5]. Machine learning has shown promise in creating models that can learn from historical data and make accurate predictions, reducing the workload of healthcare professionals and improving patient outcomes [6].

There has been a growing body of research exploring the application of AI in healthcare. Early work focused on using rule-based systems [7] for diagnostics and care planning, which were limited by their need for explicit programming and inability to learn from new data. More recent efforts have employed machine learning algorithms, such as support vector machines, decision trees, and neural networks, to automate complex tasks like disease prediction [8], imaging analysis [9], and patient risk stratification [10]. These models have been integrated into clinical workflows, providing decision support and improving the speed and accuracy of diagnoses in several medical fields [11].

The literature demonstrates significant advancements in machine learning models for healthcare, particularly with the emergence of more sophisticated techniques like deep learning and ensemble methods. LightGBM [12] and XGBoost [13], two of the most popular gradient boosting algorithms, have been widely used in healthcare for their ability to handle large datasets and produce highly accurate models. These techniques, combined with natural language processing (NLP) for analyzing unstructured text, have been applied to a range of healthcare problems, from predicting patient deterioration [6] to optimizing treatment plans [1]. The increasing availability of healthcare data has accelerated the development of these models, allowing for continuous learning and improvement in performance.

However, there has been limited work specifically targeting the identification of trauma-related cases in EDs using AI. Some studies have explored the use of AI for broader emergency care applications, such as triaging ED admissions [14] or identifying sepsis [15]. Several studies utilized NLP methods to process free text on ED admission description to predict different outcomes such as predicting admission at time of triage, prediction of critical illness, and prediction of triage score [16]. One study aimed to utilize NLP methods on clinical documents to enable automated injury scoring for trauma cases [17]. However, few limited numbers of publications focused on the challenge of automating manual ED description by clinicians to build a registry for trauma cases. The manual nature of trauma registry building, combined with the variability in EMR systems and data quality across hospitals, has made it difficult to standardize this process. This work seeks to address this gap by developing machine learning models specifically designed to identify traffic accidents within trauma cases using ED data.

In this paper, we present a method for automating traffic crash identification within pre-identified trauma ED admissions using machine learning models developed in collaboration with the Clinical and Business Intelligence (CBI) department at eHealth Queensland. We describe the collection and preprocessing of ED data, the development of three machine learning models to identify traffic-related injuries and classify injury severity, and the deployment of these models in a real-time clinical environment. This paper makes the following important contributions: 1) providing an example of deployed ML model for healthcare use, showing the impact of integrating ML models and how they can save invaluable clinical time, 2) addressing the ML model ability to produce accurate results using simple free text added by clinicians to ED description and diagnosis fields, and 3) validating the developed model using a real dataset.

2   Method

2.1   Data Collection

For this study, we utilized a comprehensive dataset that includes all Emergency Department (ED) trauma admissions across 122 hospitals in Queensland. The primary data sources used for model development and evaluation were triage codes and free-text descriptions from ED electronic medical records. These free-text inputs were critical for building machine learning models, as they provided a more nuanced understanding of the clinical context of each admission beyond the structured data.

The dataset consisted of 167,541 trauma ED presentations, of which 4,676 records were labeled as traffic accident-related injuries. This represents approximately 2.8% of the total dataset, highlighting a significant imbalance in the class distribution. To handle this imbalance, we employed techniques such as oversampling of the minority class (traffic crash cases), as well as advanced decision-tree-based algorithms which inherently manage imbalanced datasets better by assigning greater weight to minority class observations during the training process [17–20]. The imbalance observed in the dataset posed a challenge, but through careful feature engineering and the use of advanced machine learning techniques, the models achieved high accuracy and performance levels, effectively supporting clinicians in real-time trauma screening.

2.2   Data Preparation

The data preparation process for building the machine learning models involved several steps to ensure the dataset was clean, structured, and ready for ML model training. These steps are essential for effective feature extraction and model performance, particularly when dealing with free-text inputs and imbalanced datasets.

Data Cleansing. The initial step in data preparation was removing records that contained null or empty values in the "presenting problem" field, as these records lacked the necessary information for identifying trauma cases. This step reduced noise in the dataset, ensuring that only relevant records were included. After that, we performed comprehensive text cleaning on the free-text descriptions. This involved several sub-steps including the removal of stop words, whitespace, empty lines, special characters, and punctuation, lemmatization, and lowercasing. These preprocessing steps helped streamline the text data and make it suitable for further feature extraction.

Feature Extraction. Once the data is cleaned, the next step was converting the free-text data into features that could be used by machine learning algorithms. To extract features, we used a bag-of-words model with unigram representation, where each word is treated as a unique feature. To optimize the feature space and reduce noise, we limited the vocabulary by applying frequency thresholds. Specifically, Minimum Frequency, as we included only words that appeared in at least 100 records, and Maximum Frequency where words that appeared in more than 95% of the records were excluded, as they were too common to provide useful information. These frequency thresholds were chosen based on experiments to balance the trade-off between including too many irrelevant terms and retaining sufficient information for classification tasks. We have tested more than 100 combinations of different thresholds and selected the threshold values which produced the best results.

TF-IDF Representation. To represent the text data, we employed the Term Frequency-Inverse Document Frequency (TF-IDF) method. This approach assigns higher weights to words that are frequent in individual records but rare across the entire dataset, allowing us to capture the most distinctive terms for each presentation. TF-IDF helped us reduce the influence of common but uninformative words while emphasizing more relevant terms for trauma identification.

$$TF(t, d) = \frac{\text{Number of times term t appears in document d}}{\text{Total number of terms in document d}} \tag{1}$$

$$IDF(t,D) = \log\left(\frac{\text{Total number of documents in the corpus N}}{\text{Number of documents containing term t}}\right) \tag{2}$$

$$TF - IDF(t, d, D) = TF(t, d) \times IDF(t,D) \tag{3}$$

Handling Imbalanced Datasets. To address the significant class imbalance in the traffic accidents model, we tested various sampling techniques to balance the dataset and improve model performance. We experimented with a range of oversampling methods including SMOTE (Synthetic Minority Over-sampling Technique) [18], SMOTENC (SMOTE for Nominal and Continuous data) [18], SVMSMOTE (Support Vector Machine SMOTE) [19], BorderlineSMOTE [20], and ADASYN (Adaptive Synthetic Sampling) [21]. Oversampling methods are used to increase the number of minority class instances (e.g., traffic crash and major injury cases) in the training data. These techniques generate synthetic samples of the minority class, helping to prevent the model from being biased toward the majority class.

In contrast, under-sampling techniques are used to reduce the majority class to reach into a balance in the dataset. We didn't test any under-sampling techniques as they have a clear disadvantage of possibility of losing important information from the dataset, especially when the dataset dimensionality is high. However, we also tested hybrid approaches like SMOTETomek [22] and SMOTEEN [23], which combine oversampling with under-sampling by generating synthetic minority instances and removing specific majority class samples.

These methods aim to enhance the model's ability to distinguish between the minority and majority classes while reducing noise from redundant majority samples. Through extensive experimentation, we identified the best sampling strategy for each model, balancing the dataset effectively and improving the overall performance of the classification tasks. The results section shows the performance of different implemented methods. As we will show in the Results section, we collected results of different performance metrics to compare the implemented balancing techniques and select the best performing one.

By following these steps in data preparation, we created a robust and balanced dataset that was well-suited for the machine learning models used in this study, ultimately enabling accurate and reliable identification of trauma cases in near real-time.

2.3 Feature Selection

We conducted a thorough feature selection process, testing various methods to identify the most relevant features to include in our final model. Not all features are useful to build a reliable and accurate ML model. In many cases, having more features could lead to decreased model performance. To confirm the importance of the selected features, we performed statistical analysis, ensuring that all features included in the final models had a p-value of less than 0.05 when tested against the outcome variables. This statistical significance test reinforced the relevance of each feature in relation to the model's objectives.

We experimented with different feature selection techniques to isolate the most important predictors for each model such as SelectFromModel method which was used with tree-based estimator, XGBoost, to automatically select the most informative features based on feature importance scores. This allowed us to focus on the most impactful predictors while discarding less relevant variables. We also tested Recursive Feature Elimination (RFE) [24] which recursively removes features and selects a subset that contributes the most to model performance. This method helped refine the feature set by evaluating model accuracy as features were eliminated.

In addition to algorithmic feature selection, we collaborated with subject matter experts (SMEs) in trauma and emergency medicine to identify and include features that might have clinical relevance. Their insights helped ensure that the selected features were not only statistically significant but also meaningful in a clinical context.

After applying these feature selection techniques and incorporating SME feedback, the final list of features used in the models included 49 features, focusing on keywords related to vehicle accidents, injury mechanisms, and specific trauma descriptions. The selected features provided the model with the most relevant and statistically significant predictors, contributing to the high accuracy of the traffic crash models.

2.4 Model Development and Algorithm Selection

To develop robust machine learning models for identifying traffic-related injuries, general injuries, and predicting injury severity, we employed a systematic approach that involved testing multiple algorithms and validation techniques. The model development process focused on exploring various methods and balancing strategies to determine the optimal solution for each task. Given the healthcare context, our goal was not only to maximize accuracy but also to ensure that the models were interpretable, reliable, and aligned with clinical requirements.

We implemented a stratified 5-fold cross-validation to evaluate model performance. This method ensured that each fold contained a similar proportion of trauma and non-trauma cases, preserving the distribution of the minority and majority classes across all splits. Stratified cross-validation is particularly important when working with imbalanced datasets, such as those in this study, where traffic-related injury cases and major injuries were significantly underrepresented compared to non-traffic and minor injuries. This approach enabled us to evaluate models under consistent conditions and obtain reliable estimates of model accuracy, minimizing the risk of overfitting while providing a comprehensive view of performance across different subsets of data.

Algorithm Selection. We tested a variety of machine learning algorithms, each offering unique advantages for handling structured data and text features. The algorithms tested included:

Logistic Regression. A linear baseline model for binary classification

Random Forest. [25] A powerful ensemble method that builds multiple decision trees and combines their predictions. This model is known for handling large numbers of features and providing robust performance on tabular data. Additionally, it offers a degree of interpretability through feature importance scores, which is valuable in understanding which factors contribute most to classification.

Gradient Boosting. [26] An ensemble technique that sequentially builds trees, optimizing each one based on the errors of previous iterations. This method is effective at reducing bias and variance, leading to higher performance.

LightGBM. A highly efficient implementation of gradient boosting designed for large-scale datasets, offering faster training times and lower memory consumption compared to traditional gradient boosting methods.

XGBoost. Another gradient boosting method known for its speed and performance. XGBoost includes regularization techniques to prevent overfitting and is well-suited for handling imbalanced datasets.

Stochastic Gradient Descent (SGD). [27] Used with linear classifiers, particularly Support Vector Machines (SVM) [28], to optimize decision boundaries for classification. SVMs are effective for high-dimensional data and work well with text-based features, making them suitable for handling the diverse feature set in this study.

Despite the high-performance potential of neural network models, we chose not to implement them in this study due to the specific requirements of healthcare-related applications. Neural networks, especially deep learning models, are often considered "black box" models, making it challenging to interpret their decision-making processes. In healthcare, where model transparency and explainability are critical, the ability to understand and explain model predictions is essential for gaining clinician trust and ensuring patient safety.

Metrics and Experiment Design. To evaluate the performance of each model, we employed a comprehensive set of metrics, including accuracy, precision, recall, F1-score, and the Area Under the Curve (AUC) of the Receiver Operating Characteristic (ROC). These metrics provided a holistic view of model performance, enabling us to assess the models' ability to correctly classify injury cases, balance between sensitivity and specificity, and handle class imbalances effectively. The use of multiple evaluation criteria ensured that we captured various aspects of model quality, such as its robustness, discriminatory power, and clinical applicability.

3   Results

The comparison of machine learning methods and data balancing techniques in terms of precision and recall reveals several key findings as they appear in Fig. 1. XGBoost demonstrates superior overall performance compared to other methods, achieving consistently higher precision and recall values across various balancing techniques. For instance, XGBoost with SMOTE achieves a precision of 0.835 and a recall of 0.927, which surpasses the highest values attained by Random Forest and Gradient Boosting models, regardless of the balancing method used. This indicates that XGBoost is less sensitive to the choice of balancing method and performs well across different scenarios.

In terms of balancing methods, SMOTE and its variants (e.g., SVMSMOTE and BorderlineSMOTE) generally outperform other balancing techniques, such as ADASYN and SMOTEEN, in both precision and recall. For example, Logistic Regression with SMOTE achieves a precision of 0.822 and recall of 0.916, while the same model using ADASYN only reaches a precision of 0.816 and recall of 0.908. This suggests that SMOTE-based techniques are more effective at enhancing model performance by mitigating class imbalance, irrespective of the machine learning method applied.

The best-performing model for predicting traffic accidents from textual ED descriptions was achieved using the XGBoost algorithm combined with SMOTE to address class imbalance in the dataset. This model exhibited outstanding performance across multiple evaluation metrics, achieving a precision of 0.83, a recall of 0.92 as shown in Fig. 1, and an F1-score of 0.87 for the minority class (traffic-related injuries). The high recall value indicates the model's strong capability to correctly identify a substantial majority of true traffic accident cases, thereby minimizing the number of false negatives (actual traffic accidents records labelled negatively).

The model's precision score of 0.83 indicates that when it predicts a traffic-related injury, it is correct 83% of the time. This helps reduce the number of false positives, ensuring that non-traffic injury cases are not incorrectly flagged as traffic related. As a result, the number of cases that require manual review is minimized, significantly decreasing the workload on clinicians. This balance between precision and recall is represented by an F1-score of 0.87, confirming that the model provides a robust and reliable tool for identifying traffic-related trauma cases in ED presentations.

Additionally, the model's performance was further validated using the Area Under the Curve (AUC) of the Receiver Operating Characteristic (ROC) curve, which was found to be 0.96. An AUC value close to 1 suggests that the model has a high discriminatory power, meaning it can accurately differentiate between true positive cases (actual traffic-related injuries) and false positive cases (non-traffic-related injuries incorrectly classified as traffic-related). This high AUC score reflects the model's ability to balance sensitivity (recall) and specificity across various threshold levels, minimizing the rate of false positives while maintaining a high true positive rate. Such performance is crucial in this use case, where misclassifying cases can lead to unnecessary increased workload

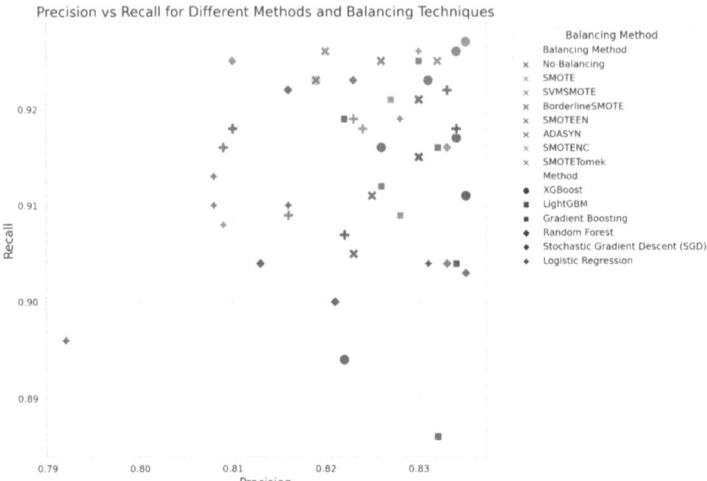

Fig. 1. A precision-recall scatter plot for the implemented methods.

for clinicians. Overall, the combination of the XGBoost algorithm with the SMOTE balancing technique proved to be effective in overcoming the class imbalance issue and enhancing the model's capacity to detect traffic-related injuries from ED data.

4   Discussion

The high-performance metrics achieved by the XGBoost model in this study have substantial clinical implications, particularly in reducing the manual screening burden on clinicians. The recall value of 0.92 ensures that the vast majority of traffic-related injury cases are correctly identified, which is critical in emergency departments where quick and accurate identification of trauma cases is essential for timely intervention. The high precision of 0.83, on the other hand, minimizes the number of non-traffic injury cases that are incorrectly flagged as traffic related. This balance between precision and recall is essential in a clinical setting because it ensures that the model not only captures most of the true traffic-related cases but also reduces the incidence of false positives, thereby optimizing clinician workload.

Clinicians reviewed the model's performance and were satisfied with its specificity and precision. Given that the specificity rate was deemed acceptable, they decided to cease manual screening for referrals that were labeled as "not traffic accident" by the model. This decision has had a profound impact on clinical operations, as clinicians are now only required to review the positive predictions made by the model. This change has led to an 80–85% reduction in the overall workload, as the need for manual verification of non-traffic-related cases has been eliminated. The significant reduction in manual screening efforts means that clinical staff can allocate more time to direct patient care and focus on critical cases that require immediate attention.

From a clinical perspective, the integration of the XGBoost model into the workflow has not only improved efficiency but also reducing manual workload helps mitigate clinician burnout, which is a common issue in high-pressure environments like emergency departments. Overall, this study demonstrates the potential of AI models in transforming trauma registry workflows. By automating the classification of ED presentations, the XGBoost model significantly reduces the administrative burden on healthcare professionals, enabling them to focus on higher-priority tasks.

5 Conclusion and Future Work

This case study demonstrates the utility of artificial intelligence (AI) tools in accurately identifying traffic-related injuries from textual Emergency Department (ED) descriptions. The successful deployment of the XGBoost model, combined with the Synthetic Minority Over-sampling Technique (SMOTE), highlights the efficiency gains and time savings for clinical teams. By automating the classification of ED presentations, the model has reduced the manual screening burden on clinicians by 80–85%, allowing them to focus on more critical cases. This integration of AI not only streamlined clinical workflows but also ensured accurate identification of trauma cases, ultimately contributing to improved patient care and operational efficiency in healthcare settings.

In future work, additional machine learning models could be developed to automate the labeling of trauma admissions for other outcomes, such as identifying general injury-related admissions and predicting injury severity. Expanding the scope of AI models in this way could further optimize the triage process and improve patient management. Moreover, incorporating more comprehensive data from patients' Electronic Health Records (EHR), including clinical notes, diagnostic results, and imaging data, could enhance the predictive power of the current models and enable the development of new models tailored to more complex clinical scenarios. Additionally, implementing a model monitoring framework would be essential to detect any potential model or data drift over time, ensuring that the AI models maintain their performance and continue to provide reliable support in dynamic clinical environments.

Acknowledgments. The authors would like to formally acknowledge the Clinical and Business Intelligence (CBI) department, eHealth Queensland, for their invaluable support in the development and hosting of the machine learning models used in this case study.

The authors have no competing interests to declare that are relevant to the content of this article.

Disclosure of Interests. The authors have no competing interests to declare that are relevant to the content of this article.

References

1. Abdel-Hafez, A., Scott, I.A., Falconer, N., Canaris, S., Bonilla, O., Marxen, S., et al.: Predicting therapeutic response to unfractionated heparin therapy: machine learning approach. Interact. J. Med. Res. **11**(2), e34533 (2022)

2. Falconer, N., Abdel-Hafez, A., Scott, I.A., Marxen, S., Canaris, S., Barras, M.: Systematic review of machine learning models for personalised dosing of heparin. Br. J. Clin. Pharmacol. **87**(11), 4124–4139 (2021)
3. Scott, I.A., De Guzman, K.R., Falconer, N., Canaris, S., Bonilla, O., McPhail, S.M., et al.: Evaluating automated machine learning platforms for use in healthcare. JAMIA open. **7**(2), ooae031 (2024)
4. Falconer, N., Scott, I.A., Abdel-Hafez, A., Cottrell, N., Long, D., Morris, C., et al.: The adverse inpatient medication event and frailty (AIME-frail) risk prediction model. Res. Soc. Admin. Pharm. **20**, 796–803 (2024)
5. Parsons, R., Blythe, R., Cramb, S., Abdel-Hafez, A., McPhail, S.: Development of an electronic medical record-based prognostic model for inpatient falls with internal-external cross-validation. J. Med. Internet Res. **26**, e59634 (2024)
6. Brankovic, A., Hassanzadeh, H., Good, N., Mann, K., Khanna, S., Abdel-Hafez, A., et al.: Explainable machine learning for real-time deterioration alert prediction to guide pre-emptive treatment. Sci. Rep. **12**(1), 11734 (2022)
7. Seto, E., Leonard, K.J., Cafazzo, J.A., Barnsley, J., Masino, C., Ross, H.J.: Developing health-care rule-based expert systems: case study of a heart failure telemonitoring system. Int. J. Med. Informatics **81**(8), 556–565 (2012)
8. Arumugam, K., Naved, M., Shinde, P.P., Leiva-Chauca, O., Huaman-Osorio, A., Gonzales-Yanac, T.: Multiple disease prediction using Machine learning algorithms. Mater. Today: Proc. **80**, 3682–3685 (2023)
9. Rana, M., Bhushan, M.: Machine learning and deep learning approach for medical image analysis: diagnosis to detection. Multimedia Tools Appl. **82**(17), 26731–26769 (2023)
10. Mohsin, S,N, Gapizov A, Ekhator C, Ain NU, Ahmad S, Khan M, et al. The role of artificial intelligence in prediction, risk stratification, and personalized treatment planning for congenital heart diseases. Cureus. 2023;15(8)
11. An, Q., Rahman, S., Zhou, J., Kang, J.J.: A comprehensive review on machine learning in healthcare industry: classification, restrictions, opportunities and challenges. Sensors. **23**(9), 4178 (2023)
12. Ke, G., Meng, Q., Finley, T., Wang, T., Chen, W., Ma, W., et al.: LightGBM: a highly efficient gradient boosting decision tree. In: Advances in Neural Information Processing Systems, vol. 30 (2017)
13. Chen, T., Guestrin, C., (eds.) XGBoost: a scalable tree boosting system. In: Proceedings of the 22nd ACM SIGKDD International Conference on Knowledge Discovery and Data Mining (2016)
14. Feretzakis, G., Sakagianni, A., Anastasiou, A., Kapogianni, I., Tsoni, R., Koufopoulou, C., et al.: Machine learning in medical triage: a predictive model for emergency department disposition. Appl. Sci. **14**(15), 6623 (2024)
15. Van Der Vegt, A.H., Scott, I.A., Dermawan, K., Schnetler, R.J., Kalke, V.R., Lane, P.J.: Deployment of machine learning algorithms to predict sepsis: systematic review and application of the SALIENT clinical AI implementation framework. J. Am. Med. Inform. Assoc. **30**(7), 1349–1361 (2023)
16. Stewart, J., Lu, J., Goudie, A., Arendts, G., Meka, S.A., Freeman, S., et al.: Applications of natural language processing at emergency department triage: a narrative review. PLoS ONE **18**(12), e0279953 (2023)
17. Kulshrestha, S., Dligach, D., Joyce, C., Baker, M.S., Gonzalez, R., O'Rourke, A.P., et al.: Prediction of severe chest injury using natural language processing from the electronic health record. Injury **52**(2), 205–212 (2021)
18. Chawla, N.V., Bowyer, K.W., Hall, L.O., Kegelmeyer, W.P.: SMOTE: synthetic minority over-sampling technique. J. Artif. Intell. Res. **16**, 321–357 (2002)

19. Nguyen, H.M., Cooper, E.W., Kamei, K.: Borderline over-sampling for imbalanced data classification. Int. J. Knowl. Eng. Soft Data Paradigms **3**(1), 4–21 (2011)
20. Han, H., Wang, W.Y., Mao, B.H.: Borderline-SMOTE: A new over-sampling method in imbalanced data sets learning. In: Huang, D.S., Zhang, X.P., Huang, G.B. (eds.) Advances in Intelligent Computing. ICIC 2005. LNCS, vol. 3644. Springer, Heidelberg (2005). https://doi.org/10.1007/11538059_91
21. He, H., Bai, Y., Garcia, E.A., Li, S., (eds.) ADASYN: Adaptive synthetic sampling approach for imbalanced learning. In: 2008 IEEE International Joint Conference on Neural Networks (IEEE World Congress on Computational Intelligence). IEEE (2008)
22. Batista, G.E., Bazzan, A.L., Monard, M.C.: Balancing training data for automated annotation of keywords: a case study. Wob. **3**, 10–18 (2003)
23. Batista, G.E., Prati, R.C., Monard, M.C.: A study of the behavior of several methods for balancing machine learning training data. ACM SIGKDD Explor. Newsl. **6**(1), 20–29 (2004)
24. Guyon, I., Weston, J., Barnhill, S., Vapnik, V.: Gene selection for cancer classification using support vector machines. Mach. Learn. **46**, 389–422 (2002)
25. Ho, T.K.: Random decision forest. In: Proceedings of the 3rd International Conference on Document Analysis and Recognition, Montreal, pp. 14–16 August 1995, 278–282 (1995)
26. Friedman, J.H.: Greedy function approximation: a gradient boosting machine. Ann. Stat. **29**, 1189–232 (2001)
27. Bottou, L.: Stochastic gradient descent tricks. In: Montavon, G., Orr, G.B., Müller, KR. (eds.) Neural Networks: Tricks of the Trade. LNCS, vol. 7700. Springer, Heidelberg (2012). https://doi.org/10.1007/978-3-642-35289-8_25
28. Cortes, C., Vapnik, V.: Support-vector networks. Mach. Learn. **20**, 273–297 (1995). https://doi.org/10.1007/BF00994018

Blockchain and Encrypted NFTs: A New Paradigm for Intellectual Property Rights Management

Trung Phan[1], Khoa Tran[1], Khiem Huynh[1], Loc Van Cao Phu[1],
Ngan Nguyen[2(✉)], Nam Tran Ba[1], Hieu Doan Minh[1], and Anh The Nguyen[1]

[1] FPT University, Can Tho, Vietnam
Trungpht@fe.edu.vn
[2] FPT polytechnic, Ho Chi Minh City, Vietnam
nganntkpc06789@fpt.edu.vn

Abstract. This research introduces an innovative digital framework for intellectual property rights administration that leverages distributed ledger architectures and cryptographically secured digital assets. The proposed system integrates three key technological components: programmable smart contracts, cryptographically enhanced non-fungible tokens (NFTs) utilizing RSA encryption, and decentralized storage solutions through the InterPlanetary File System (IPFS). The framework underwent comprehensive evaluation across multiple blockchain infrastructures compatible with the Ethereum Virtual Machine (EVM), specifically examining implementations on four major platforms: BNB Chain, Polygon Network, Fantom Opera, and Celo. This multi-platform assessment examined critical operational parameters including computational efficiency, security robustness, and resource utilization patterns. Performance metrics encompassed transaction processing capabilities, operational costs, and system responsiveness across diverse conditions.

Keywords: Intellectual property rights · Blockchain · Data Management · NFTs · IPFS · Decentralized Storage · Smart Contracts

1 Introduction

The management of intellectual property (IP) rights in the digital age presents complex challenges that demand innovative solutions. Contemporary IP administration systems frequently encounter limitations in ensuring transparent operations, maintaining efficient processes, and preventing unauthorized usage. These systemic constraints often result in compromised asset protection and reduced value realization for intellectual property holders, necessitating the development of more robust and efficient management frameworks.

Recent technological advancements have introduced new possibilities for enhancing IP rights management. Scholarly investigations have demonstrated the potential of distributed ledger technologies in revolutionizing IP administration. Research has explored various aspects of blockchain implementation in

IP management, from establishing immutable ownership records [12] to adapting legal frameworks for digital rights administration [5]. Studies have examined innovative approaches such as digital content distribution systems [10], integrity preservation models [9], and integrated security frameworks combining digital watermarking with blockchain technology [15]. Further developments include IoT integration for enhanced protection mechanisms [14] and distributed storage solutions for content integrity [1]. Comprehensive reviews have highlighted blockchain's capacity to transform IP rights management through improved transparency and operational efficiency [17]. Our research introduces an advanced digital infrastructure that combines distributed ledger systems, cryptographically secured tokens, and decentralized storage solutions. This framework implements multiple technological innovations through the integration of blockchain technology for creating immutable IP rights records, alongside the development of automated systems for rights enforcement and transaction processing. The architecture incorporates sophisticated security protocols through multiple encryption methodologies, including RSA for asymmetric encryption, RC4 for stream cipher operations, DES for block cipher functionality, and AES for advanced security measures. Additionally, the implementation of IPFS establishes robust content management capabilities, creating a comprehensive system that prioritizes security while maintaining operational efficiency and establishing new standards for IP rights management in digital environments.

The framework underwent comprehensive evaluation across multiple blockchain platforms compatible with the Ethereum Virtual Machine (EVM) [16], including BNB Chain (formerly Binance Smart Chain), Polygon Network, Fantom Opera, and Celo Platform. This multi-platform assessment examined the system's capability to leverage platform-specific features for enhanced IP management [2,8]. The evaluation process focused on critical operational aspects, encompassing digital rights documentation, encrypted token generation and management, secure asset transfer protocols, resource utilization patterns, and detailed transaction cost analysis. This thorough assessment provides valuable insights into the practical implementation of blockchain-based IP management solutions.

Our study advances the field of intellectual property rights management through several significant contributions. The development of an integrated digital framework combines blockchain technology with encrypted digital assets, establishing new paradigms for IP protection and management. The implementation of multi-layered security protocols ensures robust protection for intellectual assets, while comprehensive platform evaluation provides detailed insights into operational efficiency metrics, security implementation effectiveness, resource utilization patterns, and economic viability analyses. Through systematic assessment of encryption methodologies, we establish optimal security configurations for digital IP management systems. These advancements create a foundation for implementing secure, efficient, and transparent IP management systems in the digital age, demonstrating how technological integration can enhance traditional IP management practices while ensuring robust protection mechanisms.

2   Related Work

2.1   Digital Innovation in Intellectual Property Administration

The integration of distributed ledger technologies into IP management has sparked significant academic discourse and technological innovation. Contemporary research has demonstrated diverse approaches to enhancing IP administration through blockchain implementation. Foundational work by Kumar and Tripathi [12] established frameworks for creating verifiable IP ownership records, while subsequent investigations by Finck and Moscon [5] examined the adaptation of copyright legislation to accommodate emerging digital paradigms. Research has progressed through various technological iterations, from streamlined content distribution mechanisms [10] to sophisticated integrity preservation systems [9]. The evolution of security frameworks has led to innovative combinations of digital watermarking with blockchain architectures [15], demonstrating enhanced capabilities in rights protection and verification. The convergence of multiple technological domains has further advanced IP management capabilities. Investigations into integrated systems combining IoT infrastructures with blockchain networks have established new paradigms for intellectual property protection [14]. The development of distributed storage solutions, particularly through peer-to-peer architectures like IPFS, has addressed fundamental challenges in content integrity and accessibility [1]. Comprehensive analyses of blockchain applications in IP management have highlighted significant improvements in operational transparency and administrative efficiency [17]. Recent developments in smart contract implementation have demonstrated enhanced potential for IP rights administration. Research by Ferro et al. [3] has explored the application of programmable legal agreements in digital asset management, while investigations into blockchain-based legal frameworks have revealed promising approaches for intellectual property protection. Academic discourse has expanded to examine the intersection of distributed ledger technologies with international legal standards [4], while practical implementations have demonstrated strengthened IP rights enforcement through technological innovation [13].

2.2   Legal Framework Evolution in Digital IP Management

The transformation of intellectual property rights management in the digital era has necessitated significant adaptation of legal frameworks and administrative processes. Contemporary research has explored multifaceted approaches to addressing emerging challenges in copyright and patent protection, particularly in response to technological advancement [18]. The integration of smart legal contracts with blockchain architectures has established new paradigms for digital asset management, as demonstrated in recent studies [3]. Scholarly examination of blockchain's implications for intellectual property law has revealed complex interactions between technological innovation and legal frameworks [7]. Research has identified specific challenges and potential solutions in blockchain-related intellectual property law [11], while investigations into copyright administration on blockchain platforms have suggested transitions toward decentralized management systems [6]. These academic contributions collectively illuminate the evolving relationship between emerging technologies and intellectual property rights, establishing foundations for modernized legal practices in the digital area.

3   System Architecture and Implementation

3.1   Contemporary IP Management Framework

Contemporary intellectual property management operates within an established framework that facilitates the protection and administration of creative works and innovations (Fig. 1). The process initiates with the conceptualization and development of intellectual assets, encompassing diverse creative works from artistic productions to technological innovations. Upon creation, innovators engage with regulatory bodies through formal registration procedures, submitting comprehensive documentation for patent, trademark, or copyright consideration. These submissions undergo rigorous evaluation processes to verify compliance with established legal standards, particularly focusing on originality and practical utility requirements. Successful verification results in formal registration, establishing legal recognition of intellectual property ownership. This certification empowers creators with exclusive rights to their intellectual assets, enabling them to exercise control over usage and distribution. The framework facilitates various forms of rights management, including enforcement against unauthorized utilization and strategic licensing arrangements. These mechanisms create economic opportunities while maintaining creator control over intellectual property implementation.

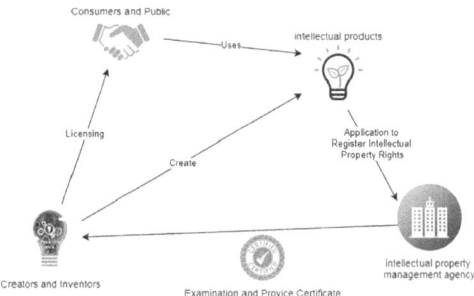

Fig. 1. Conventional Intellectual Property Management Architecture

However, contemporary IP management faces significant challenges in the digital era. International protection encounters complexities due to jurisdictional variations in legal frameworks and enforcement capabilities. Digital proliferation has intensified vulnerability to unauthorized reproduction and distribution. Additionally, stakeholder awareness regarding IP rights and protection mechanisms often remains insufficient, creating barriers to effective rights management and fair compensation distribution.

3.2   Advanced Digital Rights Management Architecture

Our proposed framework introduces an advanced digital infrastructure for intellectual property rights management, integrating distributed ledger technology, programmable smart contracts, cryptographically secured tokens, and decentralized storage solutions (Fig. 2). This architecture establishes a comprehensive system for managing digital rights throughout the intellectual property lifecycle, from initial registration through ongoing rights administration. The system architecture implements a sophisticated registration process that begins with digital asset submission through a specialized interface. Regulatory authorities utilize this platform to conduct thorough examinations, generating immutable digital certificates upon approval. These certifications are synchronized with distributed ledger systems, creating permanent, verifiable records of intellectual property rights. The blockchain approach ensures transparent documentation while maintaining data integrity throughout the verification process.

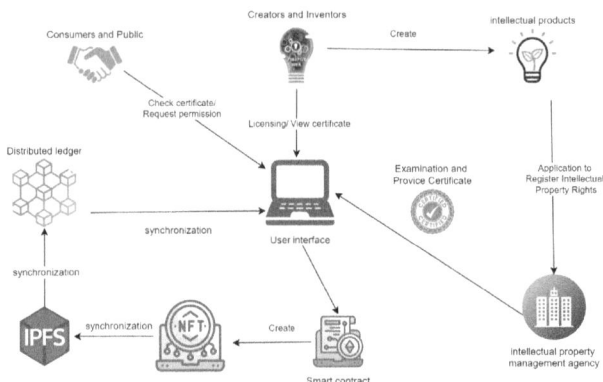

Fig. 2. Integrated Blockchain-Based Rights Management System

The framework incorporates an intuitive user interface that facilitates seamless interaction between stakeholders. Content creators access comprehensive management tools for certificate verification and licensing administration, while consumers interface with validation mechanisms and usage permission protocols. This digital environment streamlines rights management processes while enhancing transparency in intellectual property transactions. Smart contract integration automates critical aspects of rights management, establishing self-executing protocols for licensing and usage agreements. These programmable contracts, operating on blockchain infrastructure, ensure precise execution of predetermined terms while minimizing administrative overhead. The automation of contractual obligations reduces potential disputes while enhancing operational efficiency. The architecture leverages cryptographically secured non-fungible tokens to establish unique digital representations of intellectual assets. Each registered property generates an encrypted token, synchronized with decentralized storage systems through IPFS integration.

4   System Performance Analysis

4.1   Integration of Encrypted Digital Assets

The implementation of secure intellectual property management begins with the establishment of sophisticated data architectures. Our framework utilizes structured JSON formatting to encapsulate essential property information, including asset classification, detailed descriptions, temporal data, geographical indicators, and stakeholder identification (Fig. 3). This structured approach creates a foundation for implementing advanced security protocols through blockchain integration and cryptographically secured digital tokens, ensuring data integrity throughout the management process.

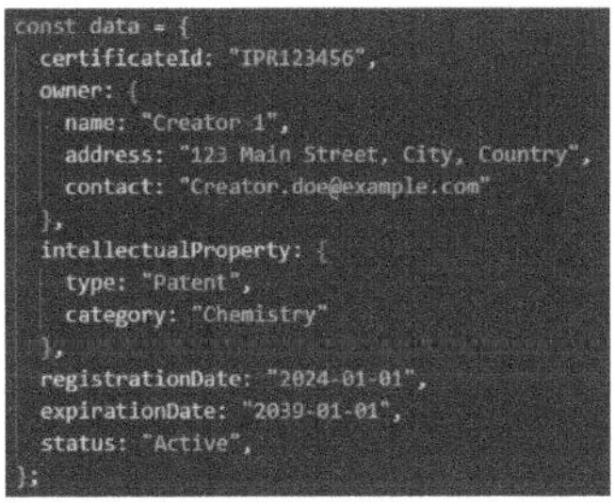

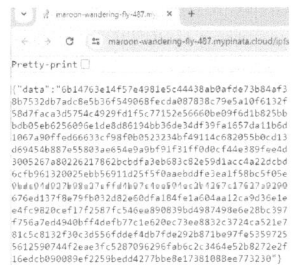

Fig. 3. Digital Asset Structure for Intellectual Property Certification

Fig. 4. Encrypted Certificate Data Retrieved from Distributed Storage

The system implements a web-based interface for accessing encrypted data stored within the IPFS network (Fig. 4). Each encrypted string represents secured metadata associated with specific intellectual property assets, requiring appropriate decryption protocols for access. This encryption-decryption mechanism ensures data integrity while maintaining accessibility for authorized stakeholders, establishing a robust foundation for digital rights management.

4.2   Transaction Cost Analysis and Platform Performance

Our research presents a detailed examination of operational costs across multiple blockchain platforms, focusing on key transactions essential for intellectual property management (Table 1). The analysis encompasses three fundamental operations: initial data registration, digital asset creation, and ownership transfer mechanisms. Transaction costs were evaluated using market rates as of March 27, 2024, 7:00:00 AM UTC.

Table 1. Cross-Platform Transaction Cost Assessment

Platform	Operation Initialization	Asset Creation	Asset Transfer
BNB Chain	0.0273134 BNB ($8.27)	0.00109162 BNB ($0.33)	0.00057003 BNB ($0.17)
Fantom	0.00957754 FTM ($0.00)	0.000405167 FTM ($0.00)	0.0002380105 FTM ($0.00)
Polygon	0.006840710 MATIC ($0.01)	0.000289405 MATIC ($0.00)	0.000170007 MATIC ($0.00)
Celo	0.007097844 CELO ($0.005)	0.0002840812 CELO ($0.000)	0.0001554878 CELO ($0.000)

The BNB Chain demonstrates robust operational capabilities with corresponding cost structures. Initial transaction creation requires 0.0273134 BNB (approximately $8.27), while digital asset generation incurs fees of 0.00109162 BNB ($0.33). Asset transfer operations cost 0.00057003 BNB ($0.17). These rates reflect the platform's established infrastructure and processing capabilities, particularly suitable for applications requiring high transaction reliability. The Fantom Opera network presents a notably efficient cost structure. Operation initialization requires 0.00957754 FTM, with digital asset creation and transfer operations costing 0.000405167 and 0.0002380105 FTM, respectively. The minimal transaction costs position Fantom as an economically advantageous platform for high-volume operations in intellectual property management systems.

Polygon's network demonstrates exceptional cost efficiency in transaction processing. Initial operations require 0.006840710 MATIC (app. $0.01), while asset creation and transfer operations cost 0.000289405 MATIC, 0.00017 MATIC respectively. These minimal fees, combined with the platform's scalability features, create favorable conditions for extensive intellectual property management operations. The Celo platform exhibits competitive operational costs, with transaction initialization requiring 0.007097844 CELO (app. $0.005). Digital asset creation and transfer operations incur fees of 0.0002840812 and 0.0001554878 CELO respectively. While these rates position slightly above certain alternatives, they align with Celo's focus on accessibility and sustainable operation.

5   Conclusion

Our research demonstrates the transformative potential of distributed ledger technologies in revolutionizing intellectual property rights administration. The integration of cryptographically secured digital assets with programmable smart contracts establishes new paradigms for managing intellectual property, addressing fundamental limitations in conventional systems. Through comprehensive evaluation across diverse blockchain infrastructures, our framework exhibits remarkable adaptability, with each platform offering unique advantages in operational efficiency and economic viability. The systematic assessment of encryption methodologies ensures robust protection mechanisms for sensitive intellectual property data, while the implementation of automated smart contracts streamlines administrative processes. This technological synthesis creates a secure, transparent, and efficient ecosystem for intellectual property management, significantly enhancing stakeholder trust and system reliability.

References

1. Benet, J.: IPFS—content addressed, versioned, p2p file system. arxiv.org (2014)
2. Duong-Trung, N., et al.: Multi-sessions mechanism for decentralized cash on delivery system. Int. J. Adv. Comput. Sci. Appl. **10**(9), 553–560d (2019)
3. Ferro, E., et al.: Digital assets rights management through smart legal contracts and smart contracts. Blockchain Res. Appl. **4**(3), 100142 (2023)
4. Fidalgo, V.P.: Blockchain (s), smart contracts and intellectual property, pp. 295–319 (2022)
5. Finck, M., Moscon, V.: Copyright law on blockchains: between new forms of rights administration and digital rights management 2.0. IIC Int. Rev. Intellect. Property Competition Law (2018)
6. Finck, M., Moscon, V.: Copyright law on blockchains: between new forms of rights administration and digital rights management 2.0. IIC - Int. Rev. Intellect. Property Competition Law **50**(1), 77–108 (2018). https://doi.org/10.1007/s40319-018-00776-8
7. Gürkaynak, et al.: Intellectual property law and practice in the blockchain realm. Comput. Law Secur. Rev. **34**(4), 847–862 (2018)
8. Ha, X.S., et al.: DEM-COD: novel access-control-based cash on delivery mechanism for decentralized marketplace. In: The 19th International Conference on Trust, Security and Privacy in Computing and Communications, pp. 71–78. IEEE (2020)
9. Halloush, Z., Yaseen, Q.: A blockchain model for preserving intellectual property. In: Proceedings of the ACM Conference (2019)
10. Kishigami, J., et al.: The blockchain-based digital content distribution system. In: 2015 IEEE Fifth International Conference on Big Data and Cloud Computing. IEEE (2015)
11. Kraus, D., Boulay, C.: Blockchains: aspects of intellectual property law. In: Blockchains, Smart Contracts, Decentralised Autonomous Organisations and the Law, pp. 240–271. Edward Elgar Publishing (2019)
12. Kumar, B., Tripathi, A.: Blockchain technology and intellectual property rights. (2018). https://nopr.niscair.res.in/
13. Lando, D.D., Miashchanava, M.V.: Strengthening intellectual property rights and blockchain technology. In: Popkova, E.G., Sergi, B.S. (eds.) ISC 2019. LNNS, vol. 198, pp. 1532–1540. Springer, Cham (2021). https://doi.org/10.1007/978-3-030-69415-9_169
14. Lin, J., Long, W., Zhang, A., Chai, Y.: Blockchain and IoT-based architecture design for intellectual property protection. Int. J. Crowd Sci. **4**, 283–293 (2020)
15. Meng, Z., et al.: Design scheme of copyright management system based on digital watermarking and blockchain. In: COMPSAC 2018. IEEE (2018)

16. Quoc, K.L., et al.: Sssb: An approach to insurance for cross-border exchange by using smart contracts. In: Awan, I., Younas, M., Poniszewska-Marańda, A. (eds.) Mobile Web and Intelligent Information Systems: 18th International Conference, pp. 179–192. Springer, Cham (2022). https://doi.org/10.1007/978-3-031-14391-5_14

17. Rambhia, V., Mehta, V., Mehta, R., Shah, R., Patel, D.: Intellectual property rights management using blockchain. In: Kaiser, M.S., Xie, J., Rathore, V.S. (eds.) Information and Communication Technology for Competitive Strategies (ICTCS 2020). LNNS, vol. 190, pp. 545–552. Springer, Singapore (2021). https://doi.org/10.1007/978-981-16-0882-7_47

18. Singh, G.: Intellectual property rights in the digital age: challenges and solutions for copyright and patent protection

Urban Computing for Disease Prediction: Type 2 Diabetes Case

Hamdi Aloulou[1]([✉]), Bessam Abdulrazak[2], and Mounir Mokhtari[1]

[1] Institut Mines Télécom, Paris, France
hamdi.aloulou@imt.fr
[2] Université de Sherbrooke, Sherbrooke, Canada

Abstract. Public health organizations play a crucial role in preventing diseases, promoting health, and addressing disparities within communities. However, their ability to monitor health trends and respond effectively to emerging threats is often obstructed by fragmented and incomplete data. This paper proposes a holistic, data-driven approach to enhance the capabilities of public health agencies in disease surveillance and community health assessment. By leveraging advanced data acquisition, AI-driven analysis, and intuitive data visualization tools, the proposed system enables public health professionals to gather, analyze, and interpret large volumes of health, environmental, and personal data in real time. The system was deployed across five cities globally, focusing on Type 2 Diabetes (T2D) as a case study. Data was collected from 1,832 participants using mobile applications, wearable devices, and environmental sensors. This approach demonstrated the potential to generate actionable insights, improve public health decision-making, and foster personalized health interventions.

Keyword: Data-driven healthcare, Type 2 Diabetes, health risk assessment, data visualization.

1 Introduction

Public health organizations are instrumental in promoting the health and well-being of communities, particularly through efforts in disease prevention, health promotion, and education. These organizations aim to monitor and manage health risks by employing epidemiological surveillance and collaborating with various stakeholders, including healthcare providers and policymakers. However, public health efforts are often hindered by fragmented data sources, limited real-time information, and challenges in data sharing, which can delay effective responses to emerging health threats. This paper proposes a holistic, data-driven approach that leverages modern tools for the acquisition, analysis, and visualization of diverse health and environmental data. By doing so, the approach aims to empower public health organizations with comprehensive insights into disease spread and community health needs, facilitating more targeted and effective interventions.

M. Barhamgi et al. (Eds.): WISE 2024, LNCS 15463, pp. 439–453, 2025.
https://doi.org/10.1007/978-981-96-1483-7_36

2   Context

Public health organizations play a vital role in safeguarding the well-being of communities by addressing health concerns. They play a pivotal role in disease prevention, health promotion, and health education initiatives, aiming to improve the overall health outcomes of individuals and communities. Through epidemiological surveillance, the public health agencies objective is to monitor the spread of diseases, identify emerging health threats, and implement strategies to contain outbreaks and mitigate risks. These agencies also collaborate with healthcare providers, policymakers, and community stakeholders to develop and implement evidence-based interventions aimed at reducing health disparities and promoting health equity.

3   Problematics

Public health organizations face several challenges in their efforts to prevent diseases and promote health within communities. One significant issue is the disparate nature of data sources, which often leads to fragmented information and gaps in understanding population health trends. Traditional data collection methods may not capture real-time or comprehensive data, resulting in delays in identifying emerging health threats or understanding community health needs. Additionally, the total volume of data generated from various sources, such as healthcare records, environmental monitoring, and behavioral surveys, can overwhelm existing systems and impede effective analysis. Without a unified approach to data collection and analysis, public health professionals may struggle to prioritize interventions, allocate resources efficiently, and tailor strategies to address specific community needs. Furthermore, the lack of standardized protocols and interoperability between data systems complicates data sharing and collaboration among different stakeholders, hindering efforts to develop holistic and coordinated public health initiatives.

4   State of the Arts

Recent advances in digital health tools and data analytics have greatly enhanced the capacity of public health organizations to collect, analyze, and respond to health data in real-time. A wide range of systems, dashboards, and mobile applications are being developed to improve disease surveillance, facilitate data-driven decision-making, and enhance public health interventions. Several notable projects in this domain highlight the evolving landscape of data-driven public health systems.

In [1], a novel Infectious Disease Surveillance (IDS) system was introduced, incorporating a mobile app and a dashboard to streamline the process of data capturing, analysis, and decision-making. The system allows outbreak data to be collected from both mobile devices and desktop PCs, and processed in real-time through a client-server architecture. The dashboard provides real-time summaries of outbreak data, enabling public health professionals to make informed decisions and plan interventions more effectively. This approach simplifies data collection and reporting, contributing to more accurate public health responses and improving the registration and analysis of outbreak information. This system represents a significant advancement in infectious disease management, enabling real-time tracking and intervention planning for future outbreaks.

Similarly, the data exploration dashboard developed at the Africa Health Research Institute (AHRI) in KwaZulu-Natal, South Africa, focuses on health and demographic indicators in the Treatment as Prevention (TasP) trial, which targets HIV prevention [3]. The dashboard provides real-time access to data through interactive touchscreens, supporting collaboration among researchers, staff, and community members. It enables users to monitor key performance indicators (KPIs) at both global and local levels via intuitive charts and maps, allowing for detailed spatial analysis while protecting participant privacy. This system's modular architecture ensures flexibility and scalability, allowing it to integrate new datasets as needed. Such a dashboard facilitates transparent, informed decision-making in public health research by providing easy access to ongoing study data.

Another example is found in the study by [4], which focused on stakeholder perspectives regarding the adoption of a dashboard to promote responsible research practices at university medical centers (UMCs). This research identified four key stakeholder groups—UMC leadership, support staff, research funders, and responsible research experts—and explored their views through online interviews. The dashboard aimed to improve transparency and establish a performance baseline for responsible research. However, stakeholders expressed concerns about the lack of a cohesive framework and the use of outdated metrics, leading to divided opinions on whether public access to the dashboard would encourage positive change or damage institutional reputations. While the dashboard was seen as a potentially valuable tool, the need for further development and a consensus on metrics was highlighted.

These examples illustrate the ongoing development of sophisticated data collection and visualization systems in public health, with a focus on real-time data access, privacy considerations, and decision-making support. While each system serves a different purpose—infectious disease tracking, HIV trial monitoring, and research performance assessment—they all underscore the importance of dashboards and mobile tools in enhancing public health data management and fostering informed, timely decision-making.

5   Approach

In this paper, a holistic approach is proposed to provide public health agencies with a global overview about the spread of diseases and understand community health needs. This approach is following a data-driven socio-economic model occurring as a result of the increased volume, velocity and variety of data. We propose to develop tools that collect, store, analyze, process and visualize large amounts of health and environment data emerging from diverse sources. Acquisition, systematization and correlation of large volumes of heterogeneous health, social, personal and environmental data is among the core pillars of the proposed approach.

The proposed approach follows three main steps as described in Fig. 1:

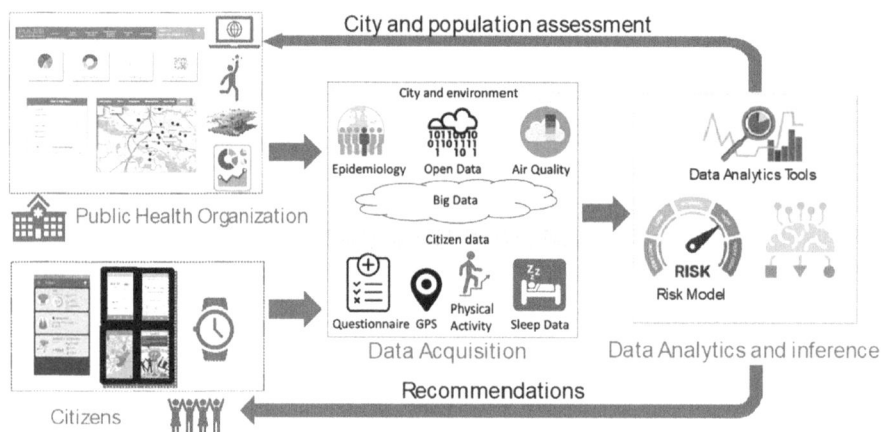

Fig. 1. Smart Health based on urban analytics overall approach.

1. **Data Acquisition :** Two levels of data are distinguished : Citizen data and city/environmental data. Citizen data are collected from diverse sources such as questionnaires, wearable sensors, medical records, etc. while environmental data are collected from deployed sensors in the city and available open data. Citizen data provide information on personal profiles of the citizens, their health status and life style (physical activity, Sleep quality, etc.), and their vision about their neighborhood while environmental and city data give information about the spread of the disease in the city and some environmental related information such as the level of pollution and the air quality.

2. **Data Analysis and Inference :** Collected data need to be cleaned and analyzed in order to extract meaningful and relevant information that will be provided for the policymakers and the public health organizations. In addition, AI models are employed to infer new information and predict possible disease outbreaks and spread within the population. Data analysis and AI models help in identifying patterns, trends, and correlations that are crucial for understanding the spread and expanse of diseases. Additionally, they help in identifying high-risk populations and predicting future outbreaks. This information allows policymakers and public health agencies to implement targeted interventions and allocate resources efficiently and ultimately.

3. **Data Visualization :** Data visualization plays a crucial role in empowering individuals and policymakers to make informed decisions and take adequate measures. On the community and public health level, dashboards are used to present complex datasets in visually intuitive formats that offer a clear and concise overview of key metrics, trends, and insights related to disease spread, healthcare utilization, and community health needs. Therefore, policymaker and public health agencies can dynamically explore data, drill down into specific areas of interest, and uncover hidden patterns or correlations. They can also rapidly identify areas requiring attention or intervention. On the individual level, data visualization provide a clear vision about citizens health and well-being. Visualization tools enable users to track their progress, identify potential health risks, and make lifestyle adjustments accordingly.

6 System Deployment and Participants Recruitment

In order to validate the proposed approach, we choose to work on an important chronic disease : Type 2 Diabetes (T2D). Based on our experience in pilot sites deployment [2], a real deployment of our system was carried out in five pilot sites in different cities around the world (Barcelona, Birmingham, New York, Paris and Singapore). The deployment showcased how it is possible to collect data from different sources and provide significant insights about these two diseases that can help public health organizations. A total of 1832 participants have been recruited to be included in our study from our five pilot sites. During the recruitment process, several steps have been followed. We started by a general presentation of the system to respective stakeholders' audience (potential participants, municipalities, local authorities, PHO, Ethics committees, etc.). This step is followed by some briefing sessions where specific deployment aspects and practical matters are discussed with volunteer participants who want to be involved in the project. Technology devices are introduced to the participants and Q&A sessions enable a good understanding of the deployment's scope. Once the participants express their willingness to be involved in the deployment, recruitment sessions are conducted to provide the Consent Forms, and the Participant Information Sheet to ensure a smooth experimentation. Starting from this step, sets of questionnaires such as Basic Socio-Demographics, Neighbourhood Environment, Health Behaviours and Habits, Physical Activity IPAQ-short, Euroqol-5d, and Wellbeing and The European Social Survey are pushed to the users through local instruments used in each pilot site during deployment interviews. At the end of the deployment, Post-pilot surveys were performed to assess the significance of the technological solution in changing behaviors and improving the Quality of Life. Table 1 presents the distribution of the participants among the five pilot sites.

Table 1. Participants distribution by pilot site

BCN	BIR	PAR	NYC	SIN	Total
407	333	320	501	271	1832
(22.21%)	(18.18%)	(17.47%)	(27.35%)	(14.79%)	(100%)

7   Data Acquisition

During the deployment in the five testbeds, data have been collected using different data sources. A mobile application has been deployed for all pilot sites' participants and used to collect data using different surveys/questionnaires (wellbeing, quality of life, lifestyle, health assessment, depression, social support environment and habits). In addition, participants were equipped by activity trackers. Those activity trackers are used to monitor and track fitness-related metrics such as distance walked or run, calorie consumption, and in some cases heartbeat and quality of sleep. The system also uses air sensors to monitor the air quality in a real-time and open-data sources to collect significant data about the pilot sites.

Over the projects' full duration of 48 months, 84 632 answers from questionnaires have been collected directly through the mobile application and surveys, 72 729 065 measured values have been collected from wearable devices (Activity Trackers). Also, a total of 4 569 490 air quality values have been collected from air sensors and open-data sources available in the five pilot sites. Table 2 describes the different sources of data employed in the pilot sites and the amount of data collected.

Table 2. Sources and amount of data collected from the different pilot sites

Questionnaires	Number of participants	1718
	Number of answers	84 632
Wearable devices	Number of participants	297
	Number of devices	404
	Measured values	72 729 065
Air Sensors	Number of air sensors	91
	Measured data values	4 569 490

8   Data Analytics and Inference

Collected data has been cleaned and organized. Following this, a detailed analysis has been performed using statistical methods and machine learning algorithms to identify patterns and insights.

8.1   Data Analytics

Different elements have been considered when working on data analytics.

Self-reported Health. We have performed analytics on data collected from the EuroQol survey and the simple question "In general, how would you describe your health?" with a grading scale from 1 to 5. The results concern two iterations as described in Fig. 2. During the first iteration, considering 1056 users data from the 5 pilots, 88,2% of all participants described their health as good or excellent, with results above 3 on the rating system from 1 to 5. During the second iteration, performed 12 months after the first one, with 1008 users who completed the questionnaires, the results were slightly different, dropping to 63,0% people describing their health as good. The most affected pilot is Birmingham with a score of self-rated "good" only for 32,2% of total respondents. Barcelona remains good with 80,0%, meanwhile all the other pilots numbers drop to 73,0% for New York pilot, 65,8% for Paris and 64,4% for Singapore. The reason is that involved users became more aware about their health condition when participating to the experimentation, thus provided more accurate feedback.

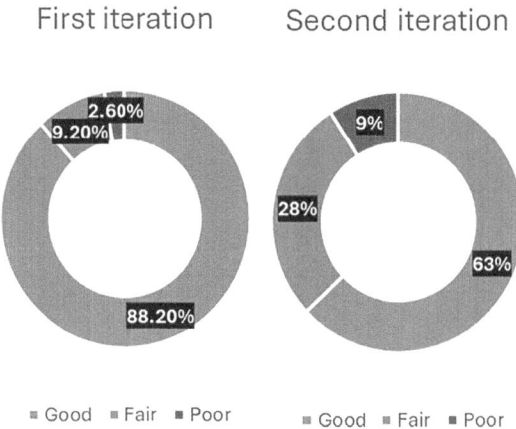

Fig. 2. All pilots health evaluation

Lifestyle (Physical Activity and Sleep Time). Data from IPAQ-short questionnaire and the simple question "Over the last week, on how many days did you engage in moderate/vigorous physical activity like heavy lifting, digging, aerobics, or fast bicycling?" have also been considered. The data is related to physical activity (days by week of moderate to vigorous effort) sleep quality (hours slept by night) as shown in Fig. 3. The result involved 1.071 users, who completed the questionnaire. Results shows a distribution of physical activity with 38% of the participants never exercising, more than a third exercising between one to three days a week. The more active group, considering exercising 4 d a week or more represents a quarter of the total cohort (26,5%). Considering the sleep quality (hours slept by night) indicator, about 10% of the total participants sleep less than 6 h per night, where the vast majority sleeping more than 6 h.

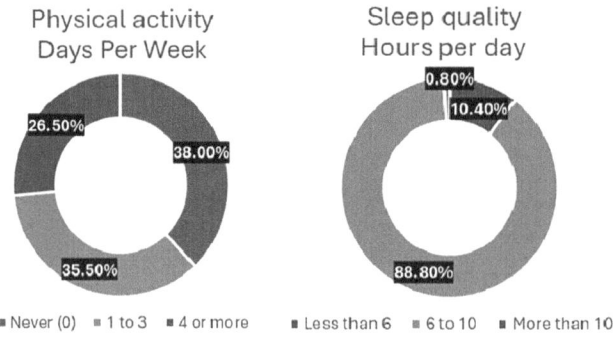

Fig. 3. All pilots physical activity and sleep time

Disease Diagnosis Analysis. The cohort of 1.832 participants included 164 persons diagnosed with Type 2 Diabetes (7 in Barcelona, 48 in Birmingham, 7 in New York City, 22 in Paris and 24 in Singapore).

Diagnosed with T2D over
total participants

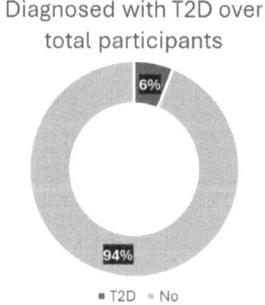

Fig. 4. Participants diagnosed with T2D over total cohort

Neighborhood Assessment. In our deployment, we intended to assess the impact of the urban environment to the health of the population. Items were compiled into 3 categories impacting the overall lifestyle of the population (Traffic, food and green groceries), this set of data was extracted from a total number

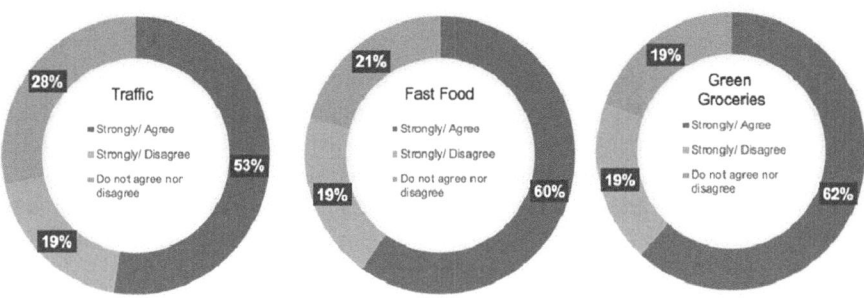

Fig. 5. Neighborhood assessment for all pilots (average)

of 1.148 participants who completed the full set of questions during our study from the partners on neighborhood's perception.

Traffic congestion is an important factor on the daily life within a specific neighborhood. On top of decreasing the overall livability of the neighborhood, it directly affects the visual perception of the streets, produces noise and direct exposure to air pollution.

For all pilots together, 53% of the participants are affected or strongly affected by traffic congestion in their neighborhood. Barcelona and Birmingham's participants feel more affected by the traffic congestion in their neighborhoods, with 64% and 61% of the total cohort respectively. New York pilot scores slightly better with 56% of the total participants having an issue with this traffic congestion, meanwhile Paris and Singapore score 43% and 35%. Those numbers are related to the exact pilot's boundaries and where our solution is deployed and may not reflect the situation at the district or city level.

Global score for fast food availability is 60% of all participants agreeing that their neighborhood have too much fast food establishments. This number varies from 83% (Birmingham) to 43% (Singapore). This is explained for example that in Singapore, population tends to eat either on the malls or at the hawker centers (food courts) from where the stalls are locals and are not large fast food companies.

Surprisingly, participants also tend to agree that the neighborhoods also have green groceries available at a footstep. Average score for all pilot is 62% of the participants agreeing that it is easy and convenient to find healthy food within their neighborhood, either from healthy restaurants or at local healthy groceries (nutrition experts chain, healthy and organic shops or either at the local fresh markets).

8.2   AI Models for Health Risk Assessment

Collected data have also been used to feed AI models that have been developed for health risk assessment. We have developed models for T2D risk assessment.

T2D Risk Assessment Model. Twelve original models for the prediction of type 2 diabetes (T2D) onset have also been developed, 6 based on survival Support Vector Machines (SVM) and 6 on Cox survival analysis (CSA). The models were trained on two retrospective datasets, namely MESA and ELSA, in 3 scenarios reflecting different degrees of information availability. Scenario 1 includes all the easily accessible variables that do not require particular measurements; scenario 2 adds to scenario 1 non-invasive measurements of health parameters (e.g. blood pressure); Scenario 3 adds to scenario 2 invasive measurements of biomarkers (e.g. fasting glucose concentration).

Performance of the models were assessed on independent test sets, extracted from the MESA and ELSA datasets. The C-index values obtained on MESA and ELSA test sets for the 12 developed models are reported in Tab. 3.

Table 3. Performance of CSA and survival SVM T2D models developed in the 3 scenarios on MESA and ELSA test datasets

Model	CSA		survSVM	
	C-index		C-index	
	MESA	ELSA	MESA	ELSA
Scenario 3	0.88	0.80	0.82	0.79
Scenario 2	0.84	0.79	0.74	0.77
Scenario 1	0.81	0.76	0.73	0.74

The 12 developed models were finally combined in a consensus T2D model that implements risk-score rescaling and weighted average to provide an average risk score. The consensus T2D model also includes 8 literature models namely, the Finnish Diabetes Risk Score (FINDRISC) model [9], the three Atherosclerosis Risk in Communities (ARIC) models [8], the Framingham model [6], the basic risk score by Kahn et al. [5], and the Diabetes Population Risk Tool (DPoRT) [7]. The risk score provided in output by the consensus T2D model represents the subject's probability of developing T2D in the next 8 years. Subjects can be categorized according to their T2D risk scores using the following thresholds:

- Low risk: risk score $\prec 0.05$
- Medium-low risk: $0.05 \leq$ risk score $\prec 0.10$
- Medium risk: $0.10 \leq$ risk score $\prec 0.15$
- Medium-high risk: $0.15 \leq$ risk score $\prec 0.20$
- High risk: $0.20 \leq$ risk score $\prec 0.25$
- Very high risk: risk score $\succeq 0.25$

The models have afterword been applied to our data set. Table 4 and Tab. 5 show the computational obtained results.

Table 4. Summary of T2D consensus risk model results dataset related to total numbers of questionnaire respondents per cities

City	Number of Computed Consensus T2D Risk Model Results for Citizens	Total Number of Citizens Submitting Filled Questionnaires
Barcelona	390	390
Birmingham	280	330
New York	234	242
Paris	266	298
Singapore	210	229

Table 5. Summary of the T2D consensus risk model results, in numbers of citizens per risk level category, per cities

City	BCN	BIR	NYC	PAR	SIN
Low Risk	358	249	181	253	197
Medium-low Risk	23	17	29	8	3
Medium Risk	6	5	10	2	2
Medium-high Risk	1	6	6	2	4
High Risk	0	1	3	0	0

9   Data Visualization (Analytics Results and Models Outputs)

The summary results of the different models (T2D risk model and Well-being model) are displayed on the Overview page a Public Health Organization (PHO) Observatory Dashboard that we have developed as shown in Fig. 6.

Fig. 6. Summary & Overview Navigation Bar on top of the content area on the main PHO Observatory Dashboard start page

This small panel and navigation item:

– provides the top-level summary and overview of the current calculated models' scores. Context provided for the diagrams on this Navigation Bar is the selected cohort context (intra-city or city context).

– initiates most analysis workflows, navigating the user (with a click/tap any-
   where on the panel surface) to the detailed Analytics pages.

Detailed Analytics page contains more elaborate interactive visualizations of
the models' outputs and explorations of predictor variable values, primarily:

– the embedded WebGIS [1] UI Control configured for displaying computed
   outputs of any selected model, or main predictor values - acquired data
   from wearable trackers or questionnaire responses – geo-localized within the
   selected city and its territorial subdivision, and in the context of the active
   cohort, and
– the T2D domain decomposition and socio-demographic stratification panel,
   containing multiple composite diagrams and featuring elementary interactive
   visual data exploration, with the user selecting and cross-stratifying variables
   of choice.

Instance of the WebGIS Interactive Data Visualization Control, displayed in
Fig. 7, is embedded in the Analytics page and coupled with the connected histogram, displays spatial distributions of different variables from T2D domain and
related datasets, within the selected city and cohort. User can select different
data variables (questionnaire response values, wearable-sensed data, imported
open data, calculated well-being domain scores...) known to affect T2D, spatial
subdivision level for their plotting (per zip/postal codes, districts, boroughs etc.
defined for each city), and data aggregation functions (average, minimum or
maximum values for continuous variables, and categorized distribution for categorized variables), on the interactive control panel above the map. For continuous
data, different colors are assigned in ascending order from red (implicit lowest)
to green (implicit best or most favourable). For categorized data, different disparate colors are automatically assigned for each possible category option, and
each granular territorial subdivision area on the map is coloured as the category
value prevalent among the values in that area.

Diagrams on the detailed T2D domain decomposition and socio-demographic
stratification panel are divided into three thematic subpanel groups:

– Sociodemographic T2D risk model stratification – visualized in categorized
   range distributions (by age, gender, ethnicity, educational level and marital
   status) on bar/histogram diagrams displaying relative percentages of citizens
   with specific score category values within the total number of citizens in the
   active cohort as shown in Fig. 8.
– Questionnaire data related to T2D – visualized as combined pie and sorted
   bar/histogram diagrams, displaying the distributions of relevant questionnaire response values, such as relatives with diagnosed diabetes, participants
   weight, people diagnosed with high blood glucose questionnaires, etc. as
   shown in Fig. 9.

---

[1] http://www.webgis.com/.

Fig. 7. WebGIS Interactive Data Visualization Control, embedded in the T2D Analytics page with the coupled histogram, showing the spatial distribution of the T2D consensus model score, per zip/postal code areas in Barcelona

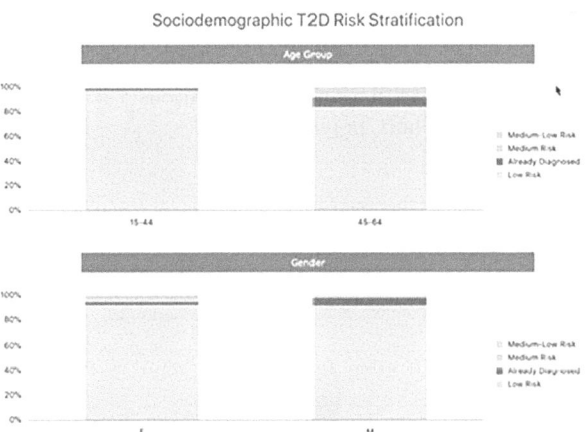

Fig. 8. Subpanel of the T2D domain decomposition and socio-demographic stratification panel, presenting the relative distributions of T2D risk stratification scores within the selected observed cohort/population

- Cross-stratifications of data – stacked or grouped bar chart visualizations enabling the user to select a variable from questionnaire data related to T2D and an additional stratifying basic socio-demographic variable (gender, age range, marital status, ethnicity, education level...), and presenting the resulting value distribution of the selected variable stratified per selected socio-demographic factor as shown in Fig. 10.

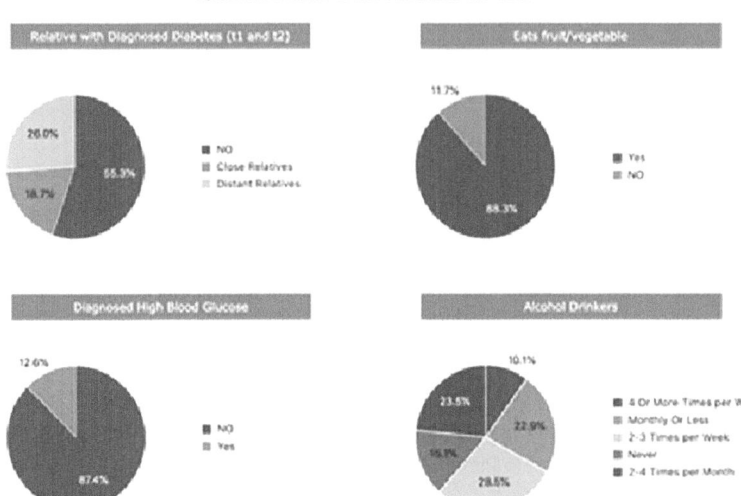

Fig. 9. Subpanel of the T2D domain decomposition and socio-demographic stratification panel, presenting the distributions of values of various T2D related questionnaires within the selected observed cohort/population

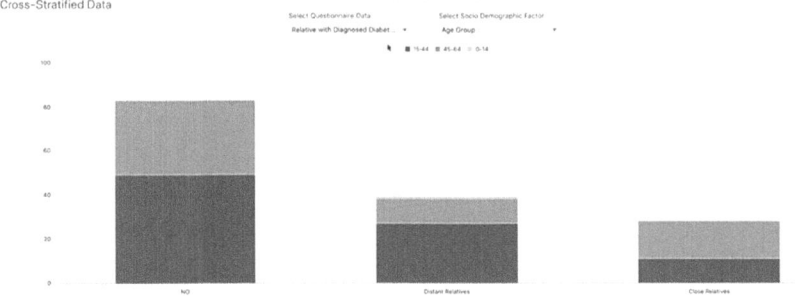

Fig. 10. Subpanel of the T2D domain decomposition and socio-demographic stratification panel, presenting the resulting selected socio-demographic stratification of a selected well-being domain score or predictor

10   Conclusion

In this paper, we have outlined a data-driven approach to improving public health management by integrating citizen, environmental, and health data. By deploying this system across five global pilot sites and focusing on Type 2 Diabetes as a case study, we demonstrated the value of real-time data collection and analysis in identifying health trends, high-risk populations, and potential disease outbreaks. The insights gained from this approach can significantly enhance the decision-making processes of public health organizations, helping them to develop more effective, targeted interventions. Ultimately, this framework holds the potential to improve public health outcomes by fostering a more connected, informed, and proactive public health system.

Acknowledgment. This work was realized as part of the European Funded project "PULSE". We would like to thank all the partners who were involved in this project and all the included pilot sites' participants.

References

1. Ahn, E., et al.: A mobile app and dashboard for early detection of infectious disease outbreaks: development study. JMIR. Public Health Surveill. **7**(3), e14837 (2021). https://doi.org/10.2196/14837
2. Aloulou, H., Mokhtari, M., Abdulrazak, B.: Pilot site deployment of an iot solution for older adults' early behavior change detection. Sensors **20**(7), 1888 (2020)
3. Concannon, D., Herbst, K., Manley, E., et al.: Developing a data dashboard framework for population health surveillance: widening access to clinical trial findings. JMIR Form. Res. **3**(2), e11342 (2019)
4. Haven, T.L., Holst, M.R., Strech, D.: Stakeholders' views on an institutional dashboard with metrics for responsible research. PLoS ONE **17**(6), e0269492 (2022)
5. Kahn, H.S., Cheng, Y.J., Thompson, T.J., Imperatore, G., Gregg, E.W.: Two risk-scoring systems for predicting incident diabetes mellitus in us adults age 45 to 64 years. Ann. Intern. Med. **150**(11), 741–751 (2009)
6. McEwan, P., et al.: Evaluating the performance of the framingham risk equations in a population with diabetes. Diabet. Med. **21**(4), 318–323 (2004)
7. Rosella, L.C., Manuel, D.G., Burchill, C., Stukel, T.A., et al.: A population-based risk algorithm for the development of diabetes: development and validation of the diabetes population risk tool (dport). J. Epidemiol. Commun. Health **65**(7), 613–620 (2011)
8. Schneider, A.L., et al.: Diabetes and prediabetes and risk of hospitalization: the atherosclerosis risk in communities (aric) study. Diabetes Care **39**(5), 772–779 (2016)
9. Vandersmissen, G.J.M., Godderis, L.: Evaluation of the finnish diabetes risk score (findrisc) for diabetes screening in occupational health care. Int. J. Occup. Med. Environ. Health **28**(3), 587–591 (2015)

Author Index

M. Barhamgi et al. (Eds.): WISE 2024, LNCS 15463, pp. 455–457, 2025.
https://doi.org/10.1007/978-981-96-1483-7

The manufacturer's authorised representative in the EU is Springer
Nature Customer Service Centre GmbH, Europaplatz 3, 69115 Heidelberg,
Germany. If you have any concerns regarding our products, please
contact ProductSafety@springernature.com

Printed and bound by CPI Group (UK) Ltd, Croydon, CR0 4YY

29/04/2026

02099551-0005